*"Information through Innovation"*

## ABOUT THE COVER

The cover of this text contains various photographs of a pipe organ. If you are wondering about the connection between pipe organs and databases, consider the following:

Before an organ is installed, an analyst representing the organ builder will interview the people who will be using the organ (from this point on called simply "the users"). This analyst will ask pertinent questions concerning the users' desires for the organ. The analyst will also study the physical environment into which the organ will be placed. Using this information, an organ designer will then design the organ. In the process, the designer will determine the particular ranks (sets of pipes) which the organ will contain as well as the placement of these ranks within the organ. The designer will produce written documentation concerning the design. Once the users have reviewed this documentation and agreed to the specifications, the components of the organ will be carefully crafted and assembled. When the organ has been completed, an organist will furnish the necessary input to the organ by manipulating the various keys, pedals, stops, couplers, pistons, and so on. Provided this is done correctly, the organ will produce the desired output (the music). The output can then be appreciated by others. Finally, the completed organ will require periodic maintenance and fine-tuning.

# DATABASE SYSTEMS
## Management and Design

SECOND EDITION

**Philip J. Pratt**
**Joseph J. Adamski**
Grand Valley State University

boyd & fraser publishing company

## Credits:

**Vice President and Publisher:** Thomas K. Walker
**Acquisitions Editor:** James H. Edwards
**Director of Production:** Becky Herrington
**Production Editor:** Pat Donegan
**Manufacturing Director:** Dean Sherman
**Cover/Book Design:** Becky Herrington
**Cover Photo:** Leslie Peart
Central Reformed Church
Grand Rapids, Michigan
**Cover Photo Retouch:** Ken Russo
**Typesetting:** Huntington & Black Typography

© 1991 by boyd & fraser publishing company
A Division of South-Western Publishing Company
Boston, MA 02116

Manufactured in the United States of America

**Library of Congress Cataloging-in-Publication Data**

2 3 4 5 6 7 8 9 MT 4 3 2 1

*Dedication*

To Judy, Randy, and Tammy — Phil
To Judy and our families — Joe

Without their love, understanding, support,
and encouragement, this project would
not have been possible.

# ORDER INFORMATION AND FACULTY SUPPORT INFORMATION

For the quickest service, refer to the map below for the South-Western Regional Office serving your area.

## 1 ORDER INFORMATION
5101 Madison Road
Cincinnati, OH 45227-1490
General Telephone–513-527-6945
Telephone: 1-800-543-8440
FAX: 513-527-6979
Telex: 214371

### FACULTY SUPPORT INFORMATION
5101 Madison Road
Cincinnati, OH 45227-1490
General Telephone–513-527-6950
Telephone: 1-800-543-8444

| | | |
|---|---|---|
| Alabama | Massachusetts | Ohio |
| Connecticut | Michigan | Pennsylvania |
| Delaware | Minnesota | Rhode Island |
| Florida | Mississippi | South Carolina |
| Georgia | Missouri | South Dakota |
| Illinois | Nebraska | Tennessee |
| Indiana | New Hampshire | Vermont |
| Iowa | New Jersey | Virginia |
| Kentucky | New York | West Virginia |
| Maine | North Carolina | Wisconsin |
| Maryland | North Dakota | District of Columbia |

## 2 ORDER INFORMATION
13800 Senlac Drive
Suite 100
Dallas, TX 75234
General Telephone–214-241-8541
Telephone: 1-800-543-7972

### FACULTY SUPPORT INFORMATION
5101 Madison Road
Cincinnati, OH 45227-1490
General Telephone–513-527-6950
Telephone: 1-800-543-8444

| | | |
|---|---|---|
| Arkansas | Louisiana | Texas |
| Colorado | New Mexico | Wyoming |
| Kansas | Oklahoma | |

## 3 ORDER INFORMATION and FACULTY SUPPORT INFORMATION
6185 Industrial Way
Livermore, CA 94550
General Telephone–415-449-2280
Telephone: 1-800-543-7972

| | | |
|---|---|---|
| Alaska | Idaho | Oregon |
| Arizona | Montana | Utah |
| California | Nevada | Washington |
| Hawaii | | |

# CONTENTS

The past few years have produced a number of dramatic developments that make the process of managing a database accessible to a wide variety of users. These developments include commercial relational model systems, microcomputer database systems, the fourth-generation environment, and the integration of database software with other types of software such as spreadsheets and graphics. Since its inception, database management has always been an important area. It is even more important now, with an ever-increasing audience needing to be familiar with database concepts.

## ABOUT THIS BOOK

This book is intended to be used as the textbook for a course in database management. The vast majority of people who will take a serious course in database management in the coming years will eventually be users of database management systems. That is, they will *use* a database management system to create application software, either for themselves or for others. Thus the book is an appropriate text for a database course in an information systems, business or a computer science curriculum in which applications are important.

Students using this text should have experience with some programming language and with the basics of file processing. They should be familiar with the terms *files*, *records*, and *fields*. They should be at least minimally familiar with the general characteristics of modern computing equipment (e.g., the fact that files are stored on disk, the role of CRTs, and the role of microcomputers). Students with this background should certainly be able to successfully use this text.

To receive maximum benefit from the text, it would be helpful for students to have a good background in the file organization and data structures concepts covered in the Appendix of this textbook. This background ideally will have been obtained from a prior course. If that is not possible, then the material in the Appendix can be presented near the beginning of the database course. (Many textbooks in database management cover such material in two or three chapters early in the book. If desired, this book can be used in a similar fashion; i.e., the material in the Appendix can be taught near the beginning of the database course, immediately following the introduction.) The time spent covering this material will, of course, mean that less of the book can be covered in the remainder of the course. If the course is part of a two-term sequence, this will not be a problem. In a single course, however, some of the later material will need to be omitted.

## CHANGES IN THE SECOND EDITION

Users of the first edition will find three types of changes in this second edition. First, existing material has been changed to reflect changes that have occurred in the field in the last few years. For example, the SQL material now includes a discussion of the Integrity Enhancement Feature; the popular QBE implementation in Paradox (a product of Borland International) is used to illustrate the concepts in Query-By-Example; the material on the fourth-generation tools includes illustrations of visually-oriented report generators as well as facilities for incorporating windows into applications; and so on.

Second, new material has been added. The second edition features an entire chapter devoted to microcomputer DBMS's including an extensive discussion of dBASE IV (a product of Ashton-Tate). The second edition includes new material on object-oriented databases. It also includes a discussion of knowledge-based systems.

Finally, the second edition incorporates some helpful suggestions from users of the first edition. The detailed design examples from Appendix B of the first edition, for example, have been incorporated into the database design chapters within the text. The design methodology given in the text now incorporates a graphic element. In addition, there are new figures illustrating the use of a computerized design tool in the construction and documentation of Entity-Relationship diagrams.

## DISTINGUISHING FEATURES

### The Relational Model Emphasized

The relational model is given a special place of prominence befitting its importance, both today and in the future. It is the first model covered, with three complete chapters devoted to exploring its basic structure, methods of manipulating relational databases and the relational model's impact on database design. In addition, two major commercial implementations of the model are presented and discussed.

### The CODASYL and Hierarchical Models

The CODASYL and hierarchical models also receive detailed coverage. In each case, the coverage includes the basic and advanced features of the model as well as details of a significant commercial implementation of the model.

Study of these additional models is motivated by the fact that many commercial implementations of them still exist. Additionally, a comparative analysis of the various models can be quite instructive.

The book is designed in a modular fashion to allow the instructor the maximum flexibility regarding the order in which the models are to be presented. Chapters concerning the CODASYL and hierarchical models (chapters 9 and 10) can be taught in any sequence or completely omitted. These chapters can also be covered early in the course where students are working with systems that follow one of these models in their projects.

## Database Design Covered in Detail

The very important process of database design is covered in great detail, both the information level of database design and the physical level. In the two chapters (7 and 8) devoted to the information level, a methodology is presented that has the relational model as its foundation. In chapter 11, after all of the models have been examined, the physical level of design is examined in detail.

In attempting to master the topic of database design, examples are crucial. In addition to the examples illustrating the individual concepts, there are two detailed database design examples which emphasize all facets of the process.

## The Fourth-Generation Environment

There is a detailed discussion of the fourth-generation environment. The central component of this environment, the data dictionary, along with other components such as report writers, query languages, screen generators, program generators, teleprocessing monitors, and fourth-generation languages are also covered. The role of the fourth-generation environment in the prototyping process is examined. Large numbers of fourth-generation products are available today, and more are being developed. These easier-to-use, integrated products will be tomorrow's technology and are a required part of the database student's background.

## In-Depth Coverage of the Database Administration Function

There is a detailed discussion of the role of database administration in computing today. Central and distributed databases require central management, coordination and control, and database administration is assigned this responsibility. In addition to a review of the organizational placement and structure of database administration, there is detailed coverage of the characteristics of successful database administration groups and of their administrative, application and technical functions.

### Early Treatment of DBMS Functions

The functions that should be provided by a full-scale DBMS are presented early in the book (chapter 2), immediately following the general introduction to database management. There are three important benefits to the early treatment of DBMS functions. First, to satisfy the natural curiosity of students about the overall capabilities of DBMS. Second, an understanding of this material provides students with an excellent foundation for the remaining material in the text. Finally, when the various commercial systems are discussed later in the text, students gain an appreciation for the manner in which these systems furnish the required functions.

### Detailed Coverage of Important Commercial Systems

Some of the most significant of today's commercial systems, DB2, INGRES, IDMS/R, IMS and dBASE IV, are examined in the text along with the manner in which these systems provide the features expected from a full-scale commercial DBMS.

### Numerous Realistic Examples

The book contains numerous examples illustrating each of the concepts covered. The examples presented throughout the text are based on two hypothetical organizations, Marvel College and Premiere Products. The examples are realistic and representative of the kinds of problems that professionals encounter in designing, manipulating and administering databases.

### Questions and Exercises

**Q&As**  At key points within the chapters, there are Q&As. These are questions for students to answer to ensure they understand the material before proceeding further. The answers to these questions are given immediately following the questions themselves.

**Review Questions**  At the end of each chapter, there are Review Questions, which test the student's recall of the important points in the chapter. The answers to all of the odd-numbered review questions are given at the end of the text. The answers to the even-numbered review questions are given in the Instructor's Manual.

**Exercises**   There are also Exercises in which the students must apply what they have learned. The answers to all of the exercises are given in the accompanying Instructor's Manual.

## Projects

Projects in which the students actually use a DBMS are essential in a database course. We suggest assigning a single project with several parts to run throughout the semester. Eight such projects are presented in the Instructor's Manual together with tips for administering the projects. These projects vary in size and can be implemented by students working in either microcomputer or mainframe environments. These projects can also be used as the basis for database design exercises by students.

## ANCILLARY MATERIALS

A comprehensive instructors' support package accompanies *Database Systems Management and Design*, *Second Edition*. These ancillaries are available to instructors upon request from our publisher, boyd & fraser.

## Instructor's Manual

Material in the Instructor's Manual follows the organization of the text. Chapters of the Instructor's Manual include:

- Purpose
- Vocabulary Words
- Chapter Objectives
- Lecture Outlines [keyed to Transparency Masters]
- Teaching Suggestions [keyed to Lecture Outline]
- Answers to Exercises [found in the text]
- Test Questions
- Answers to Test Questions
- Database Design (and/or Implementation) Projects

## Transparency Masters

An extensive set of over 250 transparency masters is also available. These masters include figures, program segments and tables from the text.

## COMPANION TEXTS

### A Guide to SQL

Many instructors will find the substantial material on SQL contained in *Database Systems Management and Design, Second Edition* to be more than sufficient for their needs. Some instructors, however, prefer to cover all aspects of SQL in great detail. *A Guide to SQL* is available at a reduced price as a companion text to *Database Systems Management and Design, Second Edition*. *A Guide to SQL*, which contains over 100 examples, covers all facets of the SQL language.

### Using dBASE III PLUS

Instructors who would like to use dBASE III PLUS as a vehicle for project work in their courses should consider *Using dBASE III PLUS*. This text covers the Assistant, the dot prompt, the report facility, the labels facility, the view facility, and the screen generator. It also contains three chapters devoted to programming in dBASE. After mastering the material in this text, students should be able to use dBASE to develop sophisticated application systems. This text is also available from boyd & fraser at a reduced price as a companion text to *Database Systems Management and Design, Second Edition*.

## ORGANIZATION OF THIS BOOK

The textbook contains 14 chapters and an appendix which are organized as follows.

### Introduction

Chapter 1 provides a general introduction to the field of database management.

### The Functions of a DBMS

Chapter 2 discusses the features that should be provided by a full-functioned database management system. In later chapters, the manner in which the commercial systems examined in the text furnish these functions is explored.

## The Relational Model

Chapters 3, 4, and 6 concern the relational model. In chapter 3, the general model is presented along with methods for manipulating relational databases. Chapter 4 covers advanced features of the model together with a discussion of two of the major implementations of the relational model: DB2 and INGRES. Chapter 6 deals with normalization, the contribution of the relational model to the field of database design.

## Microcomputer DBMS's

Chapter 5 contains a detailed discussion of Microcomputer DBMS's. It also contains extensive coverage of dBASE IV.

## Database Design (Information Level)

Chapters 7 and 8 deal with database design. Chapter 7 introduces the information level of database design together with a specific methodology for performing database design. Chapter 8 expands on this material with some specific tips. It also presents another design methodology, the entity-relationship model, which is compared and contrasted with the methodology of the text. A method for converting between the two methodologies is also presented.

## The CODASYL Model

Chapter 9 covers the CODASYL model. The basics and advanced features of the model are presented in this chapter. It also includes a discussion of a prime example of the CODASYL model: IDMS. Along with the discussion of IDMS is a discussion of IDMS/R, an enhancement of IDMS that includes relational-like features.

## The Hierarchical Model

Chapter 10 covers the hierarchical model and the major hierarchical system: IMS.

## Database Design (Physical Level)

Chapter 11 completes the discussion of database design by covering the physical part of the design process; i.e., the implementation of the information-level design on a specific database management system. A methodology is given for this process.

### The Fourth-Generation Environment

Chapter 12 examines the fourth-generation environment. The data dictionary and other major components of this environment are covered along with the information center, prototyping and emerging fifth-generation software.

### Database Administration

Chapter 13 covers the role of database administration. Major emphasis is devoted to an examination of the administrative, application and technical functions of database administration.

### Distributed Systems and Other Current Trends

Chapter 14 presents a discussion of some current trends: distributed systems, database computers, object-oriented systems, and knowledge-based systems.

### File Organization and Data Structures

The Appendix presents material on file organization and data structures that relate to database management.

### Answers to Odd-Numbered Review Questions

Answers to the odd-numbered review questions are given at this point in the text.

### Glossary

There is a glossary containing definitions to over 300 of the most important terms in the text. Important terms, which are printed in **boldface** within the text, are either defined on the page on which they appear or in the glossary.

## TO THE STUDENT

### Boldfaced Terms

Terms that are printed in **boldface** are either defined where they appear or are defined in the glossary. If you encounter a term in boldface whose definition does not accompany the term, it has been defined earlier in the text and you should be familiar with it. If you are not, you could look it up in the glossary.

### Embedded Questions

There are a number of places in the text where special questions have been embedded. Sometimes the purpose of these questions is to ensure that you understand some crucial material before you proceed. In other cases, the questions are designed to give you the chance to consider some special concept in advance of its actual presentation. In all cases, the answer to the question is given immediately after the question. You could simply read the question and its answer. To receive maximum benefit, however, you should take the time to work out your own answer and then check it against the one given in the text.

### End-of-Chapter Material

The end-of-chapter material consists of three elements: a summary, review questions and exercises. The summary briefly describes the material covered in the chapter. The review questions require you to recall the important material in the chapter. The answers to the odd-numbered review questions are given in the text. The exercises require you to apply what you have learned.

We suggest that, upon completion of a chapter, you read the summary to make sure that you are generally familiar with the main concepts of the chapter. Next, answer the review questions and compare your answers to the odd-numbered questions with those given in the text. Finally, work whatever exercises your instructor has assigned.

### A Final Note

We wish you the best in your study of the exciting, important, and rapidly changing field of database management. We hope that you find it as interesting, challenging, and rewarding as we do.

## ACKNOWLEDGEMENTS

We would like to acknowledge several individuals for their contributions in the preparation of this book.

We are grateful to our students in the database course at Grand Valley State University who used preliminary versions of this text. We appreciate not only their many helpful suggestions but also their support and encouragement.

We also greatly appreciate the efforts of the following individuals who class-tested or reviewed the first edition of the text and made many helpful suggestions: John M. Atkins, West Virginia University; Madeline Baugher, Southwestern Oklahoma State University; C. Andrew Belew, Ferris State College; Alfred Boals, Western Michigan University; Donald Dawley, Miami University; John Demel, Ohio State University; Gary Heisler, Lansing Community College; Carl Penziul, Corning Community College; Darleen V. Pigford, Western Illinois University; Phil Prins, Calvin College; David D. Riley, University of Wisconsin-LaCrosse; Constantine Ruossos, Lynchburg College; and Marguerite Summers, University of North Carolina.

We would also like to thank the following reviewers for their comments and suggestions during the preparation of this second edition: Thomas Case, Georgia Southern College; Kent Foster, Winthrop College; Patricia Green, Temple Junior College; Herbert R. Haynes, Corpus Christi State University; Timothy Heintz, Marquette University; David Russell, Western New England College; Chris Schmidt, Wartburg College; Ken Shaw, Metropolitan State College; Laurette Simmons, Loyola College of Maryland; Kar Yan Tam, University of Texas at Austin; and David Chi-Chung Yen, Miami University.

The efforts of the following members of the staff of boyd & fraser have been invaluable: Tom Walker, president; Pat Donegan, production editor; Becky Herrington, director of production; Ginny Harvey, editorial assistant; and the entire production department for all their hard work. We also express our thanks and appreciation to our copy editor, Jackie Cowlishaw, for her many helpful suggestions.

Allendale, Michigan                                              Philip J. Pratt
January 1991                                                 Joseph J. Adamski

# Introduction to Database Management

## INTRODUCTION

We begin by looking at some special needs at Marvel College.

1. **Mike (Payroll).** Mike works in the Payroll department of Marvel College. One of the crucial reports that he uses is the Departmental Earnings Report (Figure 1.1a). The two files in the payroll system that are used to support this report are a department file that contains a record for each department and a faculty master file that contains a record for each faculty member. Included in the faculty record, among other things, is the number for the department in which the faculty member works. (See Figure 1.1b on the next page for details concerning these files.)

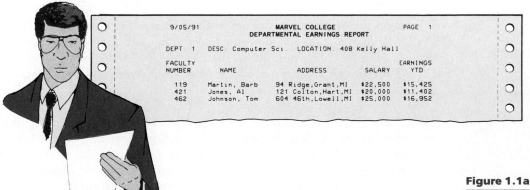

```
    9/05/91                MARVEL COLLEGE              PAGE   1
                      DEPARTMENTAL EARNINGS REPORT

    DEPT: 1   DESC: Computer Sci.  LOCATION: 408 Kelly Hall

    FACULTY                                        EARNINGS
    NUMBER      NAME           ADDRESS      SALARY     YTD

       119   Martin, Barb   94 Ridge,Grant,MI   $22,500   $15,425
       421   Jones, Al     121 Colton,Hart,MI   $20,000   $11,402
       462   Johnson, Tom  604 46th,Lowell,MI   $25,000   $16,952
```

**Figure 1.1a**

Departmental
earnings report

1

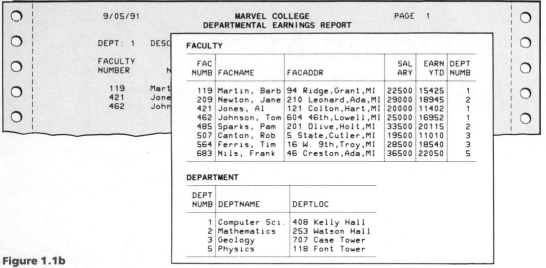

**Figure 1.1b**

Files for depart-
mental earnings
report

# Q & A

**Question:**    Using Mike's files, how can you tell which faculty members are assigned to the Mathematics department?

**Answer:**    Look up the department number of the Mathematics department in the *DEPARTMENT* file (table). Once you find the number (2), look up all the employees who have this number in the *DEPTNUMB* field (column) in the *FACULTY* file. In this case, the employees are Jane Newton and Pam Sparks.

2. **Maria (Personnel).** Maria works in the Personnel department. She oversees the medical insurance for the college. One of the reports she uses is the Insurance Plan Report shown in Figure 1.2a. This report uses the two files from the Personnel system shown in Figure 1.2b. These are an insurance policy file that gives information on the possible insurance plans available to the faculty at Marvel, and a faculty master file.

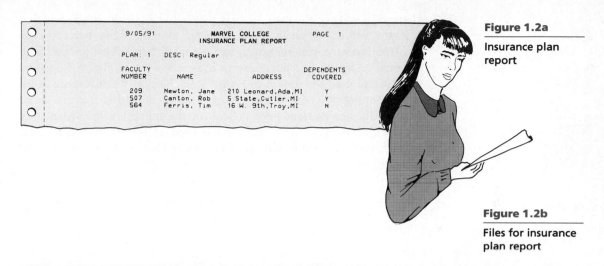

**Figure 1.2a**

Insurance plan report

**Figure 1.2b**

Files for insurance plan report

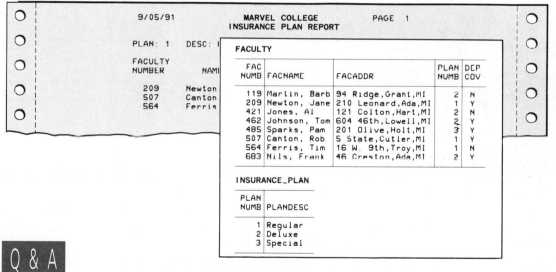

**FACULTY**

| FAC NUMB | FACNAME | FACADDR | PLAN NUMB | DEP COV |
|---|---|---|---|---|
| 119 | Martin, Barb | 94 Ridge,Grant,MI | 2 | N |
| 209 | Newton, Jane | 210 Leonard,Ada,MI | 1 | Y |
| 421 | Jones, Al | 121 Colton,Hart,MI | 2 | N |
| 462 | Johnson, Tom | 604 46th,Lowell,MI | 2 | Y |
| 485 | Sparks, Pam | 201 Olive,Holt,MI | 3 | Y |
| 507 | Canton, Rob | 5 State,Cutler,MI | 1 | Y |
| 564 | Ferris, Tim | 16 W. 9th,Troy,MI | 1 | N |
| 683 | Nils, Frank | 46 Creston,Ada,MI | 2 | Y |

**INSURANCE_PLAN**

| PLAN NUMB | PLANDESC |
|---|---|
| 1 | Regular |
| 2 | Deluxe |
| 3 | Special |

## Q & A

Question:    What are the differences between this faculty master file and the one used for the Departmental Earnings Report?

Answer:         The other contains the department number, salary and earnings year-to-date, which this one doesn't. This one contains the insurance plan number and a code called *DEPCOV*. (**Note:** If the value for this code is "Y," dependents are covered by the faculty member's policy. If it is "N," they are not.)

3. **George (Speakers' Bureau).** George works for a group on campus that is in the process of setting up a Speakers' Bureau. They want to keep information on topics on which various faculty members are prepared to speak. The main report George uses is shown in Figure 1.3a, and the files he uses are shown in Figure 1.3b. Notice the difference in his faculty master file. He doesn't need some of the fields that the other groups do, but he does need a field for the highest degree earned by the faculty member and one for the field in which the degree was earned. Neither of the other faculty master files we have encountered so far have such fields.

**Figure 1.3a**

Speaking topics report

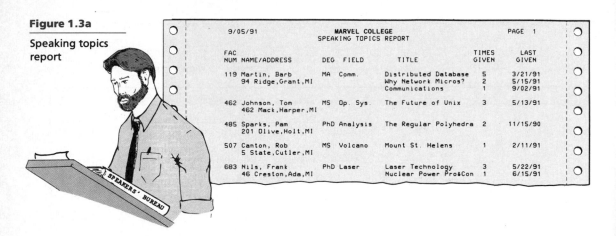

**Figure 1.3b**

Files for speaking topics report

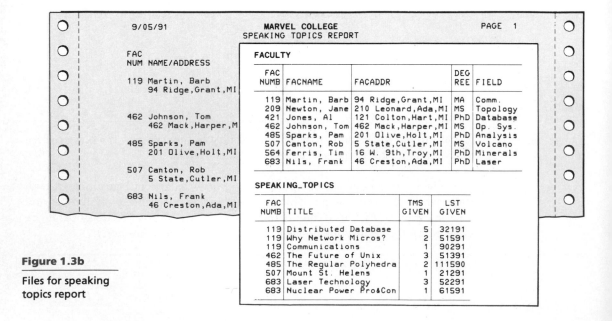

Q & A

**Question:**     Using George's files, how can you find the titles of the various talks given by Frank Nils?

**Answer:**     Look up the faculty number of Frank Nils in the *FACULTY* file. Once you find the number (683), look up all the records (rows) in the *SPEAKING_ TOPICS* file that have this number in the *FACNUMB* field. In this case, the titles are "Laser Technology" and "Nuclear Power Pro&Con."

4. **Thanh (Personnel).** Thanh is the chair of the Personnel committee at Marvel College. As part of his duties, he needs to know when each faculty member was promoted and to what rank. The main report he uses for this purpose is shown in Figure 1.4a. The files used to produce this report are shown in Figure 1.4b on the next page. Notice the differences in his faculty master file. He needs the highest degree attained, just as George does, but he doesn't need the field in which the degree was attained. He also needs the current rank of the faculty member, which none of the rest have.

| 9/05/91 | | MARVEL COLLEGE JOB HISTORY REPORT | | | | PAGE  1 |
|---|---|---|---|---|---|---|
| FAC NUM | NAME | ADDRESS | DEGREE | CURRENT RANK | RANK | DATE ATTAINED |
| 119 | Martin, Barb | 94 Ridge,Grant,MI | MA | Asst | Asst | 9/15/81 |
| 209 | Newton, Jane | 210 Leonard,Ada,MI | MS | Asso | Asst | 9/01/76 |
| | | | | | Asso | 9/13/83 |
| 421 | Jones, Al | 121 Colton,Hart,MI | PhD | Asst | Asst | 8/15/83 |
| 462 | Johnson, Tom | 604 46th,Lowell,MI | MS | Asso | Asst | 4/12/71 |
| | | | | | Asso | 9/14/81 |
| 485 | Sparks, Pam | 201 Olive,Holt,MI | PhD | Prof | Asst | 4/02/65 |
| | | | | | Asso | 9/12/74 |
| | | | | | Prof | 9/13/83 |
| 507 | Canton, Rob | 5 State,Cutler,MI | MS | Asst | Asst | 9/12/81 |
| 564 | Ferris, Tim | 16 W. 9th,Troy,MI | PhD | Asso | Asst | 5/21/76 |
| | | | | | Asso | 9/01/91 |
| 683 | Nils, Frank | 46 Creston,Ada,MI | PhD | Prof | Asst | 6/11/66 |
| | | | | | Asso | 8/02/74 |
| | | | | | Prof | 8/12/83 |

**Figure 1.4a**

Job history report

|  | 9/05/91 | | MARVEL COLLEGE<br>JOB HISTORY REPORT | | PAGE  1 |
|--|--|--|--|--|--|

FAC
NUM     NAME              AI

119 Martin, Barb    94 Ridge

209 Newton, Jane    210 Leor

421 Jones, Al       121 Colt

462 Johnson, Tom    604 46th

485 Sparks, Pam     201 Oliv

507 Canton, Rob     5 State,

564 Ferris, Tim     16 W. 91

683 Nils, Frank     46 Crest

**FACULTY**

| FAC<br>NUMB | FACNAME | FACADDR | DEG<br>REE | CURR<br>RANK |
|--|--|--|--|--|
| 119 | Martin, Barb | 94 Ridge,Grant,MI | MA | Asst |
| 209 | Newton, Jane | 210 Leonard,Ada,MI | MS | Asso |
| 421 | Jones, Al | 121 Colton,Hart,MI | PhD | Asst |
| 462 | Johnson, Tom | 604 46th,Lowell,MI | MS | Asso |
| 485 | Sparks, Pam | 201 Olive,Holt,MI | PhD | Prof |
| 507 | Canton, Rob | 5 State,Cutler,MI | MS | Asst |
| 564 | Ferris, Tim | 16 W. 9th,Troy,MI | PhD | Asso |
| 683 | Nils, Frank | 46 Creston,Ada,MI | PhD | Prof |

**JOB_HISTORY**

| FAC<br>NUME | RANK | DATEATT |
|--|--|--|
| 119 | Asst | 91581 |
| 209 | Asst | 90176 |
| 209 | Asso | 91383 |
| 421 | Asst | 81583 |
| 462 | Asst | 41271 |
| 462 | Asso | 91481 |
| 485 | Asst | 40265 |
| 485 | Asso | 91274 |
| 485 | Prof | 91383 |
| 507 | Asst | 91281 |
| 564 | Asst | 52176 |
| 564 | Asso | 90191 |
| 683 | Asst | 61166 |
| 683 | Asso | 80274 |
| 683 | Prof | 81283 |

**Figure 1.4b**

Files for job history
report

# Q & A

Question:        What problems do you notice as you look at the various reports and files?

Answer:                    First, you probably noticed the duplication. Each faculty file contained a
faculty member's number, name, and address. Thus, this information would
be stored four times for each faculty member! In fact, there may be still other
places it is stored that we are not even aware of at this point.

The common term for such duplication is **redundancy**. We say that we
have redundancy or that the data is stored redundantly. One obvious problem
with redundancy is that it wastes a lot of space. Wasted space is only the
beginning, however. Think about what happens when a faculty member
moves. The address must be changed in each place it occurs.

There's still another problem associated with redundancy. Look at the
address for Tom Johnson on the Departmental Earnings Report, then look at
his address on the Speaking Topics Report. The two addresses are different,
yet they are for the same person. When addresses are stored in several different places, such discrepancies are always possible.

There is still another problem. Consider the following.

5. **Juan (Personnel).** Juan is a programmer/analyst at Marvel College. The Personnel department asked Juan to develop a special report, grouping the full professors, the associate professors, and the assistant professors in each department. The report is to show when each faculty member was promoted to each rank. It is also to include the topics on which these professors are prepared to speak. Unfortunately, the data Juan needs is not contained in any one system. Rather it crosses systems boundaries. (See Figure 1.5.) Drawing this data together can be cumbersome to say the least.

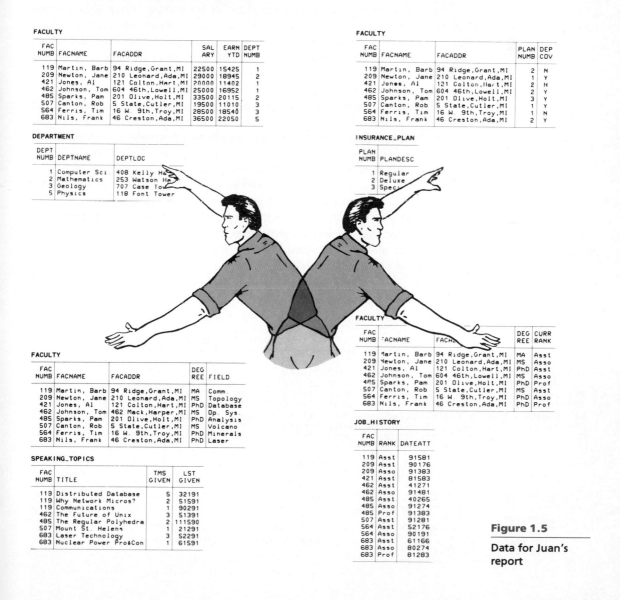

FACULTY

| FAC NUMB | FACNAME | FACADDR | SAL ARY | EARN YTD | DEPT NUMB |
|---|---|---|---|---|---|
| 119 | Martin, Barb | 94 Ridge,Grant,MI | 22500 | 15425 | 1 |
| 209 | Newton, Jane | 210 Leonard,Ada,MI | 29000 | 18945 | 2 |
| 421 | Jones, Al | 121 Colton,Hart,MI | 20000 | 11402 | 1 |
| 462 | Johnson, Tom | 604 46th,Lowell,MI | 25000 | 16952 | 1 |
| 485 | Sparks, Pam | 201 Olive,Holt,MI | 33500 | 20115 | 2 |
| 507 | Canton, Rob | 5 State,Cutler,MI | 19500 | 11010 | 3 |
| 564 | Ferris, Tim | 16 W. 9th,Troy,MI | 28500 | 18540 | 3 |
| 683 | Nils, Frank | 46 Creston,Ada,MI | 36500 | 22050 | 5 |

DEPARTMENT

| DEPT NUMB | DEPTNAME | DEPTLOC |
|---|---|---|
| 1 | Computer Sci. | 408 Kelly Ha |
| 2 | Mathematics | 253 Watson Ha |
| 3 | Geology | 707 Case To |
| 5 | Physics | 118 Font Tower |

FACULTY

| FAC NUMB | FACNAME | FACADDR | DEG REE | FIELD |
|---|---|---|---|---|
| 119 | Martin, Barb | 94 Ridge,Grant,MI | MA | Comm. |
| 209 | Newton, Jane | 210 Leonard,Ada,MI | MS | Topology |
| 421 | Jones, Al | 121 Colton,Hart,MI | PhD | Database |
| 462 | Johnson, Tom | 462 Mack,Harper,MI | MS | Op. Sys. |
| 485 | Sparks, Pam | 201 Olive,Holt,MI | PhD | Analysis |
| 507 | Canton, Rob | 5 State,Cutler,MI | MS | Volcano |
| 564 | Ferris, Tim | 16 W. 9th,Troy,MI | PhD | Minerals |
| 683 | Nils, Frank | 46 Creston,Ada,MI | PhD | Laser |

SPEAKING_TOPICS

| FAC NUMB | TITLE | TMS GIVEN | LST GIVEN |
|---|---|---|---|
| 119 | Distributed Database | 5 | 32191 |
| 119 | Why Network Micros? | 2 | 51591 |
| 119 | Communications | 1 | 90291 |
| 462 | The Future of Unix | 5 | 51391 |
| 485 | The Regular Polyhedra | 2 | 111590 |
| 507 | Mount St. Helens | 1 | 21291 |
| 683 | Laser Technology | 3 | 52291 |
| 683 | Nuclear Power ProbCon | 1 | 61591 |

FACULTY

| FAC NUMB | FACNAME | FACADDR | PLAN NUMB | DEP COV |
|---|---|---|---|---|
| 119 | Martin, Barb | 94 Ridge,Grant,MI | 2 | N |
| 209 | Newton, Jane | 210 Leonard,Ada,MI | 1 | Y |
| 421 | Jones, Al | 121 Colton,Hart,MI | 2 | N |
| 462 | Johnson, Tom | 604 46th,Lowell,MI | 2 | Y |
| 485 | Sparks, Pam | 201 Olive,Holt,MI | 3 | Y |
| 507 | Canton, Rob | 5 State,Cutler,MI | 1 | Y |
| 564 | Ferris, Tim | 16 W. 9th,Troy,MI | 1 | N |
| 683 | Nils, Frank | 46 Creston,Ada,MI | 2 | Y |

INSURANCE_PLAN

| PLAN NUMB | PLANDESC |
|---|---|
| 1 | Regular |
| 2 | Deluxe |
| 3 | Spec |

FACULTY

| FAC NUMB | FACNAME | FACA | DEG REE | CURR RANK |
|---|---|---|---|---|
| 119 | Martin, Barb | 94 Ridge,Grant,MI | MA | Asst |
| 209 | Newton, Jane | 210 Leonard,Ada,MI | MS | Asso |
| 421 | Jones, Al | 121 Colton,Hart,MI | PhD | Asst |
| 462 | Johnson, Tom | 604 46th,Lowell,MI | MS | Asso |
| 485 | Sparks, Pam | 201 Olive,Holt,MI | PhD | Prof |
| 507 | Canton, Rob | 5 State,Cutler,MI | MS | Asst |
| 564 | Ferris, Tim | 16 W. 9th,Troy,MI | PhD | Asso |
| 683 | Nils, Frank | 46 Creston,Ada,MI | PhD | Prof |

JOB_HISTORY

| FAC NUMB | RANK | DATEATT |
|---|---|---|
| 119 | Asst | 91581 |
| 209 | Asst | 90176 |
| 209 | Asso | 91383 |
| 421 | Asst | 81583 |
| 462 | Asst | 41271 |
| 462 | Asso | 91481 |
| 485 | Asst | 40265 |
| 485 | Asso | 91274 |
| 485 | Prof | 91383 |
| 507 | Asst | 91281 |
| 564 | Asst | 52176 |
| 564 | Asso | 90191 |
| 683 | Asst | 61166 |
| 683 | Asso | 80274 |
| 683 | Prof | 81283 |

**Figure 1.5**

Data for Juan's report

A solution is to build a single pool of data, rather than separate collections of files. Such a pool is a **database**. Basically the idea of a database is pretty simple. Instead of holding information about a single **entity**, such as employees, customers, parts, or whatever, the way a normal file does, a database holds information about many different *types* of entities. In a single database, for example, we could have information about sales reps, customers, orders, parts, and so on. In the database for the users at Marvel College, we would have information about such entities as faculty members, departments, insurance plans, job history information, and speaking topics.

There is another special characteristic of databases: They also contain information about *relationships*. A database containing information about sales reps and customers could also contain information that indicates which sales rep represents which customer. You could then start with a customer and find the sales rep who represents this customer, or you could start with a sales rep and find all of the customers he or she represents.

In a database for the college, we would have information not only about departments and faculty members, but also about which faculty member works in which department. We would also have information relating insurance plans and faculty members as well as information relating faculty members to their job history records and speaking topics.

In this database, each faculty member would be stored only once, thus eliminating the problems associated with redundancy. (See Figure 1.6.) The Departmental Earnings Report would use faculty members and departments and the relationship between them. (See Figure 1.7.) The Insurance Plan Report, on the other hand, would use faculty members and insurance plans. (See Figure 1.8 on page 10.)

**Figure 1.6**

Marvel College
database

FACULTY

| FAC NUMB | FACNAME | FACADDR | SAL ARY | EARN YTD | DEPT NUMB | DEG REE | FIELD | CURR RANK | PLAN NUMB | DEP COV |
|---|---|---|---|---|---|---|---|---|---|---|
| 119 | Martin, Barb | 94 Ridge,Grant,MI | 22500 | 15425 | 1 | MA | Comm. | Asst | 2 | N |
| 209 | Newton, Jane | 210 Leonard,Ada,MI | 29000 | 18945 | 2 | MS | Topology | Asso | 1 | Y |
| 421 | Jones, Al | 121 Colton,Hart,MI | 20000 | 11402 | 1 | PhD | Database | Asst | 2 | N |
| 462 | Johnson, Tom | 604 46th,Lowell,MI | 25000 | 16952 | 1 | MS | Op. Sys. | Asso | 2 | Y |
| 485 | Sparks, Pam | 201 Olive,Holt,MI | 33500 | 20115 | 2 | PhD | Analysis | Prof | 3 | Y |
| 507 | Canton, Rob | 5 State,Cutler,MI | 19500 | 11010 | 3 | MS | Volcano | Asst | 1 | Y |
| 564 | Ferris, Tim | 16 W. 9th,Troy,MI | 28500 | 18540 | 3 | PhD | Minerals | Asso | 1 | N |
| 683 | Nils, Frank | 46 Creston,Ada,MI | 36500 | 22050 | 5 | PhD | Laser | Prof | 2 | Y |

DEPARTMENT

| DEPT NUMB | DEPTNAME | DEPTLOC |
|---|---|---|
| 1 | Computer Sci. | 408 Kelly Hall |
| 2 | Mathematics | 253 Watson Hall |
| 3 | Geology | 707 Case Tower |
| 5 | Physics | 118 Font Tower |

INSURANCE_PLAN

| PLAN NUMB | PLANDESC |
|---|---|
| 1 | Regular |
| 2 | Deluxe |
| 3 | Special |

**SPEAKING_TOPICS**

| FAC NUMB | TITLE | TMS GIVEN | LST GIVEN |
|---|---|---|---|
| 119 | Distributed Database | 5 | 32191 |
| 119 | Why Network Micros? | 2 | 51591 |
| 119 | Communications | 1 | 90291 |
| 462 | The Future of Unix | 3 | 51391 |
| 485 | The Regular Polyhedra | 2 | 111590 |
| 507 | Mount St. Helens | 1 | 21291 |
| 683 | Laser Technology | 3 | 52291 |
| 683 | Nuclear Power Pro&Con | 1 | 61591 |

**JOB_HISTORY**

| FAC NUMB | RANK | DATEATT |
|---|---|---|
| 119 | Asst | 91581 |
| 209 | Asst | 90176 |
| 209 | Asso | 91383 |
| 421 | Asst | 81583 |
| 462 | Asst | 41271 |
| 462 | Asso | 91481 |
| 485 | Asst | 40265 |
| 485 | Asso | 91274 |

**Figure 1.6**

(continued)

**Figure 1.7**

Portion of database used to produce departmental earnings report

**FACULTY**

| FAC NUMB | FACNAME | FACADDR | SAL ARY | EARN YTD | DEPT NUMB |
|---|---|---|---|---|---|
| 119 | Martin, Barb | 94 Ridge,Grant,MI | 22500 | 15425 | 1 |
| 209 | Newton, Jane | 210 Leonard,Ada,MI | 29000 | 18945 | 2 |
| 421 | Jones, Al | 121 Colton,Hart,MI | 20000 | 11402 | 1 |
| 462 | Johnson, Tom | 604 46th,Lowell,MI | 25000 | 16952 | 1 |
| 485 | Sparks, Pam | 201 Olive,Holt,MI | 33500 | 20115 | 2 |
| 507 | Canton, Rob | 5 State,Cutler,MI | 19500 | 11010 | 3 |
| 564 | Ferris, Tim | 16 W. 9th,Troy,MI | 28500 | 18540 | 3 |
| 683 | Nils, Frank | 46 Creston,Ada,MI | 36500 | 22050 | 5 |

| FIELD | CURR RANK | PLAN NUMB | DEP COV |
|---|---|---|---|
| Comm. | Asst | 2 | N |
| Topology | Asso | 1 | Y |
| Database | Asst | 2 | N |
| Op. Sys. | Asso | 2 | Y |
| Analysis | Prof | 3 | Y |
| Volcano | Asst | 1 | Y |
| Minerals | Asso | 1 | N |
| Laser | Prof | 2 | Y |

**DEPARTMENT**

| DEPT NUMB | DEPTNAME | DEPTLOC |
|---|---|---|
| 1 | Computer Sci. | 408 Kelly Hall |
| 2 | Mathematics | 253 Watson Hall |
| 3 | Geology | 707 Case Tower |
| 5 | Physics | 118 Font Tower |

**INSURANCE_PLAN**

| PLAN NUMB | PLANDESC |
|---|---|
| 1 | Regular |
| 2 | Deluxe |
| 3 | Special |

**SPEAKING_TOPICS**

| FAC NUMB | TITLE | TMS GIVEN | LST GIVEN |
|---|---|---|---|
| 119 | Distributed Database | 5 | 32191 |
| 119 | Why Network Micros? | 2 | 51591 |
| 119 | Communications | 1 | 90291 |
| 462 | The Future of Unix | 3 | 51391 |
| 485 | The Regular Polyhedra | 2 | 111590 |
| 507 | Mount St. Helens | 1 | 21291 |
| 683 | Laser Technology | 3 | 52291 |
| 683 | Nuclear Power Pro&Con | 1 | 61591 |

**JOB_HISTORY**

| FAC NUMB | RANK | DATEATT |
|---|---|---|
| 119 | Asst | 91581 |
| 209 | Asst | 90176 |
| 209 | Asso | 91383 |
| 421 | Asst | 81583 |
| 462 | Asst | 41271 |
| 462 | Asso | 91481 |
| 485 | Asst | 40265 |
| 485 | Asso | 91274 |

FACULTY

| FAC NUMB | FACNAME | FACADDR | SAL ARY | EARN YTD | DEPT NUMB | DEG REE | FIELD | CURR RANK | PLAN NUMB | DEP COV |
|---|---|---|---|---|---|---|---|---|---|---|
| 119 | Martin, Barb | 94 Ridge,Grant,MI | | | | | | | 2 | N |
| 209 | Newton, Jane | 210 Leonard,Ada,MI | 2500 | 15425 | 1 | MA | Comm. | Asst | 1 | Y |
| 421 | Jones, Al | 121 Colton,Hart,MI | 3000 | 18945 | 2 | MS | Topology | Asso | 2 | N |
| 462 | Johnson, Tom | 604 46th,Lowell,MI | 0000 | 11402 | 1 | PhD | Database | Asst | 2 | Y |
| 485 | Sparks, Pam | 201 Olive,Holt,MI | 5000 | 16952 | 1 | MS | Op. Sys. | Asso | 3 | Y |
| 507 | Canton, Rob | 5 State,Cutler,MI | 3500 | 20115 | 2 | PhD | Analysis | Prof | 1 | Y |
| 564 | Ferris, Tim | 16 W. 9th,Troy,MI | 9500 | 11010 | 3 | MS | Volcano | Asst | 1 | N |
| 683 | Nils, Frank | 46 Creston,Ada,MI | 9500 | 18540 | 3 | PhD | Minerals | Asso | 2 | Y |
| | | | 6500 | 22050 | 5 | PhD | Laser | Prof | | |

DEPARTMENT

| DEPT NUMB | DEPTNAME | DEPTLOC |
|---|---|---|
| 1 | Computer Sci. | 408 Kelly Hall |
| 2 | Mathematics | 253 Watson Hall |
| 3 | Geology | 707 Case Tower |
| 5 | Physics | 118 Font Tower |

INSURANCE_PLAN

| PLAN NUMB | PLANDESC |
|---|---|
| 1 | Regular |
| 2 | Deluxe |
| 3 | Special |

SPEAKING_TOPICS

| FAC NUMB | TITLE | TMS GIVEN | LST GIVEN |
|---|---|---|---|
| 119 | Distributed Database | 5 | 32191 |
| 119 | Why Network Micros? | 2 | 51591 |
| 119 | Communications | 1 | 90291 |
| 462 | The Future of Unix | 3 | 51391 |
| 485 | The Regular Polyhedra | 2 | 111590 |
| 507 | Mount St. Helens | 1 | 21291 |
| 683 | Laser Technology | 3 | 52291 |
| 683 | Nuclear Power Pro&Con | 1 | 61591 |

JOB_HISTORY

| FAC NUMB | RANK | DATEATT |
|---|---|---|
| 119 | Asst | 91581 |
| 209 | Asst | 90176 |
| 209 | Asso | 91383 |
| 421 | Asst | 81583 |
| 462 | Asst | 41271 |
| 462 | Asso | 91481 |
| 485 | Asst | 40265 |
| 485 | Asso | 91274 |

**Figure 1.8**

Portion of database used to produce insurance plan report

In addition, the special report Juan was asked to develop, which included departments, faculty members, job history information, and speaking topics, would be much easier using this approach. All the information he needs is in the database.

Question:            Where is the information Juan needs?

Answer:                  The basic information about each faculty member, including the faculty
member's current rank is in the *FACULTY* table. The names of the departments are contained in the *DEPARTMENT* table. The information concerning
when each faculty member was promoted to each rank is contained in the
*JOB_HISTORY* table. The information on the topics on which each faculty
member is prepared to speak is in the *SPEAKING_TOPICS* table.

There is a problem maintaining a database, however. The actual structure
of a database can be quite complex. To efficiently manage a database, you
typically must utilize such strategies as **hashing, linked lists, inverted files, B-
tree indexes**, and so on. (**Note:** You do not need to be familiar with these terms
for the purposes of this discussion. If you are interested in the details of these
strategies, see the appendix.)

These strategies certainly don't present any insurmountable problems.
They do, however, make every program more complicated than if the program were accessing simple files. Also, if even a single program functions
incorrectly, it can potentially destroy the whole structure of the database for
everyone. Fortunately, there is a tool, called a **database management system**,
or simply a **DBMS**, that does all this work.

This textbook deals with the topic of database management. We will
examine a variety of these database management systems. We will look at the
various categories, or models, into which these systems are grouped. We will
study the process of database design (i.e., how a database is structured to
meet the needs of a given organization). We will look at the people involved
in database management. We will also look at what is happening in the world
of database management today, and what is likely to happen tomorrow. In
this chapter, we begin our study of this very important topic.

First, we look at some background material and terminology concerning
database management. Next we will study the history of the topic. Finally we
will examine some of the advantages and disadvantages of using database
management systems.

## BACKGROUND

This section introduces some crucial background terminology and ideas. You are probably familiar with some of the terms from previous work you have done with files.

### Entities, Attributes, and Relationships

Among the most fundamental terms are entity, attribute, and relationship. An **entity** is really just like a noun; it is a person, place, or thing. The entities of interest to the group from Marvel College are faculty members, departments, insurance plans, job history records, and speaking topics. We will soon meet another organization, called Premiere Products, which is interested in entities like sales reps, customers, orders, and parts.

An **attribute** is a property of an entity. The term is used here exactly as it is used in everyday English. You might speak of the attributes of a person, such as eye color and height. At Marvel College, on the other hand, for the entity called faculty member, the attributes of interest are faculty number, name, address, and so on. While these properties may not be as physical as eye color or height, they are indeed properties of faculty members.

Figure 1.9 shows two entities, department and faculty. It also shows a number of attributes. The department entity has three attributes: department number, description, and location. The faculty entity has five attributes: faculty number, name, address, salary, and earnings year-to-date.

**Figure 1.9**

Entities and attributes

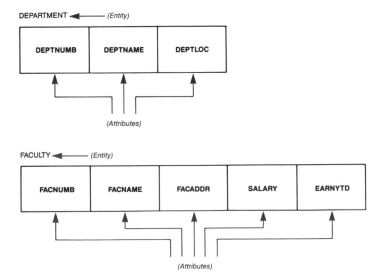

When we speak of **relationship**, we really mean an association between entities. There is a relationship between departments and faculty members, for example. A department is related to all of the faculty members who work in the department, and a faculty member is related to the department in which he or she works.

Figure 1.10 shows the relationship between the department and faculty entities. The arrow represents the relationship. In this case, it is a **one-to-many** relationship; i.e., one department is associated with many faculty members, but each faculty member is associated with only one department. (In this type of relationship, "many" is used in a slightly different manner than in everyday English. It would actually be better to state that a department is associated with *any number* of faculty members. This number can even be zero! Certainly this is not the normal use of the word "many.")

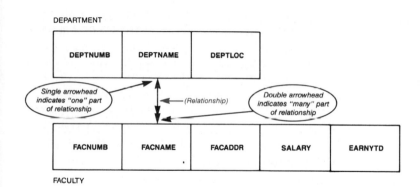

**Figure 1.10**

One-to-many
relationship

In the type of drawing shown in the figure, a single arrowhead is used to indicate the "one" part of the relationship and a double arrowhead is used to indicate the "many" part. In another common type of drawing used in the database environment, the same type of relationship is indicated by having only a single arrowhead indicating the "many" part and no arrowhead for the "one" part. This type of diagram is shown in Figure 1.11 on the next page and represents the style that will be encountered most often in this text. Fortunately, when examining either type of diagram, it is usually clear which style has been used.

**Figure 1.11**

One-to-many
relationship

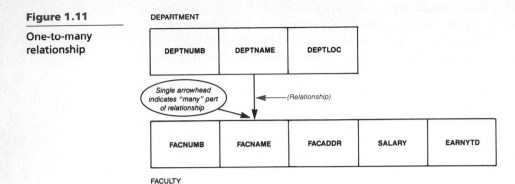

## Files, Records, and Fields

In a file-processing environment, the critical terms are field, record, and file. The smallest amount of data that can be stored is the bit. Bits are grouped into bytes (or characters). Collections of characters form a **field**. Collections of fields form a **record**. Collections of occurrences of a specific type of record form a **file**.

For example, consider the data needed by Mike for faculty members as shown in Figure 1.1. The fields shown are *FACNUMB, FACNAME, FACADDR, SALARY, EARNYTD,* and *DEPTNUMB*. Collectively, all these fields form a record (technically, a record type). The collection of all the occurrences of this record type (one for each faculty member) forms a file. Both the file and the record type would be given names, of course. We might choose to call the file *EMPFILE* and the record type *EMPREC*, for example.

How are entities, attributes, and relationships handled in a file-processing environment? As you might expect, for each entity, we will have a separate file. For each attribute of that entity in which we are interested, we will have a field. Relationships will be implemented by having fields within one file identify records in another.

Consider, for example, Mike's requirements. There were two entities: departments and faculty members. The attributes of interest for departments were department number, description, and location. The attributes of interest for faculty members were employee number, name, address, salary, and year-to-date earnings. We thus have two files: a department file and a faculty file. The attributes become the fields in these records. In addition, there was a relationship between departments and faculty members in which each department was related to all faculty members who worked in the department, and each faculty member was related to the unique department in which he or she worked (the same relationship shown pictorially in Figures 1.10 and 1.11). This relationship is accomplished by placing the department number, which is the key to the department file, as one of the fields in the faculty file record.

Given a specific faculty member, the value in this field indicates the number of the department in which the faculty member works. If we want further information about the department, using this value as the key to the department file enables us to find any information about the department we desire. On the other hand, if we wish to find all the faculty members who work in a given department, say department 3, we search through the faculty member file looking for any faculty records that have the number 3 in the department number field.

## Databases

In a typical file-processing environment, each user area, such as payroll, personnel, and the speakers' bureau, has its own collection of files and programs that access these files. (See Figure 1.12.) This type of environment leads to the problems mentioned in the discussion of Marvel College. Since there is usually overlap of data between user areas, there is **redundancy** in the system. The address of a faculty member can occur in many places, for example. While this is certainly wasteful of space, the problems it causes for updates are potentially much more serious. In addition, trying to produce reports or respond to queries that span user areas can be extremely difficult. These problems lead to the idea of a pool of data, or database, rather than separate collections of individual files.

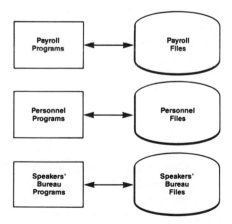

**Figure 1.12**

Classical file approach

Is a database the next step in the progression? (Fields -> records -> files -> database?) Is a database merely a collection of files? Although there is some justification for viewing a database in this way, it is insufficient. Some mention must be made of relationships among the records in these files.

*Definition:* A **database** is a structure that can house information about multiple types of entities, as well as relationships among the entities.

Note that this definition doesn't indicate that all the entities must be housed within the same actual physical file on disk. While a database may be contained in a single file, it can also be stored within a number of different files, one for each entity, for example. The crucial point is that there must be some way of implementing relationships among the records.

Different definitions of a database exist. Some definitions include the word **self-describing**. This means a database contains within it a *description of itself*. This would be analogous to a file containing its record description as part of the contents of the file. It makes the database a logically complete structure (i.e., it does not rely on a separate structure for information about itself). Every DBMS discussed in this text has this property. Another word often used is **integrated**. This simply means that the database contains the relationships mentioned in our definition. The final word that is sometimes included is **shared**, which means that more than one user has access to the data. After all, if a database is not shared, its full potential value will not be available to the organization.

We could eliminate the problems associated with a straight file-processing environment by moving to a database environment. One way to do this would be to have a single database that users from each area would access, as shown in Figure 1.13. In this database, an individual faculty member would be found only once. This faculty member would somehow be related to the department in which he or she worked, the insurance plan covering that faculty member, that faculty member's job history information, and the lectures that faculty member would be willing to give. With this structure, all the programmers at Marvel would be able to complete their tasks.

**Figure 1.13**

Database (user-maintained)

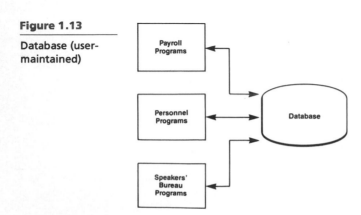

Managing a database is a complicated task, however. The underlying structure is inherently more involved than a simple file. Whether we use hashing, linked lists, inverted files, B-tree indexes, or anything else to accomplish the task, we've added complexity to the structure. If we are to manage this structure ourselves, each program in the system will be more complex than a comparable program in a corresponding file-processing environment. In addition, a failure on the part of any of these programs could actually destroy the structure of the database.

### Database Management Systems

Fortunately, software packages called **database management systems** can do the job of manipulating actual databases for us. A database management system, or **DBMS**, at its simplest is a software product through which users interact with a database. The actual manipulation of the underlying database structures is handled by the DBMS. (See Figure 1.14.) Using a DBMS, we can request the system to find department 3, for example, and the system will either locate the desired department or tell us that no such department exists. All the work in accomplishing this task is done by the system. We don't have to worry about hashing, indexing, or any other mechanisms used to accomplish the task. We could then ask for the faculty members in the department and again the system would perform all the work of locating these faculty members. Likewise, when we store a new faculty member in the database, the DBMS performs all the tasks necessary to ensure that the faculty member is, in fact, connected to the appropriate department and insurance plan.

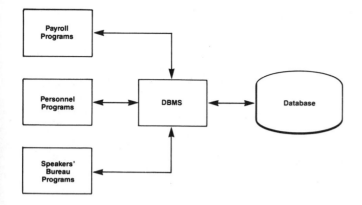

**Figure 1.14**

Database (using a database management system)

In addition to manipulating a database for us, there are several things a good DBMS can do. One important feature of a DBMS is that it allows each user to each have his or her own **view** of the database. Figure 1.15, for example, shows the view of the database that would be used in producing the Departmental Earnings Report. Figure 1.15a shows the portion of the database included in this view. Figure 1.15b shows the view as it would be perceived by the user. Figure 1.16a on page 20 shows the view that would be used in producing the Speakers' Bureau Report.

**Figure 1.15a**

View for departmental earnings report as a portion of the database

FACULTY

| FAC NUMB | FACNAME | FACADDR | SAL ARY | EARN YTD | DEPT NUMB |
|----------|---------|---------|---------|----------|-----------|
| 119 | Martin, Barb | 94 Ridge,Grant,MI | 22500 | 15425 | 1 |
| 209 | Newton, Jane | 210 Leonard,Ada,MI | 29000 | 18945 | 2 |
| 421 | Jones, Al | 121 Colton,Hart,MI | 20000 | 11402 | 1 |
| 462 | Johnson, Tom | 604 46th,Lowell,MI | 25000 | 16952 | 1 |
| 485 | Sparks, Pam | 201 Olive,Holt,MI | 33500 | 20115 | 2 |
| 507 | Canton, Rob | 5 State,Cutler,MI | 19500 | 11010 | 3 |
| 564 | Ferris, Tim | 16 W. 9th,Troy,MI | 28500 | 18540 | 3 |
| 683 | Nils, Frank | 46 Creston,Ada,MI | 36500 | 22050 | 5 |

| FIELD | CURR RANK | PLAN NUMB | DEP COV |
|-------|-----------|-----------|---------|
| Comm. | Asst | 2 | N |
| Topology | Asso | 1 | Y |
| Database | Asst | 2 | N |
| Op. Sys. | Asso | 2 | Y |
| Analysis | Prof | 3 | Y |
| Volcano | Asst | 1 | Y |
| Minerals | Asso | 1 | N |
| Laser | Prof | 2 | Y |

DEPARTMENT

| DEPT NUMB | DEPTNAME | DEPTLOC |
|-----------|----------|---------|
| 1 | Computer Sci. | 408 Kelly Hall |
| 2 | Mathematics | 253 Watson Hall |
| 3 | Geology | 707 Case Tower |
| 5 | Physics | 118 Font Tower |

INSURANCE_PLAN

| PLAN NUMB | PLANDESC |
|-----------|----------|
| 1 | Regular |
| 2 | Deluxe |
| 3 | Special |

SPEAKING_TOPICS

| FAC NUMB | TITLE | TMS GIVEN | LST GIVEN |
|----------|-------|-----------|-----------|
| 119 | Distributed Database | 5 | 32191 |
| 119 | Why Network Micros? | 2 | 51591 |
| 119 | Communications | 1 | 90291 |
| 462 | The Future of Unix | 3 | 51391 |
| 485 | The Regular Polyhedra | 2 | 111590 |
| 507 | Mount St. Helens | 1 | 21291 |
| 683 | Laser Technology | 3 | 52291 |
| 683 | Nuclear Power Pro&Con | 1 | 61591 |

JOB_HISTORY

| FAC NUMB | RANK | DATEATT |
|----------|------|---------|
| 119 | Asst | 91581 |
| 209 | Asst | 90176 |
| 209 | Asso | 91383 |
| 421 | Asst | 81583 |
| 462 | Asst | 41271 |
| 462 | Asso | 91481 |
| 485 | Asst | 40265 |
| 485 | Asso | 91274 |

FACULTY

| FAC NUMB | FACNAME | FACADDR | SAL ARY | EARN YTD | DEPT NUMB |
|---|---|---|---|---|---|
| 119 | Martin, Barb | 94 Ridge,Grant,MI | 22500 | 15425 | 1 |
| 209 | Newton, Jane | 210 Leonard,Ada,MI | 29000 | 18945 | 2 |
| 421 | Jones, Al | 121 Colton,Hart,MI | 20000 | 11402 | 1 |
| 462 | Johnson, Tom | 604 46th,Lowell,MI | 25000 | 16952 | 1 |
| 485 | Sparks, Pam | 201 Olive,Holt,MI | 33500 | 20115 | 2 |
| 507 | Canton, Rob | 5 State,Cutler,MI | 19500 | 11010 | 3 |
| 564 | Ferris, Tim | 16 W. 9th,Troy,MI | 28500 | 18540 | 3 |
| 683 | Nils, Frank | 46 Creston,Ada,MI | 36500 | 22050 | 5 |

DEPARTMENT

| DEPTNUMB | DEPTNAME | DEPTLOC |
|---|---|---|
| 1 | Computer Sci. | 408 Kelly Hall |
| 2 | Mathematics | 253 Watson Hall |
| 3 | Geology | 707 Case Tower |
| 5 | Physics | 118 Font Tower |

**Figure 1.15b**

View for departmental earnings report as perceived by the user

(There is another name often used for views. Sometimes they are called **subschemas**. In the systems that use the term subschema, the overall description of the entire database is called a **schema**, as in *schema*tic diagram. The term subschema then refers to an individual user's *sub*set of the *schema*.)

Views have several benefits. Since a view typically has a much simpler structure than the entire database, things seem simpler to the user of the view. Consider the view for the Departmental Earnings Report as shown in Figure 1.15, for example. Certainly the view as perceived by the user (see Figure 1.15b) is simpler than the entire database (see Figure 1.15a).

Another important benefit to views concerns security. If a given user is not to be allowed to access faculty salaries, we simply don't include *SALARY* in that user's view. As far as a user of the view for the Speakers' Bureau (see Figure 1.16b on page 21) is concerned, for example, there isn't even a field called *SALARY* in the database.

FACULTY

| FAC NUMB | FACNAME | FACADDR | SALARY | EARN YTD | DEPT NUMB | DEGREE | FIELD | CURR RANK | PLAN NUMB | DEP COV |
|---|---|---|---|---|---|---|---|---|---|---|
| | | | | | | MA | Comm. | | | |
| 119 | Martin, Barb | 94 Ridge,Grant,MI | :500 | 15425 | 1 | MS | Topology | Asst | 2 | N |
| 209 | Newton, Jane | 210 Leonard,Ada,MI | )000 | 18945 | 2 | PhD | Database | Asso | 1 | Y |
| 421 | Jones, Al | 121 Colton,Hart,MI | :000 | 11402 | 1 | MS | Op. Sys. | Asst | 2 | N |
| 462 | Johnson, Tom | 604 46th,Lowell,MI | :000 | 16952 | 1 | PhD | Analysis | Asso | 2 | Y |
| 485 | Sparks, Pam | 201 Olive,Holt,MI | :500 | 20115 | 2 | MS | Volcano | Prof | 3 | Y |
| 507 | Canton, Rob | 5 State,Cutler,MI | )500 | 11010 | 3 | PhD | Minerals | Asst | 1 | Y |
| 564 | Ferris, Tim | 16 W. 9th,Troy,MI | )500 | 18540 | 3 | PhD | Laser | Asso | 1 | N |
| 683 | Nils, Frank | 46 Creston,Ada,MI | )500 | 22050 | 5 | | | Prof | 2 | Y |

DEPARTMENT

| DEPT NUMB | DEPTNAME | DEPTLOC |
|---|---|---|
| 1 | Computer Sci. | 408 Kelly Hall |
| 2 | Mathematics | 253 Watson Hall |
| 3 | Geology | 707 Case Tower |
| 5 | Physics | 118 Font Tower |

INSURANCE_PLAN

| PLAN NUMB | PLANDESC |
|---|---|
| 1 | Regular |
| 2 | Deluxe |
| 3 | Special |

SPEAKING_TOPICS

| FAC NUMB | TITLE | TMS GIVEN | LST GIVEN |
|---|---|---|---|
| 119 | Distributed Database | 5 | 32191 |
| 119 | Why Network Micros? | 2 | 51591 |
| 119 | Communications | 1 | 90291 |
| 462 | The Future of Unix | 3 | 51391 |
| 485 | The Regular Polyhedra | 2 | 111590 |
| 507 | Mount St. Helens | 1 | 21291 |
| 683 | Laser Technology | 3 | 52291 |
| 683 | Nuclear Power Pro&Con | 1 | 61591 |

JOB_HISTORY

| FAC NUMB | RANK | DATEATT |
|---|---|---|
| 119 | Asst | 91581 |
| 209 | Asst | 90176 |
| 209 | Asso | 91383 |
| 421 | Asst | 81583 |
| 462 | Asst | 41271 |
| 462 | Asso | 91481 |
| 485 | Asst | 40265 |
| 485 | Asso | 91274 |
| • | • | • |

**Figure 1.16a**

View for speaking topics report as a portion of the database

A final benefit concerns changes to the structure of a database. Occasionally, it's necessary to change the overall structure of the database, either because of a change in requirements or perhaps to make the system run more efficiently. Provided we didn't do something that would invalidate a given user's view, such as remove one of the fields the user needs to access, we don't need to change the user's programs at all.

What do we do, however, about users who are allowed to *see* faculty members' salaries but not change them? If we don't include salary in a user's view, the user couldn't even see a salary. Yet, if you do include it, the user would be able to make changes to faculty salaries. This is where another nice feature of a DBMS is helpful. Most DBMS's allow an additional level of protection. Even though the salary field is included in a given view, a user accessing the database via this view can be forced to furnish a certain password to even see the salary, and perhaps a different password to be able to both see the salary and change it.

**FACULTY**

| FAC NUMB | FACNAME | FACADDR | DEGREE | FIELD |
|---|---|---|---|---|
| 119 | Martin, Barb | 94 Ridge,Grant,MI | MA | Comm. |
| 209 | Newton, Jane | 210 Leonard,Ada,MI | MS | Topology |
| 421 | Jones, Al | 121 Colton,Hart,MI | PhD | Database |
| 462 | Johnson, Tom | 462 Mack,Harper,MI | MS | Op. Sys. |
| 485 | Sparks, Pam | 201 Olive,Holt,MI | PhD | Analysis |
| 507 | Canton, Rob | 5 State,Cutler,MI | MS | Volcano |
| 564 | Ferris, Tim | 16 W. 9th,Troy,MI | PhD | Minerals |
| 683 | Nils, Frank | 46 Creston,Ada,MI | PhD | Laser |

**SPEAKING_TOPICS**

| FACNUMB | TITLE | TMSGIVEN | LSTGIVEN |
|---|---|---|---|
| 119 | Distributed Database | 5 | 32191 |
| 119 | Why Network Micros? | 2 | 51591 |
| 119 | Communications | 1 | 90291 |
| 462 | The Future of Unix | 3 | 51391 |
| 485 | The Regular Polyhedra | 2 | 111590 |
| 507 | Mount St. Helens | 1 | 21291 |
| 683 | Laser Technology | 3 | 52291 |
| 683 | Nuclear Power Pro&Con | 1 | 61591 |

**Figure 1.16b**

View for speaking topics report as perceived by the user

With a DBMS offering such a feature, you can also specify what are termed **integrity constraints**. You can say that a given field must contain only numeric data, or that another field must be in the range 100 to 500. You can specify that the department for a given faculty member must exist in order for the faculty member to be stored in the database. You could prevent deletions of departments that contain any faculty members. The DBMS will then enforce these things.

We have just begun to touch on the features of a complete DBMS. We will discuss these and other features in detail in chapter 2 and will encounter such features throughout the remainder of the text.

## Data Models

Database management systems are characterized by the model of data they follow. A **data model** has two components: structure and operations. The **structure** refers to the way the system structures data or, at least, the way the users of the DBMS feel the data is structured. The **operations** are the facilities given to the users of the DBMS to manipulate data within the database. What is crucial is the way things *feel* to the user. It doesn't matter how the designers of the DBMS choose to implement these facilities behind the scenes.

There are three models, or categories, for the vast majority of DBMS's: the relational model, the network model, and the hierarchical model. These models will be investigated in detail in later chapters of the text. At this point, we just wish to give a brief introduction to them and to the sample databases we'll use throughout the text. Although we need to touch on some of the terminology at this point to present the ideas of the models, don't be overly concerned with it. It will all be covered in detail later.

**Relational Model.**   A **relational model** database is perceived by the user as being just a collection of tables. Formally, these **tables** are called **relations**, and this is where the relational model gets its name. Relationships are implemented through common columns in two or more tables. Consider the relational database for Marvel College in Figure 1.17. In this database, we have a table for each entity: faculty members, departments, insurance plans, speaking topics, and job history records. If you examine the department and faculty tables, you will see they both contain a *DEPTNUMB* column. This column allows us to relate a department to the faculty members in the department.

**Figure 1.17**

Marvel College
relational database
structure

FACULTY

| FAC NUMB | FACNAME | FACADDR | SAL ARY | EARN YTD | DEPT NUMB | DEG REE | FIELD | CURR RANK | PLAN NUMB | DEP COV |
|---|---|---|---|---|---|---|---|---|---|---|
| | | | | | | | | | | |

DEPARTMENT

| DEPT NUMB | DEPTNAME | DEPTLOC |
|---|---|---|
| | | |

INSURANCE_PLAN

| PLAN NUMB | PLANDESC |
|---|---|
| | |

SPEAKING_TOPICS

| FAC NUMB | TITLE | TMS GIVEN | LST GIVEN |
|---|---|---|---|
| | | | |

JOB_HISTORY

| FAC NUMB | RANK | DATEATT |
|---|---|---|
| | | |

There are many ways of manipulating a relational database. These will be discussed in detail in chapter 3. One of the most prevalent of these is a language called **SQL (Structured Query Language)** which was developed by IBM. The basic form of an SQL command is simply SELECT ... FROM ... WHERE .... We list the columns we wish to see printed after the word SELECT. After the word FROM, we list all tables that contain these columns. Finally, we list any restrictions to be applied after the word WHERE. For example, if we wish to print the number, name, and address of all faculty members whose salary is over $25,000, we would type

```
SELECT FACNUMB, FACNAME, FACADDR
    FROM FACULTY
    WHERE SALARY > 25000
```

and the computer would respond with

```
FACNUMB  FACNAME        FACADDR
    209  Newton, Jane   210 Leonard,Ada,MI
    485  Sparks, Pam    201 Olive,Holt,MI
    564  Ferris, Tim    16 W. 9th,Troy,MI
    683  Nils, Frank    46 Creston,Ada,MI
```

**Network Model.** A **network model** database is perceived by the user as a collection of record types and relationships between these record types. Such a structure is called a **network**, and it's from this that the model takes its name. In contrast to the relational model, in which relationships were *implicit* (being derived from matching columns in the tables), in the network model the relationships are *explicit* (presented as part of the structure itself). Consider the database in Figure 1.18. The rectangles represent the record types in the database. There is one for each of the entities: departments, faculty members, insurance plans, job history information, and speaking topics. The arrows represent the relationships. In particular, they represent the one-to-many relationship, which was discussed earlier. The arrow goes from the "one" part of the relationship to the "many" part. (Each department is related to *many* faculty members, but each faculty member is related to exactly *one* department.)

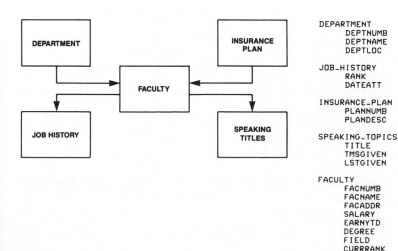

DEPARTMENT
    DEPTNUMB
    DEPTNAME
    DEPTLOC

JOB-HISTORY
    RANK
    DATEATT

INSURANCE-PLAN
    PLANNUMB
    PLANDESC

SPEAKING-TOPICS
    TITLE
    TMSGIVEN
    LSTGIVEN

FACULTY
    FACNUMB
    FACNAME
    FACADDR
    SALARY
    EARNYTD
    DEGREE
    FIELD
    CURRRANK
    DEPCOV

**Figure 1.18**

Marvel College network database structure

We manipulate a network model database by essentially *following the arrows*. This procedure is often referred to as **database navigation**. Arrows may be followed in either direction. Suppose we need to print a list of all of the faculty members in department 3. We first ask the DBMS to FIND department 3. Assuming there is such a department, we then repeatedly ask to FIND the NEXT faculty member within this department until reaching the end of the list of faculty members in this department. While we are on a given faculty member, we can ask to find the insurance plan related to that faculty member. Here we would be following the arrow from insurance plan to faculty member in the reverse direction. If we also wanted to print all the faculty member's job history information, we could repeatedly ask the DBMS to FIND the NEXT job history record for this faculty member until there were no more.

Note that we find the department to which a faculty member is related by following the arrow, not by looking at a department number field in a faculty record. There is thus no need for such a field. In general, there is no need to have fields in network model records to implement the relationships.

**Hierarchical Model.**   A **hierarchical model** database is perceived by a user as a collection of hierarchies, or trees. A **hierarchy** is really a network with an added restriction: no box can have more than one arrow entering the box. (It doesn't matter how many arrows leave a box.) A hierarchy is thus a more restrictive structure than a network. Since two arrows enter the faculty box in the Marvel College database shown in Figure 1.18, it is not a hierarchy and cannot be implemented directly in a hierarchical model DBMS.

## Premiere Products

It is time to meet Premiere Products, the other organization we will use as an example throughout the text. A distributor of appliances and sporting goods, Premiere Products needs to maintain the following information:

1. For sales representatives, they need to store the rep's number, name, address, total commission, and commission rate.
2. For customers, they need to store the customer's number, name, address, current balance, credit limit, and the number of the sales rep who represents the customer.
3. For parts, they need to store the part number, description, units on hand, item class, the number of the warehouse in which the item is stored, and the unit price.

Premiere Products also must store information on orders. A sample order is shown in Figure 1.19.

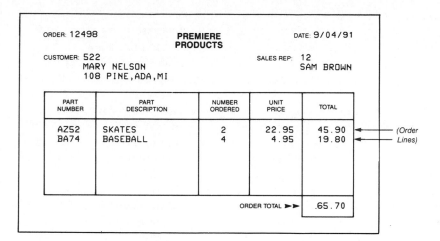

**Figure 1.19**

Premiere Products
order

Note that there are three parts to the order. The heading (top) of the order contains the order number, date, customer number, name, address, sales rep number, and sales rep name. The body of the order contains a number of order lines, sometimes called line items. Each order line contains a part number, part description, the number of the part that was ordered, and the quoted price for the part. It also contains a total (often called an extension), which is the product of the number ordered and the quoted price. Finally, the footing (bottom) of the order contains the order total. The following are the additional items Premiere Products must store concerning orders:

4.  For orders, they need to store the order number, date the order was placed, and the number of the customer who placed the order. Note that the customer's name, address, and the number of the sales rep who represents the customer are stored with customer information. In addition, the name of the sales rep is stored with sales rep information.
5.  For each order line, they need to store the order number, part number, number ordered, and the quoted price. Note that the part description is stored with part information. The product of number ordered and quoted price is not stored, since it can easily be computed when needed.
6.  The overall order total is not stored but will be computed when the order is produced.

Figure 1.20 on the next page represents a relational model database for Premiere Products. Figure 1.21 on page 27 shows the same database, but filled in with sample data that will be used throughout the book.

**Figure 1.20**

Premiere Products
relational database
structure

SLSREP

| SLSRNUMB | SLSRNAME | SLSRADDR | TOTCOMM | COMMRATE |
|----------|----------|----------|---------|----------|
|          |          |          |         |          |

CUSTOMER

| CUSTNUMB | CUSTNAME | CUSTADDR | BALANCE | CREDLIM | SLSRNUMB |
|----------|----------|----------|---------|---------|----------|
|          |          |          |         |         |          |

ORDERS

| ORDNUMB | ORDDTE | CUSTNUMB |
|---------|--------|----------|
|         |        |          |

ORDLNE

| ORDNUMB | PARTNUMB | NUMBORD | QUOTPRCE |
|---------|----------|---------|----------|
|         |          |         |          |

PART

| PARTNUMB | PARTDESC | UNONHAND | ITEMCLSS | WRHSNUMB | UNITPRCE |
|----------|----------|----------|----------|----------|----------|
|          |          |          |          |          |          |

For sales reps, we have columns for the number, name, address, total commission earned, and commission rate. For customers, we have the number, name, address, balance, and credit limit. In addition, we have a column for the number of the sales rep who represents the customer. Using it, we can find the one sales rep who represents a particular customer. Thus, we see that customer 256 (Ann Samuels) is represented by sales rep 6 (William Smith). On the other hand, by looking for all of the customers who have some specific number in this column, we can find all the customers a given sales rep serves. Thus, we see that sales rep 12 (Sam Brown) represents customers 311 (Don Charles), 405 (Al Williams), and 522 (Mary Nelson).

For orders, we have the number and date of the order. In addition, we have a column for the customer who placed an order. This column relates orders to customers in the same way the sales rep column in the customer table related customers to sales reps. For parts, we have columns for the part number, description, number of units on hand, the item class the part belongs in (housewares, sporting goods, or appliances), the number of the warehouse in which the part is stored, and the price.

**Note:** In many situations, the word "ORDER" has special meaning to a DBMS or to a programming language. This means that there are potential problems with using *ORDER* as the name of the table containing orders. To avoid these problems, we will instead use *ORDERS* as the name of this table.

In the *ORDLNE* table, we have columns for the order number that a given order line corresponds to, the number of the part that is present on that order line, the number of units of that part that were ordered, and the price that was quoted for that part on that order. The sixth row of the *ORDLNE* table tells us, for example, that there is a line on order 12498 on which four units of part BA74 (BASEBALL) were ordered at a price of $4.95 each.

To test your understanding of the relational model database for Premiere Products, answer the following questions using the data in Figure 1.21.

**SLSREP**

| SLSRNUMB | SLSRNAME | SLSRADDR | TOTCOMM | COMMRATE |
|---|---|---|---|---|
| 3 | Jones, Mary | 123 Main,Grant,MI | 2150.00 | .05 |
| 6 | Smith, William | 102 Raymond,Ada,MI | 4912.50 | .07 |
| 12 | Brown, Sam | 419 Harper,Lansing,MI | 2150.00 | .05 |

**CUSTOMER**

| CUSTNUMB | CUSTNAME | CUSTADDR | BALANCE | CREDLIM | SLSRNUMB |
|---|---|---|---|---|---|
| 124 | Adams, Sally | 481 Oak,Lansing,MI | 418.75 | 500 | 3 |
| 256 | Samuels, Ann | 215 Pete,Grant,MI | 10.75 | 800 | 6 |
| 311 | Charles, Don | 48 College,Ira,MI | 200.10 | 300 | 12 |
| 315 | Daniels, Tom | 914 Cherry,Kent,MI | 320.75 | 300 | 6 |
| 405 | Williams, Al | 519 Watson,Grant,MI | 201.75 | 800 | 12 |
| 412 | Adams, Sally | 16 Elm,Lansing,MI | 908.75 | 1000 | 3 |
| 522 | Nelson, Mary | 108 Pine,Ada,MI | 49.50 | 800 | 12 |
| 567 | Baker, Joe | 808 Ridge,Harper,MI | 201.20 | 300 | 6 |
| 587 | Roberts, Judy | 512 Pine,Ada,MI | 57.75 | 500 | 6 |
| 622 | Martin, Dan | 419 Chip,Grant,MI | 575.50 | 500 | 3 |

**ORDERS**

| ORDNUMB | ORDDTE | CUSTNUMB |
|---|---|---|
| 12489 | 90291 | 124 |
| 12491 | 90291 | 311 |
| 12494 | 90491 | 315 |
| 12495 | 90491 | 256 |
| 12498 | 90591 | 522 |
| 12500 | 90591 | 124 |
| 12504 | 90591 | 522 |

**ORDLNE**

| ORDNUMB | PARTNUMB | NUMBORD | QUOTPRCE |
|---|---|---|---|
| 12489 | AX12 | 11 | 14.95 |
| 12491 | BT04 | 1 | 402.99 |
| 12491 | BZ66 | 1 | 311.95 |
| 12494 | CB03 | 4 | 175.00 |
| 12495 | CX11 | 2 | 57.95 |
| 12498 | AZ52 | 2 | 22.95 |
| 12498 | BA74 | 4 | 4.95 |
| 12500 | BT04 | 1 | 402.99 |
| 12504 | CZ81 | 2 | 108.99 |

**PART**

| PARTNUMB | PARTDESC | UNONHAND | ITEMCLSS | WRHSNUMB | UNITPRCE |
|---|---|---|---|---|---|
| AX12 | IRON | 104 | HW | 3 | 17.95 |
| AZ52 | SKATES | 20 | SG | 2 | 24.95 |
| BA74 | BASEBALL | 40 | SG | 1 | 4.95 |
| BH22 | TOASTER | 95 | HW | 3 | 34.95 |
| BT04 | STOVE | 11 | AP | 2 | 402.99 |
| BZ66 | WASHER | 52 | AP | 3 | 311.95 |
| CA14 | SKILLET | 2 | HW | 3 | 19.95 |
| CB03 | BIKE | 44 | SG | 1 | 187.50 |
| CX11 | MIXER | 112 | HW | 3 | 57.95 |
| CZ81 | WEIGHTS | 208 | SG | 2 | 108.99 |

**Figure 1.21**

Premiere Products sample data

**Q & A**

**Question:**

1. Give the numbers of all the customers represented by Mary Jones.
2. Give the name of the customer who placed order 12491. Give the name of the sales rep who represents this customer.
3. List all of the parts that appear on order 12491. For each part, give the description, number ordered, and quoted price.
4. Why is the column *QUOTPRCE* part of the *ORDLNE* table? Can't we just take the *PARTNUMB* and look up the price in the *PART* table?

**Answer:**

1. 124, 412, and 622. (Look up the number of Mary Jones in the *SLSREP* table and obtain the number 3. Then find all customers in the *CUSTOMER* table who have the number 3 in the *SLSRNUMB* column.)

2. Don Charles. Sam Brown. (Look up the customer number in the *ORDERS* table and obtain the number 311. Then find the customer in the *CUSTOMER* table who has customer number 311. Using this customer's sales rep number of 12, find the name of the sales rep in the *SLSREP* table.)

3. BZ66, WASHER, 1, $311.95. BT04, STOVE, 1, $402.99. (Look up each *ORDLNE* table row in which the order number is 12491. Each of these rows contains a part number, the number ordered, and the quoted price. The only thing missing is the description of the part. Use the part number to look up the corresponding description in the *PART* table.)

4. If we don't have the *QUOTPRCE* column in the *ORDLNE* table, the price for a part on an order line must be obtained by looking up *UNITPRCE* in the *PART* table. While this may not be bad, it does prevent Premiere Products from charging different prices to different customers for the same part. Since Premiere Products wants the flexibility to quote different prices to different customers, we include the *QUOTPRCE* column in the *ORDLNE* table. (**Note:** If you examine the *ORDLNE* table, you will see cases in which the *QUOTPRCE* value matches the actual price in the *PART* table and cases in which it differs.)

Figure 1.22 shows a network model database for Premiere Products.

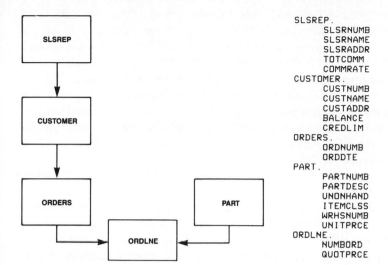

```
SLSREP.
     SLSRNUMB
     SLSRNAME
     SLSRADDR
     TOTCOMM
     COMMRATE
CUSTOMER.
     CUSTNUMB
     CUSTNAME
     CUSTADDR
     BALANCE
     CREDLIM
ORDERS.
     ORDNUMB
     ORDDTE
PART.
     PARTNUMB
     PARTDESC
     UNONHAND
     ITEMCLSS
     WRHSNUMB
     UNITPRCE
ORDLNE.
     NUMBORD
     QUOTPRCE
```

**Figure 1.22**

**Premiere Products network database structure**

## HISTORY OF DATABASE MANAGEMENT

Although it is difficult to pinpoint exactly when the area of database management began, there is good reason to place its beginnings with the APOLLO project of the 1960s, which was launched in response to President John F. Kennedy's stated goal of landing a man on the moon by the end of the decade. Since, at the time, no available systems were capable of handling the coordination of the vast amounts of data required, North American Rockwell, the prime contractor for the project, asked IBM to develop one. In response, IBM developed the Generalized Update Access Method (GUAM), which went into production in 1964.

It soon became clear to IBM that this product was useful in other environments and in 1966 the company made the product available to the general public under the name Data Language/I (DL/I). This product is actually the data management component of the Information Management System (IMS), which was certainly one of the most important of the early database management systems. IMS has been enhanced over the years and is still offered by IBM.

Another development taking place in the mid-1960s was a system called Integrated Data Store (I-D-S), developed at General Electric by a team headed by Charles Bachman. This system led to a whole class of database management systems — the CODASYL systems — which are still popular and influential today.

In the late 1960s, **CODASYL**, the COnference on DAta SYstems Languages, the group responsible for COBOL, tackled the problem of providing a standard for database management systems. CODASYL charged a task group, the DataBase Task Group (**DBTG**), with the job of developing specifications for database management systems. The DBTG did this and in 1971, CODASYL presented these specifications to the American National Standards Institute (**ANSI**) for adoption as a national standard. Although these specifications were not accepted as a standard by ANSI, a number of systems were developed following the CODASYL guidelines. These systems are usually called CODASYL systems or DBTG systems.

In 1970, Dr. E. F. Codd presented a paper that was to have a profound impact on the database community. In it, he proposed a new and, at the time, radically different approach to the management of data: the relational model. Throughout the decade of the 1970s, the relational model was the subject of intense research. In addition to purely theoretical research, prototype systems were developed, the most important being a system called System R, which was developed by IBM. It was not until the 1980s, however, that commercial relational DBMS's began to appear. Systems that are at least partly relational now exist in abundance on computers ranging from the smallest micro to the largest mainframe. While System R never became a commercial system, it led to IBM's commercial relational offering, DB2.

The 1970s and 1980s have seen the development of a number of support products to go along with DBMS's. **Data dictionaries**, **report generators**, **query facilities**, and **nonprocedural languages** have all been developed and, along with the DBMS, are now a part of an entire environment, the so-called **fourth-generation environment**. We speak of systems that contain all of these facilities as **fourth-generation languages** (4GL) or as **application generators**. They represent a tremendous increase in productivity. (This environment will be discussed in chapter 13.) In addition, the 1980s have seen the development of microcomputer DBMS's. As the decade has progressed, these systems have increased greatly in functionality, to the point where they rival their mainframe counterparts in a number of areas.

For an excellent account of the early history of database management, see the March 1976 issue of the *ACM Computing Surveys*; in this issue, [6] gives the history of database management and an overview of the various models; [4] discusses the relational model; [11] discusses the CODASYL approach; [12] examines the hierarchical model; and [10] presents a comparison between the relational and CODASYL approaches.

## *ADVANTAGES OF DATABASE PROCESSING*

There are a number of advantages to the database approach to processing, particularly when a powerful, full-functioned DBMS is used. These advantages are listed in Figure 1.23.

## Advantages of Database Processing

1. Economy of scale
2. Getting more information from same amount of data
3. Sharing of data
4. Balancing conflicting requirements
5. Enforcement of standards
6. Controlled redundancy
7. Consistency
8. Integrity
9. Security
10. Flexibility and responsiveness
11. Increased programmer productivity
12. Improved program maintenance
13. Data independence

**Figure 1.23**

Advantages of database processing

## 1. Economy of Scale

The concentration of applications in one location allows for the possibility of smaller numbers of larger and more powerful computers, which usually results in an *economy of scale*. The same economy of scale may be realized by the concentration of technical expertise. Furthermore, since many users are sharing the database, any improvement in the database will potentially benefit many different users. In general, economy of scale refers to the fact that the collective cost of several combined operations may be less than the sum of the cost of the individual operations. Database processing makes this type of combination possible.

## 2. Getting More Information From the Same Amount of Data

The primary goal of a computer system is to turn data (recorded facts) into information (knowledge gained by processing these facts). Even though all the data Juan needed for a requested report was in computer files, he could not easily access it and thus could not obtain the desired information. If, however, that data were in a common database, he would be able to access it (provided, of course, he were authorized to do so). Thus, this added *information* would now be available even though the database might not contain additional *data* not already present in the files.

## 3. Sharing of Data

The data can be shared among authorized users, allowing users access to more of the data. Several users might have access to the same piece of data (e.g., a faculty member's address), but use it in a variety of ways. When a faculty member's address is changed, the change is immediately available to all users. In addition, new applications can be developed using the existing data in the database without the added burden of creating separate collections of files.

### 4. Balancing Conflicting Requirements

For the database approach to function adequately, there must be a person or group within the organization in charge of the database itself. This group is often called Database Administration (**DBA**). By keeping the overall needs of the organization in mind, DBA can structure the database to the benefit of the entire organization, not just a single user group. While this may potentially mean that an individual user group is served less well than it might have been if it had its own isolated system, the overall organization will benefit. If the organization benefits, then, ultimately, so will the individual user groups.

### 5. Enforcement of Standards

With the central control mentioned in the previous paragraph, DBA can ensure that standards for such things as data names, usages, and formats are followed uniformly throughout the organization.

### 6. Controlled Redundancy

Since data that was kept separate in a file-oriented system is now integrated into a single database, we no longer have multiple copies of the same data. We saw that at Marvel College there were at least four separate *FACULTY* files. Each contained a faculty member's address. Thus the address of each faculty member appeared in at least four different places. In the database approach, since there is only one occurrence of each faculty member, this redundancy is eliminated. In practice, there are places we might actually introduce some limited amount of redundancy into a database for performance reasons. But, even in these cases, we're able to keep it under tight control. This is why it's better to say that we *control* redundancy rather than *eliminate* it.

### 7. Consistency

Consistency follows from the control or elimination of redundancy. For example, if a faculty member's address appears in only one place, there is no possibility that faculty member 111 will have the address 123 Main at one spot within our data and 466 Willow in another.

## 8. Integrity

An **integrity constraint** is a rule that data in the database must follow. Here is an example of an integrity constraint: The department number given for a faculty member must be that of a department that *actually exists*. A database has **integrity** if data in the database satisfies all integrity constraints that have been established. In the database approach, DBA can define validation procedures that will ensure the integrity of the database.

## 9. Security

**Security** is the prevention of access to the database by unauthorized users. Since DBA has control over the operational data, it can define authorization procedures to ensure that only legitimate users access the data. DBA can further allow different users to have different types of access to the same data. The Payroll department at Marvel College may be able to view and change the salary of a faculty member. The Insurance department may be able to view the salary of a faculty member but not change it. The Speakers' Bureau may not even be able to view a salary.

One way DBA achieves this security is through user views. Any data items not included in the user view for a given user will not be accessible to that user. Another means of achieving security is through the use of sophisticated password schemes.

## 10. Flexibility and Responsiveness

Since the data that was previously kept in several different files by several different user areas is now in the same database, it is possible to respond to requests for data from multiple areas in a much easier and more flexible way. Even within a single user area, the flexibility furnished by the DBMS to locate and access data in a number of different ways aids programmers in developing new programs to satisfy user requests. The use of high-level languages allows users to do some of their own programming easily. A user who employs one such language, for example, to find all the faculty members who are assigned to department 3, who are covered by insurance plan 2, and who have a salary under $20,000, need only type

```
SELECT FACNUMB, FACNAME
      FROM FACULTY
      WHERE DEPTNUMB = 3
            AND PLANNUMB = 2
            AND SALARY < 20000
```

Employing yet another language, called a **natural language**, a user may actually be able to type

```
Give me the names and numbers of all faculty members who
are in department 3, covered by plan 2, and make less than
20000.
```

In both cases, the user can get a response to a question concerning data in the database rapidly and easily, without having to submit a request for the creation of a special program to the Information Systems department.

## 11. Increased Programmer Productivity

Since programmers accessing a database do not have to worry about the mundane data manipulation activities, as they would when accessing files, they will be more productive. Studies have shown that on the average they will be two to four times more productive (i.e., a new application can be developed in one-quarter to one-half of the time it would take if it were a straight file-oriented application). In addition, with the advent of fourth-generation languages built around database management systems, the productivity increases can be much more dramatic. Ten- to twentyfold increases (and more) in productivity are not uncommon.

## 12. Improved Program Maintenance

When interacting with a DBMS, programs are relatively independent of the actual data in the database. This means that many changes to the structure of the data itself may not require maintenance to existing application programs. In a straight file environment this is not true. Even simple changes to file layouts can require substantial changes in every program that accesses the file. In addition, since the low-level data manipulation is handled by the DBMS, details concerning this manipulation do not appear in programs. Thus, the complexity of maintaining such logic is not a concern in a DBMS environment.

## 13. Data Independence

While improving program maintenance is one important advantage of having programs independent of the structure of the database, this independence has other advantages as well. Without such independence, changes to the database structure to improve performance and to meet changing corporate requirements become very complex. The fact that all of the programs in the system need maintenance every time a change is made to the database structure would be a strong incentive not to make any of these changes. **Data independence** removes this obstacle to changing the structure.

Data independence occurs when the structure of the database can change without requiring the programs that access the database to change. Data independence is achieved in the database environment through the use of **external views** or **subschemas**. Each program accesses data through an external view. The underlying structure of the database can change without requiring a change in the external view. Thus, programs would not have to change. (There is an obvious stipulation. If the change to the database structure invalidated a user view, then the user view, and consequently any programs using the view, would have to change. An example of such a change would be the removal of a required field from the database structure.)

To address the independence issue in a general way, the American National Standards Institute/Committee X3/Standards Planning And Requirements sub-Committee (ANSI/X3/SPARC or **ANSI/SPARC**), proposed the model illustrated in Figure 1.24. The **external schemas** are views of data furnished to application programs. The **conceptual schema** is the overall global organizational view of data. Finally, the **internal schema** is the view of the database as seen by the computer. It is the responsibility of the DBMS to map one view to another.

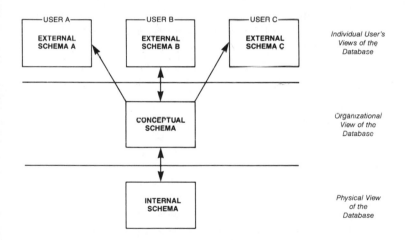

**Figure 1.24**

ANSI/SPARC model

The only requirement imposed on the external schemas is that they can be derived from what is in the conceptual schema. Certainly, if there is no *SALARY* field within the conceptual schema, there can be no *SALARY* field within an external schema. If there is no relationship between customers and employees in a conceptual schema, for example, there can be no relationship between them in any external schema. The important point is that the conceptual schema could change (fields added, relationships added, formats changed) without affecting the external schemas. Obviously, an external schema would need to be changed if some field that it required were deleted from the conceptual schema.

Similarly, an internal schema can be changed without affecting the conceptual schema. Storage details or access strategies could change, for example. Where a given field was stored as zoned decimal, we may now wish to store it as packed decimal or, perhaps, in a binary format. Where direct access to a faculty member had previously been accomplished through one scheme, say hashing, we may now wish to use another scheme, perhaps some kind of index, for this purpose. (Don't worry about the technical terminology at this point.)

DBA could thus make changes to the internal schema to improve the performance of the database. DBA could also make changes to the conceptual schema to respond to new requirements within the organization. In both cases, the external schemas could remain the same (subject, of course, to the stipulation that the data they require is still present in the new structure). In this way the independence described earlier is achieved.

Most DBMS's support the external schemas of the ANSI/SPARC model. CODASYL systems call them subschemas. Many relational model systems call them views. In any case, the idea is the same: Users can have their own views of what the database looks like.

Likewise, most DBMS's support, in general, the conceptual and internal schemas. In this case, however, the support is often not as complete as it could be. In the ANSI/SPARC model, logical details about the structure of the database belong in the conceptual schema. Physical details about such things as the actual storage and access methods for the database belong in the internal schema. Many DBMS products do not have this clear of a breakdown. Their designers may not have attempted to separate the logical from the physical or, if they have, the separation may not be nearly as complete as the ANSI/SPARC model requires. This is the direction in which systems are moving, however, and we have already discussed why it is a worthy goal.

## DISADVANTAGES OF DATABASE PROCESSING

As you would expect, if there are advantages to doing something a certain way, there are also disadvantages. The database area is no exception. There are several disadvantages regarding database processing, which are listed in Figure 1.25.

**Figure 1.25**

Disadvantages of database processing

**Disadvantages of Database Processing**

1. Size
2. Complexity
3. Cost
4. Additional hardware requirements
5. Higher impact of a failure
6. Recovery more difficult

## 1. Size

To support all the complex functions it must provide to users, a database management system must, by its very nature, be a large program occupying megabytes of disk space, as well as a substantial amount of internal memory.

## 2. Complexity

Again, the complexity and breadth of the functions furnished by a DBMS make it a complex product. Programmers and analysts must understand the features of the system to take full advantage of it. There is a great deal for them to learn. In addition, with many choices to make when designing and implementing a new system using a DBMS, it's possible to make these choices incorrectly, especially if the understanding of the system is not thorough enough. Unfortunately, a few incorrect choices can spell disaster for the whole project.

## 3. Cost

A good mainframe DBMS is an expensive product. By the time all the appropriate components related to the DBMS are purchased for a major mainframe system, the total price can easily run into the $100,000 to $400,000 range. (Such is not the case on microcomputers, however. Some good microcomputer DBMS's cost well under $1,000.)

## 4. Additional Hardware Requirements

Because of the size and complexity of a DBMS, greater hardware resources are required than would be necessary without the DBMS. This means that if the hardware resources are not increased when a DBMS is purchased, users of the system may very well notice a severe degradation in performance. Purchasing (or leasing) additional hardware resources represents yet another added cost.

## 5. Higher Impact of a Failure

Since many of the information systems resources are now concentrated in the database, a failure of any component has a much more far-reaching effect than in a nondatabase environment.

### 6. Recovery More Difficult

Because of the added complexity, the process of recovering the database in the event of a catastrophe is a more complicated one, particularly if the database is being updated by a large number of users **concurrently** (i.e., at the same time).

## SUMMARY

While a conventional file is capable of housing information concerning only a single type of entity (such as customers), a database is capable of housing information concerning several different types of entities (such as customers, sales reps, orders, and parts). In addition, a database also contains information concerning relationships among the various entities (such as the relationship between a sales rep and all of the customers he or she represents). In contrast to the file approach to processing, the database approach offers the possibility of controlling or eliminating redundancy; it also offers greater flexibility in drawing relationships among diverse entities.

A database management system (DBMS) is a software product that manages a database. Any interaction between users and the database is through the DBMS. The DBMS takes all responsibility for the actual storage and retrieval of data.

Database management systems began to appear in the mid-1960s. They are classified by the model of data they support. There are three basic models of data: the relational model, the network model (which includes systems following the specifications proposed by CODASYL), and the hierarchical model.

Taking the database approach to processing involves pooling data into a common database and managing this database with a DBMS. Some advantages of this approach include the ability to control redundancy, share data among users, get more information from the same data, and increase programmer productivity. Some disadvantages of this approach include the cost of the DBMS and related additional hardware, the complexity of a DBMS, and the higher potential impact of any type of failure.

For other information concerning the background of database processing, along with the advantages and disadvantages, see numbers [1], [2], [3], [5], [7], [8], [9], and [13] in the references section at the end of this chapter.

# REVIEW QUESTIONS

1. Define redundancy. What redundancy currently exists in systems at Marvel College? What are the problems associated with redundancy?
2. Why is satisfying the request made to Juan by the Personnel department difficult with the present system? Would it be easier to satisfy this request if Marvel were currently using a database approach? Why or why not?
3. Define entity, attribute, and relationship.
4. Explain how entities, attributes, and relationships are implemented in a straight file environment.
5. Define database.
6. What does it mean to say a database is self-describing? Why is this a desirable feature?
7. What does it mean to say a database is integrated? Why is this a desirable feature?
8. What does it mean to say a database is shared? Why is this a desirable feature?
9. What is a DBMS? What is the fundamental function of a DBMS?
10. What is a data model? What are the three main data models?
11. If the beginning of database technology could be traced to a single event, which event would that be?
12. What contribution did CODASYL make to the database area?
13. What contribution did Dr. E. F. Codd make to the database area?
14. Describe what is meant by "economy of scale." How does database processing achieve an economy of scale?
15. How is it possible to get more information from the same amount of data when a database approach is used as opposed to a file approach?
16. What is DBA? What are the responsibilities of DBA in a database environment?
17. How does consistency result from controlling or eliminating redundancy?
18. What is meant by integrity as it is used in this chapter?
19. What is meant by security? Explain how it is achieved in the database environment.
20. How does the database approach furnish additional flexibility and responsiveness.
21. Why are programmers more productive in the database environment?
22. What is meant by data independence? How is it achieved in the database environment?
23. How does the ANSI/X3/SPARC model relate to data independence?
24. How can the size of a DBMS be a disadvantage to using one?

25. How can the complexity of a DBMS be a disadvantage?
26. Why could the impact of a failure in the database environment be more serious than in a file environment?
27. Why could recovery be more difficult in the database environment?

## EXERCISES

1. Using the data for Marvel College as shown in Figure 1.26, answer each of the following questions:
   a. How many faculty members in the Computer Science department have a salary of at least $25,000?
   b. How many faculty members covered by the regular insurance plan have coverage for dependents?
   c. What are the names of the faculty members who have at least two different speaking topics?
   d. What are the names of the faculty members who are still at the rank at which they were hired?
   e. How many talks have been given by members of the Computer Science department?
   f. Give all of the information currently in the database concerning Barb Martin.
2. Using the data for Premiere Products as shown in Figure 1.27, answer each of the following questions.
   a. Give the names of all customers represented by William Smith.
   b. How many customers have a balance that is over their credit limit?
   c. Which sales reps represent customers whose balance is over their credit limit?
   d. Which customers placed orders on 9/05/91?
   e. Which sales reps represent any customers who placed orders on 9/05/91?
   f. Which customers currently have a stove on order?
   g. List the number and description of all parts that are currently on order by any customer represented by William Smith.
3. Indicate the changes that should be made to the Marvel College relational database structure shown in Figure 1.26 to satisfy the following additional requirements:
   a. Store the date of birth of each faculty member.
   b. Store the name of the secretary of each department.
   c. Store the number, name, and address of each student of Marvel College. In addition, there is a relationship between faculty and students in which each faculty member advises many students but each student is advised by exactly one faculty member.

d. Store the number and description of each course offered at Marvel College, as well as the number of credits each course is worth. Each course is offered by exactly one department. Each department offers many courses.

e. Store the grade each student received in each course taken by the student. (This one is a little tricky.)

**FACULTY**

| FAC NUMB | FACNAME | FACADDR | SAL ARY | EARN YTD | DEPT NUMB | DEG REE | FIELD | CURR RANK | PLAN NUMB | DEP COV |
|---|---|---|---|---|---|---|---|---|---|---|
| 119 | Martin, Barb | 94 Ridge,Grant,MI | 22500 | 15425 | 1 | MA | Comm. | Asst | 2 | N |
| 209 | Newton, Jane | 210 Leonard,Ada,MI | 29000 | 18945 | 2 | MS | Topology | Asso | 1 | Y |
| 421 | Jones, Al | 121 Colton,Hart,MI | 20000 | 11402 | 1 | PhD | Database | Asst | 2 | N |
| 462 | Johnson, Tom | 604 46th,Lowell,MI | 25000 | 16952 | 1 | MS | Op. Sys. | Asso | 2 | Y |
| 485 | Sparks, Pam | 201 Olive,Holt,MI | 33500 | 20115 | 2 | PhD | Analysis | Prof | 3 | Y |
| 507 | Canton, Rob | 5 State,Cutler,MI | 19500 | 11010 | 3 | MS | Volcano | Asst | 1 | Y |
| 564 | Ferris, Tim | 16 W. 9th,Troy,MI | 28500 | 18540 | 3 | PhD | Minerals | Asso | 1 | N |
| 683 | Nils, Frank | 46 Creston,Ada,MI | 36500 | 22050 | 5 | PhD | Laser | Prof | 2 | Y |

**DEPARTMENT**

| DEPT NUMB | DEPTNAME | DEPTLOC |
|---|---|---|
| 1 | Computer Sci. | 408 Kelly Hall |
| 2 | Mathematics | 253 Watson Hall |
| 3 | Geology | 707 Case Tower |
| 5 | Physics | 118 Font Tower |

**INSURANCE_PLAN**

| PLAN NUMB | PLANDESC |
|---|---|
| 1 | Regular |
| 2 | Deluxe |
| 3 | Special |

**SPEAKING_TOPICS**

| FAC NUMB | TITLE | TMS GIVEN | LST GIVEN |
|---|---|---|---|
| 119 | Distributed Database | 5 | 32191 |
| 119 | Why Network Micros? | 2 | 51591 |
| 119 | Communications | 1 | 90291 |
| 462 | The Future of Unix | 3 | 51391 |
| 485 | The Regular Polyhedra | 2 | 111590 |
| 507 | Mount St. Helens | 1 | 21291 |
| 683 | Laser Technology | 3 | 52291 |
| 683 | Nuclear Power Pro&Con | 1 | 61591 |

**JOB_HISTORY**

| FAC NUMB | RANK | DATEATT |
|---|---|---|
| 119 | Asst | 91581 |
| 209 | Asst | 90176 |
| 209 | Asso | 91383 |
| 421 | Asst | 81583 |
| 462 | Asst | 41271 |
| 462 | Asso | 91481 |
| 485 | Asst | 40265 |
| 485 | Asso | 91274 |

**Figure 1.26**

Marvel College database

4. Indicate the changes that should be made to the Premiere Products relational database structure shown in Figure 1.27 on the next page to satisfy the following additional requirements:
   a. Store the phone number for each customer.
   b. Premiere Products is divided into territories. For each territory, store the number and description. Each sales rep is located in a single territory. Many sales reps can be located in the same territory.
   c. Each customer is located in a single territory.
   d. What change should be made if the territory in which a customer is located must be the same as the territory in which his or her sales rep is located?

**Figure 1.27**

Premiere Products
database

SLSREP

| SLSRNUMB | SLSRNAME | SLSRADDR | TOTCOMM | COMMRATE |
|---|---|---|---|---|
| 3 | Jones, Mary | 123 Main,Grant,MI | 2150.00 | .05 |
| 6 | Smith, William | 102 Raymond,Ada,MI | 4912.50 | .07 |
| 12 | Brown, Sam | 419 Harper,Lansing,MI | 2150.00 | .05 |

CUSTOMER

| CUSTNUMB | CUSTNAME | CUSTADDR | BALANCE | CREDLIM | SLSRNUMB |
|---|---|---|---|---|---|
| 124 | Adams, Sally | 481 Oak,Lansing,MI | 418.75 | 500 | 3 |
| 256 | Samuels, Ann | 215 Pete,Grant,MI | 10.75 | 800 | 6 |
| 311 | Charles, Don | 48 College,Ira,MI | 200.10 | 300 | 12 |
| 315 | Daniels, Tom | 914 Cherry,Kent,MI | 320.75 | 300 | 6 |
| 405 | Williams, Al | 519 Watson,Grant,MI | 201.75 | 800 | 12 |
| 412 | Adams, Sally | 16 Elm,Lansing,MI | 908.75 | 1000 | 3 |
| 522 | Nelson, Mary | 108 Pine,Ada,MI | 49.50 | 800 | 12 |
| 567 | Baker, Joe | 808 Ridge,Harper,MI | 201.20 | 300 | 6 |
| 587 | Roberts, Judy | 512 Pine,Ada,MI | 57.75 | 500 | 6 |
| 622 | Martin, Dan | 419 Chip,Grant,MI | 575.50 | 500 | 3 |

ORDERS

| ORDNUMB | ORDDTE | CUSTNUMB |
|---|---|---|
| 12489 | 90291 | 124 |
| 12491 | 90291 | 311 |
| 12494 | 90491 | 315 |
| 12495 | 90491 | 256 |
| 12498 | 90591 | 522 |
| 12500 | 90591 | 124 |
| 12504 | 90591 | 522 |

ORDLNE

| ORDNUMB | PARTNUMB | NUMBORD | QUOTPRCE |
|---|---|---|---|
| 12489 | AX12 | 11 | 14.95 |
| 12491 | BT04 | 1 | 402.99 |
| 12491 | BZ66 | 1 | 311.95 |
| 12494 | CB03 | 4 | 175.00 |
| 12495 | CX11 | 2 | 57.95 |
| 12498 | AZ52 | 2 | 22.95 |
| 12498 | BA74 | 4 | 4.95 |
| 12500 | BT04 | 1 | 402.99 |
| 12504 | CZ81 | 2 | 108.99 |

PART

| PARTNUMB | PARTDESC | UNONHAND | ITEMCLSS | WRHSNUMB | UNITPRCE |
|---|---|---|---|---|---|
| AX12 | IRON | 104 | HW | 3 | 17.95 |
| AZ52 | SKATES | 20 | SG | 2 | 24.95 |
| BA74 | BASEBALL | 40 | SG | 1 | 4.95 |
| BH22 | TOASTER | 95 | HW | 3 | 34.95 |
| BT04 | STOVE | 11 | AP | 2 | 402.99 |
| BZ66 | WASHER | 52 | AP | 3 | 311.95 |
| CA14 | SKILLET | 2 | HW | 3 | 19.95 |
| CB03 | BIKE | 44 | SG | 1 | 187.50 |
| CX11 | MIXER | 112 | HW | 3 | 57.95 |
| CZ81 | WEIGHTS | 208 | SG | 2 | 108.99 |

# REFERENCES

1] Atre, S., *Data Base: Structured Techniques for Design, Performance, and Management*, 2nd ed. John Wiley & Sons, Inc., 1988.

2] Bradley, James, *Introduction to Data Base Management in Business*, 2d ed. Holt, Rinehart & Winston, 1987.

3] Cardenas, Alfonso F., *Data Base Management Systems*, 2d ed. Allyn & Bacon, 1984.

4] Chamberlin, Donald D., "Relational Data-Base Management Systems." *ACM Computing Surveys* 8, no. 1 (March 1976).

5] Date, C. J., *Introduction to Database Systems, Volume I*, 4th ed. Addison-Wesley, 1986.

6] Fry, James P., and Sibley, Edgar H., "Evolution of Data-Base Management Systems." *ACM Computing Surveys* 8, no. 1 (March 1976).

7] Goldstein, Robert C., *Database Technology and Management*. John Wiley & Sons, 1985.

8] Kroenke, David, and Dolan, Kathleen A., *Database Processing: Fundamentals, Design, Implementation*. 3d ed. SRA, 1988.

9] McFadden, Fred R., and Hoffer, Jeffrey A., *Data Base Management*, 2d ed. Benjamin Cummings, 1988.

10] Michaels, Ann S., Mittman, Benjamin, and Carlson, J. Robert, "A Comparison of the Relational and CODASYL Approaches to Data-Base Management." *ACM Computing Surveys* 8, no. 1 (March 1976).

11] Taylor, Robert W., and Frank, Randall L., "CODASYL Data-Base Management Systems." *ACM Computing Surveys* 8, no. 1 (March 1976).

12] Tsichritzis, D. C., and Lochovsky, F. H., "Hierarchical Data-Base Management: A Survey." *ACM Computing Surveys* 8, no. 1 (March 1976).

13] Vasta, Joseph A., *Understanding Data Base Management Systems*. Wadsworth, 1985.

# Functions of a Database Management System

## INTRODUCTION

In chapter 1, we discussed the concepts of a database and a database management system (DBMS). Throughout the remainder of the text, we'll be investigating various aspects of database management in detail. We will look at the various models that DBMS's follow, as well as some specific DBMS implementations. We'll study the process of database design, and we will discuss the people involved in the management of databases, especially those who handle database administration (DBA) functions. Before beginning any of this study, however, we need to know more about what a DBMS is supposed to do.

The main function of a DBMS, as we learned in chapter 1, is to store, update, and retrieve data in a database. Several other functions were mentioned briefly. In this chapter, we'll examine these and other functions in some detail to set the stage for the remainder of the text. As we study various DBMS implementations, we'll see to what degree these functions are actually present and how they are implemented.

In [4], Dr. E. F. Codd lists eight capabilities, or services, that should be provided by any full-scale DBMS. This list has found general acceptance and forms the basis of our study of the functions of a database management system. In addition, there are two important services not covered in Dr. Codd's list, which we will also investigate. In the following list, the first eight services are those presented by Codd.

1. **Data storage, retrieval, and update**. A DBMS must furnish users with the ability to store, retrieve, and update data in the database.
2. **A user-accessible catalog**. A DBMS must furnish a catalog in which descriptions of data items are stored and which is accessible to users.

3. **Transaction support.** A DBMS must furnish a mechanism which will ensure that either all the updates corresponding to a given transaction are made or that none of them are made.
4. **Concurrency control services.** A DBMS must furnish a mechanism to ensure that the database is updated correctly when multiple users are updating the database concurrently.
5. **Recovery services.** A DBMS must furnish a mechanism for recovering the database in the event the database is damaged in any way.
6. **Authorization services.** A DBMS must furnish a mechanism to ensure that only authorized users can access the database.
7. **Support for data communication.** A DBMS must be capable of integrating with communication software.
8. **Integrity services.** A DBMS must furnish a means to ensure that both the data in the database and changes to the data follow certain rules.
9. **Services to promote data independence.** A DBMS must include facilities to support the independence of programs from the actual structure of the database.
10. **Utility services.** A DBMS should provide a set of utility services.

The preceding list is summarized in Figure 2.1.

| **Figure 2.1** | **Functions of a DBMS** |
|---|---|
| Functions of a DBMS | 1. Data storage, retrieval, and update |
| | 2. A user-accessible catalog |
| | 3. Transaction support |
| | 4. Concurrency control services |
| | 5. Recovery services |
| | 6. Authorization services |
| | 7. Support for data communication |
| | 8. Integrity services |
| | 9. Services to promote data independence |
| | 10. Utility services |

## DATA STORAGE, RETRIEVAL, AND UPDATE (Function 1)

It almost goes without saying that a DBMS must allow its users to store, retrieve, and update data in a database. This is the fundamental capability. Without it, there is no point in talking about anything else. In storing, retrieving, and updating data, the user should *not* have any need to be aware of the system's internal structures (such as **linked lists**, **inverted files**, **indexes**, or the use of **hashing**) or the procedures used to manipulate these structures. (The specific meaning of these terms is not important for this discussion. If you would like information concerning them, see the appendix.)

Consider Figure 2.2. In Figure 2.2a, the user is adding customer 124, whose name is Sally Adams, to the database. To add this data, the DBMS will handle all the work of maintaining the necessary underlying structures. The DBMS, for example, might use hashing to determine where to position the customer in the database, then connect the customer to a link list that is sorted by name. The user need not be concerned with any of this activity, however.

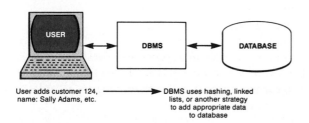

**Figure 2.2a**

Adding data

In Figure 2.2b, the user is now attempting to determine the name of customer 256. The DBMS will locate the customer using the same strategy as when it added the customer to the database in the first place. If hashing was the scheme it used, for example, it will use hashing again to determine exactly where the customer is located. Once it has done so, it will find the desired customer, then return the name to the user.

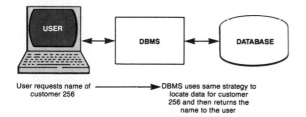

**Figure 2.2b**

Retrieving data

In Figure 2.2c on the next page, the user is changing the name of a customer. Again the DBMS will use the same strategy to locate the customer. It will make the indicated change to the name. This change might require further changes on the part of the DBMS, however. If, for example, the customers are part of a linked list that is sorted by customer name, the new name would place this customer at a different position on the list. Once again the user does not need to be aware of these details. The DBMS handles all the details of this repositioning.

**Figure 2.2c**

**Updating data**

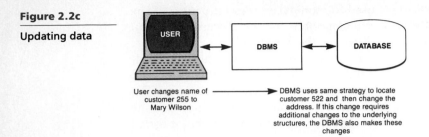

User changes name of customer 255 to Mary Wilson ——→ DBMS uses same strategy to locate customer 522 and then change the address. If this change requires additional changes to the underlying structures, the DBMS also makes these changes

## A USER-ACCESSIBLE CATALOG (Function 2)

It is very important for those who are responsible for a given database to have a catalog they can access to determine what the database "looks like," and how various programs access the database. In particular, they need to be able to easily get answers to such questions as:

1. What records and fields are included in the current structure?
2. What are the characteristics of these fields? Is the *CUSTNAME* field within the *CUSTOMER* record twenty characters long or thirty?
3. What are the possible values for the various fields? Are there any restrictions on the possibilities for *CREDLIM*, for example?
4. What is the meaning of the various fields? For example, what, exactly, is *ITEMCLSS*? What does an item class of "HW" mean?
5. What relationships are present? What is the meaning of each of the relationships? Must the relationship always exist? Does a customer, for example, have to have a sales rep?
6. Which programs in the system access which data in the database? How do they access it? Do they merely retrieve it or do they actually update it? What kinds of updates do they do? Can a certain program add a new customer, for example, or can it merely make changes to existing customers? When it makes a change to a customer, can it change all the fields or only the address?

Providing answers to these questions is crucial if a complex database is to be managed effectively. Since the DBMS uses the layout of the database to function, some of this information is available from the DBMS itself. In general, however, the information available from the DBMS may be limited to such things as record names, field names, and field characteristics (such as the fact that the sales rep number is a two-digit number).

What the DBMS "knows" does not necessarily include meanings of records, fields, and relationships, or the relationship between the data in the database and the programs that access the database. This additional information is often furnished by a software tool called a **data dictionary system**. This product, which complements the DBMS to furnish a highly useful catalog, can be a module of the DBMS itself or a separate software product.

For additional discussion of the catalog, see [10] and [11].

## TRANSACTION SUPPORT *(Function 3)*

A **logical transaction** (often simply called a *transaction*) is a sequence of steps that will accomplish a single task (or, at least, what feels to the user like a single task). The following are some examples of logical transactions: add a customer, enter an order, enroll a student in a course, deactivate an employee, increase the units on hand of a particular part by 50. To a user, these all seem to be single tasks. As we'll soon see, accomplishing a "single task" may require many changes to be made to the database. Provided all the changes are indeed made, everything is fine. We would have *severe* problems if some were made and others were not. A DBMS should furnish services that will ensure this does not happen. If it does, the database will not be consistent with reality.

Suppose in the Premiere Products database there are some additional columns, as shown in Figure 2.3. In the *SLSREP* table, there is a column labeled *ONORD*. This column contains the total dollar value of all the orders currently on file for each customer of the given sales rep. There is also a similar column in the *CUSTOMER* table, which represents the total dollar value of all the orders for each customer. Finally, there is a column labeled *ALLOC* in the *PART* table, which represents the number of units of a given part that are currently on order (allocated).

**SLSREP**

| SLSRNUMB | SLSRNAME | SLSRADDR | TOTCOMM | COMMRATE | ONORD |
|---|---|---|---|---|---|
| 3 | Jones, Mary | 123 Main,Grant,MI | 2150.00 | .05 | 567.44 |
| 6 | Smith, William | 102 Raymond,Ada,MI | 4912.50 | .07 | 815.90 |
| 12 | Brown, Sam | 419 Harper,Lansing,MI | 2150.00 | .05 | 998.62 |

**CUSTOMER**

| CUSTNUMB | CUSTNAME | CUSTADDR | BALANCE | CREDLIM | SLSRNUMB | ONORD |
|---|---|---|---|---|---|---|
| 124 | Adams, Sally | 481 Oak,Lansing,MI | 418.75 | 500 | 3 | 567.44 |
| 256 | Samuels, Ann | 215 Pete,Grant,MI | 10.75 | 800 | 6 | 115.90 |
| 311 | Charles, Don | 48 College,Ira,MI | 200.10 | 300 | 12 | 714.94 |
| 315 | Daniels, Tom | 914 Cherry,Kent,MI | 320.75 | 300 | 6 | 700.00 |
| 405 | Williams, Al | 519 Watson,Grant,MI | 201.75 | 800 | 12 | .00 |
| 412 | Adams, Sally | 16 Elm,Lansing,MI | 908.75 | 1000 | 3 | .00 |
| 522 | Nelson, Mary | 108 Pine,Ada,MI | 49.50 | 800 | 12 | 283.68 |
| 567 | Baker, Joe | 808 Ridge,Harper,MI | 201.20 | 300 | 6 | .00 |
| 587 | Roberts, Judy | 512 Pine,Ada,MI | 57.75 | 500 | 6 | .00 |
| 622 | Martin, Dan | 419 Chip,Grant,MI | 575.50 | 500 | 3 | .00 |

**Figure 2.3**

**Premiere Products sample data**

*(continued)*

**Figure 2.3**

(continued)

**ORDERS**

| ORDNUMB | ORDDTE | CUSTNUMB |
|---|---|---|
| 12489 | 90291 | 124 |
| 12491 | 90291 | 311 |
| 12494 | 90491 | 315 |
| 12495 | 90491 | 256 |
| 12498 | 90591 | 522 |
| 12500 | 90591 | 124 |
| 12504 | 90591 | 522 |

**ORDLNE**

| ORDNUMB | PARTNUMB | NUMBORD | QUOTPRCE |
|---|---|---|---|
| 12489 | AX12 | 11 | 14.95 |
| 12491 | BT04 | 1 | 402.99 |
| 12491 | BZ66 | 1 | 311.95 |
| 12494 | CB03 | 4 | 175.00 |
| 12495 | CX11 | 2 | 57.95 |
| 12498 | AZ52 | 2 | 22.95 |
| 12498 | BA74 | 4 | 4.95 |
| 12500 | BT04 | 1 | 402.99 |
| 12504 | CZ81 | 2 | 108.99 |

**PART**

| PARTNUMB | PARTDESC | UNONHAND | ITEMCLSS | WRHSNUMB | UNITPRCE | ALLOC |
|---|---|---|---|---|---|---|
| AX12 | IRON | 104 | HW | 3 | 17.95 | 11 |
| AZ52 | SKATES | 20 | SG | 2 | 24.95 | 2 |
| BA74 | BASEBALL | 40 | SG | 1 | 4.95 | 4 |
| BH22 | TOASTER | 95 | HW | 3 | 34.95 | 0 |
| BT04 | STOVE | 11 | AP | 2 | 402.99 | 2 |
| BZ66 | WASHER | 52 | AP | 3 | 311.95 | 1 |
| CA14 | SKILLET | 2 | HW | 3 | 19.95 | 0 |
| CB03 | BIKE | 44 | SG | 1 | 187.50 | 4 |
| CX11 | MIXER | 112 | HW | 3 | 57.95 | 2 |
| CZ81 | WEIGHTS | 208 | SG | 2 | 108.99 | 2 |

With these changes, let's consider what would happen when a user enters an order, a single logical transaction. Suppose the user enters order 12506, with a date of 9/06/91, for customer 405. This order is for 2 AX12s at $17.95 each and 3 CZ81s at $100.00 each. Behind the scenes, the steps described in Figure 2.4 must take place.

**Figure 2.4**

Sample logical transaction

### A Logical Transaction

1. The customer's balance and credit limit are checked to ensure that the new order will not raise the balance over the credit limit.

    Assuming we can proceed...

2. The order total, $335.90 (2 * $17.95 + 3 * $100.00), must be added to the value in the *ONORD* column for customer 405. In addition, depending on how soon the order is to be shipped, it may also be added to the customer's .balance.
3. This same total must be added to the value in the *ONORD* column for sales rep 12 (the sales rep who represents customer 405).
4. Order 12506 must be added to the *ORDERS* table with a date of 9/06/91 and a customer number of 405.

Figure 2.4

(continued)

5. Two order lines must be added to the *ORDLNE* table. They both will have an order number of 12506. One will have part number AX12, number ordered 2, quoted price $17.95 and the other will have part number CZ81, number ordered 3, quoted price $100.00.
6. The allocated column for part AX12 must be increased by 2 and the allocated column for part CZ81 must be increased by 3.

All of these steps must be performed when a user submits the single logical transaction, enter an order. While they do not necessarily have to happen in the order stated, they had better all happen or we'll have problems. Consider a hypothetical situation, for example, in which the *ONORD* figures in the *CUSTOMER* and *SLSREP* tables are updated but, for some reason, perhaps a hardware or software failure, the order itself is never added to the database!

What must a DBMS do about this problem? First, realize that a program accomplishing these updates can be processing more than just a single logical transaction. This may have been the forty-third of the many transactions it must process, for example, with 151 transactions to go. Each of these transactions may require several updates to the database. The DBMS has no inherent way of knowing which updates are grouped together in response to a single transaction. Thus, it must furnish the programmer with a mechanism to communicate this information to the DBMS.

It could, for example, allow a programmer to issue a command, BEGIN TRANSACTION, when the program is ready to begin a series of updates in response to a single logical transaction, and END TRANSACTION when the last of the updates has been completed. When the DBMS receives END TRANSACTION, it knows these updates can be made permanent and available to other users. (The technical term is that the transaction is **committed**.) If a problem occurs before the END TRANSACTION is received, we say that the transaction is to be **aborted**. The DBMS should then undo all the changes made since the last BEGIN TRANSACTION was received. (The technical term is that the database has been **rolled back**.) In addition to accomplishing this task, the DBMS should also notify the user that this has happened. Once a transaction has been committed, the updates caused by the transaction should be available to all programs accessing the database (i.e., they should see the new data). If, on the other hand, a transaction is aborted, no program should see the results of *any* of the updates that were accomplished along the way.

For additional discussion of logical transactions, see [6], [10], and [11].

## CONCURRENCY CONTROL SERVICES (Function 4)

By **concurrent update**, or **shared update**, we mean two or more users involved in making updates to the database at the same time. We say that these users are updating the database **concurrently**, or that *concurrent update* is taking place. On the surface, it may seem as though shared update is no problem. Why can't two or three (or fifty, for that matter) different users update the database at the same time? What's the problem?

### The Problem

To illustrate the problems involved in shared update, let's assume we have two users: Tom and Mary. Tom is currently accessing the database to process orders and, among other things, to increase customers' balances by the amount of the orders. In particular, let's assume customer 124's balance is to be increased by $100.00. Mary is accessing the database to post payments and, among other things, to decrease customers' balances by the amount of the payments. As it happens, customer 124 (Sally Adams) has just made a $100.00 payment, so her balance is to be decreased by $100.00. The balance of customer 124 was $418.75 prior to the start of this activity and, since the amount of the increase exactly matches the amount of the decrease, it should still be $418.75 after the activity has been completed. Will it? That depends.

How exactly does Tom make the required update? First, the data concerning customer 124 is read from the database into Tom's work area. Second, any changes are made to the data in the work area; in this case, $100.00 is added to the current balance of $418.75, bringing it up to $518.75. This change has *not* yet taken place in the database, *only* in Tom's work area. Finally, the information is written to the database and the change is now made in the database itself. (See Figure 2.5.)

**Figure 2.5**

Tom updates
database

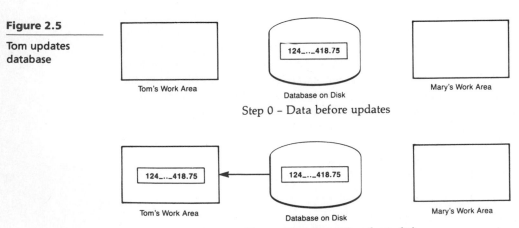

Tom's Work Area          Database on Disk          Mary's Work Area

Step 0 – Data before updates

Step 1 – Tom reads information from disk

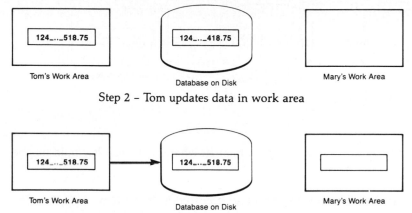

**Figure 2.5**

(continued)

Step 2 – Tom updates data in work area

Step 3 – Tom updates database with data in work area

Suppose Mary begins her update at this point. The data for customer 124 would be read from the database, including the new balance of $518.75. The amount of the payment, $100.00, would then be subtracted from the balance, thus giving a balance of $418.75 *in Mary's work area*. Finally, this new information is written to the database, and customer 124's balance is what it should be. (See Figure 2.6.)

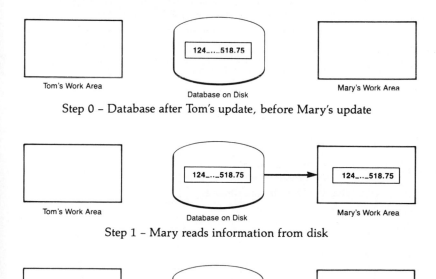

**Figure 2.6**

Mary updates
database

Step 0 – Database after Tom's update, before Mary's update

Step 1 – Mary reads information from disk

Step 2 – Mary updates data in work area

*(continued)*

**Figure 2.6**

**(continued)**

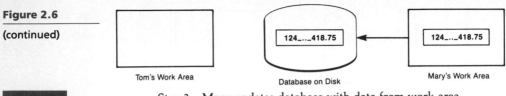

Tom's Work Area                    Database on Disk                    Mary's Work Area

Step 3 – Mary updates database with data from work area

# Q & A

**Question:**    Do you see another way for things to happen whereby the result would not be correct?

**Answer:**    Suppose the following scenario had occurred instead. Tom reads the data from the database into his work area. Mary reads the data from the database into her work area. At this point, both Tom and Mary have the data for customer 124, including a balance of $418.75. Tom adds $100.00 to the balance in his work area, and Mary subtracts $100.00 from the balance in her work area. At this point, in Tom's work area the balance reads $518.75, while in Mary's work area it reads $318.75. Tom now writes to the database. At this moment, customer 124 has a balance of $518.75 in the database. Finally, Mary writes to the database. Now, customer 124's balance in the database is *$318.75!* (A very good deal for Sally Adams. Unfortunately, not such a good deal for Premiere Products, the company paying our salary; see Figure 2.7.) Had the updates taken place in the reverse order, the final balance would have been $518.75. In either case, we now have incorrect data in our database (one of the updates has been *lost*). This cannot be permitted to happen.

**Figure 2.7**

**Tom and Mary update database in manner that leads to inconsistent data**

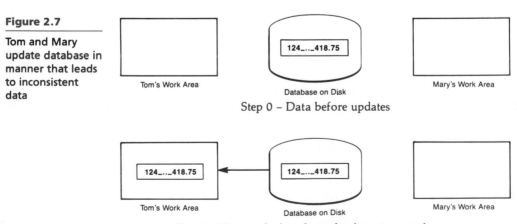

Tom's Work Area                    Database on Disk                    Mary's Work Area

Step 0 – Data before updates

Tom's Work Area                    Database on Disk                    Mary's Work Area

Step 1 – Tom reads data from database into work area

**Figure 2.7**

(continued)

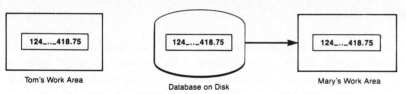

Tom's Work Area          Database on Disk          Mary's Work Area

Step 2 – Mary reads data from database into work area

Tom's Work Area          Database on Disk          Mary's Work Area

Step 3 – Tom updates data in work area

Tom's Work Area          Database on Disk          Mary's Work Area

Step 4 – Mary updates data in work area

Tom's Work Area          Database on Disk          Mary's Work Area

Step 5 – Tom updates database with data from work area

Tom's Work Area          Database on Disk          Mary's Work Area

Step 6 – Mary updates database with data from work area
Tom's update is lost!

### Avoiding the Problem

One way to prevent this situation from occurring is to prohibit the opportunity for shared update. While this may seem a little drastic, it is not quite as far-fetched as it may appear. We could permit several users to access the database, but for *retrieval* only (i.e., they would be able to read information from the database, but would not be able to write anything to the database). When these users entered some kind of transaction to update the database (like posting a payment), the database would not really be updated at all. Instead, a record would be placed in a separate file of transactions. A record in this file might indicate, for example, that $100.00 had been received from customer 124 on a certain date. Periodically, a single update program would read the records in these transaction files and actually perform the appropriate updates to the database. Since this program would be the only program actually updating the database, we would not have the problems associated with shared update.

Using this approach avoids one set of problems, those associated with shared update, but creates another. From the time users start updating (placing records in the update files) until the time the update program actually runs, the information in the database is out of date. Where a customer's balance in the database is $49.50, it may in fact be $649.50, if a transaction has been entered that would increase the balance by $600.00. Assuming the customer has an $800.00 credit limit, we should prohibit him or her from charging, say, a $200.00 item. However, as far as the data currently in the database is concerned, this should be no problem. After all, the customer has $750.50 of available credit ($800.00 – $49.50). If we are in such a situation, where the data in the database must be current, then this scheme for avoiding the problems of shared update will not work.

### Locking

Assuming we cannot solve the shared update problem by avoidance, we need a mechanism for dealing with the problem. We need to be able to keep Mary from even beginning the update on customer 124 until Tom has completed his update (or vice versa). This could be accomplished by some kind of **locking** scheme. Suppose once Tom had read customer 124's record, the record became locked (no other user could access it) and remained locked until he had completed the update. During the duration of the lock, any attempt by Mary to read the record would be rejected. Mary would be notified that the record was locked. Mary could, if desired, keep attempting to read the record until it was no longer locked, at which time her update could be completed. Thus, we have a scenario as shown in Figure 2.8. In at least this simple case, the problem of a "lost update" seems to have been solved.

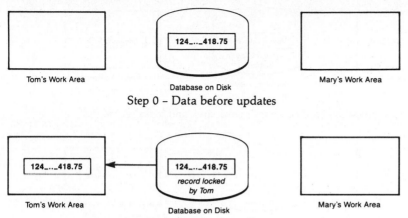

Step 0 – Data before updates

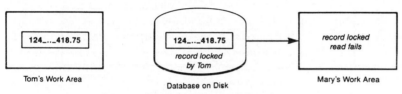

Step 1 – Tom reads data from database into work
area and locks record

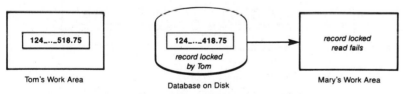

Step 2 – Mary tries to read data from
database into work area

Step 3 – Tom updates data in work area
Mary again tries to read data from database and again fails

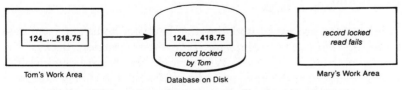

Step 4 – Tom updates database with data from work area
Mary again tries to read data from database and again fails

**Figure 2.8**

Tom and Mary
update database.
Locking prevents
inconsistent data

*(continued)*

**Figure 2.8**

(continued)

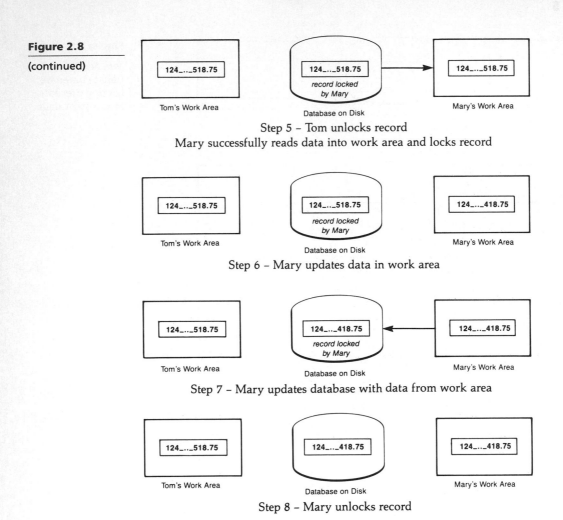

Step 5 – Tom unlocks record
Mary successfully reads data into work area and locks record

Step 6 – Mary updates data in work area

Step 7 – Mary updates database with data from work area

Step 8 – Mary unlocks record

## Two-Phase Locking

Suppose Tom is in the process of updating the database; he has updated customer 405's record, but has not completed the entire transaction. Because the record has been updated, it is locked. When should the record be unlocked? Suppose it was unlocked at this time and Mary proceeded to change customer 405's balance to $300.00. Now suppose, for whatever reason, Tom's transaction is aborted. As indicated in the discussion of logical transactions, all the activity he completed thus far must be undone. The database must be rolled back to the state it was in before the transaction was performed. In particular, the data for customer 405 reverts to its original state, *with its original balance*. Mary's update is *lost* even though we are using a locking mechanism.

Obviously, Tom gave up the lock on customer 405 too early. Until his transaction has actually been committed (completed successfully), the possibility of this problem exists. Thus, he should retain all of his locks until the last update for the given transaction has actually been made. At this point, *all* locks should be released. This approach is called **two-phase locking**. There is a **growing phase** in which more and more records are being locked but none are being released, and a **shrinking phase** in which all locks are released and no new ones added. This two-phase approach solves the lost update problem.

## Deadlock

There is another problem to deal with, however. Suppose Tom has completed steps 1 through 5 of a series of updates for a single transaction and is about to complete step 6. One part of step 6 involves updating part AX12. Suppose this record is locked by another user, Mary. Tom must wait for this record until Mary is done with it. As it turns out, Mary needs to update customer 405 in order to finish the updates for the transaction on which she is working. Since Tom currently has this record locked, Mary must wait until Tom is done. Thus, Tom cannot proceed until Mary is done and Mary cannot proceed until Tom is done! This situation is called **deadlock**, or the **deadly embrace**. (See Figure 2.9a.)

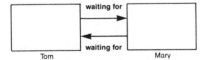

**Figure 2.9a**

Two users each waiting for resources held by the other — DEADLOCK!

The final problem then is: What do we do about deadlock? One possible scheme is to make each user lock all the records he needs to update at the beginning, before any updates have actually taken place. If he encounters a record that another user currently has locked, he must release *all* of his locks and try again. While this scheme technically works, it is difficult to implement in the database environment, since the collection of records that needs to be updated is often not known until the update is already under way. This approach is designed to prevent deadlock.

Another approach that is, in general, more workable is to let users lock records as they need them, thus allowing deadlock to occur, but then to detect and break any deadlocks that actually take place. To detect deadlock, the system must keep track of the collection of records each user has locked, as well as the records each user is waiting for. If two users are each waiting for records held by the other, a deadlock has occurred. Actually, more than two users could be involved. Tom might be waiting for a record held by Mary, while Mary is waiting for a record held by Juan, who is in turn waiting for Tom. (See Figure 2.9b on the next page.) This situation, however, is rare.

**Figure 2.9b**

Three users each
waiting for
resources held by
the other —
DEADLOCK!

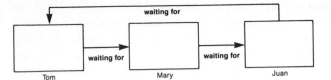

Once a deadlock has been detected, it must be broken. To break the deadlock, one of the deadlocked users is chosen to be the **victim**. This user's transaction is aborted (i.e., all the updates already accomplished are undone). In addition, all locks are released and the program is notified that this has taken place. Each program in the system should be prepared to take appropriate action in the event that a transaction has been aborted in this way. The action taken may be as simple as retrying all the updates. In this case, the only divergence from normal processing that the user would notice would be a delay in the time the update takes to complete. In other situations, the program may need to notify the user that there has been a problem. If this happens, the user must indicate what action he or she wishes to take.

### Lock Granularity

So far, it has been assumed that any locking that took place occurred at the *record level* (i.e., it was individual records that were locked). This need not be the case. Locking can occur at the field level, in which individual fields can be locked, or at the block (or page) level. A database, like any file, is organized in blocks or pages, which is the amount that is physically accessed when data is read from or written to the disk. If customer 405 is found on page 13 of the database, then the lock would actually be placed on the entire page, not just on customer 405. While this effectively locks many records that are not being accessed (the page might contain 4K bytes' worth of various kinds of data, for example), it is often easier to administer than field-level locks or record-level locks. Finally, the lock might take place at the file or database level, allowing only one user to update anything at all in the database.

The level of the lock is called the **lock granularity**. As we have seen, the lock level could be:

1. The whole file or database
2. A block or page
3. A record
4. An individual field

The larger the amount of data locked, the easier the locks are for the DBMS to administer. The smaller the amount, the less contention ("bumping heads") there will be among users. If the locking occurs at the page level, for example, two users attempting to access records on the same page will be in contention, even though they might be attempting to update *totally different records*. If locking occurs at the record level, the same two users would not be in contention. In actual practice, locking at the page level is the most common, especially when the files are large.

## Shared and Exclusive Locks

A locking scheme in which users obtain an **exclusive lock** on a record when they read it is unduly harsh: As long as they hold this type of lock, no other user can gain any kind of lock. The act of reading in itself does not cause any problems. It is only an eventual update that brings about difficulties. One hundred different users all reading the same record would not cause any problems. In general, granting exclusive locks every time any record is read can create performance problems, with far too much of the database locked at any time. Picture those 100 users all standing in line waiting for their turn to read and exclusively lock the one record they all are interested in. Each must wait until the previous user gives up his lock before being able to access it. While the likelihood of 100 users all wanting precisely the same record at the same time is obviously very slim, we think you get the point about how the use of only exclusive locks can tie up the database.

In practice, there are usually two different types of locks: shared and exclusive. A user reading a record holds a **shared lock** on the record, thus allowing other users to also read the record. To update a record, the lock must be *promoted* to exclusive. Once the user holds an exclusive lock, no other users may obtain even a shared lock on the record until this user has released the lock. If, when the user attempts to gain an exclusive lock, other users currently hold shared locks on the same record, the user must wait until the other users release their shared locks. This brings up another deadlock possibility, of course. Suppose both Tom and Mary hold shared locks on customer 405 and part BT04. If Tom attempts to gain an exclusive lock on customer 405, he must wait until Mary releases her shared lock. If instead of doing this, Mary attempts to gain an exclusive lock on part BT04, we again have two users waiting for each other: DEADLOCK!

## Lock Duration

When we discussed Tom's update to customer 124, we said that Tom should lock the record for customer 124 as soon as he reads it (really as soon as the program he is running reads it). Tom will have the record locked until he completes the update. This approach is ideal for preventing the lost update problem. Unfortunately, it is not always practical.

Suppose the program that Tom is running works this way: Tom first enters 124 as the customer number. At this point, current data will be read from the database and displayed on his screen. Tom now makes his change on the screen and presses Enter. At this point the database is updated with the new data and the record can be unlocked. Normally everything is fine. But what if Tom is interrupted by a phone call before he has completed filling in the new data? What if he goes to lunch? The record might remain locked for an extended period of time. If the update involves several records, all must be locked, making the problem that much worse. Clearly, this cannot be permitted to occur.

While using shared and exclusive locks helps in this problem, they still don't completely solve it. A user holding a shared lock on a record for an extended period of time can still interfere with other users who want to lock the record. For this reason, we often encounter situations where we don't want records to be locked any longer than is absolutely necessary.

One way to accomplish this is for programs to read the information they need at the beginning of the update, then immediately *release all locks*. After the user has entered all the new data, the update takes place as described earlier (the contents of the record are read into the work area and the record is locked; the data is updated in the work area; the data from the work area is written back to the database; and the record is unlocked).

This poses a problem, however. Suppose Tom and Mary were both updating the database, running programs that worked exactly as described in the previous paragraph. Suppose Tom's program read the data for customer 124, then released its lock on this customer while Tom was filling in new data on the screen. What if Mary updated customer 124 in the meantime and completed her update before Tom finished filling in his new data? If Tom then were to finish filling in the new data, and the program he was running blindly went ahead to update the row for customer 124 with his data, Mary's update would be lost, that is; it would be over-written with Tom's data. This is the problem we were trying to prevent!

Each program must take a further precautionary step. Before blindly updating the database with the new data, the program should make sure that nobody else has updated the data in the meantime. If someone has, the program cannot update the database with the new data; instead, the user of the program must be informed of the situation and permitted to decide whether he or she wants to redo the update or move on to something else.

How will a program know whether another user has updated the row for customer 124? Several methods can be used to provide the answer. One is to store a special field, called a *timestamp*, in each record. Whenever a program updates the contents of a record, it also updates the timestamp by changing it to the time of the update. This timestamp can then be used to detect whether a record has been changed. When a program initially reads a record, it saves the current value of the timestamp in some variable. Later, when it reads the record a second time in preparation for the update, it compares the new value of the timestamp with the one it saved. If they are the same, the record was evidently not changed in the meantime and so the program can complete the update. If they are different, another user must have changed the record. In this case, the program cannot complete the update.

One problem with timestamps is that they typically occupy about ten bytes of storage, thus adding ten bytes to the length of every record. An alternative that occupies substantially less space would be to include an additional field, such as a three-digit number, that serves as an update counter. Suppose we call this field *UPDCOUNT*. Every time a program updates a row in any way, it should also update *UPDCOUNT* by adding 1 to it. (If the previous value was 999, the new value produced by adding one to the old value would be too big for the column. In such a case, the program would have set *UPDCOUNT* back to zero.) Assuming every program in the system were to adhere to this approach, we could use the following logic:

1. Read all the data from the record for customer 124, including the value of *UPDCOUNT*. (Assume the current value is 478.) Store this value in some variable for future reference. Unlock the row.
2. Get all the new data from the user.
3. When it's time to do the update, lock the record for customer 124, read the current data, and examine the value of *UPDCOUNT*. If it is still the same (in our case, 478), the record has not been updated and we can finish our update. If it is different (479 or 480, for example), we know that at least one other program has updated the data in the meantime and we cannot complete our update.
4. If we have to lock multiple records, the same procedure is followed for each one; that is, for each of the records involved, store its update count in some variable. When it is time to do the update, lock all the records, read each record's update count, and compare them with the counts we have stored. If all of the counts agree, we can perform the update. If they don't agree, the update cannot take place.

## Locking on Microcomputer DBMS's

The facilities we've been discussing are common to mainframe DBMS's. Microcomputer DBMS's, on the other hand, usually provide much more limited facilities. These limitations, in turn, put an additional burden on the programmers who write programs that allow several users to update the same database simultaneously.

Although the features for handling these problems vary from one microcomputer DBMS to another, the following list is fairly typical of the types of facilities provided.

1. Programs can lock a whole table or an individual row within a table (but only one). As long as one program has a row or table locked, no other program may access it.
2. Programs can release any of the locks they currently hold.
3. Programs can inquire whether a given row or table is locked.

This list, though short, comprises the complete set of facilities provided by many systems. Consequently, the following guidelines have been devised for writing programs for a shared-update environment:

1. If more than one row in the same table must be locked during an update, the *entire table* must be locked.
2. When a program attempts to read a locked row, it may wait a short period, then try to read the row again. This process could continue until the row becomes unlocked. It is usually preferable, however, to impose a limit on the number of times a program may attempt to read the row. In this case, reading is done in a loop, which proceeds until either (a) the read is successful, or (b) the maximum number of times the program can repeat the operation is reached. Programs vary in terms of what action is taken should the loop be terminated without the read being successful. One possibility is to notify the user of the problem and let him or her decide whether to try the same update again or move on to something else.
3. Since there is no facility to detect and handle deadlocks, we must try to *prevent* them. A common approach to this problem is for every program in the system to attempt to lock all the rows and/or tables it needs before beginning an update. Assuming it is successful in this attempt, each program can then perform the required updates. If any row or table that the program needs is already locked, it should immediately release *all* of the locks it currently holds, wait a specified period, then try the entire process again. (In some cases, it may be better to notify the user of the problem and see whether he or she wants to try again.) Effectively, this means that any program that encounters a problem will immediately get out of the way of all other programs, rather than be involved in a deadlock.

For additional discussion of the shared update, see [3], [6], [9], [10], [11], [13], and [15].

## RECOVERY SERVICES (Function 5)

There are, of course, many different occurrences that could result in a damaged database. Programs could abort or behave incorrectly. There could be problems with the disk or disks on which the database resides. The computer could suffer a hardware failure as the database is being processed. The DBMS must be able to restore the database to its correct state following any kind of catastrophe. This process is called **recovery**.

In a straight batch environment, where master files are updated by running update programs that access files of transactions, the process is fairly simple. A copy, called a **backup**, or **save**, of the master file is made before the update takes place. If the updated master is destroyed or damaged in any way, it can be recreated by copying the backup over the actual master file, then rerunning the update program against the same transaction file. In the database environment, however, we have many different users updating the database, typically interactively. If the database is destroyed at 2:00 P.M. and the backup copy was made at 10:00 P.M. the previous evening, what do we do about all the transactions the users have entered since they came on-line at 8:00 A.M. this morning? Do we phone each of these users and ask them to repeat the entire day's worth of activity? Clearly, this is not acceptable. The DBMS must furnish a mechanism to recover the database in a much simpler fashion.

To facilitate this recovery, the DBMS should provide features to:

1. Back up the database
2. Maintain a journal (or log)
3. Recover the database

## Backup

The DBMS should provide the facility to make a **backup**, or **save**, copy of the database. This copy will be used to recover the database if the active copy of the database is destroyed. This operation should take place on a regular basis.

## Journaling

The process of **journaling** involves maintaining a **log**, or **journal**, of all the activity that updates the database. Several types of information are typically kept in the log for each transaction. This includes the transaction ID and the time and date of each individual update, together with a record of what the data in the database looked like before the change (called a **before image**) and a record of what the data looked like after the change (called an **after image**). In addition, a record will be kept in the log indicating the beginning of a transaction as well as a record indicating the end (**COMMIT**) of a transaction.

To illustrate the use of such a log, consider the sample transactions shown in Figure 2.10 on the next page. There are four transactions. Three of them, CST1, PRT1, and PRT2, represent single-update transactions, that is, transactions requiring that only a single update be made to the database. One of them, ORD1, involves several updates. (This transaction is, in fact, the logical transaction described in Figure 2.4.) Assume that these four transactions are the first transactions in a given day and that they all complete successfully. In this case the log might look like the sample log shown in Figure 2.11.

**Figure 2.10**

Sample transactions

| TRANSACTION ID | TRANSACTION DESCRIPTION |
|---|---|
| CST1 | 1. Change the balance of customer 256 |
| ORD1 | 1. Change the ONORD value for customer 405<br>2. Change the ONORD value for sales rep 12<br>3. Add order ( order number - 12506 , date  -<br>   90691, customer -  405)<br>4. Add order line (order - 12506, part - AX12,<br>   number ordered - 2, quoted price - 17.95)<br>5. Add order line (order - 12506, part - CZ81,<br>   number ordered - 3, quoted price - 100.00)<br>6. Change ALLOC value for part AX12<br>7. Change ALLOC value for part CZ81 |
| PRT1 | 1. Add part BV57 |
| PRT2 | 1. Delete part BH22 |

**Figure 2.11**

Sample log (all transactions committed normally)

| TRANS ID | TIME | ACTION | OBJECT OF ACTION | BEFORE IMAGE | AFTER IMAGE |
|---|---|---|---|---|---|
| CST1 | 8:00 | START | | | |
| PRT1 | 8:02 | START | | | |
| CST1 | 8:03 | MODIFY | CUSTOMER (256) | (old values) | (new values) |
| ORD1 | 8:05 | START | | | |
| CST1 | 8:06 | COMMIT | | | |
| ORD1 | 8:08 | MODIFY | CUSTOMER (405) | (old values) | (new values) |
| PRT2 | 8:09 | START | | | |
| PRT1 | 8:12 | INSERT | PART (BV57) | | (new values) |
| ORD1 | 8:13 | MODIFY | SLSREP (12) | (old values) | (new values) |
| PRT1 | 8:14 | COMMIT | | | |
| ORD1 | 8:16 | INSERT | ORDERS (12506) | | (new values) |
| ORD1 | 8:18 | INSERT | ORDLNE (12506,AX12) | | (new values) |
| PRT2 | 8:19 | ERASE | PART (BH22) | (old values) | |
| ORD1 | 8:20 | INSERT | ORDLNE (12506,CZ81) | | (new values) |
| ORD1 | 8:22 | MODIFY | PART (AX12) | (old values) | (new values) |
| PRT2 | 8:23 | COMMIT | | | |
| ORD1 | 8:24 | MODIFY | PART (CZ81) | (old values) | (new values) |
| ORD1 | 8:26 | COMMIT | | | |

Before investigating how the log is used in the recovery process, let's examine the log itself. Each record in the log includes the ID of the trans-action, as well as the time the particular event occurred. (The actual time recorded in a log would be much more precise than in this example, and would also include the date the event occurred. For the sake of simplicity in the example, the time is only given to the nearest minute.) The event can be START, indicating that a transaction has begun, or COMMIT, indicating that a transaction has successfully completed. In addition, the event can be an actual update to the database: an INSERT (add data), a MODIFY (change data), or an ERASE (delete data). For the updates, the log record also contains the before image and the after image. For an INSERT, there is effectively no before image, since the data did not exist in the database prior to the operation. Similarly, for an ERASE, there is effectively no after image.

This particular log indicates, for example, that transaction ORD1 began at 8:05. The updates necessary to accomplish the complete transaction occurred at 8:08 (customer 405 is modified); 8:13 (slsrep 12 is modified); 8:16 (order 12506 is inserted); 8:17 (the first order line is inserted); 8:20 (the second order line is inserted); 8:22 (the first part is modified); and 8:24 (the other part is modified). Finally, at 8:26, the transaction is committed. During this same period of time, other transactions were also processed.

To illustrate the use of before images, suppose that the MODIFY for transaction ORD1 at 8:24 is unsuccessful. Instead, the transaction aborts at this time and all previous updates must be undone. This is accomplished by changing the database to match the before images of all the updates for transaction ORD1 in reverse order (technically, before images are **applied** to the database.) Thus, the first update undone will be the MODIFY of part AX12 that occurred at 8:22. This is followed by undoing the insert of the order line for order 12506, part CZ81 that occurred at 8:20. Note that since the before image for an insert is nonexistent, this action will delete the order line. Each of the updates is undone in this fashion. The process is complete when the system has worked back to the START for ORD1, which occurred at 8:05. (Incidentally, this is one reason the START must be recorded. Without it, the system would have to look all the way back to the beginning of the log for updates for transaction ORD1. In this small example, this may not seem so bad. With an actual log in a heavily used system, this would take a prohibitive amount of time.)

To illustrate the use of after images, suppose a system crash occurs at 8:21, as shown in Figure 2.12 on the next page. Suppose further that the actual database is destroyed in some way. In this case, we copy the most recent backup version of the database over the live database. We now can recreate the updates that have taken place, since this backup was made by applying the after images stored in the log in chronological order. Thus the after image of the MODIFY that occurred at 8:03 for transaction CST1 would be the first to be applied. This would recreate the effect of the MODIFY command. Next the after image for the MODIFY for transaction ORD1 that occurred at 8:08 would be applied. The process proceeds in this fashion.

**Figure 2.12**

Sample log (mal-
function occurs at
8:21)

| TRANS ID | TIME | ACTION | OBJECT OF ACTION | BEFORE IMAGE | AFTER IMAGE |
|----------|------|--------|------------------|--------------|-------------|
| CST1 | 8:00 | START  |                        |              |              |
| PRT1 | 8:02 | START  |                        |              |              |
| CST1 | 8:03 | MODIFY | CUSTOMER (256)         | (old values) | (new values) |
| ORD1 | 8:05 | START  |                        |              |              |
| CST1 | 8:06 | COMMIT |                        |              |              |
| ORD1 | 8:08 | MODIFY | CUSTOMER (405)         | (old values) | (new values) |
| PRT2 | 8:09 | START  |                        |              |              |
| PRT1 | 8:12 | INSERT | PART (BV57)            |              | (new values) |
| ORD1 | 8:13 | MODIFY | SLSREP (12)            | (old values) | (new values) |
| PRT1 | 8:14 | COMMIT |                        |              |              |
| ORD1 | 8:16 | INSERT | ORDERS (12506)         |              | (new values) |
| ORD1 | 8:18 | INSERT | ORDLNE (12506,AX12)    |              | (new values) |
| PRT2 | 8:19 | ERASE  | PART (BH22)            | (old values) |              |
| ORD1 | 8:20 | INSERT | ORDLNE (12506,CZ81)    |              | (new values) |

/\/\/\/\/\/\/\/\/\/\/\/\/\/\/\/\
/\/\/\/\/\/\/\/\/\/\/\/\/\/\/\/\  ◄—— CRASH!!
/\/\/\/\/\/\/\/\/\/\/\/\/\/\/\/\

There is, however, a serious question that needs to be resolved concerning the application of after images. *Exactly when does the process stop?* If we apply all the after images, we are left with two transactions, PRT2 and ORD1, that are technically still in progress, but there is no practical way to continue them. (The programs that were processing these transactions aborted when the system crashed.) The answer is that we only apply the after images of transactions that had successfully completed prior to the crash (i.e., transactions for which there is a COMMIT in the log). This can be accomplished by applying *all* after images, then undoing the transactions for which there is no COMMIT, using the before images in the manner described earlier. It can also be accomplished be prescanning the log to determine which transactions have actually been committed, then selectively applying only the after images of these transactions.

## Write-Ahead Log

For each change made to the database, we now have extra activity to perform: The log must be updated. Which should be done first: the update to the database or the update to the log? If everything completes successfully, it makes no difference. What if, however, there is a failure partway through an update? If the database is updated first, then, before the log can be updated, the system fails, we have changes in the database *that have never been recorded in the log*. Thus, there is no way for the system to undo these changes. As , far as the log is concerned, *they don't even exist!* If, on the other hand, the log is updated first, then, before the database is updated, the system fails, there will be enough information in the log to allow the database to be returned to a correct state. Thus, it is crucial that the log be updated first.

## Recovery

**Recovery** means returning the database to a state that is known to be correct from a state known to be incorrect. With the facilities listed above, all the pieces necessary for recovery are in place. The way they will be used depends on the kind of recovery that must be accomplished, which in turn depends on the kind of problem that occurred. Let's examine the different types of problems that might be encountered to see what process would be necessary to recover the database.

**Forward Recovery.**   If all or part of the database has actually been destroyed, then the recovery must begin with the most recent backup copy of the database. Since this copy is no longer current, it must be brought up to date. This can be accomplished by applying the after images of updates from committed (completed) transactions to this copy of the database. In its simplest form this consists of copying the after image of a given record or page over the actual record or page in the database in chronological order. This process can be improved by realizing that if a given page were updated ten times, this page would be changed ten times in the process just described. In reality, the first nine of those would be unnecessary. The tenth after image actually includes all the changes accomplished in the first nine. Thus, we can improve things considerably by scanning the log before the recovery and only applying the most recent after image.

**Backward Recovery.**   If the database has not actually been destroyed, then the problem must involve transactions that were either incorrect or, more likely, transactions that were stopped in midstream. The database is currently not in a valid state, but we can return it to a valid state by undoing the transactions that are currently in progress. This can be accomplished by processing the log backward, using the before images to undo changes that have been made.

   The actual problem may be systemwide: A hardware or software problem may have caused the whole system to go down and there were many transactions halted in progress. In this case, the before images of all transactions could be used to roll the database back to the most recent correct state. At that point, the database would be brought forward by applying the after images of those transactions that had completed before the problem occurred.

   The problem could involve only a single transaction. In this case, the individual transaction would be undone by using its before images.

**Checkpoint.**   In the rollback of the full database, the procedure was to use the before images to roll the database back to its most recent correct state. What was the time of this most recent correct state? With large numbers of transactions from large numbers of users in various stages of progress, it is not clear exactly when everything is known to be correct. We would want a point where we were sure that the database and the log matched and, ideally, where no transactions were currently in progress. Do we have to go all the way back to the most recent backup to achieve this state? Fortunately not. Most systems incorporate a feature known as **checkpoint**. When this feature is used, the system will periodically refuse to accept any new requests and will complete any updates of the database and the log that are currently in progress. Once this has been completed, the system will again accept new requests. These checkpoints do not involve much overhead and are usually employed frequently, perhaps every fifteen minutes or so. They then help identify the correct states.

**Recovery Through Offsetting Transactions.**    Suppose a transaction is erroneous (i.e., it puts faulty data in the database). The transaction runs to completion and, on the surface, everything seems fine. Because of a program or user error, however, the database is now actually in an incorrect state. Suppose, for example, that a user inadvertently enters a $100 payment for customer 315 when the payment was really made by customer 311. If the problem is not discovered in time, rolling back the transaction will not be effective. The only alternative is to enter another transaction (or other transactions) to correct the data in the database. In our example, we could enter a payment of $100 for customer 311 and a negative $100 payment (or adjustment) for customer 315 to offset the payment entered earlier.

**Differential Files.**    The problem of recovery is not difficult if the database is not being updated on-line (i.e., if the update is done in a batch type of environment). If the data in the database must be up-to-date, however, batch update is probably not appropriate. There is a way, however, of obtaining the ease of recovery that is present in a batch update environment while making the data in the database seem up-to-date. This approach uses a separate file that contains the changes to the database. This file is called a **differential file** (see [12]).

Under this scheme, an update entered by a user does not actually update the database at all. Instead, an entry is made in the differential file to indicate the change. When a user retrieves data from the database, the differential file must first be scanned, in reverse order, to determine whether any changes have been made to the appropriate record. Once this has been done, the appropriate data can be presented to the user, whether it be data directly from the database or from the differential file. The user will not know the difference.

Periodically, a program will actually update the database with data from the differential file in a fashion similar to ordinary batch update programs.

Thus, recovery can be accomplished with the same relative ease found in a batch update environment. Yet, since the differential file is scanned whenever data is retrieved from the database, the data feels up-to-date to the user. It would seem that this approach provides the best of both worlds. Unfortunately, if the volume of updates is at all large, the overhead of continually having to access the differential file is often more than can be tolerated.

For additional discussion of recovery, see [1], [3], [6], [9], [10], [11], [12], [13], and [14].


## AUTHORIZATION SERVICES (Function 6)

The term **security** refers to the protection of the database against unauthorized (or even illegal) access, either intentional or accidental. For this reason, the features of a DBMS that provide for security are often called **authorization services**. These include:

1. Encryption
2. Subschemas or views
3. Authorizations
4. User-defined procedures


### Encryption

**Encryption** refers to the storing of the data in the database in an encrypted format. Any time a user stores or modifies data in the database, the DBMS will encrypt the data before actually updating the database. When any legitimate user retrieves the data via the DBMS, it will be decrypted before the user sees it. The whole encryption process is transparent to a legitimate user (i.e., he or she is not aware it is happening). However, if an unauthorized user attempts to bypass all the controls of the DBMS and get to the database directly, he or she will only be able to see the encrypted version of the data.


### Subschemas or Views

A DBMS should furnish a **subschema** or **view** facility (external schemas in the terminology of ANSI/SPARC). While this facility encompasses more than strictly security, it plays an important role in this area.

If, for example, a given user is not to be able to see or change the balance of any of the customers, we simply do not include the balance field in his or her view. As far as this user is concerned, there is no balance field in the database. Thus, he or she cannot access it. A different user may be able to access all information about a customer, but only for customers of sales rep 3. This user can be furnished a view that contains all the fields within the customer record, but, as far as this user is concerned, the only customers in the database are those represented by sales rep 3. Thus, it would not be possible for this sales rep to see any information about customer 405, for example, much less change it, since this customer is represented by sales rep 12.

## Authorizations

In [8], Fernandez, Summers, and Wood proposed a model for database security using a table of **Authorization Rules**. An authorization rule has four parts: a subject, an object, an action, and a constraint. An example of an authorization rule would be that Jane (subject) is allowed to delete (action) customers (object) whose balance is 0 (constraint).

The subject of an authorization rule can be any entity that can access the database. It could be a person, a department, a program, or some specific kind of transaction. Subjects are identified in a variety of ways. Usually they are identified by a password, or a password in conjunction with an account number. Occasionally, where more stringent controls are required, they may be identified through such things as fingerprints or voiceprints.

The object of an authorization rule is the set of database entities that can be updated by the subject. These usually are records, although they could be individual fields or, at the other extreme, the entire database.

The action referred to in the authorization rule is really the action that the subject can take on the object. The actions typically permitted are read, insert, modify, and delete. An action of read allows the subject to retrieve information about the object. Insert allows the subject to add new occurrences of the object. Modify allows the subject to change data for existing occurrences. Delete allows the subject to delete existing occurrences of the object. It is permissible, of course, to assign multiple actions to a given subject. Jane may be able, for example, to read, modify, and delete customers. In this case, Jane could retrieve information about existing customers. She could also change or delete customers. She would not, however, be able to add new customers.

The constraint specifies limitations on when the subject can take the action on the object. In the authorization rule listed earlier, Jane can only delete a customer *if the balance is 0*. The fact that the balance must be 0 is a constraint on Jane's taking the indicated action. It is possible to have a constraint of "none," indicating that the subject can take the action without any restriction. It is also possible to have complicated constraints. For example,

Tom may add an order provided that *the total obtained by adding the number ordered, multiplied by the quoted price on each line item, is no more than $500.00. Also, that there is enough of each part that was requested in the order available to satisfy the order.*

Most systems currently offer a limited form of support for authorization rules. Usually a given user can take a given action on a given object. It is often not possible to specify much in the way of further constraints. Most often, the actions available are *retrieve* and *update*. Retrieve corresponds to read. Update corresponds to the combination of read, insert, modify, and delete. Authorizations are usually accomplished through the combination of subschemas and passwords, although some of the relational systems offer more powerful authorization support through additional features.

## User-Defined Procedures

A **user-defined procedure** is just what it says. It is a procedure written by the users of the DBMS in a programming language. The DBMS provides a *user exit* to these procedures. When the database is accessed in a particular way, the DBMS will invoke the procedure. The procedure will, in turn, perform whatever action it was designed to take. Information about when these procedures are to be invoked will be described in the schema.

For example, suppose the only way a customer can place an order that would bring the customer's balance over his or her credit limit is if a special authorization exists for this customer. Information about these special authorizations is kept outside of the database in a separate file. A user-defined procedure could be created, which would check to see whether an order would raise the customer's balance over the credit limit and, if so, would check the information in this file to see whether the order should be accepted. This procedure would be invoked whenever an attempt was made to store an order.

User-defined procedures allow users to build a wide variety of authorization tests. They can be used to supplement the capabilities of a DBMS. Deficiencies in the security facilities of the DBMS can potentially be overcome by using these procedures. However, this means that the burden for developing and testing these procedures falls on the enterprise using the DBMS rather than on the DBMS itself. It is desirable for the DBMS to possess sophisticated enough security facilities that user-defined procedures become unnecessary.

## Privacy

While **privacy** has become a complex societal issue whose scope goes far beyond what is appropriate for a text such as this one, no discussion of security would be complete without at least a brief mention of privacy. Although the two terms are often used synonymously, in reality they are different, albeit related, concepts. Technically, privacy refers to the right of an individual to have certain information concerning him or her kept confidential. Privacy and security are related, since it is only through appropriate *security* measures that *privacy* can be ensured.

The need for privacy (or the lack thereof) can be dictated by law or, alternatively, can be a matter of organizational policy. If Marvel College is a state-supported institution, for example, it may be that employee salaries are considered to be public information, available to anyone who wishes to examine it. Even if Marvel is not state-supported, it may still be college policy that salaries are public. On the other hand, they may be considered private, with strict rules concerning who can see another's salary.

Suppose salaries at Marvel were considered private. The policy could be, for example, that an appropriate person within the payroll department could see the salary of any employee, whereas a department chairperson could only see the salaries of the faculty members within the department; an individual faculty member could not see the salaries of any other employee. Finally, suppose there were a certain employee who could not view the salary of any employee but who was allowed to see statistics (e.g., average salary within departments).

### Statistical Databases

This brings us to the interesting but tricky topic of statistical databases. A **statistical database** is a database that is intended to supply only statistical information to its users. A census database would be an example of a statistical database. Since the database at Marvel College is not only supplying statistical information, but information on individuals as well, it is technically not a statistical database. It does function in this way for the last user mentioned, however, and we will use it to illustrate a problem associated with this kind of database.

In a statistical database, the user should *not* be able to infer information about any individual. This brings up a problem. We will not discuss a solution here, but merely illustrate the problem. (For a more detailed discussion see [6] and [7].)

Suppose there were only one employee, Gus Flavian, in the Latin department. Obviously, in this case, the average salary for the Latin department would be Gus Flavian's salary. Thus, by obtaining a statistic — the average salary for faculty within the Latin department — the user could infer information about an individual, namely, Gus's salary. Similarly, if there were only one female, Diane Smith, within the History department, the average salary for females within the History department would be Diane's salary. It might seem we could avoid this problem by reporting a statistic only when there were a minimum number of values upon which the statistic was calculated. The system could potentially report an average salary, for example, only if there were at least five employees within the sample. Even this is not good enough, however. Suppose there were ten faculty members in the History department, with Diane Smith being the only female. If a user requested the average salary within the History department, the system would give an answer, since ten faculty members would be involved. It would not give an answer if the average salary of all females in the History department were requested, but it would answer if the average salary of *all males* were requested since nine faculty members would be involved. From these two figures, however, Diane's salary could be computed, thus circumventing the controls built into the system!

For additional discussion of security, see [1], [3], [5], [6], [7], [8], [9], [10], [11], [12], and [13].

## SUPPORT FOR DATA COMMUNICATION *(Function 7)*

In the typical database environment today, most users access the database through terminals, both to retrieve data from the database and to update the data. While batch users usually interface directly with the DBMS, terminal users often do not, instead interacting with a **teleprocessing (TP) monitor**. This TP monitor routes transactions from the terminal users to the appropriate application programs, which in turn interface with the DBMS. (See Figure 2.13.) The main purpose of a TP monitor is to efficiently support on-line update activity. The powerful TP monitors, such as IBM's CICS, capably support large numbers of users and heavy transaction volume.

There is an overlap in services between the DBMS and a TP monitor. For example, both provide support for concurrent update and both typically provide recovery services. For everything to function smoothly, then, these two must be carefully integrated.

**Figure 2.13**

Use of a TP monitor

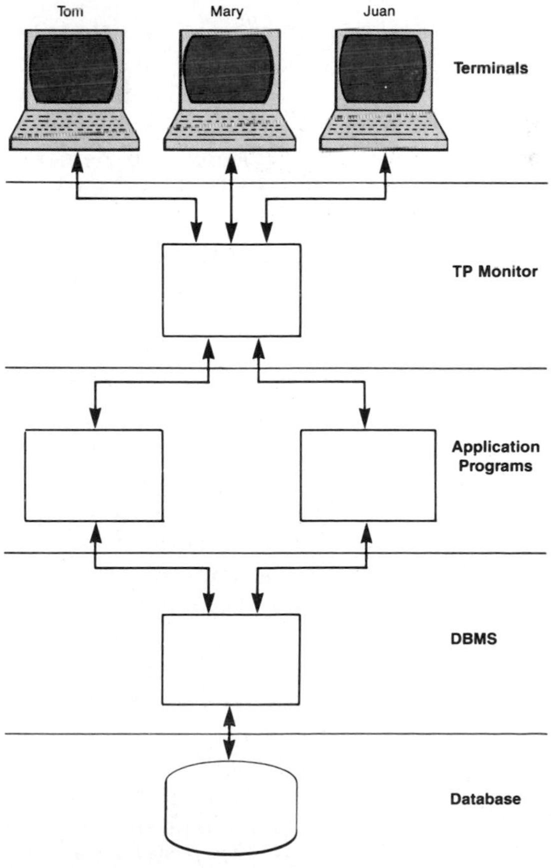

In many cases, the vendor of a DBMS will also furnish a TP monitor, designed specifically to work with the DBMS. Usually DBMS's are also designed to work with the more popular of the existing TP monitors. Organizations already using CICS for many applications, for example, will usually not want to install another TP monitor just for the activity that pertains to the DBMS. Instead they would rather continue to use CICS as their TP monitor for all activity. Such organizations may very well not consider a DBMS that is not designed to work with CICS.

For more discussion of communications, see [3], [5], [6], [7], [8], [9], [10], [11], [12], and [13].

## INTEGRITY SERVICES (Function 8)

In any database, there will be conditions, called **integrity constraints**, that must be satisfied by the data within the database. The types of constraints that may be present fall into the following four categories:

1. **Data type**. The data entered for any column should be consistent with the data type for that column. For a numeric column, only numbers should be allowed to be entered. If the column is a date, only a legitimate date (in some appropriate form, such as MMDDYY or MM/DD/YY) should be permitted. An entry such as 13/07/87 would be rejected, since it is not a legitimate date, even though it has the right form.
2. **Legal values**. It may be that for certain columns, not every possible value that is of the right type is legitimate. For example, even though CREDLIM is a numeric column, only the values 300, 500, 800, and 1,000 may be valid. It may be that only numbers between 2.00 and 800.00 are legal values for UNITPRCE.
3. **Format**. It may be that certain columns have a very special format that must be followed. Even though the column PARTNUMB is a character field, for example, only specially formatted strings of characters may be acceptable. Legitimate part numbers may have to consist of two letters followed by a hyphen, followed by a three-digit number. This is an example of a format constraint.
4. **Key constraints**. There are two types of key constraints: *primary key* constraints and *foreign key* constraints. Primary key constraints enforce the uniqueness of the primary key (the unique identifier). For example, forbidding the addition of a sales rep whose number matched the number of a sales rep already in the database would be a primary key constraint. A **foreign key** is a column, or collection of columns, in one table whose values are required to match the primary key of some specific table. An example is the SLSRNUMB column in the CUSTOMER table. Foreign key constraints enforce the fact that a

value for a foreign key must match a value for the primary key of the other table. Forbidding the addition of a customer whose sales rep *was not already in the database* is thus an example of a foreign key constraint.

An integrity constraint can be treated in one of four ways:

1. The constraint can be ignored, in which case, no attempt is made to enforce the constraint. (See Figure 2.14a.)

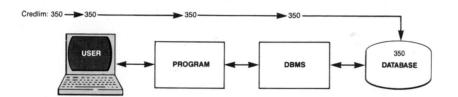

**Figure 2.14a**

Ignoring an integrity constraint (database contains a customer with a $350 credit limit)

2. The burden of enforcing the constraint can be placed on the users of the system. This means that users must be careful that any changes they make in the database do not violate the constraint. (See Figure 2.14b.)

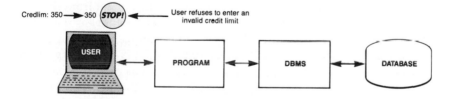

**Figure 2.14b**

User enforcing integrity constraint

3. The burden can be placed on programmers. Logic to enforce the constraint is then built into programs. Users must update the database only by means of these programs and not through any of the built-in entry facilities provided by the DBMS, since these would allow violation of the constraint. The programs are designed to reject any attempt on the part of the user to update the database in such a way that the constraint is violated. (See Figure 2.14c.)

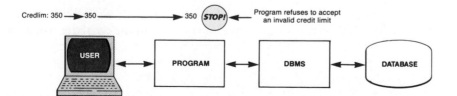

**Figure 2.14c**

Program enforcing integrity constraint

4. The burden can be placed on the DBMS. The constraint is specified to the DBMS, which then rejects any attempt to update the database in such a way that the constraint is violated. (See Figure 2.14d.)

**Figure 2.14d**

DBMS enforcing integrity constraint

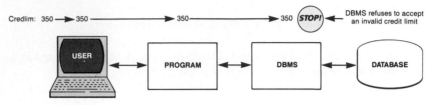

| Question: | Which of these approaches is best? |
|---|---|

Answer:         The fourth approach for the following reasons.

The first approach is undesirable, since it can lead to invalid data in the database (two customers with the same number, part numbers with an invalid format, illegal credit limits, and so on).

The second approach is a little better, since at least an attempt is made to enforce the constraints. Yet it puts the burden of enforcement on the user. Not only does this mean extra work for the user, but any mistake on the part of a single user, no matter how innocent, can lead to invalid data in the database.

The third approach removes the burden of enforcement from the user and places it on the programmers. This is better still, since it means that users will be unable to violate the constraints. The disadvantage is that all the update programs in the system are made more complex. This complexity makes the programmers less productive and makes the programs more difficult to create and modify. It also makes changing an integrity constraint more difficult, since this may mean changing all the programs that update the database. Further, any program in which the logic that is used to enforce the constraints is faulty could permit some constraint to be violated *without anyone being aware that this had happened* until some problem that occurred at a later date brought it to someone's attention. Finally, we would have to carefully guard against a user bypassing the programs in the system to enter data directly into the database (for example, by using a built-in facility of the DBMS). If this should happen, all the controls we had so diligently placed into our programs would be unable to prevent a violation of the constraints.

The best approach is the one in which we put the burden on the DBMS. We would specify constraints to the DBMS and the DBMS would ensure that they are never violated.

Unfortunately, most microcomputer DBMS's and many mainframe DBMS's don't have all the necessary capabilities to enforce the various types of integrity constraints. Usually, the approach that is taken is a combination of (3) and (4). We let the DBMS enforce any of the constraints it is capable of enforcing; other constraints are enforced by application programs. We might also create a special program whose sole purpose would be to examine the data in the database to determine whether any constraints had been violated; this program would be run periodically. Corrective action could be taken to remedy any violations that were discovered by means of this program.

For more discussion of integrity, see [3], [5], [6], [9], [10], [11], and [13].

## SERVICES TO PROMOTE DATA INDEPENDENCE (Function 9)

**Data independence** basically means that users are unaffected by changes to the logical and/or physical structure of the database. If a DBMS truly furnishes data independence, the structure of the database should be able to be changed one night and the programs that ran the preceding day will still run the next day *with no changes*. In fact, we should not even have to recompile these programs. There is, of course, an obvious stipulation that should be added: If any data used by a given program is *removed* from the database structure, then changes will certainly have to be made. If a particular program uses the credit limit field and we no longer store credit limits in the database, clearly something will have to be done to the program.

There are two types of data independence: logical and physical.

**Logical data independence** occurs when changes to the logical structure of the database do not affect the programs that access the database. Changes to the logical structure include adding, deleting, or changing fields, records, or relationships. The addition of the field *CUSTTYPE* to the customer record would be an example of such a change. This change should not affect any existing programs. Logical data independence allows us to change the structure of the database to keep pace with changes in the organization without having to continually change application programs.

**Physical data independence** occurs when changes to the underlying physical structure of the database do not affect the programs that access the database. Changes to the physical structure include changing the storage characteristics of fields, changing the placement strategies for records in the database, changing encryption schemes, changing underlying structures used to directly access records (i.e., changes to the way the database is physically stored and manipulated).

Changing the *BALANCE* field from zoned decimal to packed decimal is an example of a physical change. Another example would be changing the underlying structure used to find all the customers of a given sales rep. Physical data independence allows us to *tune* the database for performance (i.e., to make changes that will improve the overall performance of our applications without having to change the application programs themselves).

Usually in a DBMS, data independence is achieved through a **subschema** or **view** type mechanism. The level of data independence obtained by a given DBMS is determined by the kinds of changes (logical and/or physical) that can be made to the database structure without a subschema or view having to change. Most systems are quite respectable in terms of physical data independence (i.e., there are a number of kinds of changes that can be made to the physical characteristics of the database without affecting the subschemas). Virtually all nonrelational systems fall short of true logical independence. The addition of new fields and records can usually be handled, but *not* changes to relationships. While current relational systems are better at handling changes to relationships, there is still room for improvement. There is every reason to believe that improvement in this area will occur in the near future.

## UTILITY SERVICES (Function 10)

There are a number of services a DBMS can provide which would be of assistance in the general maintenance of the database. Services to facilitate the accomplishment of the physical and logical changes just described, services to gather and report on statistics involving patterns of database usage, and services to examine the data in the database to look for any irregularities (bad pointers, for example) are just a few of the utility-type services a DBMS can and should provide. To do an effective job administering and monitoring a database requires services like these. If the DBMS does not provide them, the enterprise using the DBMS must provide its own.

## SUMMARY

In this chapter, we have examined the capabilities that should be provided by any full-scale DBMS. Ten such capabilities were examined:

1. The DBMS must support data storage, retrieval, and update.
2. The DBMS must include a catalog accessible to the user and that gives descriptions of the various fields, records, and relationships in the database. In addition, the catalog contains information concerning the programs that access the database, including the set of data items accessed by each program and how that data is accessed.

3. The DBMS should provide support for logical transactions. A logical transaction is a sequence of steps that will accomplish what feels to the user like a single task. An example was given of the logical transaction of entering an order. To a user, that was a single task. For the system, however, there were many steps that had to be accomplished. Many different updates had to occur. To say a DBMS supports logical transactions means that the DBMS will ensure that either all the updates will take place or none of them will take place (i.e., we will not be left in that unacceptable middle ground where some of the updates occurred and others did not). If all the updates occur, we say the transaction has been committed. If something prevents all the updates from occurring, we say the transaction has been aborted. In this case, a rollback will be performed in which all the updates that have been made will be undone, thus returning the system to the state it was in before the transaction was started.

4. The DBMS should provide support for shared update. When two or more users update the database at the same time, there is a potential for incorrect results and lost updates. To prevent these problems, the DBMS must allow some form of locking. The amount of material to be locked, called the lock granularity, could be a field, record, page, or the entire database. A lock can either be shared, which permits other programs to read the same data, or exclusive, which prohibits other programs from accessing the data in any way. To ensure correct results, programs should use two-phase locking. In this approach, locks are first gained but never released until a transaction is complete, following which all locks are released. Locking brings up the potential problem of deadlock, which must be resolved in some way. The most common approach is to pick one of the transactions that is in deadlock and abort it (i.e., roll it back).

5. The DBMS should provide recovery services. If the database is damaged in any way, the system should be able to recover the database to a correct state. The DBMS must be capable of backing up the database; maintaining a journal, or log, of all activities that update the database, as well as before and after images of portions of the database; and, finally, using the data in the journal to recover the database. If the database is destroyed, a forward recovery is done, which starts with the backup copy, then applies after images from the journal to roll the database forward. If the database has not been destroyed, a backward recovery may be done, in which before images from the journal are applied in reverse order to roll the database back to the most recent state when the database was known to be correct. After the database has been rolled back, it may be brought forward by applying after images of only committed transactions (transactions that have completed successfully).

6. The DBMS should provide services that protect the database from unauthorized access. There are four basic features of a DBMS that provide for security. Encryption refers to storing the data in the database in an encrypted format. Users that access the database through the DBMS will see the correct information; users that bypass the DBMS will need to break the code to make sense of the data. Subschemas or views provide security by furnishing a mechanism whereby a given user can be kept from knowing about the existence of a particular field or record. If a given user does not have the salary field in his or her subschema, he or she cannot retrieve or update any salaries. In fact, as far as that user is concerned, there is no salary field in the database. Authorization rules allow us to specify that a given subject (person, department, etc.) can take a given action (read, insert, modify, delete) on a given object (record, field, etc.), subject to a given constraint. Finally, user-defined procedures allow the users of a DBMS to add security checks of their own in some programming language. This facility allows users of the DBMS to supplement the security features of the DBMS itself.

   The related topic, privacy, refers to the right of individuals to have certain information concerning themselves kept confidential. It is through appropriate security measures that privacy is ensured.

   Finally, the statistical database concept was briefly examined. A statistical database is one from which statistics (average, sum, max, etc.) are to be drawn but no information about individuals is to be available.

7. The DBMS should provide support for related communications software. In particular, since a good TP monitor provides some services that overlap the services of the DBMS, the two should be carefully integrated.

8. The DBMS should provide services to ensure that the database has integrity. An integrity constraint is a condition that the data in the database must satisfy or, alternatively, a condition that describes the kinds of processing that may or may not take place. The DBMS should ensure that none of these constraints are violated.

9. The DBMS should provide facilities to promote data independence. Data independence means that the overall physical and/or logical structure of the database can be changed without affecting the users or the programs that are accessing the database. Data independence is often divided into physical data independence and logical data independence. Logical data independence occurs when changes to the logical structure do not affect the programs that access the database, and physical data independence occurs when changes to the underlying physical structures do not affect these programs. While many systems do a creditable job of achieving physical data independence, most systems currently fall short of true logical data independence. Good relational model systems come the closest to true logical data independence.

10. The DBMS should provide utility services. There are a number of valuable services a DBMS can and should provide that do not fall into any of the preceding categories and that are more properly termed utilities. These would include services to facilitate the changes to the logical and/or physical structure of the database mentioned in the section on data independence, services to report on statistics concerning different types of database usage, and services to examine the database structure to look for any irregularities.

# REVIEW QUESTIONS

1. What do we mean when we say that a DBMS should provide facilities for storage, retrieval, and update?
2. What is the purpose of the catalog?
3. Discuss why the DBMS (or related software product) should maintain the catalog.
4. When and how is the catalog used? Give examples.
5. Define logical transaction. Give an example of a logical transaction that can be accomplished by updating a single record. Give an example of a logical transaction for which several records must be updated.
6. Why must a system support logical transactions? Why do we even need to worry about them?
7. Describe what is meant by a transaction being committed. Describe what is meant by a transaction being aborted.
8. What is a rollback?
9. Give two different reasons why a transaction might be aborted.
10. What is meant by shared update? What is another name for it?
11. What is meant by locking?
12. Describe a situation, other than the example used in the text, in which uncontrolled shared update produces incorrect results.
13. What is meant by two-phase locking? Give an example illustrating how lack of adherence to two-phase locking would cause a problem.
14. What is deadlock? Why must one transaction be rolled back instead of merely held up and allowed to continue when the other user is done?
15. What is the difference between a shared lock and an exclusive lock? Why is it better to use these two types of locks than just exclusive locks?
16. What is meant by lock granularity? What are the possibilities?
17. How long should records be locked? Why might we need to lock them for a shorter time? How do we prevent the lost update problem from occurring in such situations?

18. Describe the facilities for shared update present on many microcomputer DBMS's.
19. What is meant by recovery?
20. What kinds of events might precipitate the need for a recovery?
21. If the database is updated by a single batch program running once a day, how could recovery be accomplished?

For questions 22 through 28, assume that the database is being updated interactively.

22. What activities must the DBMS perform to be able to do a recovery?
23. What is the journal? What kind of information is kept in the journal?
24. Which should be updated first, the database or the journal? Why?
25. Describe forward recovery. How is it accomplished? When is it appropriate?
26. Describe backward recovery. How is it accomplished? When is it appropriate?
27. If an erroneous transaction has produced invalid data in the database, how may the situation be corrected?
28. What is a differential file? What purpose does it serve?
29. What is meant by security?
30. What is encryption? How does it promote security?
31. How does the subschema facility relate to security?
32. What is an authorization rule? What are the four components of an authorization rule? Give three examples of authorization rules.
33. What types of authorization rules are most commonly supported by current DBMS's? How are they most often supported?
34. What is a user-defined procedure? How does it relate to security?
35. What is privacy? How does it relate to security?
36. What is a statistical database?
37. What is meant by integrity? What is an integrity constraint?
38. What is meant by physical data independence? What benefit is achieved by having a high level of physical data independence?
39. What is meant by logical data independence? What benefit is achieved by having a high level of logical data independence?
40. How does the subschema facility relate to data independence?
41. Give two examples of utility services that a DBMS should provide.

# EXERCISES

For questions 1 through 6, assume that the log shown in Figure 2.11 has been expanded to include the time when records are read and that the result is shown in Figure 2.15.

**Figure 2.15**

Sample log
(including READ
operations)

| TRANS ID | TIME | ACTION | OBJECT OF ACTION | BEFORE IMAGE | AFTER IMAGE |
|---|---|---|---|---|---|
| CST1 | 8:00 | START | | | |
| CST1 | 8:01 | READ | CUSTOMER (256) | | |
| PRT1 | 8:02 | START | | | |
| CST1 | 8:03 | MODIFY | CUSTOMER (256) | (old values) | (new values) |
| ORD1 | 8:05 | START | | | |
| CST1 | 8:06 | COMMIT | | | |
| ORD1 | 8:07 | READ | CUSTOMER (405) | | |
| ORD1 | 8:08 | MODIFY | CUSTOMER (405) | (old values) | (new values) |
| PRT2 | 8:09 | START | | | |
| ORD1 | 8:10 | READ | SLSREP (12) | | |
| PRT1 | 8:12 | INSERT | PART (BV57) | | (new values) |
| ORD1 | 8:13 | MODIFY | SLSREP (12) | (old values) | (new values) |
| PRT1 | 8:14 | COMMIT | | | |
| PRT2 | 8:15 | READ | PART (BH22) | | |
| ORD1 | 8:16 | INSERT | ORDERS (12506) | | (new values) |
| ORD1 | 8:17 | READ | PART (AX12) | | |
| ORD1 | 8:18 | INSERT | ORDLNE (12506,AX12) | | (new values) |
| PRT2 | 8:19 | ERASE | PART (BH22) | (old values) | |
| ORD1 | 8:20 | READ | PART (CZ81) | | |
| ORD1 | 8:21 | INSERT | ORDLNE (12506,CZ81) | | (new values) |
| ORD1 | 8:22 | MODIFY | PART (AX12) | (old values) | (new values) |
| PRT2 | 8:23 | COMMIT | | | |
| ORD1 | 8:24 | MODIFY | PART (CZ81) | (old values) | (new values) |
| ORD1 | 8:26 | COMMIT | | | |

1. Assume that the DBMS being used issues locks whenever a READ, MODIFY, INSERT, or ERASE command is given and releases all locks held by a transaction when a COMMIT command is executed. Assume also that locking occurs at the record level. Indicate the locks held by each transaction at each point in time throughout the session shown in Figure 2.15 using the following format.

| Time | Trans. | Locks Held |
|------|--------|------------|
| 8:00 |        |            |
| 8:01 | CST1   | CUSTOMER 256 |
| 8:02 | CST1   | CUSTOMER 256 |
| 8:03 | CST1   | CUSTOMER 256 |
| 8:05 | CST1   | CUSTOMER 256 |
| 8:06 |        |            |
| 8:07 | ORD1   | CUSTOMER 405 |
| .    | .      | .          |
| .    | .      | .          |
| .    | .      | .          |

2. Some systems, in particular many microcomputer systems, will issue a lock to a transaction when a READ command is executed and will release the lock as soon as a MODIFY or ERASE command is executed for the same record. In addition, the lock will be released if another record of the same type is read. (Two separate *PART* records could not be locked by the same transaction at the same time, for example.) No record is locked for an INSERT command. Indicate the locks that would be held if the DBMS being used operates in such a fashion.

| Time | Trans. | Locks Held |
|------|--------|------------|
| 8:00 |        |            |
| 8:01 | CST1   | CUSTOMER 256 |
| 8:02 | CST1   | CUSTOMER 256 |
| 8:03 |        |            |
| 8:05 |        |            |
| 8:06 |        |            |
| 8:07 | ORD1   | CUSTOMER 405 |
| .    | .      | .          |
| .    | .      | .          |
| .    | .      | .          |

3. Assume that the DBMS being used issues shared locks whenever a READ command is issued and promotes the locks to exclusive when a subsequent MODIFY, INSERT, or ERASE command is issued. All other assumptions are the same as in question 1. Indicate the locks held by each transaction at each point in time throughout the session shown in Figure 2.14. For each lock, indicate whether it is shared or exclusive. Use (S) for shared and (E) for exclusive.

| Time | Trans. | Locks Held |
|------|--------|------------|
| 8:00 |        |            |
| 8:01 | CST1   | CUSTOMER 256 (S) |
| 8:02 | CST1   | CUSTOMER 256 (S) |
| 8:03 | CST1   | CUSTOMER 256 (E) |
| 8:05 | CST1   | CUSTOMER 256 (E) |
| 8:06 |        |            |
| 8:07 | ORD1   | CUSTOMER 405 (S) |
| .    | .      | .          |
| .    | .      | .          |
| .    | .      | .          |

4. Suppose another transaction, CST2, started at 8:04, read customer 405 at 8:06:30, modified customer 405 at 8:08:30, and committed at 8:11. What effect, if any, would this have on the sequence of operations shown in the log?

5. Suppose transaction PRT2 erased PART "CZ81" rather than PART "BH22." What effect, if any, would this have on the sequence of operations shown in the log?

6. Suppose transaction CST1 read and modified customer 405 rather than 256. Suppose further that transaction CST1 did not commit at 8:06 but, instead, read sales rep 12 and later, at 8:15:30, attempted to modify sales rep 12. What effect, if any, would this have on the sequence of operations shown in the log?

7. What problems would the absence of the COMMIT records in the log cause for backward and forward recovery?

8. Indicate the subject, object, action, and constraint associated with each of the following:

   a. Sales reps may retrieve customer data for their own customers but may not update this data.

   b. The order entry staff may add orders and order lines.

   c. Tom may delete customers who do not have any orders on file and whose balance is zero.

   d. Mary may perform any type of update on any item in the database.

9. Give three examples of integrity constraints that pertain to data in the database.

10. Give an example of an integrity constraint that gives conditions under which a given type of processing *may not* take place. Give an example of an integrity constraint that gives conditions under which a given type of processing *must* take place.

## REFERENCES

1] Atre, S., *Data Base: Structured Techniques for Design, Performance, and Management*, 2nd ed. John Wiley & Sons, Inc., 1988.

2] Bradley, James, *Introduction to Data Base Management in Business*, 2d ed. Holt, Rinehart & Winston, 1987.

3] Cardenas, Alfonso F., *Data Base Management Systems*, 2d ed. Allyn & Bacon, 1984.

4] Codd, E. F., "Relational Database: A Practical Foundation for Productivity." *Communications of the ACM 25*, no. 2 (February 1982).

5] Date, C. J., *Introduction to Database Systems, Volume I*, 4th ed. Addison-Wesley, 1986.

6] Date, C. J., *Introduction to Database Systems, Volume II*, Addison-Wesley, 1983.

7] Denning, D. E., and Denning, P. J., "Data Security." *ACM Computing Surveys* 11, no. 3 (September 1979).

8] Fernandez, Eduardo B., Summers, Rita C., and Wood, Christopher, *Database Security and Integrity*. Addison-Wesley, 1980.

9] Goldstein, Robert C., *Database Technology and Management*, John Wiley & Sons, 1985

10] Kroenke, David., and Dolan, Kathleen A., *Database Processing: Fundamentals, Design, Implementation*, 3d ed. SRA, 1988.

11] McFadden, Fred R., and Hoffer, Jeffrey A., *Data Base Management*, 2d ed. Benjamin Cummings, 1988.

12] Teorey, Toby J., and Fry, James P., *Design of Database Structures*, Prentice-Hall, 1982.

13] Vasta, Joseph A., *Understanding Data Base Management Systems*, Wadsworth, 1985.

14] Wood, J. Chris, "Restart and Recovery in DBMS's." In *A Practical Guide to Data Base Management*, ed. John Hannan. Auerbach, 1982.

15] Young, John W., Jr., "Concurrency in DBMS's." In *A Practical Guide to Data Base Management*, ed. John Hannan. Auerbach, 1982.

# Introduction to the Relational Model

## INTRODUCTION

In a landmark paper in 1970, Dr. E. F. Codd proposed "...a relational model of data for large shared databanks." (See [3].) Throughout the '70s, this **relational model** was the subject of a great deal of theoretical research activity. Prototype relational systems were being developed, most notably a system called "System R" from IBM. With the advent of the 1980s, commercial relational systems began appearing, first in the mainframe environment and then in the microcomputer environment. These have now proliferated to the extent that there are large numbers of systems which are, at least in some sense, relational.

When compared to the other DBMS models, the **hierarchical model** and the **network model**, the relational model offers the following advantages:

1. The logical and physical characteristics of the database are separated.
2. The model is much more easily understood. Data is viewed in a more natural way, with no complex paths to be followed.
3. There are powerful operators available, which enable even complex operations to be accomplished with brief commands.
4. The model provides a sound framework for the design of databases. Until the introduction of the relational model, database design was definitely a "seat of the pants" process in which designs were used simply because they felt right. On occasion, reasonably correct designs were produced in this manner. Usually, however, designs were incorrect, problem-ridden, and the direct cause of some major computing disasters. The relational model provides important tools that allow us to determine whether there are potential problems in a design. If such problems do exist, it provides a mechanism for correcting the design.

Like the other models, the relational model has its proponents and critics. Even its critics will admit that relational model systems are much easier to use and more flexible than nonrelational systems. The critics claim, however, that relational model systems are not nearly as efficient as some of the good hierarchical and network systems and that this makes them inappropriate for large applications. Its proponents respond that there is no reason a relational model system cannot be as efficient as any other. The view of the authors of this text is that while at the present time the relational model systems are in general less efficient than some of the best of the nonrelational model systems, the gap is narrowing. When the time comes, and it will, that the relational systems are comparable in efficiency, new application development will, with rare exceptions, take place only with regard to relational systems. The other systems will continue to exist for a number of years, owing to the sheer volume of current applications that have been developed with them, but they will not be the subject of many new applications.

In this chapter we study the basic relational model. We first look at the model itself and some of the important terminology. We then examine how various types of relationships are implemented within the relational model. The remaining sections deal with various approaches to the problem of manipulating data within the relational model, including both updating what is currently in the database (**data manipulation**) and producing reports using the data in the database (**data retrieval**).

## *TERMINOLOGY*

In its simplest terms, a relation is just a two-dimensional table. Figure 3.1 shows the five tables, or relations, for Premiere Products that were discussed in chapter 1.

In examining these tables, we can see that there are certain restrictions we would probably want to place on relations. Each column should have a unique name, and entries within each column should all "match" this column name (i.e., if the column name is *CREDLIM* (credit limit), all entries in that column should actually be credit limits). Also, each row should be unique. After all, if two rows are absolutely identical, the second row does not give us any information that we didn't already have. In addition, for maximum flexibility, the ordering of the columns and the rows should be immaterial. Finally, the table will be simplest if each position is restricted to a single entry (i.e., if we do not allow repeating groups or arrays in an individual location in the table). These ideas lead to the following definitions:

**SLSREP**

| SLSRNUMB | SLSRNAME | SLSRADDR | TOTCOMM | COMMRATE |
|---|---|---|---|---|
| 3 | Jones, Mary | 123 Main,Grant,MI | 2150.00 | .05 |
| 6 | Smith, William | 102 Raymond,Ada,MI | 4912.50 | .07 |
| 12 | Brown, Sam | 419 Harper,Lansing,MI | 2150.00 | .05 |

**CUSTOMER**

| CUSTNUMB | CUSTNAME | CUSTADDR | BALANCE | CREDLIM | SLSRNUMB |
|---|---|---|---|---|---|
| 124 | Adams, Sally | 481 Oak,Lansing,MI | 418.75 | 500 | 3 |
| 256 | Samuels, Ann | 215 Pete,Grant,MI | 10.75 | 800 | 6 |
| 311 | Charles, Don | 48 College,Ira,MI | 200.10 | 300 | 12 |
| 315 | Daniels, Tom | 914 Cherry,Kent,MI | 320.75 | 300 | 6 |
| 405 | Williams, Al | 519 Watson,Grant,MI | 201.75 | 800 | 12 |
| 412 | Adams, Sally | 16 Elm,Lansing,MI | 908.75 | 1000 | 3 |
| 522 | Nelson, Mary | 108 Pine,Ada,MI | 49.50 | 800 | 12 |
| 567 | Baker, Joe | 808 Ridge,Harper,MI | 201.20 | 300 | 6 |
| 587 | Roberts, Judy | 512 Pine,Ada,MI | 57.75 | 500 | 6 |
| 622 | Martin, Dan | 419 Chip,Grant,MI | 575.50 | 500 | 3 |

**ORDERS**

| ORDNUMB | ORDDTE | CUSTNUMB |
|---|---|---|
| 12489 | 90291 | 124 |
| 12491 | 90291 | 311 |
| 12494 | 90491 | 315 |
| 12495 | 90491 | 256 |
| 12498 | 90591 | 522 |
| 12500 | 90591 | 124 |
| 12504 | 90591 | 522 |

**ORDLNE**

| ORDNUMB | PARTNUMB | NUMBORD | QUOTPRCE |
|---|---|---|---|
| 12489 | AX12 | 11 | 14.95 |
| 12491 | BT04 | 1 | 402.99 |
| 12491 | BZ66 | 1 | 311.95 |
| 12494 | CB03 | 4 | 175.00 |
| 12495 | CX11 | 2 | 57.95 |
| 12498 | AZ52 | 2 | 22.95 |
| 12498 | BA74 | 4 | 4.95 |
| 12500 | BT04 | 1 | 402.99 |
| 12504 | CZ81 | 2 | 108.99 |

**PART**

| PARTNUMB | PARTDESC | UNONHAND | ITEMCLSS | WRHSNUMB | UNITPRCE |
|---|---|---|---|---|---|
| AX12 | IRON | 104 | HW | 3 | 17.95 |
| AZ52 | SKATES | 20 | SG | 2 | 24.95 |
| BA74 | BASEBALL | 40 | SG | 1 | 4.95 |
| BH22 | TOASTER | 95 | HW | 3 | 34.95 |
| BT04 | STOVE | 11 | AP | 2 | 402.99 |
| BZ66 | WASHER | 52 | AP | 3 | 311.95 |
| CA14 | SKILLET | 2 | HW | 3 | 19.95 |
| CB03 | BIKE | 44 | SG | 1 | 187.50 |
| CX11 | MIXER | 112 | HW | 3 | 57.95 |
| CZ81 | WEIGHTS | 208 | SG | 2 | 108.99 |

**Figure 3.1**

Premiere Products
sample data

*Definition:* A **relation** is a two-dimensional table in which...

- the entries in the table are single-valued.
- each column has a distinct name (called the attribute name).
- all the values in a column are values of the same attribute (namely, the attribute identified by the column name).
- the order of columns is immaterial.
- each row is distinct.
- the order of rows is immaterial.

*Definition:* A **relational database** is a collection of relations.

Each row of the relation is technically called a **tuple**, and each column is technically called an **attribute**. Thus, we have two different sets of terms: relation, tuple, attribute and table, row, column. There is actually a third set. The table could be viewed as a file. (In fact, this is how relational databases are often, but not always, stored, with each relation, or table, in a separate file.) In this case, we would call the rows records and the columns fields. We now have *three* different sets of terms! Their correspondence is shown below.

| FORMAL TERMS | ALTERNATIVE ONE | ALTERNATIVE TWO |
|:---:|:---:|:---:|
| relation | table | file |
| tuple | row | record |
| attribute | column | field |

Of these three sets of choices, the one that is the most popular is Alternative One: tables, rows, and columns. One reason for its popularity is that it seems the most natural to the nontechnical user. A second reason is that many of the commercial relational DBMS's, including IBM's offering in the relational database market, use these terms. In this text, as well as many other references, the formal terms and the corresponding terms from the first alternative will be used interchangeably.

As a sort of shorthand representation of the structure of these tables, we write the name of the table and then within parentheses list all the columns in the table. Thus, this sample database consists of:

```
SLSREP (SLSRNUMB, SLSRNAME, SLSRADDR, TOTCOMM, COMMRATE)
CUSTOMER (CUSTNUMB, CUSTNAME, CUSTADDR, BALANCE, CREDLIM,
          SLSRNUMB)
ORDERS (ORDNUMB, ORDDTE, CUSTNUMB)
ORDLNE (ORDNUMB, PARTNUMB, NUMBORD, QUOTPRCE)
PART (PARTNUMB, PARTDESC, UNONHAND, ITEMCLSS, WRHSNUMB,
      UNITPRCE)
```

Notice that there is some duplication of names. The attribute *SLSRNUMB* appears in *both* the *SLSREP* relation *and* the *CUSTOMER* relation. If a situation exists wherein the two might be confused, we **qualify** the names by placing the relation name in front of the attribute name, separated by a period. Therefore, we would write *CUSTOMER.SLSRNUMB* or *SLSREP.SLSRNUMB*. It is always acceptable to qualify data names, even if there is no possible confusion. There will be times, however, when it is absolutely essential to do so.

The **primary key** of a relation is the attribute (column) or collection of attributes that uniquely identifies a given tuple (row). In the *SLSREP* relation, for example, the sales rep's number uniquely identifies a given row. (Sales rep 6 occurs in only one row of the table, for example.) Thus *SLSRNUMB* is the primary key. As indicated in the shorthand representation, the common practice is to underline the primary keys.

Q & A

---

**Question:**       Why does the primary key to the *ORDLNE* relation consist of two attributes, not just one?

**Answer:**          No single attribute uniquely identifies a given row. It requires two: *ORDNUMB* and *PARTNUMB*.

---

There is another kind of key that is extremely important. An attribute in one relation that is required to match the primary key of another relation is called a **foreign key**. As an example, the *SLSRNUMB* in the customer relation should match a real sales rep (i.e., the *SLSRNUMB* of an actual sales rep in the *SLSREP* table). We say the sales rep number in the *CUSTOMER* table (*CUSTOMER.SLSRNUMB*) is a foreign key that identifies *SLSREP*. This provides a mechanism for explicitly specifying relationships between two different relations, as well as a mechanism for ensuring integrity. It tells us there is a relationship between customers and their sales reps. It also indicates that we should not enter a customer in the *CUSTOMER* table whose sales rep is not already in the *SLSREP* table. For example, given the current data for Premiere Products, as shown in Figure 3.1, we should not enter a customer whose sales rep number is 4.

A word about repeating groups is in order. A structure that satisfies all the properties listed earlier is often called a **normalized** relation. A structure that satisfies all but property 1 (i.e., repeating groups are allowed) is sometimes called an **unnormalized** relation. Thus, according to the definition, an unnormalized relation is technically not a relation at all!

It is always possible to replace an unnormalized relation with a normalized relation that is equivalent (i.e., that represents the same information).

Consider the following unnormalized relation, for example.

ORDERS(<u>ORDNUMB</u>, ORDDTE, PARTNUMB, NUMBORD)

(This notation indicates an unnormalized relation, called *ORDERS*, consisting of a primary key, *ORDNUMB*, an attribute, *ORDDTE*, and a repeating group containing two attributes, *PARTNUMB* and *NUMBORD*.) Figure 3.2 gives a sample of this relation. To **normalize** this relation, the repeating group is removed, giving the following:

ORDERS(<u>ORDNUMB</u>, ORDDTE, <u>PARTNUMB</u>, NUMBORD)

**Figure 3.2**

Unnormalized
*ORDER* relation

ORDERS

| ORDNUMB | ORDDTE | PARTNUMB | NUMBORD |
|--------:|-------:|----------|--------:|
| 12489 | 90291 | AX12 | 11 |
| 12491 | 90291 | BT04<br>BZ66 | 1<br>1 |
| 12494 | 90491 | CB03 | 4 |
| 12495 | 90491 | CX11 | 2 |
| 12498 | 90591 | AZ52<br>BA74 | 2<br>4 |
| 12500 | 90591 | BT04 | 1 |
| 12504 | 90591 | CZ81 | 2 |

The corresponding sample of the new relation is shown in Figure 3.3. Note that the second row of the unnormalized relation indicated that part BT04 and part BZ66 were both present for order 12491. In the normalized relation, this information is represented by *two* rows, the second and third. Notice also that the primary key of the new relation is no longer just the order number, but the combination of the order number and the part number. (Technically, it is called the **concatenation** of the order number and part number.)

**ORDERS**

| ORDNUMB | ORDDTE | PARTNUMB | NUMBORD |
|--------:|-------:|----------|--------:|
| 12489 | 90291 | AX12 | 11 |
| 12491 | 90291 | BT04 | 1 |
| 12491 | 90291 | BZ66 | 1 |
| 12494 | 90491 | CB03 | 4 |
| 12495 | 90491 | CX11 | 2 |
| 12498 | 90591 | AZ52 | 2 |
| 12498 | 90591 | BA74 | 4 |
| 12500 | 90591 | BT04 | 1 |
| 12504 | 90591 | CZ81 | 2 |

**Figure 3.3**

Normalized *ORDER* relation

## EXPRESSING RELATIONSHIPS

A database contains not only information about several different types of entities (sales reps, customers, orders), but also information about relationships between these entities. A sales rep is related to the customers he or she represents. A customer is related to the orders he or she has placed. In the relational model, these relationships are achieved by having common attributes in separate tables. The relationship between sales reps and the customers they represent, for example, is achieved by having the sales rep number in both the *SLSREP* table and the *CUSTOMER* table.

The two most common types of relationships with which we must contend are one-to-many and many-to-many. If the relationship between entity A and entity B is *one-to-many*, every occurrence of A is related to many occurrences of B, but every occurrence of B is related to one occurrence of A. For example, at Premiere Products the relationship between sales reps and customers is one-to-many, since one sales rep represents many customers, but each customer is represented by exactly one sales rep. If the relationship between entity A and entity B is *many-to-many*, every occurrence of A is related to many occurrences of B, and every occurrence of B is related to many occurrences of A. At Premiere Products, for example, the relationship between orders and parts is many-to-many since an order contains many different parts and each part can appear on many different orders.

We will now examine the manner in which each of these types of relationships may be implemented in the relational model.

### One-to-Many Relationship

Suppose that at Premiere Products each customer is represented by only one sales rep, but each sales rep represents many customers. In this case, we will have one table for sales reps and a separate table for customers. We will include the primary key of the "one" part of the relationship, in this case sales reps, as a foreign key in the "many" part of the relationship. (See Figure 3.4.)

**Figure 3.4**

One-to-many relationship implemented by including the primary key of the "one" as a foreign key in the "many"

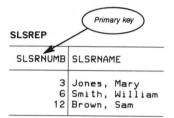

SLSREP

| SLSRNUMB | SLSRNAME |
|---|---|
| 3 | Jones, Mary |
| 6 | Smith, William |
| 12 | Brown, Sam |

CUSTOMER

| CUSTNUMB | CUSTNAME | SLSRNUMB |
|---|---|---|
| 124 | Adams, Sally | 3 |
| 256 | Samuels, Ann | 6 |
| 311 | Charles, Don | 12 |
| 315 | Daniels, Tom | 6 |
| 405 | Williams, Al | 12 |
| 412 | Adams, Sally | 3 |
| 522 | Nelson, Mary | 12 |
| 567 | Baker, Joe | 6 |
| 587 | Roberts, Judy | 6 |
| 622 | Martin, Dan | 3 |

Since each customer appears in only one row in the *CUSTOMER* relation and this row contains a single sales rep number, each customer is associated with exactly one sales rep. On the other hand, since the *SLSREP* relation itself contains no customer number column, the only way to find the customer or customers a given sales rep represents is to find those rows within the *CUSTOMER* relation that contain the desired sales rep number. Since an individual sales rep number can occur in many rows within the *CUSTOMER* relation, a given sales rep is associated with many customers.

## Many-to-Many Relationship

Suppose that at Premiere Products each order contains lines for many differ-ent parts, and each part is found on lines in many different orders. We will need an *ORDERS* table and a *PART* table. To implement the many-to-many relationship between orders and parts, we introduce a third table containing as its key the concatenation (combination) of the keys of the original tables. In this case, the key is the concatenation of *ORDNUMB* and *PARTNUMB*. In addition, there may be other columns in this new table if there are any attrib-utes that depend on both *ORDNUMB* and *PARTNUMB*. Here, the number of units of a given part that were ordered and the quoted price could be the third and fourth columns in the relation. In this case, the third table effectively represents lines within the orders and we call it *ORDLNE*. The relations are shown in Figure 3.5.

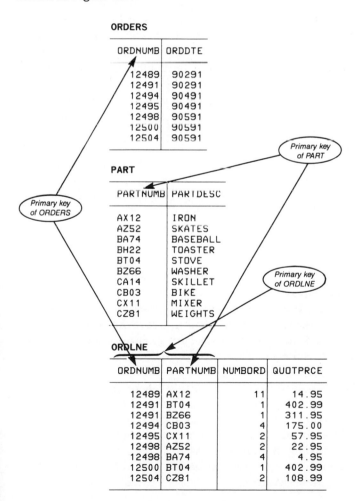

**Figure 3.5**

Implementation of a many-to-many relationship

To find the parts that are related to a given order, we find the part numbers that appear in any row in the *ORDLNE* relation that contains the appropriate order number. Since any number of such rows is possible, an order is related to many parts. Likewise, to find the orders that are related to a given part, we find the order numbers that appear in any row in the *ORDLNE* relation that contains the appropriate part number. Again, any number of such rows is possible and a part is related to many orders.

## *SQL*

The remaining sections of this chapter are devoted to studying a variety of approaches to data manipulation within the relational model (i.e., relational **data manipulation language**, or **DML**). The examples throughout these sections will use the database described in Figure 3.1. Most of the examples will involve retrieval, or getting information out of the database for either a printed report or for display on a screen. Obtaining this information from the data in the database is also called **querying the database**. We refer to the commands that request this information as "queries."

From a theoretical standpoint, perhaps the most important approach to manipulating relational databases is the **relational calculus**, which is based on the *predicate calculus*, a term whose origin is the discipline known as mathematical logic. The idea of a relational calculus was first proposed by Codd (see [4]), who also presented a language called ALPHA, which was based on this calculus (see [5]). Although this language was never implemented, a language with a similar flavor, called QUEL, is used as the manipulation language in the relational DBMS, INGRES, which will be examined in chapter 5. Basically, the importance of the relational calculus is in the theoretical arena, and we will not discuss it here. The only other point we wish to make regarding the relational calculus concerns the concept of *relational completeness*, a concept defined by Codd. (See [4].) A language is said to be **relationally complete** if any relation that can be retrieved by using the relational calculus can also be retrieved using that other language. In other words, if the other language is as "powerful" as the relational calculus. Thus, the relational calculus forms a yardstick by which other languages for relational data manipulation can be measured. For further information on the relational calculus, see [2], [6], and [11].

Other relational DML approaches to be studied here are SQL, the relational algebra, and Query-by-Example. In this section we examine the language called **SQL** (Structured Query Language), which is perhaps the most important relational DML of all. Many, if not most, relational DBMS's use a version of SQL, or something similar to it, as their data manipulation language. In addition, there is every reason to believe that this trend will continue as new systems are developed.

SQL is an example of a *transform-oriented* language, or a language designed to use relations to transform inputs into desired outputs. It does bear some similarity to the relational calculus mentioned earlier. It was developed under the name SEQUEL at the IBM San Jose research facilities as the DML for IBM's prototype relational model DBMS, System R, in the mid-1970s. In 1980, it was renamed SQL to avoid confusion with an unrelated hardware product called SEQUEL. It is used as the DML for IBM's current production offerings in the relational DBMS arena, SQL/DS and DB2.

Before beginning our study of SQL, we should note that even though we have referred to it as a relational DML, it is really more than that. It also contains facilities to *define* data, that is, to describe the structure of the database. This facility is usually called a **data definition language (DDL)**. Thus, SQL is both a DML and a DDL.

Some points concerning these examples should be made before we begin. As you might expect, SQL, like most modern languages, is basically free-format. The purpose of the indenting scheme shown in this chapter is strictly readability. Commas, where used, are essential, however.

In the examples that follow, we will investigate the manner in which tables may be described, data may be retrieved, new data may be added, data may be changed, and data may be deleted.

## Database Creation

We must describe the layout of each table in the database before we can begin loading and accessing data.

**Example 1:** Describe the layout of the sales rep table to the DBMS.

The SQL statement used to describe the layout of a table is CREATE TABLE. The word TABLE is followed by the name of the table to be created and then by the names and data types of the columns that comprise the table. The rules for naming tables and columns vary slightly from one version of SQL to another. If you have any doubts about the validity of any of the names you have chosen, you should consult a manual. Typical restrictions are:

1. The name can be no longer than 18 characters.
2. The name must start with a letter.
3. The name can contain letters, numbers, and underscores (_).
4. The name cannot contain spaces.

The names used in this text should work on any SQL implementation.

In example 1, the appropriate statement is:

```
CREATE TABLE SLSREP
    (SLSRNUMB      DECIMAL(2),
     SLSRNAME      CHAR(15),
     SLSRADDR      CHAR(25),
     TOTCOMM       DECIMAL(7,2),
     COMMRATE      DECIMAL(3,2))
```

In this SQL statement, which uses the data definition features of SQL, we're describing a table that will be called *SLSREP*. It contains five columns: *SLSRNUMB*, *SLSRNAME*, *SLSRADDR*, *TOTCOMM*, and *COMMRATE*. *SLSRNUMB* is a two-digit number. *SLSRNAME* is a fifteen-character alphanumeric field and *SLSRADDR* is a twenty-five-character alphanumeric field. *TOTCOMM* is numeric and is seven digits long, including two decimal places. Similarly, *COMMRATE* is three digits long, and two of those are decimal places. We can visualize this statement as setting up for us a blank table with appropriate column headings. (See Figure 3.6.)

**Figure 3.6**

Blank *SLSREP* table

**SLSREP**

| SLSRNUMB | SLSRNAME | SLSRADDR | TOTCOMM | COMMRATE |
|----------|----------|----------|---------|----------|
|          |          |          |         |          |
|          |          |          |         |          |

**Note:** In SQL, commands are free-format. No rule says that a particular word must begin in a particular position on the line. The previous SQL command could have been written:

```
CREATE TABLE SLSREP (SLSRNUMB DECIMAL(2), SLSRNAME
CHAR(15)  SLSRADDR CHAR(25), TOTCOMM DECIMAL(7,2), COMMRATE
DECIMAL(2,2))
```

The manner in which it was actually written simply makes the command more readable. Throughout the text, we will strive for such readability when we write SQL commands.

## Data Types

Besides the data types DECIMAL (numeric) and CHAR (text), there are other types. While the actual data types will vary somewhat from one implementation of SQL to another, the following list indicates the types that are often encountered.

1. **INTEGER.** Integers, or numbers without a decimal part. Range is –2147483648 to 2147483647.
2. **SMALLINT.** Like INTEGER but does not occupy as much space. Range is –32768 to 32767. This is a better choice than INTEGER if you are certain that numbers will be in the indicated range.
3. **DECIMAL (p,q).** Decimal number $p$ digits long with $q$ of these being decimal places. For example, DECIMAL (5,2) represents a number with three places to the left of the decimal and two to the right.
4. **CHAR (n).** Character string $n$ characters long.
5. **DATE.** Dates in the form DD-MON-YY or MM/DD/YYYY. For example, May 12, 1991 could be stored as 12-MAY-91 or 5/12/1991.

### Simple Retrieval

The basic form of an SQL expression is quite simple: SELECT-FROM-WHERE. After the SELECT, we list those columns we wish to display. After the FROM, we list the table or tables involved in the query. Finally, after the WHERE, we list any conditions that apply to the data we want to retrieve.

There are no special format rules in SQL. In this text, we place the word FROM on a new line indented five spaces, then place the word WHERE (when it is used) on the next line indented five spaces. This makes the commands more readable.

**Example 2:** List the number, name, and balance of all customers.

Since we want all customers listed, there is no need for the WHERE clause (we have no restrictions). The query is thus:

```
SELECT CUSTNUMB, CUSTNAME, BALANCE
     FROM CUSTOMER
```

The computer responds with:

| CUSTNUMB | CUSTNAME | BALANCE |
|---|---|---|
| 124 | Adams, Sally | 418.75 |
| 256 | Samuels, Ann | 10.75 |
| 311 | Charles, Don | 200.10 |
| 315 | Daniels, Tom | 320.75 |
| 405 | Williams, Al | 201.75 |
| 412 | Adams, Sally | 908.75 |
| 522 | Nelson, Mary | 49.50 |
| 567 | Baker, Joe | 201.20 |
| 587 | Roberts, Judy | 57.75 |
| 622 | Martin, Dan | 575.50 |

**Example 3:** List the complete part table.

We could certainly use the same approach as in example 2. However, there is a shortcut. Instead of listing all the column names after SELECT, we can use the "*" symbol. This indicates that we want all columns listed (in the order in which we described them to the system during data definition). If we want all the columns, but in a different order, we would have to type the names of the columns in the order we want them to appear. In this case, assuming the normal order is appropriate, the query would be:

```
SELECT *
    FROM PART
```

| PARTNUMB | PARTDESC | UNONHAND | ITEMCLSS | WRHSNUMB | UNITPRCE |
|----------|----------|----------|----------|----------|----------|
| AX12 | IRON | 104 | HW | 3 | 17.95 |
| AZ52 | SKATES | 20 | SG | 2 | 24.95 |
| BA74 | BASEBALL | 40 | SG | 1 | 4.95 |
| BH22 | TOASTER | 95 | HW | 3 | 34.95 |
| BT04 | STOVE | 11 | AP | 2 | 402.99 |
| BZ66 | WASHER | 52 | AP | 3 | 311.95 |
| CA14 | SKILLET | 2 | HW | 3 | 19.95 |
| CB03 | BIKE | 44 | SG | 1 | 187.50 |
| CX11 | MIXER | 112 | HW | 3 | 57.95 |
| CZ81 | WEIGHTS | 208 | SG | 2 | 108.99 |

**Example 4:** What is the name of customer 124?

We use the WHERE clause to restrict the output of the query to customer 124 as follows:

```
SELECT CUSTNAME
    FROM CUSTOMER
    WHERE CUSTNUMB = 124
```

| CUSTNAME |
|----------|
| Adams, Sally |

The condition in the preceding WHERE clause is called a simple condition. A **simple condition** has the form: column name, comparison operator, then either another column name or a value. The possible comparison operators are shown in Figure 3.7. Note that there are two different versions for "not equal to" (< > and ! =). You must use the one that is right for your particular implementation of SQL. (If you use the wrong one, your system will instantly let you know. Simply use the other.)

| Comparison Operator | Meaning |
|---|---|
| = | Equal to |
| < | Less than |
| > | Greater than |
| <= | Less than or equal to |
| >= | Greater than or equal to |
| <> | Not equal to (used by most implementations of SQL) |
| != | Not equal to (used by some implementations of SQL) |

**Figure 3.7**

Comparison operators

In example 4, the WHERE clause compared a numeric column, *CUSTNUMB*, to a number, 124. In that command, we simply used the number 124. No special action had to be taken. When the query involves a character column, such as *CUSTNAME*, the value to which the column is being compared must be surrounded by single quote marks, as illustrated in example 5.

**Example 5:** Find the customer number for any customer whose name is Sally Adams.

Remember that the names are stored in the database with the last name followed by a comma, then the first name. The query is thus:

```
SELECT CUSTNUMB
     FROM CUSTOMER
     WHERE CUSTNAME = 'Adams, Sally'
```

```
CUSTNUMB
```
```
    124
    412
```

The conditions we've seen so far are called simple conditions. The next examples require compound conditions. **Compound conditions** are formed by connecting two or more simple conditions using AND, OR, and NOT. When simple conditions are connected by the word AND, all the simple conditions must be true in order for the compound condition to be true. When simple conditions are connected by the word OR, the compound condition will be true whenever any of the simple conditions are true. Preceding a condition by NOT reverses the truth or falsity of the original condition. That is, if the original condition is true, the new condition will be false; if the original condition is false, the new one will be true.

**Example 6:** List the descriptions of all parts in warehouse 3, and have more than 100 units on hand.

In this example, we want those parts for which *both* the warehouse number is equal to 3 *and* the number of units on hand is greater than 100. Thus, we form a compound condition using the word AND as follows:

```
SELECT PARTDESC
     FROM PART
     WHERE WRHSNUMB = 3
     AND UNONHAND > 100
```

```
PARTDESC

IRON
MIXER
```

As you would expect, we form compound conditions involving OR in the same fashion. We simply use the word OR instead of the word AND.

**Example 7:** List the descriptions of all parts that are not in warehouse 3.

For this example, we could use a simple condition with the condition operator "not equal to." As an alternative, we could use EQUALS in the condition, but precede the whole condition with the word NOT, as follows:

```
SELECT PARTDESC
     FROM PART
     WHERE NOT (WRHSNUMB = 3)
```

```
PARTDESC

SKATES
BASEBALL
STOVE
BIKE
WEIGHTS
```

It is possible to use computed columns in SQL queries. By a **computed column**, we mean one that does not exist in the database but can be computed from columns that do. Such computations can involve any of the arithmetic operators shown in Figure 3.8. The query in example 8, for instance, uses subtraction.

| Arithmetic Operator | Meaning |
|---|---|
| + | Addition |
| - | Subtraction |
| * | Multiplication |
| / | Division |

**Figure 3.8**

Arithmetic operators

**Example 8:** Find the available credit for all customers who have a credit limit of at least $800.

There is no column for available credit in our database. It is, however, computable from two columns that are present, *CREDLIM* and *BALANCE* (*AVAILABLE_CREDIT* = *CREDLIM* − *BALANCE*). In this case, we would have:

```
SELECT CUSTNUMB, CUSTNAME, (CREDLIM - BALANCE)
     FROM CUSTOMER
     WHERE CREDLIM >= 800
```

| CUSTNUMB | CUSTNAME | CREDLIM - BALANCE |
|---|---|---|
| 256 | Samuels, Ann | 789.25 |
| 405 | Williams, Al | 598.25 |
| 412 | Adams, Sally | 91.25 |
| 522 | Nelson, Mary | 750.50 |

The parentheses around the calculation (*CREDLIM* − *BALANCE*) are not essential but improve readability.

## Sorting

Recall that the order of rows in a table is considered to be immaterial. From a practical standpoint, this means that in querying a relational database, there are no guarantees concerning the order in which the results will be displayed. It may be in the order in which the data was originally entered, but even this is not certain. Thus, if the order in which the data is displayed is important, we should *specifically* request that the results be displayed in the desired order. In SQL, this is done with the ORDER BY clause, as shown in example 9.

**Example 9:** List the number, name, and address of all customers. Order the output by name.

The column on which data is to be sorted is called a **sort key**, or simply a **key**. In this case, since the output is to be ordered (sorted) by name, the key is *CUSTNAME*. To sort the output, we include the words ORDER BY, followed by the sort key. Thus, the appropriate query is:

```
SELECT CUSTNUMB, CUSTNAME, CUSTADDR
    FROM CUSTOMER
    ORDER BY CUSTNAME
```

| CUSTNUMB | CUSTNAME | CUSTADDR |
|---|---|---|
| 124 | Adams, Sally | 481 Oak,Lansing,MI |
| 412 | Adams, Sally | 16 Elm,Lansing,MI |
| 567 | Baker, Joe | 808 Ridge,Harper,MI |
| 311 | Charles, Don | 48 College,Ira,MI |
| 315 | Daniels, Tom | 914 Cherry,Kent,MI |
| 622 | Martin, Dan | 419 Chip,Grant,MI |
| 522 | Nelson, Mary | 108 Pine,Ada,MI |
| 587 | Roberts, Judy | 512 Pine,Ada,MI |
| 256 | Samuels, Ann | 215 Pete,Grant,MI |
| 405 | Williams, Al | 519 Watson,Grant,MI |

### Built-in Functions

SQL has built-in functions to calculate such things as sums, averages, and so on. The list of built-in functions is shown in Figure 3.9.

**Figure 3.9**

Built-in functions

| Built-in Function | Meaning |
|---|---|
| COUNT | Count of the number of rows satisfying the WHERE clause. |
| SUM | Sum of the values in a column for all rows satisfying the WHERE clause (column must be numeric). |
| AVG | Average of the values in a column for all rows satisfying the WHERE clause (column must be numeric). |
| MAX | Largest value in a column for all rows satisfying the WHERE clause. (If column is numeric, will be largest number. If not, will be highest entry based on collating sequence. If column contains names, for example, will be last name alphabetically.) |
| MIN | Smallest value in a column for all rows satisfying WHERE clause. (If column is numeric, will be smallest number. If not, will be lowest entry based on collating sequence. If column contains names, for example, will be first name alphabetically.) |

**Example 10:** How many parts are in item class HW?

In this query, we're interested in the number of rows in the table produced by selecting only those parts that are in item class HW. We could count the number of part numbers in this table, or the number of descriptions, or the number of entries in any other column. It doesn't make any difference. Rather than requiring us to pick one of these arbitrarily, some versions of SQL allow us to use the "*" symbol. In such a version, we could formulate the query as:

```
SELECT COUNT(*)
      FROM PART
      WHERE ITEMCLSS = 'HW'
```

```
COUNT(*)
```
---
```
    4
```

If this is not allowed, we would formulate it as:

```
SELECT COUNT(PARTNUMB)
      FROM PART
      WHERE ITEMCLSS = 'HW'
```

```
COUNT(PARTNUMB)
```
---
```
      4
```

**Example 11:** Find the number of customers and the total of their balances.

The only differences between COUNT and SUM — other than the obvious fact that they are computing different statistics — are that (1) in the case of SUM, we *must* specify the column for which we want a total and (2) the column must be numeric. (How could you calculate a sum of names or addresses?) This query is:

```
SELECT COUNT(CUSTNUMB), SUM(BALANCE)
      FROM CUSTOMER
```

| COUNT(CUSTNUMB) | SUM(BALANCE) |
---
| 10 | 2944.80 |

The use of AVG, MAX, and MIN is similar to SUM. The only difference is that a different statistic is calculated.

## Nesting Queries

It is possible to place one query inside another. The inner query is called a **subquery**.

**Example 12:** List the customer number and name of all customers of Premiere Products who have a credit limit that is equal to the largest credit limit awarded to any customer of sales rep 3.

We could do this in two steps. We could first find the largest credit limit awarded to any customer of sales rep 3 as follows:

```
SELECT MAX(CREDLIM)
     FROM CUSTOMER
     WHERE SLSRNUMB = 3


MAX(CREDLIM)
_____
     1000
```

After viewing the answer (1000), we could use the following SELECT statement:

```
SELECT CUSTNUMB, CUSTNAME
     FROM CUSTOMER
     WHERE CREDLIM = 1000

CUSTNUMB CUSTNAME
_____ _____
     412 Adams, Sally
```

We can actually accomplish this in one step, however, by using subqueries. In this case, the query would be:

```
SELECT CUSTNUMB, CUSTNAME
     FROM CUSTOMER
     WHERE CREDLIM IN
          (SELECT MAX(CREDLIM)
               FROM CUSTOMER
               WHERE SLSRNUMB = 3)

CUSTNUMB CUSTNAME
_____ _____
     412 Adams, Sally
```

The portion in parentheses is called a **subquery**. This subquery is evaluated first, producing a temporary table. In this case the table has one column called *MAX(CREDLIM)* and a single row containing the number 1,000. (See Figure 3.10.)

TEMPORARY TABLE

| MAX(CREDLIM) |
| --- |
| 1000 |

Figure 3.10

Temporary table produced by evaluating subquery

The outer query can now be evaluated. We will only obtain the names of customers whose credit limit is in the result produced by the subquery. Since that table contains only the maximum credit limit for the customers of sales rep 3, we will obtain the desired list of customers. Incidentally, since the subquery in this case will produce a table containing only a single value (the maximum credit limit), this query could have been formulated in another way:

```
SELECT CUSTNUMB, CUSTNAME
      FROM CUSTOMER
      WHERE CREDLIM =
            (SELECT MAX(CREDLIM)
                  FROM CUSTOMER
                  WHERE SLSRNUMB = 3)
```

| CUSTNUMB | CUSTNAME |
| --- | --- |
| 412 | Adams, Sally |

In this formulation we are asking for those customers whose credit limit *is equal to* the one credit limit obtained by the subquery. In general, unless you know that the subquery *must* produce a single value, the prior formulation using IN would be the one to use.

## Grouping

**Example 13:** List the order total for each order.

The order total is equal to the total of the products of number ordered and quoted price for all the order lines within the order. These queries thus involve the sum of computed fields. However, there is a little more to it than just including SUM(*NUMBORD * QUOTPRCE*) in the query. This would only give us the grand total over all order lines; the grand total would not be broken down by order. To get individual totals we use the GROUP BY clause. In this case, GROUP BY *ORDNUMB* will cause the order lines for each order to be "grouped together," that is, all order lines with the same order number will form a group. Any statistics, such as totals, requested in the SELECT clause will be calculated for each of these groups. It is important to note that the GROUP BY clause does not imply that the information will be sorted. To produce the report in a particular order, the ORDER BY clause must be used. Assuming that the report is to be ordered by order number, we would have the following formulation:

```
SELECT ORDNUMB, SUM(NUMBORD * QUOTPRCE)
    FROM ORDLNE
    GROUP BY ORDNUMB
    ORDER BY ORDNUMB
```

| ORDNUMB | SUM(NUMBORD * QUOTPRCE) |
|---------|-------------------------|
| 12489   | 164.45                  |
| 12491   | 714.94                  |
| 12494   | 700.00                  |
| 12495   | 115.90                  |
| 12498   | 65.70                   |
| 12500   | 402.99                  |
| 12504   | 217.98                  |

When rows are grouped, one line of output is produced for each group. The only things that may be displayed are statistics calculated for the group or columns whose values are the same for all rows in a group.

## Q & A

**Question:**   Would it be appropriate to display the order number?

**Answer:**   Yes, since the output is grouped by order number; thus, the order number on one row in a group must be the same as the order number on any other row in the group.

**Question:**   Would it be appropriate to display a part number?

**Answer:**   No, since the part number will vary from one row in a group to another. (SQL could not determine which part number to display for the group.)

**Example 14:** List the order total for those orders amounting to more than $200.

This example is like the previous one. The only difference is that there is a restriction; namely, we only want to display totals for those orders that amount to more than $200. This restriction does not apply to individual rows, but rather to *groups*. Since the WHERE clause applies only to rows, it is not the appropriate clause to accomplish the kind of selection we have here. Fortunately, there is a facility that is to groups what WHERE is to rows. It is the following HAVING clause.

```
SELECT ORDNUMB, SUM(NUMBORD * QUOTPRCE)
    FROM ORDLNE
    GROUP BY ORDNUMB
    HAVING SUM(NUMBORD * QUOTPRCE) > 200
    ORDER BY ORDNUMB
```

| ORDNUMB | SUM(NUMBORD * QUOTPRCE) |
|---------|------------------------|
| 12491 | 714.94 |
| 12494 | 700.00 |
| 12500 | 402.99 |
| 12504 | 217.98 |

In this case, the row created for a group will be displayed only if the sum calculated for the group is larger than $200.

## Joining Tables

One common way to access data from more than one table is to **join** the tables together; that is, to find rows in the two tables that have identical values in matching columns. This is accomplished through appropriate conditions in the WHERE clause.

**Example 15:** List the number and name of each customer together with the number and name of the sales rep who represents the customer.

Since the numbers and names of customers are in the *CUSTOMER* table, while the numbers and names of sales reps are in the *SLSREP* table, we need to access both tables in our SQL command:

1. In the SELECT clause, we indicate all columns we wish displayed.
2. In the FROM clause, we list all tables involved in the query.
3. In the WHERE clause, we give the condition that will restrict the data to be retrieved to only those rows from the two tables that match; that is, to the rows that have common values in matching columns.

We have a problem, however. The matching columns are both called *SLSRNUMB*: There is a column in *SLSREP* called *SLSRNUMB*, as well as a column in *CUSTOMER* called *SLSRNUMB*. In this case, if we merely mention *SLSRNUMB*, it will not be clear which one we mean. It is necessary to **qualify** *SLSRNUMB*, or to specify which column we are referring to. We do this by preceding the name of the column with the name of the table, followed by a period. The *SLSRNUMB* column in the *SLSREP* table is *SLSREP.SLSRNUMB*. The *SLSRNUMB* column in the *CUSTOMER* table then becomes *CUSTOMER.SLSRNUMB*. The query follows.

```
SELECT CUSTNUMB, CUSTNAME, SLSREP.SLSRNUMB, SLSRNAME
    FROM CUSTOMER, SLSREP
    WHERE CUSTOMER.SLSRNUMB = SLSREP.SLSRNUMB
```

| CUSTNUMB | CUSTNAME | SLSRNUMB | SLSRNAME |
|---|---|---|---|
| 124 | Adams, Sally | 3 | Jones, Mary |
| 256 | Samuels, Ann | 6 | Smith, William |
| 311 | Charles, Don | 12 | Brown, Sam |
| 315 | Daniels, Tom | 6 | Smith, William |
| 405 | Williams, Al | 12 | Brown, Sam |
| 412 | Adams, Sally | 3 | Jones, Mary |
| 522 | Nelson, Mary | 12 | Brown, Sam |
| 567 | Baker, Joe | 6 | Smith, William |
| 587 | Roberts, Judy | 6 | Smith, William |
| 622 | Martin, Dan | 3 | Jones, Mary |

Note that whenever there is potential ambiguity, we *must* qualify the columns involved. It is permissible to qualify other columns as well, even if there is no confusion. Some people prefer to qualify all columns and this is certainly not a bad approach. In this text, we will only qualify columns when it is necessary to do so.

**Example 16:** List the number and name of each customer whose credit limit is $800, together with the number and name of the sales rep who represents the customer.

In example 15, the condition in the WHERE clause served only to relate a customer to a sales rep. While relating a customer to a sales rep is essential in this example as well, we also want to restrict the output to only those customers whose credit limit is $800. This is accomplished by a compound condition, as follows:

```
SELECT CUSTNUMB, CUSTNAME, SLSREP.SLSRNUMB, SLSRNAME
    FROM CUSTOMER, SLSREP
    WHERE CUSTOMER.SLSRNUMB = SLSREP.SLSRNUMB
    AND CREDLIM = 800
```

| CUSTNUMB | CUSTNAME | SLSRNUMB | SLSRNAME |
|---|---|---|---|
| 124 | Adams, Sally | 3 | Jones, Mary |
| 256 | ANN JONES | 6 | Smith, William |
| 405 | Williams, Al | 12 | Brown, Sam |
| 522 | Nelson, Mary | 12 | Brown, Sam |

## Union

SQL supports the union operation. The **union** of two tables is a table containing all rows that are in either the first table, the second, or both. There is an obvious restriction on union. It does not make sense, for example, to talk about the union of the *CUSTOMER* table and the *ORDERS* table. What would rows in this union look like? The two tables *must* have the same structure. The formal term is union-compatible. Two tables are **union-compatible** if they have the same number of columns and if their corresponding columns have identical data types and lengths.

　　Note that the definition does not state that the column headings of the two tables must be identical, but rather that the columns must be of the same type. Thus, if one is CHAR(20), the other must also be CHAR(20).

**Example 17:** List the number and name of all customers who are either represented by sales rep 12, or who currently have orders on file, or both.

We can create a table containing the number and name of all customers who are represented by sales rep 12 by selecting customer numbers and names from the *CUSTOMER* table in which the sales rep number is 12. Then we can create another table containing the number and name of all customers who currently have orders on file by creating a join of the customer table and the order table. The two tables created by this process have the same structure: two columns, a customer number, and a name. Since they are thus union-compatible, it is legitimate to take the union of these two tables. This is accomplished in SQL by:

```
SELECT CUSTNUMB, CUSTNAME
     FROM CUSTOMER
     WHERE SLSRNUMB = 12
UNION
SELECT CUSTOMER.CUSTNUMB, CUSTNAME
     FROM CUSTOMER, ORDERS
     WHERE CUSTOMER.CUSTNUMB = ORDERS.CUSTNUMB
```

```
CUSTNUMB CUSTNAME
-------- --------
     124 Adams, Sally
     256 Samuels, Ann
     311 Charles, Don
     315 Daniels, Tom
     405 Williams, Al
     522 Nelson, Mary
```

If an implementation truly supports the union operation, it will remove any duplicate rows (i.e., any customers who are represented by sales rep 12 *and* who currently have orders on file will not appear twice). Some implementations of SQL have a "union" operation but will not remove such duplicates.

## Update

The following examples illustrate the way SQL can be used to update data in a database.

**Example 18:** Change the name of customer 256 to "Jones, Ann."

The SQL command to make changes to existing data is the UPDATE command. The formulation is:

```
UPDATE CUSTOMER
        SET CUSTNAME = 'Jones,Ann'
        WHERE CUSTNUMB = 256
```

The results of this command are shown in Figure 3.11.

**BEFORE:**

**Figure 3.11**

Name has been changed

**CUSTOMER**

| CUSTNUMB | CUSTNAME | CUSTADDR | BALANCE | CREDLIM | SLSRNUMB |
|---|---|---|---|---|---|
| 124 | Adams, Sally | 481 Oak,Lansing,MI | 418.75 | 500 | 3 |
| 256 | Samuels, Ann | 215 Pete,Grant,MI | 10.75 | 800 | 6 |
| 311 | Charles, Don | 48 College,Ira,MI | 200.10 | 300 | 12 |
| 315 | Daniels, Tom | 914 Cherry,Kent,MI | 320.75 | 300 | 6 |
| 405 | Williams, Al | 519 Watson,Grant,MI | 201.75 | 800 | 12 |
| 412 | Adams, Sally | 16 Elm,Lansing,MI | 908.75 | 1000 | 3 |
| 522 | Nelson, Mary | 108 Pine,Ada,MI | 49.50 | 800 | 12 |
| 567 | Baker, Joe | 808 Ridge,Harper,MI | 201.20 | 300 | 6 |
| 587 | Roberts, Judy | 512 Pine,Ada,MI | 57.75 | 500 | 6 |
| 622 | Martin, Dan | 419 Chip,Grant,MI | 575.50 | 500 | 3 |

**AFTER:**

**CUSTOMER**

| CUSTNUMB | CUSTNAME | CUSTADDR | BALANCE | CREDLIM | SLSRNUMB |
|---|---|---|---|---|---|
| 124 | Adams, Sally | 481 Oak,Lansing,MI | 418.75 | 500 | 3 |
| 256 | Jones, Ann | 215 Pete,Grant,MI | 10.75 | 800 | 6 |
| 311 | Charles, Don | 48 College,Ira,MI | 200.10 | 300 | 12 |
| 315 | Daniels, Tom | 914 Cherry,Kent,MI | 320.75 | 300 | 6 |
| 405 | Williams, Al | 519 Watson,Grant,MI | 201.75 | 800 | 12 |
| 412 | Adams, Sally | 16 Elm,Lansing,MI | 908.75 | 1000 | 3 |
| 522 | Nelson, Mary | 108 Pine,Ada,MI | 49.50 | 800 | 12 |
| 567 | Baker, Joe | 808 Ridge,Harper,MI | 201.20 | 300 | 6 |
| 587 | Roberts, Judy | 512 Pine,Ada,MI | 57.75 | 500 | 6 |
| 622 | Martin, Dan | 419 Chip,Grant,MI | 575.50 | 500 | 3 |

To add data, we use the INSERT command as shown in example 19.

**Example 19:** Add sales rep data (14, "Crane,Ann," "123 River,Ada,MI," 0, 0.05) to the database.

Addition of new data is accomplished through the INSERT command. If we have specific data, as in this example, we can use the insert command as follows:

```
INSERT INTO SLSREP
     VALUES
     (14,'Crane,Ann','123 River,Ada,MI',0.00,0.05)
```

The results of this insertion are shown in Figure 3.12.

**BEFORE:**

**SLSREP**

| SLSRNUMB | SLSRNAME | SLSRADDR | TOTCOMM | COMMRATE |
|---|---|---|---|---|
| 3 | Jones, Mary | 123 Main,Grant,MI | 2150.00 | .05 |
| 6 | Smith, William | 102 Raymond,Ada,MI | 4912.50 | .07 |
| 12 | Brown, Sam | 419 Harper,Lansing,MI | 2150.00 | .05 |

**AFTER:**

**SLSREP**

| SLSRNUMB | SLSRNAME | SLSRADDR | TOTCOMM | COMMRATE |
|---|---|---|---|---|
| 3 | Jones, Mary | 123 Main,Grant,MI | 2150.00 | .05 |
| 6 | Smith, William | 102 Raymond,Ada,MI | 4912.50 | .07 |
| 12 | Brown, Sam | 419 Harper,Lansing,MI | 2150.00 | .05 |
| 14 | Crane, Ann | 123 River,Ada,MI | 0.00 | .05 |

**Figure 3.12**

New sales rep has been added

**Example 20:** Delete from the database the customer whose name is Al Williams.

To delete data from the database, use the DELETE command, as in the following:

```
DELETE CUSTOMER
     WHERE CUSTNAME = 'Williams, Al'
```

Figure 3.13 on the next page shows the effect of this deletion on the *CUSTOMER* table.

**Figure 3.13**

Customer has been deleted

BEFORE:

CUSTOMER

| CUSTNUMB | CUSTNAME | CUSTADDR | BALANCE | CREDLIM | SLSRNUMB |
|---|---|---|---|---|---|
| 124 | Adams, Sally | 481 Oak,Lansing,MI | 418.75 | 800 | 3 |
| 256 | Jones, Ann | 215 Pete,Grant,MI | 10.75 | 800 | 6 |
| 311 | Charles, Don | 48 College,Ira,MI | 200.10 | 300 | 12 |
| 315 | Daniels, Tom | 914 Cherry,Kent,MI | 320.75 | 300 | 6 |
| 405 | Williams, Al | 519 Watson,Grant,MI | 201.75 | 800 | 12 |
| 412 | Adams, Sally | 16 Elm,Lansing,MI | 908.75 | 1000 | 3 |
| 522 | Nelson, Mary | 108 Pine,Ada,MI | 49.50 | 800 | 12 |
| 567 | Baker, Joe | 808 Ridge,Harper,MI | 201.20 | 300 | 6 |
| 587 | Roberts, Judy | 512 Pine,Ada,MI | 57.75 | 800 | 6 |
| 622 | Martin, Dan | 419 Chip,Grant,MI | 575.50 | 500 | 3 |

AFTER:

CUSTOMER

| CUSTNUMB | CUSTNAME | CUSTADDR | BALANCE | CREDLIM | SLSRNUMB |
|---|---|---|---|---|---|
| 124 | Adams, Sally | 481 Oak,Lansing,MI | 418.75 | 800 | 3 |
| 256 | Jones, Ann | 215 Pete,Grant,MI | 10.75 | 800 | 6 |
| 311 | Charles, Don | 48 College,Ira,MI | 200.10 | 300 | 12 |
| 315 | Daniels, Tom | 914 Cherry,Kent,MI | 320.75 | 300 | 6 |
| 412 | Adams, Sally | 16 Elm,Lansing,MI | 908.75 | 1000 | 3 |
| 522 | Nelson, Mary | 108 Pine,Ada,MI | 49.50 | 800 | 12 |
| 567 | Baker, Joe | 808 Ridge,Harper,MI | 201.20 | 300 | 6 |
| 587 | Roberts, Judy | 512 Pine,Ada,MI | 57.75 | 800 | 6 |
| 622 | Martin, Dan | 419 Chip,Grant,MI | 575.50 | 500 | 3 |

Note that this type of deletion can be dangerous. If there happens to be another customer whose name is also Al Williams, this customer would also be deleted in the process. The safest type of deletion occurs when the condition involves the primary key 9 (for example, deleting customer 124). In such a case, since the primary key is unique, we are certain we will not accidentally delete other rows in the table.

## Creating a New Table From an Existing Table

**Example 21:** Create a new table called *SMALLCUST* containing the same columns as *CUSTOMER*, but only the rows for which the credit limit is $500 or less.

The first thing to do is to describe this new table using the data definition facilities of SQL, as follows.

```
CREATE TABLE SMALLCUST
     (CUSTNUMB      DECIMAL(4),
      CUSTNAME      CHAR(15),
      CUSTADDR      CHAR(25),
      BALANCE       DECIMAL(7,2),
      CREDLIM       DECIMAL(4),
      SLSRNUMB      DECIMAL(2))
```

Once this is done, we can use the same INSERT command we encountered earlier. Here, however, we use a SELECT command to indicate what is to be inserted into this new table. The exact formulation is:

```
INSERT INTO SMALLCUST
     SELECT *
     FROM CUSTOMER
     WHERE CREDLIM <= 500
```

For other examples of SQL queries, see [1], [2], [6], [8], [10], and [11].


## THE RELATIONAL ALGEBRA

Like the **relational calculus**, the **relational algebra** is a theoretical way of manipulating a relational database. In the relational algebra, there are operations that act on relations to produce new relations, just as the operations of + and – act on numbers to produce new numbers in the algebra with which you are familiar. Retrieving data from a relational database through the use of the relational algebra involves issuing relational algebra commands to operate on existing relations to form a new relation that contains the desired information. It may be that successive commands will be required to form intermediate relations before the final result is obtained, as some of the following examples demonstrate. As you will notice in these examples, each command ends with a clause that reads GIVING, followed by a relation name. This clause is requesting that the result of the execution of the command is to be placed in a relation with the name we have specified.

The relational algebra is **relationally complete**; that is, anything that can be accomplished using the relational calculus can also be accomplished using the relational algebra. In fact, many people use the relational algebra as an alternate standard for relational completeness. In this section, we will briefly consider the operations of the relational algebra and will give a few examples of their use.

### Select

The SELECT command within the relational algebra takes a horizontal subset of a relation; that is, it causes only certain rows to be included in the new relation. (It should not be confused with the SQL SELECT command, which is considerably more powerful.) This SELECT causes a new table to be created, including rows of a single table that meet some specified criteria.

**Example 1:** List all information from the *CUSTOMER* relation concerning customer 256.

Relational algebra:

```
SELECT CUSTOMER WHERE CUSTNUMB = 256 GIVING ANSWER
```

**Example 2:** List all information from the *CUSTOMER* relation concerning those customers who have an $800 credit limit.

Relational algebra:

```
SELECT CUSTOMER WHERE CREDLIM = 800 GIVING ANSWER
```

### Project

The PROJECT command within the relational algebra takes a vertical subset of a relation (i.e., it causes only certain columns to be included in the new relation).

**Example 3:** List the number and name of all customers.

Relational algebra:

```
PROJECT CUSTOMER OVER (CUSTNUMB, CUSTNAME) GIVING ANSWER
```

**Example 4:** List the number and name of all customers who have an $800 credit limit.

This is accomplished in a two-step process. We first use a SELECT command to create a new relation that contains only those customers with the appropriate credit limit. Then we project that relation to restrict the result to only the indicated columns.

Relational algebra:

```
SELECT CUSTOMER WHERE CREDLIM = 800 GIVING TEMP
PROJECT TEMP OVER (CUSTNUMB, CUSTNAME) GIVING ANSWER
```

## Join

The JOIN operation is at the heart of the relational algebra. It is the command that allows us to pull together data from more than one relation. In the most usual form of the JOIN, we **join** two tables together, based on a common attribute. A new table is formed containing the columns of both the tables that have been joined. Rows in this new table will be the concatenation of a row from the first table and a row from the second that match on the common attribute (often called the JOIN column). For example, suppose we wish to JOIN the following tables on *SLSRNUMB* (the join column), creating a new relation called *TEMP*:

**CUSTOMER**

| CUSTNUMB | CUSTNAME | SLSRNUMB |
|---|---|---|
| 124 | Adams, Sally | 3 |
| 256 | Samuels, Ann | 6 |
| 311 | Charles, Don | 12 |
| 315 | Daniels, Tom | 6 |
| 405 | Williams, Al | 12 |
| 412 | Adams, Sally | 3 |
| 522 | Nelson, Mary | 12 |
| 567 | Baker, Joe | 6 |
| 587 | Roberts, Judy | 6 |
| 622 | Martin, Dan | 3 |
| 701 | Peters, Art | 5 |

and

**SLSREP**

| SLSRNUMB | SLSRNAME |
|---|---|
| 3 | Jones, Mary |
| 6 | Smith, William |
| 12 | Brown, Sam |
| 15 | Lewis, Joan |

The result of the join would be:

**TEMP**

| CUSTNUMB | CUSTNAME | SLSRNUMB | SLSRNAME |
|---|---|---|---|
| 124 | Adams, Sally | 3 | Jones, Mary |
| 256 | Samuels, Ann | 6 | Smith, William |
| 311 | Charles, Don | 12 | Brown, Sam |
| 315 | Daniels, Tom | 6 | Smith, William |
| 405 | Williams, Al | 12 | Brown, Sam |
| 412 | Adams, Sally | 3 | Jones, Mary |
| 522 | Nelson, Mary | 12 | Brown, Sam |
| 567 | Baker, Joe | 6 | Smith, William |
| 587 | Roberts, Judy | 6 | Smith, William |
| 622 | Martin, Dan | 3 | Jones, Mary |

Note that the column on which the tables are joined appears only once. Other than that, all columns from both tables are present in the result. Two points need to be emphasized concerning this join operation:

1. If there is a row in one table that does not match any row in the other table, it will not appear in the result of the join. Thus, sales rep 15, Joan Lewis, and customer 701, Art Peters, do not appear, since they do not match anything.
2. In this case, since sales rep number is the primary key, there cannot be two rows in the *SLSREP* relation on which there is the same sales rep number. Consequently, each customer will appear on one row at most in the new relation created by the join. If, however, for some reason the sales rep table were allowed to have multiple rows with the same sales rep number, each customer could appear several times. If the SLSREP relation also contained a row in which the sales rep number were 3 and the name were Bob Johnson, the relation created would be:

**TEMP**

| CUSTNUMB | CUSTNAME | SLSRNUMB | SLSRNAME |
|---|---|---|---|
| 124 | Adams, Sally | 3 | Jones, Mary |
| 124 | Adams, Sally | 3 | Johnson, Bob |
| 256 | Samuels, Ann | 6 | Smith, William |
| 311 | Charles, Don | 12 | Brown, Sam |
| 315 | Daniels, Tom | 6 | Smith, William |
| 405 | Williams, Al | 12 | Brown, Sam |
| 412 | Adams, Sally | 3 | Jones, Mary |
| 412 | Adams, Sally | 3 | Johnson, Bob |
| 522 | Nelson, Mary | 12 | Brown, Sam |
| 567 | Baker, Joe | 6 | Smith, William |
| 587 | Roberts, Judy | 6 | Smith, William |
| 622 | Martin, Dan | 3 | Jones, Mary |
| 622 | Martin, Dan | 3 | Johnson, Bob |

The output from the join relation can be restricted to include only desired columns by using the project command, as the following example illustrates.

**Example 5:** List the number and name of all customers together with the number and name of the sales rep who represents each customer.

Relational algebra:

```
JOIN CUSTOMER SLSREP
    WHERE CUSTOMER.SLSRNUMB = SLSREP.SLSRNUMB
    GIVING TEMP
PROJECT TEMP OVER (CUSTNUMB, CUSTNAME, SLSRNUMB,
    SLSRNAME) GIVING ANSWER
```

Although this is by far the most common kind of join, there are other possibilities worth mentioning. If we are distinguishing between different types of joins, the one described above is called the **natural join**. In this form of the join, the column on which the table was joined appeared only once. If we follow the same process but leave both copies of the join column in the table that is created, we have the **equijoin**. In the preceding example, an equi-join would have contained two *SLSRNUMB* columns, one for the *SLSRNUMB* from the *CUSTOMER* relation and the other for the *SLSRNUMB* from the *SLSREP* relation. If we join on a condition other than equality, we have the **theta-join**. For example, we could join each customer to any sales rep whose commission was more than 10 percent of the customer's balance. The final type of join, the **outer join**, differs from the natural join only for rows in the original relations that do not match any row in the other relation. Recall that in the natural join these rows are eliminated. In the outer join they are maintained, and values of the columns from the other table are left vacant, or **null**. In the case of the original example from this section, the outer join operation would give:

**TEMP**

| CUSTNUMB | CUSTNAME | SLSRNUMB | SLSRNAME |
|---|---|---|---|
| 124 | Adams, Sally | 3 | Jones, Mary |
| 256 | Samuels, Ann | 6 | Smith, William |
| 311 | Charles, Don | 12 | Brown, Sam |
| 315 | Daniels, Tom | 6 | Smith, William |
| 405 | Williams, Al | 12 | Brown, Sam |
| 412 | Adams, Sally | 3 | Jones, Mary |
| 522 | Nelson, Mary | 12 | Brown, Sam |
| 567 | Baker, Joe | 6 | Smith, William |
| 587 | Roberts, Judy | 6 | Smith, William |
| 622 | Martin, Dan | 3 | Jones, Mary |
| 701 | Peters, Art | 5 | |
| | | 15 | Lewis, Joan |

## Union

The UNION operation is conceptually identical to the SQL union encountered earlier. As you might expect, the same requirement for **union compatibility** exists here.

**Example 6:** List all customers who either have orders or are represented by sales rep 12, or both.

We can form the list of all customers who have orders by projecting the *ORDERS* relation over customer number. We can form the list of all customers represented by sales rep 12 by first selecting those rows in the

*CUSTOMER* relation where the sales rep number is 12 and then projecting that result over the customer number. Finally, taking the union of these two intermediate results will satisfy the query. Since both relations consist only of a customer number, they are union-compatible; thus, forming the union is a legitimate operation.

Relational algebra:

```
PROJECT ORDERS OVER (CUSTNUMB) GIVING TEMP1
SELECT CUSTOMER WHERE SLSRNUMB = 12 GIVING TEMP2
PROJECT TEMP2 OVER (CUSTNUMB) GIVING TEMP3
UNION TEMP1 WITH TEMP3 GIVING ANSWER
```

## Intersection

**Example 7:** List all the customers who have orders *and* are represented by sales rep 12.

This process is virtually identical to the one encountered in the UNION example. Here, however, at the end, we should INTERSECT the two tables, not take their union. The structure is thus:

Relational algebra:

```
PROJECT ORDERS OVER (CUSTNUMB) GIVING TEMP1
SELECT CUSTOMER WHERE SLSRNUMB = 12 GIVING TEMP2
PROJECT TEMP2 OVER (CUSTNUMB) GIVING TEMP3
INTERSECT TEMP1 WITH TEMP3 GIVING ANSWER
```

## Difference

The DIFFERENCE operation is performed by the SUBTRACT statement in the relational algebra.

**Example 8:** List all customers who have orders but are not represented by sales rep 12.

Relational algebra:

```
PROJECT ORDERS OVER (CUSTNUMB) GIVING TEMP1
SELECT CUSTOMER WHERE SLSRNUMB = 12 GIVING TEMP2
PROJECT TEMP2 OVER (CUSTNUMB) GIVING TEMP3
SUBTRACT TEMP3 FROM TEMP1 GIVING ANSWER
```

## Product

The PRODUCT of two relations (mathematically called the Cartesian product) is the relation obtained by concatenating every row in the first relation with every row in the second relation. Thus, the product of

**ORDERS**

| ORDNUMB | ORDDTE |
|---------|--------|
| 12489 | 90291 |
| 12491 | 90291 |
| 12494 | 90491 |

and

**PART**

| PARTNUMB | PARTDESC |
|----------|----------|
| BT04 | STOVE |
| BZ66 | WASHER |

would be

**ANSWER**

| ORDNUMB | ORDDTE | PARTNUMB | PARTDESC |
|---------|--------|----------|----------|
| 12489 | 90291 | BT04 | STOVE |
| 12491 | 90291 | BT04 | STOVE |
| 12494 | 90491 | BT04 | STOVE |
| 12489 | 90291 | BZ66 | WASHER |
| 12491 | 90291 | BZ66 | WASHER |
| 12494 | 90491 | BZ66 | WASHER |

Every row of *ORDERS* is matched with every row of *PART*. If *ORDERS* has $m$ rows and *PART* has $n$ rows, there would be $mn$ rows in the product. If, as is typically the case, the tables have a large number of rows, the number of rows in the product can be so great that it is not practical to form the product. Usually, we would only want combinations that satisfy certain restrictions and so we would virtually always use the join operation instead of product.

## Division

The DIVISION process is best illustrated by considering the division of a relation with two columns by a relation with a single column. As an example, let's divide the relation

**ORDLNE**

| ORDNUMB | PARTNUMB |
|---------|----------|
| 12489   | AX12     |
| 12491   | BT04     |
| 12491   | BZ66     |
| 12494   | CB03     |
| 12495   | CX11     |
| 12498   | AZ52     |
| 12498   | BA74     |
| 12500   | BT04     |
| 12504   | CZ81     |

by the relation

**PART**

| PARTNUMB |
|----------|
| BZ66     |
| BT04     |

The quotient will be a new relation with a single column *ORDNUMB*. The rows in this new relation will consist of those order numbers from *ORDLNE* which are "matched" to *all* of the parts appearing in the *PART* relation. For an order number to appear in the quotient, there must be a row in *ORDLNE* with this order number in the *ORDNUMB* column and "BZ66" in the *PARTNUMB* column. There must also be a row in *ORDLNE* with this same order number in the *ORDNUMB* column and "BT04" in the *PARTNUMB* column. It doesn't matter if there are other rows in *ORDLNE* containing the same order number as long as the rows with "BZ66" and "BT04" are present. With our sample data, only order 12491 qualifies. Thus the result would be

**ANSWER**

| ORDNUMB |
|---------|
| 12491   |

Before leaving the relational algebra, it is worth noting that of the eight operations listed, not all are necessary. The five operations — SELECT, PROJECT, PRODUCT, UNION, and DIFFERENCE — are the "primitive" operations (i.e., the other operations can be specified in terms of these five). To do a JOIN, for example, we could first take a PRODUCT, followed by a SELECT, followed by a PROJECT. The other three operations, especially the JOIN operation, are so useful in practice that they are usually included in any list of operations within the relational algebra.

For more discussion of the relational algebra, see [1], [2], [6], [8], and [10].

## QBE

In this section, we will investigate an approach to manipulating relational databases that is very different from the approaches discussed earlier in this chapter. It is called **Query-By-Example (QBE)** and was developed by M. M. Zloof at the IBM Yorktown Heights Research Laboratory. (See [12] and [13].) Not only are results displayed on the screen in tabular form, but users actually enter their requests by filling in portions of the displayed tables. Studies have shown (see [7]) that in regard to the time it takes to learn QBE, the time it takes to formulate a query using QBE, and the accuracy with which these queries are formulated, the figures for the use of QBE are as good as, if not better than, those obtained for other approaches.

**Note:** We will illustrate QBE by using a particular implementation of it. The version we'll look at is found in the microcomputer DBMS called Paradox, a product of Borland International. Although the various versions of QBE are certainly not identical, the differences are relatively minor. If you have mastered one version of it, you should be able to easily learn another.

In using QBE we first identify the table we wish to query. We are then presented with a blank form corresponding to the table we have chosen. In Figure 3.14 on the next page, for example, we have selected the *PART* table.

We will now investigate the manner in which we can retrieve data, as well as update our database, using Query-by-example.

**Figure 3.14**

Query-by-Example
(QBE) screen

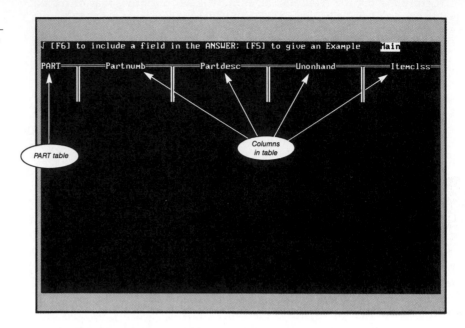

## Retrieving All Rows

**Example 1:** List the part number and description of all parts.

(In the general QBE approach, we indicate that we wish the contents of a specific column printed by typing the letter *P* followed by a period in the column. In the Paradox version, instead of the letter, we place a check mark in the column. We do so by moving the cursor to the column and pressing F6 as indicated at the top of the screen. From now on, we will focus on the Paradox approach. Remember that other versions may differ on this point.)

For this example, we place check marks in both the *PARTNUMB* and *PARTDESC* columns as shown in Figure 3.15. We then execute the query. (In Paradox, we do so by pressing F2.) The results are shown in Figure 3.16.

**Figure 3.15**

QBE screen

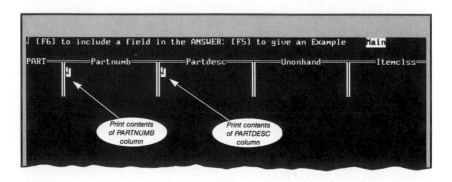

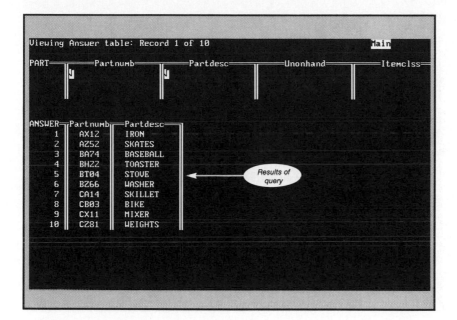

**Figure 3.16**

QBE screen with results

**Example 2:** List the complete part table.

We could certainly put a check mark in each column in the table to obtain this result. There is a simpler method, however. Place the cursor in the first column (the one headed by the name of the table) and press F6. Paradox automatically places check marks in all the other columns. (See Figure 3.17.) The results are shown in Figure 3.18 on the next page.

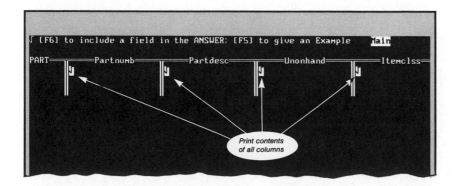

**Figure 3.17**

QBE screen

**Figure 3.18**

QBE screen with
results

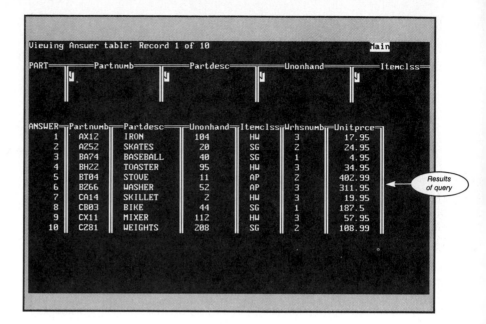

**Simple Conditions**

**Example 3:** List the part numbers of all parts in item class HW.

We use the check marks, as before, to indicate the columns to be printed. We can also place a specific value in a column as shown in Figure 3.19. This indicates that the part numbers to be printed should only be those for which the item class is HW. The results are shown in Figure 3.20.

**Figure 3.19**

QBE screen

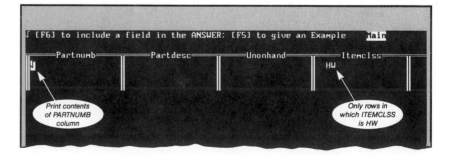

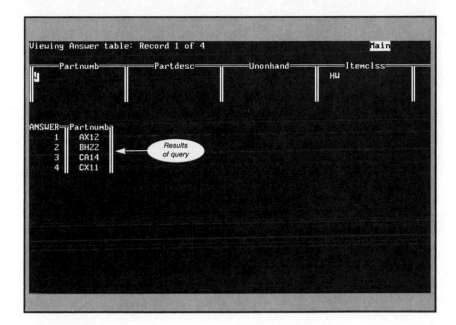

**Figure 3.20**

QBE screen with
results

**Note:** From this point on, we will show both the query and the result in the same figure.

## Compound Conditions

**Example 4:** List the part numbers for all parts that are in item class SG and are located in warehouse 2.

As you might expect, we can put specific values in more than one column. Further, QBE also supports the normal comparison operators ( = , > , > = , < , < = ), as well as NOT = (NOT EQUAL). It is common in QBE to omit the " = " symbol in "equal" and "not equal" comparisons, although it may be used if desired. (See Figure 3.21 on the next page.) In this case, we have requested those parts for which the item class is SG *and* the warehouse is 2.

**Figure 3.21**

QBE screen with
"AND" condition

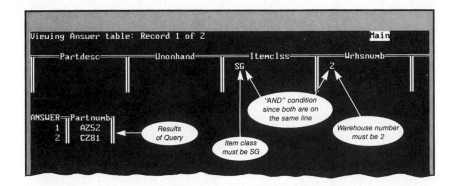

**Example 5:** List the part descriptions for those parts that are in item class SG or warehouse 2.

What we essentially have in this query is two queries. We want the descriptions of all parts that are in class SG. We also want the descriptions of all parts that are in warehouse 2. This is effectively how we enter our request, as two queries. (See Figure 3.22.) The first row in the query indicates that we want all parts in class SG. The second row indicates that we also want all parts that are in warehouse 2.

**Figure 3.22**

QBE screen with
"OR" condition in
separate columns

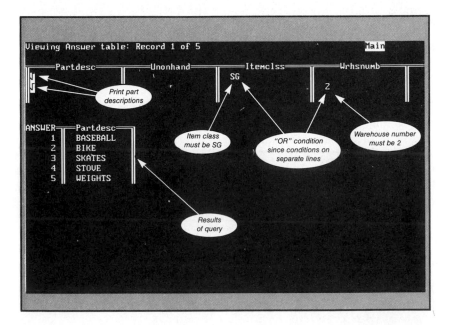

**Example 6:** List the number and names of all customers who have a credit limit of $300 or $800.

This query involves the *CUSTOMER* table, so we first bring this to the screen. Once we have done so, we again need to enter an "OR" condition. We could do so in the same manner as in the previous example. Since both individual conditions involve the same column, there is a slightly simpler approach we can use. We simply enter both values, separated by the word OR, in the *CREDLIM* column. (See Figure 3.23.)

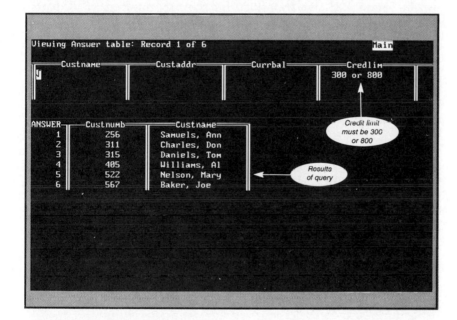

**Figure 3.23**

QBE screen with "OR" condition in single column

**Example 7:** List the part numbers of all parts that are not in item class HW.

For this query, we simply use the word NOT as shown in Figure 3.24.

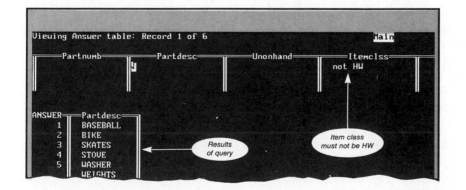

**Figure 3.24**

QBE screen with "NOT" condition

In each of the previous examples, we could have used a feature of the QBE language from which it draws its name: an example. The prior queries were simple enough, so there was no real need to use an example, but it would certainly have been legitimate to do so. To use an example, we pick a sample response that the computer could give to the query and actually enter it in the table. To indicate that it is merely an example in Paradox, we press F5 before we make the entry. It will then be displayed in reverse video. In the query shown in Figure 3.25, we are asking for the part numbers of all parts for which there are more than 100 units on hand.

**Figure 3.25**

QBE screen with example

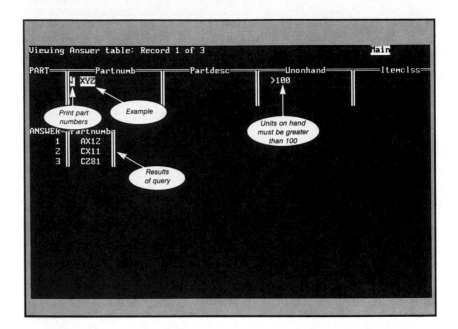

We are indicating that XYZ is an example of the response we are expecting. It does *not* have to be an actual response that would be generated in response to this query. In this case, in fact, there is not even a part XYZ in the database. Notice the difference between the part number XYZ and the number 100. The XYZ is shown in reverse video, indicating that it is strictly an example. The 100 is not, indicating that it is an actual value in which we are interested.

In this case, there was no good reason for using an example. In the next query, however, the use of an example is essential.

## Joining Tables

**Example 8:** List the name and number of those customers who placed an order on 9/02/91.

This query cannot be satisfied using a single table. The customer name is in the customer table, whereas the order date is in the orders table. We need the equivalent of a **join** operation. To do this, we first need to bring both tables to the screen. (See Figure 3.26.) We then make the entries shown in Figure 3.27.

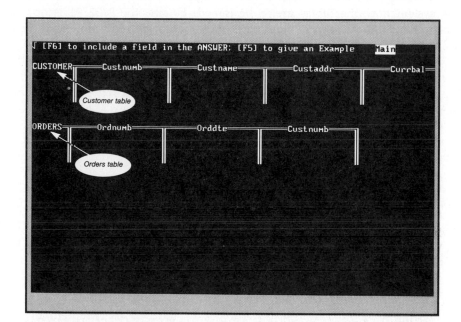

**Figure 3.26**

QBE screen with two tables

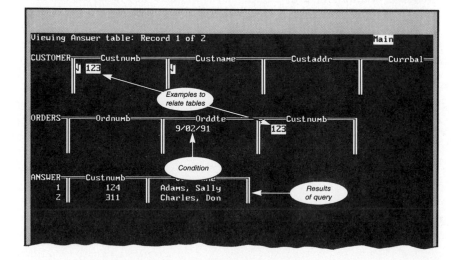

**Figure 3.27**

QBE screen with two tables

In this example, there is a check mark in both the *CUSTNUMB* and *CUSTNAME* columns of the *CUSTOMER* table, indicating that these are the columns whose values are to be printed. Further, there is an example, 123, in the CUSTOMER number column of the customer table, as well as *the same* example in the *CUSTNUMB* column of the *ORDERS* table. These examples are necessary, and the fact that they are the same is crucial. This is what tells the system how the tables are to be joined. Finally, the 9/02/91 is not an example (it is not in reverse video), but rather a specific restriction. In words, we are telling the system to:

PRINT the number and name of any customers in the *CUSTOMER* table for whom there is a row in the *ORDERS* table where the customer number matches the customer number in the *CUSTOMER* table and the order date is 90291.

**Example 9:** For each order, list the sales rep number, the sales rep name, the customer number, the customer name, the order number, and the order date.

This query involves three tables, *SLSREP, CUSTOMER,* and *ORDERS,* so we first bring all three tables to the screen. We need to relate the *SLSREP* and *CUSTOMER* tables by indicating that the values in the *SLSRNUMB* columns in both tables must match. Similarly we need to relate the *CUSTOMER* and *ORDERS* tables by indicating that the values in the *CUSTNUMB* columns in both tables must match. As you would expect, we do so through examples. Let's use 11 as an example of sales rep numbers and 123 as examples of customer numbers.

In Figure 3.28 we have placed check marks in the *SLSRNUMB* and *SLSRNAME* columns of the *SLSREP* table and also in the *CUSTNUMB* and *CUSTNAME* columns of the *CUSTOMER* table, indicating that values in these columns are to be printed. We have also entered 11 as an example in the *SLSRNUMB* column of the *SLSREP* table, and 123 as an example in the *CUSTNUMB* column of the *CUSTOMER* table. We are not done, however.

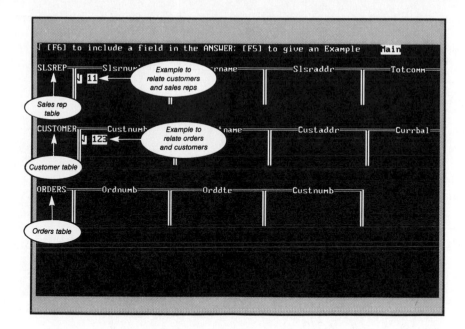

**Figure 3.28**

QBE screen with
three tables

In Figure 3.29, we have entered the other example of 11 in the
*SLSRNUMB* column of the *CUSTOMER* table. In Figure 3.30 on the next
page, we have entered the other example of 123 in the *CUSTNUMB* column of
the *ORDERS* table. We have also placed check marks in the *ORDNUMB* and
*ORDDTE* columns of the *ORDERS* table indicating that these columns are to
be printed as well.

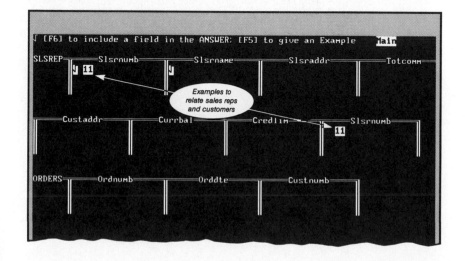

**Figure 3.29**

QBE screen with
three tables

**Figure 3.30**

QBE screen with
three tables

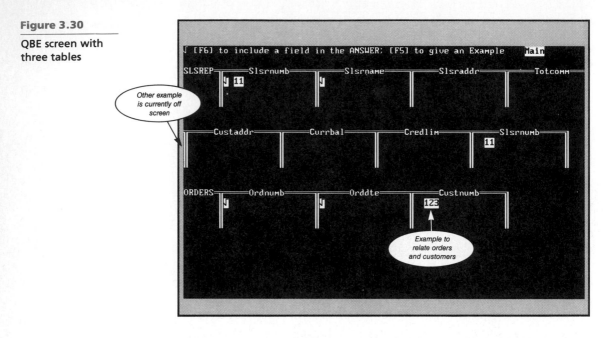

The query is now complete. The results are shown in Figure 3.31.

**Figure 3.31**

QBE screen with
three tables

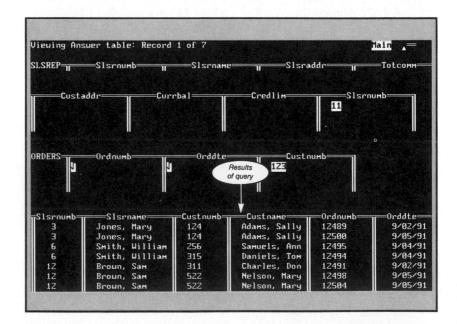

## Built-in Functions

**Example 10:** Find the average of the balances of each sales rep.

There is the usual collection of built-in functions in QBE. These are COUNT, SUM, AVERAGE, MAX, and MIN. We can use these in conditions or simply request that the values be calculated. To indicate that we want an average calculated, we enter the words "calc average." (See Figure 3.32.) The check mark in the *SLSRNUMB* column indicates that we want sales rep numbers printed. It also indicates that the rows should be grouped by sales rep number to calculate the averages. As you can see in the results, for example, the average for all the rows on which the sales rep number is 3 is 634.33. The average for all the rows on which the sales rep number is 12 is 150.45.

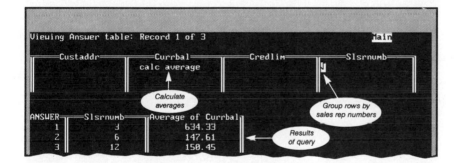

**Figure 3.32**

QBE screen with calculation

## Update

The remaining examples deal with the update facilities of QBE.

**Example 11:** Add order 12520 (date – 90691, customer – 256) to the database.

To add a record, we first bring the appropriate table to the screen (in this case the *ORDERS* table). We then place the word "insert" under the name of the table and the desired values in the other columns. (See Figure 3.33.)

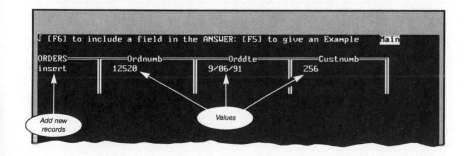

**Figure 3.33**

QBE screen

**Example 12:** Change the credit limit of customer 256 to $1,000.

To accomplish this change, we place the number 256 in the *CUSTNUMB* column. (See Figure 3.34.) We then put the special word "changeto" and the new value in the *CREDLIM* column. (See Figure 3.35.)

**Figure 3.34**

QBE screen

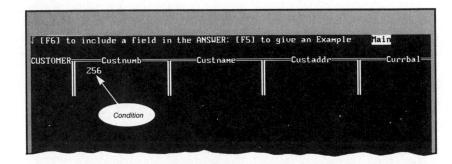

**Figure 3.35**

QBE screen

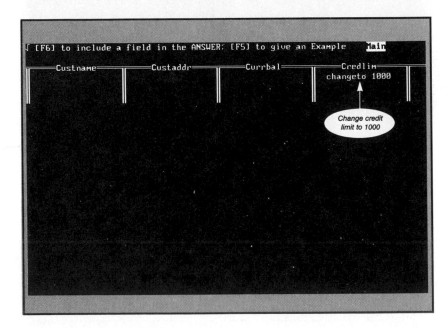

**Example 13:** Change the credit limit of all customers who currently have a $300 limit to $350.

In this case, we have both a condition and a "changeto" clause to place in the same column. To do so, we simply separate these entries with a comma as shown in Figure 3.36.

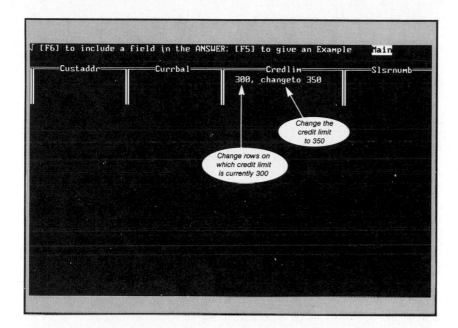

**Figure 3.36**

QBE screen

**Example 14:** Add $50 to the credit limit of all customers of sales rep 12.

We can accomplish this through an example as shown in Figure 3.37. Note that the 123 is in reverse video, which emphasizes that it is an example, not a specific value. The entry after "changeto," 123 + 50, indicates that the old value, whatever it was, is to be increased by 50. The 12 is a restriction, i.e., the process of increasing the credit limit will be applied only to customers of sales rep 12.

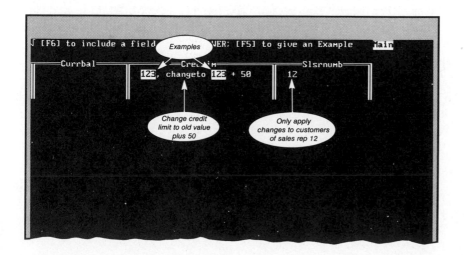

**Figure 3.37**

QBE screen

**Example 15:** Delete customer 256.

To delete records, we place the word "delete" under the name of the table, then enter our conditions as before. In this case, we enter the number 256 in the *CUSTNUMB* column. (See Figure 3.38.)

**Figure 3.38**

QBE screen

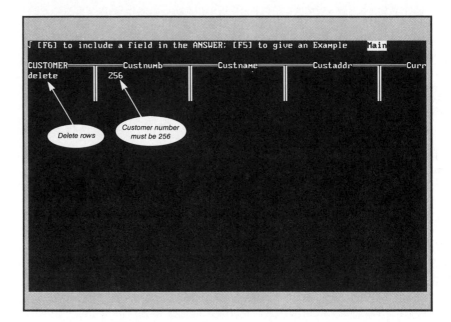

As with SQL, the examples just described are certainly not intended to be a complete treatment of QBE but rather are presented to give you the flavor of this very different and very important approach to manipulating relational databases. For further examples of QBE, see [1], [2], [6], [9], [10], and [11].

## SUMMARY

In this chapter, we began the study of the relational model of data. A relational model database consists of a collection of relations. Relations are simply two-dimensional tables that are subject to some restrictions:

1. The entries in the table are single-valued.
2. Each column has a distinct name (called the attribute name).
3. Each column contains values about the same attribute (namely, the attribute identified by the column name).
4. The order of columns is immaterial.

5. Each row is distinct.
6. The order of rows is immaterial.

Each row is technically called a tuple, and each column is called an attribute (although the terms *table*, *row*, and *column* are finding widespread use themselves).

Some critical relational model terms were discussed. The primary key of a relation is the attribute or collection of attributes that uniquely identifies a given tuple. A foreign key is an attribute in one relation that is required to match an attribute in another relation. A structure that satisfies all the properties just listed for a relation, except property one, is called an unnormalized relation. One that satisfies all the properties is sometimes called a normalized relation.

Next, the relational model implementation of one-to-many and many-to-many relationships was discussed. In implementing a one-to-many relationship, the key of the "one" table is an attribute (specifically a foreign key) in the "many" table. In implementing a many-to-many relationship, a third table is constructed whose key is the concatenation of the keys of the original tables.

Finally, a variety of approaches to the manipulation of relational databases was discussed. The relational calculus, a form of manipulation based on the predicate calculus of mathematical logic, was discussed only briefly. It is of theoretical importance as a standard by which other approaches are judged. That is, a language is relationally complete if it is as "powerful" as the relational calculus. The language SQL, Structured Query Language, is perhaps the most important approach of all because of its widespread use. It is an example of a transform-oriented language, which uses relations to transform inputs into desired outputs. Many features of this very important language were illustrated through examples. The relational algebra, an approach in which operations act on relations to produce new relations, and QBE (Query-by-Example), a language in which users visually fill in forms on the screen to manipulate the data in the database, were also discussed.

## REVIEW QUESTIONS

1. Define relation.
2. Define domain.
3. Define primary key and foreign key. What is the difference between the two?
4. What is the difference between a normalized and an unnormalized relation? How can an unnormalized relation be converted to an equivalent normalized relation?

5. How can a one-to-many relationship be implemented using relations?
6. How can a many-to-many relationship be implemented using relations?
7. Define union-compatible. Which of the relational algebra commands require union-compatibility? Why?
8. Describe four different types of joins. What are the differences between them? Where might each be used?

## EXERCISES

Questions 1 through 16 are based on the sample database of Figure 3.1 and deal with the language SQL. For each question, give both the appropriate SQL formulation and the result that would be produced.

1. Find the part number and description of all parts.
2. List the complete sales rep table.
3. Find the names of all the customers who have a credit limit of at least $800.
4. Give the order numbers of the orders placed by customer 124 on 9/05/91.
5. Give the part number, description, and on-hand value (units on hand * price) for each part in item class "AP." (On-hand value is really units on hand * cost, but we do not have a cost column in the *PART* table.)
6. List all details about parts. The output should be sorted by item class.
7. Find out how many customers have a balance that exceeds their credit limit.
8. Find the total of the balances for all customers represented by sales rep 12.
9. List the number, name, and balance of each customer, together with the number, name, and commission rate of each customer's sales rep.
10. Find the order number and date for all orders that contain a line for an IRON.
11. List the order number and date for all orders placed by any customer who is represented by the sales rep whose name is William Smith.
12. Change the description of part "BT04" to "OVEN."
13. Add $100 to the credit limit of all customers represented by sales rep 6.
14. Add order 12600 (date – 90691, customer – 311) to the database.
15. Delete all customers whose balance is 0 and who are represented by sales rep 12.
16. Describe a new relation to the database called "SPGOOD." It contains only part number, description, and price. Once this has been done, insert the part number description and price of all parts whose item class is "SG" into this new relation.

17. ***** COMPUTER PROJECT *******

    If you have access to a relational database management system, do each of the following:

    a. Create each of the five tables shown in Figure 3.1.

    b. Enter the sample data from Figure 3.1 into your database. For *SLSREP*, *ORDERS*, *ORDLNE*, and *PART* use whatever default type of features are included in your system for entering the data. If your system allows you to design your own forms, use this feature to enter the data for the *CUSTOMER* table. Finally, determine whether it is possible in your system to ensure, first, that a customer will not be added if the corresponding sales rep does not exist and, second, that a customer will not be deleted if he or she has any orders currently on file. Use whatever features of your system that you need to accomplish this. (It may very well mean writing a program in an appropriate language.)

    c. Actually do each of the queries in problems 1 through 16. Point out how the formulation in your system differs from the answers you gave earlier. If any of these queries cannot be satisfied in your system, explain why.

Questions 18 through 24 are also based on the sample database of Figure 3.1 but deal with the relational algebra. For each question, give both the appropriate relational algebra formulation and an equivalent SQL formulation.

18. List all information from the part relation concerning part BT04.
19. List the number and name of all sales reps.
20. List the order number, order date, customer number, and customer name for each order.
21. List the order number, order date, customer number, and customer name for each order placed by any customer represented by Mary Jones.
22. List all orders that were either placed on 90291 or placed by a customer with a $1,000 credit limit.
23. List all orders that were placed on 90291 by a customer with a $1,000 credit limit.
24. List all orders that were placed on 90291 but not by a customer with a $1,000 credit limit.

Questions 25 through 35 are also based on the sample database of Figure 3.1, but deal with QBE. For each question, give the appropriate QBE formulation.

25. List the number and name of all sales reps.
26. List the complete *CUSTOMER* table.
27. List the number and name of all customers who are represented by sales rep 3 and whose balance is at least $500.
28. List the number and name of all customers who are either represented by sales rep 3 or whose balance is at least $500.
29. List the number and name of all customers who do not have a credit limit of $1,000.

30. List the number and name of all customers who are represented by Mary Jones.
31. Find the total number of units on hand in warehouse 3.
32. Add sales rep 11 (name – Joan Thomas, address – 10 Maple,Grant,MI, commission – 0, commission rate – 7 percent) to the database.
33. Change the description of part "BT04" to "OVEN."
34. Add 10 percent to the price of all parts that are in item class "HW."
35. Delete all parts that are in item class "SG."

# REFERENCES

1] Bradley, James, *Introduction to Data Base Management in Business*, 2d ed. Holt, Rinehart & Winston, 1987.

2] Cardenas, Alfonso F., *Data Base Management Systems*, 2d ed. Allyn & Bacon, 1984.

3] Codd, E. F., "A Relational Model of Data for Large Shared Databanks." *Communications of the ACM* 13, no. 6 (June 1970).

4] Codd, E. F., "Relational Completeness of Data Base Sublanguages." In *Data Base Systems, Courant Computer Science Symposia Series*, vol. 6. Prentice-Hall, 1972.

5] Codd, E. F., "A Data Base Sublanguage Founded on the Relational Calculus." Proceedings of the ACM SIGFIDET Workshop on Data Description, Access and Control, 1971.

6] Date, C. J., *Introduction to Database Systems, Volume I,* 4th ed. Addison-Wesley, 1986.

7] Greenblatt, D., and Waxman, J., "A Study of Three Database Query Languages." In *Databases: Improving Usability and Responsiveness*, ed. B. Schneideman. Academic Press, 1978.

8] Kroenke, David, and Dolan, Kathleen A., *Database Processing: Fundamentals, Design, Implementation*, 3d ed. SRA, 1988.

9] Martin, James, *Managing the Database Environment*, Prentice-Hall, 1983.

10] McFadden, Fred R., and Hoffer, Jeffrey A., *Data Base Management*, 2d ed. Benjamin Cummings, 1988.

11] Ullman, Jeffrey D., *Principles of Database Systems*, 2d ed. Computer Science Press, Prentice-Hall, 1982.

12] Zloof, M. M., "Query By Example." Proceedings of the NCC 44, May 1975.

13] Zloof, M. M., "Design Aspects of the Query-by-Example Data Base Management Language." In *Databases: Improving Usability and Responsiveness*, ed. B. Schneideman, Academic Press, 1978.

# Relational Model: Advanced Topics and Implementation

## INTRODUCTION

In this chapter, we continue our study of the relational model. We begin by investigating some advanced concepts within the general model. We will look at the following:

- the issues involved in supporting nulls
- the use of views and their relationship to subschemas
- security within relational model systems
- the use of indexes to improve performance
- the process of changing the structure of a relational database
- the system catalog and the manner in which it can be accessed
- integrity within the relational model

We will also consider the question, *What does it take to be relational?* We then turn our attention to the manner in which SQL can be embedded in programs in languages like COBOL.

The remainder of the chapter will be spent discussing two major relational model implementations. The first of these, DB2, a product of IBM, will be examined in some detail. We will see that much of what we have been discussing applies directly to DB2. We will also investigate the way in which DB2 supports the functions of a DBMS that were described in chapter 2. Finally, we will discuss INGRES, which is a major alternative to the systems that support SQL and is marketed by Relational Technology, Inc.

## ADVANCED TOPICS

In this section, we investigate a number of advanced topics in the relational model. In many cases, we will use SQL as a vehicle for illustrating the topic. Systems that do not support SQL may well support the same concept, but in a slightly different fashion. The basic ideas are quite similar, however.

### Nulls

Occasionally, when a new row is entered into a database or an existing row is modified, the values for one or more columns are unknown. They may be merely unavailable for the moment; a customer may not yet have been assigned a sales rep or a credit limit. In other cases, these values may never be known; perhaps a customer may exist without ever having a sales rep. This concept of unknown (or nonapplicable) values is supported by many systems. Such values are called **null data values**, or simply **nulls**.

In any system that supports null values, the choice of whether to allow them must be made for each column. This choice should be made carefully, since null values can present problems.

It makes no sense to allow null values for the primary key. The wisdom of storing a customer whose customer number is unknown is questionable at best.

Null values in numeric fields can cause strange results when statistics are computed. Suppose that *BALANCE* accepts null values. Suppose, further, that there are currently four customers on file, with respective balances of $100, $200, and $300, and one whose balance is null (unknown). When the average balance is calculated, most implementations will ignore the null value and obtain $200 (($100 + $200 + $300)/ 3). Similarly, if the total of the balances is calculated, the null value will be ignored and a total of $600 will be obtained. If a count of the number of rows in the table is made, however, the row containing the null will be included, yielding a result of 4. Thus the total balance ($600) divided by the number of customers (4) is not equal to the average balance ($200)!

Another problem occurs when tables are joined on columns that are allowed to be null. Suppose that in the Marvel College database the column indicating the field of specialization of a faculty member is allowed to be null. Suppose further that we are attempting to find pairs of faculty members who are in the same area of specialization by joining the *FACULTY* table to itself, based on matching fields of specialization. What happens when the areas of specialization of two faculty members are both null? Are these two faculty members to be joined or not? Both specializations seem to be the same — null — but on the other hand, null means we don't know what their specializations really are. To claim that they are the same would certainly seem strange.

In addition, what happens if we request a list of all faculty members whose area of specialization is "TOPOLOGY" or whose salary is greater than $25,000? In SQL, this would be formulated as:

```
SELECT * FROM FACULTY
     WHERE SALARY > 25000
     OR FIELD = 'TOPOLOGY'
```

Is the condition considered true for a faculty member whose salary is $30,000 and for whom the value of *FIELD* is null? In particular, what about the single condition FIELD = 'TOPOLOGY'? Is it to be considered true or false? It certainly cannot be considered true; yet we can't say it is false either. We need a third possibility, perhaps called "unknown." Once we allow this third possibility for simple conditions, we need a way to assign values for compound conditions. If SALARY > 25000 is true, for example, and FIELD = 'TOPOLOGY' is unknown, what value should be assigned to the compound condition SALARY > 25000 OR FIELD = 'TOPOLOGY'? In this case, since the first condition in an OR is true, the overall condition should be true independently of the truth or falsity of the second condition, and thus it makes sense to assign it the value true.

We can, in fact, construct a new set of truth tables, as shown in Figure 4.1. These truth tables represent the net result of combining two simple conditions with AND or OR or taking the negation (NOT) of an individual simple condition. They give the resulting values based on the values of the simple conditions themselves. Thus, for example, if condition A is unknown and condition B is false, condition A AND B will be false, condition A OR B will be unknown, condition NOT A will be unknown, and condition NOT B will be true.

| AND | T | U | F |
|-----|---|---|---|
| T | T | U | F |
| U | U | U | F |
| F | F | F | F |

| OR | T | U | F |
|-----|---|---|---|
| T | T | T | T |
| U | T | U | U |
| F | T | U | F |

| NOT | |
|-----|---|
| T | F |
| U | U |
| F | T |

```
T - true
F - false
U - unknown
```

**Figure 4.1**

Three-way logic

This is not to imply that relational model systems (or any others, for that matter) actually implement this **three-way logic**, nor that implementing such logic is even desirable. It is, however, at least a theoretical way around some of the problems caused by nulls.

A final comment is in order before leaving the subject of nulls. As indicated earlier, nulls can be used when values are either unknown or nonapplicable. It is the "unknown" use of nulls that causes many of the problems just described. If nulls are used only to support nonapplicable values, at least some of the problems disappear. These same problems do not arise, for example, if a null sales rep number in the *CUSTOMER* relation means specifically that a customer has no sales rep, not that we don't know who represents the customer; they also do not arise if a null value in *FIELD* indicates that the faculty member has no area of specialization. It is clear that when customers are related to sales reps, a customer whose sales rep number is null should not be related to any sales reps. It is equally clear that for a faculty member for whom the value of *FIELD* is null, the value of the condition FIELD = 'TOPOLOGY' is false.

In any implementation of SQL that supports **nulls**, there must be a mechanism to indicate which columns can accept null values and which cannot. This is usually accomplished through the clause NOT NULL. Those columns whose description includes NOT NULL are not allowed to accept null values. Other columns may accept such values.

For example, suppose the sales rep number and name cannot accept null values but all other columns in the *SLSREP* table can. The corresponding CREATE TABLE command is shown in Figure 4.2. Any attempt to store a null value in either the sales rep number or name columns will be rejected by the system.

**Figure 4.2**

SQL create statement that involves nulls

```
CREATE TABLE SLSREP
     (SLSRNUMB          INTEGER        NOT NULL,
      SLSRNAME          CHAR(15)       NOT NULL,
      SLSRADDR          CHAR(25),
      TOTCOMM           DECIMAL(7,2),
      COMMRATE          DECIMAL(3,2)
```

The only new aspect of data manipulation that will be discussed here is the impact of nulls. Two aspects must be covered: setting a given column to null, and testing a given column to determine whether it is or is not null.

To set a given column to null, we merely use the word null in the appropriate assignment. To set the address of customer 124 to null, for example, we would enter:

```
UPDATE CUSTOMER
     SET CUSTADDR = NULL
     WHERE CUSTNUMB = 124
```

We can also test to see whether a given column is null. The syntax for the test is not CUSTADDR = NULL, as you might expect, but rather

CUSTADDR IS NULL. To obtain a list of the customer numbers and names of all the customers whose address is null, we would type

```
SELECT CUSTNUMB, CUSTNAME
     FROM CUSTOMER
     WHERE CUSTADDR IS NULL
```

For other perspectives on nulls, see [5], [6], and [9].


## Views

A good DBMS is capable of giving each user his or her own picture of the database. The existing, permanent tables in a relational database are often called **base tables**. A **view** is a pseudotable. This means that it appears to the user to be an actual table. The data doesn't really exist in this fashion, however. Rather, SQL will derive its contents from data in existing base tables whenever users attempt to access the view. The manner in which this data is to be derived is stored as part of the view definition.

A view is defined through a **defining query** as illustrated in example 1.

**Example 1:** Define a view, *HSEWRES*, that consists of the part number, description, units on hand, and unit price of all parts of item class HW.

This would be accomplished as follows:

```
CREATE VIEW HSEWRES AS
     SELECT PARTNUMB, PARTDESC, UNONHAND, UNITPRCE
          FROM PART
          WHERE ITEMCLSS = 'HW'
```

Given the current data in the Premiere Products database, this view will contain the data shown in Figure 4.3. The data does not actually exist in this form, however, nor will it *ever* exist in this form. It is tempting to think that when this view is used, the query will be executed and will produce some sort of temporary table, called *HSEWRES*, which the user will then access. This is *not* what happens. Instead, the query acts as a sort of "window" into the database (see Figure 4.4 on the next page). As far as a user of this view is concerned, the whole database consists of the dark portion of the *PART* table.


**HSEWRES**

| PARTNUMB | PARTDESC | UNONHAND | UNITPRCE |
|----------|----------|----------|----------|
| AX12 | IRON | 104 | 17.95 |
| BH22 | TOASTER | 95 | 34.95 |
| CA14 | SKILLET | 2 | 19.95 |
| CX11 | MIXER | 112 | 57.95 |

**Figure 4.3**

*HSEWRES* view

**Figure 4.4**

Premiere Products
sample data

PART

| PARTNUMB | PARTDESC | UNONHAND | ITEMCLSS | WRHSNUMB | UNITPRCE |
|----------|----------|----------|----------|----------|----------|
| AX12 | IRON | 104 | HW | 3 | 17.95 |
| AZ52 | SKATES | 20 | SG | 2 | 24.95 |
| BA74 | BASEBALL | 40 | SG | 1 | 4.95 |
| BH22 | TOASTER | 95 | HW | 3 | 34.95 |
| BT04 | STOVE | 11 | AP | 2 | 402.99 |
| BZ66 | WASHER | 52 | AP | 3 | 311.95 |
| CA14 | SKILLET | 2 | HW | 3 | 19.95 |
| CB03 | BIKE | 44 | SG | 1 | 187.50 |
| CX11 | MIXER | 112 | HW | 3 | 57.95 |
| CZ81 | WEIGHTS | 208 | SG | 2 | 108.99 |

The way this is implemented is clever. Suppose, for example, a user of this view typed the following query:

```
SELECT *
    FROM HSEWRES
    WHERE UNONHAND > 100
```

Rather than being executed directly, this query is first merged with the query that defines the view, producing:

```
SELECT PARTNUMB, PARTDESC, UNONHAND, UNITPRCE
    FROM PART
    WHERE ITEMCLSS = 'HW'
    AND UNONHAND > 100
```

Note that the selection is from the *PART* table, rather than the *HSEWRES* view; the "*" is replaced by just those columns in the *HSEWRES* view; and the condition involves the condition in the query entered by the user, together with the condition stated in the view definition. This new query is the one that is actually executed.

The user, however, is unaware that this kind of activity is taking place. It seems there actually is a table called *HSEWRES* being accessed. One advantage of this approach is that since *HSEWRES* never exists in its own right, any update to the *PART* table is *immediately* felt by someone accessing the database through the *HSEWRES* view. If *HSEWRES* were an actual stored table, this would not be the case.

The form of a view definition is illustrated in the *HSEWRES* view. It is CREATE view-name AS query. The query, which is called the **defining query**, can be any legitimate SQL query. (This is not technically true for all relational model implementations. Some forbid the use of UNION in the query, for example.) Optionally the view-name can be followed by the names for columns in the view, as in the following.

```
CREATE VIEW HSEWRES (PARTNUMB, PARTDESC, UNONHAND,
        UNITPRCE) AS
    SELECT PARTNUMB, PARTDESC, UNONHAND, UNITPRCE
        FROM PART
        WHERE ITEMCLSS = 'HW'
```

This feature can also be used to rename columns, as shown in example 2.

**Example 2:** Define a view, *HSEWRES*, that consists of the part number, description, units on hand, and unit price of all parts of item class HW. In this view, the part number column is to be called *PNUM*, the part description column is to be called *DESC*, the units on hand column is to be called *ONHAND*, and the unit price column is to be called *PRICE*.

We simply include the desired column names in parentheses, as follows:

```
CREATE VIEW HSEWRES (PNUM, DESC, ONHAND, PRICE) AS
    SELECT PARTNUMB, PARTDESC, UNONHAND, UNITPRCE
        FROM PART
        WHERE ITEMCLSS = 'HW'
```

In this case, anyone accessing the *HSEWRES* view will refer to *PARTNUMB* as *PNUM*, *PARTDESC* as *DESC*, *UNONHAND* as *ONHAND*, and *UNITPRCE* as *PRICE*.

The *HSEWRES* view is an example of a row-and-column subset view, that is, it consists of a subset of the rows and columns in some base table, in this case the *PART* table. Since the query can be any SQL query, a view could involve the join of two or more tables. It could also involve statistics. Example 3 involves a join.

**Example 3:** Define a view, *SLSCUST*, that consists of the sales rep number (called *SNUMB*), sales rep name (called *SNAME*), customer number (called *CNUMB*), and customer name (called *CNAME*) for all sales reps and matching customers in the *SLSREP* and *CUSTOMER* tables.

The command to create this view would be:

```
CREATE VIEW SLSCUST (SNUMB, SNAME, CNUMB, CNAME) AS
    SELECT SLSREP.SLSRNUMB, SLSREP.SLSRNAME,
        CUSTOMER.CUSTNUMB, CUSTOMER.CUSTNAME
        FROM SLSREP, CUSTOMER
        WHERE SLSREP.SLSRNUMB = CUSTOMER.SLSRNUMB
```

Given the current data in the Premiere Products database, this view is the table shown in Figure 4.5 on the next page.

Example 4 is a view that involves statistics.

**Figure 4.5**

*SLSCUST* view

**SLSCUST**

| SNUMB | SNAME | CNUMB | CNAME |
|-------|-------|-------|-------|
| 3 | Jones, Mary | 124 | Adams, Sally |
| 3 | Jones, Mary | 412 | Adams, Sally |
| 3 | Jones, Mary | 622 | Martin, Dan |
| 6 | Smith, William | 256 | Samuels, Ann |
| 6 | Smith, William | 315 | Daniels, Tom |
| 6 | Smith, William | 567 | Baker, Joe |
| 6 | Smith, William | 587 | Roberts, Judy |
| 12 | Brown, Sam | 311 | Charles, Don |
| 12 | Brown, Sam | 405 | Williams, Al |
| 12 | Brown, Sam | 522 | Nelson, Mary |

**Example 4:** Define a view, *CREDCST*, that consists of a credit limit (*CREDLIM*) and the number of customers who have this limit (*NUMBCUST*).

To create this view, we would use the following command:

```
CREATE VIEW CREDCST (CREDLIM, NUMBCUST) AS
     SELECT CREDLIM, COUNT(CUSTNUMB)
          FROM CUSTOMER
          GROUP BY CREDLIM
```

Given the current data in the Premiere Products database, this view is the table shown in Figure 4.6.

**Figure 4.6**

*CREDCST* view

**CREDCST**

| CREDLIM | NUMBCUST |
|---------|----------|
| 300 | 3 |
| 500 | 3 |
| 800 | 3 |
| 1000 | 1 |

**Advantages of Views.**    The use of views furnishes several advantages:

1. Views provide data independence. If the database structure is changed (columns added, relationships changed, etc.) in such a way that the view can still be derived from existing data, the user can still access the same view. If adding extra columns to tables in the database is the only change, and these columns are not required by this user, the defining query may not even need to be changed. If relationships are changed, the defining query may be different, but since users need not even be aware of the defining query, this difference is unknown to them. They continue to access the database through the same view, as

though nothing has changed. For an example of the type of change that requires modification of the defining query, consider the following:

a. Customers are assigned to territories.
b. Each territory is assigned to a single sales rep.
c. A sales rep can have more than one territory.
d. A customer is represented by the sales rep who covers the territory to which the customer is assigned.

To implement these changes, we might choose to restructure the database as follows:

```
SLSREP(SLSRNUMB, SLSRNAME, SLSRADDR, TOTCOMM, COMMRATE)
TERRIT(TERRNUMB, TERRDESC, SLSRNUMB)
CUSTOMER(CUSTNUMB, CUSTNAME, CUSTADDR, BALANCE, CREDLIM,
     TERRNUMB)
```

Assuming the *SLSCUST* view shown earlier is still required, the defining query could be reformulated as follows:

```
CREATE VIEW SLSCUST (SNUMB, SNAME, CNUMB, CNAME) AS
     SELECT SLSREP.SLSRNUMB, SLSREP.SLSRNAME,
          CUSTOMER.CUSTNUMB, CUSTOMER.CUSTNAME
          FROM SLSREP, TERRIT, CUSTOMER
          WHERE SLSREP.SLSRNUMB = TERRIT.SLSRNUMB
          AND TERRIT.TERRNUMB = CUSTOMER.TERRNUMB
```

The user of this view will still be presented with the number and name of a sales rep, together with the number and name of customers the sales rep represents. Such a user will be unaware of the new structure in the database.

2. Since each user has his or her own view, the same data can be viewed by different users in different ways.
3. A view should contain only those columns required by a given user. This practice accomplishes two things. First, since the view will, in all probability, contain far fewer columns than the overall database and since the view is effectively a single table, rather than a collection of tables, it greatly simplifies the user's perception of the database. Second, it furnishes a measure of security. Columns that are not included in the view are not accessible to this user. Omitting the *BALANCE* column from the view will ensure that a user of this view cannot access any customer's balance. Likewise, rows that are not included in the view are not accessible. A user of the *HSEWRES* view, for example, cannot obtain any information about sporting goods, even though both housewares and sporting goods are stored in the same base table, *PART*.

The advantages just described hold when views are used for retrieval purposes only; the story is a little different when it comes to updates. The issues involved in updating data through a view depend on the type of view.

1. **Row and Column Subsets.** Consider the row and column subset view *HSEWRES*. There are columns in the underlying base table, *PART*, which are not present in the view. Therefore, if we attempt to add a row ('BB99','PAN',50,14.95), somehow the system must determine how to fill in the remaining columns from *PART*: *ITEMCLSS* and *WRHSNUMB*. In this case, it is clear how to fill in *ITEMCLSS*. According to the definition of the view, it should be HW. But it is not at all clear how to fill in *WRHSNUMB*. The only possibility would be NULL. Thus, provided that any columns not included in a view may accept nulls, we can add new rows in the fashion previously indicated. There is another problem, however. Suppose the user attempts to add the row ('AZ52','POT',25,9.95). This attempt *must* be rejected, since there is already a part numbered AZ52 in the *PART* table. This rejection will certainly seem strange to the user, since there is no such part in this user's view! (It has a different item class.)

Updates or deletions cause no particular problem in this view. If the description of part CA14 is changed from skillet to pan, this change will be made in the *PART* table. If part CX11 is deleted, this deletion will occur in the *PART* table. One peculiar change could take place, however. Suppose *ITEMCLSS* were included as a column in the *HSEWRES* view, and suppose a user changed the item class of part CX11 from HW to AP. Since this item would no longer satisfy the criterion for being included in the *HSEWRES* view, it would effectively disappear as far as this user were concerned!

While some problems do have to be overcome, it seems possible to update the database through the *HSEWRES* view. This does not imply that *any* row and column subset view is updatable, however. Consider the following view:

```
CREATE VIEW SLSCRED AS
     SELECT DISTINCT CREDLIM, SLSRNUMB
          FROM CUSTOMER
```

(The word DISTINCT is used to omit duplicate rows in the resulting table.) This view currently contains the data shown in Figure 4.7. It shows the relationship between sales reps and the credit limits of customers they represent.

**SLSCRED**

| CREDLIM | SLSRNUMB |
|---------|----------|
| 500     | 3        |
| 800     | 6        |
| 300     | 12       |
| 300     | 6        |
| 800     | 12       |
| 1000    | 3        |
| 500     | 6        |

**Figure 4.7**

*SLSCRED* view

How would we add the row (1000,6) to this view? In the underlying base table, *CUSTOMER*, at least one customer must be added whose credit limit is $1,000 and whose sales rep is 6, but who? We can't leave the other columns null in this case, especially since one of them is *CUSTNUMB*, which is the primary key. What would it mean to change the row (800,12) to (1000,12)? Would it mean changing the credit limit of all the customers who are represented by sales rep 12 and who currently have a credit limit of $800 to $1,000? Would it mean changing the credit limit of one of these customers and deleting the rest? What would it mean to delete the row (500,3)? Would it mean deleting all customers whose credit limit is $500 and whose sales rep is 3? Or would it mean assigning these customers a different sales rep or a different credit limit? Potentially, we could also set their credit limit and/or their sales rep numbers to null.

Why does the view *SLSCRED* involve a number of serious problems that are not present in *HSEWRES*? The basic reason is that *HSEWRES* includes, as one of its columns, the primary key of the underlying base table, and *SLSCRED* does not. This is true in general. A row and column subset view that contains the primary key of the underlying base table is updatable (subject, of course, to some of the concerns we have discussed).

2. **Joins.** In general, views that involve joins of base tables can cause real problems at update. Consider the relatively simple view *SLSCUST*, for example, described earlier. (See Figure 4.5.) The fact that some columns in the underlying base tables are not seen in this view certainly presents some of the same problems discussed earlier. Even assuming that these problems can be overcome through the use of nulls, there are more serious problems inherent in the attempt to update the database through this view. On the surface, changing the row (6,'Smith, William',256,'Samuels, Ann') to (6,'Baker, Nancy',256, 'Samuels, Ann') might not appear to pose any problems other than some inconsistency in the data. (In the new version of the row, the name of sales rep 6 is Nancy Baker; on the next row in the table, the name of sales rep 6 is William Smith.) The problem is actually more

serious than that. It is not possible to make only this change! Since the name of the sales rep is stored just once in the underlying sales rep table, changing the name from William Smith to Nancy Baker on this one row of the view will cause the same change to be made on all the other rows. Although in this case that would probably be a good thing, in general, the unexpected changes caused by an update are definitely not desirable.

Before leaving the topic of views that involve joins, note that not all joins create the preceding problem. If two base tables happen to have the same primary key and this primary key is used as the join field, updating the database will not be a problem. For example, what if the actual database contains not a single *SLSREP* table but two (see Figure 4.8):

```
SLSRDEMO(SLSRNUMB, SLSRNAME, SLSRADDR)
```

and

```
SLSRFIN(SLSRNUMB, TOTCOMM, COMMRATE)
```

**Figure 4.8**

Slsrep data split across two relations

**SLSRDEMO**

| SLSRNUMB | SLSRNAME | SLSRADDR |
|---|---|---|
| 3 | Jones, Mary | 123 Main,Grant,MI |
| 6 | Smith, William | 102 Raymond,Ada,MI |
| 12 | Brown, Sam | 419 Harper,Lansing,MI |

**SLSRFIN**

| SLSRNUMB | TOTCOMM | COMMRATE |
|---|---|---|
| 3 | 2150.00 | .05 |
| 6 | 4912.50 | .07 |
| 12 | 2150.00 | .05 |

In this case, what was a single table in the Premiere Products database has been divided into two. Any user who expected to see a single table could be accommodated through a view that joined these two tables together on *SLSRNUMB*. We could, in fact, call the view *SLSREP*. The view definition would be:

```
CREATE VIEW SLSREP AS
     SELECT SLSRDEMO.SLSRNUMB, SLSRNAME, SLSRADDR,
            TOTCOMM, COMMRATE
       FROM SLSRDEMO, SLSRFIN
       WHERE SLSRDEMO.SLSRNUMB = SLSRFIN.SLSRNUMB
```

This view would contain the data shown in Figure 4.9.

**SLSREP**

| SLSRNUMB | SLSRNAME | SLSRADDR | TOTCOMM | COMMRATE |
|---|---|---|---|---|
| 3 | Jones, Mary | 123 Main,Grant,MI | 2150.00 | .05 |
| 6 | Smith, William | 102 Raymond,Ada,MI | 4912.50 | .07 |
| 12 | Brown, Sam | 419 Harper,Lansing,MI | 2150.00 | .05 |

**Figure 4.9**

*SLSREP* as a view that is a join of *SLSRDEMO* and *SLSRFIN*

No difficulty is encountered in updating this view. Adding a row simply involves adding a row to each of the underlying base tables. A change to any row in the view requires only a change to the appropriate base table. To delete any row from the view, we delete the corresponding rows from both underlying base tables.

Q & A

Question:         How would you add the row (10,'Peters, Jean','14 Brink,Hart,MI',107.50,.05)?

Answer:            Add the row (10,'Peters, Jean','14 Brink,Hart,MI') to *SLSRDEMO* and the row (10,107.50,.05) to *SLSRFIN*.

Question:         How would you change sales rep 3's name to Mary Lewis?

Answer:            Change the name in *SLSRDEMO*.

Question:         How would you change her commission rate to .06?

Answer:            Make the change in *SLSRFIN*.

Question:         How would you delete sales rep 6 from *SLSREP*?

Answer:            Delete sales rep 6 from *both SLSRDEMO and SLSRFIN*.

The previously discussed view *SLSREP* is updatable. None of the types of updates (add, change, or delete) cause any problems. The main reason that this view is updatable and other views involving joins are not is that this view is derived from the joining of two base tables *on the primary key of each*. In contrast, the view *SLSCUST* is derived from joining two tables using the primary key of one table and a matching foreign primary key in the other. Even more severe problems are encountered if neither of the columns used in the join is a primary key.

3. **Statistics.** A view that involves statistics calculated from one or more base tables is the most troublesome of all. Consider *CREDCST*, for example. (See Figure 4.6.) How would we add the row (600,3)? We would somehow have to add to the database three customers, each of whose credit limit is $600. Likewise, changing the row (500,3) to (500,6) means adding three customers, each of whose credit limit is $500. Clearly these are impossible tasks.

**Current Systems.**   The preceding discussion concerned what is *theoretically possible*, not what is actually implemented on current commercial systems. Many current systems support update of views that are row and column subsets. (In performing this kind of update, keep in mind some of the pitfalls we've discussed.) Views involving statistics are not even *theoretically* updatable. Views involving joins form the middle ground. Some such views are not theoretically updatable, others are. *Most current implementations will not support update of the database through any view that involves a join, even views that are updatable in theory.* Someday systems will support this type of update, however; progress is being made.

**Views and Subschemas.**   In chapters 1 and 2, we discussed the concept of a subschema, or individual user's view of the database. While it may seem that the relational model "view" is really what we termed a subschema, this is not quite accurate. The basic problem is that a view, even though it may be derived by joining more than one base table, is still essentially a single table. For some users, this will not be enough. If a given user required access to all the columns in all the tables of the Premiere Products database, it would not be practical to attempt to present this user with a single table that was the result of joining all existing tables together. The database is generally far more involved than the sample we have been using for Premiere Products, so an attempt to join all the tables together in one view would be even less practical, if not impossible. Further, since some views involving joins are not updatable using today's systems, and others are not even theoretically updatable, such an approach would not be feasible for any user updating the database.

In reality, a subschema in a relational model system will consist of some combination of base tables and views. For some users, a single view may suffice. Others may require a combination. In general, views rather than base tables should be used wherever possible in order to obtain the advantages described earlier.

For other information on views, see [5], [6], [8], [9], and [10].

## Security

**Security** is the prevention of unauthorized access to the database. Within an organization, some person or group will determine the types of access various users can have to the database. Some users might be able to retrieve and update anything in the database. Other users may be able to retrieve any data from the database but not make any changes to the data. Still other users may only be able to access a portion of the database. For example, Bill may be able to retrieve and update customer data, but not retrieve sales reps, orders, order lines, or parts. Mary may be able to retrieve data on parts and nothing else. Sam may be able to retrieve and update data on parts in item class HW, but no others.

Once these rules have been determined, it's up to the DBMS to enforce them. In particular, it's up to whatever security mechanism the DBMS provides. In SQL systems, there are two security mechanisms. We have already seen that views furnish a certain amount of security. (If someone is accessing the database through a view, they cannot access any data that is not part of the view.) The main mechanism, however, is the GRANT facility. The basic idea is that different types of privileges can be granted to users and, if necessary, later revoked. These privileges include such things as the right to select rows from a table, the right to insert new rows, the right to update existing rows, and so on. Granting and revoking these privileges is accomplished through GRANT and REVOKE statements. Following are some examples of the GRANT statement.

**Example 5:** User Jones must be able to retrieve data from the *SLSREP* table.

```
GRANT SELECT ON SLSREP TO JONES
```

**Example 6:** Users Smith and Brown must be able to add new parts.

```
GRANT INSERT ON PART TO SMITH, BROWN
```

**Example 7:** User Jones is no longer allowed to retrieve data from the *SLSREP* table.

```
REVOKE SELECT ON SLSREP FROM JONES
```

GRANT and REVOKE can also be applied to views. This provides the capability of restricting access only to certain rows within tables.

For other information on security, see [1], [5], [6], [8], [9], and [10].

## Indexes

**Purpose of an Index.**   Much of what we do when we manipulate a database involves finding a row or collection of rows that satisfies some condition. Examining every single row in a table looking for the desired rows often takes far too long to be practical. Fortunately, there is an alternative approach that can greatly speed up the process. This approach involves the use of what is called an **index**. You are probably already familiar with the idea. If you wanted to find a discussion of a given topic in a book, you could scan the entire book from start to finish, looking for references to the topic you had in mind. More than likely, however, you wouldn't have to resort to this technique. If the book had a good *index,* you would use it to rapidly locate the pages on which your topic was discussed.

Within relational model systems on both mainframes and microcomputers, the main mechanism for increasing the efficiency with which data is retrieved from the database is the use of indexes. These indexes are very much like the index in a book. Consider Figure 4.10, for example, which shows the *CUSTOMER* table for Premiere Products together with one extra column, *REC*. This extra column gives the number of each record within the file. (Customer 124 is on record 1; customer 256 is on record 2; and so on.) These record numbers are used by the DBMS to allow it to go directly to a specific row. They are not used by the users of the DBMS, and that is why we do not normally show them. Here, however, we are dealing with the manner in which the DBMS works, so we do need to be aware of them.

**Figure 4.10**

*CUSTOMER* table with record numbers

CUSTOMER

| REC | | CUSTNAME | CUSTADDR | BALANCE | CREDLIM | SLSRNUMB |
|---|---|---|---|---|---|---|
| 1 | 124 | Adams, Sally | 481 Oak,Lansing,MI | 418.75 | 500 | 3 |
| 2 | 256 | Samuels, Ann | 215 Pete,Grant,MI | 10.75 | 800 | 6 |
| 3 | 311 | Charles, Don | 48 College,Ira,MI | 200.10 | 300 | 12 |
| 4 | 315 | Daniels, Tom | 914 Cherry,Kent,MI | 320.75 | 300 | 6 |
| 5 | 405 | Williams, Al | 519 Watson,Grant,MI | 201.75 | 800 | 12 |
| 6 | 412 | Adams, Sally | 16 Elm,Lansing,MI | 908.75 | 1000 | 3 |
| 7 | 522 | Nelson, Mary | 108 Pine,Ada,MI | 49.50 | 800 | 12 |
| 8 | 567 | Baker, Joe | 808 Ridge,Harper,MI | 201.20 | 300 | 6 |
| 9 | 587 | Roberts, Judy | 512 Pine,Ada,MI | 57.75 | 500 | 6 |
| 10 | 622 | Martin, Dan | 419 Chip,Grant,MI | 575.50 | 500 | 3 |

In order to rapidly access a customer on the basis of his or her number, we might choose to create and use an index as shown in Figure 4.11. The index is a separate file that has two columns. The first column contains a customer number, and the second column contains the number of the record on which the customer is found. To find a customer, we look up the customer's number in the first column in the index. The value in the second column indicates which record we should retrieve from the *CUSTOMER* table. We proceed directly to the desired record and we have the customer we want.

**CUSTNUMB INDEX**

| CUSTNUMB | REC |
|----------|-----|
| 124 | 1 |
| 256 | 2 |
| 311 | 3 |
| 315 | 4 |
| 405 | 5 |
| 412 | 6 |
| 522 | 7 |
| 567 | 8 |
| 587 | 9 |
| 622 | 10 |

**Figure 4.11**

Index for *CUSTOMER* table on *CUSTNUMB* column

**CUSTOMER**

| REC | CUSTNUMB | CUSTNAME | CUSTADDR | BALANCE | CREDLIM | SLSRNUMB |
|-----|----------|----------|----------|---------|---------|----------|
| 1 | 124 | Adams, Sally | 481 Oak,Lansing,MI | 418.75 | 500 | 3 |
| 2 | 256 | Samuels, Ann | 215 Pete,Grant,MI | 10.75 | 800 | 6 |
| 3 | 311 | Charles, Don | 48 College,Ira,MI | 200.10 | 300 | 12 |
| 4 | 315 | Daniels, Tom | 914 Cherry,Kent,MI | 320.75 | 300 | 6 |
| 5 | 405 | Williams, Al | 519 Watson,Grant,MI | 201.75 | 800 | 12 |
| 6 | 412 | Adams, Sally | 16 Elm,Lansing,MI | 908.75 | 1000 | 3 |
| 7 | 522 | Nelson, Mary | 108 Pine,Ada,MI | 49.50 | 800 | 12 |
| 8 | 567 | Baker, Joe | 808 Ridge,Harper,MI | 201.20 | 300 | 6 |
| 9 | 587 | Roberts, Judy | 512 Pine,Ada,MI | 57.75 | 500 | 6 |
| 10 | 622 | Martin, Dan | 419 Chip,Grant,MI | 575.50 | 500 | 3 |

Since customer numbers are unique, there will be a single record number in each row in the index. This need not always be the case, however. Suppose we wanted to be able to rapidly access all customers who have a given credit limit. We would also like to be able to rapidly access all customers who are represented by a given sales rep. In this case, we might choose to create and use an index on credit limit (Figure 4.12a on the next page), as well as an index on sales rep number. (See Figure 4.12b on the next page.) In the index on credit limit, the first column contains a credit limit and the second column contains the numbers of *all* the records on which that credit limit is found. The index on sales rep number is similar, only the first column contains a sales rep number.

**Figure 4.12a**

Index for
*CUSTOMER* table
on *CREDLIM*
column

**CREDLIM INDEX**

| CREDLIM | RECs |
|---------|------|
| 300 | 3, 4, 8 |
| 500 | 1, 9, 10 |
| 800 | 2, 5, 7 |
| 1000 | 6 |

**CUSTOMER**

| REC | CUSTNUMB | CUSTNAME | CUSTADDR | BALANCE | CREDLIM | SLSRNUMB |
|-----|----------|----------|----------|---------|---------|----------|
| 1 | 124 | Adams, Sally | 481 Oak,Lansing,MI | 418.75 | 500 | 3 |
| 2 | 256 | Samuels, Ann | 215 Pete,Grant,MI | 10.75 | 800 | 6 |
| 3 | 311 | Charles, Don | 48 College,Ira,MI | 200.10 | 300 | 12 |
| 4 | 315 | Daniels, Tom | 914 Cherry,Kent,MI | 320.75 | 300 | 6 |
| 5 | 405 | Williams, Al | 519 Watson,Grant,MI | 201.75 | 800 | 12 |
| 6 | 412 | Adams, Sally | 16 Elm,Lansing,MI | 908.75 | 1000 | 3 |
| 7 | 522 | Nelson, Mary | 108 Pine,Ada,MI | 49.50 | 800 | 12 |
| 8 | 567 | Baker, Joe | 808 Ridge,Harper,MI | 201.20 | 300 | 6 |
| 9 | 587 | Roberts, Judy | 512 Pine,Ada,MI | 57.75 | 500 | 6 |
| 10 | 622 | Martin, Dan | 419 Chip,Grant,MI | 575.50 | 500 | 3 |

**Figure 4.12b**

Index for
*CUSTOMER* table
on *SLSRNUMB*
column

**SLSRNUMB INDEX**

| SLSRNUMB | RECs |
|----------|------|
| 3 | 1, 6, 10 |
| 6 | 2, 4, 8, 9 |
| 12 | 3, 5, 7 |

**CUSTOMER**

| REC | CUSTNUMB | CUSTNAME | CUSTADDR | BALANCE | CREDLIM | SLSRNUMB |
|-----|----------|----------|----------|---------|---------|----------|
| 1 | 124 | Adams, Sally | 481 Oak,Lansing,MI | 418.75 | 500 | 3 |
| 2 | 256 | Samuels, Ann | 215 Pete,Grant,MI | 10.75 | 800 | 6 |
| 3 | 311 | Charles, Don | 48 College,Ira,MI | 200.10 | 300 | 12 |
| 4 | 315 | Daniels, Tom | 914 Cherry,Kent,MI | 320.75 | 300 | 6 |
| 5 | 405 | Williams, Al | 519 Watson,Grant,MI | 201.75 | 800 | 12 |
| 6 | 412 | Adams, Sally | 16 Elm,Lansing,MI | 908.75 | 1000 | 3 |
| 7 | 522 | Nelson, Mary | 108 Pine,Ada,MI | 49.50 | 800 | 12 |
| 8 | 567 | Baker, Joe | 808 Ridge,Harper,MI | 201.20 | 300 | 6 |
| 9 | 587 | Roberts, Judy | 512 Pine,Ada,MI | 57.75 | 500 | 6 |
| 10 | 622 | Martin, Dan | 419 Chip,Grant,MI | 575.50 | 500 | 3 |

Q & A

---

Question:         How would you find all customers who have a $500 credit limit?

Answer:              Look up 500 in the credit limit index. This will give you a collection of record numbers (1, 9, and 10). Use these record numbers to find the corresponding customers (Sally Adams, Judy Roberts, and Dan Martin).

Question:         How would you find all customers who are represented by sales rep 6?

Answer:              Look up 6 in the sales rep number index. This will give you a collection of record numbers (2, 4, 8, and 9). Use these record numbers to find the corresponding customers (Ann Samuels, Tom Daniels, Joe Baker, and Judy Roberts).

---

The actual structure of these indexes is a bit more complicated than what we have been looking at here, although what we have seen is fine for our purposes. (Indexes typically use the B-tree structure. If you are interested in information on B-trees, see the appendix.) Fortunately, we don't have to be concerned with the details of manipulating and using these indexes. The DBMS will do all this for us. We merely decide which columns indexes should be built on. Typically, an index can be created and maintained for any column or combination of columns in any table. Once an index has been created, the DBMS can use it to facilitate retrieval. In powerful relational systems, the decision concerning which index or indexes to use (if any) during a particular type of retrieval is one function of a part of the DBMS called an **optimizer**. (No reference is made to any index by the user; rather, the system makes the decision behind the scenes.)

As you would expect, the use of any index is not purely advantageous or disadvantageous. The advantage was already mentioned: an index makes certain types of retrieval more efficient. There are two disadvantages. First, an index occupies space that could be used for something else. Any retrieval that can be made using an index can also be made without the index. The process may be less efficient, but it is still possible. So an index, while it occupies space, is technically unnecessary. Second, the index must be updated whenever corresponding data in the database is updated. Without the index, these updates would not have to be performed. The main question to ask when considering whether to create an index is, Do the benefits derived during retrieval outweigh the additional storage required and the extra processing involved in update operations?

Indexes can be added and dropped at will. The final decision concerning the columns or combination of columns on which indexes should be built does not have to be made at the time the database is first implemented. If the pattern of access to the database later indicates that overall performance would benefit from the creation of a new index, it can easily be added. Likewise, if it appears that an existing index is unnecessary, it can easily be dropped.

**Creating and Dropping Indexes.**   The commands used to create an index are CREATE INDEX and CREATE UNIQUE INDEX. Following are examples of the use of these commands for creating indexes for the Premiere Products database.

**Example 8:** Create a unique index on the *CUSTNUMB* column within the *CUSTOMER* table. The index is to be called *CUSTIND*.

The word UNIQUE indicates that the system is to maintain uniqueness of customer numbers (i.e., the system will not permit two customers with the same number to exist in the database). This index will be used to support direct retrieval based on the primary key, *CUSTNUMB*.) The command to create this index is:

```
CREATE UNIQUE INDEX CUSTIND ON CUSTOMER (CUSTNUMB)
```

**Example 9:** Create a unique index called *ORDLIND* on the *ORDNUMB*, *PARTNUMB* combination, which is the primary key of the *ORDLNE* table.

To create an index on more than one field, simply list the fields as in:

```
CREATE UNIQUE INDEX ORDLIND
        ON ORDLNE (ORDNUMB, PARTNUMB)
```

The command used to drop an index is DROP INDEX.

**Example 10:** Delete the index called *CUSTIND*. The command is:

```
DROP INDEX CUSTIND
```

**Index Discussion.**   These indexes are efficient and, if a given type of retrieval is going to be performed with any frequency, an index to facilitate the process is usually worthwhile. The added efficiency, in such situations, will usually offset the additional storage required and the extra overhead in processing incurred when updating the database. The ability to create and drop indexes easily, together with an efficient optimizer, provides a great deal of flexibility. If an index were created on a given date that would increase the efficiency of a given type of retrieval, the optimizer should immediately begin making use of the index. No program needs to change. The only difference a user might notice is that certain types of retrieval would be faster and certain types of updates might be slower. Likewise, if an index were dropped on a particular date, the optimizer would find new ways of satisfying any request that utilized that index. Again, no program needs to change. In this case, the only notice-able difference is that certain types of retrieval would be slower and certain types of update might be faster. The flexibility to make this type of change "on the fly" is one of the real benefits of the relational model systems, which is not shared by systems following other models.

For other information on the use of indexes, see [1], [5], [8], [9], and [10].

## Changing the Database Structure

In relational model systems, it is possible to easily alter the structure of an existing table. In contrast, such a change to the structure of existing databases in a nonrelational system is a much more complex process, involving not only changing the description of the structure but using utility programs to unload the data from the current structure and then reload it with the new structure.

Changing a table in SQL is accomplished through the ALTER table command, as illustrated in the following examples.

**Example 11:** Premiere Products decides to maintain a customer type for each customer in the database. This type is R for regular customers, D for distribu-tors, and S for special customers. Add this as a new column in the customer table.

Columns are added using the ADD option of the ALTER command, as follows:

```
ALTER TABLE CUSTOMER
     ADD CUSTTYPE        CHAR(1)
```

The *CUSTOMER* table now contains an extra column, *CUSTTYPE*. Any rows added from this point on will have this extra column. Existing records contain this extra column, effective immediately. The data in any existing row will be changed to reflect the new column the next time the row is updated. However, any time a row is selected for any reason, the system will treat the row as though the column is actually present. Thus, to the user, it will feel as though the structure was changed immediately.

For rows added from this point on, the value of *CUSTTYPE* will be assigned as the row is added. For existing rows, some value of *CUSTTYPE* must be assigned. The simplest approach (from the point of view of the DBMS, *not* the user) is to assign the value NULL as a *CUSTTYPE* on all existing rows. This requires that *CUSTTYPE* accept null values, and some systems actually insist on this. That is, any column added to a table definition *must* accept nulls; the user has no choice in the matter. A more flexible approach and one that is supported by some systems is to allow the user to specify an initial value. In our example, if most customers are of type R, we might set all the customer types for existing customers to R and later change those customers of type D or type S to the appropriate value. To change the structure and set the value of *CUSTTYPE* to R for all existing records, we would type:

```
ALTER TABLE CUSTOMER
     ADD CUSTTYPE        CHAR(1)      INIT = 'R'
```

Note that if a system will only set new columns to null, the above initialization can still be accomplished by following the ALTER command with an update command:

```
UPDATE CUSTOMER
     SET CUSTTYPE = 'R'
```

While this is not particularly difficult, it still is an extra step. Further, it is desirable for a user to determine whether to allow nulls rather than have the system require them. Thus, it is preferable for the system to support initial values for added columns.

While some systems automatically position newly added columns at the end, others allow users to determine where to put them. If *CUSTTYPE* is to be positioned before *BALANCE* in such systems, the ALTER statement would read something like:

```
ALTER TABLE CUSTOMER
     ADD CUSTTYPE        BEFORE BALANCE
                         CHAR(1)    INIT = 'R'
```

or, assuming *BALANCE* is the forth column:

```
ALTER TABLE CUSTOMER
     ADD CUSTTYPE        BEFORE 4
                         CHAR(1)    INIT = 'R'
```

Note that this column ordering becomes important only when a feature such as SELECT * FROM table-name is used (i.e., where the system lists all columns in the order in which they are stored.)

**Example 12:** The *WRHSNUMB* column is no longer needed in the *PART* table, so delete it.

Deleting a column is accomplished through the DELETE option of the ALTER command. In this case, the formulation is:

```
ALTER TABLE PART
    DELETE WRHSNUMB
```

**Example 13:** The length of the *CUSTNAME* column is too short. Increase it to thirty characters.

Characteristics of existing columns can be changed using the CHANGE option of the ALTER command. To change *CUSTNAME* so that it is now a character field of length 30 (it was a character field of length 15), the command would be:

```
ALTER TABLE CUSTOMER
    CHANGE COLUMN CUSTNAME TO CHAR(30)
```

Interestingly enough, many mainframe systems currently do not support this useful type of change, while many microcomputer systems do.

A table that is no longer needed can be deleted with the DROP command.

**Example 14:** The *SLSREP* table is no longer needed in the Premiere Products database, so delete it.

To delete a table, we simply write DROP TABLE, followed by the name of the table. In this case, the command would be:

```
DROP TABLE SLSREP
```

## The Catalog

Information concerning the tables known to the system is kept in the system **catalog**. In the following description of the catalog, the exact structure has been somewhat oversimplified, but it is representative of the basic ideas.

The catalog contains several tables of its own. We will focus on three of the most important: *SYSTABLES* (information about the tables known to SQL), *SYSCOLUMNS* (information about the columns within these tables), and *SYSINDEXES* (information about indexes defined on these tables.) While these tables have many columns, only a few are of concern to us here.

*SYSTABLES* (see Figure 4.13) contains columns *NAME, CREATOR,* and *COLCOUNT*. The *NAME* column identifies the name of a table. The *CREATOR* column contains an identification of the person or group who created the table. The *COLCOUNT* column contains the number of columns within the table being described. If, for example, user Brown created the sales rep table and the sales rep table had five columns, there would be a row in the *SYSTABLES* table in which *NAME* was SLSREP, *CREATOR* was BROWN, and *COLCOUNT* was 5. Similar rows would exist for all tables known to the system.

**Figure 4.13**

*SYSTABLES* table

**SYSTABLES**

| NAME | CREATOR | COLCOUNT |
|------|---------|----------|
| CUSTOMER | BROWN | 6 |
| ORDERS | BROWN | 3 |
| ORDLNE | BROWN | 4 |
| PART | BROWN | 6 |
| SLSREP | BROWN | 5 |

**Figure 4.14**

*SYSCOLUMNS* table

**SYSCOLUMNS**

| NAME | TBNAME | COLTYPE |
|------|--------|---------|
| COMMRATE | SLSREP | DECIMAL(3,2) |
| CREDLIM | CUSTOMER | DECIMAL(4) |
| BALANCE | CUSTOMER | DECIMAL(7,2) |
| CUSTADDR | CUSTOMER | CHAR(25) |
| CUSTNAME | CUSTOMER | CHAR(15) |
| CUSTNUMB | CUSTOMER | DECIMAL(3) |
| CUSTNUMB | ORDERS | DECIMAL(3) |
| ITEMCLSS | PART | CHAR(2) |
| NUMBORD | ORDLNE | DECIMAL(3) |
| ORDDTE | ORDERS | DECIMAL(6) |
| ORDNUMB | ORDERS | DECIMAL(5) |
| ORDNUMB | ORDLNE | DECIMAL(5) |
| PARTDESC | PART | CHAR(10) |
| PARTNUMB | PART | CHAR(4) |
| PARTNUMB | ORDLNE | CHAR(4) |
| QUOTPRCE | ORDLNE | DECIMAL(6,2) |
| SLSRADDR | SLSREP | CHAR(25) |
| SLSRNAME | SLSREP | CHAR(15) |
| SLSRNUMB | CUSTOMER | DECIMAL(2) |
| SLSRNUMB | SLSREP | DECIMAL(2) |
| TOTCOMM | SLSREP | DECIMAL(7,2) |
| UNITPRCE | PART | DECIMAL(6,2) |
| UNONHAND | PART | DECIMAL(4) |
| WRHSNUMB | PART | DECIMAL(2) |

*SYSCOLUMNS* (see Figure 4.14) contains columns *NAME, TBNAME,* and *COLTYPE*. The *NAME* column identifies the name of a column in one of the tables. The table in which the column is found is stored in *TBNAME*, and the data type for the column is found in *COLTYPE*. For example, there is a row in *SYSCOLUMNS* for each column in the *SLSREP* table. On each of these rows, *TBNAME* will be SLSREP. On one of these rows, *NAME* will be SLSRNUMB and *COLTYPE* will be DECIMAL (2). On another row, *NAME* will be SLSRNAME and *COLTYPE* will be CHAR(15). Similar rows would exist for all columns known to the system.

SYSINDEXES contains columns *NAME, TBNAME,* and *CREATOR*. The name of the index is found in the *NAME* column. The name of the table on which the index was built is found in the *TBNAME* column. The ID of the person or group that created the index is found in the *CREATOR* column.

The system catalog is a relational database of its own. Consequently, in general, the same types of queries that are used to retrieve information from relational databases can be used to retrieve information from the system catalog. The following examples illustrate this process.

**Example 15:** List the name and creator of all tables known to the system.

```
SELECT NAME, CREATOR
    FROM SYSTABLES
```

**Example 16:** List all the columns in the *CUSTOMER* table as well as their associated data types.

```
SELECT NAME, COLTYPE
    FROM SYSCOLUMNS
    WHERE TBNAME = 'CUSTOMER'
```

**Example 17:** List all tables that contain a column called *SLSRNUMB*.

```
SELECT TBNAME
    FROM SYSCOLUMNS
    WHERE NAME = 'SLSRNUMB'
```

Thus, information concerning the tables in our relational database, the columns they contain, and the indexes built on them can be obtained from the catalog by using the same SQL syntax used to query any other relational database.

Updating the tables that constitute the catalog occurs automatically when users CREATE, ALTER, or DROP tables or when they CREATE or DROP indexes. Users should not update the catalog directly using the update features of SQL, because inconsistent results may be produced. If a user were to delete the row in the *SYSCOLUMNS* table for the *CUSTNUMB* column, the system would no longer have any knowledge of this column, which is the primary key, yet all the rows in the database would still contain a customer number. The system might now treat those customer numbers as names, since, as far as it is concerned, *CUSTNAME* is the first column in the *CUSTOMER* table.

For other perspectives on SQL, see [1], [5], [8], [9], and [10].

## Relational Integrity Rules

In [2], Codd presents some extensions to the basic relational model in an attempt to capture more of the semantics, or meaning, of the actual data that is being modeled. His paper contains a summary of the main features of the model, together with a statement of two integrity rules. While the ideas behind these integrity rules appeared in his original paper on the subjects as discussed in chapter 3, they were not listed explicitly.

**Entity Integrity.** Since the function of the primary key is to uniquely identify a particular row in the relation, it does not make sense for the primary key to be null. The usefulness of storing a customer without a customer number, a part without a part number, or an employee without an employee number would certainly be questionable. Refusing to allow null values for any portion of the primary key is the property that Codd termed entity integrity.

> *Definition:* **Entity integrity** is the rule that no attribute which participates in the primary key may accept null values.

This property guarantees that entities do indeed have an identity. There will be a way to distinguish one from another, namely, through the primary key. Entity integrity guarantees that the primary key can, indeed, serve this function.

**Referential Integrity.**   A **foreign key** is an attribute (or collection of attributes) in one relation whose values are required to match the primary key of another relation. The example given was that the *SLSRNUMB* in the *CUSTOMER* relation is a foreign key that must match the primary key of the *SLSREP* relation. In practice this simply means that the sales rep number for any customer must be that of a *real* sales rep.

There is one possible exception to this. In some organizations a customer might exist *without* a sales rep. This could be indicated in the *CUSTOMER* table by setting such a customer's sales rep number to null. A null sales rep number would, however, violate the restrictions that we have indicated for a foreign key. Thus, we modify the definition of foreign keys to include the possibility of nulls. In doing so, we are describing the property that Codd called referential integrity.

> *Definition:* **Referential integrity** is the rule that if a relation, A, contains a foreign key matching the primary key of a relation, B, then values of this foreign key must either match the value of the primary key for some row in relation B or be null.

Without foreign keys, the relational model suffers from two serious deficiencies. The first is that relationships are hidden. We have to notice the existence of a *SLSRNUMB* column in the *SLSREP* table and a *SLSRNUMB* column in the *CUSTOMER* table to be aware that there is a relationship between sales reps and customers. Even then we are not sure. The identical names could be a coincidence. Further, if the names happened to be different, say, *SLSRNUMB* in the *SLSREP* table and *SRNUMB* in the *CUSTOMER* table, we might not even be aware that the relationship existed. Foreign keys make such relationships explicit. Even if the names are different, indicating that the *SRNUMB* within the *CUSTOMER* table is a foreign key which must match *SLSRNUMB* within the *SLSREP* table leaves no doubt about the relationship.

The second deficiency concerns integrity. There is nothing about the basic relational model that would prevent us from storing a row in the *CUSTOMER* table, in which the *SLSRNUMB* were 11 even though there were no sales rep 11 in the database. Foreign keys solve this problem through the restrictions stated previously.

The DEFINE PERMIT command has some interesting options, as the following example illustrates:

```
DEFINE PERMIT RETRIEVE, REPLACE
     ON   CUSTOMER (CUSTNUMB, CUSTOMER_CUSTNAME)
     TO   MARY_JONES
     AT   VT100-3
     FROM 13:00 TO 16:00
     ON   THU   TO FRI
     WHERE CUSTOMER.SLSRNUMB = 3
```

In this example, Mary Jones is allowed to retrieve or update the number and name of any customer represented by sales rep 3. This activity can take place, however, only at terminal VT100-3 between 1:00 and 4:00 in the afternoon on Thursday or Friday. Of course, any DEFINE PERMIT command does not have to use all the features just illustrated.

When a user who has been issued a PERMIT accesses an INGRES database, the QUEL command is modified to include the conditions in the permit. If Mary Jones, for example, issued the query:

```
RETRIEVE (CUSTOMER.CUSTNUMB, CUSTOMER.CUSTNAME)
        WHERE CUSTOMER.CREDLIM = 500
```

the query actually executed would be:

```
RETRIEVE (CUSTOMER.CUSTNUMB, CUSTOMER.CUSTNAME)
     WHERE CUSTOMER.CREDLIM = 500
     AND CUSTOMER.SLSRNUMB = 3
```

Integrity is supported through the DEFINE INTEGRITY command. As commands are modified for security, so in a similar way are commands modified to include the integrity constraint. Suppose, for example, that the following integrity constraint has been defined:

```
DEFINE INTEGRITY
     ON CUSTOMER
     IS CREDLIM = 300
     OR CREDLIM = 500
     OR CREDLIM = 800
     OR CREDLIM = 1000
```

and a user attempts to add $200 to the credit limit for all customers of sales rep 3. According to the constraint, this should be permitted only if the customer's credit limit is $300 or $800. (Adding $200 to a credit limit of $500 or $1,000 will produce an invalid credit limit.) INGRES enforces this constraint by converting the command the user would enter from:

```
REPLACE CUSTOMER (CREDLIM = CUSTOMER.CREDLIM + 200)
     WHERE CUSTOMER.SLSRNUMB = 3
```

to

```
REPLACE CUSTOMER (CREDLIM = CUSTOMER.CREDLIM + 200)
    WHERE CUSTOMER.SLSRNUMB = 3
    AND (    CUSTOMER.CREDLIM + 200 = 300
        OR CUSTOMER.CREDLIM + 200 = 500
        OR CUSTOMER.CREDLIM + 200 = 800
        OR CUSTOMER.CREDLIM + 200 = 1000 )
```

Certainly, many constraints cannot be handled in this simple way, and these constraints are not supported by INGRES. However, many other systems do not currently support such restrictions, either.

For other information on INGRES, see [5], [7], or the manuals from Relational Technology, Inc.


## SUMMARY

In this chapter, we have examined some of the advanced topics within the relational model. We discussed the problems that pertain to the use of nulls. We discussed views, (derived, virtual tables), how they are defined, how they are manipulated, which types of views may be updated, and the role that views play in logical data independence and in security. We also discussed another typical security feature in relational model systems, the ability to grant various types of authorizations to different users. We discussed the use of indexes to improve performance.

We looked at the ALTER statement, which allows users to add columns to an existing table, change the characteristics of columns in a table, or delete columns from a table. We looked at the type of information stored in the catalog and how information can be retrieved from the catalog.

We also looked at the integrity rules: entity integrity, which states that no attribute that is a part of the primary key may accept null values, and referential integrity, which states that if the value for a foreign key is not null, it must match the value of the primary key for some row in the relation identified by the foreign key. We investigated the integrity features in SQL. We also listed some criteria that systems must satisfy to be considered fully relational systems. We looked at the issues involved in embedding SQL in a program in a language like COBOL. We discussed the problem created when an SQL command retrieves several rows that are then passed to a language designed to handle a single row (or record) at a time. We saw how this problem is solved through the use of cursors.

Next, we investigated the relational system DB2, a product of IBM that grew out of the prototype System R. Since much of the previous discussion in the text concerning SQL and advanced features of the relational model also pertained to DB2, we listed the ways in which DB2 differed. We saw the manner in which DB2 furnished the ten functions of a DBMS.

In the final section, we examined an alternative relational product, INGRES, that is not SQL based. (Although SQL is now supported in INGRES, it is not the principal language.) INGRES supports a language called QUEL. We examined the data definition and manipulation features of QUEL, together with the manner in which QUEL can be embedded in application programs using the EQUEL (Embedded QUEL) processor. Finally, we examined the manner in which INGRES handles security and integrity restrictions.

## R E V I E W   Q U E S T I O N S

1. What are nulls? What problems are associated with nulls?
2. What is a view? What is the difference between a view and a base table? Does the data described in a view definition ever exist in that form? What happens when a user accesses a database through a view?
3. Name three advantages of using views.
4. Which types of views are theoretically updatable? Which types are not? Which types are updatable in most current systems? Which types are not?
5. What is the relationship between a view and a subschema?
6. Describe the GRANT mechanism and explain how it relates to security. What types of privileges may be granted? How are they revoked?
7. What are the advantages of using indexes? What are the disadvantages?
8. How can the structure of a table be changed in SQL? What types of changes are possible in general?
9. Why should users not be able to update the catalog directly?
10. State the two integrity rules. Indicate why it is desirable to enforce each rule.
11. What types of integrity support are provided by SQL? Do all versions of SQL furnish this support.
12. List the two basic properties specified by Codd that a system must satisfy to be considered relational.
13. List the four categories of systems proposed by Date. Describe the characteristics of systems in each category.
14. List and briefly describe the twelve rules that a true relational DBMS should follow.
15. How are SQL commands that are embedded in a COBOL program identified to the precompiler? What are host variables? How are column names distinguished from host variables in an embedded SQL command?
16. What is the SQLCA? What function does it serve? How is it included in a COBOL program?
17. Why does a select that produces more than one row cause a problem for a language like COBOL? How do cursors solve this problem?
18. How do COMMIT and ROLLBACK relate to the support of logical transactions?

19. How do COMMIT and ROLLBACK relate to the support of shared update?
20. Describe how a user-defined procedure could be used for integrity support. What are the limitations involved in user-defined procedures in DB2?
21. Describe the major features through which DB2 furnishes logical and physical data independence.
22. What is EQUEL? How is the problem of retrieving multiple rows handled in EQUEL?
23. How is security handled in INGRES? What happens when a user for whom some security restrictions have been defined enters a QUEL command?
24. How is integrity handled in INGRES? What happens when an update occurs that would affect a column for which an integrity constraint has been defined?

## EXERCISES

1. In the ORDERS table, ORDNUMB is the primary key and CUSTNUMB is a foreign key that identifies the CUSTOMER table. The ORDDTE column can contain a null value, but ORDNUMB and CUSTNUMB cannot.
   a. Write a CREATE TABLE command for the ORDERS table.
   b. Write a SQL command to set the order date for order 12345 to null.
   c. Write a SQL command to find all orders where the order date is null.
2. A view, SMLLCUST, is to be defined. It consists of the customer number, name, address, balance, and credit limit for all customers whose credit limit is $500 or less.
   a. Write the view definition for SMLLCUST.
   b. Write an SQL query to retrieve the number and name of all customers in SMLLCUST whose balance is over their credit limit.
   c. Convert the query from (b) to the query that will actually be executed.
   d. Are any problems created by updating the database through this view? If so, what are they? If not, why not?
3. A view, CUSTORD, is to be defined. It consists of the customer number, name, balance, order number, and order date for all orders currently on file.
   a. Write the view definition for CUSTORD.
   b. Write an SQL query to retrieve the customer number, name, order number, and order date for all orders in CUSTORD for customers whose balance is more than $100.

   c. Convert the query from (b) to the query that will actually be executed.

   d. Are any problems created by updating the database through this view? If so, what are they? If not, why not?

4. A view, *ORDTOT*, is to be defined. It consists of the order number and order total for each order currently on file in which the total is more than $100. (The order total is the sum of the number ordered times the quoted price on each of the order lines for the order.)

   a. Write the view definition for *ORDTOT*.

   b. Write an SQL query to retrieve the order number and order total for all orders whose total is over $100.

   c. Convert the query from (b) to the query that will actually be executed.

   d. Are any problems created by updating the database through this view? If so, what are they? If not, why not?

5. Give the SQL command to create an index called NAMEIND on the *CUSTNAME* column in the *CUSTOMER* table. Should this be a unique index? For what types of operations would this index be beneficial?

6. Give the syntax required to add the column *MTDSALES* to the *CUSTOMER* table. *MTDSALES* is a dollar figure that will be less than $10,000. It should be placed before the *CREDLIM* column. *MTDSALES* for current customers should be set to zero.

7. Give the syntax required to delete the column *ITEMCLSS* from the *PART* table.

8. Give the syntax required to expand *PARTDESC* to thirty characters.

9. Describe the information stored in the catalog. Give an SQL query that will access the catalog to determine the creator of the *SLSREP* table. Give an SQL query that will access the catalog to determine all columns in all tables created by JONES.

10. Assuming that the appropriate entries have been made in the DATA DIVISION of a COBOL program, give the procedure division code for each of the following:

   a. Obtain the description and unit price of the part whose part number is currently stored in *W-PARTNUMB*. Place these values in the variables *W-PARTDESC* and *W-UNITPRCE*, respectively.

   b. Obtain the order date, customer number, and name for the order whose number is currently stored in *W-ORDNUMB*. Place these values in the variables *W-ORDDTE*, *W-CUSTNUMB*, and *W-CUSTNAME*, respectively.

   c. Add a row to the *PART* table. The data is currently stored in the fields within the *W-PART* record.

   d. Change the description of the part whose number is stored in *W-PARTNUMB* to the value currently found in *W-PARTDESC*.

   e. Increase the price of all parts in item class 'HW' by 5 percent.

   f. Delete the part whose number is stored in *W-PARTNUMB*.

11. Let's assume we wish to retrieve all parts located in the warehouse whose number is stored in *W-WRHSNUMB*.

   a. Write an appropriate cursor description.

b. Give all statements that will be included in the PROCEDURE DIVISION and that relate to processing the database through this cursor.

c. Write the additional PROCEDURE DIVISION code that will update any of these parts that are in item class 'HW' by adding 5 percent to the unit price and any parts in item class 'SG' by adding 10 percent to the unit price. (The cursor must be used in the answer.)

12. Give an INGRES view definition for the *SMLLCUST* view described in exercise 1.

13. Give QUEL commands for the following:

a. List the part number, description, and unit price for all parts.

b. List the complete *SLSREP* table.

c. List the description of part "BT04."

d. Find the on-hand value (units on hand times the unit price) for all parts in warehouse 3.

e. Count the number of customers of sales rep 3.

f. Change the number of units on hand of part "BT04" to 15.

g. Add order (12506, 90691, 124) to the database.

h. Delete from the database all orders placed by customer 522.

# REFERENCES

1] Bradley, James, *Introduction to Data Base Management in Business*, 2d ed. Holt, Rinehart & Winston, 1987.

2] Codd, E. F., "Extending the Relational Database Model to Capture More Meaning." *ACM TODS* 4, no. 4 (December 1979).

3] Codd, E. F., "Relational Database: A Practical Foundation for Productivity." *Communications of the ACM* 25, no. 2 (February 1982).

4] Codd, E. F., "Is Your DBMS Really Relational." *ComputerWorld*, October 14, 1985.

5] Date, C. J., *Introduction to Database Systems, Volume I*, 4th ed. Addison-Wesley, 1986.

6] Date, C. J., *Introduction to Database Systems, Volume II*. Addison-Wesley, 1983.

7] Date, C. J., *A Guide to INGRES*, Addison-Wesley, 1987.

8] Date, C. J., and White, Colin J., *A Guide to DB2*, 3d ed. Addison-Wesley, 1989.

9] Kroenke, David, and Dolan, Kathleen A., *Database Processing: Fundamentals, Design, Implementation*. 3d ed. SRA, 1988.

10] McFadden, Fred R., and Hoffer, Jeffrey A., *Data Base Management*, 2d ed. Benjamin Cummings, 1988.

# Microcomputer Database Management

## INTRODUCTION

In this chapter, we will investigate database management systems on micro-computers. We will talk about such systems in general, but will also illustrate the ideas involved by looking at a specific microcomputer DBMS called dBASE IV. This DBMS, a product of Ashton-Tate, is one of the leaders in the field. There are many other excellent systems, however, that accomplish many of the same things, although often the manner in which we accomplish those things may vary slightly.

We'll look at the way databases can be created and updated, as well as the way we can change the structure of an existing database. We'll investigate the way we can create and use both reports and labels. We'll discuss the manner in which users can query databases using either SQL or QBE. We'll see that many such systems support the concept of views. We will also examine the way we can create custom forms to be used during the data-entry process.

We next turn to a special tool called an applications generator that many microcomputer systems furnish. Such a tool allows us to develop a complete application system quickly and easily. We will also see that most of these systems contain a complete programming language we can use to enhance these applications. Finally we turn to the way in which typical microcomputer DBMS's furnish the functions of a DBMS as discussed in chapter 2.

For a general introduction to dBASE III PLUS or dBASE IV, see either [4] or [5]. For detailed coverage of dBASE III PLUS, R:Base System V, or dBASE IV, see [1], [2], or [3]. In addition, many fine texts concerning a variety of microcomputer database management systems should be available at your local book store.

## CREATING A DATABASE

A typical microcomputer DBMS contains a facility for easily defining the structure of a database. In dBASE IV, for example, we use a screen, called the Database Design screen, to define the various tables (in dBASE IV, they are called *database files*) that make up our database. This screen is shown in Figure 5.1. To define a column in a table (dBASE IV uses the term *field* rather than column), we enter the name, the type, the width, and so on, as shown in Figure 5.2. dBASE IV assists us in the process in several ways. dBASE IV will ensure, for example, that the field names we enter follow the rules. When we select a field type, all we need to do is repeatedly press the space bar until the type we want is displayed on the screen. We can easily change entries that we have made incorrectly.

**Figure 5.1**

Database Design
screen

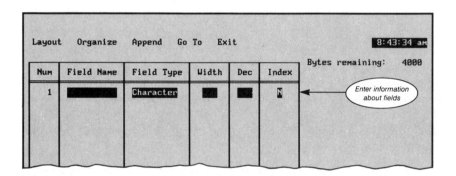

**Figure 5.2**

Database Design
screen

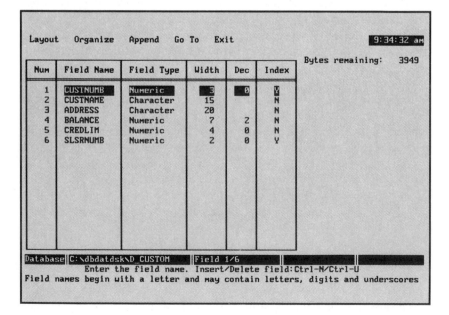

The typical microcomputer DBMS furnishes an easy-to-use user interface that allows us to tap its power by selecting options from menus or by pressing appropriate key combinations. In dBASE IV this interface is called the Control Center. (See Figure 5.3.) As you can see in this figure, we have already created the five tables for the Premiere Products database and called them *D_CUSTOM, D_ORDERS, D_ORDLNE, D_PART*, and *D_SLSREP*.

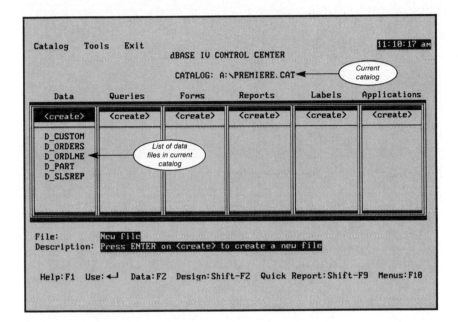

**Figure 5.3**

**Control Center**

## POPULATING A DATABASE

Once we have defined the structure of our database, we need to populate it. This simply means we need to add our initial data. Most microcomputer systems allow you to enter data in at least two different ways. One approach is to use a form. (See Figure 5.4 on the next page.) In dBASE IV, this screen is called the Edit screen. While the appearance of this form is not particularly pleasing, it does furnish a simple way to enter data. Further, no additional work was required to develop this form. As we will see, with just a little extra work we can greatly improve the appearance of the form.

**Figure 5.4**

Edit screen

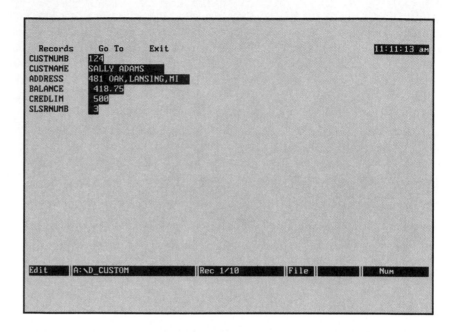

The other approach is to use a screen that looks more like a table. (See Figure 5.5.) In dBASE IV, this is called the Browse screen. The advantage to this type of screen is that you can view several records at the same time.

**Figure 5.5**

Browse screen

| Records | Fields | Go To | Exit | | | 11:11:07 am |
|---|---|---|---|---|---|---|
| CUSTNUMB | CUSTNAME | ADDRESS | BALANCE | CREDLIM | SLSRNUMB | |
| 124 | SALLY ADAMS | 481 OAK,LANSING,MI | 418.75 | 500 | 3 | |
| 256 | ANN SAMUELS | 215 PETE,GRANT,MI | 10.75 | 800 | 6 | |
| 311 | DON CHARLES | 48 COLLEGE,IRA,MI | 200.10 | 300 | 12 | |
| 315 | TOM DANIELS | 914 CHERRY,KENT,MI | 320.75 | 300 | 6 | |
| 405 | AL WILLIAMS | 519 WATSON,GRANT,MI | 201.75 | 800 | 12 | |
| 412 | SALLY ADAMS | 16 ELM,LANSING,MI | 908.75 | 1000 | 3 | |
| 522 | MARY NELSON | 108 PINE,ADA,MI | 49.50 | 800 | 12 | |
| 567 | JOE BAKER | 808 RIDGE,HARPER,MI | 201.20 | 300 | 6 | |
| 587 | JUDY ROBERTS | 512 PINE,ADA,MI | 57.75 | 500 | 6 | |
| 622 | DAN MARTIN | 419 CHIP,GRANT,MI | 575.50 | 500 | 3 | |

Browse   A:\D_CUSTOM           Rec 1/10          File           Num

View and edit fields

## *CHANGING THE STRUCTURE*

One of the big advantages of relational model systems is the ease with which the structure of a database can be changed. The same holds true for most of the good microcomputer systems. Suppose, for example, that we decide it would be more convenient to have separate columns for first and last names, rather than the single *CUSTNAME* column.

To make these changes, we return to the Database Design screen. In Figure 5.6, we have made room for one of the new fields and in Figure 5.7, we have added the field for last name. We would add the field for the first name in a similar fashion. We could delete the *CUSTNAME* field at this time, but it's simpler to keep this field until we have filled in the new ones.

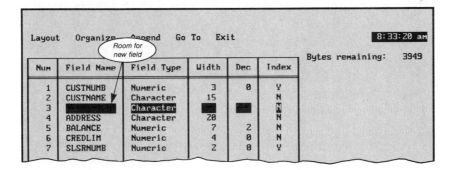

**Figure 5.6**

Database Design screen

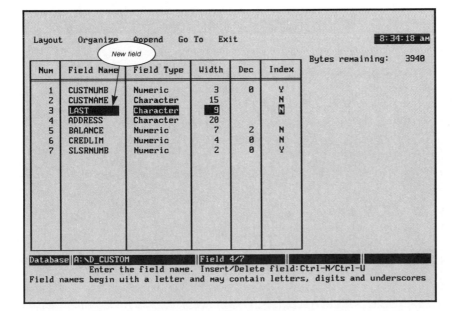

**Figure 5.7**

Database Design screen

As you can see in Figure 5.8, *LAST* and *FIRST* have been added to the database structure. We have not yet filled in the data for these fields, however. Once we have filled in this data (see Figure 5.9), the *CUSTNAME* field is no longer required so we can return to the Database Design screen and delete it. The final results are shown in Figure 5.10.

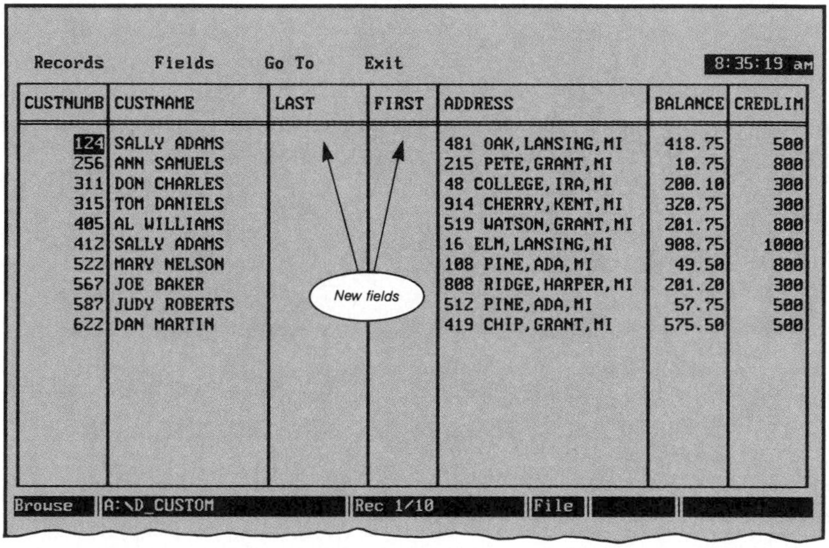

**Figure 5.8**

Browse screen

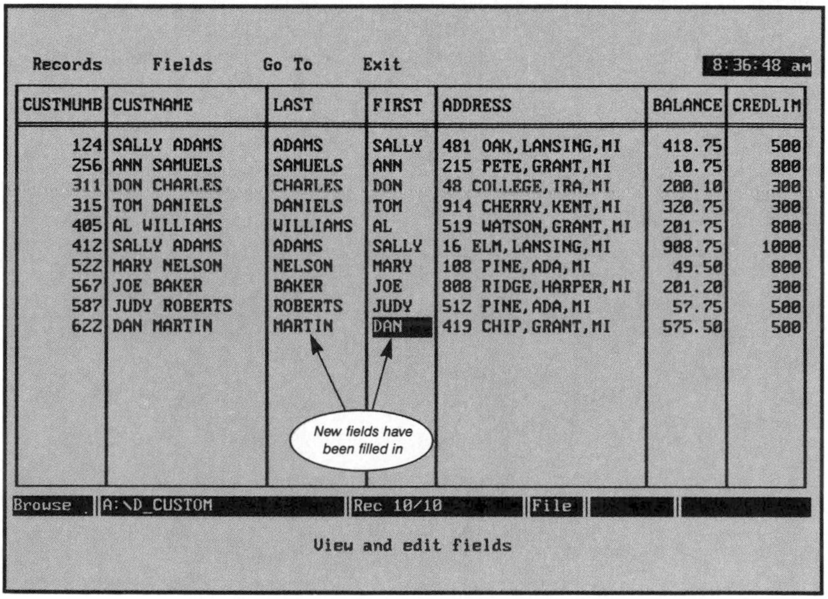

**Figure 5.9**

Browse screen

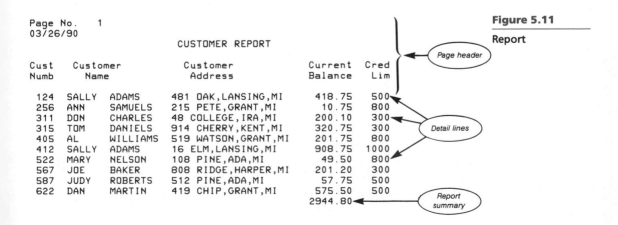

**Figure 5.10**

Browse screen

## CREATING REPORTS

### Introduction to Report Generators

Any decent microcomputer DBMS contains a **report generator**, a facility for producing reports. Before we look at the way such tools function, we need to be familiar with some terms that pertain to reports in general. Consider the report shown in Figure 5.11. The portion at the top of the report is called a **page header**. A page header appears at the top of each page in the report. The body of the report consists of **detail lines**. One of these is printed for each record. The final line, the one containing the total of the current balances, is called a **report footer**. It appears once at the end of the report. Even if this report were fifty pages long, there would still be only one of these, at the very end.

```
Page No.   1
03/26/90
                        CUSTOMER REPORT

Cust    Customer            Customer            Current   Cred
Numb      Name               Address            Balance   Lim

 124    SALLY   ADAMS     481 OAK,LANSING,MI      418.75   500
 256    ANN     SAMUELS   215 PETE,GRANT,MI        10.75   800
 311    DON     CHARLES   48 COLLEGE,IRA,MI       200.10   300
 315    TOM     DANIELS   914 CHERRY,KENT,MI      320.75   300
 405    AL      WILLIAMS  519 WATSON,GRANT,MI     201.75   800
 412    SALLY   ADAMS     16 ELM,LANSING,MI       908.75  1000
 522    MARY    NELSON    108 PINE,ADA,MI          49.50   800
 567    JOE     BAKER     808 RIDGE,HARPER,MI     201.20   300
 587    JUDY    ROBERTS   512 PINE,ADA,MI          57.75   500
 622    DAN     MARTIN    419 CHIP,GRANT,MI       575.50   500
                                                 2944.80
```

**Figure 5.11**

Report

*Page header*

*Detail lines*

*Report summary*

The report generators in microcomputer DBMS's take many different approaches to the task of producing reports. **Band-oriented** report generators, however, are becoming increasingly more common, so that is the approach we will discuss here. With a band-oriented facility, such as the report generator in dBASE IV, we have a **band** for each portion of the report. Figure 5.12 shows the dBASE IV Report Design screen. Note that there is a page header band, a detail band, and a report summary band, which correspond to sections of the report you wish to create. There are also two others, a report intro band and a page footer band. A report intro appears once at the beginning of a report, regardless of how many pages the report contains. A page footer appears at the bottom of each page. Neither the report intro nor the page footer are commonly used, but it's nice to have them available in case you run into a report that requires them.

**Figure 5.12**

Reports screen

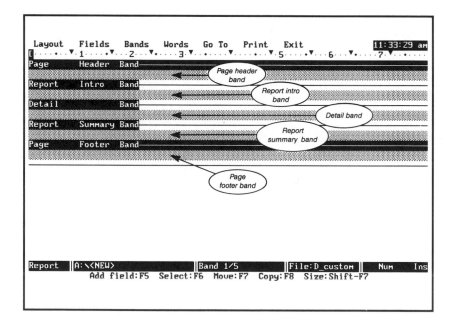

### Defining a Report

We could now begin defining the report. To do so, we work on the various bands making them look the way we want them to appear on our report. There is, however, a quick way to get started, called the "Quick layouts" option. When we pick that option, dBASE IV will create an initial report layout for us. Figure 5.13 shows such a layout. Let's examine this layout before we discuss how to change it to match the report layout we want.

**Figure 5.13**

Reports screen

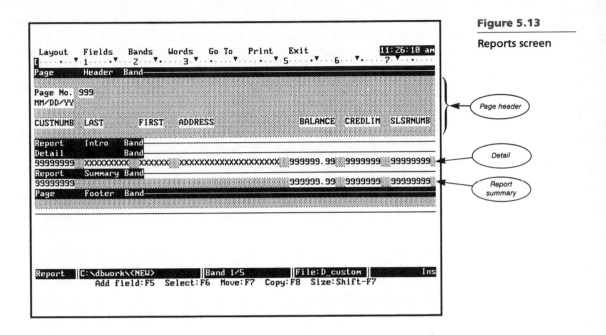

The block of lines that follow "Page Header Band" is the page header that prints at the top of each page. There is currently no report intro band. The detail band consists of a single line that is printed once for each record. Finally, there is a report summary band that prints once at the end of the report.

In the page header band, you see things like "Page No.," "CUSTNUMB," and so on. These are printed on the page heading exactly as they are shown here in exactly the same position. Thus "Page No." prints on the second line of the page starting in the first column; "CUSTNUMB" prints on the fifth line on the page starting in the first column; and so on.

There's something else in the page header, however. You also see "999" and "MM/DD/YY." It certainly doesn't make sense to print "Page No. 999" at the top of each page and then "MM/DD/YY" on the next line. Similarly you don't want each detail line to start with "99999999" and then be followed by "XXXXXXXXXXXXXXX." Fortunately this is not what these symbols mean. They indicate the position at which the data in some particular field will be printed and what it will look like.

The 9s and the X's give some important information about the field that is to be displayed. The 9 indicates that the field is numeric. The X indicates that the field is a character field. The number of 9s or X's indicate how many positions the field will occupy. A decimal point in a group of 9s indicates the position at which the decimal point will appear when the field is displayed on the report.

You may have wondered how you can tell whether "99999999" is indicating that the data in some field will be inserted in the report at this spot or that the report is going to contain eight 9s. Also, if it's the data from some field, which field? Fortunately there's an easy way to tell. When you move the cursor into the group of 9s, a description of the corresponding field appears on the last line of the screen. This indicates that it is the contents of the field that are displayed at this position, rather than a series of 9s.

At this point, we modify the layout, transforming it into the one we want. We can move fields, add fields, delete fields, and change the characteristics of fields. We can add lines to a band or remove lines. We can add text to any band or remove text that is already there. If we wanted to produce the report shown in Figure 5.11, for example, we would modify the "quick layout" to look like the one shown in Figure 5.14.

**Figure 5.14**

Reports screen

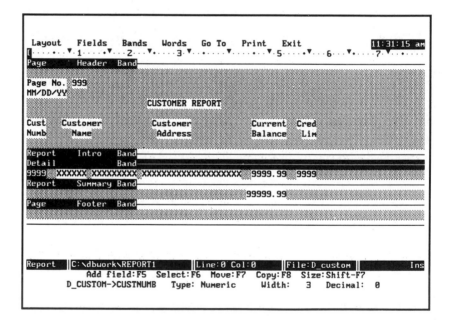

### Grouping in a Report

Next, consider the report shown in Figure 5.15. This report contains a page header, detail lines, and a report summary just like the previous one. It also contains the following additional features:

1. There is a column (available credit) that is not in the database. When we create this report, we indicate that this column is to be computed by subtracting the credit limit from the balance.

2. The records are grouped by sales rep number. The first group consists of those customers (124, 412, 622) represented by sales rep 3; the next group consists of those customers (256, 315, 567, 587) represented by sales rep 6; and so on.

3. Before each group, there is a *group intro*. This is a line or collection of lines that *introduces* the *group*. In this report, the group intro gives the number and name of the sales rep who represents all the customers in the group.

4. After each group, there is a *group summary*. This is a line or collection of lines that provides *summary* information about the *group*. In this report, the group summary gives subtotals of current balances and available credit amounts for all the customers in the group.

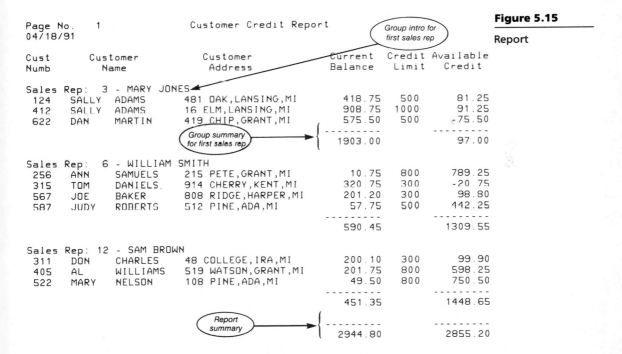

```
Page No.    1              Customer Credit Report      [ Group intro for
04/18/91                                                 first sales rep ]

Cust      Customer           Customer            Current  Credit  Available
Numb        Name             Address             Balance   Limit   Credit

Sales Rep:  3 - MARY JONES
  124   SALLY  ADAMS    481 OAK,LANSING,MI       418.75    500      81.25
  412   SALLY  ADAMS    16 ELM,LANSING,MI        908.75   1000      91.25
  622   DAN    MARTIN   419 CHIP,GRANT,MI        575.50    500     -75.50
                        [ Group summary          ---------         ---------
                          for first sales rep ]  1903.00            97.00

Sales Rep:  6 - WILLIAM SMITH
  256   ANN    SAMUELS  215 PETE,GRANT,MI         10.75    800     789.25
  315   TOM    DANIELS  914 CHERRY,KENT,MI       320.75    300     -20.75
  567   JOE    BAKER    808 RIDGE,HARPER,MI      201.20    300      98.80
  587   JUDY   ROBERTS  512 PINE,ADA,MI           57.75    500     412.25
                                                 ---------         ---------
                                                  590.45           1309.55

Sales Rep: 12 - SAM BROWN
  311   DON    CHARLES  48 COLLEGE,IRA,MI        200.10    300      99.90
  405   AL     WILLIAMS 519 WATSON,GRANT,MI      201.75    800     598.25
  522   MARY   NELSON   108 PINE,ADA,MI           49.50    800     750.50
                                                 ---------         ---------
                                                  451.35           1448.65
                        [ Report                 ---------         ---------
                          summary ]              2944.80           2855.20
```

**Figure 5.15**

Report

Figure 5.16 on the next page shows the way the report layout screen would look for this report. Notice the additional bands for the group intro and the group summary.

**Figure 5.16**

Reports screen

```
   Layout   Fields   Bands   Words   Go To   Print   Exit        9:06:17 am
[ . . . . ▼ 1 . . . ▼ . . 2 . . ▼ . . 3 ▼ . . . . ▼ . . . . ▼ 5 . . ▼ . . 6 . . ▼ . . 7 ▼ . ▼ . .
 Page        Header  Band
 Page No. 999                    Customer Credit Report
 MM/DD/YY
 Cust      Customer           Customer           Current Credit Available
 Numb      Name               Address            Balance Limit  Credit
 Report    Intro   Band
 Group 1   Intro   Band
 Sales Rep: 99 - XXXXXXXXXXXXX
 Detail            Band
 9999   XXXXXX XXXXXXXXX XXXXXXXXXXXXXXXXXXXX 999999.99  9999  999999.99
 Group 1   Summary Band
                                             ----------        ----------
                                              999999.99         999999.99
 Report    Summary Band
                                             ----------        ----------
                                              999999.99         999999.99
 Report  ║A:\CREDRPT          ║Line:0 Col:73  ║View:CUSTSLS          ║   Ins
         Add field:F5  Select:F6  Move:F7  Copy:F8  Size:Shift-F7
```

## Mailmerge

Some report facilities support *mailmerge*, the process of producing a document that incorporates data from a database (dBASE IV includes such support). In Figure 5.17, we have written a letter that is to include the customer's first name, last name, address, balance, and credit limit. This letter will then be printed to each customer whose balance currently exceeds the credit limit. In each customer's letter, the appropriate data from the customer's record will be inserted at the correct locations. (See Figure 5.18.)

**Figure 5.17**

Reports screen

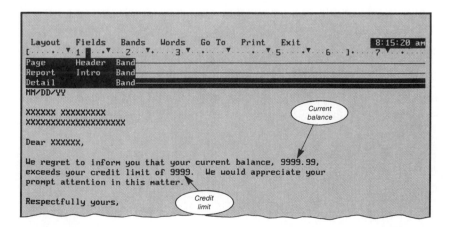

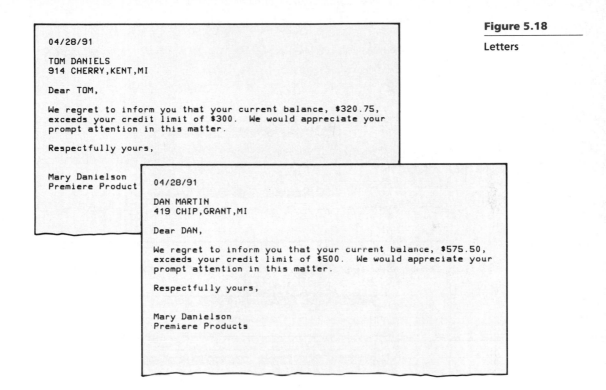

**Figure 5.18**

Letters

## CREATING LABELS

Printing mailing labels is a common requirement. In some systems, there is no separate utility for producing labels. In such systems, we typically use the report facility. Many systems, however, contain a tool designed specifically for producing labels.

Figure 5.19 on the next page shows the Labels screen in dBASE IV. Using menu options, we can specify such things as label dimensions, number of labels across a page, and so on. We describe the contents of a label by using the box in the middle of the screen. We simply position the fields that we want to appear on the label at the appropriate positions in the box. In Figure 5.20 on the next page, we are in the process of adding the *CUSTNUMB* field to the label.

**Figure 5.19**

Labels screen

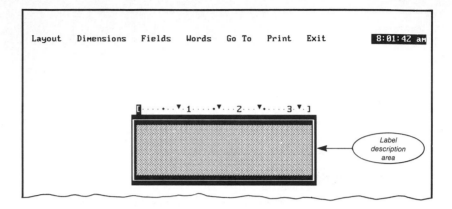

**Figure 5.20**

Labels screen

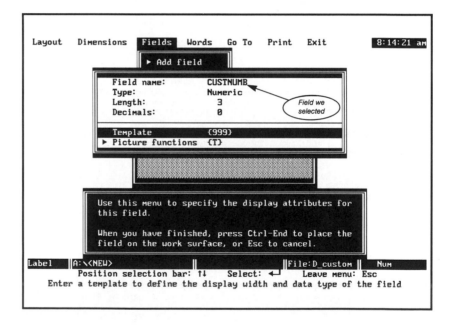

Figure 5.21 shows the Labels screen with all the fields added. When it is time to actually print labels, we simply instruct dBASE IV to use the label design we created. Figure 5.22 shows labels printed using the design we created. In addition, we can use other features of the DBMS to produce the labels sorted in some particular order. We can also, if we wish, print labels for only those records that satisfy some condition. Perhaps, for example, we have a mailing to be sent to customers of sales rep 6. We may create a custom letter and print a copy of it for each such customer using mailmerge. We could then print a label for each of these customers using the Labels facility.

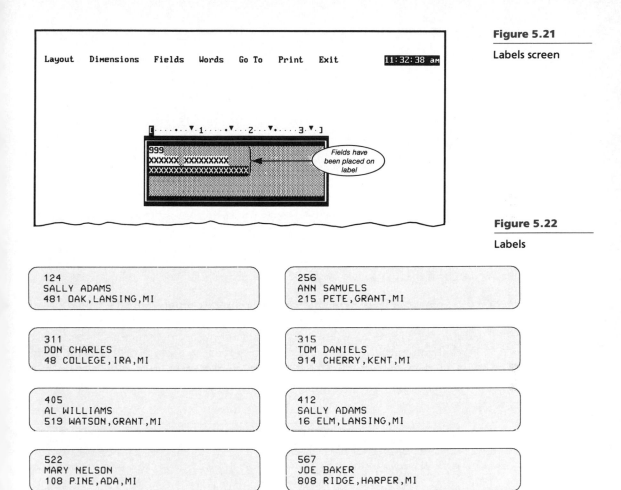

**Figure 5.21**

Labels screen

**Figure 5.22**

Labels

## QUERYING A DATABASE

### Using SQL

Many microcomputer systems now allow users to query a database using SQL commands. In dBASE IV, you can type a SQL command directly, then press Enter to see the results. (See Figure 5.23 on the next page.) In this mode you have a single line on which to type the command. The command can actually be longer than one line. If so, when you reach the right-hand edge of the screen, the previous portion of the command is moved to the left, giving you room to finish the command.

**Figure 5.23**

SQL mode

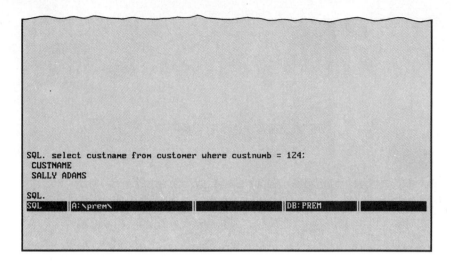

```
SQL. select custname from customer where custnumb = 124;
  CUSTNAME
  SALLY ADAMS

SQL.
SQL      ||A:\prem\                              ||DB:PREM         ||
```

Sometimes the command can be complex enough that this would prove very cumbersome. In this case, you can use a full-screen editor to enter your command. Figure 5.24 shows an example of such a command. Once you are certain you have the command correctly typed, you can instruct dBASE IV to execute the command. If at that point you discover an error, you can return to this screen, correct the error, then have dBASE IV re-execute the command.

**Figure 5.24**

Full-screen editor

```
   Layout   Words   Go To   Print   Exit                    12:10:33 PM
· · · · · · [1 · · · · ▼ · 2 · · · ▼ · · · 3 · ▼ · · · · · 4▼ · · · ▼5 · · · · · ▼ · · 6 · · · · ▼ · · · · 7 · ▼ · · · · · ]
   select ordlne.partnumb, numbord, ordlne.ordnumb, orders.custnumb,
          custname, slsrname
          from ordlne, orders, customer, slsrep
          where orders.ordnumb = ordlne.ordnumb
          and customer.custnumb = orders.custnumb
          and slsrep.slsrnumb = customer.slsrnumb;




   SQL      ||A:\prem\                  ||Line:6 Col:49 ||DB:PREM      ||         CapsIns
               Zoom window command editor, CTRL-END exits to dot prompt
```

## Using QBE

Another common approach in microcomputer systems is Query-by-Example (QBE). When we discussed QBE in chapter 3, we illustrated its use with a microcomputer DBMS called Paradox, a product of Borland International. Paradox was the first microcomputer system to support QBE but there are now several others, including dBASE IV.

Figure 5.25 shows the Query Design screen in dBASE IV. This represents the dBASE IV implementation of QBE. At the top of the screen is the *file skeleton*, the portion we use to enter conditions. Near the bottom of the screen is the *view skeleton*, the portion that indicates which fields are to be included in our query. In the Paradox implementation of QBE, we indicate which fields are to be displayed by putting check marks in the desired columns. In the dBASE IV implementation, we make sure the view skeleton contains precisely the fields we want.

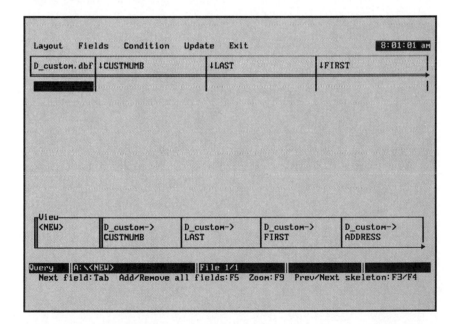

**Figure 5.25**

Query Design screen

We enter conditions in the dBASE IV implementation in the usual way. For example, to select only those customers whose credit limit is $300, we type 300 in the *CREDLIM* column as shown in Figure 5.26 on the next page. The results of this query are shown in Figure 5.27 on the next page.

**Figure 5.26**

Query Design
screen

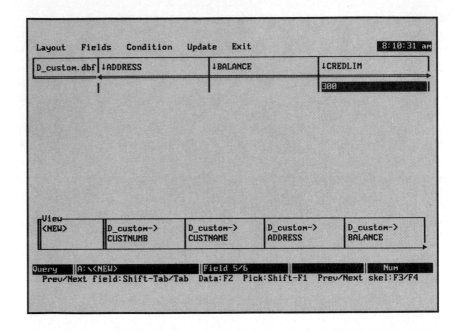

**Figure 5.27**

Browse screen

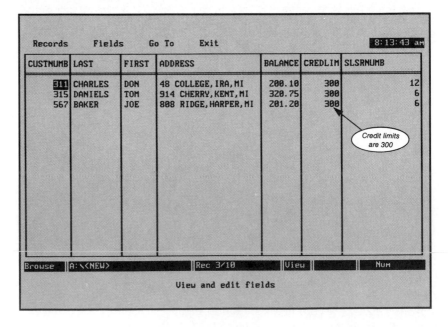

Credit limits
are 300

In Figure 5.28 we have done two things. We have entered a condition of 6 in the *SLSRNUMB* column. We have also changed the view skeleton to include only the *CUSTNUMB*, *LAST*, and *FIRST* columns. The results are shown in Figure 5.29.

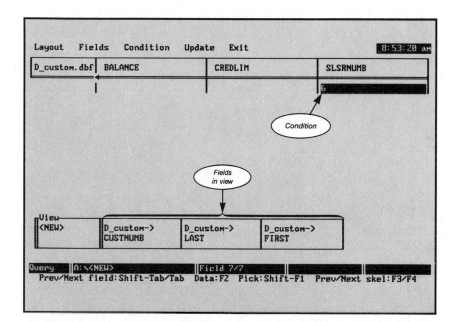

**Figure 5.28**

Query Design screen

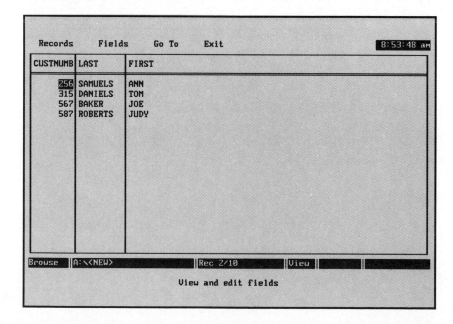

**Figure 5.29**

Browse screen

To join database files in dBASE IV, we first create file skeletons for each of the files to be joined. In Figure 5.30, we have file skeletons for both the *CUSTOMER* file and the *SLSREP* file. To link the files, we use a special option called "Create link by pointing." (See Figure 5.31.) When we use this option, we identify the fields in the two database files that must match. We can also change the view skeleton to include fields from both database files. Assuming we have changed the view skeleton to include *CUSTNUMB, LAST, FIRST,* and *SLSRNUMB* from *CUSTOMER*, as well as *SLSRNAME* from *SLSREP*, the results would look like the ones shown in Figure 5.32.

**Figure 5.30**

Query Design
screen

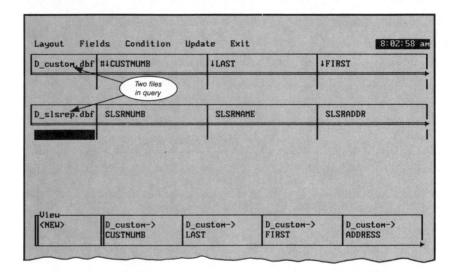

**Figure 5.31**

Query Design
screen

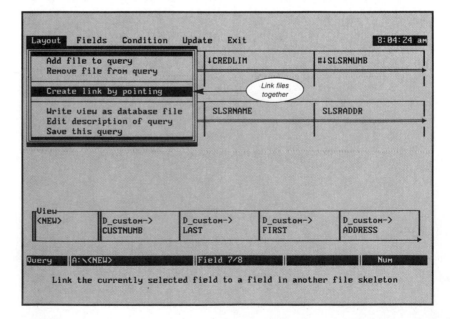

**Figure 5.32**

Browse screen

```
┌─────────────────────────────────────────────────────────────────────────┐
│ Records      Fields       Go To      Exit              ┌8:12:40 am┐      │
│ ┌────────┬──────────┬────────┬────────┬─────────────────────────────────┐│
│ │CUSTNUMB│ LAST     │ FIRST  │SLSRNUMB│ SLSRNAME                        ││
│ ├────────┼──────────┼────────┼────────┼─────────────────────────────────┤│
│ │  124   │ ADAMS    │ SALLY  │    3   │ MARY JONES                      ││
│ │  256   │ SAMUELS  │ ANN    │    6   │ WILLIAM SMITH                   ││
│ │  311   │ CHARLES  │ DON    │   12   │ SAM BROWN                       ││
│ │  315   │ DANIELS  │ TOM    │    6   │ WILLIAM SMITH                   ││
│ │  405   │ WILLIAMS │ AL     │   12   │ SAM BROWN                       ││
│ │  412   │ ADAMS    │ SALLY  │    3   │ MARY JONES                      ││
│ │  522   │ NELSON   │ MARY   │   12   │ SAM BROWN                       ││
│ │  567   │ BAKER    │ JOE    │    6   │ WILLIAM SMITH                   ││
│ │  587   │ ROBERTS  │ JUDY   │    6   │ WILLIAM SMITH                   ││
│ │  622   │ MARTIN   │ DAN    │    3   │ MARY JONES                      ││
│ │        │          │        │        │                                 ││
│ ├────────┴──────────┴────────┴────────┴─────────────────────────────────┤│
│ │Browse  │A:\<NEW>   o          │Rec 1/10        │View │ReadOnly│  Num   ││
│ └──────────────────────────────────────────────────────────────────────┘│
│                          View and edit fields                            │
└─────────────────────────────────────────────────────────────────────────┘
```

## UPDATING A DATABASE

We can update a database using the same facilities we used to initially add records. In dBASE IV, for example, we can use either the Edit screen (Figure 5.4) or the Browse screen (Figure 5.5) to add, change, or delete records. These are fine for individual changes. Sometimes, however, we would like to make mass changes to a database.

For example, suppose we wish to increase the credit limit of every customer of sales rep 6 by $100. It would be cumbersome to have to manually change each of these credit limits, especially if the number of customers represented by sales rep 6 is large. Fortunately, most good microcomputer DBMS's have facilities to allow us to easily make this type of change.

In dBASE IV, this is done through QBE. Figure 5.33 on the next page shows the entries we would make on the Query Design screen in order to accomplish this update. Notice the word "Replace" under the name of the database file, indicating that we are going to make a change. The number 6 in the *SLSRNUMB* column indicates that the replacement only applies to records on which the sales rep number is 6. Finally the "WITH CREDLIM + 100" indicates that the value in the *CREDLIM* column is to be replaced with the old value plus 100. This is all it takes to make the change. We can also use this feature to rapidly delete all records that satisfy some condition.

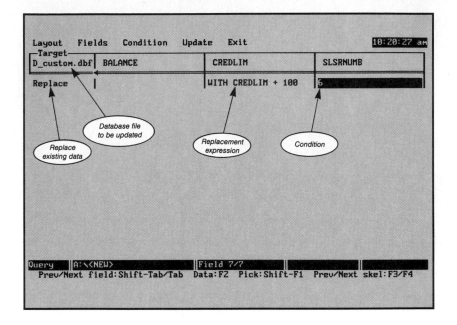

## CREATING AND USING VIEWS

The leading microcomputer DBMS's all support the concept of a view. Remember that a **view** is a pseudotable. It appears to the user to be an actual table. The data doesn't really exist in this form, however. Rather, the DBMS derives its contents from data in existing base tables whenever users attempt to access the view.

Most microcomputer systems support views that are row-and-column subsets, as well as views involving joins. Some also support views that involve statistics. Some allow users to update the underlying database through a view; many do not.

In dBASE IV, views are defined through QBE. To create a view, we use QBE to create a query describing the data to be in the view, then simply save the query. In the process, we will assign the view a name. Whenever we want to use this view, we activate it by name. From that point on, we will be accessing the data in the database through this view.

Unfortunately, dBASE IV is one of the systems that does not allow us to update the database through the view. We can use it in all other ways, however. We can do further queries with it. We can print reports using the view. We can use it for mailmerge and for labels.

## CREATING CUSTOM FORMS

We already saw that microcomputer DBMS's include a built-in form that can be used to update the database. These forms are not particularly pleasing in appearance (see Figure 5.4) nor do they include any special features for ensuring that only valid data is entered. Fortunately, virtually all microcomputer systems include tools for creating custom forms that can be used in place of such built-in forms. Such a tool is usually called a **screen generator** or **screen painter**.

In dBASE IV, we design custom forms on the Form Design screen. We typically begin with the built-in form (see Figure 5.34), then modify it, gradually changing it into the form we want. In Figure 5.35, we've added some blank lines to separate the form into functional groupings.

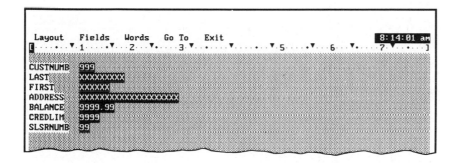

**Figure 5.34**

Form Design screen

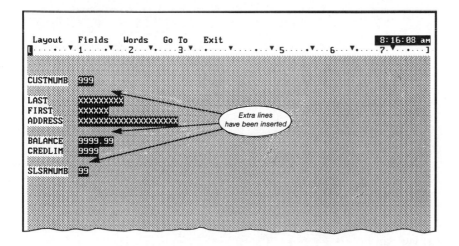

**Figure 5.35**

Form Design screen

In Figure 5.36, two things have been done. The portions of the form where data is to be entered have been moved so they are roughly centered on the form. In addition, the names of the fields have been replaced with names that are more descriptive. We have also included colons after each name. This is common in custom forms. The colon further emphasizes that the user is to enter the indicated data. For example, "Customer number:" makes it much clearer that the user is to enter a customer number at this point than "CUSTNUMB" does.

In Figure 5.37, we have moved these names so that they immediately precede the data to be entered. We have also typed the words "last" and "first" under the fields where the user is to enter the last and first names. This should make it clear to the user that the last name is to be entered first.

**Figure 5.36**

Form Design screen

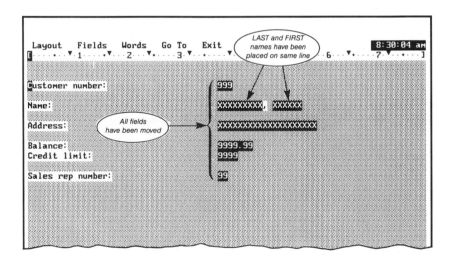

**Figure 5.37**

Form Design screen

Finally, in Figure 5.38, we have added boxes to improve the appearance of the form. Figure 5.39 illustrates the use of the form. In this figure we are using the form to update the data for customer 124.

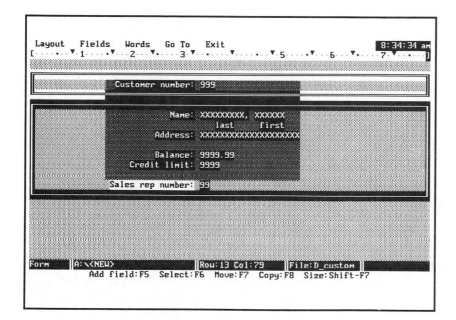

**Figure 5.38**

Form Design screen

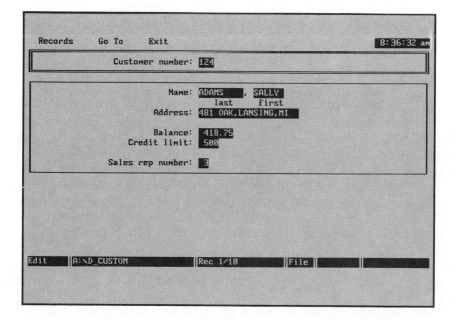

**Figure 5.39**

Edit screen

The things we have done so far have improved the appearance of the form. There are other improvements we can make, however. The most important is the ability to specify integrity constraints for the fields on the form. We can, for example, specify that the value for *CREDLIM* must be 300, 500, 800, or 1,000, in which case the DBMS will not accept any other value. We can also enter an error message that will be displayed in the event the user attempts to violate this rule.

Some microcomputer DBMS's allow us to construct forms involving more than one table. Using one of these systems, we could, for example, construct a single form to allow us to enter both orders and order lines. Entering an order and all its order lines on the same screen is a natural way to enter orders. Unfortunately many microcomputer systems (including dBASE IV) do not support such forms. In these systems we would need two separate forms: one to enter the order and another to enter the associated order lines.

## *GENERATING APPLICATIONS*

### Introduction to Applications

We have seen a number of things we can do easily using a microcomputer DBMS. It is easy to create a database, to add new data to the database, to change existing data, and to delete data from the database. It is also easy to query your database in a variety of ways, to create reports and labels, and to create custom forms. We can also create and use views.

Even though the menu-driven interface in the DBMS makes it relatively easy to do all these things, we still need to use it. We need to remember the correct series of steps to execute any time we want to do something with our database. It would be nice if we could create our own menu system, in which all we need to do is select an option from a menu. This way we could put all our updates, reports, etc. together in one single system. Such a system is called an **application system**, or simply an **application**.

Fortunately most microcomputer DBMS's contain tools, called **applications generators**, whose sole purpose is to enable us to create such application systems quickly and easily. We will illustrate the ideas behind these tools by briefly examining the applications generator in dBASE IV.

Suppose, for example, we wish to create an application system whose main menu consists of five choices: Updates, Reports, Labels, Utilities, and Exit. Each of these choices leads to another menu. Thus there will be an Updates menu, a Reports menu, and so on.

Let's organize the menu as shown in Figure 5.40. The main menu is called a *horizontal bar* menu, since all the options within it are arranged in a single horizontal strip. At any point in time, one of these options will be highlighted.

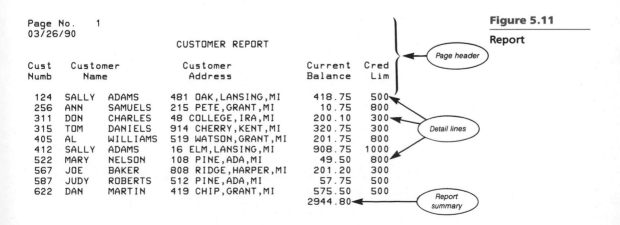

Figure 5.10

Browse screen

*(Browse screen image shows:)*

```
 Records      Fields      Go To     Exit                    8:38:12 am

 CUSTNUMB LAST       FIRST  ADDRESS               BALANCE CREDLIM SLSRNUMB

    124  ADAMS      SALLY  481 OAK,LANSING,MI      418.75    500         3
    256  SAMUELS    ANN    215 PETE,GRANT,MI        10.75    800         6
    311  CHARLES    DON    48 COLLEGE,IRA,MI       200.10    300        12
    315  DANIELS    TOM    914 CHERRY,KENT,MI      320.75    300         6
    405  WILLIAMS   AL     519 WATSON,GRANT,MI     201.75    800        12
    412  ADAMS      SALLY  16 ELM,LANSING,MI       908.75   1000         3
    522  NELSON     MARY   108 PINE,ADA,MI          49.50    800        12
    567  BAKER      JOE    808 RIDGE,HARPER,MI     201.20    300         6
    587  ROBERTS    JUDY   512 PINE,ADA,MI          57.75    500         6
    622  MARTIN     DAN    419 CHIP,GRANT,MI       575.50    500         3
```

*CUSTNAME field has been deleted*

# CREATING REPORTS

## Introduction to Report Generators

Any decent microcomputer DBMS contains a **report generator**, a facility for producing reports. Before we look at the way such tools function, we need to be familiar with some terms that pertain to reports in general. Consider the report shown in Figure 5.11. The portion at the top of the report is called a **page header**. A page header appears at the top of each page in the report. The body of the report consists of **detail lines**. One of these is printed for each record. The final line, the one containing the total of the current balances, is called a **report footer**. It appears once at the end of the report. Even if this report were fifty pages long, there would still be only one of these, at the very end.

Figure 5.11

Report

```
Page No.   1
03/26/90
                         CUSTOMER REPORT                         Page header

Cust    Customer            Customer           Current   Cred
Numb      Name               Address           Balance    Lim

 124    SALLY   ADAMS     481 OAK,LANSING,MI     418.75    500
 256    ANN     SAMUELS   215 PETE,GRANT,MI       10.75    800
 311    DON     CHARLES   48 COLLEGE,IRA,MI      200.10    300         Detail lines
 315    TOM     DANIELS   914 CHERRY,KENT,MI     320.75    300
 405    AL      WILLIAMS  519 WATSON,GRANT,MI    201.75    800
 412    SALLY   ADAMS     16 ELM,LANSING,MI      908.75   1000
 522    MARY    NELSON    108 PINE,ADA,MI         49.50    800
 567    JOE     BAKER     808 RIDGE,HARPER,MI    201.20    300
 587    JUDY    ROBERTS   512 PINE,ADA,MI         57.75    500
 622    DAN     MARTIN    419 CHIP,GRANT,MI      575.50    500
                                                2944.80              Report
                                                                    summary
```

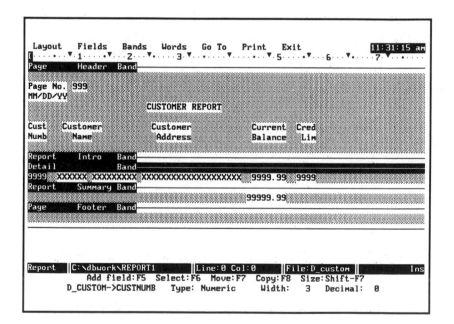

**Figure 5.16**

Reports screen

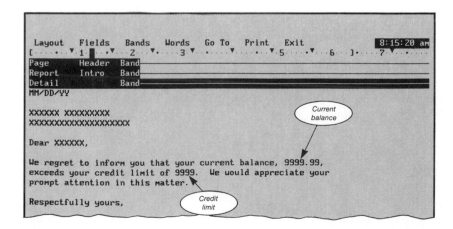

```
  Layout   Fields   Bands   Words   Go To   Print   Exit          9:06:17 am
[····▼·1····▼····2··▼····3·▼····▼·····▼·5····▼··6···▼····7·▼···
Page        Header  Band
Page No. 999                    Customer Credit Report
MM/DD/YY

Cust       Customer          Customer          Current Credit Available
Numb         Name            Address           Balance Limit  Credit
Report    Intro   Band
Group  1  Intro   Band
Sales Rep: 99 - XXXXXXXXXXXXXX
Detail            Band
9999   XXXXXX XXXXXXXX  XXXXXXXXXXXXXXXXXXX  999999.99  9999  999999.99
Group  1  Summary Band
                                          ---------         ---------
                                          999999.99         999999.99

Report    Summary Band
                                          ---------         ---------
                                          999999.99         999999.99
Report   A:\CREDRPT            Line:0 Col:73    View:CUSTSLS           Ins
           Add field:F5  Select:F6  Move:F7  Copy:F8  Size:Shift-F7
```

## Mailmerge

Some report facilities support *mailmerge*, the process of producing a document that incorporates data from a database (dBASE IV includes such support). In Figure 5.17, we have written a letter that is to include the customer's first name, last name, address, balance, and credit limit. This letter will then be printed to each customer whose balance currently exceeds the credit limit. In each customer's letter, the appropriate data from the customer's record will be inserted at the correct locations. (See Figure 5.18.)

**Figure 5.17**

Reports screen

```
  Layout   Fields   Bands   Words   Go To   Print   Exit          8:15:20 am
[····▼·1··▼····2··▼····3·▼···▼·····▼·5····▼··6···]····7·▼···
Page        Header  Band
Report    Intro   Band
Detail            Band
MM/DD/YY

XXXXXX XXXXXXXX
XXXXXXXXXXXXXXXXXX

Dear XXXXXX,

We regret to inform you that your current balance, 9999.99,
exceeds your credit limit of 9999.  We would appreciate your
prompt attention in this matter.

Respectfully yours,
```

( Current balance )

( Credit limit )

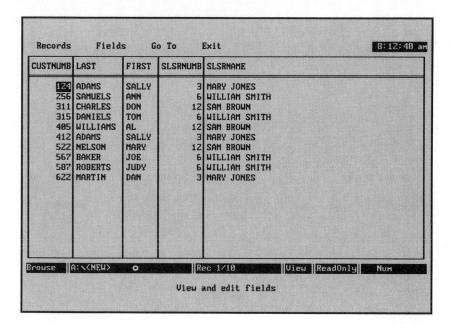

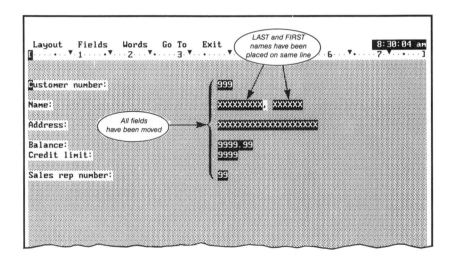

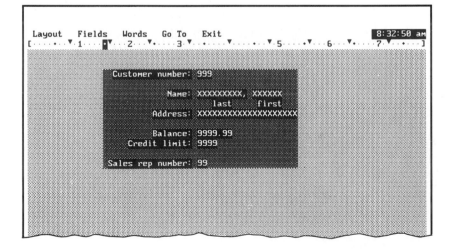

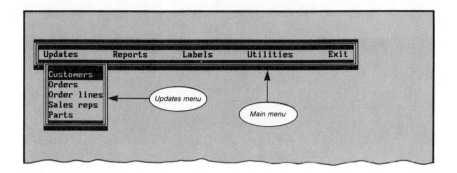

**Figure 5.40**

Updates menu

The menu corresponding to the highlighted selection will automatically be displayed underneath the option. Such a menu is called a *pull-down* menu, since highlighting the corresponding selection in the menu seems to "pull down" the menu. In Figure 5.40, the Updates choice is highlighted, so the Updates pull-down menu is displayed on the screen. To move from one option on the main menu to another, we use the left or right arrows. Pressing the right arrow once, for example, moves the highlight to Reports and consequently the Reports pull-down menu will be displayed. (See Figure 5.41.)

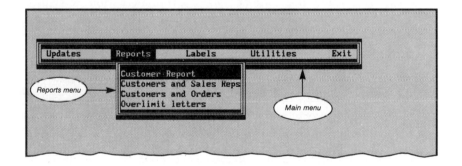

**Figure 5.41**

Reports menu

To select an option from one of the pull-down menus, we first use the left or right arrows to bring the pull-down menu to the screen. We next use the up or down arrows to move the highlight in the pull-down menu to the desired selection. Once this has been done, we press Enter. At this point we have made our selection.

Sometimes when we make such a selection, some action is taken immediately. A report may begin to print, for example. In other cases, we might still need to make a further selection. In these situations another menu will appear on the screen. This type of menu is called a *pop-up* menu, since making a selection seems to make this menu "pop up" onto the screen. An example of a pop-up menu is shown in Figure 5.42 on the next page. In this figure we have selected the "Customers" option of the Updates menu. We would then make a selection from the pop-up menu to indicate how we wish to update customers.

**Figure 5.42**

Customers
submenu

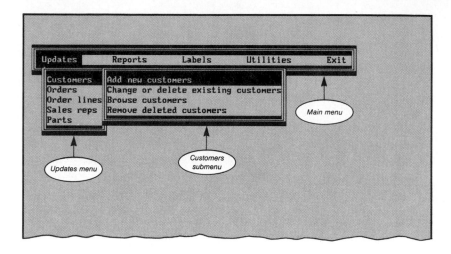

## Using an Applications Generator

We begin creating our application by selecting an option that allows us to create a horizontal bar menu. We then enter the options we want for our menu as shown in Figure 5.43. We next use appropriate options to create and position the various pull-down menus. In Figure 5.44, for example, we've created and positioned the Updates menu.

**Figure 5.43**

Application Design
screen

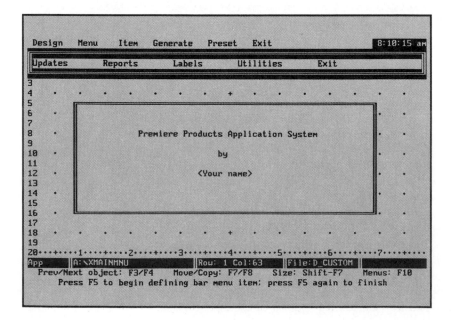

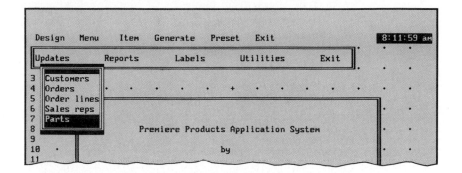

**Figure 5.44**

Application Design screen

So far, we have created the menus and entered the appropriate options. We have only indicated the wording of the options, however. We have not yet assigned the actions to be taken when the user selects the various options. The next step is to indicate these actions.

In Figure 5.45, we have indicated that when the user selects Updates from the main menu, we will activate the menu called XUPDMNU, which is the name we have given to the Updates menu. In Figure 5.46 on the next page, we are assigning an action to one of the options on the Reports menu. We are indicating that the action is to print a report following the layout given in the file called *CUSTRPT1*. In a similar manner, we assign actions to all the options.

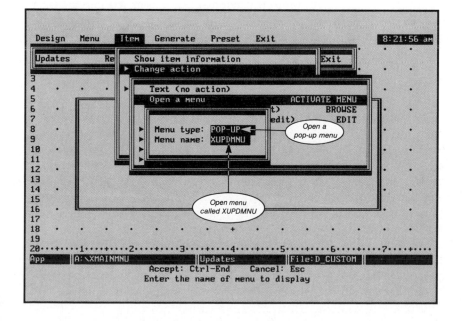

**Figure 5.45**

Application Design screen

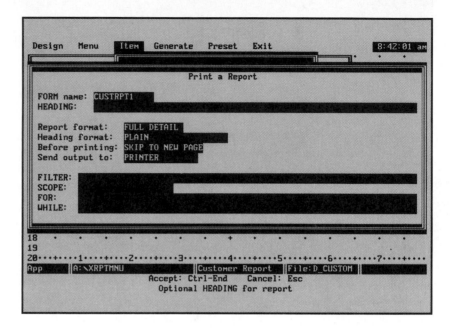

Once we have created all the menus and assigned all the actions, we have completely specified our application. At this point, we simply select an option called "generate the application," and dBASE IV will create the application system we have specified. From this point on, any user wishing to access the database can simply run this application system, greatly simplifying the process.

## PROGRAMMING

### Programming Languages

The leading microcomputer DBMS's all include a full-scale programming language. Such languages include the typical structures you expect to find in a complete programming environment, such as IF-THEN-ELSE structures, loops, and performed procedures. They also include features to simplify access to a database. Some even allow SQL commands to be embedded in programs.

Sometimes programs in such languages can be extremely short. The program in Figure 5.47 allows users to update customer data using a special form we have created. Some of the commands within the language are so powerful that we have actually accomplished a great deal with a small number of statements.

```
******************************************************************
* Program..: UPDCUST                                             *
* Author...: PHILIP PRATT                                        *
* Date.....: 10/01/91                                            *
* Notes....: Procedure to update records in D_CUSTOM             *
******************************************************************

CLEAR
USE d_custom
SET ORDER TO CUSTNUMB
SET FORMAT TO CUSTFORM
EDIT
CLOSE DATABASES
CLEAR
RETURN
```

**Figure 5.47**

Program *UPDCUST*

## Need for Programming

You may wonder why we even need the ability to write programs. We've already seen how much we can accomplish using the built-in facilities of the DBMS. We can even create complete application systems using the Applications Generator. Given the power of these tools, where does programming fit in?

Current microcomputer DBMS's are so powerful that many users will never have a need to write programs. No matter how complete a tool, however, there will always be some situations in which it is not appropriate. Perhaps we need a certain feature in a report that the report generator simply cannot produce. Perhaps we need a certain type of validation to take place during data entry that is beyond the scope of the screen generator. Perhaps we need a form that includes data from two tables, and we have a DBMS that does not support this.

In such cases, we turn to the programming language. Figure 5.48 gives a sample of a program written in the dBASE IV programming languages. (We will not get into details of the language here. If you are interested in further details, see [1] or [3].)

```
******************************************************************
* Program..: RPTCSSR2                                            *
* Author...: PHILIP PRATT                                        *
* Date.....: 10/01/91                                            *
* Notes....: Program to produce a detailed customer and          *
*    sales rep report.  Program does not use REPORT              *
*    facility but uses @...SAY commands to display               *
*    output.  Program is like RPTCSSR except that                *
*    the sales rep table is used so that we can find the         *
*    name of the sales rep of the given customer.  In addition,  *
*    program is fully commented.                                 *
******************************************************************

CLEAR
```

**Figure 5.48**

Program *RPTCSSR2*

*(continued)*

**Figure 5.48**

(continued)

```
* Activate customer table in area 1.  Order by last name, first
*    name by using index called "nameind."  Activate sales rep
*    table in area 2.  Order by index built on slsrnumb.
*    Make area containing customer table the active area.
SELECT 1
USE d_custom
SET ORDER TO nameind
SELECT 2
USE d_slsrep
SET ORDER TO slsrnumb
SELECT d_custom

* Initialize page number to 1.  Initialize line number to a
*    large number to force a page header immediately.
pagenum = 1
linenum = 70

* Direct output to printer.
SET DEVICE TO PRINT

* Loop until end of file.
DO WHILE .NOT. EOF()

     * If more then 55 lines have been printed, put out page
     *    heading, set line number to 7, and increment page
     *    number.
     IF linenum > 55
          @  1,   2  SAY DATE()
          @  1,  25  SAY "Premiere Products"
          @  1,  72  SAY "Page"
          @  1,  77  SAY pagenum PICTURE "99"
          @  2,  23  SAY "Customer Master List"
          @  4,   0  SAY "Cust"
          @  4,   8  SAY "Customer"
          @  4,  27  SAY "Customer"
          @  4,  44  SAY "Current"
          @  4,  53  SAY "Cred"
          @  4,  59  SAY "Sls"
          @  4,  68  SAY "Slsrep"
          @  5,   0  SAY "Numb"
          @  5,  10  SAY "Name"
          @  5,  28  SAY "Address"
          @  5,  44  SAY "Balance"
          @  5,  54  SAY "Lim"
          @  5,  59  SAY "Num"
          @  5,  69  SAY "Name"
          linenum = 7
          pagenum = pagenum + 1
     ENDIF

* Make the area containing the sales rep file the active
*    area.  Try to find matching sales rep.  If one exists,
*    set m_slsrname to slsrname.  If not, set slsrname to
*    "*** NO SLSREP ***".  Make the area containing the
*    customer file the active area once again.
SELECT d_slsrep
SEEK d_custom->slsrnumb
IF FOUND()
     m_slsrname = d_slsrep->slsrname
   ELSE
     m_slsrname = "*** NO SLSREP ***"
ENDIF
SELECT d_custom
```

```
     * Print detail line
     @ linenum,  0  SAY  d_custom->custnumb
     @ linenum,  5  SAY  d_custom->first
     @ linenum, 12  SAY  d_custom->last
     @ linenum, 22  SAY  d_custom->address
     @ linenum, 44  SAY  d_custom->balance
     @ linenum, 53  SAY  d_custom->credlim
     @ linenum, 59  SAY  d_custom->slsrnumb
     @ linenum, 63  SAY  m_slsrname

     * Increment line number and read next record
     linenum = linenum + 1
     SKIP
ENDDO

* Eject page, close all open databases, direct output
*   back to screen and return to calling program.
EJECT
CLOSE DATABASES
SET DEVICE TO SCREEN
RETURN
```

**Figure 5.48**

(continued)

This program produces the report shown in Figure 5.49. Notice the sales rep name for customer 311 is listed as "*** NO SLSREP ***" indicating that the sales rep number for this customer doesn't match that of any sales rep. The ability to include such a message is beyond the bounds of some (but not all) report tools. If we were using such a tool and needed to have this message appear on our report, we would have to write a program (or have someone else write the program for us).

**Figure 5.49**

Customer master
list

```
10/03/91                    Premiere Products          Customer has              Page   1
                           Customer Master List        invalid sales
                                                       rep number

Cust     Customer               Customer           Current   Cred  Sls    Slsrep
Numb       Name                 Address            Balance   Lim   Num     Name

124   SALLY   ADAMS      481 OAK,LANSING,MI         418.75   300    6 WILLIAM SMITH
412   SALLY   ADAMS      16 ELM,LANSING,MI          908.75  1000    3 MARY JONES
567   JOE     BAKER      808 RIDGE,HARPER,MI        201.20   300    6 WILLIAM SMITH
311   DON     CHARLES    48 COLLEGE,IRA,MI          200.10   300   21 *** NO SLSREP ***
315   TOM     DANIELS    914 CHERRY,KENT,MI         320.75   300    6 WILLIAM SMITH
622   DAN     MARTIN     419 CHIP,GRANT,MI          575.50   500    3 MARY JONES
522   MARY    NELSON     108 PINE,ADA,MI             49.50   800   12 SAM BROWN
587   JUDY    ROBERTS    512 PINE,ADA,MI             57.75   500    6 WILLIAM SMITH
256   ANN     SAMUELS    215 PETE,GRANT,MI           10.75   800    6 WILLIAM SMITH
405   AL      WILLIAMS   519 WATSON,GRANT,MI        201.75   800   12 SAM BROWN
```

## Debugging

Most good microcomputer systems include a number of special features that help in the debugging process. The most useful of these is an on-line debugger. (See Figure 5.50.) This type of tool allows us to do a number of things interactively, such as:

1.  We can step through the program one line (or a given number of lines) at a time.
2.  At any point, we can look at the contents of any of the variables in the program.
3.  We can set breakpoints. These are points at which the program will automatically pause and allow us to take whatever action we desire. If we have set breakpoints, we will usually choose to let the program run until it encounters the next breakpoint, rather than stepping a line at a time.

**Figure 5.50**

Debugger

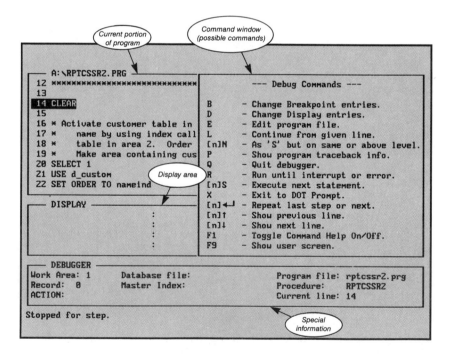

There are a number of other things we can do when using such a tool, although we need not cover them here. With just the features we have listed, you should have a good idea of how useful such a tool can be.

## Relationship with Other Tools

The relationship between programming and the other tools in a DBMS varies from one tool to another and one DBMS to another. We'll use the report generator as an example. The ideas are similar for label and screen generators.

Some report generators have no relationship with the programming language. With this type of generator, if we need to produce a report that is beyond its capabilities, we must write a program *from scratch*. In such situations, the report generator does us no good at all.

There are other report generators, including the one in dBASE IV, that produce a program during the report generation process. Running this program will then print the report. Most users are unaware of this distinction, since they can run this program by simply selecting the report from the list of available reports. There is no need for them to know that there is a special program that is actually producing the report. All they care about is the fact that the report is printed.

Suppose we want to create a report that is beyond the capabilities of such a report generator. In that case, we could define a report that is as close as possible to the one we want, yet is still within the scope of reports the generator can produce. We can then take the program created by the tool and modify it to add whatever additional features are necessary. Thus, rather than writing a lengthy program from scratch, we should only need to make a few modifications to an existing program. In such cases, it is clearly preferable to have a generator that produces a program.

## Relationship with the Applications Generator

Applications generators create programs. To make use of the application system we have created, users run these programs. There are several possible ways we can use programming in conjunction with the applications generator. The two most common are:

1. Create a program to take some special action. Then assign the running of this program as the action for one of the options in a menu in the application system.
2. Describe as much as you can about your application system to the applications generator, then let it create the corresponding program or programs. Once you have done so, you can modify these programs to incorporate any features you were not able to include with the applications generator.

## THE FUNCTIONS OF A DBMS

In this section, we will investigate the manner in which microcomputer DBMS's typically furnish some of the DBMS functions we discussed in chapter 2.

### Catalog

Most microcomputer DBMS's have at least a minimal catalog. You can easily see a list of all the tables, columns, indexes, reports, and so on that are associated with a particular database. In many it is possible to enter a description for each table, index, and so on, then display these descriptions as part of various reports and displays. You can obtain information concerning the structure of any table. Included in this information is the name of each column, together with the type of data the column will contain.

Unfortunately, most of these systems do not let you enter a description for the columns. Nor do they allow you to relate a column in a database to the screens, reports, or programs that access the column. Thus, although they provide some of the support for user-accessible catalogs we discussed in chapter 2, there is still room for improvement in this area.

### Shared Update

There are typically two ways of working in a shared update environment when we use a microcomputer DBMS: automatic locking and program locking. With automatic locking, the DBMS automatically locks and unlocks records. A user who attempts to access a locked record cannot do so. Instead, the user receives a message indicating that the record is locked. In some systems, a user can even determine which other user has locked the record.

Although automatic locking is desirable in many ways and is easy to implement in a program, sometimes it's not appropriate. If transactions are particularly complex, requiring many updates that involve many tables, it may be better for programmers to build appropriate locking into the program. It gives them much better control and can, if done correctly, improve overall performance. Typical capabilities in microcomputer systems for program locking allow us to do the following:

1. We can determine whether the record we have attempted to access is currently locked. It is up to us to determine the appropriate action to take in the event a record is locked. A typical response would be to try repeatedly to access the record. The process would continue until either the user successfully accessed the record, or some preset number of tries was reached. In the latter case, the user would have to move on to some other transaction and return later to try this one again.

2. We can lock an entire table. As long as we have a lock on the table, no other user can access the file in any way.
3. We can lock a single row. As long as we have a lock on the row, no other user can access it.
4. We can unlock a row or table.

There are no facilities for detecting and handling deadlocks in most of these systems. Thus, if we are writing programs for this environment, we should follow the steps discussed in chapter 2 in the section on lock duration.

## Recovery

The typical microcomputer DBMS contains a facility for making backup copies of live databases and a facility for copying a backup copy over the live database. It does *not* usually include facilities for maintaining and using a journal that contains a record of changes made in the database.

Some include a limited version of the journal, however. These are particularly useful in situations where a particular set of updates (i.e., all the updates necessary for entering an order) must be done together; that is, either all must be made or none must be made. If our database is left in a state where some of the updates have been made and others haven't, we have real problems.

To use these facilities, a program will execute a special statement, such as

```
BEGIN TRANSACTION
```

before making such a set of updates. At this point, the DBMS begins keeping a journal of all updates made to the database file. Once the updates have all been made, the program will execute a statement like

```
END TRANSACTION
```

At this point, the DBMS deletes the journal. (The whole process can then begin again, if necessary.)

If everything goes smoothly, there is no need to use the journal. If there is a problem — for example, an abnormal program termination or a power failure — we have the situation we wanted to avoid. Some, but not all, of the updates have been made to the database, and there is no practical way to make the rest. To rectify this, we execute a command like

```
ROLLBACK
```

either directly or within a program. This command uses the data in the journal to restore the database to the state it was in immediately prior to the last BEGIN TRANSACTION.

## Security

Many microcomputer DBMS's have fairly sophisticated security facilities. The DBMS allows us to make password assignments and also to use encryption.

There are several types of privileges (permitted actions) that may be associated with passwords. Some of the privileges pertain to a whole table. The **table-access privileges** are

1.  Add new rows to a table.
2.  Delete rows from a table.
3.  Read rows from a table.
4.  Change rows in a table.

Others pertain to individual columns. The **column-access privileges** are

1.  Read and write the column (user can see and change the data in the column).
2.  Read but not write the column (user can see but cannot change the data in the column).
3.  Neither read nor write the column (user cannot even see the data in the column).

## Integrity

Support for integrity in many microcomputer DBMS's (as well as many mainframe DBMS's), is somewhat limited. The only true integrity support that some DBMS's furnish is that the data entered for a given field must agree with the field type. For example, a field that has been specified as numeric will not be allowed to contain nonnumeric data. If custom screen forms are used for data entry, however, further support is available. We can specify that certain fields on a form may only accept data that satisfies certain conditions.

Some microcomputer systems, however, offer a much greater level of support. In R:BASE, a product of Microrim, we can specify rules that the data in the database must follow. Associated with each rule, we can specify an error message that will be displayed on the screen in the event any user attempts to update the database in a way that would violate the rule.

## Data Independence

It is easy to change the structure of a database in most microcomputer DBMS's. We can add new columns, delete existing columns, or change the characteristics of existing columns. By far the most common change to a column would be to change the length. Certainly a report or custom form that displayed a column whose length had been increased might have to be changed to accommodate the new length. Other than this obvious type of change, though, changes in the structure of a database file are easy to make and exert a minimal impact on existing programs.

Creating a new index is a simple matter. In some microcomputer systems, the DBMS will automatically use the new index. Others, including dBASE IV, will not, however. Program code must be changed to take advantage of the new index. Thus, contrary to the way it is in mainframe systems, changes need to be made in the programs in order to take advantage of the new index.

The other type of change involves changes in relationships. If a user is not employing views, implementation of any relationships must be built directly into programs, and these programs need to be changed to accommodate the change in the relationship. For someone who is using the view facility, this might not be the case. If the view definition could be changed to handle the change in the relationship itself, a user *might* not need to make any changes. The reason we say *might* instead of *would* is that views cause problems in many update situations. In fact, some microcomputer systems do not allow any views to be used for update, even simple row-and-column subsets. Thus, although a user who was interested only in retrieval would probably not be affected by such a change in a relationship, a user who also needed to be able to update the database would, in all probability, need to make changes to programs.

## SUMMARY

In this chapter we have investigated the characteristics of microcomputer database management systems. We have seen that they offer an easy way to initially create a database and to populate that database; that is, add the initial data to it. If we later determine that the structure of the database needs to be changed, we can change the structure in the same fashion we initially created it.

We discussed the process of creating reports using a microcomputer DBMS. We saw that the most common type of report generator is band-oriented. In this type of facility, there is a band for each portion of a report (page headers, detail lines, report summaries, and so on). To describe the layout of a report, we simply make each band appear the way we want it to be on the report. We also saw that it is possible to add columns on a report that are computed from other columns, as well as to do grouping. In addition to the standard type of reports, some microcomputer DBMS's offer mailmerge. Using mailmerge, we can create documents that include data from our database. We could, for example, create a custom letter that we'll send to each of our customers. We also discussed the feature included in many systems to print labels.

We next turned to the process of querying a database. We saw that many systems allow users to access the data in the database through SQL commands. We also discussed the fact that more and more such systems are offering support for some form of QBE (Query-by-Example). In chapter 3, we saw the implementation of QBE included in the microcomputer DBMS called Paradox. In this chapter we looked at the dBASE IV implementation of QBE and saw that, while the two are basically similar, there are some differences.

We saw that many microcomputer systems support the concept of a view. We also saw that creating a view in dBASE IV involves simply creating a query using QBE, which describes the view, then saving the query. Once the view has been created, we can access it for retrieval just as if it were an actual table in our database. Many systems, including dBASE IV, will not allow us to use a view for update purposes.

We next turned to the process of creating custom forms. We discussed the manner in which they can be created and saw an example of the process that is used in dBASE IV. We also discussed the fact that we can impose conditions on the data that is to be entered in the various fields on the form. This helps ensure that users enter only valid data.

At this point, we turned to the process of putting all the various forms, reports, labels, and so on, together in a single menu-driven system, called an **application system**. Many microcomputer DBMS's contain a tool called an **applications generator** that assists us in rapidly developing such a system. We discussed the process and looked at how an application would be developed using the applications generator in dBASE IV.

We next saw that many of these microcomputer DBMS's contain complete programming languages. We discussed the fact that we need a good programming language to supplement the built-in features of the DBMS. We saw that a good DBMS contains facilities to assist us in debugging our programs. Included in these facilities should be a good on-line debugger that allows us to step through our programs interactively, pausing wherever we wish, to examine the contents of our variables. We also discussed the relationship of the programming language to other tools within the DBMS.

Finally, we turned our attention to the functions that should be provided by a good DBMS. We saw that microcomputer systems offer a decent user-accessible catalog. We also saw that, while they do provide support for shared update, it is not as extensive as the support provided by mainframe systems. Similarly, there is some support for recovery, although not nearly as extensive as that provided by a good mainframe DBMS. Support for both encryption and passwords is provided by the security facilities of microcomputer DBMS's. While many microcomputer systems provide only rudimentary support for integrity, some, such as R:BASE, provide extensive support through the use of rules. Microcomputer systems also provide good support for data independence. Changes to the database structure are easy to make and typically have minimal impact. Indexes can easily be created and removed. In some systems, unfortunately, the creation or removal of an index requires changes to be made in programs.

## REVIEW QUESTIONS

1. How do the features in a typical microcomputer DBMS assist in the creation of a database? How do they assist in populating the database? How do they assist in the process of changing the structure of a database?
2. What is a report generator? What is a band-oriented report generator? Describe the various types of bands. Describe the process of creating a report using dBASE IV.
3. What is meant by grouping in a report? What is a group intro? What is a group summary?
4. What is mailmerge? How does it relate to database management?
5. Do all microcomputer systems have a separate facility for creating labels? If not, what facility would you use to create labels? What is the advantage to having a separate labels facility?
6. What mechanisms were discussed in this chapter for querying a database?
7. How do you update a database if you want to make a change to only a single row? How would you do it if you needed to make the same change to all rows that satisfy some condition?
8. Do microcomputer database management systems typically support views? If so, are there any restrictions on these views? How do you create a view in dBASE IV?
9. Give two reasons why we might want to create a custom form. Describe the process of creating a custom form using dBASE IV.
10. What is meant by an application system? What is an applications generator? Describe the process of generating an application using dBASE IV.

11. Why is it desirable for a microcomputer DBMS to include a programming language? Why might we need to write programs?
12. What is an on-line debugger? How does it assist in the debugging process?
13. How can we use programming in conjunction with an applications generator?
14. Describe how microcomputer DBMS's support each of the following. In each case, compare the support provided with the support provided by their mainframe counterparts.
    a. The catalog
    b. Shared update
    c. Recovery
    d. Security
    e. Integrity
    f. Data independence

## EXERCISES

The following exercises require access to a microcomputer DBMS.

1. Create the tables for the Premiere Products database.
2. Populate the tables with the Premiere Products data.
3. Change the structure of the *CUSTOMER* table so there are separate columns for street address, city, and state.
4. Fill in the new columns. When you have done so, delete the *CUSTADDR* column.
5. Create a report listing all the data in the *PART* table. Include an additional field for the on-hand value (price * units on hand). Give a total of the on-hand value column at the bottom of the report. The report should contain a title, date, and page number. There should be two lines of column headings.
6. Create a second report. This report should be just like the first, except that the records should be grouped by item class. In addition, after all the parts in a given item class, there should be a subtotal of the on-hand values.
7. Produce a mailmerge document to be sent to all sales reps. Included in the document should be the sales rep's number, name, address, and commission rate. You can type whatever contents you wish, as long as all these fields are included. Once you have created the document, print a copy for each sales rep in the database.
8. Create labels for sales reps. The label should include the sales rep's number, name, and address. Print a label for each sales rep in the database.

9. Do the queries found in questions 1 through 23 of chapter 3. Use SQL if your DBMS supports it. If not, use whatever query facility is available.
10. If your DBMS supports QBE, do the queries found in questions 25 through 35 of chapter 3.
11. If your DBMS contains a feature to allow you to update several rows at once, use it to increase the price of all parts in item class HW by 5 percent.
12. Create the views described in exercises 2, 3, and 4 of chapter 4.
13. Create custom forms for each of the tables in the database. The form for the *CUSTOMER* table should ensure that credit limits are 300, 500, 800, or 1,000. The form for the *PART* table should ensure that item classes are AP, HW, or SG.
14. Create an application system that ties together the custom forms, reports, and labels you have created.
15. Discuss the relationship between programming and the other tools in the DBMS you are using.
16. Compare the support your DBMS provides for the various DBMS functions with that discussed in the text. In what areas is your DBMS particularly strong? In what areas is it weak?

## REFERENCES

1] Pratt, Philip J., *Microcomputer Database Management Using dBASE III PLUS*, boyd & fraser, 1988.
2] Pratt, Philip J., *Microcomputer Database Management Using R:Base System V*, boyd & fraser, 1988.
3] Pratt, Philip J., *Microcomputer Database Management Using dBASE IV*, boyd & fraser, 1990.
4] Shelly, Gary B., Cashman, Thomas J., and Pratt, Philip J., *Learning to Use dBASE III PLUS*, boyd & fraser, 1989.
5] Shelly, Gary B., Cashman, Thomas J., and Pratt, Philip J., *Learning to Use dBASE IV*, boyd & fraser, 1990.

# Normalization

## INTRODUCTION

We have discussed the basic relational model, its structure, and the various ways of manipulating data within a relational database. In this chapter, we discuss the **normalization** process and its underlying concepts and features. Normalization enables us to analyze the design of a relational database to see whether it is bad; that is, normalization gives us a method for identifying the existence of potential problems, called **update anomalies**, in the design. The normalization process also supplies methods for correcting these problems.

The process involves various types of **normal forms**. **First normal form** (1NF), **second normal form** (2NF), and **third normal form** (3NF) are three of these types. It is these three that will be of the greatest use to us during database design. They form a progression in which a relation that is in 1NF is better than a relation that is not in 1NF; a relation that is in 2NF is better yet; and so on. The goal of this process is to allow us to start with a relation or collection of relations and produce a new collection of relations equivalent to the original collection (i.e., that represents the same information) but is free of problems. For practical purposes, this means that relations in the new collection will be at least in 3NF.

We begin by discussing two crucial concepts that are fundamental to the understanding of the normalization process: functional dependence and keys. We then discuss first, second, and third normal forms. Following this, we examine the issues involved in fourth normal form. We briefly discuss higher normal forms. Finally, we look at the application of normalization to database design. We will then be ready to begin our study of the database design process in the next chapter.

Many of the examples in this chapter use data from the Premiere Products example. (See Figure 6.1 on the next page.)

Figure 6.1

Premiere Products
sample data

**SLSREP**

| SLSRNUMB | SLSRNAME | SLSRADDR | TOTCOMM | COMMRATE |
|---|---|---|---|---|
| 3 | Jones, Mary | 123 Main,Grant,MI | 2150.00 | .05 |
| 6 | Smith, William | 102 Raymond,Ada,MI | 4912.50 | .07 |
| 12 | Brown, Sam | 419 Harper,Lansing,MI | 2150.00 | .05 |

**CUSTOMER**

| CUSTNUMB | CUSTNAME | CUSTADDR | BALANCE | CREDLIM | SLSRNUMB |
|---|---|---|---|---|---|
| 124 | Adams, Sally | 481 Oak,Lansing,MI | 418.75 | 500 | 3 |
| 256 | Samuels, Ann | 215 Pete,Grant,MI | 10.75 | 800 | 6 |
| 311 | Charles, Don | 48 College,Ira,MI | 200.10 | 300 | 12 |
| 315 | Daniels, Tom | 914 Cherry,Kent,MI | 320.75 | 300 | 6 |
| 405 | Williams, Al | 519 Watson,Grant,MI | 201.75 | 800 | 12 |
| 412 | Adams, Sally | 16 Elm,Lansing,MI | 908.75 | 1000 | 3 |
| 522 | Nelson, Mary | 108 Pine,Ada,MI | 49.50 | 800 | 12 |
| 567 | Baker, Joe | 808 Ridge,Harper,MI | 201.20 | 300 | 6 |
| 587 | Roberts, Judy | 512 Pine,Ada,MI | 57.75 | 500 | 6 |
| 622 | Martin, Dan | 419 Chip,Grant,MI | 575.50 | 500 | 3 |

**ORDERS**

| ORDNUMB | ORDDTE | CUSTNUMB |
|---|---|---|
| 12489 | 90291 | 124 |
| 12491 | 90291 | 311 |
| 12494 | 90491 | 315 |
| 12495 | 90491 | 256 |
| 12498 | 90591 | 522 |
| 12500 | 90591 | 124 |
| 12504 | 90591 | 522 |

**ORDLNE**

| ORDNUMB | PARTNUMB | NUMBORD | QUOTPRCE |
|---|---|---|---|
| 12489 | AX12 | 11 | 14.95 |
| 12491 | BT04 | 1 | 402.99 |
| 12491 | BZ66 | 1 | 311.95 |
| 12494 | CB03 | 4 | 175.00 |
| 12495 | CX11 | 2 | 57.95 |
| 12498 | AZ52 | 2 | 22.95 |
| 12498 | BA74 | 4 | 4.95 |
| 12500 | BT04 | 1 | 402.99 |
| 12504 | CZ81 | 2 | 108.99 |

**PART**

| PARTNUMB | PARTDESC | UNONHAND | ITEMCLSS | WRHSNUMB | UNITPRCE |
|---|---|---|---|---|---|
| AX12 | IRON | 104 | HW | 3 | 17.95 |
| AZ52 | SKATES | 20 | SG | 2 | 24.95 |
| BA74 | BASEBALL | 40 | SG | 1 | 4.95 |
| BH22 | TOASTER | 95 | HW | 3 | 34.95 |
| BT04 | STOVE | 11 | AP | 2 | 402.99 |
| BZ66 | WASHER | 52 | AP | 3 | 311.95 |
| CA14 | SKILLET | 2 | HW | 3 | 19.95 |
| CB03 | BIKE | 44 | SG | 1 | 187.50 |
| CX11 | MIXER | 112 | HW | 3 | 57.95 |
| CZ81 | WEIGHTS | 208 | SG | 2 | 108.99 |

## FUNCTIONAL DEPENDENCE

The concept of functional dependence is critical to the material in the rest of this chapter. Functional dependence is a fancy name for what is basically a simple idea. To illustrate, suppose the *SLSREP* table for Premiere Products is as shown in Figure 6.2. The only difference between this *SLSREP* table and the one we had been looking at previously is the addition of an extra column, *PAYCLASS* (pay class). Let's suppose further that one of the policies at Premiere Products is that all sales reps in any given pay class get the same commission rate. If you were asked to describe this policy in another way, you might say something like, "A sales rep's pay class *determines* his or her commission rate." Or you might say, "A sales rep's commission rate *depends on* his or her pay class." If you said either of these things, you would be using the word *determines* or the words *depends on* in exactly the fashion we will be using them. If we wanted to be formal, we would precede either expression with the word *functionally*. Thus, we might say, "A sales rep's pay class *functionally determines* his or her commission rate," or "A sales rep's commission rate *functionally depends on* his or her pay class." The formal definition of functional dependence is as follows:

*Definition:* An attribute, B, is **functionally dependent** on another attribute, A (or possibly a collection of attributes), if a value for A determines a single value for B at any one time.

**SLSREP**

| SLSRNUMB | SLSRNAME | SLSRADDR | TOTCOMM | PAYCLASS | COMMRATE |
|---|---|---|---|---|---|
| 3 | Jones, Mary | 123 Main,Grant,MI | 2150.00 | 1 | .05 |
| 6 | Smith, William | 102 Raymond,Ada,MI | 4912.50 | 2 | .07 |
| 12 | Brown, Sam | 419 Harper,Lansing,MI | 2150.00 | 1 | .05 |

**Figure 6.2**

*SLSREP* table with additional column, *PAYCLASS*

We can think of this as follows. If we are given a value for A, do we know that we will be able to find a single value for B? If so, B is functionally dependent on A (often written as A --> B). If B is functionally dependent on A, we also say that A **functionally determines** B.

For example, in the *CUSTOMER* relation, is the *CUSTNAME* functionally dependent on *CUSTNUMB*? The answer is yes. If we are given customer number 124, for example, we would find a *single* name, Sally Adams, associated with it.

In the same *CUSTOMER* relation, is *CUSTADDR* functionally dependent on *CUSTNAME*? Here the answer is no, since, given the name Sally Adams, we would not be able to find a single address.

In the *FACULTY* relation at Marvel College, is *DEPTNUMB* (the number of the department in which a faculty member works) functionally dependent on *FACNUMB*? Given a faculty number, say 123, do we know that we can find a single department number? The answer is yes, since at Marvel College each faculty member must be assigned to a single department. If joint appointments were allowed, the answer would be no.

In the relation *ORDLNE*, is the *NUMBORD* functionally dependent on *ORDNUMB*? No. *ORDNUMB* does not give enough information. Is it functionally dependent on *PARTNUMB*? No. Again, not enough information is given. In reality, *NUMBORD* is functionally dependent on the **concatenation** (combination) of *ORDNUMB* and *PARTNUMB*.

At this point, a question naturally arises: How do we determine functional dependencies? Can we determine them by looking at sample data, for example? The answer is no.

Consider Figure 6.3, in which customer names happen to be unique. It is tempting to say that *CUSTNAME* functionally determines *CUSTADDR* (or equivalently that *CUSTADDR* is functionally dependent on *CUSTNAME*). After all, given the name of a customer, we can find the single address. But what happens when customer 412, whose name also happens to be Sally Adams, is added to the database? We then have the situation exhibited in Figure 6.4.

**Figure 6.3**

*CUSTOMER* relation

CUSTOMER

| CUSTNUMB | CUSTNAME | CUSTADDR | BALANCE | CREDLIM | SLSRNUMB |
|---|---|---|---|---|---|
| 124 | Adams, Sally | 481 Oak,Lansing,MI | 418.75 | 500 | 3 |
| 256 | Samuels, Ann | 215 Pete,Grant,MI | 10.75 | 800 | 6 |
| 311 | Charles, Don | 48 College,Ira,MI | 200.10 | 300 | 12 |
| 315 | Daniels, Tom | 914 Cherry,Kent,MI | 320.75 | 300 | 6 |
| 405 | Williams, Al | 519 Watson,Grant,MI | 201.75 | 800 | 12 |
| 522 | Nelson, Mary | 108 Pine,Ada,MI | 49.50 | 800 | 12 |
| 567 | Baker, Joe | 808 Ridge,Harper,MI | 201.20 | 300 | 6 |
| 587 | Roberts, Judy | 512 Pine,Ada,MI | 57.75 | 500 | 6 |
| 622 | Martin, Dan | 419 Chip,Grant,MI | 575.50 | 500 | 3 |

**Figure 6.4**

*CUSTOMER* relation with second Sally Adams

CUSTOMER

| CUSTNUMB | CUSTNAME | CUSTADDR | BALANCE | CREDLIM | SLSRNUMB |
|---|---|---|---|---|---|
| 124 | Adams, Sally | 481 Oak,Lansing,MI | 418.75 | 500 | 3 |
| 256 | Samuels, Ann | 215 Pete,Grant,MI | 10.75 | 800 | 6 |
| 311 | Charles, Don | 48 College,Ira,MI | 200.10 | 300 | 12 |
| 315 | Daniels, Tom | 914 Cherry,Kent,MI | 320.75 | 300 | 6 |
| 405 | Williams, Al | 519 Watson,Grant,MI | 201.75 | 800 | 12 |
| 412 | Adams, Sally | 16 Elm,Lansing,MI | 908.75 | 1000 | 3 |
| 522 | Nelson, Mary | 108 Pine,Ada,MI | 49.50 | 800 | 12 |
| 567 | Baker, Joe | 808 Ridge,Harper,MI | 201.20 | 300 | 6 |
| 587 | Roberts, Judy | 512 Pine,Ada,MI | 57.75 | 500 | 6 |
| 622 | Martin, Dan | 419 Chip,Grant,MI | 575.50 | 500 | 3 |

If the name we are given is Sally Adams, we can no longer find a single address. Thus we were misled by our original sample data. The only way to really determine the functional dependencies that exist is to examine the user's policies.

## KEYS

A second underlying concept of the normalization process is that of the primary key. It builds on functional dependence, and it completes the background required for an understanding of the normal forms.

> *Definition:* Attribute A (or a collection of attributes) is the **PRIMARY KEY** for a relation, R, if
>
> 1. *All* attributes in R are functionally dependent on A.
> 2. No subcollection of the attributes in A (assuming A is a collection of attributes and not just a single attribute) also has property 1.

For example, is *CUSTNAME* the primary key for the *CUSTOMER* relation? No, since the other attributes are not functionally dependent on name. (Note that the answer would be different in an organization that had a policy enforcing uniqueness of customer names.)

Is *CUSTNUMB* the primary key for the *CUSTOMER* relation? Yes, since all attributes in the *CUSTOMER* relation are functionally dependent on *CUSTNUMB*.

Is *ORDNUMB* the primary key for the *ORDLNE* relation? No, since it does not uniquely determine *NUMBORD* or *QUOTPRCE*.

Is the combination of the *ORDNUMB* and the *PARTNUMB* the primary key for the *ORDLNE* relation? Yes, since all attributes can be determined by this combination, and nothing less will do.

Is the combination of the *PARTNUMB* and the *PARTDESC* the primary key for the *PART* relation? No. Though it is true that all attributes of the *PART* relation can be determined by this combination, something less, namely, the *PARTNUMB* alone, also has this property.

Occasionally (but not often) there might be more than one possibility for the primary key. For example, in an *EMPLOYEE* relation, either the *EMPNUMB* or the *SSNUMB* (Social Security number) could serve as the key. In this case, one of these is designated as the primary key. The other is referred to as a **candidate key**. A candidate key is a collection of attributes that has the same properties presented in the definition of the primary key. (Technically, the definition given for primary key really defines candidate key. From all the candidate keys one is chosen to be the primary key. The candidate keys that are not chosen to be the primary key are often referred to as **alternate keys**.)

**Note:** The primary key is frequently simply called the *key* in other studies on database management and the relational model. We will continue to use the term *primary key* to clearly distinguish among the several different concepts of a key we will encounter.

## FIRST, SECOND, AND THIRD NORMAL FORMS

The first three of the normal forms were defined by Codd in 1972. (See [3].) Subsequently, it was discovered that in some situations the definition of third normal form was inadequate. A revised, and stronger, definition was given by Boyce and Codd in 1974. (See [4].) It is this new definition of third normal form (often called **Boyce-Codd normal form**) that we shall examine later in this section.

### First Normal Form

A relation that contains a repeating group is called an **unnormalized relation**. (Technically, it is not a relation at all.) Removal of repeating groups is the starting point in our quest for relations that are as free of problems as possible. Relations without repeating groups are said to be in first normal form.

> *Definition:* A relation is in **first normal form** (1NF) if it does not contain repeating groups.

As an example, consider the following *ORDERS* relation, in which there is a repeating group consisting of *PARTNUMB* and *NUMBORD*. As the example shows, there is one row per order with *PARTNUMB* and *NUMBORD* repeated as many times as is necessary.

ORDERS(<u>ORDNUMB</u>,ORDDTE, PARTNUMB, NUMBORD)

(This notation indicates a relation called *ORDERS*, consisting of a primary key, *ORDNUMB*, an attribute, *ORDDTE*, and a repeating group containing two attributes, *PARTNUMB* and *NUMBORD*.) Figure 6.5 shows a sample of this relation.

**Figure 6.5**

**Sample unnormalized relation**

ORDERS

| ORDNUMB | ORDDTE | PARTNUMB | NUMBORD |
|---------|--------|----------|---------|
| 12489 | 90291 | AX12 | 11 |
| 12491 | 90291 | BT04<br>BZ66 | 1<br>1 |
| 12494 | 90491 | CB03 | 4 |
| 12495 | 90491 | CX11 | 2 |
| 12498 | 90591 | AZ52<br>BA74 | 2<br>4 |
| 12500 | 90591 | BT04 | 1 |
| 12504 | 90591 | CZ81 | 2 |

To convert this relation to 1NF, the repeating group is removed, giving the following:

```
ORDERS(ORDNUMB, ORDDTE, PARTNUMB, NUMBORD)
```

The corresponding example of the new relation is shown in Figure 6.6.

**ORDERS**

| ORDNUMB | ORDDTE | PARTNUMB | NUMBORD |
|---------|--------|----------|---------|
| 12489   | 90291  | AX12     | 11      |
| 12491   | 90291  | BT04     | 1       |
| 12491   | 90291  | BZ66     | 1       |
| 12494   | 90491  | CB03     | 4       |
| 12495   | 90491  | CX11     | 2       |
| 12498   | 90591  | AZ52     | 2       |
| 12498   | 90591  | BA74     | 4       |
| 12500   | 90591  | BT04     | 1       |
| 12504   | 90591  | CZ81     | 2       |

**Figure 6.6**

Result of normalization (conversion to 1NF)

Note that the second row of the unnormalized relation indicates that part BZ66 and part BT04 are both present for order 12491. In the normalized relation, this information is represented by *two* rows, the second and third. The primary key to the unnormalized *ORDERS* relation was the *ORDNUMB* alone. The primary key to the normalized relation is now the combination of *ORDNUMB* and *PARTNUMB*. In general it will be true that the primary key will expand in converting a non-1NF relation to 1NF. It will typically include the original primary key concatenated with the key to the repeating group (i.e., the attribute that distinguishes one occurrence of the repeating group from another within a given row in the relation). In this case, *PARTNUMB* is the key to the repeating group and thus becomes part of the primary key of the 1NF relation.

## Second Normal Form

Even though the following relation is in 1NF, problems exist within the relation that will cause us to want to restructure it. Consider the relation:

```
ORDERS(ORDNUMB, ORDDTE, PARTNUMB, PARTDESC, NUMBORD, QUOTPRCE)
```

with the functional dependencies

```
ORDNUMB--> ORDDTE
PARTNUMB --> PARTDESC
ORDNUMB, PARTNUMB --> NUMBORD, QUOTPRCE
```

Thus *ORDNUMB* determines *ORDDTE, PARTNUMB* determines *PARTDESC,* and the concatenation of *ORDNUMB* and *PARTNUMB* determines *NUMBORD* and *QUOTPRCE.* Consider the sample of this relation shown in Figure 6.7.

**Figure 6.7**

Sample *ORDERS* relation

ORDERS

| ORDNUMB | ORDDTE | PARTNUMB | PARTDESC | NUMBORD | QUOTPRCE |
|---|---|---|---|---|---|
| 12489 | 90291 | AX12 | IRON | 11 | 14.95 |
| 12491 | 90291 | BT04 | STOVE | 1 | 402.99 |
| 12491 | 90291 | BZ66 | WASHER | 1 | 311.95 |
| 12494 | 90491 | CB03 | BIKE | 4 | 175.00 |
| 12495 | 90491 | CX11 | MIXER | 2 | 57.95 |
| 12498 | 90591 | AZ52 | SKATES | 2 | 22.95 |
| 12498 | 90591 | BA74 | BASEBALL | 4 | 4.95 |
| 12500 | 90591 | BT04 | STOVE | 1 | 402.99 |
| 12504 | 90591 | CZ81 | WEIGHTS | 2 | 108.99 |

As you can see in the example, the description of a specific part, BT04 for instance, occurs several times in the table. This redundancy causes several problems. It is certainly wasteful of space, but that in itself is not nearly as serious as some of the other problems, called **update anomalies**, which fall into four categories:

1. **UPDATE.** A change to the description of part BT04 requires not one change but several—we have to change each row in which BT04 appears. This certainly makes the update process more cumbersome; it is more complicated logically and takes more time to update.
2. **INCONSISTENT DATA.** There is nothing about the design that would prohibit part BT04 from having two different descriptions in the database. In fact, if it occurs in twenty rows, it could conceivably have twenty *different* descriptions in the database!
3. **ADDITIONS.** We have a real problem when we try to add a new part and its description to the database. Since the primary key for the table consists of both *ORDNUMB* and *PARTNUMB,* we need values for both of these in order to add a new row. If we have a part to add but there are as yet no orders for it, what do we use for an *ORDNUMB?* Our only solution would be to make up a dummy order number, then replace it with a real *ORDNUMB* once an order for this part had actually been received. Certainly this is not an acceptable solution.

4. **DELETIONS.** In the sample relation, if we delete order 12489 from the database, we also *lose* the fact that part AX12 is called IRON.

The problems just described occur because we have an attribute, *PART-DESC*, that is dependent on only a portion of the primary key, *PARTNUMB*, and *not* on the complete primary key. This leads to the definition of second normal form. Second normal form represents an improvement over first normal form because it eliminates these update anomalies in these situations. First, we need to define non-key attribute.

*Definition:* An attribute is a **non-key attribute** if it is not a part of the primary key.

We can now provide a definition for second normal form.

*Definition:* A relation is in **second normal form** (2NF) if it is in first normal form and no non-key attribute is dependent on only a portion of the primary key.

For another perspective on 2NF, consider Figure 6.8. This type of diagram, sometimes called a **dependency diagram**, indicates all the functional dependencies present in the *ORDERS* relation through arrows. The arrows above the boxes indicate the normal dependencies that should be present; that is, the primary key functionally determines all other attributes. (In this case, the concatenation of *ORDNUMB* and *PARTNUMB* determines all other attributes.) It is the arrows below the boxes that prevent the relation from being in 2NF. These arrows represent what is often termed **partial dependencies**, or dependencies on something less than the key. In fact, an alternative definition for 2NF is that a relation is in 2NF if it is in 1NF but contains no partial dependencies.

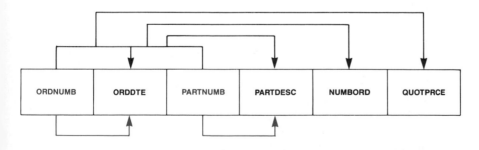

**Figure 6.8**

Dependencies in *ORDERS* relation (blue arrows represent partial dependencies)

Either way we view 2NF, we can now name the fundamental problem with the *ORDERS* relation: it is *not* in 2NF. While it may be pleasing to have a name for the problem, what we really need, of course, is a method to *correct* it. Such a method follows.

First, for each subset of the set of attributes that make up the primary key, begin a relation with this subset as its primary key. For the *ORDERS* relation, this would give:

```
(ORDNUMB,
(PARTNUMB,
(ORDNUMB, PARTNUMB,
```

Next, place each of the other attributes with the appropriate primary key; that is, place each one with the minimal collection on which it depends. For the *ORDERS* relation this would yield:

```
(ORDNUMB, ORDDTE)
(PARTNUMB, PARTDESC)
(ORDNUMB, PARTNUMB, NUMBORD, QUOTPRCE)
```

Each of these relations can now be given a name that is descriptive of the meaning of the relation, such as *ORDERS, PART,* or *ORDLNE,* for example. Figure 6.9 shows samples of the relations involved.

**Figure 6.9**

Conversion to 2NF

ORDERS

| ORDNUMB | ORDDTE | PARTNUMB | PARTDESC | NUMBORD | QUOTPRCE |
|---|---|---|---|---|---|
| 12489 | 90291 | AX12 | IRON | 11 | 14.95 |
| 12491 | 90291 | BT04 | STOVE | 1 | 402.99 |
| 12491 | 90291 | BZ66 | WASHER | 1 | 311.95 |
| 12494 | 90491 | CB03 | BIKE | 4 | 175.00 |
| 12495 | 90491 | CX11 | MIXER | 2 | 57.95 |
| 12498 | 90591 | AZ52 | SKATES | 2 | 22.95 |
| 12498 | 90591 | BA74 | BASEBALL | 4 | 4.95 |
| 12500 | 90591 | BT04 | STOVE | 1 | 402.99 |
| 12504 | 90591 | CZ81 | WEIGHTS | 2 | 108.99 |

is replaced by

ORDERS

| ORDNUMB | ORDDTE |
|---|---|
| 12489 | 90291 |
| 12491 | 90291 |
| 12494 | 90491 |
| 12495 | 90491 |
| 12498 | 90591 |
| 12500 | 90591 |
| 12504 | 90591 |

PART

| PARTNUMB | PARTDESC |
|---|---|
| AX12 | IRON |
| AZ52 | SKATES |
| BA74 | BASEBALL |
| BH22 | TOASTER |
| BT04 | STOVE |
| BZ66 | WASHER |
| CA14 | SKILLET |
| CB03 | BIKE |
| CX11 | MIXER |
| CZ81 | WEIGHTS |

ORDLNE

| ORDNUMB | PARTNUMB | NUMBORD | QUOTPRCE |
|---|---|---|---|
| 12489 | AX12 | 11 | 14.95 |
| 12491 | BT04 | 1 | 402.99 |
| 12491 | BZ66 | 1 | 311.95 |
| 12494 | CB03 | 4 | 175.00 |
| 12495 | CX11 | 2 | 57.95 |
| 12498 | AZ52 | 2 | 22.95 |
| 12498 | BA74 | 4 | 4.95 |
| 12500 | BT04 | 1 | 402.99 |
| 12504 | CZ81 | 2 | 108.99 |

Note that the update anomalies have been eliminated. A description appears only once, so we do not have the redundancy we did in the earlier design. Changing the description of part BT04 to OVEN is now a simple process involving a single change. Since the description for a part occurs in one single place, it is not possible to have multiple descriptions for a single part in the database at the same time. To add a new part and its description, we create a new row in the *PART* relation and thus there is no need to have an order exist for that part. Also, deleting order 12489 does not cause part number AX12 to be deleted from the *PART* relation, and so we still have its description (IRON) in the database. Finally, we have not lost any information in the process. The data in the original design can be reconstructed from the data in the new design.

## Third Normal Form

Problems can still exist with relations that are in 2NF. Consider the following *CUSTOMER* relation:

```
CUSTOMER(CUSTNUMB, CUSTNAME, CUSTADDR, SLSRNUMB, SLSRNAME)
```

with the functional dependencies:

```
CUSTNUMB --> CUSTNAME, CUSTADDR, SLSRNUMB, SLSRNAME
SLSRNUMB --> SLSRNAME
```

(*CUSTNUMB* determines all the other attributes. In addition, *SLSRNUMB* determines *SLSRNAME*.)

If the primary key of a table is a single column, the table is automatically in second normal form. (If the table were not in 2NF, some column would be dependent on only a *portion* of the primary key, which is impossible when the primary key is just one column.) Thus, the *CUSTOMER* table is in second normal form.

As the sample of this relation demonstrates (Figure 6.10 on the next page), this relation possesses problems similar to those encountered earlier, even though it is in second normal form. In this case it is the name of a sales rep that can occur many times in the table; see sales rep 12 (Sam Brown), for example. This redundancy results in the same set of problems that was described in the previous *ORDERS* relation. In addition to the problem of wasted space, we have similar update anomalies, as follows:

1. **UPDATE.** A change to the name of a sales rep requires not one change but several. Again the update process becomes very cumbersome.

2. **INCONSISTENT DATA.** There is nothing about the design that would prohibit a sales rep from having two different names in the database. In fact, if the same sales rep represents twenty different customers (and thus would be found on twenty different rows), he or she could have twenty different names in the database.

3. **ADDITIONS.** To add sales rep 47, whose name is Mary Daniels, to the database, we must have at least one customer whom she represents. If she has not yet been assigned any customers, then either we cannot record the fact that her name is Mary Daniels, or we have to create a fictitious customer for her to represent. Again, this is not a very desirable solution to the problem.

4. **DELETIONS.** If we were to delete all the customers of sales rep 6 from the database, we would also lose the name of sales rep 6.

**Figure 6.10**

Sample *CUSTOMER* relation

CUSTOMER

| CUSTNUMB | CUSTNAME | CUSTADDR | SLSRNUMB | SLSRNAME |
|---|---|---|---|---|
| 124 | Adams, Sally | 481 Oak,Lansing,MI | 3 | Jones, Mary |
| 256 | Samuels, Ann | 215 Pete,Grant,MI | 6 | Smith, William |
| 311 | Charles, Don | 48 College,Ira,MI | 12 | Brown, Sam |
| 315 | Daniels, Tom | 914 Cherry,Kent,MI | 6 | Smith, William |
| 405 | Williams, Al | 519 Watson,Grant,MI | 12 | Brown, Sam |
| 412 | Adams, Sally | 16 Elm,Lansing,MI | 3 | Jones, Mary |
| 522 | Nelson, Mary | 108 Pine,Ada,MI | 12 | Brown, Sam |
| 567 | Baker, Joe | 808 Ridge,Harper,MI | 6 | Smith, William |
| 587 | Roberts, Judy | 512 Pine,Ada,MI | 6 | Smith, William |
| 622 | Martin, Dan | 419 Chip,Grant,MI | 3 | Jones, Mary |

These update anomalies are due to the fact that *SLSRNUMB* determines *SLSRNAME* but *SLSRNUMB* is not the primary key. As a result, the same *SLSRNUMB*, and consequently the same *SLSRNAME*, can appear on many different rows.

We've seen that 2NF is an improvement over 1NF, but to eliminate 2NF problems, we need an even better strategy for creating tables in our database. Third normal form gives us that strategy. Before we look at third normal form, however, we need to become familiar with the special name given to any column that determines another column (such as the *SLSRNUMB* column in the *CUSTOMER* table).

*Definition:* Any attribute (or collection of attributes) that determines another attribute is called a **determinant**.

Certainly the **primary key** in a relation will be a determinant. In fact, by definition, any **candidate key** will be a determinant. (Remember that a candidate key is an attribute or collection of attributes which could have functioned as the primary key.) In this case, *SLSRNUMB* is a determinant, but is certainly not a candidate key, and that is the problem.

*Definition:* A relation is in **third normal form** (3NF) if it is in second normal form and if the only determinants it contains are candidate keys.

Again, for an additional perspective, we will consider a dependency diagram, as shown in Figure 6.11. As before, the arrows above the boxes represent the normal dependencies of all attributes on the primary key. It is the arrow below the boxes that causes the problem. The presence of this arrow makes *SLSRNUMB* a determinant. If there were arrows from *SLSRNUMB* to all the attributes, *SLSRNUMB* would be a candidate key and we would not have a problem. The absence of these arrows indicates that this relation possesses a determinant that is not a candidate key. Thus, the relation is not in 3NF.

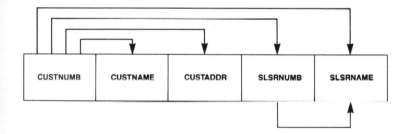

**Figure 6.11**

Dependencies in *CUSTOMER* relation (*SLSRNUMB* is a determinant since it functionally determines *SLSRNAME*)

**Note:** The definition given above is not the original definition of third normal form. This more recent definition, which is preferable to the original, is often referred to as **Boyce-Codd normal form** (BCNF) when it is important to make a distinction between this definition and the original. We will not make such a distinction but will take this to be *the* definition of 3NF.

We have now named the problem with the *CUSTOMER* relation: It is not in 3NF. What we need is a scheme to correct the deficiency in the *CUSTOMER* relation and in all relations having similar deficiencies. Such a method follows.

First, for each determinant that is not a candidate key, remove from the relation the attributes that depend on this determinant. Next, create a new relation containing all the attributes from the original relation that depend on this determinant. Finally, make the determinant the primary key of this new relation.

In the *CUSTOMER* relation, for example, SLSRNAME is removed since it depends on the determinant *SLSRNUMB*, which is not a candidate key. A new relation is formed, consisting of *SLSRNUMB* as the primary key and *SLSRNAME*. Specifically,

```
CUSTOMER(CUSTNUMB, CUSTNAME, CUSTADDR, SLSRNUMB, SLSRNAME)
```

is replaced by

```
CUSTOMER(CUSTNUMB, CUSTNAME, CUSTADDR, SLSRNUMB)
```

and

```
SLSREP(SLSRNUMB, SLSRNAME)
```

Figure 6.12 shows samples of the relations involved.

**Figure 6.12**

Conversion to 3NF

CUSTOMER

| CUSTNUMB | CUSTNAME | CUSTADDR | SLSRNUMB | SLSRNAME |
|---|---|---|---|---|
| 124 | Adams, Sally | 481 Oak,Lansing,MI | 3 | Jones, Mary |
| 256 | Samuels, Ann | 215 Pete,Grant,MI | 6 | Smith, William |
| 311 | Charles, Don | 48 College,Ira,MI | 12 | Brown, Sam |
| 315 | Daniels, Tom | 914 Cherry,Kent,MI | 6 | Smith, William |
| 405 | Williams, Al | 519 Watson,Grant,MI | 12 | Brown, Sam |
| 412 | Adams, Sally | 16 Elm,Lansing,MI | 3 | Jones, Mary |
| 522 | Nelson, Mary | 108 Pine,Ada,MI | 12 | Brown, Sam |
| 567 | Baker, Joe | 808 Ridge,Harper,MI | 6 | Smith, William |
| 587 | Roberts, Judy | 512 Pine,Ada,MI | 6 | Smith, William |
| 622 | Martin, Dan | 419 Chip,Grant,MI | 3 | Jones, Mary |

is replaced by

CUSTOMER

| CUSTNUMB | CUSTNAME | CUSTADDR | SLSRNUMB |
|---|---|---|---|
| 124 | Adams, Sally | 481 Oak,Lansing,MI | 3 |
| 256 | Samuels, Ann | 215 Pete,Grant,MI | 6 |
| 311 | Charles, Don | 48 College,Ira,MI | 12 |
| 315 | Daniels, Tom | 914 Cherry,Kent,MI | 6 |
| 405 | Williams, Al | 519 Watson,Grant,MI | 12 |
| 412 | Adams, Sally | 16 Elm,Lansing,MI | 3 |
| 522 | Nelson, Mary | 108 Pine,Ada,MI | 12 |
| 567 | Baker, Joe | 808 Ridge,Harper,MI | 6 |
| 587 | Roberts, Judy | 512 Pine,Ada,MI | 6 |
| 622 | Martin, Dan | 419 Chip,Grant,MI | 3 |

SLSREP

| SLSRNUMB | SLSRNAME |
|---|---|
| 3 | Jones, Mary |
| 6 | Smith, William |
| 12 | Brown, Sam |

Have we now corrected all previously identified problems? A sales rep's name appears only once, thus avoiding redundancy and making the process of changing a sales rep's name a very simple one. It is not possible with this design for the same sales rep to have two different names in the database. To add a new sales rep to the database, we add a row in the *SLSREP* relation so that it is not necessary to have a customer whom the sales rep represents. Finally, deleting all the customers of a given sales rep will not remove the sales rep's record from the *SLSREP* relation, so we do retain the sales rep's name; all the data in the original relation can be reconstructed from the data in the new collection of relations. All previously mentioned problems have indeed been solved.

### Incorrect Decompositions

It is important to note that the decomposition of a relation into two or more 3NF relations *must* be accomplished by the method indicated, even though there are other possibilities that might seem at first glance to be legitimate. Let us examine two other decompositions of the *CUSTOMER* relation into 3NF relations in order to understand the difficulties they pose.

What if, in the decomposition process,

    CUSTOMER(CUSTNUMB, CUSTNAME, CUSTADDR, SLSRNUMB, SLSRNAME)

is replaced by

    CUSTOMER(CUSTNUMB, CUSTNAME, CUSTADDR, SLSRNUMB)

and

    SLSREP(CUSTNUMB, SLSRNAME)

Samples of these relations are shown in Figure 6.13 on the next page.

Both new relations are in 3NF. In addition, by joining these two relations together on *CUSTNUMB* we can reconstruct the original *CUSTOMER* relation. The result, however, still suffers from some of the same kinds of problems that the original *CUSTOMER* relation did. Consider, for example, the redundancy in the storage of sales reps' names, the problem encountered in changing the name of sales rep 12, and the difficulty of adding a new sales rep for whom there are as yet no customers. In addition, since the sales rep number is in one relation and the sales rep name is in another, we have actually *split a functional dependence across two different relations*. Thus, this decomposition, while it may appear to be valid, is definitely not a desirable way to create 3NF relations.

**Figure 6.13**

Incorrect
decomposition

CUSTOMER

| CUSTNUMB | CUSTNAME | CUSTADDR | SLSRNUMB | SLSRNAME |
|---|---|---|---|---|
| 124 | Adams, Sally | 481 Oak,Lansing,MI | 3 | Jones, Mary |
| 256 | Samuels, Ann | 215 Pete,Grant,MI | 6 | Smith, William |
| 311 | Charles, Don | 48 College,Ira,MI | 12 | Brown, Sam |
| 315 | Daniels, Tom | 914 Cherry,Kent,MI | 6 | Smith, William |
| 405 | Williams, Al | 519 Watson,Grant,MI | 12 | Brown, Sam |
| 412 | Adams, Sally | 16 Elm,Lansing,MI | 3 | Jones, Mary |
| 522 | Nelson, Mary | 108 Pine,Ada,MI | 12 | Brown, Sam |
| 567 | Baker, Joe | 808 Ridge,Harper,MI | 6 | Smith, William |
| 587 | Roberts, Judy | 512 Pine,Ada,MI | 6 | Smith, William |
| 622 | Martin, Dan | 419 Chip,Grant,MI | 3 | Jones, Mary |

is replaced by

CUSTOMER

| CUSTNUMB | CUSTNAME | CUSTADDR | SLSRNUMB |
|---|---|---|---|
| 124 | Adams, Sally | 481 Oak,Lansing,MI | 3 |
| 256 | Samuels, Ann | 215 Pete,Grant,MI | 6 |
| 311 | Charles, Don | 48 College,Ira,MI | 12 |
| 315 | Daniels, Tom | 914 Cherry,Kent,MI | 6 |
| 405 | Williams, Al | 519 Watson,Grant,MI | 12 |
| 412 | Adams, Sally | 16 Elm,Lansing,MI | 3 |
| 522 | Nelson, Mary | 108 Pine,Ada,MI | 12 |
| 567 | Baker, Joe | 808 Ridge,Harper,MI | 6 |
| 587 | Roberts, Judy | 512 Pine,Ada,MI | 6 |
| 622 | Martin, Dan | 419 Chip,Grant,MI | 3 |

SLSREP

| CUSTNUMB | SLSRNAME |
|---|---|
| 124 | Jones, Mary |
| 256 | Smith, William |
| 311 | Brown, Sam |
| 315 | Smith, William |
| 405 | Brown, Sam |
| 412 | Jones, Mary |
| 522 | Brown, Sam |
| 567 | Smith, William |
| 587 | Smith, William |
| 622 | Jones, Mary |

There is another decomposition we might choose. That is to replace

CUSTOMER(<u>CUSTNUMB</u>, CUSTNAME, CUSTADDR, SLSRNUMB, SLSRNAME)

by

CUSTOMER(<u>CUSTNUMB</u>, CUSTNAME, CUSTADDR, SLSRNAME)

and

```
SLSREP(SLSRNUMB, SLSRNAME)
```

Samples of these relations are shown in Figure 6.14.

**CUSTOMER**

| CUSTNUMB | CUSTNAME | CUSTADDR | SLSRNUMB | SLSRNAME |
|---|---|---|---|---|
| 124 | Adams, Sally | 481 Oak,Lansing,MI | 3 | Jones, Mary |
| 256 | Samuels, Ann | 215 Pete,Grant,MI | 6 | Smith, William |
| 311 | Charles, Don | 48 College,Ira,MI | 12 | Brown, Sam |
| 315 | Daniels, Tom | 914 Cherry,Kent,MI | 6 | Smith, William |
| 405 | Williams, Al | 519 Watson,Grant,MI | 12 | Brown, Sam |
| 412 | Adams, Sally | 16 Elm,Lansing,MI | 3 | Jones, Mary |
| 522 | Nelson, Mary | 108 Pine,Ada,MI | 12 | Brown, Sam |
| 567 | Baker, Joe | 808 Ridge,Harper,MI | 6 | Smith, William |
| 587 | Roberts, Judy | 512 Pine,Ada,MI | 6 | Smith, William |
| 622 | Martin, Dan | 419 Chip,Grant,MI | 3 | Jones, Mary |

**Figure 6.14**

Second incorrect decomposition

is replaced by

**CUSTOMER**

| CUSTNUMB | CUSTNAME | CUSTADDR | SLSRNAME |
|---|---|---|---|
| 124 | Adams, Sally | 481 Oak,Lansing,MI | Jones, Mary |
| 256 | Samuels, Ann | 215 Pete,Grant,MI | Smith, William |
| 311 | Charles, Don | 48 College,Ira,MI | Brown, Sam |
| 315 | Daniels, Tom | 914 Cherry,Kent,MI | Smith, William |
| 405 | Williams, Al | 519 Watson,Grant,MI | Brown, Sam |
| 412 | Adams, Sally | 16 Elm,Lansing,MI | Jones, Mary |
| 522 | Nelson, Mary | 108 Pine,Ada,MI | Brown, Sam |
| 567 | Baker, Joe | 808 Ridge,Harper,MI | Smith, William |
| 587 | Roberts, Judy | 512 Pine,Ada,MI | Smith, William |
| 622 | Martin, Dan | 419 Chip,Grant,MI | Jones, Mary |

**SLSREP**

| SLSRNUMB | SLSRNAME |
|---|---|
| 3 | Jones, Mary |
| 6 | Smith, William |
| 12 | Brown, Sam |

This seems to be a possibility. Not only are both relations in 3NF, but joining them together based on *SLSRNAME* seems to reconstruct the data in the original relation. Or does it? Suppose the name of sales rep 6 is also Mary Jones. In that case, when we join the two new relations together, we will get a row in which customer 124 (Sally Adams) is associated with sales rep 3 (Mary

Jones) and *another* row in which customer 124 is associated with sales rep 6 (William Smith). Since we obviously want decompositions that preserve the original information (called **nonloss decompositions**), this scheme is not appropriate.

## Q & A

**Question:**

Using the types of entities found in a college environment (faculty, students, departments, courses, etc.), create an example of a relation that is in 1NF but not in 2NF, and an example of a relation that is in 2NF but not in 3NF. In each case justify the answers and show how to convert to the higher forms.

**Answer:**

There are many possible solutions. If your solution differs from the one we will look at, this does not mean it is an unsatisfactory solution.

To create a 1NF relation that is not in 2NF, we need a relation that (a) has no repeating groups and (b) has at least one attribute that is dependent on only a portion of the primary key. For an attribute to be dependent on a portion of the primary key, the key must contain at least two attributes. Following is a picture of what we need:

( __1__ , __2__ , 3 , 4 )

This relation contains four attributes, numbered 1, 2, 3, and 4, in which attributes 1 and 2 functionally determine both attributes 3 and 4. In addition, neither attribute 1 nor 2 can determine *all* other attributes, otherwise the key would contain only this one attribute. Finally, we want part of the key, say, attribute 2, to determine another attribute, say, attribute 4. Now that we have the pattern we need, we would like to find attributes from within the college environment to fit it. One example would be:

(<u>STUNUMB</u>, <u>CRSENUMB</u>, GRADE, CRSEDESC)

In this example, the concatenation of *STUNUMB* (student number) and *CRSENUMB* (course number) determines both *GRADE* and *CRSEDESC* (course description). Both of these are required to determine *GRADE*, and thus the primary key consists of their concatenation (nothing less will do). The *CRSEDESC*, however, is only dependent on the *CRSENUMB*. This violates second normal form. To convert this relation to 2NF we would replace it by the two relations

(<u>STUNUMB</u>, <u>CRSENUMB</u>, GRADE)

and

(<u>CRSENUMB</u>, CRSEDESC)

We would of course now give these relations appropriate names.

To create a relation that is in 2NF but not in 3NF, we need a 2NF relation in which there is a determinant that is *not* a candidate key. If we choose a relation that has a single attribute as the primary key, it is automatically in 2NF, so the real problem is the determinant. We need a relation like the following:

( _____1_____ ,       2      ,       3       )

This relation contains three attributes, numbered 1, 2, and 3, in which attribute 1 determines each of the others and is thus the primary key. If, in addition, attribute 2 determines attribute 3, it is a determinant. If it does not also determine attribute 1, then it is not a candidate key. One example that fits this pattern would be:

(STUNUMB, ADVNUMB, ADVNAME)

Here the student number (*STUNUMB*) determines both the student's advisor's number (*ADVNUMB*) and advisor's name (*ADVNAME*). *ADVNUMB* determines *ADVNAME* but *ADVNUMB* does not determine *STUNUMB*, since one advisor can have many advisees. This relation is in 2NF but not in 3NF. To convert it to 3NF, we replace it by

(STUNUMB, ADVNUMB)

and

(ADVNUMB, ADVNAME)

Question:

Convert the following relation to 3NF:

STUDENT(STUNUMB, STUNAME, NUMBCRED, ADVNUMB, ADVNAME,
        CRSENUMB, CRSEDESC, GRADE)

In this relation, *STUNUMB* determines *STUNAME, NUMBCRED, ADVNUMB*, and *ADVNAME*. *ADVNUMB* determines *ADVNAME*. *CRSENUMB* determines *CRSEDESC*. The combination of a *STUNUMB* and a *CRSENUMB* determines a *GRADE*.

Answer:

**Step 1.** Remove the repeating group to convert to 1NF. This yields:

STUDENT(STUNUMB, STUNAME, NUMBCRED, ADVNUMB, ADVNAME,
        CRSENUMB, CRSEDESC, GRADE)

This relation is now in 1NF, since it has no repeating groups. It is not, however, in 2NF, since *STUNAME* is dependent only on *STUNUMB*, which is only a portion of the primary key.

*(continued)*

*(continued)*

**Step 2.** Convert the 1NF relation to 2NF. First, for each subset of the primary key, start a relation with that subset as its key yielding:

```
(STUNUMB,
(CRSENUMB,
(STUNUMB, CRSENUMB,
```

Next, place the rest of the attributes with the minimal collection on which they depend, giving:

```
(STUNUMB, STUNAME, NUMBCRED, ADVNUMB, ADVNAME)
(CRSENUMB, CRSEDESC)
(STUNUMB, CRSENUMB, GRADE)
```

Finally, we assign names to each of the newly created relations:

```
STUDENT(STUNUMB, STUNAME, NUMBCRED, ADVNUMB, ADVNAME)
COURSE(CRSENUMB, CRSEDESC)
GRADE(STUNUMB, CRSENUMB, GRADE)
```

While these relations are all in 2NF, both *COURSE* and *GRADE* are also in 3NF. The *STUDENT* relation is not, however, since it contains a determinant, *ADVNUMB*, that is not a candidate key.

**Step 3:** Convert the 2NF *STUDENT* relation to 3NF by removing the attribute that depends on the determinant *ADVNUMB* and placing it in a separate relation:

```
(STUNUMB, STUNAME, NUMBCRED, ADVNUMB)
(ADVNUMB, ADVNAME)
```

**Step 4:** Name these relations and put the entire collection together, giving:

```
STUDENT(STUNUMB, STUNAME, NUMBCRED, ADVNUMB)
ADVISOR(ADVNUMB, ADVNAME)
COURSE(CRSENUMB, CRSEDESC)
GRADE(STUNUMB, CRSENUMB, GRADE)
```

For more on the normalization process, see [1], [2], [5], [6], and [8].

## MULTIVALUED DEPENDENCIES AND
## FOURTH NORMAL FORM

By converting a given collection of relations to an equivalent 3NF collection, we remove any problems arising from functional dependencies. Usually this means that the types of anomalies discussed in the previous section have been eliminated. This is not always the case, however. There is a different kind of dependency that can also lead to the same types of difficulties.

To illustrate the problem, suppose we are interested in faculty members at Marvel College, the students they advise, and the committees on which the faculty members serve. Any faculty member can advise many students. A student can have more than one faculty member as an advisor, since students can have more than one major. Any faculty member can serve on more than one committee (some don't serve on any). Suppose that, as an initial relational design for this situation, we chose the following unnormalized relation:

```
FACULTY(FACNUMB, STUNUMB, COMMCODE)
```

The single relation *FACULTY* has a primary key of *FACNUMB* (faculty number) and two separate repeating groups, *STUNUMB* (student number) and *COMMCODE* (committee code). To convert this relation to 1NF, we might be tempted to merely remove the two repeating groups and expand the primary key to include both *STUNUMB* and *COMMCODE*. This solution would give the relation:

```
FACULTY(FACNUMB, STUNUMB, COMMCODE)
```

Samples of these relations are shown in Figure 6.15 on the next page. (The committee codes are codes for the various committees. They include such things as ADV for the advisory committee, PER for the personnel committee, CUR for the curriculum committee, HSG for the housing committee, and so on.)

**Figure 6.15**

Incorrect way to
remove repeating
groups

FACULTY

| FACNUMB | STUNUMB | COMMCODE |
|--------:|--------:|----------|
| 123 | 12805 | ADV |
|  | 24139 | PER |
|  |  | HSG |
| 456 | 37573 | CUR |
|  | 24139 |  |
|  | 36273 |  |
| 444 | 57384 | HSG |

is replaced by

FACULTY

| FACNUMB | STUNUMB | COMMCODE |
|--------:|--------:|----------|
| 123 | 12805 | ADV |
| 123 | 24139 | ADV |
| 123 | 12805 | PER |
| 123 | 24139 | PER |
| 123 | 12805 | HSG |
| 123 | 24139 | HSG |
| 456 | 37573 | CUR |
| 456 | 24139 | CUR |
| 456 | 36273 | CUR |
| 444 | 57384 | HSG |

You may already have spotted some problems with this approach. If so, you are correct. It is a strange way to normalize the original relation. Yet, it is precisely this approach to the removal of repeating groups that leads to the problems alluded to in the beginning of this section concerning multivalued dependencies. We will later examine how this relation should have been normalized to avoid the problems altogether. Let us for the moment, however, push ahead with the relation we have created and discuss what kinds of problems are present.

The first thing we should observe about this relation is that it is in 3NF, since there are no repeating groups; no attribute is dependent on only a portion of the primary key; and there are no determinants that are not candidate keys. There are several problems, however, with this 3NF relation:

1. **UPDATE.** Changing the code of a committee for faculty member 123 requires more than one change. If we change the code from ADV to CUR, the change should be made in both of the first two rows in the table. After all, it doesn't make sense to say that the committee is ADV when associated with student 12805 and CUR when associated with

student 24139. It is the same committee served on by the same faculty member. The faculty member does not serve on one committee when advising one student and a different committee when advising another.

2. **ADDITIONS.** Suppose that faculty member 666 joins the faculty at Marvel. Also suppose that this faculty member does not yet serve on any committee. When this faculty member begins to advise student 44332, we have a problem, since *COMMCODE* is part of the primary key. We would need to enter a fictitious committee code in this situation.

3. **DELETIONS.** If faculty member 444 no longer advises student 57384 and we delete the appropriate row from the table, we lose the information that faculty member 444 serves on the HSG (housing) committee.

These problems are certainly reminiscent of those encountered in the discussions of both 2NF and 3NF, but there are *no* functional dependencies among the attributes in this relation. A given faculty member is not associated with *one* student, as he or she would be if this were a functional dependence. Each faculty member, however, is associated with a *specific* collection of students. More importantly, this association is *independent* of any association with committees. It is this independence that causes the problem.

We can now define multivalued dependency and fourth normal form.

*Definition:* In a relation with attributes A, B, and C, there is a **multivalued dependence** of attribute B on attribute A (also read as "B is **multidependent** on A" or "A **multidetermines** B"), if a value for A is associated with a specific collection of values for B, independent of any values for C. (This is usually written A -->-> B.)

*Definition:* A relation is in **fourth normal form** (4NF) if it is in 3NF (really BCNF) and there are no multivalued dependencies.

As might be expected, converting a relation to 4NF is similar to the normalization process encountered in the treatments of 2NF and 3NF. We split the relation into separate relations, each containing the attribute that multidetermines the others, in this case the faculty number. This means we replace

```
FACULTY(FACNUMB, STUNUMB, COMMCODE)
```

with

```
FACSTU(FACNUMB, STUNUMB)
```

and

        FACCOMM(<u>FACNUMB</u>, <u>COMMCODE</u>).

Figure 6.16 shows samples of these relations. As before, the problems have disappeared. There is no problem with changing the committee code ADV to CUR, since it occurs only in one place. To add the information that faculty member 666 advises student 44332, we need only add a row to the *FACSTU* relation. It does not matter whether this faculty member serves on a committee. Finally, to delete the information that faculty member 444 advises student 57384, we need only remove a row from the *FACSTU* table. In this case, we do not lose the information that this faculty member serves on the HSG committee.

**Figure 6.16**

Conversion to 4NF

FACULTY

| FACNUMB | STUNUMB | COMMCODE |
|--------:|--------:|----------|
| 123 | 12805 | ADV |
| 123 | 24139 | ADV |
| 123 | 12805 | PER |
| 123 | 24139 | PER |
| 123 | 12805 | HSG |
| 123 | 24139 | HSG |
| 456 | 37573 | CUR |
| 456 | 24139 | CUR |
| 456 | 36273 | CUR |
| 444 | 57384 | HSG |

is replaced by

FACULTY

| FACNUMB | STUNUMB |
|--------:|--------:|
| 123 | 12805 |
| 123 | 24139 |
| 456 | 37573 |
| 456 | 24139 |
| 456 | 36273 |
| 444 | 57384 |

FACULTY

| FACNUMB | COMMCODE |
|--------:|----------|
| 123 | ADV |
| 123 | PER |
| 123 | HSG |
| 456 | CUR |
| 444 | HSG |

## Avoiding the Problem

While it is certainly true that a relation that is not in 4NF suffers some serious problems, there is a way to avoid dealing with the issue. What we need is a methodology for normalizing relations that will prevent this situation from occurring in the first place. We already have most of such a methodology in place from the discussion of the 1NF, 2NF, and 3NF normalization process. All we need is to expand the method for converting an unnormalized relation to 1NF.

The conversion of an unnormalized relation to 1NF requires the removal of repeating groups. When this was first demonstrated, we merely removed the repeating group symbol and expanded the key. You will recall, for example, that

```
ORDERS(ORDNUMB, PARTNUMB, NUMBORD)
```

became

```
ORDERS(ORDNUMB, PARTNUMB, NUMBORD)
```

The primary key was expanded to include the primary key of the original relation together with the key to the repeating group.

What if there are two or more repeating groups, however? The method we have just alluded to is inadequate for such situations. Instead we must remove each separate repeating group and place each in a separate relation. Each relation will contain all the attributes that make up a given repeating group, as well as the primary key to the original unnormalized relation. The primary key to each new relation will be the concatenation of the primary key of the original relation and the key to the repeating group.

For example, consider the following unnormalized relation containing two separate repeating groups:

```
FACULTY(FACNUMB, FACNAME, STUNUMB, STUNAME, COMMCODE, COMMDESC)
```

where *FACNAME* is the name of the faculty member and *STUNAME* is the name of the student. The attributes *COMMCODE* and *COMMDESC* refer to the committee code and committee description. (For example, one row in this table would have PER in the *COMMCODE* column and "Personnel Committee" in the *COMMDESC* column.) Applying this new method to create 1NF relations would produce

```
FACULTY(FACNUMB, FACNAME)
FACSTU(FACNUMB, STUNUMB, STUNAME)
FACCOMM(FACNUMB, COMMCODE, COMMDESC)
```

As you can see, the problems with multivalued dependencies have been avoided. At this point we have a collection of 1NF relations and we still need to convert them to 3NF. By using the process just described, however, we are guaranteed that the result will also be in 4NF.

### 4NF and Primary Keys

Some people mistakenly believe that a relation is not in 4NF if its primary key consists of three or more attributes. That is *not* the problem. The problem is the independence mentioned earlier. For example, suppose we wish to keep track of the number of items each customer has purchased from each sales rep. In this example, we assume that a customer can be represented by more than one sales rep. An appropriate relation for this example is:

SALES(<u>SLSRNUMB</u>, <u>CUSTNUMB</u>, <u>PARTNUMB</u>, NUMBSOLD)

Consider the sample of this relation shown in Figure 6.17. In this relation, we do not have the independence discussed earlier. It is certainly not true that a given sales rep is associated with the same set of customers *independent of parts*, for example. Specifically, sales rep 3 sold part AX12 to customers 124 and 412, but sold part CB03 to customer 256. Similarly, the association between a sales rep and a collection of parts depends on customers. Specifically, to customer 412, sales rep 3 sold AX12, BZ66, and CZ81, but to customer 256, sales rep 3 sold only CB03. Likewise, the relationship between a customer and a given collection of parts depends on the sales rep. Specifically, customer 412 purchased parts AX12, BZ66, and CZ81 from sales rep 3, but purchased parts AX12 and BT04 from sales rep 6. Since there is no independence among the three attributes that make up the key, we are in 4NF and thus there is no problem. The *independence* is the root of the problem, not the fact that the key consists of the concatenation of more than two attributes.

**Figure 6.17**

4NF relation with concatenation of three attributes as the key

SALES

| SLSRNUMB | CUSTNUMB | PARTNUMB | NUMBSOLD |
|---|---|---|---|
| 3 | 124 | AX12 | 15 |
| 3 | 256 | CB03 | 3 |
| 3 | 412 | AX12 | 21 |
| 3 | 412 | BZ66 | 2 |
| 3 | 412 | CZ81 | 5 |
| 6 | 124 | CZ81 | 7 |
| 6 | 412 | BT04 | 1 |
| 6 | 412 | AX12 | 4 |

## HIGHER NORMAL FORMS

Higher normal forms have been defined. These are currently the subject of a great deal of research and thus deserve mention. But at least at the present time, they do not appear to hold much value for the design process.

The first of these is fifth normal form (5NF), which involves yet another kind of dependency, a join dependency. This is an assertion that a relation can be constructed by the join of its projections. A relation is in **fifth normal form** (sometimes called project-join normal form) if every join dependency is "implied" by the candidate keys. For information concerning fifth normal form, see [5] and [9].

The other higher normal form was defined by Fagin [7] and is called domain-key normal form (DK/NF). A relation is in **domain-key normal form** if every constraint on the relation is a logical consequence of the definitions of keys and domains. In the same paper in which he defined DK/NF, Fagin also showed that a relation that is in DK/NF will suffer from no insertion or deletion anomalies. This fact then creates a boundary for the definition of normal forms; no higher normal forms will be needed. Unfortunately, no obvious general means is known for converting a relation to DK/NF. For further information on DK/NF, see [7] and [8].

## APPLICATION TO DATABASE DESIGN

The normalization process used to convert an unnormalized relation or collection of relations to an equivalent collection in 3NF is a crucial part of the database design process. By following a careful and appropriate normalization methodology, normal forms higher than 3NF will not need to be considered. There are two aspects of this methodology that warrant further discussion.

1. Conversion to 3NF should be done sensibly and not blindly. Consider the *CUSTOMER* relation

```
CUSTOMER(CUSTNUMB, CUSTNAME, CUSTADDR, CITY, STATE, ZIP, ...)
```

In addition to the functional dependencies that all the attributes have on the *CUSTNUMB*, there are two other functional dependencies. *ZIP* determines *STATE* and, at least in most regions of the country, *ZIP* also determines *CITY*. Does this mean that we should replace this relation with

```
CUSTOMER(CUSTNUMB, CUSTNAME, CUSTADDR, ZIP, ...)
```

and

```
ZIPCODES(ZIP, CITY, STATE)
```

If we are determined to ensure that every relation is in 3NF, then we should do this, but it is probably overkill. If you review the list of problems normally associated with relations that are not in 3NF, you will see that they really don't apply here. Are we likely to need to change the state in which zip code 49428 is located? Do we need to add the fact that zip code 49401 corresponds to Allendale, Michigan, if we have no customers with that zip code? In addition, if we leave the relation in its original non-3NF format, it is much more natural.

2. By splitting relations to achieve 3NF, we create the need to express interrelation constraints. In the example given earlier for converting to 3NF, we created the two relations

CUSTOMER(<u>CUSTNUMB</u>, CUSTNAME, CUSTADDR, SLSRNUMB)

and

SLSREP(<u>SLSRNUMB</u>, SLSRNAME)

There is nothing about these two relations by themselves that would force the *SLSRNUMB* in a row of the *CUSTOMER* relation to actually match a *SLSRNUMB* in the *SLSREP* relation. Requiring this to take place is an example of an **interrelation constraint**, that is, a condition that involves two or more relations. We cannot determine whether this condition has been satisfied merely by looking at the *CUSTOMER* relation. This type of interrelation constraint (there are others) is handled by FOREIGN KEY rules, which are discussed in chapter 7, the first chapter on database design. It is mentioned here only because the problem surfaces when relations are split in the normalization process.

## SUMMARY

In this chapter we have examined the relational model's normalization process. We began by discussing functional dependence. Attribute B is functionally dependent on attribute (or collection of attributes) A if a value for A determines a specific value for B. We next defined the primary key of a relation. An attribute (or collection of attributes), A, is the primary key for a relation if all attributes of the relation are dependent on A and if no subcollection of the attributes in A also has this property.

Next, the various normal forms were discussed. A first normal form relation contains no repeating groups. A second normal form relation is a relation that is in first normal form and has no attribute dependent on only a portion of the primary key. A third normal form relation is a relation that is in second normal form and has no determinants that are not also candidate keys. (Technically this is called Boyce-Codd normal form, or BC/NF.) A fourth normal form relation is a relation that is in third normal form and has no multivalued dependencies. A fifth normal form relation is one in which every join dependency is "implied" by its candidate keys. Finally, a domain/key normal form relation is one in which every constraint on the relation is a consequence of the definitions of keys and domains.

A methodology was presented for converting unnormalized relations (those not in first normal form) to third normal form in such a way that the end result will also be in fourth normal form. Since the higher forms (fifth and domain/key) are of theoretical interest but not particularly applicable to the design process, reaching fourth normal form is the goal.

## REVIEW QUESTIONS

1. Define functional dependence.
2. Give an example of an attribute, A, and an attribute, B, such that B is functionally dependent on A. Give an example of an attribute, C, and an attribute, D, such that D is not functionally dependent on C.
3. Define candidate key.
4. Define primary key.
5. Define first normal form. What is the relationship between first normal form and "normalized" relations as defined in chapter 3?.
6. Define second normal form. What types of problems are encountered in relations that are not in second normal form?
7. Define third normal form. What types of problems are encountered in relations that are not in third normal form?
8. Define multivalued dependency. How does this concept differ from functional dependency?
9. Define fourth normal form.

## EXERCISES

1. Consider a student relation containing student number, student name, student's major department, student's advisor number, student's advisor's name, student's advisor's office, student's advisor's phone, student's number of credits, and student's class standing (freshman, sophomore, etc.). List the functional dependencies that exist together with the assumptions that would support these dependencies. Change one or two of your assumptions and indicate the change this produces in the list of functional dependencies.

2. In the *CUSTOMER* relation of the example presented at the beginning of the chapter, the primary key is *CUSTNUMB*. Give an assumption under which the primary key would be the concatenation of *CUSTNUMB* and *SLSRNUMB*.

3. In the *ORDERS* relation of the example presented at the beginning of the chapter, the primary key is *ORDNUMB*. Give an assumption under which the primary key would be the concatenation of *ORDNUMB* and *CUSTNUMB*.

4. In the *ORDLNE* relation of the example presented at the beginning of the chapter, the primary key is the concatenation of *ORDNUMB* and *PARTNUMB*. Give an assumption under which the primary key would be the *ORDNUMB* alone.

5. In the *PART* relation of the example presented at the beginning of the chapter, the primary key is *PARTNUMB*. Give an assumption under which the primary key would be the concatenation of *PARTNUMB* and *WRHSNUMB*.

6. Using the types of entities found in a distribution environment (sales reps, customers, orders, parts, etc.), create an example of a relation that is in 1NF but not in 2NF and an example of a relation that is in 2NF but not in 3NF. In each case justify the answers and show how to convert to the higher forms.

7. Convert the following relation to an equivalent collection of relations that is in 3NF.

PATIENT(HHNUMB, HHNAME, HHADDR, HHBAL, <u>PATNUMB</u>, PATNAME,

SERVCODE, SERVDESC, SERVFEE, SERVDATE)

This is a relation concerning information about patients of a dentist. Each patient belongs to a household. The head of the household is designated as HH in the relation. The following dependencies exist in *PATIENT*:

```
PATNUMB --> HHNUMB, HHNAME, HHADDR, HHBAL, PATNAME
HHNUMB --> HHNAME, HHADDR, HHBAL
SERVCODE --> SERVDESC, SERVFEE
PATNUMB, SERVCODE --> SERVDATE
```

8. List the functional dependencies in the following relation, subject to the specified conditions. Convert this relation to an equivalent collection of relations that are in 3NF.

```
INVOICE(INVNUMB, CUSTNUMB, CUSTNAME, CUSTADDR, INVDATE

       PARTNUMB, PARTDESC, UNITPRCE, NUMBSHIP)
```

This relation concerns invoice information. For a given invoice (identified by the invoice number) there will be a single customer. The customer's number, name, and address appear on the invoice as well as the invoice date. Also, there may be several different parts appearing on the invoice. For each part that appears, the part number, description, price, and number shipped will be displayed. The price is from the current master price list.

9. Using your knowledge of a college environment, determine the functional dependencies that exist in the following relation. After these have been determined, convert this relation to an equivalent collection of relations that are in 3NF.

```
STUDENT(STUNUMB, STUNAME, NUMBCRED, ADVNUMB, ADVNAME,
        DEPTNUMB, DEPTNAME,

        CRSENUMB, CRSEDESC, CRSETERM, GRADE)
```

10. Determine the multivalued dependencies in the following relation. Convert this relation to an equivalent collection of relations that are in 4NF.

```
COURSE(CRSENUMB, TEXTBOOK, INSTNUMB)
```

Each course is associated with a specific set of textbooks independently of the instructors who are teaching the course (i.e., even though many instructors may be teaching the course, they will all use the same set of textbooks).

11. The following unnormalized relation is similar in content to the relation in the previous problem. Convert it to 4NF. Did you encounter the relation from the previous problem along the way?

```
COURSE(CRSENUMB, CRSEDESC, NUMBCRED,

       TEXTBOOK, INSTNUMB, INSTNAME)
```

Note that this relation has two separate repeating groups, one listing the textbooks used for the course and the other listing the instructors who are teaching the course.

12. In the customer-sales rep example, we discussed the interrelation constraint that a customer cannot be added to the database unless the corresponding sales rep already exists. List two other related constraints we might wish to impose. (**Hint:** Suppose customers represented by sales rep 6 are currently in the database. Consider the deletion of sales rep 6. Consider the process of changing sales rep 6's number to 5.)

## REFERENCES

1] Cardenas, Alfonso F., *DataBase Management Systems*, 2d ed. Allyn & Bacon, 1984.

2] Chamberlin, D. D., "Relational Data-Base Management Systems," *ACM Computing Surveys* 8, no. 1 (March 1976).

3] Codd, E. F., "Further Normalization of the Data Base Relational Model," In *Data Base Systems*, *Courant Computer Science Symposia Series*, vol. 6, Prentice-Hall, 1972.

4] Codd, E. F., "Recent Investigations into Relational Data Base Systems," Proceedings of the IFIP Congress, 1974.

5] Date, C. J., *An Introduction to Database Systems*, *Volume I*, 4th ed. Addison-Wesley, 1986.

6] Date, C. J. and White, Colin, *A Guide to DB2*, 2d ed. Addison-Wesley, 1989.

7] Fagin, Ronald, "A Normal Form for Relational Databases That is Based on Domains and Keys," *Transactions on Database Systems* 6, no. 3 (September 1981).

8] Kroenke, David, and Dolan, Kathleen A., *Database Processing: Fundamentals, Design, Implementation*, 3d ed. SRA, 1988.

9] Ullman, Jeffrey D., *Principles of Database Systems*, 2d ed. Computer Science Press, 1982; Prentice Hall, 1981.

# Introduction to Database Design

## INTRODUCTION

In all the examples we have studied thus far, the design of the databases had already been completed. The decisions had already been made regarding the collection of relations that made up the database, as well as the collection of attributes contained in these relations.

In this chapter we begin the study of database design, the process of determining the content and arrangement of data needed to support some activity on behalf of a user or group of users. **Database design** is really a two-step process. In the first step, user requirements are gathered together and a database is designed to meet these requirements as cleanly as possible. This step is called **information-level design**, and is *independent* of any individual DBMS. In the second step, this information-level design is transformed into a design for the specific DBMS that will be used to implement the system in question. In this step, which is called **physical-level design**, we are concerned with the characteristics of the specific DBMS that will be used. We are also concerned with the adequate performance of the system. Though the concept of adequate performance is difficult to define precisely, it will involve taking some measure of the space occupied by the database and some measure of processing performance, such as response time and throughput.

Both of these database design steps are critical. A poor effort made with regard to the information-level design is extremely difficult to counteract when it comes to the physical-level design. On the other hand, even an excellent information-level design is not enough to avoid a poorly performing system if the physical-level design is not done well.

Various approaches, or methodologies, have been proposed for the information level of database design. Among them are the canonical schema of James Martin [7], the entity-relationship model of Dr. Peter Chen [1], and the semantic data model of Hammer and McLeod ([4] and [6]). In this text, another methodology is presented, one that depends heavily on the relational model. While it differs in a number of ways, the methodology in the text has been heavily influenced by the methodology described by C. J. Date in [2] and also uses some of the ideas he suggests in [3]. Some of the terminology is the same as that proposed by Date.

The information-level database design process is such an important topic that two chapters of this text are devoted to it. In this chapter, we will study the basic information-level design methodology and will work through a number of examples. In chapter 8, we will go into greater detail regarding several issues within the information-level design process. In chapter 11, we will discuss the physical level of database design. At that point, we will show that even though the information-level methodology is heavily grounded in the relational model, it can still be used quite successfully when a given DBMS follows another model.

## DATABASE DESIGN GOALS

Database design is a process that takes a set of user requirements as input and produces database structures capable of supporting these requirements as output. As database designers, we have certain expectations of the user requirements and certain goals for the database structures.

First, we expect the user requirements to be as complete as possible. Specifically, this means that the user requirements for the system should address both the *functional requirements* and the *physical constraints* of the target system. The functional requirements must include:

- all reports that must be produced
- all inquiries that must be supported
- all other outputs that must be sent to other systems or to external destinations
- all update transactions that must be processed
- all calculations that must be performed

- all restrictions that the system must enforce (for example, not allowing a customer to be added for whom there is no matching sales rep and not allowing the deletion of a customer who currently has orders on file)
- all synonyms that are used for each attribute (synonyms are different names used by different users for the same attribute—for example, part number, product code, model number, and item number may all be used by different people in the same organization to refer to the same attribute)

When we turn our attention to the physical design process, we also need the user requirements to provide information about processing volumes and performance measurements. We call these volumes and measurements *physical constraints*. These would include, for example, the following estimates and constraints:

- the number of occurrences of each type of entity (sales reps, orders, customers, etc.)
- the frequency with which each report will be printed
- the length in number of lines for each report
- the response-time requirements for each query
- the response-time requirements for each update transaction
- the special security constraints that define who can access which data and in what way

Taking these user requirements as input, the information-level and physical-level design processes should produce a database design for a specific DBMS which supports these requirements and performs in an acceptable manner. The information-level design process does not entail the physical constraints from the user requirements. Instead, the information-level design is based on all other user requirements. This process results in a logical design that cleanly supports the user requirements and is independent of the characteristics of any individual DBMS. The physical-level design process utilizes this design, the physical constraints from the user requirements, and information concerning the particular DBMS involved to produce the final database structure. The overall process is illustrated in Figure 7.1 on the next page.

**Figure 7.1**

Database design
process

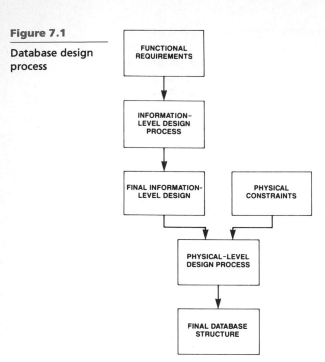

We must keep certain goals in mind as we proceed through the information-level and the physical-level design processes. The information-level design process must result in a design that is complete. That is, *all* user functional requirements must be satisfied by this design. The design itself should enforce as many of the requirements as possible, rather than force programs to do so. Among other things, this means that the design should be in 3NF or 4NF unless there is a good reason for it not to be. Any requirements that the design cannot enforce should be noted in the form of a list of requirements that the programs in the system will have to enforce. Note that efficiency of processing is not a primary goal during this step; the ultimate goal is a clean, redundancy-free design that will enforce as many of the stated requirements as possible.

Using the output of step one along with the physical requirements, the physical-level design process must result in a DBMS-specific design that still meets the user requirements. Here, however, we are concerned about system efficiency in terms of storage space, processing time, and response time. The goals of this step can and often do conflict with the goals of the information-level design. We may, for example, be able to make processing more efficient by introducing some redundancy. We may not be able to achieve 3NF with the efficiency required. It may even be necessary to use a repeating group that was removed during the process of converting to 1NF. However, any changes we make should be executed with the utmost care and in a controlled way. In addition, the need for any deviation from the information-level design must be clearly documented. Since the physical-level design may not be able to enforce all the requirements and constraints that the information-level design did, documentation must include a list of all additional restrictions that must be enforced by individual programs.

## USER VIEWS

Design of a complete database that will satisfy the requirements is not a one-step process. Unless the requirements are exceptionally simple, it is usually necessary to subdivide the overall task of database design into smaller tasks. This is often done through consideration of individual user views. A **user view** is the view of data necessary to support the operations of a particular user. For each user view, a database structure to support the view must be designed, then merged into a cumulative design. Each user view, in general, will be much simpler than the total collection of requirements, so working on individual tasks will be much more manageable than attempting to turn the design of the entire database into one task.

These user views are obtained through a variety of methods. In addition to interviewing users, we can examine reports, forms, and procedures. We can study existing file structures. We can also observe the processing that is actually taking place. We will discuss the information-gathering process to some extent in chapter 8; a complete description of this process as a means of determining these user views can be found in a systems analysis and design text. It is worth noting that the smaller the unit we work with, the easier the design of the database structures to support this unit will be. Thus, if one user requires three different reports, we might well consider each report as a separate user view, unless, of course, the design of the structure for simultaneously supporting all three reports is obvious to us.

## THE BASIC DATABASE DESIGN METHODOLOGY

The database design methodology we present involves representing individual user views, refining them to eliminate any problems, then merging them into a cumulative design. A "user" could be an actual person or group who will use the system, a report the system must produce, or a type of transaction the system must support. In the last two instances, you might think of the user as the person who will use the report or enter the transaction.

For this design methodology, we assume the users have been interviewed, that report and transaction requirements have been gathered and analyzed, and that any ambiguities have been resolved. In other words, we are assuming that the requirements needed to begin the design process are in hand.

Another "must" is that appropriate documentation will be created and maintained during the design process. Some types of documentation are addressed in the description of the methodology, but these are certainly not the only types that would be created during the design phase. Such documentation as program specifications, test plans, training plans, conversion plans, screen layouts, and printer spacing charts are also crucial.

We now turn to the methodology itself. For each user view, we need to complete the following five steps:

1. Represent the user view as a collection of relations.
2. Normalize these relations.
3. Represent all keys.
4. Determine any special restrictions.
5. Merge the result of the previous steps into the design.

We will now examine each of these steps in detail.

### Represent the User View as a Collection of Relations

When given a user view or some sort of stated requirement, we must develop a collection of relations that will support it. In some cases, the collection of relations may be obvious to us. Let's suppose, for example, that a given user view involves departments and employees. Let's assume further that each department can employ many employees but that each employee is assigned to exactly one department (a typical restriction). The design

```
DEPT (DEPTNUMB, DEPTNAME, DEPTLOC)
EMPLOYEE (EMPNUMB, EMPNAME, EMPADDR, WAGERATE, SSNUMB,
          DEPTNUMB)
```

may have naturally occurred to you and is an appropriate design. You will undoubtedly find that the more designs you have done, the easier it will be for you to develop such a collection without resorting to any special procedure. The real question is, *What procedure should be followed if a correct design is not so obvious?* In this case, we can take the following four steps:

**Step 1. Determine the entities involved and create a separate relation for each type of entity.** At this point, you do not need to do anything more than give the relation a name. For example, if a user view involves departments and employees, we can create a *DEPT* relation and an *EMPLOYEE* relation. At this point, we will write down something like this:

```
DEPT (
EMPLOYEE (
```

That is, we will write down the name of a relation and a left parenthesis, *and that is all*. Later steps will fill in the attributes in these relations.

**Step 2. Determine the primary key for each of these relations.** This will fill in one or two attributes (depending on how many attributes make up the primary key). Other attributes will not be filled in until a later step. It may seem strange, but even though we have yet to determine the attributes in the relation, we can usually determine the primary key. For example, the primary key to an *EMPLOYEE* relation will probably be the employee number, and the primary key to a *DEPT* relation will probably be the department number.

The primary key is the unique identifier, so the essential question here is, *What does it take to uniquely identify an employee or a department?* Even if we are in the process of trying to automate a system that was previously manual, some unique identifier can still usually be found in the manual system. If not, it is probably time to assign one. Let's say, for example, that in a particular manual system customers did not have numbers. The customer base was small enough that the organization felt they were not needed. Now is a good time to assign them, however, since the company is computerizing. These numbers would then be the unique identifier we are seeking.

Now, let's add these primary keys to what we have written down already. At this point, we will have something like the following:

```
DEPT (DEPTNUMB,
EMPLOYEE (EMPNUMB,
```

That is, we will have the name of the relation and the primary key, but that's all. Later steps will fill in the other attributes.

**Note:** As you have probably noticed, we will use relatively short names (eight characters or less) for the relations and attributes. This makes the designs much more concise. We will of course need to describe the meaning of these attributes in more detail at some point. We will see how to do this later in this chapter.

**Step 3. Determine the properties for each of these entities.** We can look at the user requirements, then determine the other properties of each entity which are required. These properties, along with the key identified in Step 2, will become attributes in the appropriate relations. For example, an employee entity may require *EMPNAME, EMPADDR, WAGERATE,* and *SSNUMB*

(Social Security number). The department entity may require *DEPTNAME* (department name) and *DEPTLOC* (department location). Adding these to what is already in place would produce the following:

```
DEPT (DEPTNUMB, DEPTNAME, DEPTLOC)
EMPLOYEE (EMPNUMB, EMPNAME, EMPADDR, WAGERATE, SSNUMB)
```

**Step 4. Determine relationships among the entities.** The basic relationships are one-to-many, many-to-many, and one-to-one. We will now see how to handle each of these types of relationships.

**One-to-many.** A one-to-many relationship is implemented by including the primary key of the "one" relation as a foreign key in the "many" relation. Let's suppose, for example, that each employee is assigned to a single department, but that a department can have many employees. Thus *one* department is related to *many* employees. In this case, we would include the primary key of the *DEPT* relation (the "one") as a foreign key in the *EMPLOYEE* relation (the "many"). Thus, the relations would now look like this:

```
DEPT (DEPTNUMB, DEPTNAME, DEPTLOC)
EMPLOYEE (EMPNUMB, EMPNAME, EMPADDR, WAGERATE, SSNUMB,
          DEPTNUMB)
```

**Many-to-many.** A many-to-many relationship is implemented by creating a new relation whose key is the combination of the keys of the original relations. Let's suppose that each employee can be assigned to multiple departments and that each department can have many employees. In this case, we would create a new relation whose primary key would be the combination of *EMPNUMB* and *DEPTNUMB*. Since the new relation represents the fact that an employee *works in* a department, me might choose to call it *WORKSIN*, in which case the collection of relations is as follows:

```
DEPT (DEPTNUMB, DEPTNAME, DEPTLOC)
EMPLOYEE (EMPNUMB, EMPNAME, EMPADDR, WAGERATE, SSNUMB)
WORKSIN (EMPNUMB, DEPTNUMB)
```

In some situations, no other attributes will be required in the new relation. The other attributes in the *WORKSIN* relation would be those attributes that depended on both the employee and the department, if such attributes existed. One possibility, for example, would be the date when the employee was first assigned to the department, since it depends on *both* the employee *and* the department.

**One-to-one.** If each employee is assigned to a single department and each department consists of only one employee, the relationship between employees and departments is one-to-one. Surprisingly, although the one-to-one relationships may seem like they should be the easiest kind to implement, they are not. We will discuss the issues involved in the next chapter. For now, the simplest way for us to implement a one-to-one relationship is to treat it as a one-to-many relationship. But which is the "one" part of the relationship and which is the "many" part? Sometimes looking to the future helps. For instance, in the example we are discussing, we might ask, *If the relationship changes in the future, is it more likely that one employee will be assigned to many departments, or that one department may consist of several employees rather than just one?* If we feel, for example, it is more likely that a department would be allowed to contain more than one employee, we would make *EMPLOYEE* the "many" part of the relationship. If the answer is that both things might very well happen, we might even treat the relationship as many-to-many. If neither change were likely to occur, we could actually resort to flipping a coin in order to choose the "many" part of the relationship.

## Normalize These Relations

Normalize each relation, with the target being third normal form. The target is actually fourth normal form; but a little care in the early phases of the normalization process will usually alleviate the need to consider fourth normal form.

## Represent All Keys

Identify all keys. The types of keys we must identify are primary keys, alternate keys, secondary keys, and foreign keys.

1. *Primary:* The primary key has already been determined in the earlier steps.
2. *Alternate:* An **alternate key** is an attribute or collection of attributes that could have been chosen as primary key but was not. It is not common to have alternate keys; but if they do exist, and if the system is to enforce their uniqueness, they should be so noted.
3. *Secondary:* If there are any **secondary keys** (attributes that are of interest strictly for the purpose of retrieval), they should be represented at this point. If a user were to indicate, for example, that rapidly retrieving an employee on the basis of his or her name was important, we would designate *EMPNAME* as a secondary key.
4. *Foreign:* This is in many ways the most important category, since it is through **foreign keys** that relationships are established and that certain types of integrity constraints are enforced in the database. Remember that a foreign key is an attribute (or collection of attributes) in one relation that is required to either match the value of the primary key

for some row in another relation or be null. (This is the property called **referential integrity**.) Consider, for example, the following relations:

```
DEPT (DEPTNUMB, DEPTNAME, DEPTLOC)
EMPLOYEE (EMPNUMB, EMPNAME, EMPADDR, WAGERATE, SSNUMB,
          DEPTNUMB)
```

As before, *DEPTNUMB* in the *EMPLOYEE* relation indicates the department to which the employee is assigned. We say that *DEPTNUMB* in the *EMPLOYEE* relation is a foreign key that *identifies DEPT*. Thus, the number in this attribute on any row in the *EMPLOYEE* relation must either be the number of a department that is already in the database, or be null. (Null would indicate that, for whatever reason, the employee is not assigned to a department.)

For each foreign key, we have some special decisions to make. The issues to address are as follows:

**Nulls.** Are nulls allowed? Can we store an employee without having a department number for that employee? The issue is not whether a department number must match. That is already settled by **referential integrity**, which guarantees that a department number that is actually entered must match the number of some department already in the database. The issue is whether a department number must actually be entered. Usually the answer to this question will be that nulls are not to be allowed.

**Update.** What are the rules for updating a department's number in the *DEPT* relation? If no employees are currently assigned to that department, there is no problem. If there is a row in the *EMPLOYEE* relation indicating that Jones is in department 12, however, and we decide to change the *DEPTNUMB* of department 12 to 21 in the *DEPT* relation, what do we do about Jones? Do we even permit the operation? The answer, of course, depends on the circumstances. It depends on the policies of the organization for which we are designing the database. The possible answers to the question are summarized below:

a. One possibility is to forbid this change. In this case we would say that *update is restricted*.

b. A second possibility is to allow the update but indicate that the *DEPTNUMB* for any employee in the old department had to be changed to the new department number. In this case we would say that *update cascades*.

c. The third possibility is not nearly as common as the other two. The idea here would be to allow the update but change the department number to null for those employees who were in the old department (provided, of course, that nulls were even allowed). In this case we would say that *update nullifies*.

In general, the most common choice is update cascades.

**Deletion.** What are the rules for deleting a department? Again, if no employees are currently assigned to that department, there is no problem. If there is a row in the employee relation indicating that Jones is in department 12 and we decide to delete department 12, what do we do about Jones? Do we even permit the operation? The answer, as in the case of update, depends on the policies of the organization for which we are designing the database. The possible answers to the question are summarized below:

a. One possibility is to forbid the operation. In this case we would say that *delete is restricted*.

b. A second possibility is to allow the delete and also to delete any employee who was assigned to this department. In this case we would say that *delete cascades*.

c. The third possibility is again not nearly as common as the other two. Here the deletion would be allowed but the department number for those employees who were in the old department would be changed to null (provided again, of course, that nulls were even allowed). In this case we would say that *delete nullifies*.

In general, the most common choice is delete restricted.

## Database Design Language (DBDL)

We need a mechanism for representing the relations and keys together with the restrictions just discussed. The standard mechanism for representing relations is fine but it does not go far enough. There is no routine way to represent alternate, secondary, or foreign keys, nor is there a way of representing foreign key restrictions. There is no way of indicating that a given field or attribute can accept null values. Since the methodology is based on the relational model, however, it is desirable to represent relations with the standard method. We will add additional features capable of representing additional information. The end result is **Database Design Language** (or **DBDL**).

Figure 7.2 on the next page shows sample DBDL documentation for the *EMPLOYEE* relation. In DBDL, relations and their primary keys are represented in the usual manner. Any field that is allowed to be null, such as the *EMPADDR* attribute in the *EMPLOYEE* relation, is followed by an asterisk. Underneath the relation, the various types of keys are listed. Each is preceded by an abbreviation indicating the type of key (AK – alternate key, SK – secondary key, FK – foreign key). It is sufficient to list the attribute or collection of attributes that forms an alternate or secondary key. In the case of foreign keys, however, additional restrictions must also be represented.

For each foreign key, we must represent the relation identified by the foreign key; that is, the relation whose primary key the foreign key must match. This is accomplished in DBDL by following the foreign key with an arrow pointing to the relation that the foreign key identifies. (This is the same type of notation, incidentally, that we use for functional dependencies. A functional dependence of the primary key in this relation on the foreign key really does exist, and so this is an appropriate mechanism for documenting that fact.)

If a foreign key accepts nulls, the attribute will be followed by an asterisk. Delete restrictions are documented by following the foreign key description with DLT NLF (delete nullifies), DLT RSTR (delete restricted), or DLT CSCD (delete cascades). Update restrictions are documented by following the foreign key description with UPD NLF (update nullifies), UPD RSTR (update restricted), or UPD CSCD (update cascades). The choices that were described as the most common (update cascades and delete restricted) are considered the default choices. Since the representation in Figure 7.2a happens to utilize the default choices, the representation shown in Figure 7.2b. is equally valid.

**Figure 7.2a**

DBDL for
*EMPLOYEE* relation
(all choices listed)

```
EMPLOYEE (EMPNUMB, EMPNAME, EMPADDR*, SSNUMB, DEPTNUMB,...)
        AK    SSNUMB
        SK    EMPNAME
        FK    DEPTNUMB --> DEPT DLT RSTR UPD CSCD
```

**Figure 7.2b**

DBDL for
*EMPLOYEE* relation
(default choices
listed)

```
EMPLOYEE (EMPNUMB, EMPNAME, EMPADDR*, SSNUMB, DEPTNUMB,...)
        AK    SSNUMB
        SK    EMPNAME
        FK    DEPTNUMB --> DEPT
```

Figure 7.2c summarizes the details of DBDL. Examples of DBDL will be presented in this chapter and later ones. The only feature of DBDL not listed is actually more of a tip than a rule. When several relations are listed, a relation containing a foreign key should be listed after the relation that the foreign key identifies, if possible.

**Figure 7.2c**

Summary of DBDL

### DBDL (Database Design Language)

1. Relations, attributes, and primary keys are represented in the usual way.
2. Attributes that are allowed to be null are followed by an asterisk.
3. Alternate keys are identified by the letters AK followed by the attribute(s) that comprise the alternate key.
4. Secondary keys are identified by the letters SK followed by the attribute(s) that comprise the secondary key.

| | |
|---|---|
| **Figure 7.2c**<br><br>(continued) | DBDL (continued) |

5. Foreign keys are identified by the letters FK followed by the attribute(s) that comprise the foreign key.
    a. Foreign keys are followed by an arrow pointing to the  relation identified by the foreign key.
    b. Delete rules are specified as
        DLT NLF – DELETE NULLIFIES
        DLT RSTR – DELETE RESTRICTED (default)
        DLT CSCD – DELETE CASCADES
    c. Update rules are specified as
        UPD NLF – UPDATE NULLIFIES
        UPD RSTR – UPDATE RESTRICTED
        UPD CSCD – UPDATE CASCADES (default)

In the example shown in Figures 7.2a and 7.2b, we are saying that there is a relation called *EMPLOYEE*, consisting of fields *EMPNUMB*, *EMPNAME*, *EMPADDR*, *SSNUMB* (Social Security number), *DEPTNUMB*, and so on. The *EMPADDR* field is the only one that can accept null values. The primary key is *EMPNUMB*. Another possible key is *SSNUMB*. We are interested in being able to retrieve information efficiently, based on the employee's name, so we have designated *EMPNAME* as a secondary key. The *DEPTNUMB* is a foreign key identifying the department to which the employee is assigned (it identifies the appropriate department in the *DEPT* relation). Each employee must be assigned to an actual department so *DEPTNUMB* may not be null. We are not to be able to delete a department that contains any employees, so deleting of *DEPT* is restricted. It is legitimate to change the *DEPTNUMB* in the *DEPT* relation, provided the *DEPTNUMB* of the employees who are in that department is also changed, and thus update cascades.

Note that we have just provided an example in which questions were answered in one particular way. With a different organizational policy, we would have a different example. For instance, nulls might be allowed or update might be restricted.

## A Pictorial Representation of the Database

For many people, a pictorial representation of the structure of the database is quite useful. (As the saying goes, "A picture is worth a thousand words.") Fortunately, there is an easy procedure for including a diagram representing the database structure in DBDL. The type of diagram we will use is often called a **data structure diagram**, and is similar to the type of diagram used in the Entity-Relationship (E-R) model that we will see in the next chapter. The procedure for constructing such a diagram from relations represented in DBDL follows.

1. Draw a rectangle for each relation in the DBDL design. Label the rectangle with the name of the corresponding relation.
2. For each foreign key, draw an arrow from the rectangle that corresponds to the relation being identified to the rectangle that corresponds to the relation containing the foreign key.
3. In the rare event that you have two arrows joining the same two rectangles, label the arrows with names that are indicative of the meaning of the relationships represented by the arrows.
4. If the diagram you have drawn is cluttered or messy, redraw the diagram. If possible, avoid crossing arrows, since this makes the diagram more difficult to understand.

Figure 7.3 shows the DBDL from Figure 7.2b and a corresponding data structure diagram. Notice that there is a *DEPT* rectangle and an *EMPLOYEE* rectangle. Further, since the *EMPLOYEE* relation contains a foreign key identifying the *DEPT* relation, there is an arrow from *DEPT* to *EMPLOYEE*. This arrow visually emphasizes the relationship between departments and employees. Such arrows represent one-to-many relationships (*one* department to *many* employees) with the arrow pointing to the "many" part of the relationship.

**Figure 7.3**

DBDL with data structure diagram

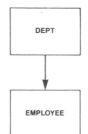

```
DEPT (DEPTNUMB, DEPTNAME)

EMPLOYEE (EMPNUMB, EMPNAME, EMPADDR*, SSNUMB, DEPTNUMB,...)
         AK    SSNUMB
         SK    EMPNAME
         FK    DEPTNUMB --> DEPT
```

## Determine Any Special Restrictions

Determine and document any special restrictions in addition to the ones already documented that involve keys. For example, perhaps a department number must be less than fifty, or employees with earnings greater than zero may not be deleted, or the state must be Ohio, Michigan, or Indiana.

It may be that many of the restrictions documented in steps 3 and 4 cannot be enforced by the DBMS and that programs will have to assume the burden for enforcing them instead. It is still critical and appropriate, however, to address these problems during the design phase. As we noted earlier, the information-level design, in this case, will produce a list of restrictions that must be enforced by programs which process the data in this database. These restrictions may simply be written in sentence form.

## Merge the Result into the Design

As soon as we have completed steps 1 through 4 for a given user view, we can merge these results into the overall design. If the view on which we have been working happens to be the first user view, then the cumulative design will be identical to the design for this first user. Otherwise, we add all the relations for this user to those which are currently in the cumulative design. We combine relations that have the same primary key to form a new relation. This relation has the same primary key as those relations which have been combined. The new relations also contain all the attributes from both relations. In the case of duplicate attributes, we remove all but one copy of the attribute. For example, if the cumulative collection already contained the following:

```
EMPLOYEE (EMPNUMB, EMPNAME, WAGERATE, SSNUMB, DEPTNUMB)
```

and the user view just completed contained the following:

```
EMPLOYEE (EMPNUMB, EMPNAME, EMPADDR)
```

then the two relations would be combined, since they would have the same primary key. All the attributes from both relations would appear in the new relation, but without duplicates. Thus, *EMPNAME* would appear only once, even though it is in each of the individual relations. The result would be:

```
EMPLOYEE (EMPNUMB, EMPNAME, WAGERATE, SSNUMB, DEPTNUMB,
          EMPADDR)
```

If we wanted to, we could reorder the attributes at this point. We might feel, for example, that placing *EMPADDR* immediately after *EMPNAME* would put it in a more natural position. This would give the following:

```
EMPLOYEE (EMPNUMB, EMPNAME, EMPADDR, WAGERATE, SSNUMB,
          DEPTNUMB)
```

We would then check the new design to ensure that it was still in third normal form. If it weren't, we would convert it to 3NF before proceeding.

We also merge the special restrictions for the user view with the list of special restrictions in the cumulative design. If a restriction from the user view is already in the design, we do not need to add it to the list. Otherwise the restriction is added to those already in place.

The process, which is summarized in Figure 7.4 on the next page, is repeated for each user view until all user views have been examined. At that point, the design is reviewed to resolve any remaining problems, and to ensure that the needs of all individual users can indeed be met. Once this has been done, the information-level design is complete.

**Figure 7.4**

Information-
level design
methodology

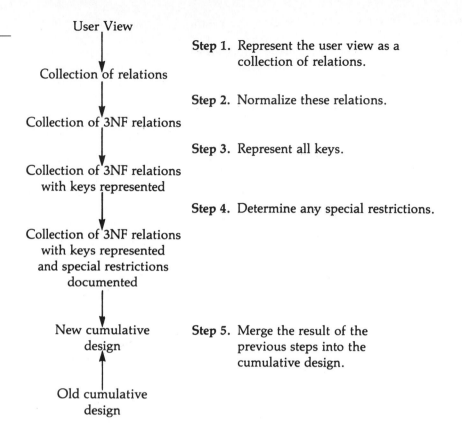

User View

Step 1. Represent the user view as a
collection of relations.

Collection of relations

Step 2. Normalize these relations.

Collection of 3NF relations

Step 3. Represent all keys.

Collection of 3NF relations
with keys represented

Step 4. Determine any special restrictions.

Collection of 3NF relations
with keys represented
and special restrictions
documented

New cumulative
design

Step 5. Merge the result of the
previous steps into the
cumulative design.

Old cumulative
design

## DATABASE DESIGN EXAMPLES

Let's now look at some examples of database design.

**EXAMPLE 1:**

For an initial example of the design methodology, let's complete an information-level design for a database that must satisfy the following constraints and requirements:

1. For a sales rep, store the sales rep's number, name, address, total commission and commission rate.
2. For a customer, store the customer's number, name, address, balance, and credit limit. In addition, store the number and name of the sales rep who represents this customer. Upon further checking with the user, we determine that a sales rep can represent many customers but a

customer must have exactly one sales rep (i.e., a customer *must have* a sales rep and cannot have more than *one*). We also determine that the only legal credit limits are 300, 500, 800, and 1,000.

3. For a part, store the part's number, description, units on hand, item class, the number of the warehouse in which the part is located, and the price. Item class must be AP (appliances), HW (housewares), and SG (sporting goods).

4. For an order, store the order number, order date, the number, name, and address of the customer who placed the order, and the number of the sales rep who represents that customer. In addition, for each line item within the order, store the part number and description, the number of the part that was ordered, and the quoted price. The following information has also been obtained from the user:

   a. Each order must be placed by a customer who is already in the customer file.

   b. There is only one customer per order.

   c. On a given order, there is at most one line item for a given part. For example, part BT04 cannot appear on several lines within the same order.

   d. The quoted price may be the same as the current price in the part master file, but it need not be. This allows the enterprise the flexibility to sell the same parts to different customers for different prices. It also allows us to change the basic price for a part without necessarily affecting orders that are currently on file.

What are the user views in the preceding example? In particular, how should the design proceed if we are given requirements that are not specifically stated in the form of user views? We might actually be lucky enough to be confronted with a series of well-thought-out user views in a form that can readily be merged into our design. On the other hand, we might only be given a set of requirements like the set we have encountered in this example. Or we might be given a list of reports and updates that a system must support. If we happen to be given the job of interviewing users and documenting their needs as a preliminary to the design process, we can make sure that their views are specified in a form that will be easy to work with when the design process starts. On the other hand, we may just have to take this information as we get it.

If the user views are not spelled out as user views per se, then we should consider each requirement that is specified to be a user view. Thus, each report or update transaction that the system must support, as well as any other requirement, such as any of those just stated, can be considered an individual user view. In fact, even if the requirements are presented as user views, we may wish to split up a particularly complex user view into smaller pieces and consider each piece a user view for the design process.

Let us now proceed with the example.

*User view 1:* This requirement, or user view, poses no particular difficulty. Only one relation is required to support this view:

SLSREP (<u>SLSRNUMB</u>, SLSRNAME, SLSRADDR, TOTCOMM, COMMRATE)

This relation is in 3NF. Since there are no foreign, alternate, or secondary keys, the DBDL representation of the relation is precisely the same as the relational model representation.

Notice we have assumed that the sales rep's number (*SLSRNUMB*) is the primary key to the relation. This is a fairly reasonable assumption, but since this information was not given in the first requirement, we would need to verify its accuracy with the user. In each of the following requirements, we shall assume that the obvious attribute (customer number, part number, and order number) is the primary key. Since this is the first user view, the "merge" step of the design methodology will produce a cumulative design consisting of this one relation. (See Figure 7.5.)

**Figure 7.5**

Cumulative design
after first user view

SLSREP

SLSREP (<u>SLSRNUMB</u>, SLSRNAME, SLSRADDR, TOTCOMM, COMMRATE)

*User view 2:* Because the first user view was relatively simple, we were able to come up with the necessary relation without having to go through the steps mentioned in the discussion of the design methodology. The second user view is a little more complicated, however, so let's use the steps suggested earlier to determine the relations. (If you've already spotted what the relations should be, you have a natural feel for the process. If so, please be patient while we work through the process.)

We'll take two different approaches to this requirement so we can see how they can both lead to the same result. The only difference between the two approaches concerns the entities that we initially identify. In the first approach, suppose we identify two entities, *sales reps* and *customers*. We would then begin with the two following relations:

SLSREP (
CUSTOMER (

After determining the unique identifiers, we add the primary keys, which would give:

```
SLSREP (SLSRNUMB,
CUSTOMER (CUSTNUMB,
```

Adding attributes for the properties of each of these entities would yield:

```
SLSREP (SLSRNUMB, SLSRNAME
CUSTOMER (CUSTNUMB, CUSTNAME, CUSTADDR, CURRBAL, CREDLIM
```

Finally, we would deal with the relationship: *one* sales rep is related to *many* customers. To implement this one-to-many relationship, we would include the key of the "one" relation in the "many" relation as a foreign key. In this case, we would include *SLSRNUMB* in the *CUSTOMER* relation. Thus, we would have the following:

```
SLSREP (SLSRNUMB, SLSRNAME)
CUSTOMER (CUSTNUMB, CUSTNAME, CUSTADDR, CURRBAL, CREDLIM,
          SLSRNUMB)
```

Both relations are in 3NF, so we can move on to representing the keys. Before doing that, however, let's investigate another approach that could have been used to determine the relations.

Suppose we didn't realize that there were really two entities and thought there was only a single entity: *customers*. We would thus begin only the single relation as follows:

```
CUSTOMER (
```

Adding the unique identifier as the primary key would give this:

```
CUSTOMER (CUSTNUMB,
```

Finally, adding the other properties as additional attributes would yield:

```
CUSTOMER (CUSTNUMB, CUSTNAME, CUSTADDR, CURRBAL, CREDLIM,
          SLSRNUMB, SLSRNAME)
```

A problem appears, however, when we examine the functional dependencies that exist in *CUSTOMER*. *CUSTNUMB* determines all the other fields, as it should. But *SLSRNUMB* determines *SLSRNAME*, yet

*SLSRNUMB* is not a candidate key. This relation, which is in 2NF, since no attribute depends on a portion of the key, is not in 3NF. Thus, converting to 3NF would produce the following two relations:

```
CUSTOMER (CUSTNUMB, CUSTNAME, CUSTADDR, CURRBAL, CREDLIM,
          SLSRNUMB)
SLSREP (SLSRNUMB, SLSRNAME)
```

Note that these are precisely the same relations we determined with the other approach. It just took us a little longer to get there.

It is these two relations that we merge into the design. Besides the obvious primary keys, *CUSTNUMB* for *CUSTOMER* and *SLSRNUMB* for *SLSREP*, the *CUSTOMER* relation now contains a foreign key, *SLSRNUMB*. We need to determine the rules pertaining to this foreign key. Since the requirement for this user is that each customer must have a sales rep, this foreign key cannot be null. We would have to check with the user to determine whether a sales rep who represented customers currently on file could be deleted or could have his or her number changed. Let's assume for the purposes of this example that both of these possibilities are forbidden. Then the DBDL for this user view would be as shown in Figure 7.6. Both update and delete are restricted for the foreign key (*SLSRNUMB*) in the *CUSTOMER* relation. Note that UPD RSTR (update restricted) must be listed, since the default is UPD CSCD. DLT RSTR (delete restricted), on the other hand, is the default and thus does not need to appear. In addition, the restriction that *CREDLIM* must be 300, 500, 800, or 1,000 is listed as a special restriction.

**Figure 7.6**

DBDL for second user view

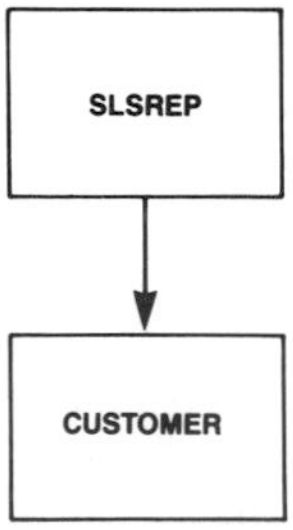

```
SLSREP (SLSRNUMB, SLSRNAME)

CUSTOMER (CUSTNUMB, CUSTNAME, CUSTADDR, CURRBAL, CREDLIM, SLSRNUMB)
     FK   SLSRNUMB --> SLSREP     UPD RSTR

Special Restrictions:
1.   CREDLIM must be 300, 500, 800, or 1000
```

There are no alternate keys, nor did the requirements state anything that would lead to a secondary key. If there were a requirement to retrieve the customer based on his or her name, for example, we would probably choose to make *CUSTNAME* a secondary key. (Since names are not unique, *CUSTNAME* is not an alternate key.)

At this point, we could represent the relation *SLSREP* in DBDL in preparation for merging this collection of relations into the collection we already have. Looking ahead, however, we see that since this relation has the same primary key as the relation *SLSREP* from the first user view, the two relations will be merged. A single relation will be formed that has the common key *SLSRNUMB* as its primary key, and that contains all the other attributes from both relations without duplication. For this second user view, the only attribute in *SLSREP* besides the primary key is *SLSRNAME*. This attribute is the same as the attribute called *SLSRNAME* already present in *SLSREP* from the first user view. Thus, nothing will be added to the *SLSREP* relation that is already in place. The cumulative design now contains the two relations *SLSREP* and *CUSTOMER*, as shown in Figure 7.7, as well as the special restriction on *CREDLIM*.

**Figure 7.7**

Cumulative design after second user view

```
SLSREP (SLSRNUMB, SLSRNAME, SLSRADDR, TOTCOMM, COMMRATE)

CUSTOMER (CUSTNUMB, CUSTNAME, CUSTADDR, CURRBAL, CREDLIM, SLSRNUMB)
     FK   SLSRNUMB --> SLSREP     UPD RSTR

Special Restrictions:
1.   CREDLIM must be 300, 500, 800, or 1000
```

*User view 3:* Like the first user view, this one poses no special problems. Only one relation is required to support it:

```
PART (PARTNUMB, PARTDESC, UNONHAND, ITEMCLSS, WRHSNUMB,
          UNITPRCE)
```

This relation is in 3NF. The DBDL representation is identical to the relational model representation.

Since *PARTNUMB* is not the primary key of any relation we have already encountered, merging this relation into the cumulative design produces a design with the three relations *SLSREP*, *CUSTOMER*, and *PART*. (See Figure 7.8.) Notice that the restriction on *ITEMCLSS* has been added to the list of special restrictions.

**Figure 7.8**

Cumulative design after third user view

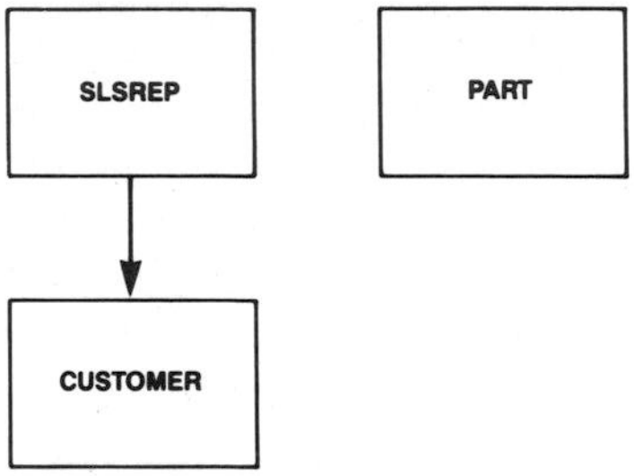

```
SLSREP (SLSRNUMB, SLSRNAME, SLSRADDR, TOTCOMM, COMMRATE)

CUSTOMER (CUSTNUMB, CUSTNAME, CUSTADDR, CURRBAL, CREDLIM, SLSRNUMB)
      FK    SLSRNUMB --> SLSREP     UPD RSTR

PART (PARTNUMB, PARTDESC, UNONHAND, ITEMCLSS, WRHSNUMB, UNITPRCE)

Special Restrictions:
1.    CREDLIM must be 300, 500, 800, or 1000
2.    ITEMCLSS must be "AP", "HW", or "SG"
```

*User view 4:* This user view is a bit more complicated, and we could approach it in several ways. Suppose we felt that only a single entity was being mentioned, namely *ORDERS*. In that case, we would create a single relation, as follows:

```
ORDERS (
```

Since orders are uniquely identified by order numbers, we would add *ORDNUMB* as the primary key, giving:

```
ORDERS (ORDNUMB,
```

Examining the various properties of an order, such as the date, the customer number, and so on, as listed in the requirement, we would add appropriate attributes, giving:

```
ORDERS (ORDNUMB, ORDDTE, CUSTNUMB, CUSTNAME, CUSTADDR,
        SLSRNUMB,
```

What about the fact that we are supposed to store the part number, description, number ordered, and quoted price for each order line on this order? One way of doing this would be to include all these attributes within the *ORDERS* relation as a repeating group (since there can be many order lines on an order). This would yield:

```
ORDERS (ORDNUMB, ORDDTE, CUSTNUMB, CUSTNAME, CUSTADDR, SLSRNUMB,
        PARTNUMB, PARTDESC, NUMBORD, QUOTPRCE)
```

At this point, we have a relation that does contain all the necessary attributes. Now we must convert this relation to an equivalent collection of relations that are in 3NF. Since this relation is not even in 1NF, we would remove the repeating group and expand the key to produce the following:

```
ORDERS (ORDNUMB, ORDDTE, CUSTNUMB, CUSTNAME, CUSTADDR, SLSRNUMB,
        PARTNUMB, PARTDESC, NUMBORD, QUOTPRCE)
```

In the new *ORDERS* relation, we have the following functional dependencies:

```
ORDNUMB --> ORDDTE, CUSTNUMB, CUSTNAMF, CUSTADDR, SLSRNUMB
CUSTNUMB --> CUSTNAME, CUSTADDR, SLSRNUMB
PARTNUMB --> PARTDESC
ORDNUMB, PARTNUMB --> NUMBORD, QUOTPRCE
```

From the discussion of the quoted price in the statement of the requirement, it should be noted that quoted price does indeed depend on *both* the order number and the part number, not on the part number alone. Since some attributes depend on only a portion of the primary key, the *ORDERS* relation is not in 2NF. Converting to 2NF would yield the following:

```
ORDERS (ORDNUMB, ORDDTE, CUSTNUMB, CUSTNAME, CUSTADDR,
        SLSRNUMB)
PART (PARTNUMB, PARTDESC)
ORDLNE (ORDNUMB, PARTNUMB, NUMBORD, QUOTPRCE)
```

The relations *PART* and *ORDLNE* are in 3NF. The *ORDERS* relation is not in 3NF, since *CUSTNUMB* determines *CUSTNAME*, *CUSTADDR*, and *SLSRNUMB*, but *CUSTNUMB* is not a candidate key. Converting the *ORDERS* relation to 3NF and leaving the other relations untouched would produce the following design for this requirement.

```
ORDERS (ORDNUMB, ORDDTE, CUSTNUMB)
CUSTOMER (CUSTNUMB, CUSTNAME, CUSTADDR, SLSRNUMB)
PART (PARTNUMB, PARTDESC)
ORDLNE (ORDNUMB, PARTNUMB, NUMBORD, QUOTPRCE)
```

This is the collection of relations that will be represented in DBDL and then merged into the cumulative design. Again, however, we can look ahead and see that *CUSTOMER* will be merged with the existing *CUSTOMER* relation, and *PART* will be merged with the existing *PART* relation. In neither case will anything new be added to the *CUSTOMER* and *PART* relations already in place, so the *CUSTOMER* and *PART* relations for this user view will not affect the overall design. To represent *ORDERS* and *ORDLNE* in DBDL, we need more information than was given concerning the foreign keys: *CUSTNUMB* in *ORDERS* and *both ORDNUMB* and *PARTNUMB* in *ORDLNE*. Let's assume that this needed information was obtained from the user and that Figure 7.9a is an accurate representation. The representation given in Figure 7.9b is identical to that in Figure 7.9a except that default choices are not listed. From this point on, we will follow the style shown in Figure 7.9b; that is, we will not list default choices.

**Figure 7.9a**

DBDL for *ORDERS* and *ORDLNE* relations (default choices listed)

```
CUSTOMER (CUSTNUMB, CUSTNAME, CUSTADDR, SLSRNUMB)

PART (PARTNUMB, PARTDESC)

ORDERS (ORDNUMB, ORDDTE, CUSTNUMB)
     FK    CUSTNUMB --> CUSTOMER    DLT RSTR    UPD CSCD

ORDLNE (ORDNUMB, PARTNUMB, NUMBORD, QUOTPRCE)
     FK    ORDNUMB --> ORDERS    DLT CSCD    UPD CSCD
     FK    PARTNUMB --> PART     DLT RSTR    UPD CSCD
```

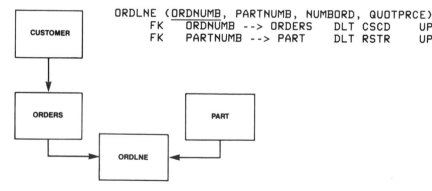

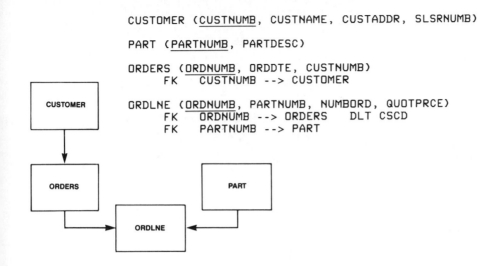

**Figure 7.9b**

DBDL for *ORDERS* and *ORDLNE* relations (default choices omitted)

```
CUSTOMER (CUSTNUMB, CUSTNAME, CUSTADDR, SLSRNUMB)

PART (PARTNUMB, PARTDESC)

ORDERS (ORDNUMB, ORDDTE, CUSTNUMB)
    FK    CUSTNUMB --> CUSTOMER

ORDLNE (ORDNUMB, PARTNUMB, NUMBORD, QUOTPRCE)
    FK    ORDNUMB --> ORDERS    DLT CSCD
    FK    PARTNUMB --> PART
```

The foreign key restrictions for *ORDERS* state that no order can exist without a customer (since *CUSTNUMB* cannot be null), that a customer with orders on file cannot be deleted (since delete is restricted), and that we can change a customer's number but that the change should cascade (since update cascades). Note that the foreign key restrictions in *ORDLNE* are a little different. Here we are saying that no *ORDLNE* can exist without both the order and the part existing. We cannot delete a part for which line items exist on some order. On the other hand, we can delete an order for which there are line items but we will automatically delete all these line items. We can change either an order number or a part number for which line items exist, provided these changes cascade.

At this point, we have completed the process for each user. We should now review the design to make sure that it will cleanly fulfill all the requirements. If problems are encountered or new information comes to light, the design must be modified accordingly. Based on the assumption that we do not have to further modify the design here, the final information-level design is shown in Figure 7.10 on the next page.

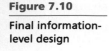

**Figure 7.10**

Final information-
level design

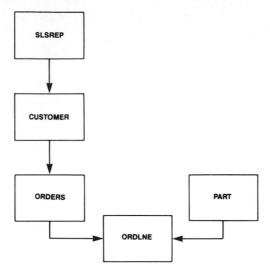

```
SLSREP (SLSRNUMB, SLSRNAME, SLSRADDR, TOTCOMM, COMMRATE)

CUSTOMER (CUSTNUMB, CUSTNAME, CUSTADDR, CURRBAL, CREDLIM, SLSRNUMB)
     FK    SLSRNUMB --> SLSREP   UPD RSTR

PART (PARTNUMB, PARTDESC, UNONHAND, ITEMCLSS, WRHSNUMB, UNITPRCE)

ORDERS (ORDNUMB, ORDDTE, CUSTNUMB)
     FK    CUSTNUMB --> CUSTOMER

ORDLNE (ORDNUMB, PARTNUMB, NUMBORD, QUOTPRCE)
     FK    ORDNUMB --> ORDERS    DLT CSCD
     FK    PARTNUMB --> PART

Special Restrictions:
1.    CREDLIM must be 300, 500, 800, or 1000
2.    ITEMCLSS must be "AP", "HW", or "SG"
```

As you may have spotted from the beginning, this set of requirements was leading to the design you have seen many times already for
Premiere Products. This is so for three reasons. First, where we have
previously encountered this example, it was used to illustrate concepts,
definitions, and nondesign processes. And it is worthwhile to see the path
by which the design process would have produced this collection of relations from a set of user requirements. Second, using a design with which
you were familiar for the first example probably helped you to focus
better on the ideas of the design methodology and to be less concerned
with the ramifications of various requirements. Third, in subsequent
examples we are going to examine how changes in requirements for this
familiar design will affect it.

## EXAMPLE 2:

Suppose the requirements of Example 1 have been changed in such a way that a customer is not necessarily represented by a single sales rep, but can be represented by several sales reps. When a customer places an order, the sales rep who gets the commission on the order *must* be one of the sales reps who represents that customer. The other requirements remain the same. How would these changes affect the design? Let's consider each of the requirements in the first example in turn to arrive at the answer.

*(Old) User view 1:* No change would need to be made to the *SLSREP* relation as a result of the new requirements.

*(Old) User view 2:* The *CUSTOMER* and *SLSREP* relations created in the previous example would have to be changed. The requirements previously resulted in a one-to-many relationship between sales reps and customers. The relationship is now many-to-many. Following the tip in the design methodology for many-to-many relationships, the relations necessary to support this user view would be:

```
CUSTOMER (CUSTNUMB, CUSTNAME, CUSTADDR, CURRBAL, CREDLIM)
SLSREP (SLSRNUMB, SLSRNAME)
CUSTSLS (CUSTNUMB, SLSRNUMB)
```

As before, the *SLSREP* relation would be merged into the existing *SLSREP* relation without adding anything to the cumulative design. The relation *CUSTOMER* would no longer have any foreign keys, and thus its DBDL representation would be exactly the same as its relational model representation:

```
CUSTOMER (CUSTNUMB, CUSTNAME, CUSTADDR, CURRBAL, CREDLIM)
```

The relation *CUSTSLS* has two foreign keys, *CUSTNUMB* and *SLSRNUMB*. Let's assume that the rules for these foreign keys have been determined and that they lead to the DBDL representation shown in Figure 7.11 on the next page.

**Figure 7.11**

DBDL for *CUSTSLS*
relation

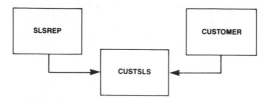

CUSTOMER (<u>CUSTNUMB</u>, CUSTNAME, CUSTADDR, CURRBAL, CREDLIM)

SLSREP (<u>SLSRNUMB</u>, SLSRNAME)

CUSTSLS (<u>CUSTNUMB</u>, SLSRNUMB)
    FK    CUSTNUMB --> CUSTOMER    DLT CSCD
    FK    SLSRNUMB --> SLSREP     DLT CSCD

*(Old) User view 3:* No changes are necessary here.

*(Old) User view 4:* The main change necessary in this requirement is due to the fact that *CUSTNUMB* no longer functionally determines *SLSRNUMB*. If we are given a customer number, we cannot now produce a unique sales rep number, since a customer can be represented by several sales reps. Consider the 2NF version of the *ORDERS* relation in the first example:

ORDERS (<u>ORDNUMB</u>, ORDDTE, CUSTNUMB, CUSTNAME, CUSTADDR,
        SLSRNUMB)

The functional dependencies would now be:

ORDNUMB --> ORDDTE, CUSTNUMB, CUSTNAME, CUSTADDR, SLSRNUMB
CUSTNUMB --> CUSTNAME, CUSTADDR (*BUT NOT* SLSRNUMB)

so that converting to 3NF would now produce:

ORDERS (<u>ORDNUMB</u>, ORDDTE, CUSTNUMB, SLSRNUMB)
CUSTOMER (<u>CUSTNUMB</u>, CUSTNAME, CUSTADDR)

The other relations in the fourth requirement, *PART* and *ORDLNE*, would not be affected by the change in requirements.

The preceding changes would take care of the new requirement that a customer could have several sales reps. What about the constraint that the sales rep who receives commission for an order must be one of the sales reps who actually represents the customer who placed the order? How do we build this constraint into the design? This is handled through an appropriate foreign key. If we say that the *CUSTNUMB* in the *ORDERS* relation is a foreign key matching *CUSTOMER*, and the *SLSRNUMB* is a foreign key matching *SLSREP*, then we are requiring only that the customer and the sales rep recorded for a given order are both currently in the database. We are *not* requiring that the sales rep actually represents that customer. Thus, we would be totally ignoring the constraint.

**Q & A**

Question:        What should be done to enforce this constraint?

Answer:                The solution is to use the concatenation of *CUSTNUMB* and *SLSRNUMB* as a foreign key which must match a tuple in the new *CUSTSLS* relation (the relation created for the second requirement in this example). A row exists in this relation only if the sales rep does indeed represent the customer. In DBDL, the *ORDERS* relation is represented in the manner shown in Figure 7.12.

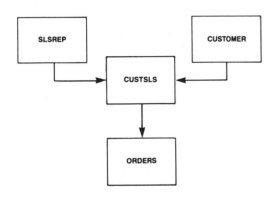

**Figure 7.12**

DBDL for *ORDERS* relation in Example 2

```
CUSTOMER (CUSTNUMB, CUSTNAME, CUSTADDR)

CUSTSLS (CUSTNUMB, SLSRNUMB)
    FK    CUSTNUMB --> CUSTOMER    DLT CSCD
    FK    SLSRNUMB --> SLSREP    DLT CSCD

ORDERS (ORDNUMB, ORDDTE, CUSTNUMB, SLSRNUMB)
    FK    CUSTNUMB, SLSRNUMB --> CUSTSLS
```

The final information-level design for this example is shown in Figure 7.13 on the next page. Let's briefly review the changes made to the design from Example 1.

Final information-
level design for
Example 2

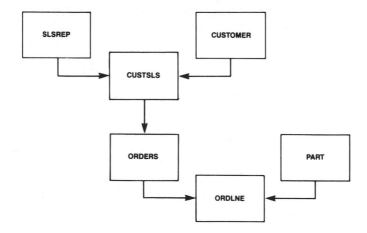

```
SLSREP (SLSRNUMB, SLSRNAME, SLSRADDR, TOTCOMM, COMMRATE)

CUSTOMER (CUSTNUMB, CUSTNAME, CUSTADDR, CURRBAL, CREDLIM, SLSRNUMB)

PART (PARTNUMB, PARTDESC, UNONHAND, ITEMCLSS, WRHSNUMB, UNITPRCE)

CUSTSLS (CUSTNUMB, SLSRNUMB)
        FK    CUSTNUMB --> CUSTOMER    DLT CSCD
        FK    SLSRNUMB --> SLSREP      DLT CSCD

ORDERS (ORDNUMB, ORDDTE, CUSTNUMB, SLSRNUMB)
        FK    CUSTNUMB, SLSRNUMB --> CUSTSLS

ORDLNE (ORDNUMB, PARTNUMB, NUMBORD, QUOTPRCE)
        FK    ORDNUMB --> ORDERS    DLT CSCD
        FK    PARTNUMB --> PART

Special Restrictions:
1.    CREDLIM must be 300, 500, 800, or 1000
2.    ITEMCLSS must be "AP", "HW", or "SG"
```

1. Since the relationship between customers and sales reps is now many-to-many, the foreign key of *SLSRNUMB* was removed from the *CUSTOMER* relation and a new relation, *CUSTSLS*, was created. The key to this relation was the concatenation of *CUSTNUMB* and *SLSRNUMB*. There were no other attributes in this relation. Note that if there had been an attribute that depended on both the customer number and the sales rep number, such as the date when a sales rep began representing a customer, or the total commission generated for the sales rep by the customer, it would have been included in this relation.

2. In the design for Example 1, we could assume that the sales rep who received credit for an order was the one and only sales rep representing the customer who placed the order. Since this is no longer the case, the sales rep number remains in the *ORDERS* relation even after converting to 3NF. (Before, it depended on the customer number and was removed.) Thus, in the *ORDERS* relation, both a customer number and a sales rep number are included.

3. We needed to ensure that the sales rep who was recorded on an order was actually the one who represented the indicated customer. To do so, we made the concatenation of *CUSTNUMB* and *SLSRNUMB* a foreign key, which is required to match the primary key of some row in the *CUSTSLS* table. In this way we ensured that the combination was meaningful, that is, that the sales rep did indeed represent the customer. Had we merely made *CUSTNUMB* a foreign key identifying *CUSTOMER* and *SLSRNUMB* a foreign key identifying *SLSREP*, we would have ensured only that both the customer and the sales rep were actually on record. It would not have ensured that that particular sales rep represented that particular customer.

## EXAMPLE 3:

The requirements of the original example have been changed in such a way that there is no relationship between customers and sales reps. When a customer places an order, it may be through any sales rep. On the order itself, however, we still need to identify both the customer placing the order and the sales rep responsible for the order. How would these changes affect the design?

*(Old) User view 1:* The new requirements would not require any changes to the *SLSREP* table.

*(Old) User view 2:* In this case, there is no relationship between customers and sales reps. We need to remove the sales rep number from the *CUSTOMER* relation, since its inclusion implies a one-to-many relationship. A new relation, as added in Example 2 to implement a many-to-many relationship, is not necessary here. To satisfy the new requirements of this example, the *CUSTOMER* relation should be:

```
CUSTOMER (CUSTNUMB, CUSTNAME, CUSTADDR, CURRBAL, CREDLIM)
```

*(Old) User view 3:* No changes are necessary here.

*(Old) User view 4:* As in Example 2, *CUSTNUMB* no longer functionally determines *SLSRNUMB*. With these new requirements there is no direct relationship between customers and sales reps. The conversion to 3NF produces:

```
ORDERS (ORDNUMB, ORDDTE, CUSTNUMB, SLSRNUMB)
CUSTOMER (CUSTNUMB, CUSTNAME, CUSTADDR)
```

The difference for this requirement between this example and the previous one appears not in the relations themselves but in the foreign keys. In Example 2, the concatenation of *CUSTNUMB* and *SLSRNUMB* was a foreign key that identified *CUSTSLS*. This ensured that the customer who was recorded for an order was actually represented by the given sales rep. In this example, we have no such constraint. We do, however, wish to ensure that the customer and the sales rep both exist. We accomplish this by making the *CUSTNUMB* a foreign key that identifies *CUSTOMER*, and *SLSRNUMB* a foreign key that identifies *SLSREP*. In DBDL, this would be represented in the manner shown in Figure 7.14.

**Figure 7.14**

DBDL for *SLSREP,*
*CUSTOMER,* and
*ORDERS* relations

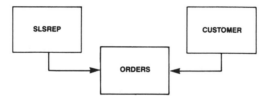

```
SLSREP (SLSRNUMB, SLSRNAME, SLSRADDR, TOTCOMM, COMMRATE)

CUSTOMER (CUSTNUMB, CUSTNAME, CUSTADDR, CURRBAL, CREDLIM)

ORDERS (ORDNUMB, ORDDTE, CUSTNUMB, SLSRNUMB)
     FK    CUSTNUMB --> CUSTOMER
     FK    SLSRNUMB --> SLSREP
```

The final information-level design for this example is shown in Figure 7.15.

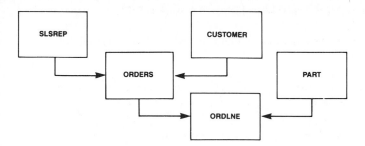

**Figure 7.15**

Final information-level design for Example 3

```
SLSREP (SLSRNUMB, SLSRNAME, SLSRADDR, TOTCOMM, COMMRATE)

CUSTOMER (CUSTNUMB, CUSTNAME, CUSTADDR, CURRBAL, CREDLIM, SLSRNUMB)
     FK    SLSRNUMB --> SLSREP   UPD RSTR

PART (PARTNUMB, PARTDESC, UNONHAND, ITEMCLSS, WRHSNUMB, UNITPRCE)

ORDERS (ORDNUMB, ORDDTE, CUSTNUMB, SLSRNUMB)
     FK   CUSTNUMB --> CUSTOMER
     FK   SLSRNUMB --> SLSREP

ORDLNE (ORDNUMB, PARTNUMB, NUMBORD, QUOTPRCE)
     FK    ORDNUMB --> ORDERS    DLT CSCD
     FK    PARTNUMB --> PART

Special Restrictions:
1.    CREDLIM must be 300, 500, 800, or 1000
2.    ITEMCLSS must be "AP", "HW", or "SG"
```

## EXAMPLE 4:

As a final example of the effect that changes in requirements can have on a design, let's suppose that the third requirement of Example 1 has been changed to the following:

3. For a part, store the part's number, description, item class, and price. In addition, for each warehouse in which the part is located, store the number of the warehouse, the description of the warehouse, and the number of units of the part that are stored in the warehouse.

It is now possible to store a part in more than one warehouse. Suppose that all the other requirements have remained the same. What changes would this bring about in the design?

The only relation in the design from Example 1 that would be affected is the *PART* relation. The initial *PART* relation in this case would be:

```
PART (PARTNUMB, PARTDESC, ITEMCLSS, UNITPRCE,
       WRHSNUMB, WRHSDESC, UNONHAND)
```

Removing the repeating group to convert to 1NF produces:

```
PART (PARTNUMB, PARTDESC, ITEMCLSS, UNITPRCE, WRHSNUMB,
        WRHSDESC, UNONHAND)
```

In the 1NF version of the *PART* relation, we have the following functional dependencies:

```
PARTNUMB --> PARTDESC, ITEMCLSS, UNITPRCE
WRHSNUMB --> WRHSDESC
PARTNUMB, WRHSNUMB --> UNONHAND
```

Using these functional dependencies to convert to 2NF produces:

```
PART (PARTNUMB, PARTDESC, ITEMCLSS, UNITPRCE)
WAREHSE (WRHSNUMB, WRHSDESC)
PARTWH (PARTNUMB, WRHSNUMB, UNONHAND)
```

These relations are also in 3NF. Note that *PARTWH* has a purpose comparable to that of *CUSTSLS* in Example 2. It is used to implement a many-to-many relationship between parts and warehouses. Besides the attributes that make up the key, there is another attribute, *UNONHAND*, in this relation. This attribute depends on both the part number and the warehouse. It is the number of units of a particular part stored in a particular warehouse. The DBDL representation for this user view is shown in Figure 7.16 and the DBDL for the final information-level design is shown in Figure 7.17.

**Figure 7.16**

DBDL for *PART,*
*WAREHSE,* and
*PARTWH* relations

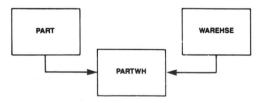

```
PART (PARTNUMB, PARTDESC, ITEMCLSS, WRHSNUMB, UNITPRCE)

WAREHSE (WRHSNUMB, WRHSDESC)

PARTWH (PARTNUMB, WRHSNUMB, UNONHAND)
     FK    PARTNUMB --> PART
     FK    WRHSNUMB --> WAREHSE
```

```
        SLSREP (SLSRNUMB, SLSRNAME, SLSRADDR, TOTCOMM, COMMRATE)

        CUSTOMER (CUSTNUMB, CUSTNAME, CUSTADDR, CURRBAL, CREDLIM, SLSRNUMB)
             FK    SLSRNUMB --> SLSREP   UPD RSTR

        ORDERS (ORDNUMB, ORDDTE, CUSTNUMB)
             FK    CUSTNUMB --> CUSTOMER

        PART (PARTNUMB, PARTDESC, ITEMCLSS, WRHSNUMB, UNITPRCE)

        WAREHSE (WRHSNUMB, WRHSDESC)

        PARTWH (PARTNUMB, WRHSNUMB, UNONHAND)
             FK    PARTNUMB --> PART
             FK    WRHSNUMB --> WAREHSE

        ORDLNE (ORDNUMB, PARTNUMB, NUMBORD, QUOTPRCE)
             FK    ORDNUMB --> ORDERS    DLT CSCD
             FK    PARTNUMB --> PART

        Special Restrictions:
        1.   CREDLIM must be 300, 500, 800, or 1000
        2.   ITEMCLSS must be "AP", "HW", or "SG"
```

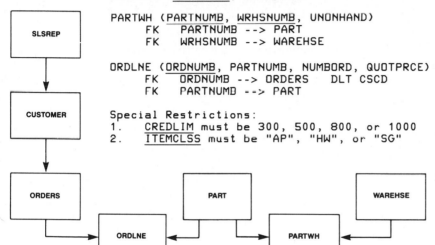

**Figure 7.17**

Final information-level design for Example 4

We could have taken another approach to determine the design for this requirement. We could have decided at the beginning of the process that two types of entities—warehouses and parts—would have a many-to-many relationship between them. Using the tips provided in the design methodology, we would be led to create a *PART* relation, a *WAREHSE* relation, and a third relation whose key would be the concatenation of the part number and the warehouse number. The *PART* relation would have part number as its primary key and also would contain the attribute description, item class, and price. The *WAREHSE* relation would have the warehouse number as its primary key and also would contain the attribute warehouse description. The function of the third relation would be to associate parts and warehouses. These decisions would lead to:

```
PART (PARTNUMB, PARTDESC, ITEMCLSS, UNITPRCE)
WAREHSE (WRHSNUMB, WRHSDESC)
PARTWH (PARTNUMB, WRHSNUMB,
```

We now would place any attribute that depends on both the part number and the warehouse number in the *PARTWH* relation. The single attribute units on hand would be the only one selected. The collection of relations now would be:

```
PART (PARTNUMB, PARTDESC, ITEMCLSS, UNITPRCE)
WAREHSE (WRHSNUMB, WRHSDESC)
PARTWH (PARTNUMB, WRHSNUMB, UNONHAND)
```

We have obtained exactly the same set of relations as we did with the previous method. In this case, however, the initial collection is in 3NF. The more experience a designer has, the more likely he or she is to create 3NF relations initially. As long as the initial collection of relations is a correct implementation of the user requirements, however, it is not so critical that this initial design be in 3NF. The second step in the methodology will still bring the design to this point.

In Examples 1 through 4, many requirements leading to the foreign key decisions were not specified. We made certain assumptions and proceeded to list the foreign key rules. In an actual design problem, these assumptions would certainly need to be discussed with and approved by the user.

We also encountered in these four examples no special restrictions that had to be documented. We will encounter some of these in the next section. There is one possible restriction we *might* wish to document in Example 4. It concerns the number of units we have on hand of a particular part in a particular warehouse. If we have none on hand, then there really is no need to store a row in the relation to record this fact. The absence of a row will imply that no units of that part are on hand in that warehouse. Thus, the restriction we would record for this user view would be that *PARTWH.UNONHAND* cannot be zero.

## FURTHER EXAMPLES OF THE METHODOLOGY

We will now turn to examples of database design in other areas.

### EXAMPLE 5:

Let's design a database for Lee. Lee is interested in movies and wants to keep information on movies, stars, and directors in a database. The only user is Lee, but we don't want to treat the whole project as a single user view: so let's assume we've asked Lee for all the reports the system is to produce, and we will treat each one as a user view. Suppose Lee has given us the following requirements.

1. For each director, list his or her number, name, the year he or she was born, and, if he or she is deceased, the year of death.
2. For each movie, list its number, title, the year the movie was made, and its type.
3. For each movie, list its number, title, the number and name of its director, the critics' rating, the MPAA rating, the number of awards the movie was nominated for, and the number it won.
4. For each movie star, list his or her number, name, birthplace, the year he or she was born, and, if he or she is deceased, the year of death.
5. For each movie, list its number and title, along with the number and name of all the stars who appeared in it.
6. For each movie star, list his or her number and name, along with the number and name of all the movies in which he or she starred.

With these six reports as the user views, let's move on to the design of Lee's database. (**Note:** We will assume that the default choices for foreign keys are appropriate throughout this design.)

*User view 1:* The only entity in this user view is *director*. The relation to support it is as follows:

DIRECTOR (<u>DIRNUMB</u>, DIRNAME, DIRBORN, DIRDIED)

This relation is in 3NF. The primary key is *DIRNUMB*. There are no alternate or foreign keys. Let's assume Lee wants to be able to access a director rapidly on the basis of his or her name. Then we will make *DIRNAME* a secondary key.

Since this is the first user view, there is no previous cumulative design. So at this point, the new cumulative design will consist solely of the design for this user view. It is shown in Figure 7.18.

```
DIRECTOR (DIRNUMB, DIRNAME, DIRBORN, DIRDIED)
    SK    DIRNAME
```

**Figure 7.18**

DBDL for *MOVIE* database after first requirement

*User view 2:* The only entity in this user view is *movie*. The relation to support it is as follows:

MOVIE (<u>MVNUMB</u>, MVTITLE, YEARMADE, MVTYPE)

This relation is also in 3NF. The primary key is *MVNUMB*, and there are no alternate or foreign keys. Let's assume Lee wants to be able to access a movie rapidly on the basis of its title. Therefore, we will make *MVTITLE* a secondary key.

Since no relation in the cumulative design has *MVNUMB* as its primary key, this relation will simply be added to the collection of relations in the cumulative design during the merge step. The result is shown in Figure 7.19.

**Figure 7.19**

DBDL for *MOVIE* database after second requirement

```
DIRECTOR (DIRNUMB, DIRNAME, DIRBORN, DIRDIED)
      SK    DIRNAME

MOVIE (MVNUMB, MVTITLE, YEARMADE, MVTYPE)
      SK    MVTITLE
```

*User view 3:* There are two entities here, *directors* and *movies,* and a one-to-many relationship between them. This leads to the following:

```
DIRECTOR (DIRNUMB, DIRNAME)
MOVIE (MVNUMB, MVTITLE, CRITRTNG, MPAARTNG, NUMNOMS,
            NUMAWRDS, DIRNUMB)
```

where *MOVIE.DIRNUMB* is a foreign key identifying director. Merging these relations with those that are already in place does not add any new attributes to the *DIRECTOR* relation, but does add some new attributes — *CRITRTNG* (critics rating), *MPAARTNG* (MPAA rating), *NUMNOMS* (number of nominations), *NUMAWRDS* (number of awards), and *DIRNUMB* — to the *MOVIE* relation. The result of the merge is shown in Figure 7.20.

**Figure 7.20**

DBDL for *MOVIE* database after third requirement

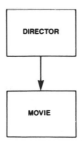

```
DIRECTOR (DIRNUMB, DIRNAME, DIRBORN, DIRDIED)
      SK    DIRNAME

MOVIE (MVNUMB, MVTITLE, YEARMADE, MVTYPE, CRITRTNG, MPAARTNG,
            NUMNOMS, NUMAWRDS, DIRNUMB)
      SK    MVTITLE
      FK    DIRNUMB --> DIRECTOR
```

*User view 4:* The only entity in this user view is *movie star.* Here is the relation to support it:

```
STAR (STARNUMB, STARNAME, BRTHPLCE, STARBORN, STARDIED)
```

Like the first two relations, this relation is in 3NF. The primary key is *STARNUMB,* and there are no alternate or foreign keys. Again, it would probably be useful to be able to retrieve a star rapidly on the basis of his or her name. Thus we will make *STARNAME* a secondary key. The result of merging this with the cumulative design is shown in Figure 7.21.

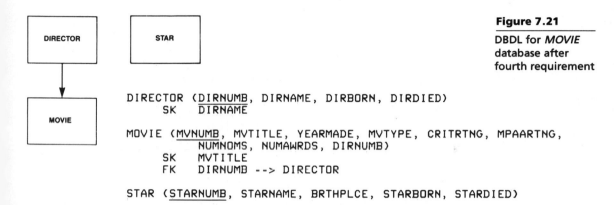

**Figure 7.21**

DBDL for *MOVIE* database after fourth requirement

```
DIRECTOR (DIRNUMB, DIRNAME, DIRBORN, DIRDIED)
     SK    DIRNAME

MOVIE (MVNUMB, MVTITLE, YEARMADE, MVTYPE, CRITRTNG, MPAARTNG,
          NUMNOMS, NUMAWRDS, DIRNUMB)
     SK    MVTITLE
     FK    DIRNUMB --> DIRECTOR

STAR (STARNUMB, STARNAME, BRTHPLCE, STARBORN, STARDIED)
```

*User view 5:* Suppose we were to decide that the only entity mentioned in this requirement was *movies.* We would then create this relation:

```
MOVIE (
```

with MVNUMB as the primary key. This would produce the following:

```
MOVIE (MVNUMB,
```

The other properties included the movie title and the number and name(s) of the movie's stars. Since movies usually have more than one star, the star number and star name will form a repeating group. We thus have the following:

```
MOVIE (MVNUMB, MVTITLE, STARNUMB, STARNAME)
```

We convert this relation to 1NF by removing the repeating group and expanding the key. This gives:

```
MOVIE (MVNUMB, MVTITLE, STARNUMB, STARNAME)
```

In this relation, we have the following functional dependencies:

```
MVNUMB --> MVTITLE
STARNUMB --> STARNAME
```

The relation is not in 2NF, since some attributes depend on just a portion of the key. Converting to 2NF gives:

```
MOVIE (MVNUMB, MVTITLE)
STAR (STARNUMB, STARNAME)
MOVSTAR (MVNUMB, STARNUMB)
```

The primary keys are indicated. In the *MOVSTAR* relation, which relates movies to the stars who performed in them, *MVNUMB* is a foreign key that identifies *MOVIE*, and *STARNUMB* is a foreign key that identifies *STAR*. In other words, for a row to exist in the *MOVSTAR* relation, *both* the movie number *and* the star number must already be in the database.

The *MOVIE* relation will merge with the existing *MOVIE* relation without adding anything new. Similarly, the *STAR* relation will not add anything new to the existing *STAR* relation. The *MOVSTAR* relation is new and will appear as part of the new cumulative design, which is given in Figure 7.22.

**Figure 7.22**

DBDL for *MOVIE* database after fifth requirement

```
DIRECTOR (DIRNUMB, DIRNAME, DIRBORN, DIRDIED)
      SK    DIRNAME

MOVIE (MVNUMB, MVTITLE, YEARMADE, MVTYPE, CRITRTNG, MPAARTNG,
           NUMNOMS, NUMAWRDS, DIRNUMB)
      SK    MVTITLE
      FK    DIRNUMB --> DIRECTOR

STAR (STARNUMB, STARNAME, BRTHPLCE, STARBORN, STARDIED)

MOVSTAR (MVNUMB, STARNUMB)
      FK    MVNUMB --> MOVIE
      FK    STARNUMB --> STAR
```

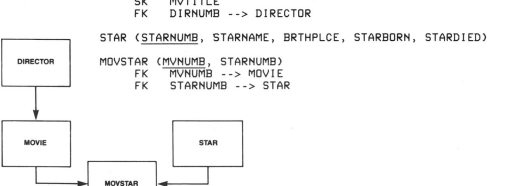

Q & A

| | |
|---|---|
| Question: | Since the only attributes in the *MOVSTAR* relation are those that make up the primary key, is the relation really necessary? Or could it be removed from the cumulative design? |
| Answer: | The function of the *MOVSTAR* relation is to relate movies to the stars who appeared in them. We cannot remove it from the cumulative design without losing this vital information; that is, we would not be able to tell which stars had appeared in which pictures. |
| Question: | How would the design for this user view have turned out if we had started out with two entities — *movie* and *star* — instead of just the single entity *movie*? |
| Answer: | In the first step, we would have these two relations: |

```
MOVIE (
STAR (
```

Adding the primary keys would give:

```
MOVIE (MVNUMB,
STAR (STARNUMB,
```

Filling in the other attributes would give:

```
MOVIE (MVNUMB, MVTITLE)
STAR (STARNUMB, STARNAME)
```

Finally, we have to implement the relationship between *MOVIE* and *STAR*. Since a movie can have many stars, and a star can appear in many movies, the relationship is many-to-many. To implement a many-to-many relationship, we add a new relation whose primary key is the combination of the primary keys of the other relations. Doing this, we produce the following:

```
MOVIE (MVNUMB, MVTITLE)
STAR (STARNUMB, STARNAME)
MOVSTAR (MVNUMB, STARNUMB)
```

Thus, we end up with exactly the same collection of relations, which illustrates a point made earlier: There's more than one way of arriving at a correct result.

*User view 6:* This user view leads to precisely the same set of relations that were created for user view 5.

We have now reached the end of the requirements, and the design shown in Figure 7.22 represents the complete information-level design. You should take a moment to review each of the requirements to make sure they can all be satisfied.

**Q & A**

---

**Question:**     What if Lee's requirements changed in such a way that, instead of simply listing the stars who appeared in a given movie, he also needed to list whether they appeared in a leading role or a supporting role?

**Answer:**          We would need a new attribute, perhaps called *TYPEROLE*, that would be used to indicate whether the role a star played was a leading role or a supporting role. Since a given movie usually has both leading and supporting roles, this attribute would not depend on *MVNUMB* alone. Further, since a given actor or actress may appear in a leading role in one movie and a supporting role in another, the attribute would not depend on *STARNUMB* alone. Rather, it would depend on the combination of *MVNUMB* and *STARNUMB*, and thus would be added to *MOVSTAR*, the relation that had this combination as its primary key. (If no relation already existed with this combination as its primary key, we would have to create one at this point.) No other changes need be made to the design.

---

## EXAMPLE 6:

As a final example of the application of the design methodology, consider the following set of requirements that must be met by a database-oriented system at Marvel College.

**Update (transaction) requirements:**

1. Enter/edit dormitory information (number and name).
2. Enter/edit faculty information (number, name, office number, phone, department number).
3. Enter/edit course information (course code, description, number of credits).
4. Enter/edit prerequisites for a given course.
5. Enter/edit sections of courses for current offerings (schedule code, course code and section letter, and the number of the faculty member who is teaching the course; e.g., schedule code 2345 is section A of course CS253 and is taught by the faculty member whose number is 3).

6. Enter/edit student information (student number, name, permanent address, status, dorm number). Status is a code indicating the type of student (full-time, part-time, continuing education, etc.), and the dorm number is the number of the dormitory in which the student resides, provided the student lives in a dorm.
7. Determine whether a student has the necessary prerequisites for a given course. If the answer is yes, enroll the student in the course.

**Report requirements:**

8. For each department, list its number and name and the number and name of each of its faculty members.
9. For each dormitory, list its number and name and the number and name of all the students living there.
10. For each course, list its code and description and the code and description of any of its prerequisites.
11. For each faculty member, list all sections of all courses he or she is currently teaching.
12. For each student, list all courses he or she has taken and the grade received.
13. For each section of each course, list the schedule code, section letter, course code, course description, the number and name of the professor who is teaching the course, and the number, name, and status of each student who is taking the course.
14. Given a student's name, list the student's number.

Each of the preceding requirements will be considered a user view.

*User view 1:* No particular problem is involved in the decision that this user view should be:

DORM (<u>DORMNUMB</u>, DORMNAME)

This relation is in 3NF. The only key of any kind is the primary key of *DORMNUMB*. Note that this user view, like many others, does not specifically state anything about one property uniquely identifying any of the others. We will assume in each case that the appropriate users have been contacted and that in each case the obvious property, in this case the *DORMNUMB*, is indeed a unique identifier. The design for user view 1 is represented in DBDL exactly as it is represented in the relational model.

*User view 2:* User view 2 is similar to user view 1 in that there is an obvious relation:

```
FACULTY (FACNUMB, FACNAME, OFFICE, PHONE, DEPTNUMB)
```

Let's assume we are not interested in the fact that *OFFICE* determines *PHONE*. Thus, this relation is in 3NF.

In reviewing the attributes in this relation, we discover the need for a further step. It certainly would seem that *DEPTNUMB* must be a foreign key identifying a row in some *DEPT* relation. So far, we have not encountered such a relation. The safest thing to do at this point is to assume that there will be a *DEPT* relation, whose key is *DEPTNUMB*, with other attributes yet to be determined. If, by the time the design is completed, no other attributes have been filled in, we could consider dropping this relation from the collection. We also would have to determine from the user the assumptions concerning the relationship between faculty and departments so that we could make the appropriate decision concerning the foreign key rules. Let's assume that this has been done and that the decisions dictate the representation shown in Figure 7.23.

**Figure 7.23**

DBDL for *FACULTY* relation

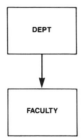

```
FACULTY (FACNUMB, FACNAME, OFFICE, PHONE, DEPTNUMB)
   FK    DEPTNUMB --> DEPT
```

In many of the following user views just the relation(s) that are involved will be described. It will be up to you to document these relations in DBDL.

*User view 3:* This view leads to the following single relation:

```
COURSE (CRSECODE, CRSEDESC, NUMBCRED)
```

*User view 4:* In this user view a many-to-many relationship really does exist between courses. A course could have many prerequisites and could itself be a prerequisite to many other courses. This is then the many-to-many relationship described earlier, except that the entities on both sides of the relationship are the *same type of entity*, namely, courses. The rules for many-to-many relationships described earlier still apply, however.

This user view thus includes the following two relations:

```
COURSE (CRSECODE, CRSEDESC)
PREREQ (CRSECODE, PRERCODE)
```

For example, if CS151 and CS153 were prerequisites for CS253, then the two rows (CS253, CS151) and (CS253, CS153) would appear in the *PREREQ* table. If CS253 were a prerequisite for CS350 and CS353, then the two rows (CS350, CS253) and (CS353, CS253) would appear in the *PREREQ* table.

You will notice that this *COURSE* relation is not a new relation. It is contained in the relation already encountered in user view 3 and is not added to the cumulative collection of relations. The relation *PREREQ* is new, however. Its representation in DBDL is shown in Figure 7.24. Notice that we have specified DLT CSCD (delete cascades) for both foreign keys. Since there are two arrows connecting the rectangles, we must name them. In the figure, we have called one *HAS_PREREQ* and the other *IS_PREREQ*, since these terms are descriptive of the relationships represented by the arrows.

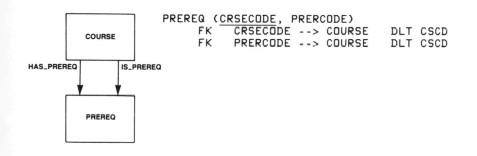

```
PREREQ (CRSECODE, PRERCODE)
      FK    CRSECODE --> COURSE    DLT CSCD
      FK    PRERCODE --> COURSE    DLT CSCD
```

**Figure 7.24**

DBDL for *PREREQ* relation

*User view 5:* The relation necessary for this user view is:

```
SECTION(SCHDCODE, CRSECODE, SECTLETT, FACNUMB)
```

In this relation, *FACNUMB* is a foreign key identifying *FACULTY*, and *CRSECODE* is a foreign key identifying *COURSE*.

*User view 6:* The relation necessary for this user view is:

```
STUDENT(STUNUMB, STUNAME, PERMADDR, STATUS, DORMNUMB)
```

Here, *DORMNUMB* is a foreign key identifying DORM. But we could have NULLS ARE ALLOWED for this foreign key to provide for the possibility of students not residing in dorms. (Remember that this is indicated by placing an asterisk after *DORMNUMB* in the DBDL representation of this relation.) We would also indicate at this point that status is restricted to values of "F" for full-time, "P" for part-time, and "C" for continuing education.

*User view 7:* Given user view 4, we have the relations necessary to determine a course's prerequisites. In addition, we must be able to determine which courses are taken by a given student. Looking ahead to user view 12, we can see that this requires listing all the courses each student has taken, along with the grade received. The combination of user view 4 and user view 12 provides the requirements for determining whether a student has the necessary prerequisites. (See the treatment of user view 12 for details concerning the relation that must be added to support this view.) The only new relation needed is one that will allow us to enroll a student in a course. The relation to support this is:

ENROLL(<u>STUNUMB</u>, SCHDCODE)

where *SCHDCODE* is the code for the particular section of the course in which the student is to be enrolled. In the exercises, you will be asked why this relation is a better choice than the following, which would be another possibility:

ENROLL(<u>STUNUMB</u>, <u>CRSECODE</u>, SCHDCODE)

Note that in this example we are assuming that a student will enroll in only one section of a given course, which means that a student number, coupled with a course code, would give us the schedule code. (Since student 123 can be enrolled in only one section of CS253, for example, the combination of this student number together with this course code will allow us to determine the unique schedule code.)

*User view 8:* The initial relation that we might try is:

DEPT (<u>DEPTNUMB</u>, DEPTNAME, FACNUMB, FACNAME)

In this relation, the attributes *FACNUMB* and *FACNAME* form a repeating group. Converting this relation to 1NF yields:

DEPT (<u>DEPTNUMB</u>, DEPTNAME, <u>FACNUMB</u>, FACNAME)

Or does it? This is what the process gives us. Let's assume, however, we have determined that *DEPTNUMB* is functionally dependent on *FACNUMB*. Then the primary key is not the combination of *DEPTNUMB* and *FACNUMB*, but merely *FACNUMB*. The correct normalization should be:

```
DEPT (DEPTNUMB, DEPTNAME, FACNUMB, FACNAME)
```

This relation violates not 2NF, as we might have guessed, but 3NF. Converting to 3NF gives:

```
DEPT (DEPTNUMB, DEPTNAME)
FAC (FACNUMB, FACNAME, DEPTNUMB)
```

You will notice that *FAC* is really a portion of the *FACULTY* relation encountered earlier; no new attributes have been added. If there were any new attributes, they would have been added to the relation already in place. You will also notice that we now have the *DEPT* relation that was discussed in user view 2.

*User view 9, user view 10, and user view 11:* All three user views are satisfied by relations already in place and will not be discussed here.

*User view 12:* This user view requires a many-to-many relationship between students and courses and adds the following relation to the collection already in place:

```
STUCRSE (STUNUMB, CRSECODE, GRADE)
```

The description in DBDL of this relation would be similar to the description of *PREREQ* in user view 4.

*User view 13:* This user view can be satisfied with relations already in place and will not be discussed here.

*User view 14:* This user view would cause us to add *STUNAME* as a secondary key in the *STUDENT* relation of user view 6.

Having reached this point, we would review the entire collection of relations. We would match the relations against all user requirements to make sure that the requirements can all be met and that the final design is in 3NF.

## *ADDITIONAL DOCUMENTATION*

The documentation we have seen so far indicates the relations and attributes that make up our database. We can easily spot the various keys in our database. We can spot relationships by looking at the foreign keys or by looking at the arrows in the diagram.

We cannot, however, tell much about the attributes. From the name of the attribute, we can guess the meaning of the attribute. Since we keep the names relatively short in order to make the relations in DBDL more concise, we still need additional information about the specific meaning of the attribute. In addition, the DBDL does not give any information about the format of the data that can be entered into the various attributes. We cannot tell, for example if an attribute is numeric (that is, it will only contain numbers), or character (it can contain any characters). Nor can we tell the size of the data the attribute will contain. We don't know the largest number that can be entered as a customer's balance or the longest name that can be entered as a customer's name. These are all important details.

To address these issues, we include the two additional pieces of documentation discussed in the following sections.

### Domain Documentation

A **domain** is a pool of possible values for a given attribute. For a DBMS to support domains, it must allow the database administrator to specify domains for each attribute of each relation in the database. The DBA gives a name and description to the domain, then specifies the values within it. The specification may be broad, stating that the domain contains a thirty-character string. On the other hand, it may be so tightly specified that a specific set of values is actually listed (for example, the domain CREDLIM contains one of four values: 300, 500, 800, or 1,000). Only values from the domains for the attributes are accepted in any updates to the database, and this must be enforced by the DBMS. Further, if users attempt to join on attributes coming from two different domains, the system either should reject the join or, perhaps better, should warn the user that the join is suspicious at best.

Without support for domains, for example, the system has no way of knowing that joining customers to sales reps where the customer's ZIP code matches the sales rep's Social Security number is not a meaningful join. Both fields are numeric. In fact, with nine-digit ZIP codes, both fields are even the same length. If domains are used, it is a simple matter for the DBMS to determine that the values for one of the fields are drawn from the domain *SOCIAL_SECURITY_NUMBER* and the values for the other are drawn from the domain *ZIP_CODES*. It does not matter that ultimately each domain is described as containing nine-digit numbers. They are still separate domains, and that is all the system needs to know.

We have described what it means for a system to support domains. At the present time, few systems provide this support to any adequate degree, but this is changing, and the next few years should bring domain support to many of the leading systems. Even though this support may not be present on the DBMS we are using, domains are an important concept in the design process and are discussed for that reason.

Domains provide valuable documentation for the type of data that can be entered for any attribute, the meaning of the attribute, and any special constraints that pertain to data in the domain. In DBDL, we represent domains as shown in Figure 7.25.

**Figure 7.25**

Sample domain definitions

```
************************* DOMAIN DEFINITIONS ****************************
    DOMAIN            TYPE      DESCRIPTION               RESTRICTIONS
--------------    ---------  -------------------    ------------------------
ADDRESS           C(40)      Addresses              Street,City,State
BALANCE           D(6,2)     Customer balances
COMMISSION        D(8,2)     Commission amounts
COMMISSION-RATE   D(2,2)     Commission rates
CREDIT-LIMIT      D(4)       Credit limits          Must be 300, 500, 800, or
                                                       1000
CUSTOMER-NUMBER   D(6)       Customer numbers
DATE              D(6)       Dates                  Stored in MMDDYY format
ITEM-CLASS        C(2)       Item classes           Must be AP (appliances),
                                                       HW (housewares), or
                                                       SG (sporting goods)
NAME              C(20)      Names
ORDER-NUMBER      D(5)       Order numbers
PRICE             D(6,2)     Item prices
PART-NUMBER       C(4)       Part numbers
PART-             C(20)      Part descriptions
   DESCRIPTION
SLSREP-NUMBER     D(2)       Sales rep numbers
UNITS             D(4)       Units (number of units
                               of a part)
WAREHOUSE-        D(2)       Warehouse numbers
   NUMBER
```

The four columns in the chart give the following information:

1. **DOMAIN.** The first column gives the name of the domain. The name should be as descriptive as possible.
2. **TYPE.** The second column gives format details. In this column, "D" stands for DECIMAL (numbers) and "C" stands for CHARACTER. The number in parentheses indicates the maximum number of positions. An entry of D(4), for example, indicates that the entries in the domain are numbers and are at most four digits in length. An entry of C(20) indicates that the field is a character field of length 20. If a decimal entry contains two numbers, the second represents the number of decimal places. An entry of D(6,2), for example, represents a

number that is at most six digits in length, the last two of which are decimal places. The biggest number that could be entered with this entry would be 9999.99 (the decimal point is not counted as one of the six positions).

3. **DESCRIPTION.** The third column describes the domain. Thus we know that the domain called *CREDIT_LIMIT* is the domain consisting of all possible credit limits.

4. **RESTRICTIONS.** The fourth column describes any restrictions on the domain. The entry in the fourth column for *CREDIT_LIMIT* indicates that the only legitimate values are 300, 500, 800, or 1,000.

### Attribute Documentation

Attributes in the relations are related to domains as shown in Figure 7.26. Entering the domain for a given attribute is then sufficient to give a description of the meaning, format details, and any restrictions placed on the column. The only thing that might be added is any description of this particular column not covered by the description of the domain itself. (See the description of the *QUOTPRCE* attribute in the *ORDLNE* relation, for example.)

**Figure 7.26**

Use of domains in table definitions

```
***************** RELATION AND ATTRIBUTE DEFINITIONS *****************
   RELATION  ATTRIBUTE       DOMAIN              COMMENTS
  ---------- ---------   -------------------   ------------------------
   CUSTOMER                                    Customer Table
             CUSTNUMB    CUSTOMER-NUMBER
             CUSTNAME    NAME
             CUSTADDR    ADDRESS
             CURRBAL     BALANCE               Current balance
             CREDLIM     CREDIT-LIMIT          Credit limit
             SLSRNUMB    SLSREP-NUMBER

   ORDERS                                      Orders Table
             ORDNUMB     ORDER-NUMBER
             ORDDTE      DATE                  Order date
             CUSTNUMB    CUSTOMER-NUMBER

   ORDLNE                                      Order Line Table
             ORDNUMB     ORDER-NUMBER
             PARTNUMB    PART-NUMBER
             NUMBORD     UNITS                 Number of units ordered
             QUOTPRCE    PRICE                 Price that was quoted for the
                                               part; could be the same as
                                               the price for the part in the
                                               PART relation, but need not
                                               be
```

```
PART                                        Part Table                Figure 7.26
            PARTNUMB    PART-NUMBER
            PARTDESC    PART-DESCRIPTION                                (continued)
            UNONHAND    UNITS                   Units on hand
            ITEMCLSS    ITEM-CLASS
            WRHSNUMB    WAREHOUSE-NUMBER        Number of the warehouse in which
                                                   the part is located  (all
                                                   units of a given part must be
                                                   located in the same
                                                   warehouse)
            UNITPRCE    PRICE                   Unit price

SLSREP                                      Sales Rep Table
            SLSRNUMB    SLSREP-NUMBER
            SLSRNAME    NAME
            SLSRADDR    ADDRESS
            TOTCOMM     COMMISSION              Total commission earned
            COMMRATE    COMMISSION-RATE
```

## SUMMARY

In this chapter, we began the study of database design, which we defined as the process of determining the structure of the underlying database that will support some collection of user requirements. This design is divided into two phases: information-level design and physical-level design. In the information-level design, we attempt to capture the essence of the requirements in as clean a structure as possible, without any regard for the DBMS that will actually be used to implement the final system. In fact, if the final system were to be implemented without using a DBMS, the design process would still be the same at the information level. In the physical-level design, we are concerned with transforming the information-level design to a design for the particular DBMS that will be used in the implementation of the system so the system will perform in an acceptable manner. Discussion of information-level design will be continued in greater detail in chapter 8. The topic of physical-level design will be explained further in chapter 11.

We described the goals of database design. The design produced during the information-level phase should be complete and should enforce, as thoroughly as possible, the constraints imposed on the system by the user requirements. We also discussed the process of classifying the requirements for the system as user views.

We presented the basic information-level design methodology, which consists of repeating several steps for each user view. These steps are as follows:

1. Represent the user view as a collection of relations.
2. Normalize these relations.
3. Represent all keys.
4. Determine any special restrictions.
5. Merge the result of the previous steps into the design.

Once these steps are completed for each user view, the final design is reviewed to ensure that each requirement can indeed be met. If problems are discovered, the design is altered as necessary to resolve them.

We presented a series of examples intended to illustrate the concepts of the methodology. Finally, we looked at domains and how they can be used in documenting database designs.

For examples of other database-design methodologies, see [1], [2], [3], [5], [6], [7], and [8].

## REVIEW QUESTIONS

1. Describe the inputs to the database design process. Which of these inputs are useful with regard to the information-level design? Which are useful with regard to the physical-level design?
2. Describe the outputs produced by the process of database design. What is the difference between the output produced during the information-level design phase and the output produced during the physical-level design phase?
3. Describe the goals of the information-level database design and the goals of the physical-level database design.
4. Define the term *user view* as it applies to database design.
5. What is the purpose of breaking down the overall design problem into the consideration of user views?
6. Under what circumstances would you not have to break down the overall design into a consideration of user views?
7. The information-level design methodology presented in this section contains a number of steps to be repeated for each user view. List the steps and briefly describe the kinds of activity that must take place at each step.
8. Describe the function of each of the following types of keys:
   a. primary
   b. alternate
   c. secondary
   d. foreign
9. What are domains? What role do they play in the documentation of database designs? How are they related to the attributes in the design?

# EXERCISES

1. Suppose a given user view contains information about employees and projects. Suppose further that each employee has a unique employee number and that each project has a unique project number. Explain how you would implement the relationship between employees and projects in each of the following scenarios:
   a. Many employees can work on a project, but each employee can only work on a *single* project.
   b. An employee can work on many projects, but each project has a *unique* employee who works on the project.
   c. An employee can work on many projects, and a project can be worked on by many employees.
2. Suppose we have a foreign key called *ADVNUMB* in a *STUDENT* relation. This foreign key identifies a relation called *ADVISOR*. In describing the foreign key, we have several options: in deciding how to treat NULLS, in determining restrictions for the deletion of an advisor, and in determining update restrictions for *ADVISOR.ADVNUMB*. In each case, list the options and describe the significance of the various possible choices.
3. A database is required to support the following requirements at a college:
   a. For a department, store its number and its name.
   b. For an advisor, store his or her number and name and the number of the department to which he or she is assigned.
   c. For a course, store the course code and the course description (e.g., MTH110, ALGEBRA).
   d. For a student, store his or her number and name. For each course the student has taken, store the course code, course description, and grade received. In addition, store the number and name of the student's advisor. Assume that an advisor may advise any number of students but that each student has exactly one advisor.

      Complete the information-level design for this set of requirements. Use your own experience to determine any assumptions you need that are not stated in the problem. Represent the answer in DBDL.
4. List the changes that would need to be made in your answer to exercise 3 if a student could have more than one advisor and an advisor could advise more than one student.

5. List the changes that would need to be made in your answer to exercise 3 if a student could have more than one advisor but an advisor could advise only one student.

6. List the changes that would need to be made in your answer to exercise 3 if a student could have at most one advisor but did not have to have an advisor.

7. Suppose that in addition to the requirements specified in exercise 3, we must also store the number of the department in which the student is majoring. Indicate the changes this would cause in the design for each of the following situations:

   a. The student must be assigned an advisor who is in the department in which the student is majoring.

   b. The student's advisor does not necessarily have to be in the department in which the student is majoring.

8. For the database-design problem given in Example 6, write in DBDL the complete collection of relations in the final information-level design.

9. Discuss the significance of the foreign key decisions that were made in this design.

10. In user view 7, explain why the relation

    ENROLL (<u>STUNUMB</u>, <u>SCHDCODE</u>)

    is a better choice than

    ENROLL (<u>STUNUMB</u>, <u>CRSECODE</u>, <u>SCHDCODE</u>)

11. Determine the relations necessary to support user view 9, user view 10, and user view 11. Normalize them and merge the results into the cumulative design to demonstrate the claim made in the example that these three views can be satisfied with relations already in place.

12. Repeat exercise 11 for user view 13.

13. In the discussion of user view 7, reference was made to user view 4 and user view 12. Write up a complete discussion of user view 7 without reference to any other user views.

14. Explain why the relation *DEPT* of user view 8 violates the restrictions of 3NF rather than 2NF, as one might expect.

15. Write the domain, relation, and attribute documentation for the design for the requirements in Example 6.

# REFERENCES

1] Chen, Peter, *The Entity-Relationship Approach to Logical Data Base Design*, QED Monograph Series, 1977.

2] Date, C. J., and White, Colin J., *A Guide to DB2*, 3d ed. Addison-Wesley, 1989.

3] Date, C. J., *Database: A Primer*, Addison-Wesley, 1983.

4] Hammer, Michael, and McLeod, Dennis, "Database Description with SDM: A Semantic Database Model," *Transactions on Database Systems* 6, no. 3 (September 1981).

5] Howe, D. R., *Data Analysis for Data Base Design*, Edward Arnold, 1983.

6] Kroenke, David, and Dolan, Kathleen A., *Database Processing: Fundamentals, Design, Implementation*, 3d ed. SRA, 1988.

7] Martin, James, *Managing the Database Environment*, Prentice-Hall, 1983.

8] Vetter, M., and Madison, R. N., *Database Design Methodology*, Prentice-Hall, 1981.

# Database Design: Advanced Topics

## INTRODUCTION

In this chapter, we continue the study of the information-level of **database design** we began in chapter 7. We start by discussing the process of obtaining **user views**, including the use of a survey form in acquiring and documenting the various types of data needed to support a user view. We also discuss a process that can be used to obtain information on user views from existing documents.

Next, we examine the process of representing user views as relations. This subject was initially discussed in chapter 7 and is reviewed and expanded here. We then turn our attention to the process of merging individual user views into the collective design.

We then offer some general comments on database design. We also look at another popular approach to database design, the **Entity-Relationship (E-R) model**, which was proposed in the mid 1970s by Peter Chen. As we will see, this model uses diagrams that are basically similar to the data structure diagrams we use in DBDL. Finally, we turn our attention to a detailed database design example that illustrates the various issues we have been examining.

## OBTAINING USER VIEWS

Obtaining information on **user views** is a critical task, but not an easy one. Procedures, documents, reports, screens, file layouts, and programs for the existing system must be reviewed. While all these provide valuable information as a starting point, they are insufficient in themselves for three reasons. First, the underlying functional dependencies may often be obvious when we study the various aspects of the current system, but in many cases they are not. Second, they only provide information about the *existing* system, whether it be manual or computerized. Third, we need information about the data requirements of the *new* system. The only source for obtaining this information is the users who will be involved in the new system. It is they who decide what changes and improvements must be incorporated into the new system.

### Survey Form

To obtain the required information from users, some sort of survey form is helpful. This form may first be filled out by the user, then reviewed by the analysts involved in the project. Alternatively, it may be filled out by an analyst as part of an interview with the user. Before beginning the interview, the analyst may fill in the survey form for all existing data that can be determined by viewing various reports, documents, and so on. In any case, it is imperative that the completed survey form contain all the information necessary for the design process.

To be truly valuable to the design process, the survey form must contain the following information:

1. **Entity information.** For each **entity** (e.g., sales reps, customers, parts) a name and description should be recorded. Any synonyms for the entity should also be identified. If the user is aware, for example, that what he or she calls "parts" are referred to as "products" by other users within the organization, this information must be noted. Any general information about the entity, such as its use within the organization, should also be recorded. Finally, for the physical end of the design process, we need to know how many times this entity is expected to occur in the database.

2. **Attribute information.** For each **attribute** of an entity, its name, description, synonyms, and physical characteristics (e.g., twenty character alphanumeric, five-digit number), along with general information concerning its use, should be listed. Any restrictions on values (e.g., must be 300, 500, 800, or 1,000; must be less than 0.25; must be greater than zero) must be listed. We should also list the place where values for the item originate (e.g., from time cards; from orders placed by customers; computed from values for other attributes, as in dividing honor points by number of credits to obtain grade point average). Finally, we should list any security restrictions that apply to the attribute.

3. **Relationships.** For any **relationship**, the survey form should include the entities involved, the type of relationship (one-to-one, one-to-many, many-to-many), and the meaning of the relationship. For example, we might list a one-to-many relationship between sales reps and customers in which each customer is related to the sales rep who represents that customer. Any restrictions on the relationship should also

be listed. In the relationship between sales reps and customers, we might state that there can be no customer without a corresponding sales rep, and that no sales rep who represents any customers may be deleted from the database. We also need volume information. For example, on the average, how many customers will be related to an individual sales rep?

4. **Functional dependencies.** We need information concerning the **functional dependencies** that exist among the attributes. The analyst would ask the user such questions as, "For a given attribute, say, the customer number, if we know a particular customer number what else do we know? Do we know the name?" (If so, the name is functionally dependent on the customer number.) "Do we know the number of the sales rep who represents the customer?" (If so, the sales rep number is functionally dependent on the customer number. If, on the other hand, a given customer can be represented by many sales reps, then we would not know the sales rep number and it would not be dependent on the customer number.)

   While we will probably not use the term *functional dependency* with the user, it is important to ask the right questions so that the functional dependencies can be identified. An accurate list of functional dependencies is absolutely essential to the design process.

5. **Processing information.** The survey form should include a description of the manner in which the various types of processing are to take place (updates to the database, reports that must be produced, etc.). The analyst would pose such questions as, "How exactly is the report to be produced? Where do the entries on the report come from? How are they calculated? When we enter a new order, where does the data come from? Precisely what entities and attributes must be updated, and how?"

   In addition, we must obtain estimates on processing volumes. To this end, the analyst would ask the user, "How often is the report produced? On the average, how long is the report? What is the maximum length of the report? How many orders do we receive per day maximum and on the average? How many invoices do we print per day maximum and on the average?"

## Obtaining Information From Existing Documents

It is virtually impossible for an analyst to look at a document and complete a corresponding survey form without input from the appropriate user. If the analyst makes a good start, however, by partially completing the survey form before meeting with the user, he or she will have in hand something concrete with which to begin the interaction. The partially completed form can be nothing more than a starting point, however. The analyst cannot create the

**Figure 8.1**

Invoice for Allied
Distributors

design merely be considering existing forms. Figure 8.1 illustrates a technique for drawing information from existing forms and also shows why, after this initial step, user involvement is essential.

```
 10/15/91                                                        Invoice 11025

                              ALLIED DISTRIBUTORS
                               146 NELSON PLACE
                              ALLENDALE, MI 49401

    SOLD                        SHIP
    TO:     SMITH RENTALS       TO:     A & B SUPPLIES
            153 MAIN ST.                2180 HALTON PL.
            SUITE 102                   ARENDVILLE, MI 49232
            GRANDVILLE, MI 49494
```

| CUSTOMER P.O. NO. | OUR ORDER NO. | ORDER DATE | SHIP DATE | SLS REP |
|---|---|---|---|---|
| 1354 | P0335 | 12424 | 10/02/91 | 10/15/91 | 10 - Brown, Sam |

| QUANTITY | | | | | | |
|---|---|---|---|---|---|---|
| ORDER | SHIP | B/O | ITEM NUMBER | DESCRIPTION | PRICE | AMOUNT |
| 6 | 5 | 1 | AT414 | LOUNGE CHAIR | 42.00 | 210.00 |
| 4 | 4 | 0 | BT222 | ARM CHAIR | 51.00 | 204.00 |
| | | | | FREIGHT | | 42.50 |

|  |  |
|---|---|
| PAY THIS AMOUNT | |
| | 456.50 |

The first step an analyst can take to obtain information from a document is to list all attributes he or she can see and give them appropriate names. This process is demonstrated in Figure 8.2. Certainly, this list may not be perfect. In all likelihood the names chosen by the user for many of these attributes will be different from the names selected by the analyst. Attributes may be required that were not evident on the document the analyst saw. For example, the ship-to address for the customer on a particular invoice happened not to require a second line, so the analyst did not list the attribute *Customer Ship to Address Line 2*. However, this attribute may be required in general. Some attributes may not be required. If *Ship Date*, for example, will always be the same as *Invoice Date*, a separate attribute is unnecessary. The user's help is needed to clarify these issues.

```
Invoice Number
Invoice Date
Customer Number
Customer Sold To Name
Customer Sold To Address Line 1
Customer Sold To Address Line 2
Customer Sold To City
Customer Sold To State
Customer Sold To Zip
Customer Ship To Name
Customer Ship To Address Line 1
Customer Ship To City
Customer Ship To State
Customer Ship To Zip
Customer PO Number
Order Number
Order Date
Ship Date
Customer Sales Rep Number
Customer Sales Rep Name
Item Number
Item Description
Item Quantity Ordered
Item Quantity Shipped
Item Quantity Backordered
Item Price
Item Amount
Freight
Invoice Total
```

**Figure 8.2**

List of attributes for the Allied Distributors invoice

Next, we need to identify functional dependencies. If the document we are examining is foreign to us, we may not be able to make much headway in determining the dependencies and may need to get all the information directly from the user. On the other hand, we can often make intelligent guesses based on our general knowledge of the type of document we are studying. We may make mistakes, of course, and these should be corrected when we interact with the user. After initially determining the functional dependencies, as shown in Figure 8.3 on the next page, we may find out, for example, that the ship-to address for a given customer will vary from one invoice to another, that is, it depends on the invoice number, not the customer number. A general ship-to address may be defined for a given customer which serves as a default in case no ship-to address is entered with an order. This would depend just on the customer. The address that actually appeared on the invoice would depend on the invoice number, however. We may also find out that a number of the attributes actually depend on the order that was initially entered. The order date, the customer, the ship-to address, and the quantities ordered on each line of the invoice may all have been entered as part of the initial order. At the time of invoicing, further information, such as quantities shipped, quantities back-ordered, and freight, may be added. We may also find that the price is not necessarily the one stored with the item, and that it can vary from one order to another. Given all these corrections, a revised list of functional dependencies might look like Figure 8.4 on the next page.

**Figure 8.3**

Tentative list of
functional
dependencies

```
Customer Number -->
         Customer Sold To Name
         Customer Sold To Address Line 1
         Customer Sold To Address Line 2
         Customer Sold To City
         Customer Sold To State
         Customer Sold To Zip
         Customer Ship To Name
         Customer Ship To Address Line 1
         Customer Ship To City
         Customer Ship To State
         Customer Ship To Zip
         Customer Sales Rep Number
         Customer Sales Rep Name

Item Number -->
         Item Description
         Item Price

Invoice Number -->
         Invoice Date
         Customer Number
         Order Number
         Order Date
         Ship Date
         Freight
         Invoice Total

Invoice Number, Item Number -->
         Item Quantity Ordered
         Item Quantity Shipped
         Item Quantity Backordered
         Item Amount
```

**Figure 8.4**

Revised list of
functional
dependencies

```
Customer Number -->
         Customer Sold To Name
         Customer Sold To Address Line 1
         Customer Sold To Address Line 2
         Customer Sold To City
         Customer Sold To State
         Customer Sold To Zip
         Customer Sales Rep Number
         Customer Sales Rep Name

Item Number -->
         Item Description
         Item Price

Invoice Number -->
         Invoice Date
         Order Number
         Ship Date
         Freight
         Invoice Total

Order Number -->
         Order Date
         Customer PO Number
         Customer Ship To Name
         Customer Ship To Address Line 1
         Customer Ship To Address Line 2
         Customer Ship To City
         Customer Ship To State
         Customer Ship To Zip
```

```
Order Number, Item Number -->
        Item Quantity Ordered  (filled in when ORDER entered)
        Item Quantity Shipped  (filled in during invoicing)
        Item Quantity Backordered     ( " )
        Item Price             (filled in when ORDER entered)
```

**Figure 8.4**

(continued)

Once the functional dependencies have been determined, even if in a preliminary manner, we can begin to determine the entities and assign attributes to them, that is, we can begin to create the relations. If the number of attributes is not too large, we may choose to initially combine all attributes into a single relation, replace this one relation with equivalent 3NF relations, then create an entity that corresponds to each of the relations thus created. The attributes from the relation will become the attributes of the corresponding entity (many times, the entities will be reasonably apparent without having to resort to such a forced approach), and we may create the tentative list of entities shown in Figure 8.5a. Generally, applying normalization techniques to this list will expand the list of entities as relations are split. The new list might look like Figure 8.5b.

```
ORDERS
CUSTOMER
SALES REP
PART
```

**Figure 8.5a**

Tentative list of entities

```
INVOICE
CUSTOMER
SALES REP
PART
ORDERS
ORDLNE
```

**Figure 8.5b**

Expanded list of entities

Thus, we can take initial steps toward listing entities, attributes, and functional dependencies. We can then also list relationships among the entities (they come from foreign-key-type restrictions, which can be discerned from the functional dependencies once entities and their keys have been identified). This kind of effort is certainly worthwhile; it gives us a better feel for the problem when we interact with the user and also a good solid starting point for both ourselves and the user. Much of what we have done may be changed during our interaction with the user. It is easy to miss things or reach false conclusions when studying a document in a vacuum. Even if our work proves to be accurate, more still needs to be added. What names does the user think are appropriate for the various entities and attributes? What synonyms are in use? What restrictions exist? What are the meanings of the various entities, attributes, and relationships?

If the organization has a computerized system, current file layouts can furnish further information on entities and attributes. Current file sizes can furnish information on volume. Examining both the logic in current programs and operational instructions can yield processing information. Again, however, this is just a starting point. We still need further information from the user. How many invoices does he or she expect to print? Exactly how are the values on the invoice calculated, or where do they come from? What updates must be made during the invoicing cycle of processing? What fields in the *PART* record must change? In the *CUSTOMER* record? In the *SLSREP* record?

For other information on obtaining user views, see [1], [2], [4], and [5].

## REPRESENTING VIEWS AS RELATIONS

The basic technique for representing user views as relations was discussed in chapter 7. In this section, we examine some of these ideas in greater detail and add some new concepts.

### Types of Relationships

Two types of relationships warrant further examination: one-to-one relationships and many-to-many relationships that involve more than two entities.

**One-to-One.** What, if anything, is wrong with implementing a one-to-one relationship by including the primary key of each relation as a foreign key in the other relation? Suppose, for example, that each customer has a single sales rep, and each sales rep represents a single customer. Applying the suggested technique to this one-to-one relationship produces two relations:

```
SLSREP(SLSRNUMB, SLSRNAME, CUSTNUMB)
CUSTOMER(CUSTNUMB, CUSTNAME, SLSRNUMB)
```

These relations would, of course, contain any additional sales rep or customer attributes of interest in the design problem. Samples of these relations are shown in Figure 8.6. This design clearly forces a sales rep to be related to a single customer. Since the number of the customer represented by the sales rep is a column in the *SLSREP* relation, there can be only one customer for each sales rep. Likewise, this design forces a customer to be related to a single sales rep.

**SLSREP**

| SLSRNUMB | SLSRNAME | CUSTNUMB |
|---|---|---|
| 3 | Jones, Mary | 124 |
| 6 | Smith, William | 256 |
| 12 | Brown, Sam | 311 |

**CUSTOMER**

| CUSTNUMB | CUSTNAME | SLSRNUMB |
|---|---|---|
| 124 | Adams, Sally | 3 |
| 256 | Samuels, Ann | 6 |
| 311 | Charles, Don | 12 |

**Figure 8.6**

One-to-one relationship implemented by including the primary key of each relation as a foreign key in the other

Question:          What is the potential problem with this solution?

Answer:                     There is no guarantee that the information will match. Consider Figure 8.7, for example. The data in the first relation indicates that sales rep 3 represents customer 124. The data in the second relation, on the other hand, indicates that customer 124 is represented by sales rep *6!* This may be the simplest way of implementing a one-to-one relationship from a conceptual standpoint, but it clearly suffers from this major deficiency. The programs themselves would have to ensure that the data in the two relations agreed, a task that the design should be able to accomplish.

**SLSREP**

| SLSRNUMB | SLSRNAME | CUSTNUMB |
|---|---|---|
| 3 | Jones, Mary | 124 |
| 6 | Smith, William | 256 |
| 12 | Brown, Sam | 311 |

**CUSTOMER**

| CUSTNUMB | CUSTNAME | SLSRNUMB |
|---|---|---|
| 124 | Adams, Sally | 6 |
| 256 | Samuels, Ann | 12 |
| 311 | Charles, Don | 3 |

**Figure 8.7**

Problem with implementation of one-to-one relationship. Information does not match

To avoid these problems, let's consider some alternative solutions. One alternative is to form a single relation, such as

```
SLSREP(SLSRNUMB, SLSRNAME, CUSTNUMB, CUSTNAME)
```

A sample of this relation is shown in Figure 8.8. What should be the key of this relation? If it is the sales rep number, then there is nothing to prevent all three rows from containing the same customer number. On the other hand, if it is the customer number, the same would hold true for the sales rep number. The solution would be to choose either the sales rep number or the customer number as the primary key and make the other an alternate key. In other words, the uniqueness of both sales rep numbers and customer numbers should be enforced. Since each sales rep and each customer will then appear on exactly one row, we have indeed implemented a one-to-one relationship between them.

**Figure 8.8**

One-to-one relationship implemented in a single table

SLSREP

| SLSRNUMB | SLSRNAME | CUSTNUMB | CUSTNAME |
|---|---|---|---|
| 3 | Jones, Mary | 124 | Adams, Sally |
| 6 | Smith, William | 256 | Samuels, Ann |
| 12 | Brown, Sam | 311 | Charles, Don |

While this solution is workable, it has two facets that are not particularly attractive. First, it combines attributes of two different entities in a single relation, although it certainly would seem more natural to have one relation with sales rep attributes and a separate relation with customer attributes. Second, if it is possible for one entity to exist without the other (e.g., if there is a customer who has no sales rep), this structure is going to cause problems. Would we leave the sales rep columns null? What about the sales rep number, which is supposed to be the key? We can't very well have a null sales rep number.

A better solution would be two separate relations, a sales rep relation and a customer relation; and the key of one of them included as a foreign key in the other. This foreign key would also be designated as an alternate key. Thus, we could choose either

```
SLSREP(SLSRNUMB, SLSRNAME, CUSTNUMB)
CUSTOMER(CUSTNUMB, CUSTNAME)
```

or

```
SLSREP(SLSRNUMB, SLSRNAME)
CUSTOMER(CUSTNUMB, CUSTNAME, SLSRNUMB)
```

Samples of these two possibilities are shown in Figure 8.9. In either case, we must enforce the uniqueness of the foreign key that we have added. In the first solution, for example, if customer numbers need not be unique, all three rows might contain customer number 124, and this would certainly violate the one-to-one relationship. We enforce the uniqueness by designating these for-eign keys as alternate keys. They will also be foreign keys, of course, since they must match an actual row in the other relation.

**SLSREP**

| SLSRNUMB | SLSRNAME | CUSTNUMB |
|---|---|---|
| 3 | Jones, Mary | 124 |
| 6 | Smith, William | 256 |
| 12 | Brown, Sam | 311 |

**CUSTOMER**

| CUSTNUMB | CUSTNAME |
|---|---|
| 124 | Adams, Sally |
| 256 | Samuels, Ann |
| 311 | Charles, Don |

or

**SLSREP**

| SLSRNUMB | SLSRNAME |
|---|---|
| 3 | Jones, Mary |
| 6 | Smith, William |
| 12 | Brown, Sam |

**CUSTOMER**

| CUSTNUMB | CUSTNAME | SLSRNUMB |
|---|---|---|
| 124 | Adams, Sally | 3 |
| 256 | Samuels, Ann | 6 |
| 311 | Charles, Don | 12 |

**Figure 8.9**

One-to-one relationship imple-mented by includ-ing the primary key of one relation as foreign key (and candidate key) in the other

How do we make a choice between the possibilities? In some cases, it really makes no difference which we choose. Suppose, however, that one of these entities can exist without the other. Suppose a customer can exist with-out a sales rep. In this case, the first alternative would be preferable, since a customer without a sales rep merely appears as a row in the customer relation. Since there is no sales rep column in the customer relation, we wouldn't have to deal with null values, as we would in the second alternative.

Another situation might lead us to prefer one alternative to the other. Suppose we anticipate the possibility that this relationship may not always be one-to-one. Suppose we feel there is a real likelihood that in the future, sales reps may represent more than one customer, but customers will still be repre-sented by exactly one sales rep. The relationship would then be one-to-many, and it would be implemented with a structure similar to the second alterna-tive. In fact, the structure would differ only in that the sales rep number in the customer relation would *not* be an alternate key. Thus, to convert from the second alternative to the appropriate structure would be a simple matter (we would merely remove the restriction that the sales rep number in the customer relation is an alternate key). This would lead us to favor the second alternative.

**Many-to-Many.** Complex issues arise when more than two entities are related in a many-to-many fashion. Let's consider some possible relationships between sales reps, customers, and parts.

Suppose initially that we want to know which sales reps sold which parts to which customers. There are no restrictions on which customers a given sales rep may sell to or on the parts that a sales rep may sell. We actually have what is termed a many-to-many-to-many relationship. The relation

SALES(<u>SLSRNUMB</u>, <u>CUSTNUMB</u>, <u>PARTNUMB</u>)

is an appropriate way to model the situation. Figure 8.10 gives a sample of this relation. Attempting to model this situation as two (or three) many-to-many relationships is not legitimate. Consider Figure 8.11, for example, in which the same data is split into three relations:

SLSCUST(<u>SLSRNUMB</u>, <u>CUSTNUMB</u>)
CUSTPART(<u>CUSTNUMB</u>, <u>PARTNUMB</u>)
SLSPART(<u>PARTNUMB</u>, <u>SLSRNUMB</u>)

**Figure 8.10**

Implementation of a many-to-many-to-many relationship

SALES

| SLSRNUMB | CUSTNUMB | PARTNUMB |
|---------:|---------:|----------|
| 3 | 124 | AX12 |
| 3 | 256 | CB03 |
| 6 | 124 | CB03 |
| 6 | 124 | BZ66 |
| 12 | 412 | AX12 |
| 12 | 256 | AX12 |

**Figure 8.11**

Result obtained by splitting *SALES* into three relations

SLSCUST

| SLSRNUMB | CUSTNUMB |
|---------:|---------:|
| 3 | 124 |
| 3 | 256 |
| 6 | 124 |
| 12 | 412 |
| 12 | 256 |

CUSTPART

| CUSTNUMB | PARTNUMB |
|---------:|----------|
| 124 | AX12 |
| 124 | CB03 |
| 124 | BZ66 |
| 256 | AX12 |
| 256 | CB03 |
| 412 | AX12 |

SLSPART

| PARTNUMB | SLSRNUMB |
|----------|---------:|
| AX12 | 3 |
| AX12 | 12 |
| CB03 | 6 |
| CB03 | 3 |
| BZ66 | 6 |

Figure 8.12 shows the result of joining these three relations together. It contains inaccurate information. The second row, for example, states that sales rep 3 has sold part CB03 to customer 124. Yet this row will be in the join, since sales rep 3 is related to customer 124 in *SLSCUST* (sales rep 3 sold some parts to customer 124), customer 124 is related to part CB03 in *CUSTPART* (customer 124 bought some CB03s), and, finally, part CB03 is related to sales rep 3 in *SLSPART* (sales rep 3 sold some CB03s). Of course, these three facts *do not* imply that sales rep 3 sold some CB03s to customer 124! The problem is that this relationship really involves all three — sales reps, customers, and parts — and splitting it any further is inappropriate.

**SALES**

| SLSRNUMB | CUSTNUMB | PARTNUMB |
|---:|---:|---|
| 3 | 124 | AX12 |
| 3 | 124 | CB03 |
| 3 | 256 | AX12 |
| 3 | 256 | CB03 |
| 6 | 124 | CB03 |
| 6 | 124 | BZ66 |
| 12 | 412 | AX12 |
| 12 | 256 | AX12 |

!!!!!  (second row)
!!!!!  (third row)

**Figure 8.12**

Result obtained by joining *SLSCUST*, *CUSTPART*, and *PARTSLS*. Second and third rows are in error!

On the other hand, let's assume the following. A sales rep represents many customers and each customer is represented by many sales reps. A sales rep sells many parts and a part can be sold by many sales reps. If this is the information we wish to model (i.e., the relationship between sales reps and the customers they represent, together with the relationship between sales reps and the parts they sell), the three-way many-to-many-to-many relationship implemented by

```
SALES(SLSRNUMB, CUSTNUMB, PARTNUMB)
```

is inappropriate. The independence that exists between these entities was not present in the prior situation. In particular, this relation would not be in 4NF. The correct method for modeling this situation would be as follows, with two relations:

```
SLSCUST(SLSRNUMB, CUSTNUMB)
SLSPART(PARTNUMB, SLSRNUMB)
```

If, in addition, there was a relationship between customers and parts that was of interest, we could include a third relation:

```
CUSTPART(CUSTNUMB, PARTNUMB)
```

The crucial issue in making the determination between a single many-to-many-to-many relationship and two (or three) many-to-many relationships is the independence. If all three entities are critical in the relationship, then the three-way relationship (like *SALES*) is appropriate. If there is independence among the individual relationships, as in the second situation (where the relationship between sales reps and the customers they represent really had nothing to do with the relationship between sales reps and the parts they sell), then separate many-to-many relationships are appropriate. Incidentally, if a many-to-many-to-many relationship is created where it is not appropriate, the conversion to 4NF will correct the problem.

## Nulls and Entity Subtypes

Remember that there are potentially serious problems involved with the use of "NULLS." We will now look at a method for avoiding them.

Let's consider a *STUDENT* relation in which one of the attributes is a foreign key, *DORMNUMB*, that identifies a *DORM* relation. We will assume that this foreign key is allowed to be null because some students do not live in a dormitory. This means that for some rows in the *STUDENT* relation, the *DORMNUMB* column was empty. To avoid this use of null values, we could remove the *DORMNUMB* attribute from the *STUDENT* relation and create a *separate* relation *STUDORM*, which contains the two attributes *STUNUMB* (the key) and *DORMNUMB*. A student would have a row in this new relation *only* if he or she was indeed living in a dorm. Students not living in a dorm would have their normal row in the *STUDENT* relation but *no* row in the *STUDORM* relation.

This change is illustrated in Figure 8.13. Note that *STUNUMB*, the primary key of *STUDORM*, will also be a foreign key that must match a student number in the *STUDENT* relation. We have created what is often termed an **entity subtype**. In this case, we say that *STUDORM* is a subtype of *STUDENT*. In other words, "students living in dorms" is a subtype (or subset) of "students." While some design methodologies have specific ways of denoting entity subtypes, this is really not necessary in **DBDL**. Entity subtypes will be recognized by the fact that the primary key is also a foreign key.

**Figure 8.13a**

*STUDENT* relation including column with nulls allowed

STUDENT

| STUNUMB | STUNAME | PERMADDR | STATUS | DORMNUMB |
|---|---|---|---|---|
| 1253 | ANN JOHNSON | 123 1ST,ADA,MI | F | 3 |
| 1662 | TOM ANDERSON | 26 FOLKS,BENSON,MI | F | 1 |
| 2108 | BILL LEWIS | 95 108TH,HOLTON,MI | C | - |
| 2546 | MARY DAVIS | 514 PETE,SPARTA,MI | P | 2 |
| 2867 | CATHY ALBERS | 878 2ND,GRANT,MI | C | 2 |
| 2992 | MARK MATTHEW | 11 COLLEGE,IONIA,MI | F | - |
| 3011 | TIM CANDELA | 27 MARTIN,ERA,MI | P | 3 |
| 3574 | SUE TALEN | 434 RAYMOND,ADA,MI | F | - |

**Figure 8.13b**

*STUDENT* relation split to avoid use of null values

STUDENT

| STUNUMB | STUNAME | PERMADDR | STATUS |
|---|---|---|---|
| 1253 | ANN JOHNSON | 123 1ST,ADA,MI | F |
| 1662 | TOM ANDERSON | 26 FOLKS,BENSON,MI | F |
| 2108 | BILL LEWIS | 95 108TH,HOLTON,MI | C |
| 2546 | MARY DAVIS | 514 PETE,SPARTA,MI | P |
| 2867 | CATHY ALBERS | 878 2ND,GRANT,MI | C |
| 2992 | MARK MATTHEW | 11 COLLEGE,IONIA,MI | F |
| 3011 | TIM CANDELA | 27 MARTIN,ERA,MI | P |
| 3574 | SUE TALEN | 434 RAYMOND,ADA,MI | F |

STUDORM

| STUNUMB | DORMNUMB |
|---|---|
| 1253 | 3 |
| 1662 | 1 |
| 2546 | 2 |
| 2867 | 2 |
| 3011 | 3 |

Two issues need to be addressed as we make the decision whether to create this type of relation. First, is it worth it? Perhaps the value of a given attribute being unknown will not cause a problem. If the attribute will never be used in any selection criteria and will never be used in joining this relation with any other, and if statistics will never be calculated on this attribute, allowing it to be null should never cause a problem. (We could still create a new relation, as we previously discussed, but it is probably unnecessary.) Another alternative might be to eliminate the problems with nulls by choosing a phony value to use in place of null. We might let a dormitory number of zero, for example, indicate that a student does not reside in a dorm. We might even store a dormitory 999, called "NONE," within our dormitory relation.

The second issue is a little trickier. Suppose several different attributes can be null as in the following *STUDENT* relation:

```
STUDENT(STUNUMB, STUNAME, ..., DORMNUMB, THSTITLE, THSAREA)
```

In this relation, the dormitory number is either the dormitory in which the student resides or null. In addition, students at this college must write a senior thesis. Once students attain senior standing, they must declare a thesis title and the area in which they will write their theses. Thus, seniors will have a thesis title and a thesis area, whereas other students will not. This can be handled by allowing the fields *THSTITLE* and *THSAREA* to be null.

We now have three different attributes — dormitory number, thesis title, and thesis area — that can be null. Dormitory will be null for students who do not reside in a dorm. Thesis title and thesis area, on the other hand, will be null for students who have not yet attained senior standing. It wouldn't make much sense to combine all three of these in a single relation. A better choice would be to create a relation

```
STUDORM (STUNUMB, DORMNUMB)
```

for students living in dorms, and another relation

```
SENSTU (STUNUMB, THSTITLE, THSAREA)
```

for students who have attained senior status (*senior stu*dents). Samples of these relations are shown in Figure 8.14 on the next page and the DBDL for these relations are shown in Figure 8.15 on the next page. Both relations represent entity subtypes. In both, the primary key, student number, will also be a foreign key matching the student number in the main student relation.

**Figure 8.14a**

*STUDENT* relation including columns with nulls allowed

STUDENT

| STU NUMB | STUNAME | PERMADDR | STATUS | DORM NUMB | THSTITLE | THSAREA |
|---|---|---|---|---|---|---|
| 1253 | ANN JOHNSON | 123 1ST,ADA,MI | F | 3 | - | - |
| 1662 | TOM ANDERSON | 26 FOLKS,BENSON,MI | F | 1 | P.D.Q. BACH | MUSIC |
| 2108 | BILL LEWIS | 95 108TH,HOLTON,MI | C | - | CLUSTER SETS | MATH |
| 2546 | MARY DAVIS | 514 PETE,SPARTA,MI | P | 2 | | |
| 2867 | CATHY ALBERS | 878 2ND,GRANT,MI | C | 2 | RAD. TREATM. | MEDICINE |
| 2992 | MARK MATTHEW | 11 COLLEGE,IONIA,MI | F | - | - | - |
| 3011 | TIM CANDELA | 27 MARTIN,ERA,MI | P | 3 | - | - |
| 3574 | SUE TALEN | 434 RAYMOND,ADA,MI | F | - | - | - |

**Figure 8.14b**

*STUDENT* relation split to avoid use of null values

STUDENT

| STUNUMB | STUNAME | PERMADDR | STATUS |
|---|---|---|---|
| 1253 | ANN JOHNSON | 123 1ST,ADA,MI | F |
| 1662 | TOM ANDERSON | 26 FOLKS,BENSON,MI | F |
| 2108 | BILL LEWIS | 95 108TH,HOLTON,MI | C |
| 2546 | MARY DAVIS | 514 PETE,SPARTA,MI | P |
| 2867 | CATHY ALBERS | 878 2ND,GRANT,MI | C |
| 2992 | MARK MATTHEW | 11 COLLEGE,IONIA,MI | F |
| 3011 | TIM CANDELA | 27 MARTIN,ERA,MI | P |
| 3574 | SUE TALEN | 434 RAYMOND,ADA,MI | F |

STUDORM

| STUNUMB | DORMNUMB |
|---|---|
| 1253 | 3 |
| 1662 | 1 |
| 2546 | 2 |
| 2867 | 2 |
| 3011 | 3 |

SENSTU

| STUNUMB | THSTITLE | THSAREA |
|---|---|---|
| 1662 | P.D.Q. BACH | MUSIC |
| 2108 | CLUSTER SETS | MATH |
| 2867 | RAD. TREATM. | MEDICINE |

**Figure 8.15**

Sample DBDL with entity subtypes

```
STUDENT (STUNUMB, STUNAME, PERM_ADDRESS, STATUS)

STUDORM (STUNUMB, DORMNUMB)
     FK    STUNUMB --> STUDENT       DLT CSCD
     FK    DORMNUMB --> DORM

SENSTU (STUNUMB, THSTITLE, THSAREA)
     FK    STUNUMB --> STUDENT       DLT CSCD
```

In general, attributes that can be null should be grouped functionally. If a given subset of the entity in question can have nulls in a certain collection of attributes, that fact should be noted. The option of splitting those attributes out in a separate relation (really an entity subtype) should be strongly considered. If we do create an entity subtype, it's a good idea to give it a name that is suggestive of the related entity type, as well as its relationship to it, for example, *SENSTU* (for *senior students*). In addition, the meaning of the entity subtype should be carefully documented, especially the conditions that will cause an occurrence of the entity itself to also be an occurrence of the entity subtype. If we do not create such an entity subtype, we must at least document precisely when the attributes might take on null as a value.

## Derived Data

Should we include an attribute in a relation that can be derived or computed from other attributes? For example, in an *INVENTORY* relation that contains attributes *UNONHAND* and *COST*, should we include the attribute *ONHNDVAL* (on hand value), which is the product of the two? Should we include in the *STUDENT* relation the attribute *TOTCRED* (total number of credits), which can be computed by summing the *NUMBCRED* (number of credits) for all courses in which the student has a passing grade? In both cases, the answer is yes for the information-level design, but we must be sure to document means of obtaining the results. The answer may very well be different in the physical-level design.

Note that including such a value means technically that the relation will not be in 3NF. (*ONHNDVAL* is functionally dependent on the combination of *UNONHAND* and *COST*, for example.) Since it is important that such an attribute be present and documented in the information-level design, we would disregard this type of functional dependency in our quest for 3NF relations.

## Encoded Data

The encoding of data is a slightly different issue. This is not enciphering, which is used for security, but rather the assignment of codes to frequently used data values. In many cases, this is done naturally and without our being particularly aware that we are encoding data. If, for example, in maintaining information on students, we have an attribute, *STANDING* (class standing), that is 1 if the student is a freshman, 2 if a sophomore, 3 if a junior, and 4 if a senior, we have actually encoded data. We have replaced one of the words "FRESHMAN," "SOPHOMORE," "JUNIOR," or "SENIOR" with a one-digit code. In this case, these codes might have been determined long before the college was ever computerized.

To illustrate the process of deciding which data to encode and how, suppose the codes described in the previous paragraph had not already been determined. Suppose the users have told us that they need to know the standing of a student and that this standing could be "FRESHMAN," "SOPHO-MORE," "JUNIOR," or "SENIOR." When we are confronted by a situation in which there is a limited set of possible values, we should consider encoding these values, that is, developing a scheme whereby each possible value is replaced by a much shorter code. The users may have some ideas at this point concerning appropriate codes. There are all sorts of possibilities. We could use the numbers 1, 2, 3, and 4, or we could choose codes that are two characters long and use "FR," "SO," "JU," and "SE."

The use of encoding entails two basic advantages. First, a substantial saving in storage space can be realized. Storing the word "SOPHOMORE" requires nine bytes, for example, whereas storing the number 2 requires only a single byte. The second advantage is felt more directly by users. Typing the number 2 requires only a single keystroke, whereas typing the word "SOPHO-MORE" requires nine.

On the other hand, there is one disadvantage: the codes, in general, will not be as readable or as easily recognizable as will the words we are encoding. But there are exceptions to this, of course. One could certainly argue that the codes "FR," "SO," "JU," and "SE" *are* both readable and recognizable as the categories for class standing by anyone working in a college environment.

To overcome this disadvantage in general, it must be easy to substitute the actual values for the codes in reports that include this field. In addition, it should be easy for users to expand the list of codes when the need arises. We can address both of these requirements by creating a new relation with the code as the key and the value for which the code stands as the other attribute. The code in the original relation becomes a foreign key matching the key of the newly created relation. In the student example, we would replace

```
STUDENT(STUNUMB, STUNAME, ..., STANDING, ...)
```

with

```
STUDENT(STUNUMB, STUNAME, ..., STNDCODE, ...)
STNDINFO(STNDCODE, STANDING)
```

Figure 8.16 contains samples of these relations. Note that in the new version of *STUDENT*, *STNDCODE* is a foreign key that matches the primary key of the *STNDINFO* relation. With this structure, obtaining the actual standing involves a join operation between the two relations. Adding a new standing involves adding a new row in the *STNDINFO* relation. By making *STNDCODE* a foreign key, we are ensuring that no student may be stored with a code that does not match the code for an actual standing. Thus, at least during the information level of design, this is a clean way of encoding data. (During the physical level, we may choose to do things differently for performance reasons.)

For additional discussion of the issues addressed in this section, see [1], [3], [4], and [5].

**STUDENT**

| STUNUMB | STUNAME | STANDING |
|---------|---------|----------|
| 1253 | ANN JOHNSON | SOPHOMORE |
| 1662 | TOM ANDERSON | SENIOR |
| 2108 | BILL LEWIS | SENIOR |
| 2546 | MARY DAVIS | FRESHMAN |
| 2867 | CATHY ALBERS | SENIOR |
| 2992 | MARK MATTHEW | FRESHMAN |
| 3011 | TIM CANDELA | SOPHOMORE |
| 3574 | SUE TALEN | JUNIOR |

**Figure 8.16a**

Student information before encoding (some columns not shown due to space limitation)

**STUDENT**

| STUNUMB | STUNAME | STNDCODE |
|---------|---------|----------|
| 1253 | ANN JOHNSON | 2 |
| 1662 | TOM ANDERSON | 4 |
| 2108 | BILL LEWIS | 4 |
| 2546 | MARY DAVIS | 1 |
| 2867 | CATHY ALBERS | 4 |
| 2992 | MARK MATTHEW | 1 |
| 3011 | TIM CANDELA | 2 |
| 3574 | SUE TALEN | 3 |

**STNDINFO**

| STNDCODE | STANDING |
|----------|----------|
| 1 | FRESHMAN |
| 2 | SOPHOMORE |
| 3 | JUNIOR |
| 4 | SENIOR |

**Figure 8.16b**

Student information after encoding

## MERGE THE RESULT INTO THE DESIGN AND REVIEW

Once user views have been represented as relations and all appropriate restrictions have been documented, the results are merged into the cumulative design. The design is reviewed at various points along the way. This section expands on these processes.

### Merge

The first step in merging is simply to add the list of relations for the user view in question to those relations already in the cumulative design. Next, relations with the same primary key are combined (i.e., two relations with the same (primary) key become a single relation, having the same primary key as the two originals and containing all the attributes from the original relations but without duplication). If the cumulative collection of relations, for example, contained the relation

```
STUDENT(STUNUMB, STUNAME, STUADDR, STATUS)
```

and the relations in a user view contained the relation

```
STUINFO(STUNUMB, STUNAME, GPA)
```

the two would be combined to form this single relation:

```
STUDENT(STUNUMB, STUNAME, STUADDR, STATUS, GPA)
```

The new relation is assigned a name that is descriptive of the entity in question. In all probability, it will be the same as the name of the relation that already existed in the cumulative design.

In one particular case, relations with identical primary keys should *not* be combined. If relations were split within an individual user view to form an **entity subtype**, combining them would destroy what we are trying to accomplish. The trick is to recognize when this has occurred so that we do not combine relations inappropriately. As we pointed out previously, such entity subtypes can be recognized by the fact that their primary key is also a foreign key. (In *STUDORM*, for example, the primary key, *STUNUMB*, is also a foreign key that must match a student in the *STUDENT* relation.) Again, such relations *should not be combined*. Further, we must be extremely careful about combining other relations with those relations that represent entity subtypes. Suppose we have the two relations, *STUDENT* and *STUDORM*, in the cumulative design already, and we have a new relation to add whose primary key is *STUNUMB*. Should the new relation be combined with *STUDENT* or *STUDORM*, or should it be left alone? If the new relation does not represent an entity subtype, it should be combined with *STUDENT*. *STUDENT* is the fundamental relation here, the one that other relations with a primary key of *STUNUMB* must match. If the new relation does represent an entity subtype, it should probably be left alone, with its primary key listed as a foreign key matching the *STUDENT* relation.

### Including Determinants

When two 3NF relations are combined, the result need not be in 3NF. Both of the following relations are in 3NF:

```
CUSTOMER(CUSTNUMB, CUSTNAME, SLSRNUMB)
CUSTINFO(CUSTNUMB, CUSTNAME, SLSRNAME)
```

When we combine them, however, we get

```
CUSTOMER(CUSTNUMB, CUSTNAME, SLSRNUMB, SLSRNAME)
```

which is not in 3NF. We would have to convert this to 3NF before proceeding to the next user view.

We can attempt to avoid the problem of obtaining a relation that is not in 3NF by being cautious when representing user views. The problem occurs when an attribute, A, in one user view **functionally determines** an attribute,

B, in a second user view. Thus, A is a **determinant** for attribute B, yet A is not an attribute in the second user view. In the preceding example, the attribute *SLSRNUMB* in the first relation determined the attribute *SLSRNAME* in the second relation, yet *SLSRNUMB* was *not* one of the attributes in the second relation. If we always attempt to determine whether determinants exist and, if they do, include them in the relations, we will go a long way toward avoiding this problem. For example, if when the second user indicates that the name of a sales rep is part of that user's view of data, we should ask whether any special way has been provided for sales reps to be uniquely identified within the organization. Even though this user evidently does not need the sales rep number, he or she might very well be aware of the existence of such a number. If so, we would include this number in the relation. Having done this, we would have a relation in this user view like the following:

```
CUSTINFO(CUSTNUMB, CUSTNAME, SLSRNUMB, SLSRNAME)
```

Now, the normalization process for this user would produce

```
CUSTINFO(CUSTNUMB, CUSTNAME, SLSRNUMB)
SLSINFO(SLSRNUMB, SLSRNAME)
```

When these two relations are merged into the cumulative design, we will not produce any non-3NF relations. Note that, effectively, the determinant *SLSRNUMB* has replaced the attribute that it determines, *SLSRNAME*, in the *CUSTINFO* relation.

## Restrictions

Basically, new foreign key restrictions, as well as others, are merely added to the cumulative design. We do need to be aware, however, of the potential for conflict. In the cumulative, design, for example, there may be a foreign key of *SLSRNUMB* within the *CUSTOMER* relation that matches the *SLSREP* relation, and for which delete is restricted. If we later encounter a user view that contains precisely the same foreign key but for which delete cascades, we have a problem. Which restriction is correct? Likewise, if a restriction in the cumulative design states that credit limits must be $300, $500, $800, or $1,000 and we later encounter a user view in which credit limits must be $500 or $1,000, we have a problem.

At this point, we must go back to the users and try to obtain agreement on what the actual restriction must be. If we are unsuccessful, we must go to someone within the organization who has the authority to make a decision. We obviously cannot enforce conflicting restrictions at the same time.

## Review

Reviews of various portions of the design take place at several stages. Each user should review the information concerning his or her view of data. Naturally, this material should be presented to users in a format that is easily understood by them. The purpose of this review is to ensure that we have correctly understood the entities, attributes, relationships, dependencies, and restrictions necessary to support this user's needs.

As each new user view is merged into the design, the new cumulative design should be reviewed to ensure that it can indeed support this new user. Once each user view has been merged into the cumulative design, the design is tentatively complete. At this point, each user view should be reviewed against the complete design to ensure not only that it can still be satisfied but that there is no better way it can be satisfied. A user view that was merged into the design later may have caused a change to the cumulative design that provides a different (and better) way of supporting the user view in question. We make changes to the cumulative design as we encounter the need for them. If along the way we have actually made some changes, then we should make another pass through all the user views. We repeatedly make these passes until there are no further changes to be made.

## THE ENTITY-RELATIONSHIP MODEL

There is another popular approach to database design which uses diagrams. The diagrams are similar to those we use with DBDL. This approach is called the **entity-relationship (E-R) model**. Since it is used in many places and also forms the basis of some computerized tools, you should be familiar with it.

The E-R model was proposed by Peter Chen of the M.I.T. Sloan School of Management in 1976 (See [2]) and has been widely accepted as a graphical approach to database design. The basic constructions in the E-R model are the familiar entities, attributes, and relationships, all of which are represented in E-R diagrams. Domains can also be represented.

In the E-R model, entities are drawn as rectangles and relationships as are drawn as diamonds, with lines connected to the entities involved. Both entities and relationships are named in the E-R model. The lines are labeled to indicate the degree of the relationship. In Figure 8.17, the relationship between sales reps and customers is "1" to "N," or one-to-many. The relationship between orders and parts is "M" to "N," or many-to-many. Finally, the many-to-many-to-many relationship between sales reps, customers, and parts discussed earlier is referred to as "M" to "N" to "P."

In the E-R model, not only can entities have attributes, but relationships can as well. Attributes are indicated in a diagram by listing them near the entity or relationship to which they correspond.

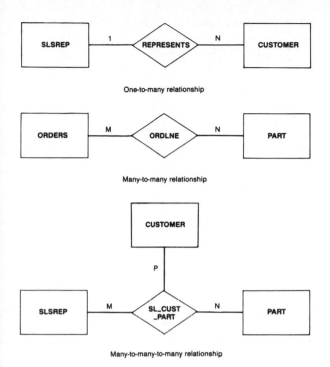

**Figure 8.17**

Representing entities and relationships in E-R model

Domains can also be represented, if desired. They are termed *value types* and are represented by circles, grouped together if possible, often at the bottom of the diagram. The attribute name is then attached to an arrow, which goes from the entity or relationship to the appropriate domain. An example of the use of domains is shown in Figure 8.18. The lower portion of the diagram, sometimes called the **lower conceptual domain**, contains a bubble for each domain. The upper portion of the diagram, termed the **upper conceptual domain**, contains the entities, attributes, and relationships.

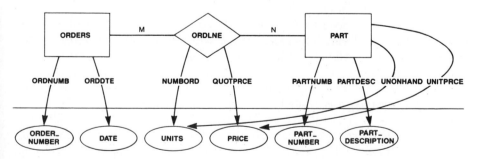

**Figure 8.18**

Representing attributes and value types (domains) in E-R model

The *ORDERS* entity, the *PART* entity, and the *ORDLNE* relationship all contain arrows to appropriate domains. Associated with each arrow is the name of the attribute. Thus, the *ORDERS* entity contains two attributes — *ORDNUMB* and *ORDDTE* — each associated with a domain of the same name. The *ORDLNE* relationship contains two attributes, *NUMBORD* and *QUOTPRCE*. *NUMBORD* is associated with a domain of the same name. *QUOTPRCE* is associated with the domain of all prices. The PART entity contains attributes *PARTNUMB*, *PARTDESC*, and *UNONHAND*, which are all associated with domains of the same name. It also contains an attribute *UNITPRCE*, which is associated with the same domain as *QUOTPRCE*, a domain called simply *PRICE*.

Often, for the sake of simplicity, any reference to domains is documented separately from the diagram. In addition, if there are many attributes, these are also listed separately. Otherwise, the diagram can rapidly become cluttered and the nice, explicit visual rendering of the relationships can easily be obscured. Wherever the attributes are listed, the attribute (or collection of attributes) that forms the primary key for an entity must be specified. Often in sample E-R diagrams this is not done, but it is absolutely critical to do so. The only possible justification for not doing it is that in certain simple diagrams, the keys may be obvious, but this is not a sufficient reason for overlooking this point. The simplest way to indicate the keys is by underlining them, as we have done with the relational model.

Two special types of dependencies are important in the E-R model: existence dependencies and ID dependencies. If the existence of one entity depends on the existence of another related entity, we have an **existence dependency**. Job history information will not be stored in the Marvel College database unless the corresponding faculty member exists. Thus, the existence of job history information *depends* on the existence of a corresponding faculty member. The relationship between faculty and job history is an existence dependency, indicated by placing an "E" in the relationship diamond, as shown in Figure 8.19. Further, an entity that depends on another entity for its existence is called a **weak entity type**, and is indicated by being enclosed in a double rectangle, as shown in Figure 8.20.

If an entity cannot be uniquely identified through its own attributes but must be identified through its relationships with other entities, we have an **ID dependency**. The attributes for job history records are rank and starting date, neither of which uniquely determines a job history record. Uniquely identifying a job history record also requires knowing the faculty member to whom the job history record is related. (The job history record for Betty Jones, on which the rank is ASST PROF and the starting date is 6/15/75, is different from a job history record for Sam Martin, which contains the same rank and starting date.) An ID dependency is indicated on an E-R diagram by including "ID" in the relationship diamond. It is possible to have a given relationship be *both* an existence dependency *and* an ID dependency, in which case the relationship diamond will contain "E & ID," as shown in Figure 8.20.

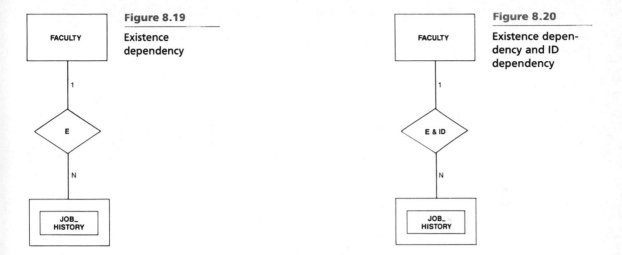

**Figure 8.19**

Existence dependency

**Figure 8.20**

Existence dependency and ID dependency

The preceding discussion of the E-R model represents the original version of the model as proposed by Chen, and the version that is probably most commonly used today. In it, both entities and relationships can have attributes. In particular, the typical many-to-many relationship is represented as a relationship which, in turn, had attributes of its own. Some confusion has existed as to whether something like *ORDLNE*, for example, should be an entity or a relationship. In other words, should the many-to-many relationship between orders and parts be represented by the diagram shown in Figure 8.21a or the one shown in Figure 8.21b? The usual response to this question was that it didn't matter.

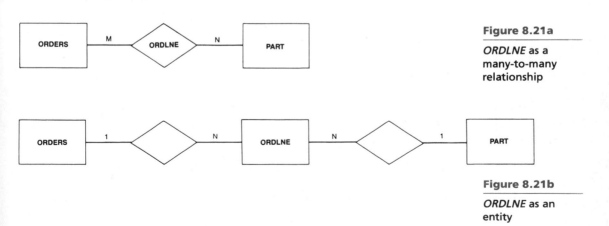

**Figure 8.21a**

*ORDLNE* as a many-to-many relationship

**Figure 8.21b**

*ORDLNE* as an entity

**Figure 8.21c**

*ORDLNE* as a composite entity

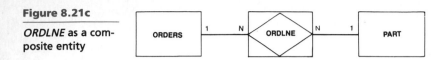

Then Chen proposed what really amounted to a slight change in the E-R approach, one which addressed this issue (see [7]). In this new version, relationships cannot have attributes; only entities can. Given this rule, Figure 8.21a is not an appropriate implementation of the relationship, since *ORDLNE* has attributes. However, Figure 8.21b does not emphasize that the entity *ORDLNE* is really implementing a many-to-many relationship between orders and parts. Chen gets around this problem by giving a special name to such an entity. It is called a **composite entity** and is represented on an E-R diagram by a diamond within a rectangle to emphasize that it is essentially both entity and relationship. Further, relations themselves no longer have special symbols. Thus, the representation that would most closely approximate Chen's most recent proposal would be Figure 8.21c. Most people, however, seem to follow Chen's original proposal. A complete E-R diagram for Premiere Products following the original approach is shown in Figure 8.22. Notice that *ORDLNE* is represented as a relationship.

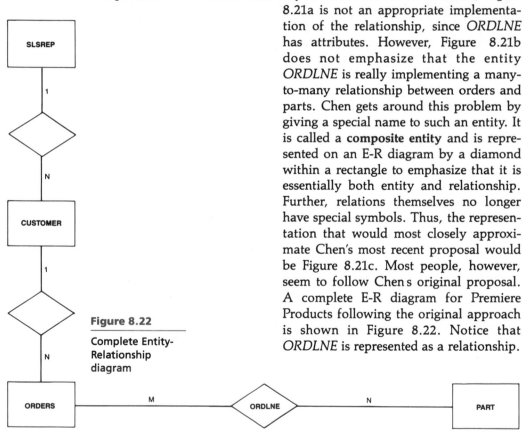

**Figure 8.22**

Complete Entity-Relationship diagram

An E-R diagram, especially one following the most recent proposals, looks very much like the data structure diagrams we use with DBDL. The only real difference is that the diagrams in DBDL use an arrow pointing from the "one" to the "many" whereas the "one" and the "many" are labeled as "1" and "n", respectively, in E-R diagrams. Converting between the two is thus a very simple process. The only thing not addressed in our approach is the idea of existence and ID dependencies. Fortunately, there are very easy ways to spot such dependencies in DBDL.

1. **Existence dependencies.** Suppose that nulls are not allowed for the *SLSRNUMB* foreign key in the *CUSTOMER* relation. Then every customer *must* have a sales rep. Put another way, a customer cannot *exist* without a sales rep. Thus, the relationship between sales reps and customers is an existence dependency. This is the way we can recognize existence dependencies in DBDL. For each arrow in our data structure diagram, we examine the foreign key to which the arrow corresponds. If nulls are not allowed for this foreign key, the relationship is an existence dependency.

2. **ID dependencies.** In the *ORDLNE* relation, *ORDNUMB* is a portion of the key. It is also a foreign key matching the *ORDERS* relation. Thus, to identify a given order line, the order number of the matching order is essential. In other words, the relationship between orders and order lines is an ID dependency (an order line cannot be identified on its own but only through its relationship with another entity). This is the general way we identify ID dependencies. If the primary key of the "many" entity type contains the foreign key identifying the "one" entity type, the relationship is an ID dependency and should be so labeled.

## GENERAL DESIGN COMMENTS

Database design problems run the gamut from designs for complex systems with large numbers of entities and relationships and large numbers of users with widely diverse needs, to designs for relatively simple, special-purpose systems with small numbers of entities, relationships, and requirements. While the basic design principles are the same for both simple systems and complex ones, many of the information-level details discussed in this chapter, as well as the physical-level details discussed in chapter 11, can be omitted in the case of simple systems. At the very least, these details will require far less attention than they would in a more complex system.

### Data Dictionary

While some forms of documentation produced during the design process have already been specified, one important form, the **data dictionary**, has not yet been mentioned. Every relation, every attribute, and every relationship should be described in great detail. To do justice to this process, an automated data dictionary is essential. These tools, which are discussed in detail in chapter 12, allow us to enter details concerning relations, attributes, and so on, in an easy and flexible way. They then allow us to produce a variety of useful reports concerning our design. As we will see in chapter 12, they have a number of other benefits as well.

## Computerization of Database Design

No matter how straightforward the application of a methodology, the process of database design can be very time-consuming, particularly for large, complex systems. Some form of computer assistance for the design process is clearly desirable. One such form was mentioned earlier, an automated data dictionary that assists in the documentation process.

CASE (Computer Aided Software Engineering) tools are becoming increasingly popular. These tools assist in various phases of the systems development life cycle. Such tools include components that relate to database design. Typically these tools provide:

1. Assistance in the creation and modification of entity-relationship or data structure diagrams.
2. A data dictionary into which we can enter information concerning entities, attributes, and relationships. Such information can then be related to the diagrams.
3. Some assistance in the normalization process.

To illustrate the way these tools work, let's look briefly at the way we would create an entity-relationship diagram and add information to the data dictionary using the CASE tool called Excelerator, a product of Index Technology.

Figure 8.23 shows the screen we use to create these diagrams. In the figure, we have placed one rectangle, the rectangle that will ultimately be labeled *SLSREP*. While we won't go into the specific mechanics here, placing the rectangle in the diagram is a very simple process.

**Figure 8.23**

Creating an E-R diagram using Excelerator

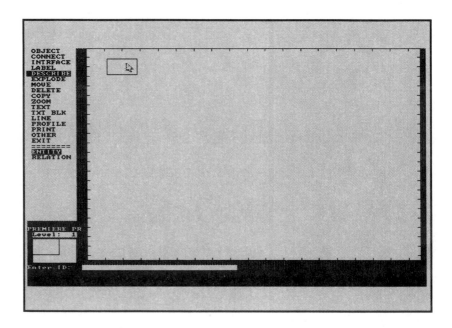

In Figure 8.24, we have placed the shapes for all the entities and relation-ships on the screen. We still need to connect the entities and the relationships. This has been done in Figure 8.25.

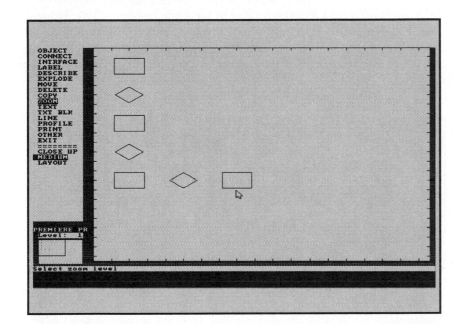

**Figure 8.24**

Creating an E-R
diagram using
Excelerator

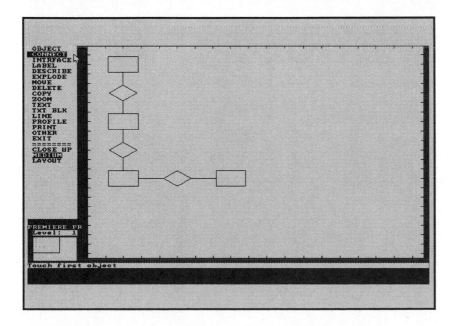

**Figure 8.25**

Creating an E-R
diagram using
Excelerator

The next step is to label the entities and relationships. This has been done in the screen shown in Figure 8.26. Notice that the relationship between *SLSREP* and *CUSTOMER* has not been given a name. The *1* and the *N* indicate that it is a one-to-many relationship. The relationship between *CUSTOMER* and *ORDERS* has been treated in the same fashion. The relationship between *ORDERS* and *PART* has been given a name, *ORDLNE*, since this relationship has attributes of its own. (For an illustration of these attributes, refer back to Figure 8.18.) The *M* and *N* indicate that it is a many-to-many relationship.

**Figure 8.26**

Creating an E-R diagram using Excelerator

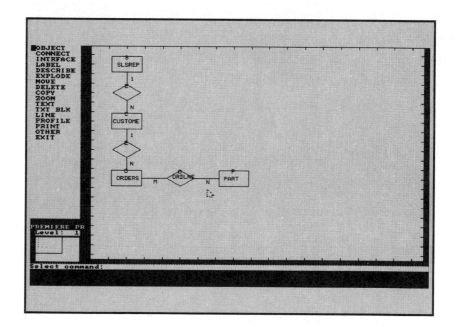

At this point, we are ready to add information concerning these entities to the dictionary. In Figure 8.27, we are beginning to describe the *PART* entity. To describe the attributes that make up the entity, we use the screen shown in Figure 8.28. In this figure, we have entered the names of each of the attributes in *PART*.

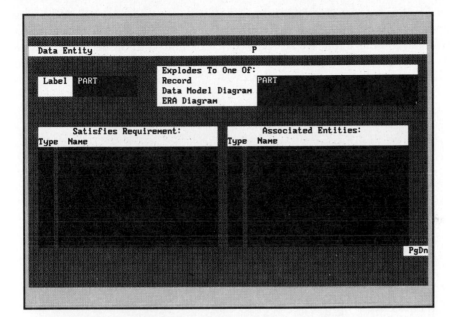

**Figure 8.27**

Entering dictionary information using Excelerator

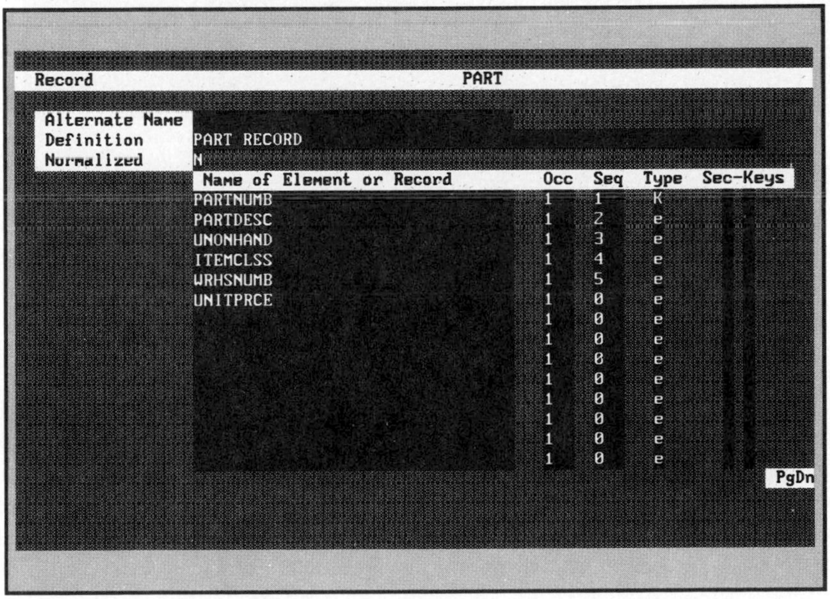

**Figure 8.28**

Entering dictionary information using Excelerator

Finally, we can describe each of the attributes in detail using the screen shown in Figure 8.29. In this figure we are describing the attribute called *ITEMCLSS*. Notice that we not only give a definition of the attribute, but we can also specify several other items, such as format details, edit rules, column headers (for reports), and so on.

**Figure 8.29**

Entering dictionary
information using
Excelerator

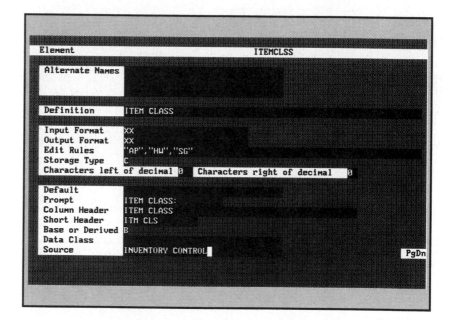

Once we have created the diagram and entered the necessary information, we can print the diagrams and associated documentation. The most important feature, however, is that we can easily modify the diagram and/or the dictionary information. It is easy to add entities, attributes, and relationships to a diagram. It is also easy to move existing entities and relationships on a diagram. It is easy to modify dictionary information.

The ease with which we can make such changes makes the process of revising a design much simpler than if we maintained the documentation by hand. This type of assistance is invaluable during the design process since these types of revision occur frequently as we treat the various user views. Such revisions are also required after designs are complete, since user requirements can change and such changes often necessitate changes in the database design.

## Synonyms

In English, a synonym is a word or expression that has the same meaning as another word or expression, or at least a meaning that is very close to it. In computing, synonyms are two different names for the same entity, attribute, or relationship. It is critical to resolve any questions concerning possible synonyms before beginning the design process. If we do not know that the attribute one user called *COURSE_CODE* is called *COURSE_NUMBER* by another user, we will probably end up having two separate attributes in the database for the same thing and will not even be aware of the problem we have created!

If the attributes in question are primary keys, which is probably the case with *COURSE_CODE* and *COURSE_NUMBER*, the problem gets worse. We will create two separate relations that really should be merged, yet we won't realize what we have done. Before assigning the primary key *COURSE_NUMBER* for a relation necessary to support a particular user, we should carefully examine the keys of the relations already in place. If we spot a relation, *COURSE*, with a primary key called *COURSE_CODE*, which sounds like a potential synonym, we should consult the users to determine whether it is a synonym, or, in fact, a different attribute. Note that this process only helps resolve synonyms involving primary keys. While unrecognized synonyms for primary keys constitute the most serious problem, any case of unrecognized synonyms is a problem.

## Top-down vs. Bottom-up

The methodology presented here is an example of a bottom-up methodology; that is, starting from specific user requirements, a design is ultimately synthesized. A top-down design methodology is one which begins with a general database design that models the overall enterprise and repeatedly refines the model until a design is achieved, which will support all the necessary applications.

Both strategies have their advantages. The top-down approach lends a more global feel to the project; we at least have some idea where we are headed, which is not so with a strictly bottom-up approach.

On the other hand, a bottom-up approach provides a rigorous way of tackling each separate requirement and ensuring that it will be met. In particular, relations are created to satisfy precisely each user view or requirement. When these relations are merged into the cumulative design, provided the merge is done correctly, we can rest assured that each user view can indeed be satisfied.

The ideal strategy would combine the best of both approaches. With a simple modification, the methodology presented here can do this. Assuming that the design problem is sufficiently complicated to warrant the benefits of the top-down approach, we can begin the design process with these steps:

1. After gathering data on all user views, review them without attempting to create any relations. In other words, try to get a general feel for the task at hand.
2. From this information, determine the basic entities of interest to the enterprise (e.g., customers, sales reps, orders, and parts). Do not be overly concerned that you might miss an entity. If you do, it will show up in later steps of the design methodology.
3. For each entity, start a relation. For example, if the entities are customers, sales reps, orders, and parts, we will have:

```
CUSTOMER (
SLSREP (
ORDERS (
PART (
```

4. Determine and fill in a primary key for each relation. In this example, we might have:

```
CUSTOMER (CUSTNUMB,
SLSREP (SLSRNUMB,
ORDERS (ORDNUMB,
PART (PARTNUMB,
```

5. (Optional) For each one-to-many relationship that can be identified among these entities, create and document an appropriate foreign key. If there is a one-to-many relationship from *SLSREP* to *CUSTOMER*, for example, add the foreign key, *SLSRNUMB* to the *CUSTOMER* relation. Again don't worry. If this is not done, or if any foreign keys are missed in the process, the situation will be rectified when we treat individual users views later.

We can now apply the methodology that has been discussed earlier for treating individual user views. We keep in mind the relations that we have created and their keys as we design each user view. When it is time to determine the primary key for a relation, for example, we find out whether such a primary key exists in our overall collection. When it is time to determine a foreign key, we find out whether the primary key it is required to match exists in the overall collection. In either case, if the primary key exists, we give it the name that has already been assigned. This ensures that the relations will merge properly. If, at the end of the design process, there are any relations that were created initially and that have not had any other attributes added to them and have no foreign keys matching them, they may be removed.

The addition of these steps to the process provides the benefits of the top-down approach. As we proceed through the design process for the individual user views, we have a general idea of the overall picture.

## COMPREHENSIVE DATABASE DESIGN EXAMPLE

### Marvel College Requirements

Now that Marvel College has entered the database age, the administration has decided to computerize more of the school's operations. Following is an explanation of the requirements the system must satisfy.

**General Description.** Marvel College is organized by department (Math, Physics, English). A department may offer more than one major; for example, the Math department might offer majors in mathematics education, applied mathematics, and statistics. Each major, however, is offered by only one department. Each faculty member is assigned to a single department. Students can have more than one major, but most have only one. Each student has a faculty member as an advisor for his or her major; students who have more than one major have a faculty advisor for each one. The faculty member may or may not be assigned to the department offering the major.

Each department is identified by a three-character code (MTH for Math, PHY for Physics, ENG for English). Each course is identified by the combination of this code and a three-digit number (MTH 201 for Calculus, ENG 102 for Creative Writing). The number of credits offered by a particular course does not vary; that is, all students who pass the same course receive the same amount of credit.

Each semester is identified by a two-character code for the term, combined with two digits that designate the year (FA91 for the fall semester of 1991). For a given semester, each section of each course is assigned a four-digit schedule code together with a section letter (schedule code 1295 for section A of MTH 201, 1297 for section B of MTH 201, and 1302 for section C of MTH 201). For a different semester, the schedule codes will be entirely different. The schedule codes are listed in the time schedule, and students use them to indicate the sections in which they wish to enroll. (The enrollment process is described in detail later in this section.)

After the enrollment process has been completed for a given semester, each faculty member receives a class list for each section he or she is teaching. In addition to listing the students who are in that particular section, the class list provides space to indicate the grade each student has earned in the course. At the end of the term, the faculty member will place the student's grades on this list and will return a copy of the list to the records office, where the grades will be entered into the computer. (At some point in the near future, the college plans to automate this part of the process.)

Once the grades have been posted, report cards are generated and sent to students. The grades become part of the student's permanent record and will appear on the student's transcript, which is generated by the computer upon request.

The preceding description of the requirements is general; the specific information requirements of the college follow.

**Report Requirements.**    The following are the report requirements for Marvel College.

1. **REPORT CARD.** At the end of each semester, report cards must be produced. A sample report card is shown in Figure 8.30.
2. **CLASS LIST.** A class list must be produced for each section of each course; a sample class list is shown in Figure 8.31. Note that space is provided for the grades. At the end of the term, the instructor will fill in the grades and return a copy of the class list. The grades will then be posted.
3. **GRADE VERIFICATION REPORT.** The grade verification report is identical to the class list shown in Figure 8.31 except that grades have been filled in. It is sent back to the section instructor after the grades have been processed. The instructor can use the report to verify that the grades were entered accurately.
4. **TIME SCHEDULE.** The time schedule, which is shown in Figure 8.32 on page 378, lists all sections of all courses to be offered during a given semester. Each section has a unique four-digit schedule code. The time schedule lists the schedule code; the department offering the course; the course number; the section letter; the title of the course; the instructor of the course; the time at which the course meets; the room in which the course meets; the number of credits generated by the course; and the prerequisites for the course. In addition to the information shown in the figure, the time schedule includes the date the semester begins; the date the semester ends; the date finals begin; the date finals end; and the last date at which students may withdraw from a course.

```
                          MARVEL COLLEGE

                  COURSE                        CREDITS CREDITS  GRADE
  DEPARTMENT      NUMBER COURSE DESCRIPTION GRADE TAKEN  EARNED  POINTS
  COMPUTER SCIENCE 153   COBOL               A     4      4      16.0
  MATHEMATICS      201   CALCULUS            B     3      3      12.0
```

```
    7       7    4.00   28.0
 CREDITS CREDITS        TOTAL             SEMESTER   WI91
  TAKEN  EARNED   GPA  POINTS
      CURRENT SEMESTER TOTALS
   44      44    3.39  149.2              STUDENT NUMBER   381124188
 CREDITS CREDITS        TOTAL
  TAKEN  EARNED   GPA  POINTS
       CUMULATIVE TOTALS
```

```
    STUDENT NAME & ADDRESS      LOCAL ADDRESS (IF DIFFERENT)
  BRIAN CONNORS
  686 FRANKLIN
  HART, MI 48282
```

**Figure 8.30**

Sample report card for Marvel College

```
                    CLASS LISTS

  DEPARTMENT: CS     COMPUTER SCIENCE      TERM: FA91
  COURSE: 153        COBOL          (4 CREDITS)
  SECTION: B
  SCHEDULE CODE: 2366

  TIME: 1:00 - 1:50 M,T,W,F
  PLACE: 118 SCR

  INSTRUCTOR: 462    DIANE JOHNSTON

  STUDENT    STUDENT              CLASS
  NUMBER     NAME               STANDING   GRADE

  000625321  ARTHUR ADAMS          4
     .          .                  .
     .          .                  .
     .          .                  .
```

**Figure 8.31**

Sample class list for Marvel College

**Figure 8.32**

Sample time
schedule for
Marvel College

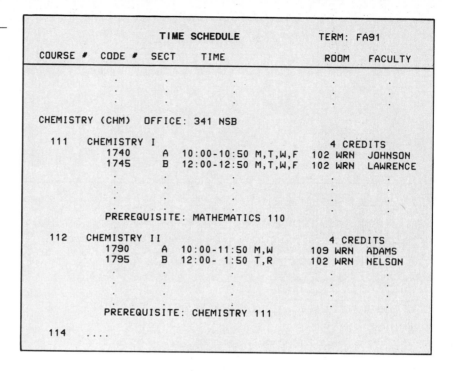

```
                        TIME  SCHEDULE            TERM: FA91

   COURSE #  CODE #  SECT    TIME                 ROOM   FACULTY

                .         .        .                .      .
                .         .        .                .      .
                .         .        .                .      .
CHEMISTRY (CHM)   OFFICE: 341 NSB

    111    CHEMISTRY I                            4 CREDITS
           1740       A   10:00-10:50 M,T,W,F  102 WRN   JOHNSON
           1745       B   12:00-12:50 M,T,W,F  102 WRN   LAWRENCE
                .         .        .                .      .
                .         .        .                .      .
                .         .        .                .      .
           PREREQUISITE: MATHEMATICS 110

    112    CHEMISTRY II                           4 CREDITS
           1790       A   10:00-11:50 M,W       109 WRN   ADAMS
           1795       B   12:00- 1:50 T,R       102 WRN   NELSON
                .         .        .                .      .
                .         .        .                .      .

           PREREQUISITE: CHEMISTRY 111

    114    ....
```

5. **REGISTRATION REQUEST FORM.** A sample registration request
   form is shown in Figure 8.33. This form is used to request classes for
   the following semester. Students indicate the sections for which they
   wish to register by entering the sections' schedule codes; for each of
   these sections, they may also enter a code for an alternate section.
   Students who cannot be placed in the section they request will be
   placed in the alternate section, provided there is room.

6. **STUDENT SCHEDULE.** A sample student schedule form is shown in
   Figure 8.34. This form shows the schedule for an individual student
   for a given semester.

7. **FULL STUDENT INFORMATION REPORT.** A sample of a full student information report is shown in Figure 8.35 on page 380. It gives
   complete information about a student, including his or her majors
   and all grades received to date.

8. **FACULTY INFORMATION REPORT.** This report lists all faculty by
   department and contains each faculty member's ID number, name,
   address, office, phone number, current rank, and starting date of
   employment. It also lists the number, name, and local and permanent address of each of the faculty member's advisees, along with the
   code number and description of the major in which the faculty member is advising each one, and the code number and description of the

department in which this major is housed. (Remember that this department need not be the one to which the faculty member is assigned.)

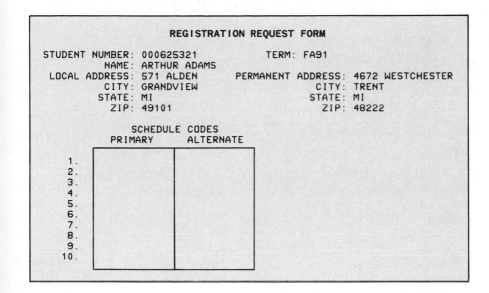

**Figure 8.33**

Sample registration request form for Marvel College

**REGISTRATION REQUEST FORM**

STUDENT NUMBER: 000625321      TERM: FA91
        NAME: ARTHUR ADAMS
LOCAL ADDRESS: 571 ALDEN      PERMANENT ADDRESS: 4672 WESTCHESTER
        CITY: GRANDVIEW           CITY: TRENT
       STATE: MI            STATE: MI
         ZIP: 49101             ZIP: 48222

              SCHEDULE CODES
        PRIMARY      ALTERNATE

1.
2.
3.
4.
5.
6.
7.
8.
9.
10.

**Figure 8.34**

Sample student schedule for Marvel College

**STUDENT SCHEDULE**

STUDENT NUMBER: 000625321      TERM: FA91
        NAME: ARTHUR ADAMS
LOCAL ADDRESS: 571 ALDEN      PERMANENT ADDRESS: 4672 WESTCHESTER
        CITY: GRANDVIEW           CITY: TRENT
       STATE: MI            STATE: MI
         ZIP: 49101            ZIP: 48222

| SCHD CODE | DEPARTMENT | CRS NUMB | COURSE DESCRIPTION | SECT | CREDITS | TIME | ROOM |
|---|---|---|---|---|---|---|---|
| 2366 | COMP. SCI. | 153 | COBOL | B | 4 | 1:00 - 1:50 M,T,W,F | 118 SCR |
| . | . | . | . | . | . | . | . |
| . | . | . | . | . | . | . | . |

                  TOTAL CREDITS      16

```
                        FULL STUDENT INFORMATION
     STUDENT NUMBER: 000625321          TERM: FA91
              NAME: ARTHUR ADAMS
     LOCAL ADDRESS: 571 ALDEN    PERMANENT ADDRESS: 4672 WESTCHESTER
              CITY: GRANDVIEW                 CITY: TRENT
             STATE: MI                       STATE: MI
               ZIP: 49101                      ZIP: 48222

     MAJOR 1: INFORMATION SYS.  DEPT: COMPUTER SCIENCE  ADVISOR: MARK LAWRENCE
     MAJOR 2: ACCOUNTING        DEPT: BUSINESS          ADVISOR: JILL THOMAS
     MAJOR 3:                   DEPT:                   ADVISOR:
```

| TERM | DEPARTMENT | COURSE NUMBER | COURSE DESCRIPTION | CREDITS | GRADE EARNED | GRADE POINTS |
|------|-----------|---------------|--------------------|---------|--------------|--------------|
| FA85: | MATHEMATICS | 110 | CALC. I | 4 | A | 16 |
| | HISTORY | 201 | WESTERN CIV | 3 | B | 9 |
| | ENGLISH | 101 | AMER. LIT. | 3 | A | 12 |
| WI86: | MATHEMATICS | 111 | CALC. II | 4 | B | 12 |
| | COMPUTER SCIENCE | 151 | PASCAL | 4 | B | 12 |
| . | . | . | . | . | . | . |
| . | . | . | . | . | . | . |
| . | . | . | . | . | . | . |
| . | . | . | . | . | . | . |
| . | . | . | . | . | . | . |

```
     CREDITS ATTEMPTED: 60
        CREDITS EARNED: 60
          GRADE POINTS: 195
      GRADE POINT AVG: 3.25
        CLASS STANDING: 2
```

**Figure 8.35**

Sample full student information report for Marvel College

9. **WORK VERSION OF THE TIME SCHEDULE.** This report is similar to the original time schedule (see Figure 8.32) but is designed for the college's internal use. It shows the current enrollments in each section of each course, as well as the maximum enrollment permitted per section. It is more up-to-date than the time schedule itself. (When students register for courses, enrollment figures are updated on the work version of the time schedule. When room or faculty assignments are changed, this information is also updated. A new version of this report that reflects the updated figures is then printed.)

10. **COURSE REPORT.** This report lists, for each course, the code and name of the department that is offering the course, the course number, the description of the course, and the number of credits awarded. Also listed is the department and course number for each prerequisite course.

**Update (Transaction) Requirements.** In addition to being able to add, change, and delete any of the entities mentioned in the report requirements, the update requirements accomplish the following.

1. **ENROLLMENT.** When a student attempts to register for a section of a course, determine whether he or she has received credit for all prerequisites to the course. If the student is eligible to enroll in the course and if the number of students currently enrolled in the section is less than the maximum enrollment, enroll the student.
2. **POST GRADES.** For each section of each course, post the grades indicated on the copy of the class list returned by the instructor, and produce a grade verification report.
3. **PURGE.** Section information, including grades assigned by the section, is retained for two semesters following the end of the semester, at which time the information is removed from the database. (Grades assigned to students are retained by course, but not by section.)

## Marvel College Information-Level Design

Some consideration should be given to overall requirements before the methodology is applied to individual user requirements. Scanning the design, we come up with the following list of possible entities: department, major, faculty member, student, course, and semester.

Your list may be different. You may have included the entity "section," for example, or "grade." On the other hand, you may not have included "semester." In the long run, as long as the list is fairly reasonable, it won't make much difference. In fact, you may remember that this step is really not even necessary. The better we do our job now, however, the simpler the process will be later on.

We now assign a primary key to each of these entities. In general, this will require some type of consultation with the user. We may need to ask the user directly for the required information, or we may be able to obtain it from some type of survey form. Let's assume that having had such a consultation, we have named a relation for each of these entities and have assigned primary keys as follows:

```
DEPT (DEPTCODE,
MAJOR (MAJNUMB,
FACULTY (FACNUMB,
STUDENT (STUNUMB,
COURSE (DEPTCODE, CRSNUMB,
SEMESTER (SEMCODE,
```

Note that the primary key for the *COURSE* relation consists of two attributes, *DEPTCODE* (such as CS) and *CRSNUMB* (such as 153). Both are required.

We now begin to examine the individual user views, create relations for them, represent any keys, and merge them into the design. First of all, we must decide exactly what the user views are. In the list of requirements, the term user view never appeared. Instead, a general description of the system was given, together with a collection of report requirements and another collection of update requirements. How do these requirements relate to user views?

Certainly, each report requirement and each update requirement can be thought of as a user view. What do we do with the general description? Do we think of each paragraph (or perhaps each sentence) in it as representing a user view, or do we use it to furnish additional information about the report and update requirements? Basically, both approaches are acceptable. The second approach is often easier, however, and we shall follow it here. We shall think of the report and update requirements as user views and use the statements in the general description to give additional information about these views wherever needed. We will also consider the general description during the review process to ensure that all the functionality it describes can be satisfied by our final design.

We now turn to the user views. First, let's take one of the simpler user views: report 10, the course report. (Technically, the user views can be examined in any order. Sometimes we take them in the order they are listed. In other cases, we may be able to come up with a better order. Often, examining some of the simpler user views first is a reasonable approach.)

Three comments are in order before we proceed with the design. First, with some of the user views, we will take a "good" approach to determining relations; that is, we will carefully determine the entities and relationships between them and use this information in creating the relations. This means that from the outset the collection of relations created will be in or close to 3NF. With other user views, we will create a single relation that potentially contains some number of repeating groups. In these cases, as we will see, the normalization process will still produce a correct design, but it will also involve more work. In practice, the more experience a designer has had, the more likely he or she is to create 3NF relations immediately. Second, many of the decisions concerning foreign key restrictions will be made arbitrarily. You can assume that appropriate users have been interviewed concerning the relationships and restrictions, and that their responses have led to the decisions found in the example. Third, the name of an entity or attribute may vary from one user view to another, and this requires resolution. We will attempt to use names that are exactly the same.

**User View 1: Course Report.**   Forgetting for the moment the requirement to list prerequisite courses, the basic relation necessary to support this report would be as follows:

```
COURSE (DEPTCODE, DEPTNAME, CRSNUMB, CRSTITLE, NUMBCRED)
```

in which the combination of *DEPTCODE* and *CRSNUMB* uniquely determines all the other attributes. In this relation, *DEPTCODE* determines *DEPTNAME*, and thus the relation is not in 2NF (an attribute depends on only a portion of the key). To correct this situation, the relation is split into:

```
COURSE (DEPTCODE, CRSNUMB, CRSTITLE, NUMBCRED)
DEPT (DEPTCODE, DEPTNAME)
```

The *DEPTCODE* in the first relation is a foreign key identifying the second.

To maintain prerequisite information, we need the relation *PREREQ*:

```
PREREQ (DEPTCODE, CRSNUMB, PRERDEPT, PRERCRS)
```

(See the discussion of the *PREREQ* relation in chapter 7 if you are not clear on the structure of this relation. The only difference between this relation and the *PREREQ* relation in that chapter is that there the attribute, *CRSCODE*, uniquely identified a course, whereas here both *DEPTCODE* and *CRSNUMB* are required.

The DBDL version of these relations is shown in Figure 8.36, and the result of merging these relations into the cumulative design is shown in Figure 8.37 on the next page. Notice that the *DEPT* and *COURSE* relations have merged with the existing *DEPT* and *COURSE* relations in the cumulative design. In the process, the attribute *DEPTNAME* was added to the *DEPT* relation, and the attributes *CRSTITLE* and *NUMBCRED* were added to the *COURSE* relation.

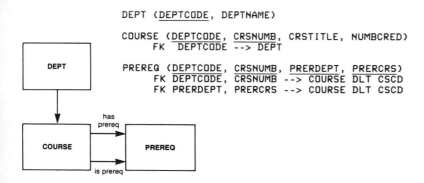

```
DEPT (DEPTCODE, DEPTNAME)

COURSE (DEPTCODE, CRSNUMB, CRSTITLE, NUMBCRED)
     FK  DEPTCODE --> DEPT

PREREQ (DEPTCODE, CRSNUMB, PRERDEPT, PRERCRS)
      FK DEPTCODE, CRSNUMB --> COURSE DLT CSCD
      FK PRERDEPT, PRERCRS --> COURSE DLT CSCD
```

**Figure 8.36**

DBDL for user
view 1

In addition, the attribute *DEPTCODE* in the *COURSE* relation was made a foreign key. Since the *PREREQ* relation was new, it was added to the cumulative collection in its entirety. Notice also that we do not yet have any relationships involving *STUDENT, MAJOR, FACULTY,* or *SEMESTER*.

**Figure 8.37**

Cumulative
collection after
user view 1

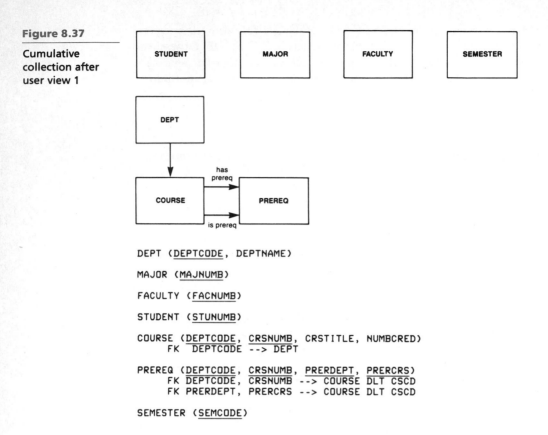

DEPT (<u>DEPTCODE</u>, DEPTNAME)

MAJOR (<u>MAJNUMB</u>)

FACULTY (<u>FACNUMB</u>)

STUDENT (<u>STUNUMB</u>)

COURSE (<u>DEPTCODE</u>, <u>CRSNUMB</u>, CRSTITLE, NUMBCRED)
        FK  DEPTCODE --> DEPT

PREREQ (<u>DEPTCODE</u>, <u>CRSNUMB</u>, <u>PRERDEPT</u>, <u>PRERCRS</u>)
        FK DEPTCODE, CRSNUMB --> COURSE DLT CSCD
        FK PRERDEPT, PRERCRS --> COURSE DLT CSCD

SEMESTER (<u>SEMCODE</u>)


**User View 2: Faculty Information Report.** This user view involves three
entities: departments, faculty, and advisees. Applying the tips from chapter 7,
we can create three relations:

        DEPT (
        FACULTY (
        ADVISEE (

The next step is to assign a primary key to each relation. Before doing so,
however, we should briefly examine the relations in the cumulative collection
and use the same names for any relations or attributes that are already there.
In this case, we would use *DEPTCODE* as the primary key for the *DEPT*
relation, and *FACNUMB* as the primary key for the *FACULTY* relation. There
is no *ADVISEE* relation in the cumulative collection, but there is a *STUDENT*
relation. Since advisees and students are the same, let's rename the *ADVISEE*
as *STUDENT* and use *STUNUMB* as the primary key, yielding

        DEPT (<u>DEPTCODE</u>,
        FACULTY (<u>FACNUMB</u>,
        STUDENT (<u>STUNUMB</u>,

(Another alternative would be to keep the names *ADVISEE* and *ADVNUMB* in this user view and record in the data dictionary the fact that these are synonyms for *STUDENT* and *STUNUMB*, respectively. In general, we avoid the use of synonyms unless there is a compelling reason to use them, and, in such cases, we make sure the reason is carefully documented.)

Next, we add the remaining attributes to these relations.

```
DEPT (DEPTCODE, DEPTNAME)
FACULTY (FACNUMB, FACNAME, FACADDR, FACCITY, FACSTATE, FACZIP,
           OFFNUMB, PHONE, CURRANK, STRTDATE, DEPTCODE)
STUDENT (STUNUMB, STUNAME, LOCADDR, LOCCITY, LOCSTATE, LOCZIP,
           PRMADDR, PRMCITY, PRMSTATE, PRMZIP,

           MAJNUMB, MAJDESC, DEPTCODE, FACNUMB, FACNAME)
```

The department code is included in the *FACULTY* relation, since there is a one-to-many relationship between departments and faculty. Since a student can have more than one major, the information concerning majors (number, description, department, and the number and name of the faculty member who advises this student in this major) is a repeating group.

Since the key to the repeating group in the student relation is the major number, removing this repeating group yields

```
STUDENT (STUNUMB, STUNAME, LOCADDR, LOCCITY, LOCSTATE, LOCZIP,
           PRMADDR, PRMCITY, PRMSTATE, PRMZIP, MAJNUMB, MAJDESC,
           DEPTCODE, FACNUMB, FACNAME)
```

Converting this relation to 2NF produces

```
STUDENT (STUNUMB, STUNAME, LOCADDR, LOCCITY, LOCSTATE, LOCZIP,
           PRMADDR, PRMCITY, PRMSTATE, PRMZIP)
MAJOR (MAJNUMB, MAJDESC, DEPTCODE, DEPTNAME)
ADVISES (STUNUMB, MAJNUMB, FACNUMB)
```

Some dependencies must be removed to create 3NF relations: *OFFNUMB* determines *PHONE* in the *FACULTY* relation, and *DEPTCODE* determines *DEPTNAME*. Removing these dependencies produces the following collection of relations:

```
DEPT (DEPTCODE, DEPTNAME)
FACULTY (FACNUMB, FACNAME, FACADDR, FACCITY, FACSTATE, FACZIP,
           OFFNUMB, CURRANK, STRTDATE, DEPTCODE)
STUDENT (STUNUMB, STUNAME, LOCADDR, LOCCITY, LOCSTATE, LOCZIP,
           PRMADDR, PRMCITY, PRMSTATE, PRMZIP)
ADVISES (STUNUMB, MAJNUMB, FACNUMB)
OFFICE (OFFNUMB, PHONE)
MAJOR (MAJNUMB, MAJDESC, DEPTCODE)
```

The DBDL representation is shown in Figure 8.38, and the result of merging these relations into the cumulative design is shown in Figure 8.39. (Note that the local address, city, state, and ZIP are allowed to be null.) The relations *STUDENT*, *FACULTY*, *MAJOR*, and *DEPT* merge into existing relations with the same primary keys and with the same names. Nothing new is added to the *DEPT* relation in the process, but the other relations all receive additional attributes.

**Figure 8.38**

*DBDL* for user
view 2

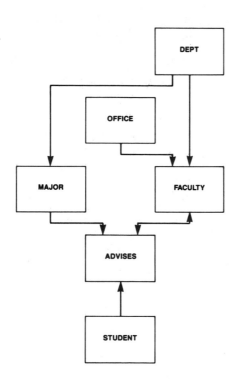

DEPT (<u>DEPTCODE</u>, DEPTNAME)

STUDENT (<u>STUNUMB</u>, STUNAME, LOCADDR*, LOCCITY*, LOCSTATE*,
      <u>LOCZIP</u>*, PRMADDR, PRMSTATE, PRMZIP)

OFFICE (<u>OFFNUMB</u>, PHONE)

FACULTY (<u>FACNUMB</u>, FACNAME, FACADDR, FACCITY, FACSTATE, FACZIP,
      OFFNUMB, CURRANK, STRTDATE, DEPTCODE)
    FK  OFFNUMB --> OFFICE
    FK  DEPTCODE --> DEPT

MAJOR (<u>MAJNUMB</u>, MAJDESC, DEPTCODE)
    FK  DEPTCODE --> DEPT

ADVISES (<u>STUNUMB</u>, FACNUMB, <u>MAJNUMB</u>)
    FK  STUNUMB --> STUDENT  DLT CSCD
    FK  FACNUMB --> FACULTY
    FK  MAJNUMB --> MAJOR

In addition, the *FACULTY* relation also receives two foreign keys, *OFFNUMB* and *DEPTCODE*. The *MAJOR* relation receives one foreign key, *DEPTCODE*. The relations *ADVISES* and *OFFICE* are new and are thus added directly to the cumulative collection of relations.

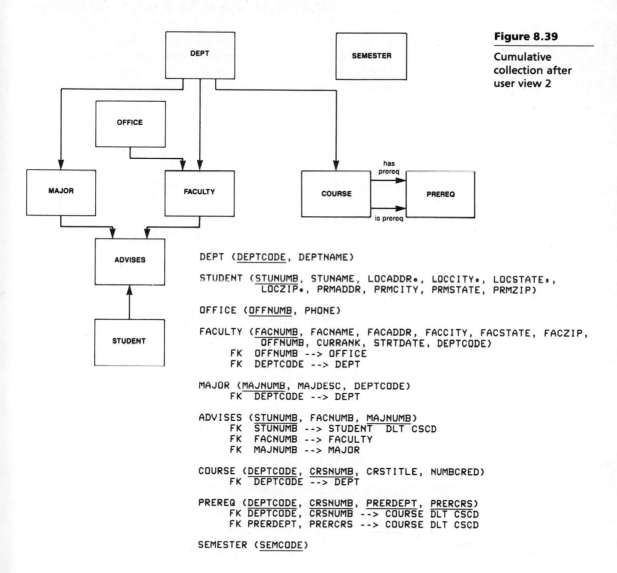

**Figure 8.39**

Cumulative collection after user view 2

DEPT (<u>DEPTCODE</u>, DEPTNAME)

STUDENT (<u>STUNUMB</u>, STUNAME, LOCADDR*, LOCCITY*, LOCSTATE*,
         LOCZIP*, PRMADDR, PRMCITY, PRMSTATE, PRMZIP)

OFFICE (<u>OFFNUMB</u>, PHONE)

FACULTY (<u>FACNUMB</u>, FACNAME, FACADDR, FACCITY, FACSTATE, FACZIP,
         OFFNUMB, CURRANK, STRTDATE, DEPTCODE)
    FK  OFFNUMB --> OFFICE
    FK  DEPTCODE --> DEPT

MAJOR (<u>MAJNUMB</u>, MAJDESC, DEPTCODE)
    FK  DEPTCODE --> DEPT

ADVISES (<u>STUNUMB</u>, <u>FACNUMB</u>, <u>MAJNUMB</u>)
    FK  STUNUMB --> STUDENT   DLT CSCD
    FK  FACNUMB --> FACULTY
    FK  MAJNUMB --> MAJOR

COURSE (<u>DEPTCODE</u>, <u>CRSNUMB</u>, CRSTITLE, NUMBCRED)
    FK  DEPTCODE --> DEPT

PREREQ (<u>DEPTCODE</u>, <u>CRSNUMB</u>, <u>PRERDEPT</u>, <u>PRERCRS</u>)
    FK  DEPTCODE, CRSNUMB --> COURSE DLT CSCD
    FK  PRERDEPT, PRERCRS --> COURSE DLT CSCD

SEMESTER (<u>SEMCODE</u>)

**User View 3: Report Card.**   Report cards are fairly complicated documents. The appropriate underlying relations are not immediately apparent. In this view, we will illustrate tips for obtaining information from existing documents.

The first step is to list all the attributes on the document and give them appropriate names. (See Figure 8.40.) After this has been done, the functional dependencies that exist between these attributes should be listed. The information necessary to determine functional dependencies must ultimately come from the user, although we can often make fairly accurate guesses for most of them. If the functional dependencies are not represented on any documentation we have been given, such as a survey form, we may well have to go directly to the users to obtain the necessary information.

Let's assume this has been done at Marvel College and that Figure 8.41 shows the results. The student number alone determines many of the other attributes. In addition to the student number, the semester must be listed to determine credits taken and earned, grade point average (GPA), and total points this semester. The combination of a department description (such as COMPUTER SCIENCE) and a course number (such as 153) determines a course title and the number of credits. Finally, the student number, the semester (season and year), and the course (discipline and course number) are required to determine an individual grade in a course, the credits earned from the course, and the grade points in a course. (The semester is required, since students can take the same course in more than one semester at Marvel College. Further, let's assume that upon checking with the users, we have learned that they want to allow for the possibility that credits offered by a course may vary from one semester to another and even, possibly, from one student to another.)

The next step is to create a collection of relations that will support this user view. A variety of approaches will work. We could combine all the attributes into a single relation, which would then be converted to 3NF. (In such a relation, the combination of discipline, course number, course title, grade, and so on would be a repeating group.) Or we could use the functional dependencies to determine the following collection of relations:

```
STUDENT (STUNUMB, STUNAME, PRMADDR, PRMCITY, PRMSTATE, PRMZIP,
         LOCADDR, LOCCITY, LOCSTATE, LOCZIP, CRDTAKEN,
         CRDEARND, GPA, TOTPNTS)
STUSEM (STUNUMB, SEMCODE, CRDTAKEN, CRDEARND, GPA, TOTPNTS)
COURSE (DEPTCODE, CRSNUMB, CRSTITLE, NUMBCRED)
STUGRADE (STUNUMB, SEMCODE, DEPTNAME, CRSNUMB, GRADE,
          CRDEARND, GRDPNTS)
```

Department Name
Course Number
Course Title
Grade
Credits Taken in Course
Credits Earned in Course
Grade Points from Course
Credits Taken this Semester
Credits Earned this Semester
GPA this Semester
Total Points this Semester
Point Credits Cumulative
Credits Taken Cumulative
Credits Earned Cumulative
GPA Cumulative
Total Points Cumulative
Semester Code
Student Number
Student Name
Address
City
State
Zip
Local Address
Local City
Local State
Local Zip

**Figure 8.40**

**Attributes on report cards for Marvel College**

Student Number -->
      Credits Taken Cumulative
      Credits Earned Cumulative
      GPA Cumulative
      Total Points Cumulative
      Student Name
      Address
      City
      State
      Zip
      Local Address
      Local City
      Local State
      Local Zip

Student Number, Semester Code -->
      Credits Taken this Semester
      Credits Earned this Semester
      GPA this Semester
      Total Points this Semester

Department Name, Course Number -->
      Course Title
      Credits Taken in Course

Student Number, Semester Code, Department Name, Course Number -->
      Grade
      Credits Earned in Course
      Grade Points from Course

**Figure 8.41**

**Functional dependencies among attributes on report cards**

These relations are all in 3NF. The only change we should make concerns the *DEPTNAME* attribute in the *STUGRADE* relation. Remember that when we encounter an attribute for which there exists a determinant not in the relation, the determinant should be added to the relation. In this case, *DEPTCODE* determines *DEPTNAME*, and we add *DEPTCODE* to the relation. In the normalization process, *DEPTNAME* will then be removed and placed in another relation whose key is *DEPTCODE*. This other relation will merge with the *DEPT* relation without the addition of any new attributes. The resulting relation *STUGRADE* is:

```
STUGRADE (STUNUMB, SEMCODE, DEPTCODE, CRSNUMB, GRADE,
          CRDEARND, GRDPNTS)
```

Before representing this design in DBDL, we will take a close look at *STUSEM*. It is true that the attributes within it, (*CRDTAKEN*, *CRDEARND*, *GPA*, and *TOTPNTS*), which all refer to the current semester, do, in fact, appear on report cards. Let's assume that after further checking we find that they are all easily calculated from other fields on the report card during the actual production of report cards. Then, rather than store them in the database, we will merely make sure that the program that produces report cards performs the necessary calculations. For this reason, we will remove the relation *STUSEM* from the collection of relations to be documented and merged. (If these attributes are also required by some other user view in which the same computations are not as practical, they may yet find their way into the database when that user view is analyzed.)

**Q & A**

Question:    Write the DBDL representation of these relations, including foreign key specifications. Note any synonyms between this user view and the cumulative design, and resolve them. Merge the result into the cumulative design.

Answer:      See Figure 8.42.

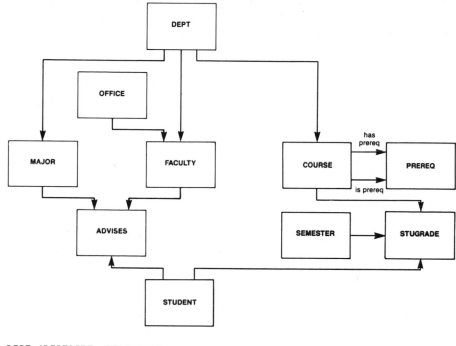

**Figure 8.42**

Cumulative design after user view 3

```
DEPT (DEPTCODE, DEPTNAME)

STUDENT (STUNUMB, STUNAME, LOCADDR*, LOCCITY*, LOCSTATE*,
         LOCZIP*, PRMADDR, PRMCITY, PRMSTATE, PRMZIP,
         CRDTAKEN, CRDEARND, GPA, TOTPNTS)

OFFICE (OFFNUMB, PHONE)

FACULTY (FACNUMB, FACNAME, FACADDR, FACCITY, FACSTATE, FACZIP,
         OFFNUMB, CURRANK, STRTDATE, DEPTCODE)
    FK   OFFNUMB --> OFFICE
    FK   DEPTCODE --> DEPT

MAJOR (MAJNUMB, MAJDESC, DEPTCODE)
    FK   DEPTCODE --> DEPT

ADVISES (STUNUMB, FACNUMB, MAJNUMB)
    FK   STUNUMB --> STUDENT   DLT CSCD
    FK   FACNUMB --> FACULTY
    FK   MAJNUMB --> MAJOR

COURSE (DEPTCODE, CRSNUMB, CRSTITLE, NUMBCRED)
    FK   DEPTCODE --> DEPT

PREREQ (DEPTCODE, CRSNUMB, PRERDEPT, PRERCRS)
    FK   DEPTCODE, CRSNUMB --> COURSE DLT CSCD
    FK   PRERDEPT, PRERCRS --> COURSE DLT CSCD

SEMESTER (SEMCODE)

STUGRADE (STUNUMB, SEMCODE, DEPTCODE, CRSNUMB, GRADE, CRDEARND,
          GRDPNTS)
    FK   STUNUMB --> STUDENT   DLT CSCD
    FK   SEMCODE --> SEMESTER
    FK   DEPTCODE, CRSNUMB --> COURSE
```

**User View 4: Class List.** Let's assume that after examining the sample class list report, we decide to create a single relation (actually an unnormalized relation) that contains all the attributes on the class list, with the student information (number, name, class standing, and grade) as a repeating group. (Applying the tips for determining the relations to support a given user view would lead more directly to the result, but, for the sake of giving the example, we'll assume we haven't done that here.) The unnormalized relation created in this fashion would be:

```
CLASSLST (DEPTCODE, DEPTNAME, SEMCODE, CRSNUMB, CRSTITLE,
         NUMBCRED, SECTLETT, SCHDCODE, TIME, ROOM,
         FACNUMB, FACNAME, STUNUMB, STUNAME, CLSSSTND, GRADE)
```

Note that we have not as yet indicated the primary key. To identify a given class within a particular semester requires either the combination of department code, course number, and section letter or, more simply, the schedule code. Taking the schedule code as the primary key, however, is not quite adequate. Since the information from more than one semester will be on file at the same time and since the same schedule code could be used in two different semesters to represent totally different courses, the primary key must also contain the semester code. When we remove the repeating group, this primary key expands to contain the key for the repeating group, in this case the student number. Thus, converting to 1NF yields:

```
CLASSLST (DEPTCODE, DEPTNAME, SEMCODE, CRSNUMB, CRSTITLE,
         NUMBCRED, SECTLETT, SCHDCODE, TIME, ROOM,
         FACNUMB, FACNAME, STUNUMB, STUNAME, CLSSSTND, GRADE*)
```

Converting to 3NF yields the following collection of relations:

```
DEPT (DEPTCODE, DEPTNAME)
SECTION (SEMCODE, SCHDCODE, DEPTCODE, CRSNUMB, SECTLETT,
         TIME, ROOM, FACNUMB)
FACULTY (FACNUMB, FACNAME)
STUCLASS (SEMCODE, SCHDCODE, STUNUMB, GRADE*)
STUDENT (STUNUMB, STUNAME, CLSSSTND)
COURSE (DEPTCODE, CRSNUMB, CRSTITLE, NUMBCRED)
```

**Q & A**

Question:        Why was the grade included?

Answer:          Although the grade is not actually printed on the class list, it will be entered on the form by the instructor and later returned for posting. A later report, called the grade verification report, differs from the class list only in that the grade is printed. Thus, the grade will ultimately be required and it is legitimate to deal with it here. Since at this point the grade is unknown, the grade field should be allowed to be null.

Question: Write the DBDL representation of these relations, including foreign key specifications. Determine the presence of any synonyms with regard to this user view and the cumulative design. Resolve such synonyms and merge the result into the cumulative design.

Answer: See Figure 8.43.

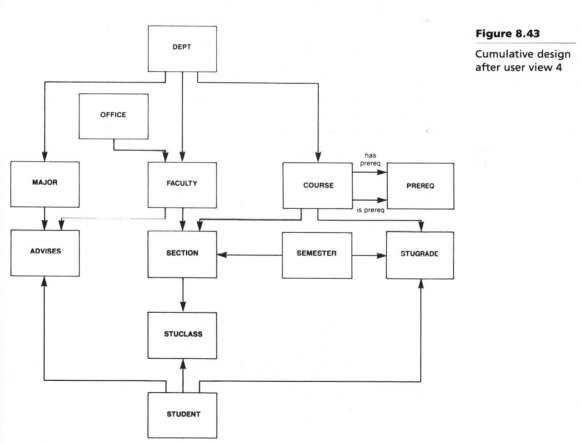

**Figure 8.43**

Cumulative design after user view 4

*(continued)*

**Figure 8.43**

(continued)

```
DEPT (DEPTCODE, DEPTNAME)

STUDENT (STUNUMB, STUNAME, LOCADDR*, LOCCITY*, LOCSTATE*,
          LOCZIP*, PRMADDR, PRMCITY, PRMSTATE, PRMZIP,
          CRDTAKEN, CRDEARND, GPA, TOTPNTS, CLSSSTND)

OFFICE (OFFNUMB, PHONE)

FACULTY (FACNUMB, FACNAME, FACADDR, FACCITY, FACSTATE, FACZIP,
          OFFNUMB, CURRANK, STRTDATE, DEPTCODE)
    FK   OFFNUMB --> OFFICE
    FK   DEPTCODE --> DEPT

MAJOR (MAJNUMB, MAJDESC, DEPTCODE)
    FK   DEPTCODE --> DEPT

ADVISES (STUNUMB, FACNUMB, MAJNUMB)
    FK   STUNUMB --> STUDENT   DLT CSCD
    FK   FACNUMB --> FACULTY
    FK   MAJNUMB --> MAJOR

COURSE (DEPTCODE, CRSNUMB, CRSTITLE, NUMBCRED)
    FK   DEPTCODE --> DEPT

PREREQ (DEPTCODE, CRSNUMB, PRERDEPT, PRERCRS)
    FK DEPTCODE, CRSNUMB --> COURSE DLT CSCD
    FK PRERDEPT, PRERCRS --> COURSE DLT CSCD

SEMESTER (SEMCODE)

STUGRADE (STUNUMB, SEMCODE, DEPTCODE, CRSNUMB, GRADE, CRDEARND,
          GRDPNTS)
    FK   STUNUMB --> STUDENT   DLT CSCD
    FK   SEMCODE --> SEMESTER
    FK   DEPTCODE, CRSNUMB --> COURSE

SECTION (SEMCODE, SCHDCODE, DEPTCODE, CRSNUMB, SECTLETT, TIME,
          ROOM, FACNUMB)
    FK   SEMCODE --> SEMESTER
    FK   DEPTCODE, CRSNUMB --> COURSE
    FK   FACNUMB --> FACULTY

STUCLASS (SEMCODE, SCHDCODE, STUNUMB, GRADE*)
    FK   SEMCODE, SCHDCODE --> SECTION   DLT CSCD
    FK   STUNUMB --> STUDENT   DLT CSCD
```

**User View 5: Grade Verification Report.** Since the only difference between the class list and the grade verification report is that the grades are printed on the latter, the user views will be quite similar. In fact, since we made provision for the grade when treating the class list, the views are identical, and no further treatment of this view is required.

**User View 6: Time Schedule.**   The attributes on the time schedule are as follows: term (which is a synonym for semester code); department code; department name; location; course number; course title; number of credits; schedule code; section letter; meeting time; meeting place; and name of instructor. The time schedule also contains the starting and ending date of the semester, the starting and ending date of the exam period, and the last withdrawal date.

   We could create a single relation containing all these attributes and then normalize the relation; or we could apply the tips presented in chapter 6 for determining the collection of relations. In either case, we ultimately create the following collection of relations:

```
DEPT (DEPTCODE, DEPTNAME, LOCATION)
COURSE (DEPTCODE, CRSNUMB, CRSTITLE, NUMBCRED)
SECTION (SEMCODE, SCHDCODE, DEPTCODE, CRSNUMB, SECTLETT,
         TIME, ROOM, FACNUMB)
FACULTY (FACNUMB, FACNAME)
SEMESTER (SEMCODE, STRTDATE, ENDDATE, EXSTDATE, EXENDATE,
         WITHDATE)
```

(Actually, given the attributes in this user view, the *SECTION* relation would contain the instructor's name (*FACNAME*). There was no mention of instructor number. In general, as we saw earlier, it's a good idea to include determinants for attributes whenever possible. In this example, since *FACNUMB* determines *FACNAME*, we would add *FACNUMB* to the *SECTION* relation, at which point the *SECTION* relation would not be in 3NF. Converting to 3NF will produce the collection of relations just shown.)

Q & A

---

**Question:**   Write the DBDL representation of these relations, including foreign key specifications. Identify any synonyms with regard to this user view and the cumulative design, and resolve them. Merge the result into the cumulative design.

**Answer:**   See Figure 8.44 on the next page.

---

**Figure 8.44**

Cumulative design
after user view 6

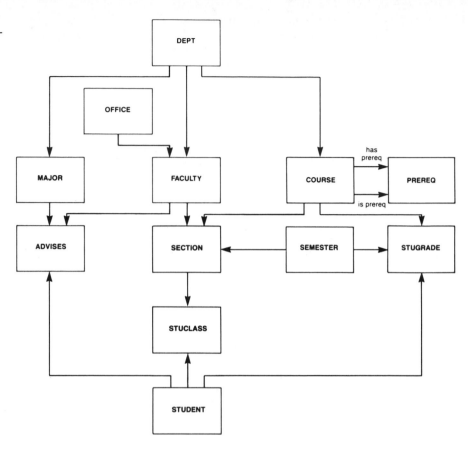

DEPT (<u>DEPTCODE</u>, DEPTNAME, LOCATION)

STUDENT (<u>STUNUMB</u>, STUNAME, LOCADDR*, LOCCITY*, LOCSTATE*,
         LOCZIP*, PRMADDR, PRMCITY, PRMSTATE, PRMZIP,
         CRDTAKEN, CRDEARND, GPA, TOTPNTS, CLSSSTND)

OFFICE (<u>OFFNUMB</u>, PHONE)

FACULTY (<u>FACNUMB</u>, FACNAME, FACADDR, FACCITY, FACSTATE, FACZIP,
         OFFNUMB, CURRANK, STRTDATE, DEPTCODE)
    FK   OFFNUMB --> OFFICE
    FK   DEPTCODE --> DEPT

MAJOR (<u>MAJNUMB</u>, MAJDESC, DEPTCODE)
    FK   DEPTCODE --> DEPT

ADVISES (<u>STUNUMB</u>, FACNUMB, <u>MAJNUMB</u>)
    FK   STUNUMB --> STUDENT   DLT CSCD
    FK   FACNUMB --> FACULTY
    FK   MAJNUMB --> MAJOR

```
COURSE (DEPTCODE, CRSNUMB, CRSTITLE, NUMBCRED)
     FK   DEPTCODE --> DEPT

PREREQ (DEPTCODE, CRSNUMB, PRERDEPT, PRERCRS)
     FK DEPTCODE, CRSNUMB --> COURSE DLT CSCD
     FK PRERDEPT, PRERCRS --> COURSE DLT CSCD

SEMESTER (SEMCODE, STRTDATE, ENDDATE, EXSTDATE, EXENDATE,
          WITHDATE)

STUGRADE (STUNUMB, SEMCODE, DEPTCODE, CRSNUMB, GRADE, CRDEARND,
          GRDPNTS)
     FK   STUNUMB --> STUDENT   DLT CSCD
     FK   SEMCODE --> SEMESTER
     FK   DEPTCODE, CRSNUMB --> COURSE

SECTION (SEMCODE, SCHDCODE, DEPTCODE, CRSNUMB, SECTLETT, TIME,
          ROOM, FACNUMB)
     FK   SEMCODE --> SEMESTER
     FK   DEPTCODE, CRSNUMB --> COURSE
     FK   FACNUMB --> FACULTY

STUCLASS (SEMCODE, SCHDCODE, STUNUMB, GRADE*)
     FK   SEMCODE, SCHDCODE --> SECTION  DLT CSCD
     FK   STUNUMB --> STUDENT  DLT CSCD
```

**Figure 8.44**

(continued)

**User View 7: Registration Request Form.**   The collection of relations to support this user view includes a *STUDENT* relation that consists of the primary key, *STUNUMB,* and all the attributes that depend only on *STUNUMB,* such as *STUNAME, LOCADDR,* and so on. Since all the attributes in this relation are already in the *STUDENT* relation in the cumulative collection, this relation will not add anything new and we will not discuss it further here.

The portion of this user view that is not already present in the cumulative collection concerns the primary and alternate schedule codes that students request. A relation to support this portion of the user view must contain both a primary and an alternate schedule code. It must also contain the number of the student making the request. Finally, to allow the flexibility of retaining this information for more than a single term, the relation must also include the term in which the request is made. This leads to the following relation:

```
REGREQ (STUNUMB, PRIMCODE, ALTCODE, SEMCODE)
```

For example, if student 123 were to request the section whose schedule code is 2345, with 2396 as an alternate for the FA91 semester, the row (123, 2345, 2396, "FA91") would be stored. The student number, the primary schedule code, and the term are required to uniquely identify a particular row. In addition, since a student is not required to furnish an alternate schedule code, the alternate schedule code must accept nulls.

# Q & A

**Question:**    Write the DBDL representation of these relations, including foreign key specifications. Identify any synonyms pertaining to this user view and the cumulative design, and resolve them. Merge the result into the cumulative design.

**Answer:**    See Figure 8.45. Notice that there are two arrows joining *SECTION* to *REGREQ*, so we must name these arrows. In this case, we use *primary* and *alternate*, indicating that one arrow relates a request to the primary section chosen, the other relates it to the alternate section if there is one.

**Figure 8.45**

Cumulative design after user view 7

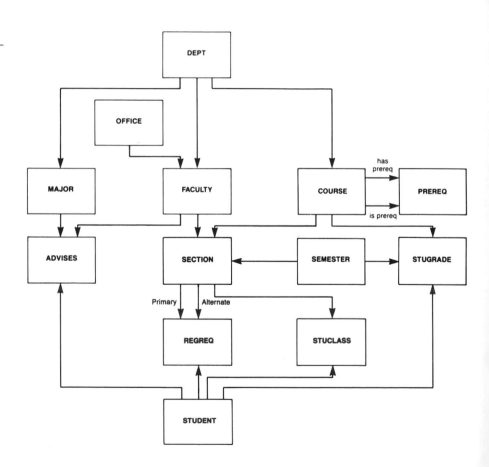

```
DEPT (DEPTCODE, DEPTNAME, LOCATION)

STUDENT (STUNUMB, STUNAME, LOCADDR*, LOCCITY*, LOCSTATE*,
         LOCZIP*, PRMADDR, PRMCITY, PRMSTATE, PRMZIP,
         CRDTAKEN, CRDEARND, GPA, TOTPNTS, CLSSSTND)
```

```
OFFICE (OFFNUMB, PHONE)

FACULTY (FACNUMB, FACNAME, FACADDR, FACCITY, FACSTATE, FACZIP,
         OFFNUMB, CURRANK, STRTDATE, DEPTCODE)
    FK  OFFNUMB --> OFFICE
    FK  DEPTCODE --> DEPT

MAJOR (MAJNUMB, MAJDESC, DEPTCODE)
    FK  DEPTCODE --> DEPT

ADVISES (STUNUMB, FACNUMB, MAJNUMB)
    FK  STUNUMB --> STUDENT  DLT CSCD
    FK  FACNUMB --> FACULTY
    FK  MAJNUMB --> MAJOR

COURSE (DEPTCODE, CRSNUMB, CRSTITLE, NUMBCRED)
    FK  DEPTCODE --> DEPT

PREREQ (DEPTCODE, CRSNUMB, PRERDEPT, PRERCRS)
    FK  DEPTCODE, CRSNUMB --> COURSE DLT CSCD
    FK  PRERDEPT, PRERCRS --> COURSE DLT CSCD

SEMESTER (SEMCODE, STRTDATE, ENDDATE, EXSTDATE, EXENDATE,
          WITHDATE)

STUGRADE (STUNUMB, SEMCODE, DEPTCODE, CRSNUMB, GRADE, CRDEARND,
          GRDPNTS)
    FK  STUNUMB --> STUDENT  DLT CSCD
    FK  SEMCODE --> SEMESTER
    FK  DEPTCODE, CRSNUMB --> COURSE

SECTION (SEMCODE, SCHDCODE, DEPTCODE, CRSNUMB, SECTLETT, TIME,
         ROOM, FACNUMB)
    FK  SEMCODE --> SEMESTER
    FK  DEPTCODE, CRSNUMB --> COURSE
    FK  FACNUMB --> FACULTY

STUCLASS (SEMCODE, SCHDCODE, STUNUMB, GRADE*)
    FK  SEMCODE, SCHDCODE --> SECTION  DLT CSCD
    FK  STUNUMB --> STUDENT  DLT CSCD

REGREQ (STUNUMB, PRIMCODE, ALTCODE*, SEMCODE)
    FK  STUNUMB --> STUDENT  DLT CSCD
    FK  SEMCODE, PRIMCODE --> SECTION DLT CSCD
    FK  SEMCODE, ALTCODE* --> SECTION DLT CSCD
```

Figure 8.45

(continued)

**User View 8: Student Schedule.**   Suppose we had created a single unnormalized relation to support the student schedule. This unnormalized relation would contain a repeating group representing the lines in the body of the schedule. The relation would thus be:

```
STUSCHED (STUNUMB, SEMCODE, STUNAME, LOCADDR, LOCCITY,
          LOCSTATE, LOCZIP, PRMADDR, PRMCITY, PRMSTATE, PRMZIP,
          _____->
          SCHDCODE, DEPTNAME, CRSNUMB, CRSTITLE, SECTLETT,
       ->_____
          NUMBCRED, TIME, ROOM)
```

At this point, we remove the repeating group to convert to 1NF, yielding the following:

```
STUSCHED (STUNUMB, SEMCODE, STUNAME, LOCADDR, LOCCITY, LOCSTATE,
          LOCZIP, PRMADDR, PRMCITY, PRMSTATE, PRMZIP, SCHDCODE,
          DEPTCODE, CRSNUMB, CRSTITLE, SECTLETT, NUMBCRED,
          TIME, ROOM)
```

Note that the key expands to include *SCHDCODE*, which is the key to the repeating group. Converting to 2NF produces:

```
STUDENT (STUNUMB, STUNAME, LOCADDR, LOCCITY, LOCSTATE, LOCZIP,
         PRMADDR, PRMCITY, PRMSTATE, PRMZIP)
STUSCHED (STUNUMB, SEMCODE, SCHDCODE)
SECTION (SEMCODE, SCHDCODE, DEPTCODE, CRSNUMB, CRSTITLE,
         SECTLETT, CREDITS, TIME, ROOM)
COURSE (DEPTCODE, CRSNUMB, CRSTITLE, NUMBCRED)
```

Removing the attributes that depend on the determinant of *DEPTCODE*, *CRSNUMB* from *SECTION* to convert to 3NF produces:

```
STUDENT (STUNUMB, STUNAME, LOCADDR, LOCCITY, LOCSTATE, LOCZIP,
         PRMADDR, PRMCITY, PRMSTATE, PRMZIP)
STUSCHED (STUNUMB, SEMCODE, SCHDCODE)
SECTION (SEMCODE, SCHDCODE, DEPTCODE, CRSNUMB, SECTLETT,
         TIME, ROOM)
COURSE (DEPTCODE, CRSNUMB, CRSTITLE, NUMBCRED)
```

Merging this collection into the cumulative design does not add anything new. In the process, *STUSCHED* will merge with *STUCLASS*.

**User View 9: Full Student Information Report.**  Suppose we attempted to place all the attributes on the student information report in a single unnormalized relation. The relation has two separate repeating groups, one for the different majors a student may have and the other for all the courses the student has taken. (**Note:** There are also several attributes, such as name, address, and so on that would not be in the repeating groups. All these attributes are already in the cumulative design, however, and we will not address them here.) The relation with repeating groups is:

```
STUDENT (STUNUMB, MAJNUMB, DEPTCODE, FACNAME,
                                                            ->
         SEMCODE, DEPTCODE, CRSNUMB, CRSTITLE, NUMBCRED,
         ->
         GRADE, GRDPNTS)
```

Separating the repeating groups produces:

```
STUMAJ (STUNUMB, MAJNUMB, DEPTCODE, FACNAME)
                                                      ->
STUCRSE (STUNUMB, SEMCODE, DEPTCODE, CRSNUMB, CRSTITLE,
       ->
           NUMBCRED, GRADE, GRDPNTS)
```

Converting these to 1NF and including *FACNUMB,* which is a determinant for *FACNAME,* produces:

```
STUMAJ (STUNUMB, MAJNUMB, DEPTCODE, FACNUMB, FACNAME)
STUCRSE (STUNUMB, SEMCODE, DEPTCODE, CRSNUMB, CRSTITLE,
        NUMBCRED, GRADE, GRDPNTS)
```

*STUCRSE* is not in 2NF, since *CRSTITLE* and *NUMBCRED* depend only on the *DEPTCODE, CRSNUMB* combination. *STUMAJ* is not in 2NF, since *DEPTCODE* depends on *MAJNUMB.* Removing these dependencies produces:

```
STUMAJ (STUNUMB, MAJNUMB, FACNUMB, FACNAME)
MAJOR (MAJOR, DEPTCODE)
STUCRSE (STUNUMB, SEMCODE, DEPTCODE, CRSNUMB, GRADE, GRDPNTS)
COURSE (DEPTCODE, CRSNUMB, CRSTITLE, NUMBCRED)
```

Other than *STUMAJ,* all these relations are in 3NF. Converting *STUMAJ* to 3NF produces the following:

```
STUMAJ (STUNUMB, MAJNUMB, FACNUMB)
FACULTY (FACNUMB, FACNAME)
```

Merging this collection into the cumulative design adds nothing new.

**User View 10: Work Version of the Time Schedule.**   The only difference between the work version of the time schedule and the time schedule itself (see user view 6) is the addition of two attributes for each section: current enrollment and maximum enrollment. Since these two attributes depend only on the combination of the term and the schedule code, they would be placed in the *SECTION* relation of user view 6 and, after the merge, would be in the *SECTION* relation in the cumulative design. The cumulative design thus far is shown in Figure 8.46 on the next page.

**Figure 8.46**

Cumulative design
after user view 10

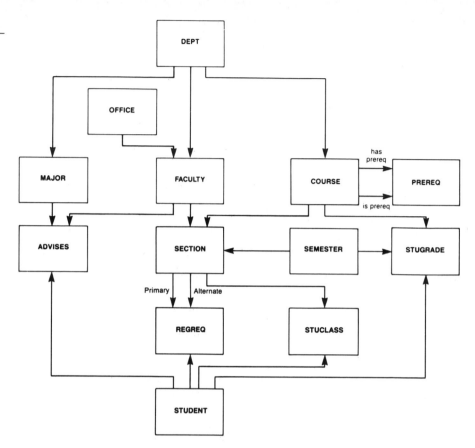

```
DEPT (DEPTCODE, DEPTNAME, LOCATION)

STUDENT (STUNUMB, STUNAME, LOCADDR*, LOCCITY*, LOCSTATE*,
         LOCZIP*, PRMADDR, PRMCITY, PRMSTATE, PRMZIP,
         CRDTAKEN, CRDEARND, GPA, TOTPNTS, CLSSSTND)

OFFICE (OFFNUMB, PHONE)

FACULTY (FACNUMB, FACNAME, FACADDR, FACCITY, FACSTATE, FACZIP,
         OFFNUMB, CURRANK, STRTDATE, DEPTCODE)
    FK  OFFNUMB --> OFFICE
    FK  DEPTCODE --> DEPT

MAJOR (MAJNUMB, MAJDESC, DEPTCODE)
    FK  DEPTCODE --> DEPT

ADVISES (STUNUMB, FACNUMB, MAJNUMB)
    FK  STUNUMB --> STUDENT  DLT CSCD
    FK  FACNUMB --> FACULTY
    FK  MAJNUMB --> MAJOR

COURSE (DEPTCODE, CRSNUMB, CRSTITLE, NUMBCRED)
    FK  DEPTCODE --> DEPT
```

```
PREREQ (DEPTCODE, CRSNUMB, PRERDEPT, PRERCRS)
     FK DEPTCODE, CRSNUMB --> COURSE DLT CSCD
     FK PRERDEPT, PRERCRS --> COURSE DLT CSCD

SEMESTER (SEMCODE, STRTDATE, ENDDATE, EXSTDATE, EXENDATE,
          WITHDATE)

STUGRADE (STUNUMB, SEMCODE, DEPTCODE, CRSNUMB, GRADE, CRDEARND,
          GRDPNTS)
     FK  STUNUMB --> STUDENT  DLT CSCD
     FK  SEMCODE --> SEMESTER
     FK  DEPTCODE, CRSNUMB --> COURSE

SECTION (SEMCODE, SCHDCODE, DEPTCODE, CRSNUMB, SECTLETT, TIME,
          ROOM, FACNUMB, CURENROL, MAXENROL)
     FK  SEMCODE --> SEMESTER
     FK  DEPTCODE, CRSNUMB --> COURSE
     FK  FACNUMB --> FACULTY

STUCLASS (SEMCODE, SCHDCODE, STUNUMB, GRADE*)
     FK  SEMCODE, SCHDCODE --> SECTION  DLT CSCD
     FK  STUNUMB --> STUDENT  DLT CSCD

REGREQ (STUNUMB, PRIMCODE, ALTCODE*, SEMCODE)
     FK  STUNUMB --> STUDENT  DLT CSCD
     FK  SEMCODE, PRIMCODE --> SECTION DLT CSCD
     FK  SEMCODE, ALTCODE* --> SECTION DLT CSCD
```

**Figure 8.46**

(continued)

Since the process of determining whether a student has had the prerequisites for a given course involves examining the grades (if any) received in these prior courses, it makes sense to analyze the user view that involves grades (post grades) before treating the user view that involves enrollment.

**User View 11: Post Grades.**   There is a slight problem with posting grades. Grades must somehow be posted by section to produce the grade report (e.g., we must record the fact that student 000625321 received an A in the section of CS 153 whose schedule code was 2366 during the fall 1991 semester). On the other hand, for the full student information report, there is no need to have any of the grades related to an *actual section* of a course. Further, since section information, including these grades, is only to be kept for two semesters (see the description of PURGE in the user requirements), grades would be lost after two semesters if they were kept by section only, since section information would be purged at that time.

A viable alternative is to post two copies of the grade; one copy would be associated with the student, the term, and the section, and the other copy would be associated only with the student and the term. The first copy would be used for the grade verification report and the second for the full student information report. Report cards would probably utilize the second copy, although not necessarily.

Thus, we would have two grade relations:

```
GRADSECT (STUNUMB, DEPTCODE, CRSNUMB, SCHDCODE, SEMCODE, GRADE)
```

and

GRADSTU (<u>STUNUMB</u>, <u>DEPTCODE</u>, <u>CRSNUMB</u>, <u>SEMCODE</u>, GRADE)

Since the *DEPTCODE* and *CRSNUMB* in *GRADSECT* depend only on the concatenation of *SCHDCODE* and *SEMCODE*, they will be removed from *GRADSECT* during the normalization process and will be placed in a relation whose primary key is the concatenation of *SCHDCODE* and *SEMCODE*. This relation will be combined with the relation *SECTION* in the cumulative design without adding new fields. The *GRADSECT* relation that is left will be merged with *STUCLASS* without adding new fields. Finally, the *GRADSTU* relation will be combined with the *STUGRADE* relation in the cumulative design without adding any new fields. Thus, treatment of this user view does not change the cumulative design.

**User View 12: Enrollment.**   With the data already in place in the overall design, we can determine what courses a student has taken. We can also determine the prerequisites for a given course. The only remaining issue is the ability to enroll a student in a course. This is similar to the problem encountered in the design exercise in chapter 7, in which we saw that what is required is another relation, *ENROLL*. In this case, since information must be retained for more than one semester, we must include the semester code in the relation. (We must have the information that student 123 enrolled in section 2345 in SU91 rather than in FA91, for example.) The additional relation is as follows:

ENROLL (<u>STUNUMB</u>, <u>SEMCODE</u>, <u>SCHDCODE</u>)

The primary key of this relation matches the primary key of the relation *STUCLASS* in the cumulative design. The fields occur in a different order here, but that makes no difference. Therefore, this relation will merge with *STUCLASS*. There are no new fields to be added, so the cumulative design remains unchanged.

**User View 13: Purge.**   Periodically, certain information that is more than two terms old is to be removed from the database. This includes all information concerning sections of courses, such as the time, the room, and the instructor, as well as information about the students in the section and their grades. The grade each student received will remain in the database by course but not by section. For example, we will always retain the fact that student 123 received an A in CS 153 during the fall semester of 1991, but, once the data for that term is purged, we will no longer know the precise section of CS 153 that awarded this grade.

If we examine the current collection of relations, we see that all the data to be purged is already included in the cumulative design and, so nothing new needs to be added at this point.

**Final Information-Level Design.** The design that has been produced is now reviewed to ensure that the user views can be met. You should conduct this review on your own to make certain you understand how the requirements of each user can indeed be satisfied. We will assume that this review has taken place and that no changes have been made. Thus, Figure 8.46 shows the final information-level design.

Figure 8.47 gives a list of the domains and Figure 8.48 on the next page gives the relationship between the relations and attributes that were defined and these domains.

```
••••••••••••••••••••••••••• DOMAIN DEFINITIONS •••••••••••••••••••••••••••
```

| DOMAIN | TYPE | DESCRIPTION | RESTRICTIONS |
|---|---|---|---|
| ADDRESS | C(25) | ADDRESSES (STREET) | |
| CITY | C(25) | CITIES | |
| CLASS_STANDING | D(1) | CLASS STANDINGS | MUST BE 1 FOR FRESHMAN, 2 FOR SOPHOMORE, 3 FOR JUNIOR OR 4 FOR SENIOR |
| COURSE_DESCRIPTION | C(25) | COURSE DESCRIPTIONS | |
| COURSE-NUMBER | D(3) | COURSE NUMBERS | |
| CREDITS | D(3) | NUMBER OF CREDITS | |
| DATE | D(6) | DATES | HAS FORM YYMMDD |
| DEPARTMENT CODE | C(3) | DEPARTMENT CODES | |
| DEPTNAME | C(25) | DEPARTMENT NAMES | |
| ENROLLMENT | D(3) | COURSE ENROLLMENTS | |
| FACULTY_NUMBER | D(4) | FACULTY NUMBERS | |
| GPA | D(3,2) | GRADE POINT AVERAGES | MUST BE BETWEEN 0.00 AND 4.00 |
| GRADE | C(1) | GRADES | MUST BE "A", "B", "C", "D", "F", OR "I" (INCOMPLETE) |
| GRADE-POINTS | D(3) | GRADE POINTS | OBTAINED BY MULTIPLYING THE NUMBER OF CREDITS OF "A" BY 4, THE NUMBER OF CREDITS OF "B" BY 3, OF "C" BY 2, OF "D" BY 1 AND ADDING THE RESULT |
| MAJOR_NUMBER | D(3) | MAJOR NUMBERS | |
| MEETING_TIME | C(20) | MEETING TIMES | IDENTIFIES START AND ENDING TIMES AND DAYS OF THE WEEK |
| NAME | C(25) | PERSON NAMES | |
| NUMBER_OF CREDITS | D(1) | NUMBER OF CREDITS GRANTED BY A COURSE | MUST BE BETWEEN 1 AND 5 |
| PHONE-NUMBER | D(4) | OFFICE PHONE NUMBERS | MUST BEGIN WITH A 3 |
| RANK | C(9) | FACULTY RANKS | MUST BE "INSTRUCTOR", "ASST PROF", "ASSO PROF", OR "PROFESSOR" |
| ROOM | C(7) | ROOM NUMBERS | CONSIST OF 3 DIGIT NUMBER AND 3 CHARACTER BUILDING ABBREVIATION, ("110 NSB") |
| SCHEDULE_CODE | D(4) | SCHEDULE CODES (CODES THAT UNIQUELY IDENTIFY: SECTIONS OF COURSES IN: A GIVEN SEMESTER | |
| SECTION_LETTER | C(1) | SECTION LETTERS | |
| SEMESTER-CODE | C(4) | SEMESTER CODES | HAS FORM SSYY WHERE SS IS EITHER FA FOR FALL, WI FOR WINTER, OR SU FOR SUMMER AND YY IS THE YEAR |
| STATE | C(2) | STATES | |
| STUDENT_NUMBER | D(9) | STUDENT NUMBERS | |
| ZIP | D(9) | ZIP CODES | |

**Figure 8.47**

Domain definitions for final design

**Figure 8.48**

Relation and
attribute defini-
tions for final
design specifying
underlying
domains

```
* * * * * * * * * * * * * * * * * * * *  RELATION AND ATTRIBUTE DEFINITIONS  * * * * * * * * * * * * * * * * * * * *
```

| RELATION | ATTRIBUTE | DOMAIN | COMMENTS |
|---|---|---|---|
| ADVISES | | | |
| | STUNUMB | STUDENT_NUMBER | |
| | FACNUMB | FACULTY_NUMBER | |
| | MAJNUMB | MAJOR_NUMBER | |
| COURSE | | | |
| | DEPTCODE | DEPARTMENT_CODE | |
| | CRSNUMB | COURSE_NUMBER | |
| | CRSTITLE | COURSE_TITLE | |
| | NUMBCRED | NUMBER_OF_CREDITS | Number of credits offered by the course |
| DEPT | | | |
| | DEPTCODE | DEPARTMENT_CODE | |
| | DEPTNAME | DEPTNAME | |
| | LOCATION | ROOM | |
| FACULTY | | | |
| | FACNUMB | FACULTY_NUMBER | |
| | FACNAME | NAME | |
| | FACADDR | ADDRESS | |
| | FACCITY | CITY | |
| | FACSTATE | STATE | |
| | FACZIP | ZIP | |
| | OFFNUMB | ROOM | |
| | CURRANK | RANK | |
| | STRTDATE | DATE | |
| | DEPTCODE | DEPARTMENT_CODE | |
| MAJOR | | | |
| | MAJNUMB | MAJOR_NUMBER | |
| | MAJDESC | MAJOR_DESCRIPTION | |
| | DEPTCODE | DEPARTMENT_CODE | Department offering the major |
| OFFICE | | | |
| | OFFNUMB | ROOM | |
| | PHONE | PHONE_NUMBER | |
| PREREQ | | | |
| | DEPTCODE | DEPARTMENT_CODE | Department for the course |
| | CRSNUMB | COURSE_NUMBER | Number for the course |
| | PRERDEPT | DEPARTMENT_CODE | Department for the prerequisite |
| | PRERCRS | COURSE_NUMBER | Number for the prerequisite |
| REGREQ | | | |
| | STUNUMB | STUDENT_NUMBER | |
| | PRIMCODE | SCHEDULE_CODE | Primary request |
| | ALTCODE | SCHEDULE_CODE | Alternate request (if one exists) |
| | SEMCODE | SEMESTER_CODE | |
| SECTION | | | |
| | SEMCODE | SEMESTER_CODE | |
| | SCHDCODE | SCHEDULE_CODE | |
| | DEPTCODE | DEPARTMENT_CODE | |
| | CRSNUMB | COURSE_NUMBER | |
| | SECTLETT | SECTION_LETTER | |
| | TIME | MEETING_TIME | |
| | ROOM | ROOM | |
| | FACNUMB | FACULTY_NUMBER | |
| | CURENROL | ENROLLMENT | |
| | MAXENROL | ENROLLMENT | |
| SEMESTER | | | |
| | SEMCODE | SEMESTER_CODE | |
| | STRTDATE | DATE | Starting date for semester |
| | ENDDATE | DATE | Ending date for semester |
| | EXSTDATE | DATE | Starting date for exams |
| | EXENDATE | DATE | Ending date for exams |
| | WITHDATE | DATE | Last date to withdraw from courses |

**Figure 8.48**

(continued)

| RELATION | ATTRIBUTE | DOMAIN | COMMENTS |
|---|---|---|---|
| STUDENT | | | |
| | STUNUMB | STUDENT-NUMBER | |
| | STUNAME | NAME | |
| | LOCADDR | ADDRESS | Local street address |
| | LOCCITY | CITY | Local city |
| | LOCSTATE | STATE | Local state |
| | LOCZIP | ZIP | Local zip code |
| | | | *Note if no local address, use permanent address as local address |
| | PRMADDR | ADDRESS | Permanent street address |
| | PRMCITY | CITY | Permanent city |
| | PRMSTATE | STATE | Permanent state |
| | PRMZIP | ZIP | Permanent zip code |
| | CRDTAKEN | CREDITS | Number of credits taken |
| | CRDEARND | CREDITS | Number of credits earned |
| | GPA | GPA | GPA (total points divided by number of credits taken) |
| | TOTPNTS | GRADE-POINTS | Total points (4 for each credit of A, 3 for each B, and so on) |
| | CLSSSTND | CLASS-STANDING | Class standing - determined by number of credits earned. If <30, standing is 1, if >= 30 and < 60, standing is 2, if >= 60 and < 90, standing is 3, if >= 90, standing is 4 |
| STUGRADE | | | |
| | STUNUMB | STUDENT-NUMBER | |
| | SEMCODE | SEMESTER-CODE | |
| | DEPTCODE | DEPARTMENT-CODE | |
| | CRSNUMB | COURSE-NUMBER | |
| | GRADE | GRADE | Grade received in course |
| | CRDEARND | CREDITS | Credits earned in course. Will be the number of credits offered by the course if grade is A, B, C, D. Will be 0 if grade is F |
| | GRDPNTS | GRADE-POINTS | Points earned in course (4 for each credit if grade is A, 3 for each credit if grade is B, and so on) |
| STUCLASS | | | |
| | SEMCODE | SEMESTER-CODE | |
| | SCHDCODE | SCHEDULE-CODE | |
| | STUNUMB | STUDENT-NUMBER | |
| | GRADE | GRADE | |

## SUMMARY

In this chapter, we have concluded our study of the information level of database design begun in chapter 7. We have discussed the process of obtaining and documenting user views. We examined the use of a survey form containing information about entities, attributes, relationships, functional dependencies, and processing information. We also investigated how to obtain information concerning user views from existing documents.

We then expanded on the topic of representing user views as relations. An analysis of various methods for representing one-to-one relationships was presented, along with the concepts pertaining to many-to-many relationships that involve more than two entities. We described the relationships between nulls and entity subtypes and proposed a method for treating nulls. We discussed the use of derived and encoded data. We investigated the process of merging relations for each user view into a cumulative design.

We next turned our attention to a popular graphical approach to database design, the Entity-Relationship (E-R) model, proposed by Peter Chen. We discussed the basic structure of the model, the use of E-R diagrams, and the types of restrictions that can be represented in such diagrams.

We made some general design comments concerning the use of data dictionaries, the computerization of database design, and the resolution of synonyms. We proposed a means of bringing the advantages of both the top-down and bottom-up approaches to database design to the methodology proposed in this text.

We finished by working through a detailed database design example. The example involved designing a database to satisfy a number of requirements for Marvel College. We will continue with this example in chapter 11 when we move to the physical level of database design.

## REVIEW QUESTIONS

1. Why is it impossible to design a system just by looking at the existing documents?
2. How may a survey form be used in the design process? What types of categories should appear on the survey form? Who should fill out the survey form?
3. Why is processing information included in the survey form? Isn't processing information used during the physical-level design phase rather than during the information-level design phase?
4. What is wrong with implementing a one-to-one relationship by including the primary key of each relation as a foreign key in the other? How should we implement such a relationship?
5. When should a three-way relationship be implemented as a three-way many-to-many-to-many relationship? How do you do so? When should such a relationship be implemented as two or three many-to-many relationships? How do you do so?
6. What does it mean for a column to allow nulls? What is an entity subtype? What is the relationship between nulls and entity subtypes? How are subtypes documented in DBDL?

7. What is derived data? Should derived data be included in an information-level design? We have not yet discussed the physical level of design, but do you think derived data should be included in a physical-level design? Why or why not?

8. What is encoded data? What are the advantages of encoding data? What are the disadvantages?

9. List the steps involved in merging the relations into the cumulative design to satisfy a given user's view. When should relations *not* be merged? In what way can foreign key restrictions become a problem?

10. What do we mean by "including determinants" in a relation? What is the benefit to doing so?

11. What features would be desirable in a computer tool to assist in the database design process?

12. What are synonyms in the computing environment? What problems do synonyms cause?

13. What is the difference between a top-down and a bottom-up design methodology? Name advantages and disadvantages of each. Into which category does the methodology we have been studying using DBDL fall? How can we modify DBDL to include the advantages of both types of methodologies?

14. Describe the entity-relationship model. Describe how entities, attributes, and relationships are represented in the original E-R model. What term in the E-R model corresponds to domains? How are they represented pictorially?

15. Describe the changes to the E-R model that were proposed by Chen. How do these changes affect relationships?

16. Describe existence dependency. Describe ID dependency. Can a relationship be both an existence dependency and an ID dependency? What is a weak entity type? What is the relationship between weak entity types and either existence or ID dependency?

---

# EXERCISES

1. Design a survey form of your own. Fill it out as it might have been filled out during the database design for Premiere Products. For any questions that you have too little information to answer, make a reasonable guess.

2. Describe two different ways of implementing one-to-one relationships. Assume we are maintaining information on offices (office number, building, phone number) and faculty (number, name, etc.). No office houses more than one faculty member. No faculty member is assigned more than

one office. Illustrate the ways of implementing one-to-one relationships using offices and faculty. Which approach would be best in each of the following situations?

   a. A faculty member must have an office and each office must be occupied by a faculty member.

   b. A faculty member must have an office, but some offices are not currently occupied. (We still need to maintain information about these unoccupied offices in an *OFFICE* relation, however.)

   c. Some faculty members do not have an office. All offices are occupied, however.

   d. Some faculty members do not have an office. Some offices are not occupied.

3. For each of the following collections of relations, give the assumptions concerning the relationship between students, courses, and faculty members which are implied by the collection. In each relation only the keys are shown.

   a. STU(<u>STUNUMB</u>, <u>CRSENUMB</u>, <u>FACNUMB</u>)

   b. STU(<u>STUNUMB</u>, <u>CRSENUMB</u>)
      FAC(<u>CRSENUMB</u>, <u>FACNUMB</u>)

   c. STU(<u>STUNUMB</u>, <u>CRSENUMB</u>)
      FAC(<u>CRSENUMB</u>, <u>FACNUMB</u>)
      STUFAC(<u>STUNUMB</u>, <u>FACNUMB</u>)

   d. STU(<u>STUNUMB</u>, <u>CRSENUMB</u>, FACNUMB)

   e. STU(<u>STUNUMB</u>, <u>CRSENUMB</u>)
      FAC(<u>CRSENUMB</u>, <u>FACNUMB</u>)
      STUFAC(<u>STUNUMB</u>, FACNUMB)

4. How is it possible to merge a collection of relations that is in 3NF into a cumulative design that is in 3NF and not obtain a collection of relations that is in 3NF? Give an example.

Discuss the effect of the following changes on the design for the Marvel College requirements.

5. A given section of a course may have more than one instructor, and each instructor is to be listed on the time schedule.

6. Each department offers only a single major.

7. Each department offers only a single major, and each faculty member may only advise students in the major that is offered by the department to which the faculty member is assigned.

8. Each department offers only a single major, and each faculty member may only advise students in the major that is offered by the department to which the faculty member is assigned. In addition, a student may only have a single major.

9. There is an additional transaction requirement: Given a student's name, find the student's number.

10. More than one faculty member may be assigned to one office.

11. The number of credits earned in a particular course may not vary from student to student or from semester to semester.

12. Instead of a course number, course codes are used to uniquely identify courses (i.e., department numbers are no longer required for this purpose). However, it is still important to know which courses are offered by which departments.

13. On the registration request, a student may designate a number of alternates along with his or her primary choice. These alternates are listed in a priority order, with the first one being the most desired and the last one being the least desired.

14. ***** SPECIAL PROJECT *****

    Complete the information-level design for the following set of requirements.

    Premiere Products has decided to expand its operation and has determined that a database should be designed to handle the new requirements. A database is needed that will satisfy the following requirements.

    **General Description.**    Premiere Products is a distributor. It buys products from its vendors and sells these products to its customers. The Premiere Products operation is divided into territories. Each customer is represented by a single sales rep, who must be assigned to the territory in which the customer resides. Although each sales rep is assigned to a single territory, more than one may be assigned to the same territory.

    When a customer places an order, the order is assigned a number. The customer number, the order number, the customer purchase order (PO) number, and date are entered. (Customers can place orders by sending in a purchase order. For orders that are placed in this fashion, the PO number is recorded.) For each part that is ordered, the part number, quantity, and quoted price are entered. (When it is time for the user to enter the quoted price, the price from the master price list for parts is displayed on the screen. If the quoted price is the same as the actual price, no special action is required. If not, the user enters the quoted price.) The order may also contain special charges, for which a description of the charge and the amount of the charge is entered. Finally, an order may include comments, in which case the comment is entered. Following this, a form is printed that is a combination order acknowledgment/picking list. This form, which is shown in Figure 8.49, is sent to the customer as a record of the order he or she has placed. A copy of the form is also used when the time comes to "pick" the merchandise that was ordered in the warehouse.

**Figure 8.49**

Order acknowledgement/ picking list for Premier Products

```
            ORDER ACKNOWLEDGEMENT/PICKING LIST

  10/15/91                                              ORDER 12424
                       PREMIERE PRODUCTS
                       146 NELSON PLACE
                       ALLENDALE, MI 49401

  SOLD                          SHIP
    TO:   SMITH RENTALS           TO:    A & B SUPPLIES
          153 MAIN ST.                   2180 HALTON PL.
          SUITE 102                      ARENDVILLE, MI 49232
          GRANDVILLE, MI 49494

  CUSTOMER  P.O. NO.   ORDER DATE    SLS REP
    1354    PO335       10/02/91     10 - SAM BROWN
```

| QUANTITY | | | | | |
|---|---|---|---|---|---|
| ORDER | SHIP | ITEM NUMBER | DESCRIPTION | PRICE | AMOUNT |
| 6 | | AT414 | LOUNGE CHAIR | 42.00 | 210.00 |
| 4 | | BT222 | ARM CHAIR | 51.00 | 204.00 |
| | | | | ORDER TOTAL | |
| | | | | | 414.00 |

Until the order is filled, it is considered to be an *open* order. When the order is filled (which may be some time later), it is said to be *released*. At this point, an invoice (bill) is printed and sent to the customer, and the customer's balance is increased by the amount of the invoice. The order may have been filled completely or it may have been partially filled (for less than the full amount originally requested). In either case, since the goods have been shipped, the order is considered to have been filled and is no longer considered an open order. (Another possibility is to allow back orders when the order cannot be completely filled. In this case, the order would remain open but only for the back-ordered portion. Premiere Products does not allow back orders, however.) When an invoice (see Figure 8.50) is generated, the order is removed from the file of open orders. Summary information is stored concerning the invoice (number, date, customer, invoice total, and freight) until the end of the month.

**Figure 8.50**

Invoice for
Premiere Products

```
                                INVOICE

  10/15/91                                            Invoice 11025

                         PREMIERE PRODUCTS
                         146 NELSON PLACE
                         ALLENDALE, MI 49401

  SOLD                        SHIP
   TO:   SMITH RENTALS         TO:    A & B SUPPLIES
         153 MAIN ST.                 2180 HALTON PL.
         SUITE 102                    ARENDVILLE, MI 49232
         GRANDVILLE, MI 49494

  CUSTOMER  P.O. NO.  OUR ORDER NO.  ORDER DATE   SHIP DATE    SLS REP
   1354     PO335        12424        10/02/91     10/15/91   10 - SAM BROWN

    QUANTITY

   ORDER   SHIP    ITEM NUMBER   DESCRIPTION      PRICE     AMOUNT

     6       5     AT414        LOUNGE CHAIR      42.00     210.00
     4       4     BT222        ARM CHAIR         51.00     204.00

                                FREIGHT                      42.50




                                        PAY THIS AMOUNT

                                              456.00
```

Companies like Premiere Products employ basically two methods for accepting payments from customers: open items and balance forward. In the open-item approach, customers make payments on specific invoices. An invoice remains on file until it is completely paid. In the balance-forward approach, customers simply have balances. When an invoice is generated, the customer's balance is increased by the amount of the invoice. When a payment is made, the customer's balance is decreased by the amount of the invoice. Premiere Products uses the balance-forward approach.

At the end of each month, customers' accounts are updated and aged. (The description of month-end processing in the requirements that follow contains details of the update and aging process.) Statements, an aged trial balance (defined under report requirements), a monthly cash receipts journal, a monthly invoice register, and a sales rep commission report are printed. Cash receipts and invoice summary records are then removed from the database. Month-to-date fields are set to zero. If it is also the end of the year, year-to-date fields are set to zero.

**Transaction Requirements.** The following are the transaction requirements.

1. Enter/edit territories (territory number and name).
2. Enter/edit sales reps (sales rep number, name, address, city, state, ZIP, MTD sales, YTD sales, MTD commission, YTD commission, and commission rate). Each sales rep represents a single territory. (MTD stands for month-to-date and YTD stands for year-to-date.)
3. Enter/edit customers (customer number, name, first line of address, second line of address, city, state, ZIP, MTD sales, YTD sales, current balance, and credit limit). A customer may have a different name and address to which goods will be shipped, called the "ship-to" address.) Each customer has a single sales rep and resides in a single territory. The sales rep must represent the territory in which the customer resides.
4. Enter/edit parts (part number, description, price, MTD and YTD sales, units on hand, units allocated, and reorder point). Units allocated are the number of units that are currently "spoken for,"; that is, the number of units of this part that are currently present on some open orders. The reorder point is the lowest value acceptable for units on hand without reordering the product. On the stock status report, which will be described later, any part for which the number of units on hand is less than the reorder point will be indicated by an asterisk.
5. Enter/edit vendors (vendor number, name, address, city, state, ZIP). In addition, for each part supplied by the vendor, enter/edit the part number, the price the vendor charges for the part, the minimum order quantity that the vendor will accept for this part, and the expected lead time for delivery of this part from this vendor.

6. Order entry (order number, date, customer, customer PO number, and the order detail lines). An order detail line consists of a part number, description, number ordered, and quoted price. Each order detail line includes a sequence number that is entered by the user. Detail lines on an order must print in order of this sequence number. The system should calculate and display the order total. After all orders for the day have been entered, order acknowledgments (see Figure 8.49) are printed. In addition, for each part ordered, the units allocated for the part must be increased by the number of units that were ordered.

7. Invoicing cycle:

   a. Enter the numbers of the orders to be released. For each order, enter the ship date for invoicing and the amount of the freight. Indicate whether the order is to be shipped in full or partially shipped. If it is to be partially shipped, enter the number shipped for each order detail line. The system will generate a unique invoice number for this invoice.

   b. Print invoices for each of the released orders. A sample invoice is shown in Figure 8.50.

   c. Update files with information from the invoices just printed. For each invoice, the invoice total is added to the current invoice total, the current balance, and MTD and YTD sales for the customer who placed the order. The total is also added to MTD and YTD sales for the sales rep who represents the customer, and the total, multiplied by the sales rep's commission rate, is added to MTD commission earned and YTD commission earned. For each part shipped, units on hand and units allocated are decremented by the number of units of the part that were shipped. MTD and YTD sales of the part are increased by the product of the number of units shipped and the quoted price.

   d. Create invoice summary record for each invoice printed. These records contain the invoice number, date, customer, sales rep, invoice total, and freight.

   e. Delete all the released orders.

8. Receive payments on account (customer number, date, amount). Each payment is assigned a number. The amount of the payment is added to the total of current payments for the customer and is subtracted from the current balance of the customer.

**Report Requirements.** The following are the report requirements.

1. **Territory list.** For each territory, list the number and name of the territory, the number, name, and address of each of the sales reps in the territory, and the number, name, and address of each of the customers represented by these sales reps.

2. **Customer master list.** For each customer, list the number and both the address and the ship-to address. Also list the number, name, address, city, state, and ZIP of the sales rep who represents the customer, and the number and name of the territory in which the customer resides.
3. **Open orders by customer.** This report lists open orders organized by customer and is shown in Figure 8.51.

**Figure 8.51**

Open orders report
(by customer)

```
10/08/91                    PREMIERE PRODUCTS                   PAGE 1
                         CUSTOMER OPEN ORDER REPORT

    ORDER     ITEM         ITEM          ORDER       ORDER      QUOTED
    NUMBER    NUMBER     DESCRIPTION      DATE         QTY        PRICE

    CUSTOMER 1354 - SMITH RENTALS

     12424    AT414      LOUNGE CHAIR    10/02/91        6        42.00
     12424    BT222      ARM CHAIR       10/02/91        4        51.00

    CUSTOMER 1358 - . . . . . . . . . . .
            .            .                .            .           .
            .            .                .            .           .
            .            .                .            .           .
            .            .                .            .           .
```

**Figure 8.52**

Open orders report
(by item)

4. **Open orders by item.** This report lists open orders organized by item and is shown in Figure 8.52.

```
10/08/91                           PREMIERE PRODUCTS                    PAGE 1
                                 ITEM OPEN ORDER REPORT

   ITEM     ITEM         CUST    CUSTOMER            ORDER    ORDER   ORDER QUOTED
   NUMBER DESCRIPTION    NUMB    NAME                NUMBER    DATE    QTY   PRICE

   AT414  LOUNGE CHAIR   1354    SMITH RENTALS       12424  10/02/91    6    42.00
                           54    KAYLAND ENTERPRISES 12489  10/03/91    8    42.00
                                               TOTAL ON ORDER -  14

   BT222  ARM CHAIR      1354    SMITH RENTALS       12424  10/02/91    4    51.00
            .              .          .                .        .       .      .
            .              .          .                .        .       .      .
            .              .          .                .        .       .      .
```

5. **Daily invoice register.** For each invoice produced on a given day, list the invoice number, the invoice date, the customer number, the customer name, the freight, and the invoice total. A sample of this report is shown in Figure 8.53.
6. **Monthly invoice register.** The monthly invoice register has the same format as the daily invoice register but includes all invoices for the month.

```
10/16/91                  PREMIERE PRODUCTS                      PAGE 1
                 DAILY INVOICE REGISTER FOR 10/15/91

INVOICE      INVOICE     CUSTOMER    CUSTOMER          SALES              INVOICE
NUMBER       DATE        NUMBER      NAME              AMOUNT   FREIGHT   AMOUNT

11025        10/15/91    1354        SMITH RENTALS     414.00    42.50    456.50
   .            .           .           .                .         .        .
   .            .           .           .                .         .        .
   .            .           .           .                .         .        .
   .            .           .           .                .         .        .
   .            .           .           .                .         .        .

                                                     2,840.50   238.20  3,078.70
```

7. **Stock status report.** For each part, list the part number, description, price, MTD and YTD sales, units on hand, units allocated, and reorder point. For each part for which the number of units on hand is less than the reorder point, an asterisk should appear at the far right of the report.
8. **Reorder point list.** This report has the same format as the stock status report. Other than the title, the only difference is that parts for which the number of units on hand is greater than or equal to the reorder point will not appear on this report.
9. **Vendor report.** For each vendor, list the vendor number, name, address, city, state, and ZIP. In addition, for each part supplied by the vendor, list the part number, description, the price the vendor charges for the part, the minimum order quantity that the vendor will accept for this part, and the expected lead time for delivery of this part from this vendor.
10. **Daily cash receipts journal.** For each payment received on a given day, list the number and name of the customer who made the payment, together with the amount of the payment. A sample of the report is shown in Figure 8.54.

**Figure 8.53**

Daily invoice register

```
10/05/91                  PREMIERE PRODUCTS              PAGE 1
                      DAILY CASH RECEIPTS JOURNAL

PAYMENT      CUSTOMER    CUSTOMER                   PAYMENT
NUMBER       NUMBER      NAME                       AMOUNT
   .            .           .                          .
   .            .           .                          .
5807         1354        SMITH RENTALS             1,000.00
   .            .           .                          .
   .            .           .                          .
   .            .           .                          .

                                                  12,235.50
```

**Figure 8.54**

Daily cash receipts journal

11. **Monthly cash receipts journal.** The monthly cash receipts journal
has the same format as the daily cash receipts journal but includes
all cash receipts for the month.

**Figure 8.55**

Customer mailing
labels

12. **Customer mailing labels.** A sample of the three-across mailing
labels the system is to print is shown in Figure 8.55.

```
SMITH RENTALS          KAYLAND ENTERPRISES       JOHN & SONS, INC.
153 MAIN ST.           267 29TH ST               5563 CRESTVIEW
SUITE 102              WYOMING, MI 48222         ADA, MI 49292
GRANDVILLE, MI 49494

         .                        .                        .
         .                        .                        .
     .   .                        .                        .
         .                        .                        .
```

13. **Statements.** Monthly statements are to be produced; a sample is
shown in Figure 8.56.

**Figure 8.56**

Statement

11/01/91

**PREMIERE PRODUCTS**
**146 NELSON PLACE**
**ALLENDALE, MI 49401**

SMITH RENTALS                CUSTOMER NUMBER: 1354
153 MAIN ST.                 SLSREP: 10 - SAM BROWN
SUITE 102
GRANDVILLE, MI 49494         LIMIT: 5,000.00

| INVOICE NUMBER | DATE | DESCRIPTION | TOTAL AMOUNT |
|---|---|---|---|
| 10945 | 10/02/91 | INVOICE | 1,230.00 |
|  | 10/05/91 | PAYMENT | 1,000.00CR |
| 11025 | 10/15/91 | INVOICE | 456.50 |
|  | 10/22/91 | PAYMENT | 500.00CR |

| OVER 90 | OVER 60 | | |
|---|---|---|---|
| .00 | 198.50 | | |
| OVER 30 | CURRENT | TOTAL DUE >>>>>> | 2,325.20 |
| 490.20 | 1,686.50 | | |

| PREVIOUS BALANCE | CURRENT INVOICES | CURRENT PAYMENTS | |
|---|---|---|---|
| 2,138.70 | 1,686.50 | 1,500.00 | |

14. **Monthly sales rep commission report.** For each sales rep, list his or her number, name, address, MTD sales, YTD sales, MTD commission earned, YTD commission earned, and the commission rate.
15. **Aged trial balance.** The aged trial balance is a report containing the same information that is printed on the statements.

**Month-End Processing.** Month-end processing consists of taking the following actions at the end of each month.

1. Update customer account information. In addition to the customer's actual balance, the system must maintain a record stating how much of what the customer owes is current debt, incurred within the last thirty days, how much is owed for more than thirty but less than sixty, more than sixty but less than ninety, and more than ninety. While the actual balance, current invoice total, and current payment total are updated whenever an invoice is produced or a payment is received, these aging figures are updated only at month end. The actual update process is as follows:
   a. The payments within the last month are credited to the over-ninety figure. Any excess is credited first to the over-sixty figure, then to the over-thirty figure, and then to the current figure. If there is still an excess, it is credited to the current month's invoices.
   b. The figures are then rolled. The over-sixty amount is added to the over-ninety amount. The over-thirty amount becomes the new over-sixty amount. The current amount becomes the new over-thirty amount. Finally, the current month's invoice total becomes the new current amount.
   c. Statements and the aged trial balance are printed.
   d. The current invoice total is set to zero, the current payment total is set to zero, and the previous balance is set to the current balance in preparation for the coming month.

To illustrate, let's assume that before the update begins, the figures for customer 1354 are as follows:

```
CURRENT BALANCE:   2,375.20    PREVIOUS BALANCE: 2,138.70
CURRENT INVOICES:  1,686.50              CURRENT:   490.20
CURRENT PAYMENTS:  1,500.00              OVER 30:   298.50
                                         OVER 60:   710.00
                                         OVER 90:   690.00
```

The current payments ($1,500.00) are subtracted from the OVER 90 figure ($690.00), reducing the OVER 90 figure to zero and leaving an excess of $810.00. This excess is subtracted from the OVER 60 figure ($710.00), reducing the OVER 60 figure to zero and leaving an excess of $100.00. This excess is subtracted from the OVER 30 figure ($298.50), reducing this figure to $198.50. At this point, all the figures are rolled and the CURRENT figure is set to the current invoice total. This produces the following:

```
CURRENT BALANCE:  2,375.20    PREVIOUS BALANCE: 2,138.70
CURRENT INVOICES: 1,686.50             CURRENT: 1,686.50
CURRENT PAYMENTS: 1,500.00             OVER 30:   490.20
                                       OVER 60:   198.50
                                       OVER 90:     0.00
```

Statements and the aged trial balance are now produced, after which the PREVIOUS BALANCE, CURRENT INVOICES, and CURRENT PAYMENTS figures are updated, yielding:

```
CURRENT BALANCE:  2,375.20    PREVIOUS BALANCE: 2,375.20
CURRENT INVOICES:     0.00             CURRENT: 1,686.50
CURRENT PAYMENTS:     0.00             OVER 30:   490.20
                                       OVER 60:   198.50
                                       OVER 90:     0.00
```

2. Print the monthly invoice register and the monthly cash receipts journal.
3. Print a monthly sales rep commission report.
4. Zero out all MTD fields. If it also happens to be year end, zero out all YTD fields.
5. Remove all cash receipts and invoice summary records. (In practice, such records would be moved to a historical type of database in order to allow for the possibility of future reference. For the purposes of this illustration, we have disregarded this fact.)

## REFERENCES

1] Atre, S., *Data Base: Structured Techniques for Design, Performance, and Management*, 2nd ed. John Wiley & Sons, Inc., 1988.
2] Chen, Peter, *The Entity-Relationship Approach to Logical Data Base Design*, Q.E.D. Information Sciences, Inc. Data Base Monograph Series, no. 6.
3] Date, C. J., *Introduction to Database Systems, Volume II*, Addison-Wesley, 1983.
4] Kroenke, David, and Dolan, Kathleen A., *Database Processing: Fundamentals, Design, Implementation*, 3d ed. SRA, 1988.
5] McFadden, Fred R., and Hoffer, Jeffrey A., *Data Base Management*, 2d ed. Benjamin Cummings, 1988.
6] Shelly, Gary B., Cashman, Thomas J., Adamski, Joseph J., and Adamski, Judy, *Systems Analysis and Design*, boyd & fraser, 1991.
7] Yao, S. Bing, *Principles of Database Design*, Prentice-Hall, 1985.

# The CODASYL Model

## INTRODUCTION

In the mid 1960s, a few commercial DBMS's began to appear, and were met with at least some acceptance within the computing community. Of these, IDS (Integrated Data Store), was one of the most influential. It was developed at General Electric by a team headed by Charles Bachman. This system proved to be the forerunner of the CODASYL model, which we will study in this chapter.

    **CODASYL** (COnference on DAta SYstems Languages) is a voluntary organization consisting of representatives from diverse areas within the computing community. Already known as the organization responsible for the development of COBOL, CODASYL turned its attention in the late 1960s to the problem of standardization of database management systems. The initial process of developing a standard was carried out by a task group within CODASYL, called the **Data Base Task Group (DBTG)**. This group studied existing systems (most notably IDS) and prepared a preliminary report on specifications for languages that define and process data. This DBTG report, published by the Association for Computing Machinery in October, 1969, drew widespread criticism, and the task group received a number of proposals from various groups suggesting changes and extensions. Many of these suggestions were accepted by the DBTG, which published an updated report in 1971. (See [8].)

    The specifications detailed in the 1971 report were considered by the American National Standards Institute (ANSI) for establishment as a standard. ANSI did not accept the specifications as a standard (neither did they reject them), but a number of vendors developed systems that followed these guidelines. Such systems have come to be called CODASYL systems or DBTG systems (the terms are synonymous). The general approach to database management proposed in the 1971 report is termed the CODASYL model, or the DBTG model.

The **CODASYL model** falls within the general category of the **network model**. A simple network is just a collection of records and one-to-many relationships. A system technically falls within the general network model if its underlying data structures are simple networks. Since this is true of the CODASYL model, it is technically a subset of the network model. There are non-CODASYL systems which also must be deemed to fall within the network model. The vast majority of network model systems are also CODASYL systems, however, so to many people within the computing community, the term network model has also come to be synonymous with CODASYL. Thus, if various individuals refer to their system as a network system or a CODASYL system or a DBTG system, they are usually talking about the same thing.

More work has been done on the specifications. The DBTG became a permanent part of CODASYL and assumed a new name (Data Description Language Committee, or DDLC) in 1972. In 1973, the DDLC published another report, one which differed in some minor aspects from the 1971 report. (See [6].) Another report, this one with more substantial changes, was published in 1978 (see [3] and [5]), and yet another one was published by ANSI in 1981. (See [4] and [7].) While the term DBTG model should technically be used only to refer to the 1971 specifications, many people use it to refer to any or all the four versions published in 1971, 1973, 1978, and 1981.

Given four different reports and the lack of a national standard, the presence of differences between CODASYL systems is not surprising; but the similarities far outnumber the differences. A person who is proficient in one CODASYL system will have no difficulty mastering another. In this chapter, we will study IDMS, one of the most popular CODASYL DBMS's. What this means, essentially, is that we will study the model that is based on the 1971–1973 specifications. We will also look at some differences between IDMS and other systems, as well as some of the changes made in the 1978–1981 specifications.

A number of CODASYL systems are commercially available, including IDMS (Cullinet Software), IDS/II (the descendant of the original IDS and now a product of Honeywell Information Systems), DMS/1100 (Univac), DBMS 10 (DEC), DMS-170 (CDC), PRIME DBMS (PRIME Computer), and PHOLAS (Phillips Electrologica of Holland). CODASYL systems are known to be powerful and capable of supporting applications with high-volume processing requirements. They are best suited to applications whose requirements can be well specified in advance. They are not particularly well-suited to applications that cannot be so tightly specified. The latter demand the flexibility that only relational model systems can provide.

We begin this chapter by studying the basic concepts and terminology of the CODASYL model. Next, we investigate the data definition language (DDL) and the data manipulation language (DML). Both of these concepts will be illustrated with the Premiere Products database. We will then look at a sample IDMS application program. We will look at IDMS/R, which represents the addition of relational features to IDMS. We next consider how IDMS furnishes the functions of a DBMS. Finally, we turn our attention to the differences between IDMS and other CODASYL systems, as well as to some of the changes alluded to in the 1978–1981 reports.

## BASIC CONCEPTS AND TERMINOLOGY

Since a database is a structure that houses not only information about different types of **entities**, but also information about **relationships** between these entities, we will begin our study of the CODASYL model by investigating how these types of information are stored in CODASYL systems. We need to examine, of course, not only how the information is stored within a CODASYL database, but also how it is manipulated. In this section we will investigate the structures within CODASYL that are used to store information about entities and relationships between them, as well as the basic facilities used within CODASYL systems to manipulate this information.

To illustrate the basic concepts, let's focus on two different entities, *faculty* and *students*, and on the one-to-many relationship between them, which we will call *ADVISES*. (A faculty member is related to the many students whom he or she advises. Each student is related to the one faculty member who advises him or her.) Thus, we need to be able to store faculty information and student information and to relate a faculty member to all the students advised by the faculty member and a student to his or her advisor.

### Entities and Attributes — Records and Fields

The terms **record** and **field** are used in the CODASYL model exactly as they are in ordinary file processing. Thus, if for the entity *STUDENT*, we are interested in the attributes *STUNUMB* (student number), *STUNAME*, and *NUMBCRED* (number of credits), we would have a *STUDENT* record with fields *STUNUMB*, *STUNAME*, and *NUMCRED*. In COBOL, this structure would be described as:

```
01    STUDENT.
      03    STUNUMB           PIC 9(4).
      03    STUNAME           PIC X(20).
      03    NUMBCRED          PIC 9(3).
```

We can picture it visually as:

```
                     STUDENT
┌──────────────┬─────────────────────┬──────────────┐
│              │                     │              │
└──────────────┴─────────────────────┴──────────────┘
  STUNUMB            STUNAME            NUMBCRED
```

It is often important to make a distinction between the structure itself, which is called the **type**, and a specific example of the structure, which is called an **occurrence**. Thus, what we have just looked at would be called a record type (we could speak of a record of type *STUDENT*, for example), whereas

| 1234 | Mary Jones | 14 |
|------|------------|----|

is a record occurrence (technically an occurrence of the record of type *STUDENT*). This distinction is not always a necessary one, but some situations make it essential. As we encounter such situations, we will point out why the distinction is necessary, and, of course, we will use the appropriate term.

## One-to-Many Relationships — Sets

Records and fields allow us to maintain information on entities and the properties of these entities, but it is another construction, called a **set**, that allows us to maintain relationships. Just as there are record types and record occurrences, there are set types and set occurrences. The set type is the general structure.

> *Definition:* A **set type** is a one-to-many association between record types.

In our example, we would have two record types, *FACULTY* and *STUDENT*. The one-to-many association between them would be represented by a set type, say, *ADVISES*. Figure 9.1 shows a pictorial way of representing these two records and the set between them. This type of diagram is often called a **data structure diagram**. Some people refer to it as a **Bachman diagram** (named for Charles Bachman). In it, we represent each record type with a box and each set type as an arrow going *from* the record type that is the "one" part of the association, *to* the record type that is the "many" part of the association. Since one faculty member is assigned to many students, the arrow goes from the record of type *FACULTY* to the record of type *STUDENT*. The record at the head of the arrow, in this case *FACULTY*, is called the **owner record type**. The record at the foot of the arrow, in this case *STUDENT*, is called the **member record type**.

**Figure 9.1**

Data structure diagram

Just as an occurrence of a record type is a specific example of that record type, an occurrence of a set type will be a specific example of that set type. But what would an example of a one-to-many association be in this case? It would be one occurrence of the owner record type (one faculty member) and many occurrences of the member record type (the many students whom this particular faculty member advises). Consider Figure 9.2, in which, for the sake of simplicity, last names represent occurrences of *FACULTY* and first names represent occurrences of *STUDENT*. The bubbles represent occurrences of *ADVISES*: one faculty member and the many students he or she advises. Thus, two occurrences of *ADVISES* are shown. In the first, Jones is the owner occurrence and Mary, Tom, and Bill are the member occurrences. In the second, Smith is the owner occurrence and Jane and Sam are the member occurrences.

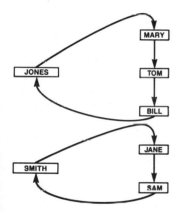

**Figure 9.2**

Occurrences of
*ADVISES*

Q & A

| | |
|---|---|
| **Question:** | How many records do you see in Figure 9.2? |
| **Answer:** | This is an ambiguous question. If, by records, we mean record types, there are two: *FACULTY* and *STUDENT*. If we mean record occurrences, there are seven: Jones, Smith, Mary, Tom, Bill, Jane, and Sam. |
| **Question:** | How many sets do you see? |
| **Answer:** | Again, this is an ambiguous question. If we mean set types, there is one: *ADVISES*. If we mean set occurrences, there are two: the two bubbles. |

## Q & A

| | |
|---|---|
| **Question:** | If we add another faculty member, Wilson, who has *no* advisees, what would the picture look like? |
| **Answer:** | There would be an additional faculty member, Wilson, in the picture and an additional bubble containing only Wilson. |
| **Question:** | If Bill is advised by both Jones *and* Smith, what would the picture look like? Would Bill have to be in an overlap of the two bubbles? |
| **Answer:** | The answer is that Bill cannot be advised by both Jones and Smith, since this would violate the relationship. (Each student is advised by exactly one faculty member.) The diagram is inappropriate for a college that allows students to have more than one advisor. |

These relationships are not actually implemented as "bubbles," as they are shown in Figure 9.2. For now, however, we do suggest that you visualize set occurrences as bubbles, each bubble containing exactly one occurrence of the owner record type and many occurrences of the member record type. In other words, each bubble will contain exactly one faculty member and the many students (possibly zero) whom this faculty member advises.

## Currency

Later in the chapter we will formally introduce a concept called **currency**, which is used in processing a CODASYL database. For now, let's picture that for each record type in our database, we are given a "finger" we can use to point at a particular occurrence of the record type. At a given instant, for example, the *FACULTY* finger could be pointing at Jones and the *STUDENT* finger could be pointing at Mary. Also, for each set type, we are given a finger we can use to point at a particular occurrence (bubble) of that set. Furthermore, this same finger will also be pointing at one of the record occurrences (owner or member) in this bubble, indicating our position within the set. These fingers are used by the system to keep track of our position within the database. Various commands utilize them in order to determine exactly what needs to be accomplished. For example, let's consider the scenario shown in Table 9.1. The STATEMENT column indicates the action we are requesting the system to perform. The EFFECT column indicates the system's response.

The *FACULTY*, *STUDENT*, and *ADVISES* columns indicate what the appropriate fingers will be pointing to *after* the action has been completed. Let's assume that initially none of the fingers are pointing to anything.

Note that the type of commands illustrated in steps one through five would serve to find a faculty member and all advisees. The commands illustrated in steps six and seven would serve to find a student and his or her advisor.

**Table 9.1   Processing a Database**

| STATEMENT | EFFECT | FACULTY | STUDENT | ADVISES |
|---|---|---|---|---|
| 1. Find faculty Jones | System locates Jones | Jones | — | bubble 1 Jones |
| 2. Find next student in ADVISES set | System locates Mary | Jones | Mary | bubble 1 Mary |
| 3. Find next student in ADVISES set | System locates Tom | Jones | Tom | bubble 1 Tom |
| 4. Find next student in ADVISES set | System locates Bill | Jones | Bill | bubble 1 Bill |
| 5. Find next student in ADVISES set | System shows no more students in set. Fingers do not change | Jones | Bill | bubble 1 Bill |
| 6. Find student Jane | System locates Jane | Jones | Jane | bubble 2 Jane |
| 7. Find owner within ADVISES set | System locates Smith | Smith | Jane | bubble 2 Smith |

## Many-to-Many Relationships — Link Records

So far, we have seen how the set construction within the CODASYL model handles the one-to-many relationship. What kind of structure is available to handle the many-to-many relationship? In particular, what about the relationship between students and the courses they have taken? Since a student has taken many courses (up to forty or so for a graduating senior; an incoming freshman, of course, has not yet taken any) and a course has been taken by many students, this is a many-to-many relationship. Figure 9.3 on the next page shows a diagram of this relationship.

**Figure 9.3**

Many-to-many
relationship

Even though the many-to-many relationship is quite common, there is no facility within the CODASYL model to handle it directly. We can, however, use a little trick to change a single many-to-many relationship into two one-to-many relationships, which can then be implemented using sets. We introduce a third record type, called a link record (in this example, named *STUCRSE*), together with a one-to-many relationship from *STUDENT* to *STUCRSE* and another one-to-many relationship from *COURSE* to *STUCRSE*. In this particular example, the *STUCRSE* record contains a single field, *GRADE*. (After discussing the concepts involved in this procedure, we will examine which types of fields this new record type will contain in general.) The one-to-many relationship between *STUDENT* and *STUCRSE* will be represented by a set, *RECEIVES*, which relates a student to the grades he or she received. The one-to-many relationship between *COURSE* and *STUCRSE* will be represented by a set, *GIVES*, which relates a course to all the grades given by that course. Figure 9.4 gives the data structure diagram for the new structure.

To demonstrate why the new structure is appropriate, we need first to examine exactly what is meant by the original structure (Figure 9.3). When we see this kind of diagram, we know we must be able to do two things:

1. Given a student, list all the courses he or she has taken.
2. Given a course, list all the students who have taken it.

**Figure 9.4**

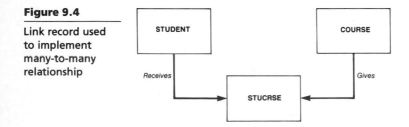

Link record used
to implement
many-to-many
relationship

If the new structure (Figure 9.4) is appropriate, we must be able to use it to accomplish at least the same two tasks. Let's see whether we can do this by examining some sample occurrences of the record types and set types.

Figure 9.5 shows sample occurrences of all three record types. If we inspect this figure, we can tell that five students (Mary, Bob, Tom, Fred, and Sue), five courses (ENG 100, MTH 110, HST 206, GEO 100, and PHY 120), and eleven grades (A, C, C, B, D, A, B, C, F, A, and B) are currently in the database. We have no idea, however, which students obtained which grades, nor do we know in which courses the grades were received.

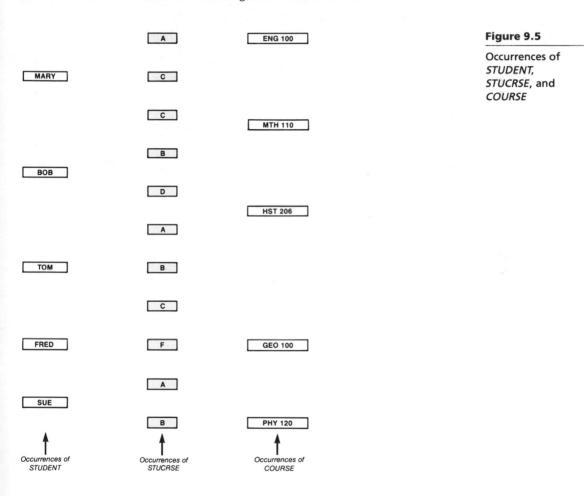

**Figure 9.5**

Occurrences of *STUDENT*, *STUCRSE*, and *COURSE*

Suppose we look at occurrences of the set *RECEIVES*. These occurrences, shown in Figure 9.6, allow us to determine which grades were received by which students. We can see, for example, that Mary received an A and two C's, whereas Tom received an A, a B, and a C. We still cannot determine in which courses these grades were earned.

**Figure 9.6**

Occurrences of
*RECEIVES*

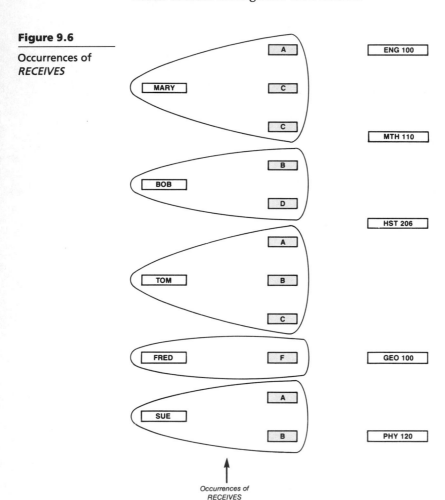

Occurrences of
RECEIVES

If, on the other hand, we look at occurrences of the set *GIVES*, shown in Figure 9.7, we can see that in ENG 100 an A was awarded, in MTH 110 a C, a B, and an A, in HST 206 a C, a D and another C, and so on, but we cannot tell which students received these grades. What we need to do, of course, is to examine occurrences of both sets at the same time. Figure 9.8 on the next page shows the complete picture, occurrences of all three record types and both set types. The occurrences of *RECEIVES* are shown in black, and occurrences of *GIVES* are shown in blue.

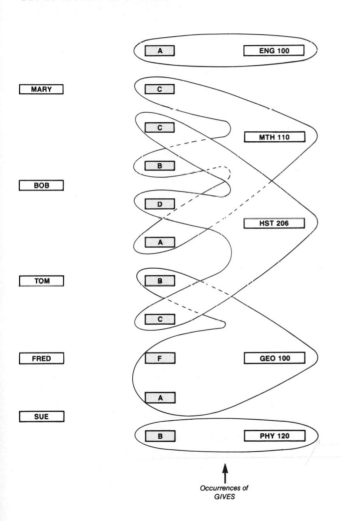

**Figure 9.7**

Occurrences of *GIVES*

Occurrences of
*GIVES*

**Figure 9.8**

Occurrences of
*RECEIVES* and
*GIVES*

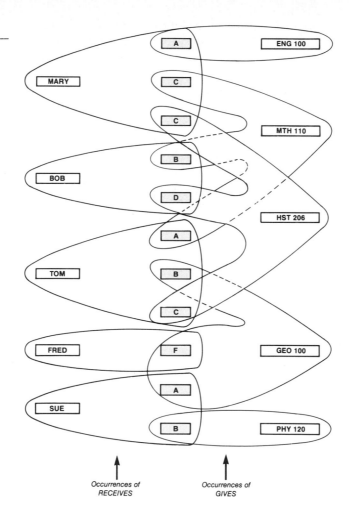

**Figure 9.8**

Occurrences of *RECEIVES* and *GIVES*

Occurrences of
RECEIVES

Occurrences of
GIVES

Now that we have access to all the information, we can see that Mary received an A in ENG 100, a C in MTH 110, and a C in HST 206. We learn this by examining all the grades that are in the *RECEIVES* bubble in which the student is Mary, and then, for each of these grades, determine the unique course that is in the same *GIVES* bubble as the grade in question. Specifically, after first finding Mary, we repeatedly find the next grade within the

*RECEIVES* set, then find this grade's owner within the *GIVES* set. This process continues until we run out of grades in Mary's set occurrence. (We will examine the exact syntax for these and other data manipulation commands, along with ways of using them, later in this chapter). We could obviously go through the same procedure for any other student. We can thus fulfill the first requirement just listed. For a given student, we can list all the courses he or she has taken. We can actually do more than was originally required: We can give the grade the student received in the course. This is a nice bonus, but what is important is that we can meet the stated requirement.

In a similar fashion, we can determine that MTH 110 gave a C to Mary, a B to Bob, and an A to Tom. Since we can do this for any course, we can fulfill the second requirement: For a given course, we can list all the students who have taken the course. Again, we can actually do more: We can list the grades these students received.

Since both of these requirements can be fulfilled by the new structure, it is a legitimate way of implementing the many-to-many relationship. It is a worthwhile exercise at this point for you to list for every student all the grades received, as well as the courses in which the grades were earned. Once you have done this, list for every course all the grades given, as well as the students to whom these grades were given. If you can get comfortable with the general concept here, things will be much easier when we look at a rigorous approach to processing CODASYL databases.

### Fields Within Link Records — Intersection Data

A natural question to ask at this point is, *Where did GRADE come from?* It was not mentioned in the original problem; we only had students and courses and a many-to-many relationship between them. In particular, suppose there was no such field. Suppose for example, that the relationship had not been between students and courses they had *taken*, but between students and courses they were *taking*. In this case, the students would not yet have received a grade. So what could we use in place of a grade? Do we really need a grade? What if every grade were replaced with some unlikely symbol, such as an asterisk, as shown in Figure 9.9 on the next page? We wouldn't be able to tell what grades students had received, since no grades would have been given. But couldn't we still tell which students were related to which courses, and which courses were related to which students in exactly the same way we did before? In fact, we could even leave the boxes blank that contained the grades, as shown in Figure 9.10 on page 435, and still be able to determine the relationship between students and courses.

**Figure 9.9**

Link records con-
taining ''*'' rather
than grades

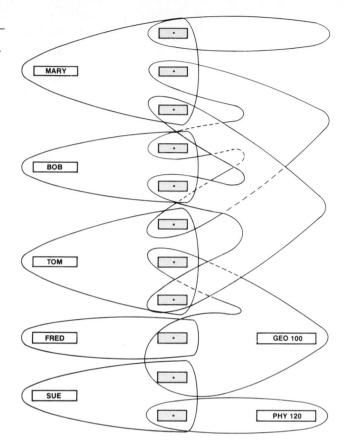

Now that we have seen why the *GRADE* field is not necessary to accomplish the many-to-many relationship, the question remains, *Where did this field come from?* This is a database design question, of course, and as such has essentially been answered in chapters 6 and 7. We will briefly review the general idea here, at least as it relates to the CODASYL model. This means we will examine the way many-to-many relationships are handled within the model.

The basic approach to dealing with a many-to-many relationship, such as the one between students and courses, involves first creating a third record type and two set types. The new record type will be the member in both sets;

the original two records will be the owners. (See Figure 9.11 on the next page.) Various terms are used for the new record type that has been introduced. It is often called a **link**, since it "links" occurrences of one record type to occurrences of the other record type. (In Figure 9.8, for example, the first occurrence of *GRADE* linked Mary to English 100.) It is also sometimes called a **cross reference**, since it serves as a "reference" from records of one record type to records of the other type. Finally, the data that this new record type contains is called **intersection data**. Looking at Figure 9.8, we see the reason for this term: the occurrences of this record are in the *intersection* of a student bubble and a course bubble.

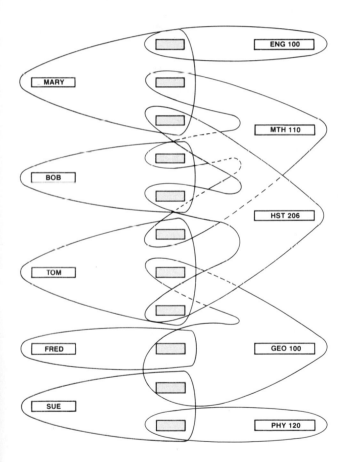

**Figure 9.10**

Link records containing no data fields

**Figure 9.11**

General link record

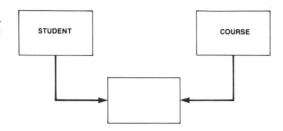

Generally speaking, the next step is to determine what type of intersection data we will have in this new record. In our example, this will be the data found in the intersection of a student and a course. We need to ask ourselves what sort of items pertain to both a student *and* a course. The student's address, for example, pertains only to the student; it has nothing to do with the courses he or she has taken. The description of a course has nothing to do with the student. These fields are not intersection data and do not belong in the link record. *GRADE*, however, pertains to both. To find an individual grade in the database, it is not enough to know that the student who received the grade was Mary or that the grade was earned by English 100. We need to know both the student and the course. Thus, *GRADE* is intersection data and should be one of the fields within the link record. (Note that this is essentially the same process discussed in chapter 6 for implementing many-to-many relationships. In that case, a new relation was created whose key was the concatenation of the keys of the original relations. The other attributes placed in this new relation were those pertaining to *both* of the original entities. These additional attributes are the intersection data.)

## Q & A

---

**Question:** Where would each of the following fields go: in the *STUDENT* record, the *COURSE* record, or the link record?
1. A student's GPA (grade point average).
2. The number of credits awarded by a course.
3. The term in which a student took the course.

**Answer:** Since a student's GPA depends only on the student, and not on the course, it will be a field within the student record. Since the number of credits depends only on the course, and not on the student, it will be a field within the *COURSE* record. Finally, the term in which a student took a course depends on both the student *and* the course and thus goes in the link record.)

---

Once the intersection data has been determined, we can give a name to the new record type. If the record type now has a special meaning, we could use the meaning as a guide to naming the record. We might also choose to name the record as we did in the example, *STUCRSE*, emphasizing its nature as a link between students and courses. Finally, we can name the two sets. In this case, we have used *RECEIVES*, since a student receives a grade, and *GIVES*, since a course gives a grade.

### Implementation of Sets

Before moving on to the specifics of the CODASYL model, we will briefly explain the actual implementation of these sets. Of course, they aren't actually implemented as bubbles, although this is a useful way to picture them. They are implemented as linked lists (you can consult the appendix for a discussion of linked lists if you are not already familiar with this topic). A pointer goes from the owner occurrence to the first member occurrence, from the first member to the second, from the second to the third, and so on. Finally, the last member occurrence points back to the owner. While the pointer is really a number, namely, the address or "database key" of the next member, it is often visualized as an arrow. Thus, the set occurrences in Figure 9.2 are implemented in the fashion shown in Figure 9.12 and those in Figure 9.8 are implemented in the fashion shown in Figure 9.13 on the next page. The processing ideas that we discussed earlier still apply, however.

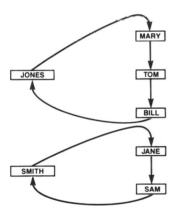

**Figure 9.12**

Implementation of *ADVISES* set

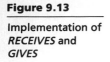

**Figure 9.13**

Implementation of
*RECEIVES* and
*GIVES*

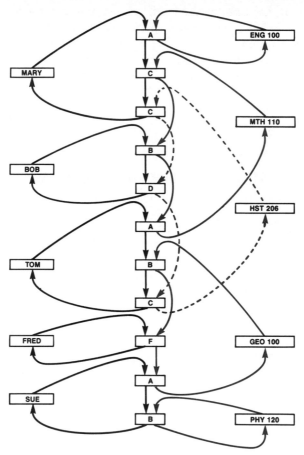

## Example Database

As an example of the preceding points, consider the entities and relationships required for the Premiere Products database described in chapter 1. The basic entities are *sales reps*, *customers*, *orders*, and *parts*, and so we have four record types, say, *SLSREP*, *CUSTOMER*, *ORDERS*, and *PART*. There is a one-to-many relationship from sales reps to customers (one sales rep represents many customers but each customer is represented by exactly one sales rep) and a one-to-many relationship between customers and orders (one customer may have many orders on file but each order was placed by exactly one customer). Therefore, we have two set types: one from *SLSREP* to *CUSTOMER* and another from *CUSTOMER* to *ORDERS*. A relationship also exists between orders and parts but it is many-to-many (one order can contain many parts and one part can be found on many orders). We thus create an additional record type, a link record, and two additional sets: one from

*ORDERS* to the link record and the other from *PART* to the link record. The fields in the link record will be the intersection data (if any); that is, the properties that pertain to both orders and parts. In this case, two properties pertain to both: quantity ordered and quoted price. Putting this all together yields the data structure diagram shown in Figure 9.14. The fields within each record are listed below the diagram.

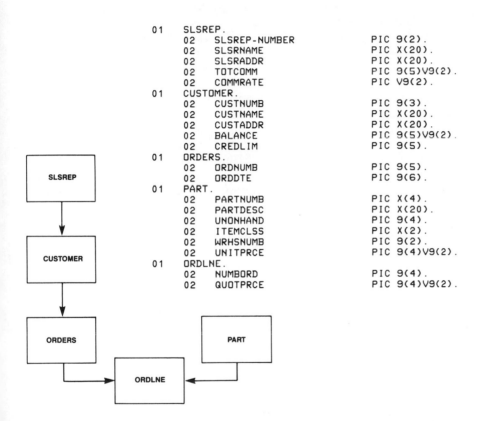

```
01   SLSREP.
     02   SLSREP-NUMBER      PIC 9(2).
     02   SLSRNAME           PIC X(20).
     02   SLSRADDR           PIC X(20).
     02   TOTCOMM            PIC 9(5)V9(2).
     02   COMMRATE           PIC V9(2).
01   CUSTOMER.
     02   CUSTNUMB           PIC 9(3).
     02   CUSTNAME           PIC X(20).
     02   CUSTADDR           PIC X(20).
     02   BALANCE            PIC 9(5)V9(2).
     02   CREDLIM            PIC 9(5).
01   ORDERS.
     02   ORDNUMB            PIC 9(5).
     02   ORDDTE             PIC 9(6).
01   PART.
     02   PARTNUMB           PIC X(4).
     02   PARTDESC           PIC X(20).
     02   UNONHAND           PIC 9(4).
     02   ITEMCLSS           PIC X(2).
     02   WRHSNUMB           PIC 9(2).
     02   UNITPRCE           PIC 9(4)V9(2).
01   ORDLNE.
     02   NUMBORD            PIC 9(4).
     02   QUOTPRCE           PIC 9(4)V9(2).
```

**Figure 9.14**

Data structure diagram for Premiere Products

No set names were given in Figure 9.14 but these sets do need to have a name. Basically, we can use two methods for assigning names to sets. We can use a name that is descriptive of the set's meaning, as we did with the *ADVISES, RECEIVES,* and *GIVES* sets earlier. The advantage of this method is that anyone looking at the name can tell the meaning of the set, provided the name was well-chosen. The disadvantage is that we cannot tell from the name which record is the owner record type and which is the member. We can guess that the owner of a set called *ADVISES* is the *FACULTY* record, but we can't be sure. The second method for naming sets doesn't require us to guess the owner and the member; we simply include the name of both the owner and the member in the set name (e.g., *FACULTY-STUDENT*). The disadvantage of this method, of course, is that we now have to guess the meaning. As you can see, there are pros and cons to both methods. For the remainder of the text, we will use the second method unless a specific situation precludes the use of the method. (Obviously, if two sets have the same owner and member, they cannot both be named in this fashion.) One benefit of this method in a data structure diagram is that there is no real need to include the set names. We know, for example, that the set from *SLSREP* to *CUSTOMER* is called *SLSREP-CUSTOMER*. Omitting the names in the diagram tends to make the diagram a little less cluttered.

If you compare the list of fields within each record for the CODASYL version of the Premiere Products database with the columns in the corresponding tables in the relational model version, you will note that for some columns that are present in the relational model version, there are no corresponding fields here. The reason is that in the relational model, relationships are determined by common columns, whereas in the CODASYL model, they are determined by sets. For the relationship between sales reps and customers, for example, we needed to include the sales rep number as part of the customer table within the relational model implementation. In the CODASYL implementation, this is not necessary. We determine which sales rep is related to a given customer by finding the sales rep who *owns* that customer within the set *SLSREP-CUSTOMER*, not by looking at the sales rep number field within the customer record.

This brings up a question: Could we include the sales rep number in the *CUSTOMER* record even though it is not necessary? We certainly could, although we usually don't. It is worth noting, however, that if we include the sales rep number in the customer record, the set *SLSREP-CUSTOMER* is technically not necessary. We could use the sales rep number in the customer record to find the given sales rep directly. Likewise, to find all the customers for a given sales rep, we could examine *all* customers looking for those customers who have the given sales rep's number in their sales rep number field. In this case, the set *SLSREP-CUSTOMER* is called an **inessential set**, since we could live without it. On the other hand, if the sales rep's number is not stored within the *CUSTOMER* record, the only way to find the sales rep who represents a given customer is through the set. In this case, the set is called an **essential set**.

The database for Premiere Products will form the basis for our discussion of the details of the CODASYL model in the sections to come.


## DATA DEFINITION

The **ANSI/SPARC model** of data includes three levels: internal (what is seen by the machine), conceptual (the global enterprise view of data), and external (the individual user view of data). Information about the internal level is defined in the **internal schema**, about the conceptual level in the **conceptual schema**, and about the external level in a number of **external schemas**, one for each separate user view. Although the recent CODASYL reports essentially support these three levels, the 1971–1973 reports and most commercial CODASYL DBMS's do not. Instead, the latter support two levels, referred to as the **schema** and **subschema**. (Actually, it is probably more accurate to refer to two and a half levels. As we will see, some of the physical details of the database are described in a third structure but many physical details are still included in the schema.) The subschema does represent an individual user view in the sense described in the ANSI/SPARC model. The schema represents the global view of the database. However, it includes both the conceptual level and some aspects of the internal level.

## Schema DDL

We begin our discussion of data definition within the CODASYL model by examining the way in which **schemas** are defined. In particular, we will look at the schema DDL (data definition language) for Premiere Products. At each step, we will examine the various options and indicate why a particular option was chosen. The complete schema DDL is shown in Figure 9.15. We will now examine each of the components to the schema.

```
ADD SCHEMA NAME IS SCHDIST
    USER IS SD00
        REGISTERED FOR ALL
        RESPONSIBLE FOR UPDATE.

ADD FILE NAME IS DISTFILE ASSIGN TO DISTFILE.

ADD AREA NAME IS DISTAREA PAGE RANGE IS 1 THRU 1000
        WITHIN FILE DISTFILE.

ADD RECORD NAME IS SLSREP
    LOCATION MODE IS CALC USING SLSRNUMB
        DUPLICATES ARE NOT ALLOWED
    WITHIN AREA DISTAREA.

    02    SLSRNUMB               PIC 9(2).
    02    SLSRNAME               PIC X(20).
    02    SLSRADDR               PIC X(20).
    02    TOTCOMM                PIC 9(5)V9(2).
    02    COMMRATE               PIC V9(2).

ADD RECORD NAME IS CUSTOMER
    LOCATION MODE IS CALC USING CUSTNUMB
        DUPLICATES ARE NOT ALLOWED
    WITHIN AREA DISTAREA.

    02    CUSTNUMB               PIC 9(3).
    02    CUSTNAME               PIC X(20).
    02    CUSTADDR               PIC X(20).
    02    BALANCE                PIC 9(5)V9(2).
    02    CREDLIM                PIC 9(5).

ADD RECORD NAME IS ORDERS
    LOCATION MODE IS CALC USING ORDNUMB
        DUPLICATES ARE NOT ALLOWED
    WITHIN AREA DISTAREA.
```

**Figure 9.15**

Schema DDL for Premiere Products

*(continued)*

**Figure 9.15**

(continued)

```
                        02    ORDNUMB                      PIC 9(5).
                        02    ORDDTE                       PIC 9(6).

            ADD RECORD NAME IS PART
                    LOCATION MODE IS CALC USING PARTNUMB
                            DUPLICATES ARE NOT ALLOWED
                    WITHIN AREA DISTAREA.

                        02    PARTNUMB                     PIC X(4).
                        02    PARTDESC                     PIC X(20).
                        02    UNONHAND                     PIC 9(4).
                        02    ITEMCLSS                     PIC X(2).
                        02    WRHSNUMB                     PIC 9(2).
                        02    UNITPRCE                     PIC 9(4)V9(2).

            ADD RECORD NAME IS ORDLNE
                    LOCATION MODE IS VIA ORDERS-ORDLNE
                    WITHIN AREA DISTAREA.

                        02    NUMBORD                      PIC 9(4).
                        02    QUOTPRCE                     PIC 9(4)V9(2).

            ADD SET NAME IS SLSREP-CUSTOMER
                    ORDER IS SORTED
                    MODE IS CHAIN          LINKED TO PRIOR
                    OWNER IS SLSREP
                    MEMBER IS CUSTOMER
                            LINKED TO OWNER
                            OPTIONAL AUTOMATIC
                    ASCENDING KEY IS CUSTNAME
                            DUPLICATES ARE LAST.

            ADD SET NAME IS CUSTOMER-ORDERS
                    ORDER IS LAST
                    MODE IS CHAIN          LINKED TO PRIOR
                    OWNER IS CUSTOMER
                    MEMBER IS ORDERS
                            LINKED TO OWNER
                            MANDATORY AUTOMATIC.

            ADD SET NAME IS ORDERS-ORDLNE
                    ORDER IS LAST
                    MODE IS CHAIN          LINKED TO PRIOR
                    OWNER IS ORDERS
                    MEMBER IS ORDLNE
                            LINKED TO OWNER
                            MANDATORY AUTOMATIC.

            ADD SET NAME IS PART-ORDLNE
                    ORDER IS LAST
                    MODE IS CHAIN          LINKED TO PRIOR
                    OWNER IS PART
                    MEMBER IS ORDLNE
                            LINKED TO OWNER
                            MANDATORY AUTOMATIC.
```

**Note:** You'll notice that each command in the schema DDL starts with the word ADD. This is because IDMS stores all the information about the structure of the database in the data dictionary and the command is really an instruction to IDMS to *add* the appropriate information to the dictionary.

## SCHEMA Entry

```
ADD SCHEMA NAME IS SCHDIST
    USER IS SD00
        REGISTERED FOR ALL
        RESPONSIBLE FOR UPDATE.
```

The first line in the schema DDL gives the name for the schema. In this case, the name SCHDIST was chosen. The SCH is included so that anyone can readily determine that this is, in fact, a schema, and the DIST was chosen as an abbreviation for the database, since it involves the distribution activities of Premiere Products. The remaining information indicates the I.D. of the user who can make changes to this schema, in this case user SD00.

## AREA Entry

```
ADD FILE NAME IS DISTFILE ASSIGN TO DISTFILE.

ADD AREA NAME IS DISTAREA PAGE RANGE IS 1 THRU 1000
    WITHIN FILE DISTFILE.
```

In general, an area is a physical file that will house a portion of or an entire database. (In IDMS, we have great flexibility in associating areas and physical files. In other systems, the two are synonymous.) This construction has been removed in the later CODASYL reports but is still found in commercial implementations. As we will see when we discuss processing the database, particularly in COBOL, there is another word, *REALM*, that is used in place of AREA. The two are synonymous. It is actually possible to have several different areas (or realms) and to indicate which record types are stored in which areas. For our purposes, one area will be sufficient.

These two clauses indicate that there will be a single area, called *DISTAREA*, and it will be assigned to the physical file, called *DISTFILE*. In fact, it will be assigned to the pages 1 through 1,000 in this file. (It is possible to have the same physical file contain portions of many areas. Usually, however, you will have a single area associated with a single database file.)

## Record Entry

For each record in the database, there is a *record entry* in the schema. The record entry gives the name of the record, as well as the name and physical characteristics of all the fields within the record. The physical characteristics are often specified through the use of COBOL picture clauses. Some systems allow the use of a TYPE clause rather than COBOL pictures. The following is the record entry for the *SLSREP* record.

```
ADD RECORD NAME IS SLSREP
        LOCATION MODE IS CALC USING SLSRNUMB
            DUPLICATES ARE NOT ALLOWED
        WITHIN AREA DISTAREA.
  02    SLSRNUMB                   PIC 9(2).
        02    SLSRNAME             PIC X(20).
        02    SLSRADDR             PIC X(20).
        02    TOTCOMM              PIC 9(5)V9(2).
        02    COMMRATE             PIC V9(2).
```

There are two other aspects of a record which must be described: the area in which occurrences of this record type are to be placed, and the record's location mode. Even though we may only mention one area within our schema, as we have done in this case, leaving no choice in terms of where to place the record, we must still specify that the record will be in that one area.

## Location Mode

A **location mode** is really a two-part strategy, one part for placing records in a database and a companion part for finding those records at some later time. Naturally, these two parts go hand-in-hand. How we place records in the database will determine what options we have for finding them later. (For a discussion of location mode and the variety of possibilities, see the appendix.) The location modes possible within a CODASYL system are as follows:

1. **DIRECT.** A location mode of DIRECT implies that the programmer will indicate exactly where in the database a record occurrence is to be placed. (Technically, the programmer will furnish the database key or address of the position to be occupied by the record.) When the programmer wants to locate the record later, he or she must know where it has been placed and ask for the record in that position. This means that the programmer must be involved at a physical level with the database. One of the goals of DBMS was to *avoid* this kind of physical involvement. The moral of the story is, *do not use a location mode of DIRECT!*

2. **CALC.** The word CALC is short for calculation, and that is exactly what happens. A record with a location mode of CALC must have one or more of its items declared to be the *key* for the record. When an occurrence of this record is stored, the position at which the record will be placed is determined by *calculating* from the value of the key. When the item is later retrieved, the same calculation is repeated, indicating to the system where to look for the record. This process is also known as randomizing, or hashing, and is discussed in the appendix.

3. **VIA SET.** The final location mode is VIA SET. The exact syntax is VIA set-name, where the set-name is the name of a set in which the

record is a *member*. In this case record occurrences will be positioned in the database as close as possible to their owner (within the set that was named in the VIA clause). There are two ramifications of this scheme. First, in contrast to the location mode CALC, we will not be able to retrieve one of these record occurrences directly. Second, retrieving an owner occurrence and all its member occurrences is a *very* efficient process if the members are stored via set. A database is divided into blocks, often called pages, which are retrieved when the disk is accessed. If the owner and member occurrences are close together, the number of pages that must be read will by minimized. For example, should an owner occurrence and its eighteen member occurrences all be placed on the same page, we will get all nineteen occurrences with a single disk access. If, on the other hand, the member record type has a location mode of CALC, the eighteen member occurrences will be distributed throughout the database and the same operation could require nineteen disk accesses!

As a rule of thumb, we will use CALC when we have a key for a record (like *SLSRNUMB* for the *SLSREP* record) on which we need to do direct access. We will use VIA SET either when there is no appropriate key or when direct access is not required. If we choose CALC, the syntax is

```
LOCATION MODE IS CALC USING data-name
     DUPLICATES ARE [NOT] ALLOWED
```

If we choose to allow duplicates, it will be possible to store in the database a second record with the same key value. If we do not allow duplicates (which is more common), a second record with the same key value will be rejected and the system will notify us of this fact. Note that even though the key is most often a single data item, it need not be; it could be a combination of several items.

In the complete schema (see Figure 9.15), you will note that *ORDLNE* is stored via the set from *ORDERS* to *ORDLNE*. This means that *ORDLNE* occurrences will be positioned physically close to the *ORDERS* to which they belong, and retrieving an order and all the associated order lines will be an efficient operation. *ORDLNE* is a member in another set, the set from *PART* to *ORDLNE*. The fact that an order line is stored close to the order that owns it will not prohibit us from retrieving a part and all the order lines associated with that part. The only difference is that this operation will be less efficient, since the order lines are not close to the part that owns them.

If a record type is a member in two or more set types and the record should have location mode VIA SET, how do we pick which set to use? We can use only one. As this is really a physical-design issue, it is discussed more thoroughly in chapter 11. In terms of a general guide, however, since processing along the set we pick will be more efficient, we try to determine the relative benefits from choosing one set as opposed to the other.

### SET Entry

For each set in the database there is a SET entry in the schema. The basic form of a set entry is very simple. It indicates the name of the set, the name of the owner, and the name of the member, as follows:

```
SET NAME IS SLSREP-CUSTOMER
    OWNER IS SLSREP
    MEMBER IS CUSTOMER.
```

The other elements in a set entry are used for the various options that we can select. The set entry for *SLSREP-CUSTOMER*, for example, is as follows.

```
ADD SET NAME IS SLSREP-CUSTOMER
    ORDER IS SORTED
    MODE IS CHAIN          LINKED TO PRIOR
    OWNER IS SLSREP
    MEMBER IS CUSTOMER
        LINKED TO OWNER
        MANDATORY AUTOMATIC
    ASCENDING KEY IS CUSTNAME
        DUPLICATES ARE LAST.
```

We will use this example to investigate the various clauses that are used in a SET entry.

### Clauses Within the SET Entry

The following clauses appear within the SET entry:

1. **ORDER IS.** The ORDER IS clause specifies what is often called the **insertion mode**. It does not affect where a record will be physically placed in the database; the **location mode** does that. Rather, it indicates where the occurrence should be positioned within the appropriate set occurrence. To see the effect of each of the various possible insertion modes, consider Figure 9.16.

**Figure 9.16**

*SET* implementation illustrating order

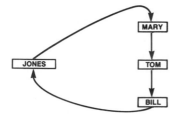

Suppose our current position within this set occurrence is Tom and we are adding a new student, Ann. The position in which the new student will be placed on the chain is determined by this insertion mode. The possibilities are as follows:

a. **FIRST.** New occurrences become the first entry on the chain; they immediately follow the owner. Thus Ann would come between Jones (the owner) and Mary.

b. **LAST.** New occurrences become the last entry on the chain; they immediately precede the owner. Ann would come between Bill and Jones.

c. **NEXT.** New occurrences come immediately after the record at which we are currently pointing. Ann would come between Tom and Bill.

d. **PRIOR.** New occurrences come immediately before the record at which we are currently pointing. Ann would come between Mary and Tom.

e. **SORTED.** For this option, a sort key must be defined and as records are added, they are placed in such a position that the occurrences around the chain are positioned in order of this sort key. Ann would be placed in whatever position the sort key indicated.

If we indicate SORTED, we must also indicate what should be done with duplicates. The possibilities are FIRST, LAST, and NOT ALLOWED. The duplication referred to, of course, is duplication on the sort key. If the set *ADVISES* were sorted by name and we attempted to add a second Ann to a set occurrence, this would be a duplicate. If we chose NOT ALLOWED, this addition would be rejected by the system. If we chose FIRST, the addition would be allowed and Ann would appear as the first of all the Anns in the chain. Likewise, if we chose LAST, Ann would appear as the last of the Anns.

## Q & A

Question:          Which is more efficient, NEXT or PRIOR?

Answer:          If you think about the work the system must do, they seem fairly similar. In the one case the system must locate the next record, in the other, the prior record. While locating the next record is easy (just follow the next pointer), locating the prior pointer may be a lengthy process. If there are no prior pointers, the only way to locate the prior record is to walk *all the way around* the chain. If the number of occurrences on the chain is large, this procedure may well be impractical. On the other hand, if we do have prior pointers, NEXT and PRIOR are virtually identical; in the one case we follow the next pointer, in the other, the prior pointer.

# Q & A

---

Question:         Is it useful to have sorted sets?

Answer:                 The answer depends on many factors. Sorted sets are convenient for retrieval. If we are producing a report in which the required order matches the order in which the set was sorted, there is no extra work to do other than retrieving the data from the database. If this is not the case, we must first retrieve the data from the database and then sort it before producing the report. Thus, sorted sets allow us to skip a step we would otherwise have to take in the reporting process. On the other hand, they incur extra overhead when the database is updated, particularly if the number of occurrences in the set is large. If a faculty member advises 1,000 students (a very busy person indeed) and we wish to add a new occurrence, Paul, to this faculty member's set occurrence, the system must first locate the position in which to insert Paul. In the normal procedure for storing sets, this would involve sequentially examining each student in the chain until we found the first student whose name came after Paul. On the average, we would expect to examine *500* records before finding the right position. More often than not, this would be a prohibitive effort.

---

Many CODASYL systems have made storing sorted sets more attractive through an alternative approach called POINTER ARRAYS. Conceptually, instead of a chain going from the owner occurrence through all the member occurrences and back, pointers come out of the owner pointing to each record. This feature is usually implemented in a B-tree-like structure (see the appendix for a discussion of B-trees) which is more complex than the normal chain and does generate some added overhead of its own. Still, it does make the updating of sorted sets much more efficient, since we can use the structure itself to rapidly determine where to place a new occurrence.

2. **MODE IS CHAIN.** This option requests the typical implementation of a set; that is, all the records in the set should be chained together.

3. **LINKED TO PRIOR.** This option requests the system to maintain prior pointers; that is, each record will contain not only a pointer to the next record in the chain but also a pointer to the *previous* record in the chain. (See Figure 9.17.) These pointers take up extra space. Any operation that involves finding the prior record, however, (such as a deletion, in which the record *prior* to the deleted record should point to the record that came *after* the deleted record), will be made more

efficient. As a general rule, prior pointers are good to have, and if they are to be used, this clause should be included in the schema. If not, the clause is omitted.

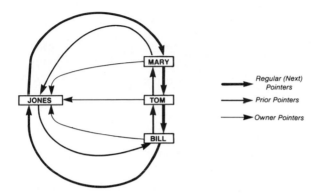

**Figure 9.17**

*SET* implementation illustrating prior and owner pointers

4. **LINKED TO OWNER.** This option requests the system to maintain pointers from each member record directly to the owner record. (See Figure 9.16.) Since it is always possible to find the owner of a given member record by following the chain until the owner is encountered, these pointers are not necessary. They do greatly facilitate the process of finding the owner, however. The tradeoff here is the added space occupied by the pointers as opposed to the added efficiency in finding the owner.

5. **Storage and removal classes.** The **storage class** is used to indicate whether a record should be connected to the set occurrence as the record is stored. The two possibilities are AUTOMATIC and MANUAL. If the choice is AUTOMATIC, the record will automatically be placed in the appropriate set occurrence as a result of the record being stored. No special action is required on the part of the programmer. If, on the other hand, the choice is MANUAL, the record will be placed in the appropriate set occurrence only when the programmer issues a special command, the CONNECT command, requesting the system to do this.

   While the storage class determines whether a record is automatically placed in a set when the record is stored, the **removal class** determines whether a record that has already been placed in a set occurrence may be removed from the occurrence. The two most common choices here are MANDATORY and OPTIONAL. If the choice is MANDATORY, once a record has been placed in a set occurrence it may not be removed. It may be moved to another occurrence, however. If the choice is OPTIONAL, the record may be removed. Other systems allow three choices: MANDATORY,

OPTIONAL, and FIXED. In these systems, FIXED implies that a record may not be moved from a set occurrence once it has been stored. MANDATORY allows a record to be moved from one set occurrence *to another*; the record *must* belong to some occurrence of this set type. OPTIONAL allows a record to be removed from a set occurrence without requiring that the record then be placed in a different occurrence; the record could "float free," so to speak.

To indicate the storage and removal classes, we simply type the desired words. The example contains MANDATORY AUTOMATIC, indicating that we have selected a storage class of AUTOMATIC and a retention class of MANDATORY.

To illustrate the differences between MANDATORY, OPTIONAL, and FIXED, consider the set *SLSREP-CUSTOMER*, the set from *SLSREP* to *CUSTOMER*. If the removal class is FIXED and customer 123 has been placed in the set owned by sales rep 12, this customer must remain with this sales rep. The only way to switch the customer to another sales rep would be to delete him or her from the database and then add him or her back in, tied to the new sales rep. At the other extreme, if the removal class is OPTIONAL, the customer could be removed from the occurrence headed by sales rep 12 and *left without a sales rep*. In between these two is MANDATORY, in which a customer could be moved from sales rep 12's chain to another sales rep's chain, but *would have to have* a sales rep.

6. **KEY IS.** If the sorted insertion mode has been specified, it is here that we define the sort key. After KEY IS we list the sort keys (there can be more than one) in order of importance. Each sort key is preceded either by the word ASCENDING or the word DESCENDING, indicating whether increasing or decreasing order is desired.

See Figure 9.15 for the complete schema for the Premiere Products database.

## Subschema DDL

Whereas the schema describes the complete database as it exists, a **subschema** describes an individual user's view of the database. It may contain all the records, fields, and sets from the database, or it may contain only a portion. Fields may appear in a different order within a record than they did in the database itself. In some systems (but not IDMS), names may be changed. Fields in the database may be treated as group items in a subschema and subdivided (e.g., a single field that is called *CUSTNAME* in the database may be subdivided into fields *FRSTNAME* and *LASTNAME* in a subschema). Conversely, fields in the database may be grouped in a subschema (e.g., if the database contained the fields *FRSTNAME* and *LASTNAME*, these fields might be grouped into a field called *CUSTNAME* in a subschema).

## Full Subschema

Figure 9.18 is a COBOL subschema that encompasses all records, fields, and sets from the Premiere Products database with no changes to either name or format. The first command, ADD SUBSCHEMA NAME, indicates the name of this subschema and the schema with which it is associated. The ADD AREA NAME command lists any areas (also referred to as realms) that are to be included. For each record to be included, there will be an ADD RECORD NAME command. The simplest way to indicate that all the fields in the record are to be included is to use the clause ELEMENTS ARE ALL. (We could also list all the fields after ELEMENTS ARE, but this is easier.) Finally, for each set to be included, there will be an ADD SET NAME command.

```
ADD SUBSCHEMA NAME IS  SSCHDIST
     OF SCHEMA NAME SCHDIST.

ADD AREA NAME IS DISTAREA.

ADD RECORD NAME    SLSREP
     ELEMENTS ARE ALL.
ADD RECORD NAME    CUSTOMER
     ELEMENTS ARE ALL.
ADD RECORD NAME    ORDERS
     ELEMENTS ARE ALL.
ADD RECORD NAME    PART
     ELEMENTS ARE ALL.
ADD RECORD NAME    ORDLNE
     ELEMENTS ARE ALL.

ADD SET NAME       SLSREP-CUSTOMER.
ADD SET NAME       CUSTOMER-ORDERS.
ADD SET NAME       ORDERS-ORDLNE.
ADD SET NAME       PART-ORDLNE.
```

**Figure 9.18**

Full subschema for Premiere Products

## Partial Subschema

Figure 9.19 represents a partial subschema that contains only portions of the *SLSREP* and *CUSTOMER* records and the set *SLSREP-CUSTOMER*. Notice that only the desired records and sets are listed. Notice also that the ELEMENTS clauses list only the desired fields.

```
ADD SUBSCHEMA NAME IS  SSCHDIST
     OF SCHEMA NAME SCHDIST.

ADD AREA NAME IS DISTAREA.

ADD RECORD NAME    SLSREP
     ELEMENTS ARE SLSRNUMB, SLSRNAME, SLSRADDR.
ADD RECORD NAME    CUSTOMER
     ELEMENTS ARE CUSTNUMB, CUSTNAME, CUSTADDR.

ADD SET NAME       SLSREP-CUSTOMER.
```

**Figure 9.19**

Partial subschema for Premiere Products

**Schema DMCL**

The schema DDL and the subschema DDL form the major portion of the data definition facility within CODASYL systems, but we'll comment briefly on another component. In commercial systems, it is usually called the DMCL (Device Media Control Language). While the DMCL was mentioned in the CODASYL report, the form for this language, as well as the specifics of what it must contain, was not. It is used to specify the physical aspects of the database. The following list represents some of the things usually specified:

1. Size of the database
2. Blocking factor (or page size)
3. Whether the database is to be encrypted
4. Whether journaling is to take place
5. Where in the database given records are to be located (ranges of pages on which records of a given type may appear)
6. Whether a given set is organized in a chain mode or uses pointer arrays (some systems include this within the schema DDL)

For further discussion of the CODASYL DDL and DMCL, see [1], [2], [9], [10], [11], [12], and [13]. For further details specific to IDMS, consult the IDMS manuals.


## DATA MANIPULATION

In this section, we will investigate the **data manipulation language (DML)** of CODASYL DBMS's. The CODASYL DML consists of a number of commands that can be used within a programming language (called a **host language**), like COBOL. COBOL, in fact, is by far the most common language used with a CODASYL system. This is why we will base the examples in this section on COBOL. If you are not familiar with the COBOL language, viewing the algorithms presented as a form of pseudocode should enable you to understand the concepts. We will not be delving deeply into the COBOL language itself, but merely using it as a vehicle for presenting the concepts.

We will examine the DML by first discussing the *user work area (UWA)*, a holding area for data being loaded to or unloaded from the database, followed by an examination of the critical concept called **currency**. Next we will briefly look at the DML commands most likely to be encountered in practice. Finally, a number of examples using these commands will be presented. The same Premiere Products database that was presented earlier will be used in these examples.

## User Work Area (UWA)

Every program accessing a CODASYL database contains a user work area (UWA). All the records (and thus all the fields) in the subschema are a part of the UWA. According to the DBTG report (see [8]), "Conceptually, the UWA is a loading and unloading zone where all data provided by the DBMS in response to a call for the data is delivered, and where all data to be picked up by the DBMS must be placed." In a COBOL program, the records from the subschema are automatically inserted into a special section at the beginning of the data division by having the following:

```
DATA DIVISION.
SUB-SCHEMA SECTION.
DB   SSCHDIST WITHIN SCHDIST.
FILE SECTION.
The rest of the DATA DIVISION would not be changed.
```

The subschema is effectively inserted during compilation at this point within the data division. (If a listing is being produced during compilation, you will actually see it here.) If you are familiar with COBOL, you will note that the records described in the subschema are identical in appearance to those described elsewhere in the DATA DIVISION. The fields and records within the subschema that have now been inserted into the program constitute the records and fields of the UWA. They may be used by the programmer just like records and fields in the other sections of the DATA DIVISION. When a record is stored or modified, the contents of the corresponding record in this subschema section are used to update the database. When information is retrieved from the database, it is placed in the appropriate records and fields within this section.

Besides the records from the subschema, the UWA contains other data: **currency indicators** and **special registers**. The currency indicators are used by the system and are normally not touched by the programmer (although it is possible to do so). The special registers are available to the programmer even though they are not explicitly listed within the subschema portion of the program. One of these, ERROR-STATUS, which is described later in this section, is absolutely crucial. It is through ERROR-STATUS that the system notifies us of any problems encountered during interaction with the database. Others, such as ERROR-RECORD and ERROR-SET, can be useful in telling us what record or set was being accessed at the time a problem arose. For the most part, however, ERROR-STATUS is the main one we will use.

## Currency Indicators

Earlier in this chapter, we mentioned that we have a variety of *fingers* that will point at various occurrences in the database. We said that we had a finger for each record type that would point at a single occurrence of that record, and a finger for each set type that would point at a single occurrence of that set. The technical term for these fingers is *currency indicator*. In practice, a currency indicator is a variable that will be maintained and used by the system and will contain the address of the record occurrence most recently manipulated in a given category of records. The record whose address is contained in this variable is called the *current of record type* or simply the *current record*.

> *Definition:* A **currency indicator** is a conceptual pointer maintained by the DBMS to establish a current record of a run unit, record type, set type, or realm (area).

A description of the various currency indicators follows.

1. **CURRENT OF RUN UNIT.** The run unit is the program. There is only one current of run unit. This will be the last occurrence of any type of record that was found or stored.
2. **CURRENT OF RECORD TYPE.** There is one of these for each record type in the subschema. The current of a given record type will be the last occurrence of that record type that was found or stored.
3. **CURRENT OF SET TYPE.** There is one of these for each set type in the subschema. The current of a given set type will be the set occurrence most recently accessed. (You will recall that a set occurrence is actually a chain containing one owner occurrence and many member occurrences.) The pointer will actually point to the last occurrence of either the owner record type or member record type in this set type that was found or stored. Thus, this pointer establishes not only which occurrence of this set is the current of set type but also a position in the set.
4. **CURRENT OF REALM.** There is one of these for each realm (or area) in the subschema. The current of a given realm will be the last record of any type that was found or stored *in* that realm. If there is only one realm, the current of realm will always be the same as the current of run-unit.

When we investigate the DML commands, we will see that these commands either use or update (or both) various currency indicators. This is how we **navigate** our way through the database.

For an example of this concept, we will expand on the discussion of currency given earlier by using the proper terminology and including the current of run unit in our comments. (The current of realm is used infrequently and we will ignore it here.) The statements described in Table 9.2 are assumed to be processing the database shown in Figure 9.12. It is the same data we used in our initial example of currency, but the set occurrences are represented realistically as chains instead of bubbles, as they were earlier.

In these examples, you may have noticed that the current of run unit was maintained but never used. The reason for this is that we did not encounter any commands that used this indicator. As we study the commands, we will see that several of them do use it.

**Table 9.2   Processing a Database, Maintaining Currencies**

| STATEMENT | EFFECT | CURRENT OF RECORD TYPE FACULTY | CURRENT OF RECORD TYPE STUDENT | CURRENT OF SET TYPE ADVISES | CURRENT OF RUN_UNIT |
|---|---|---|---|---|---|
| 1. Find faculty Jones | System locates Jones | Jones | — | Jones | Jones (faculty) |
| 2. Find next student in ADVISES set | System locates Mary | Jones | Mary | Mary | Mary (student) |
| 3. Find next student in ADVISES set | System locates Tom | Jones | Tom | Tom | Tom (student) |
| 4. Find next student in ADVISES set | System locates Bill | Jones | Bill | Bill | Bill (student) |
| 5. Find next student in ADVISES set | System shows no more students in set. Currencies do not change. | Jones | Bill | Bill | Bill (student) |
| 6. Find student Jane | System locates Jane | Jones | Jane | Jane | Jane (student) |
| 7. Find owner within ADVISES set | System locates Smith | Smith | Jane | Smith | Smith (faculty) |

## ERROR-STATUS Register

In IDMS, the special register ERROR-STATUS is really a code used by the system to inform us of any problems encountered as the database was being accessed. ERROR-STATUS is a four-digit number that is best viewed as two separate two-digit numbers. The first two digits, the major code, indicate the type of statement being executed when a problem was encountered. The last two digits, the minor code, indicate the type of problem that occurred. Some of the possibilities are shown in Table 9.3. An ERROR-STATUS of 0326, for example, would indicate that in the execution of an OBTAIN command no record was found to satisfy the record selection criteria. Table 9.3 is a greatly abridged table showing just the general format. An actual table would have many more rows.

### Table 9.3    ERROR-STATUS Codes

| MAJOR CODE | COMMAND | MINOR CODE | MEANING |
|---|---|---|---|
| 01 | FINISH | 01 | Area not ready |
| 02 | ERASE | 05 | Duplicates clause violated |
| 03 | OBTAIN | 06 | Required currency not established |
| 07 | CONNECT | 07 | End of set or realm |
| 08 | MODIFY | 11 | Space in realm exhausted |
| 09 | READY | 13 | No current of run unit |
| 11 | DISCONNECT | 16 | Record already member of set |
| 12 | STORE | 20 | Current record is of incorrect type |
| | | 22 | Record not currently member of set |
| | | 25 | Current of set not established |
| | | 26 | Record not found |
| | | 30 | Record owner of nonempty set occurrence |
| | | 31 | Statement not consistent with location mode |
| | | 32 | Calc value in UWA doesn't match current record |

## List of Commands

Table 9.4 gives a list of DML commands grouped by function. The exact syntax of these commands for use in COBOL will be demonstrated in examples given later in this section.

For further discussion of the CODASYL DML, see [1], [2], [9], [10], [11], [12], and [13]. For further details specific to IDMS, consult the IDMS manuals.

**Table 9.4   DML Commands**

| | |
|---|---|
| **OPEN AND CLOSE DATABASE** | |

READY     Opens the area(s) required by the program. The basic options are RETRIEVAL (read operations only) and UPDATE (both read and write operations are permitted).

FINISH    Closes the area(s).

**RETRIEVAL**

OBTAIN    Locates a record subject to some conditions and places the data for the located record into the UWA. The record found becomes current of run unit, current of record type, and current of set type for any set in which it is either an owner or a member. There are several forms of the OBTAIN command, the most common of which are discussed at the end of the list of commands. If no record can be found to meet the conditions, the program is notified of this fact by an appropriate ERROR-STATUS and no currencies are changed.

FIND      Is like OBTAIN, but no data is transferred to the UWA. Typically used if the CODASYL DBMS in use does not support the OBTAIN command.

GET       Retrieves the contents of the record identified as the current of run unit and places it into the UWA. The FIND command does not place any data into the user work area; it merely locates a record. The GET command is necessary to actually place the data into the appropriate fields in the UWA. Typically used with the FIND command if the CODASYL DBMS in use does not support the OBTAIN command.

**UPDATE**

STORE     Creates a new record occurrence at a position determined by the location mode of the record type using the data from the UWA. For any set in which the record type is a member that has been declared AUTOMATIC, the occurrence is inserted into the appropriate set occurrence at a position determined by the set's insertion mode. This new occurrence becomes current of its record type, current of run unit, and current of set type for any sets into which it has been inserted. If storing the new occurrence would result in the violation of any duplicates clause, then the store will *not* take place and the program will be notified of the rejection by an appropriate ERROR-STATUS.

*(continued)*

**Table 9.4    (continued)**

| | |
|---|---|
| MODIFY | Updates the current of run unit with data from the UWA. |
| ERASE | Disconnects the current of run unit from occurrences of any set in which it is a member and deletes the current of run unit, provided that the current of run unit does not own any member occurrences in any set. (A customer who has orders, for example, would not be deleted.) |
| ERASE ALL | Disconnects the current of run unit from occurrences of any set in which it is a member and deletes the current of run unit and any members of set occurrences owned by it. Note that any members deleted in this fashion, who are in turn owners in other set occurrences, cause their member occurrences to be deleted as well, and so on. Deleting a sales rep in the Premiere Products database causes all of the customers represented by that sales rep to be deleted. In turn, orders placed by any of these customers are deleted, and so on. A good description of the ERASE in this situation is LOOK OUT BELOW!!! (A customer who has orders, for example, would be deleted, as would all of the orders placed by this customer and all of the order lines on these orders.) |
| CONNECT | Connects the current of run unit into a set occurrence. The record type of the current of run unit must, of course, be a member type for this set. |
| DISCONNECT | Disconnects the current of run unit from a set occurrence. Again, the current of run unit must be a member type for this set. In addition, the set type must have RETENTION OPTIONAL. |
| RECONNECT | Disconnects the current of run unit from one occurrence of a set of a given type and connects it to another occurrence of the same set type. RECONNECT is not available in all systems. |

## FORMS OF THE OBTAIN COMMAND

**Note:** For each form of the OBTAIN command there is a corresponding form of the FIND command. The only difference is that the FIND command will not pull transfer data to the UWA. A GET command is required to do so.

| | |
|---|---|
| ANY | Locates a CALC record based on the contents of its CALC key. If duplicates have been allowed for this CALC key, the OBTAIN ANY will find the first occurrence whose CALC key matches the value in the UWA. Another form of the same command, OBTAIN DUPLICATE, can then be used to find the others. |
| NEXT | Locates the next member in the indicated set occurrence. The command is actually OBTAIN NEXT WITHIN set-name. The |

**Table 9.4   (continued)**

current of set is used to determine the present position. OBTAIN NEXT then causes the next member occurrence within that chain to be located. If the current position happens to be the last member occurrence, no new record is located and the system notifies us via an appropriate ERROR-STATUS. Related options of this command are OBTAIN FIRST (find the first member occurrence in the chain; e.g., the occurrence immediately following the owner); OBTAIN LAST (find the last member occurrence in the chain); OBTAIN PRIOR (find the member occurrence prior to the current position); OBTAIN integer (find the member occurrence in the position indicated by the integer); e.g., OBTAIN 3 would find the third member occurrence in the chain and OBTAIN identifier (identifier must be an integer variable whose contents then function as the integer in the OBTAIN integer version of the command).

OWNER    Locates the owner occurrence within the set occurrence of the indicated set. The syntax is OBTAIN OWNER WITHIN set-name.

CURRENT  Locates the current of record type. The syntax is OBTAIN CURRENT record-name. It may seem that this is a do-nothing command. If sales rep 12 is the current sales rep and we say OBTAIN CURRENT SLSREP, sales rep 12 will still be the current sales rep. It seems nothing has happened! Something important has happened, however. In addition to being the current of record type, sales rep 12 is now also the *current of run unit*. In the examples to come, we see that in certain situations the current of run unit is not the correct record type for the command we wish to issue. We can correct this by using the OBTAIN CURRENT command. The procedure is a little tricky, but don't worry about it; we will elaborate on the problem and its solution when we encounter it in the examples.

## EXAMPLES

We now examine the use of these commands through several examples, all of which refer to the database illustrated in Figures 9.14 (data structure diagram), 9.15 (schema DDL), and 9.18 (subschema DDL). For each of these examples, we will assume that the database has been opened in such a way that update is possible. This is accomplished with the following command:

```
READY  USAGE-MODE IS UPDATE.
```

If only retrieval is required, then the syntax would be:

```
READY  USAGE-MODE IS RETRIEVAL.
```

We will also assume that the database is closed when all processing has been completed. This is accomplished with the following command:

```
FINISH.
```

## The OBTAIN Command

In the following examples, the various forms of the OBTAIN command are illustrated.

**Example 1:** List the number and name of sales rep 12.

After moving 12 to the sales rep number, the CALC key, we attempt to find the sales rep. If the ERROR-STATUS is not zero, we have encountered an error and should print an error message. If it is zero, we have found the sales rep. We now have the number and name of this sales rep and can display them. The code is thus:

```
MOVE 12 TO SLSRNUMB.
OBTAIN ANY SLSREP.
IF ERROR-STATUS = '0326'
     print error message - 'NO SUCH SALES REP'
  ELSE
     print SLSRNUMB, SLSRNAME.
```

Before moving on to other examples, we need to make some general comments about how the formulations to satisfy the requirements are presented. First of all, as indicated earlier, they are presented in COBOL. If you don't know COBOL, however, you should be able to treat them as just a form of pseudocode and still obtain an understanding of the logic. Second, there may be some commands given in lower-case letters, such as "print error message." These are *not* COBOL but rather pseudocode, indicating the task that must be accomplished at that point. It is our feeling that the actual COBOL statements to accomplish these tasks are not at all relevant to the problem at hand and would just tend to obscure the overall logic. If you are familiar with COBOL, the COBOL statements necessary to accomplish these tasks should be obvious to you. Finally, it is, of course, unrealistic to build a specific sales rep number, like 12, into the COBOL program. Were we to do so, it would mean that asking the same question about a different sales rep would require changing the code and recompiling the program. Rather, this sales rep number would be in a variable, say TR-SLSRNUMB (transaction sales rep number), which would be read from a file of transactions or perhaps obtained directly from the user in some on-line session. In each example we will be dealing with specific data, but keep in mind that in actual practice we would be working with variables of the type just described.

**Example 2:** List the number and name of all the customers represented by sales rep 6.

We first attempt to find the sales rep, as we did in the previous example. If we are unsuccessful, we will again print an error message. If we are successful, we find all the customers of this sales rep by repeatedly using the OBTAIN NEXT command. This is accomplished with a priming OBTAIN NEXT command, followed by a loop, which is performed until ERROR-STATUS is not zero. This would indicate that the end of the chain has been reached. As long as the ERROR-STATUS is not zero, we have found another customer. We can then display the desired information. Once this has been done, we can attempt to find the next customer with another OBTAIN NEXT command. Thus:

```
MOVE 6 TO SLSRNUMB.
OBTAIN ANY SLSREP.
IF ERROR-STATUS = '0326'
    print error message - 'NO SUCH SALES REP'
  ELSE
    OBTAIN NEXT CUSTOMER WITHIN SLSREP-CUSTOMER
    PERFORM OBTAIN-AND-DISPLAY-CUSTOMERS
        UNTIL ERROR-STATUS = '0307'
        .
        .
        .

OBTAIN-AND-DISPLAY-CUSTOMERS.
    print CUSTNUMB, CUSTNAME.
    OBTAIN NEXT CUSTOMER WITHIN SLSREP-CUSTOMER.
```

**Example 3:** Find all orders for customer 522. For each order, list the number and date. In addition, for each order line within these orders, list the part number, the description, the quantity ordered, the quoted price, and the actual price.

Basically, the overall structure of this example is the same as that of Example 2. In this case, we are finding all the orders related to a given customer instead of all the customers for a given sales rep. Since the overall problem is similar, we would expect that the top level of logic should also be very similar, and it is. What's different in this example is what happens once we have found an order. Before moving on to another order, we will process all of the order lines for this order by repeatedly using an OBTAIN NEXT until reaching an ERROR-STATUS other than zero, which would indicate that there are no more order lines for the current order. Provided we have found an order line, we will find the part that owns it by using the OBTAIN OWNER command. Having done so, we will have gathered all the required information for the order line: the part number, description, and price are in the *PART* record, and the number ordered and quoted price are in the *ORDLNE* record. The code is:

```
MOVE 522 TO CUSTNUMB.
OBTAIN ANY CUSTOMER.
IF ERROR-STATUS = '0326'
    print error message - 'NO SUCH CUSTOMER'
  ELSE
    OBTAIN NEXT ORDERS WITHIN CUSTOMER-ORDERS
    PERFORM OBTAIN-AND-DISPLAY-ORDERS
        UNTIL ERROR-STATUS = '0307'
         .
         .
         .

OBTAIN-AND-DISPLAY-ORDERS.
    print ORDNUMB, ORDDTE.
    OBTAIN NEXT ORDLNE WITHIN ORDERS-ORDLNE.
    PERFORM OBTAIN-AND-DISPLAY-ORDER-LINES
        UNTIL ERROR-STATUS = '0307'
    OBTAIN NEXT ORDERS WITHIN CUSTOMER-ORDERS.
         .
         .
         .

OBTAIN-AND-DISPLAY-ORDER-LINES.
    OBTAIN OWNER WITHIN PART-ORDLNE.
    print PARTNUMB, PARTDESC, NUMBORD, QUOTPRCE, UNITPRCE.
    OBTAIN NEXT ORDLNE WITHIN ORDERS-ORDLNE.
```

**Example 4:** List the name and number of all customers.

We can find all customers by sequentially processing the entire database, using a version of the OBTAIN NEXT command that allows us to repeatedly find the next customer within the realm. In attempting to find all the customers in the database, the system will encounter records of types other than *CUSTOMER*: sales reps, orders, order lines, and parts. It will skip over these, however, and only stop at customers. To get the process started, we find the first customer in the realm, using the OBTAIN FIRST command. The formulation is as follows.

```
      OBTAIN FIRST CUSTOMER WITHIN DISTAREA.
      IF ERROR-STATUS = '0307'
          print error message - 'NO CUSTOMERS EXIST'
       ELSE
          PERFORM OBTAIN-AND-DISPLAY CUSTOMERS
              UNTIL ERROR-STATUS = '0307'
          .
          .
          .
  OBTAIN-AND-DISPLAY CUSTOMERS.
      print CUSTNUMB, CUSTNAME.
      OBTAIN NEXT CUSTOMER WITHIN DISTAREA.
```

**Example 5:** List the name and number of all customers using a system-owned set.

There is another alternative to sequentially scanning the entire database to find all customers, and that is the use of a **system-owned set**. This set is described like any other except that the owner is not an actual record type, but rather the special reserved word SYSTEM. Such a set is called a **singular set**. There will be only one occurrence of this set type. This occurrence will thus be a single chain that includes all member occurrences. Suppose we have included such a set, called SYSTEM-CUSTOMER, where the owner is *SYSTEM* and the member is *CUSTOMER*. We then have a chain that includes all customers. We could use this chain to answer the above query, as follows:

```
      OBTAIN FIRST CUSTOMER WITHIN SYSTEM-CUSTOMER.
      IF ERROR-STATUS = '0307'
          print error message - 'NO CUSTOMERS EXIST'
       ELSE
          PERFORM OBTAIN-AND-DISPLAY CUSTOMERS
              UNTIL ERROR-STATUS = '0307'
          .
          .
          .
  OBTAIN-AND-DISPLAY-CUSTOMERS.
      print CUSTNUMB, CUSTNAME.
      OBTAIN NEXT CUSTOMER WITHIN SYSTEM-CUSTOMER.
```

## The STORE Command

The following examples illustrate the various issues involved in storing new records.

**Example 6:** Store sales rep 14 (name "Sanchez, Maria," address "41 Crane, Ada, MI," total commission 0.00, commission rate 5 percent).

Since the sales rep record is not a member in any set type, we don't have to worry about establishing currency on any owner occurrence. The only potential problem here is that there might already be a sales rep 14 in the database. Since the sales rep record is CALC with DUPLICATES NOT ALLOWED, the system will not allow a duplicate record to be stored and will indicate through ERROR-STATUS that the record has been rejected. The code would thus be:

```
fill in all fields within SLSREP record.
STORE SLSREP.
IF ERROR-STATUS = '1205'
    print error message - 'DUPLICATE SALES REP'.
```

**Example 7:** Store customer 191 (name "Nguyen, Thanh," address "112 Long, Hart, MI," balance 0.00, credit limit $500, sales rep 3).

We do have to be concerned with storing a duplicate occurrence, as in Example 6, but we have another problem here. The *CUSTOMER* record is the member record type in the set *SLSREP-CUSTOMER*. We thus have to ensure that we are current on the correct owner occurrence, in this case sales rep 3. We first attempt to establish this currency. If we are not successful, we will issue an error message and will not complete the transaction. If we are successful, we will then attempt to store the customer. If this is rejected as a duplicate, we will again issue an error message. Thus, the code is:

```
MOVE 3 TO SLSRNUMB.
OBTAIN ANY SLSREP.
IF ERROR-STATUS = '0326'
    print error message 'NO SUCH SALES REP'
  ELSE
    fill in all fields in CUSTOMER record
    STORE CUSTOMER
    IF ERROR-STATUS = '1205'
        print error message - 'DUPLICATE CUSTOMER'.
```

Storing an *ORDERS* record is similar to storing a *CUSTOMER* record since it, too, is the member record type within a set. Storing a *PART* record is similar to storing a *SLSREP* record since it is not the member type in any set. The link record, *ORDLNE*, is different in two ways: it is the member record type in two different set types, and it is stored VIA SET instead of CALC. The fact that it is a member in more than one set type does not pose any special problem; we would merely establish currency on *all* of the appropriate owner occurrences. The fact that it is stored VIA SET (which is usually true of link records) does mean that our approach will be significantly different. The process for handling these link records is illustrated in Examples 13 through 16.

## The MODIFY Command

The following examples illustrate the use of the MODIFY command in updating the data in a database.

**Example 8:** Change the name of customer 587 to "Clark, Judy."

The command to change existing data, MODIFY, acts upon the current of run unit. We must thus establish customer 587 as the current of run unit. If we are successful, we can fill in any fields to be changed with new information, then MODIFY the record. The formulation is:

```
MOVE 587 TO CUSTNUMB.
OBTAIN ANY CUSTOMER.
IF ERROR-STATUS = '0326'
    print error message - 'NO SUCH CUSTOMER'
  ELSE
      MOVE 'Clark, Judy' TO CUSTNAME
      MODIFY CUSTOMER.
```

## The ERASE and ERASE ALL Commands

The following illustrate the use of the ERASE and ERASE ALL commands in deleting records from a database.

**Example 9:** Delete order 12491 and any order lines within this order.

The ERASE command will delete a record occurrence. It acts upon the current of run unit, so we must establish order 12491 as current of run unit. In order to also have all members (in this case all the corresponding order lines) deleted, we use the ERASE ALL MEMBERS form of the command. Thus, we have:

```
MOVE 12491 TO ORDNUMB.
OBTAIN ANY ORDERS.
IF ERROR-STATUS = '0326'
    print error message - 'NO SUCH ORDER'
  ELSE
      ERASE ORDERS ALL MEMBERS.
```

**Example 10:** Delete customer 405, provided he or she has no orders on file. If the customer does have orders on file, do not delete; print an error message indicating this fact.

The difference between this example and Example 9 is that here, if there are any members (orders), we do not want the owner (the customer) to be deleted. This is exactly what will be accomplished by the ERASE command if we *don't* include the ALL MEMBERS clause. If a customer has orders, he or she will not be deleted, and the system will inform us of this through an appropriate ERROR-STATUS. Thus:

```
MOVE 405 TO CUSTNUMB.
OBTAIN ANY CUSTOMER.
IF ERROR-STATUS = '0326'
    print error message - 'NO SUCH CUSTOMER'
  ELSE
      ERASE CUSTOMER
      IF ERROR-STATUS = '0230'
          print error message - 'CUSTOMER HAS ORDERS'.
```

## The CONNECT and DISCONNECT Commands

The following illustrate the way records can be disconnected from and connected to set occurrences.

**Example 11:** Change the sales rep for customer 124 to null (i.e., this customer no longer has a sales rep).

Since the removal class for the set *SLSREP-CUSTOMER* is OPTIONAL, it is indeed possible to disconnect the customer. The disconnect command acts upon the current of run unit, so we first establish customer 124 as current of run unit. We then attempt to disconnect the customer from the set occurrence in which the customer currently resides. If the customer has already been disconnected, we will receive an appropriate ERROR-STATUS. The code will be:

```
MOVE 124 TO CUSTNUMB.
OBTAIN ANY CUSTOMER.
IF ERROR-STATUS = '0326'
    print error message - 'NO SUCH CUSTOMER'
  ELSE
      DISCONNECT CUSTOMER FROM SLSREP-CUSTOMER
      IF ERROR-STATUS = '1122'
          print error message - 'NOT CONNECTED'.
```

**Example 12:** Assign customer 124 to sales rep 12.

To connect a record occurrence to a set occurrence, the desired set occurrence must be current of set type and the desired record occurrence must be current of run unit. Note that in the logic that follows, we first attempt to find the customer. If we are unsuccessful, we will issue an error message and will not complete the transaction. If we are successful, we will attempt to establish currency for the set type by finding the sales rep (the owner record type within *SLSREP-CUSTOMER*). If we are successful here, we will have put all the pieces in place except for the fact that customer 124 is *no longer the current of run unit.* Sales rep 12 is. Customer 124, however, is still the current of record type for the *CUSTOMER* record. The OBTAIN CURRENT command can be used to reestablish customer 124 as current of run unit. That having been done, we would be ready to issue the CONNECT command. The code for this is:

```
MOVE 124 TO CUSTNUMB.
OBTAIN ANY CUSTOMER.
IF ERROR-STATUS = '0326'
    print error message - 'NO SUCH CUSTOMER'
  ELSE
    MOVE 12 TO SLSRNUMB
    OBTAIN ANY SLSREP
    IF ERROR-STATUS = '0326'
        print error message - 'NO SUCH SALES REP'
      ELSE
        OBTAIN CURRENT CUSTOMER
        CONNECT CUSTOMER TO SLSREP-CUSTOMER
        IF ERROR-STATUS = '0716'
            print error message - 'ALREADY CONNECTED'.
```

## Processing Link Records

There are some special issues involved in processing link records as the following examples illustrate.

**Example 13:** Find the number of units of part BZ66 that were ordered on order 12491.

Since the *ORDLNE* record has no key, we cannot find it directly and must look for it. We can do this in one of two ways. We can first find order 12491, then examine each order line it owns (within *ORDERS-ORDLNE*) in turn, looking at the part that owns this order line (within *PART-ORDLNE*) to see whether it is BZ66. Alternatively, we can first find part BZ66, then examine each order line that it owns (within *PART-ORDLNE*) to see whether any of them are owned by order 12491 (within *ORDERS-ORDLNE*). (You might want to look back at the example about students and courses earlier in this chapter and ask yourself how you would find the grade for Mary in MTH 110. The logic is the same.) In theory, it doesn't matter which of these approaches we choose; they will both work. In practice, however, it may be *much* more efficient to choose one over the other. If an average order contained three order lines but an average part were found on 500 orders, for example, substantial benefits would accrue from employing the first alternative. We would have three member occurrences to examine as opposed to 500! This is the direction that has been chosen for the following.

```
MOVE 12491 TO ORDNUMB.
OBTAIN ANY ORDERS.
IF ERROR-STATUS = '0326'
    print error message - 'NO SUCH ORDER'
  ELSE
      MOVE 'NO' TO IS-THERE-A-MATCH
      OBTAIN NEXT ORDLNE WITHIN ORDERS-ORDLNE
      PERFORM OBTAIN-ORDER-LINE
            UNTIL THERE-IS-A-MATCH
            OR ERROR-STATUS = '0307'
      IF THERE-IS-A-MATCH
          print NUMBORD.
              .
              .
              .

OBTAIN-ORDER-LINE.
    OBTAIN OWNER WITHIN PART-ORDLNE.
    IF PART-NUMBER = 'BZ66'
        MOVE 'YES' TO IS-THERE-A-MATCH
      ELSE
          OBTAIN NEXT ORDLNE WITHIN ORDERS-ORDLNE.
```

**Example 14:** Add an order line for order 12491 for part AX12 with ten units ordered and a quoted price of $16.95.

This process may seem to be a relatively simple one: Find the order and the part that will own this order line, then (provided both order and part exist) fill in the order-line fields and store the record. There is a problem with this logic, however. In our example, if there already is an order-line occurrence with the same order number and part number, we should *not* store another. Could we just try to store the new occurrence and assume that the system will reject it if it is a duplicate, as we did with sales reps? In general, the answer is no. For the DBMS to reject a new occurrence as a duplicate, there must be a duplicates clause somewhere stating that duplicates are not allowed. As we have seen, there are two places where this can occur in the schema: in calc records, new occurrences that would duplicate the calc key of an existing record can be rejected; and in sorted sets, new occurrences that would duplicate the sort key of an existing record in the same set occurrence would be rejected. Is either of these possibilities relevant to our present discussion? To find the answers, let's examine each one in turn.

To reject a record based on the calc key, there must be a calc key. In the case of *ORDLNE*, the only two fields are *NUMBORD* and *QUOTPRCE*. It would certainly be strange if either of these were the calc key. Even if we chose to make one of these, say, *NUMBORD*, as a calc key and reject duplicates, the record that was rejected would have the same *NUMBORD* as an existing occurrence in the database. This is not the kind of duplication that concerns us.

To reject a record based on a sort key, some set in which the record is a member must be sorted. If we chose to sort the set *ORDERS-ORDLNE*, for example, the problem that arose in choosing a CALC key would be repeated: the only fields available would be *NUMBORD* and *QUOTPRCE*. If we chose to sort on *NUMBORD* and reject duplicates, we would now reject a new *ORDLNE* occurrence if its *NUMBORD* value matched an existing record in the same set occurrence; that is, another order line in the same order. This is not what we want either.

If the system will not detect duplicates, then the responsibility for doing so falls on our shoulders (unfortunately). This means that before we store a new order line, we must ensure that no order line for the same order and part combination already exists. In Example 11, we were given the order number and part number and required to find the number ordered and quoted price on the corresponding order line. The logic in that solution would also tell us if there were no such order line. In particular, if you examine the logic, you will see that the flag, IS-THERE-A-MATCH, will be "NO" if no such order line exists. This gives us the basis for the solution to the current problem.

We can use the same logic we used in the solution to Example 13 up to the point where we are attempting to find the number ordered and quoted price; that is, the logic that reads

```
IF THERE-IS-A-MATCH
     print NUMBORD.
```

In the current problem we *do not* want a match. If there is a match, we have a duplicate and should reject the new occurrence. If there is no match, then we can store the new occurrence. We must first be current on the appropriate order and part. Since we found the correct order at the beginning of the process and never found another, we are current on the appropriate order. We are not current on the correct part, however; we are current on the part that owned the last of the line items. Thus, we must establish currency on the correct part. Once this has been done, we can fill in the order-line fields and store the new order line. The logic for doing this would be:

```
IF THERE-IS-NOT-A-MATCH
     MOVE AX12 TO PART-NUMBER
     OBTAIN ANY PART
      IF ERROR-STATUS = '0326'
           print error message - 'NO SUCH PART'
      ELSE
            fill in order line fields
            STORE ORDLNE.
```

**Example 15:** Change the number ordered on the order line for order 12491, part BZ66 to 3.

Now, we have a problem similar to the one encountered in Example 12. Since the order line has no key, we cannot find the desired order line directly. Instead, we must search for it ourselves. Again, the necessary logic is in the solution to Example 11. There, if the desired order line existed, we

merely wanted to print the result. Here we need to use a MODIFY command to change the data for the order line. There is a problem, however,
since the MODIFY command acts upon the current of run unit. The current
of run unit, however, is not the order line, but rather the part that owned it
(it was the last thing found). In order to make the order line once again be
the current of run unit, we use the OBTAIN CURRENT command. Therefore, that portion of the solution to Example 11 which reads as follows:

```
IF THERE-IS-A-MATCH
     print NUMBORD.
```

would be changed to

```
IF THERE-IS-A-MATCH
     OBTAIN CURRENT ORDLNE
     MOVE 3 TO NUMBORD
     MODIFY.
```

The OBTAIN CURRENT ORDLNE command will make the order line on
which we are currently positioned (the one we want) the current of run unit.
Thus, once we have changed the value in *NUMBORD* to 3, we are ready to
execute the MODIFY command. This command will then update the appropriate order line.

**Example 16:** Delete the order line for order 12498, part BA74.

This problem is virtually the same as the one in Example 13. Here, we want
to delete a record (ERASE) instead of changing it (MODIFY), but we still
have to find the record ourselves, and it still has to be the current of run
unit. Thus, instead of:

```
IF THERE-IS-A-MATCH
     OBTAIN CURRENT ORDLNE
     MOVE 3 TO NUMBORD
     MODIFY.
```

we would have:

```
IF THERE-IS-A-MATCH
     OBTAIN CURRENT ORDLNE
     ERASE.
```

### Database Navigation

The following example illustrates the process called **database navigation**; that
is, the process of finding our way through the database to produce the
required results.

**Example 17:** Determine whether part BT04 is included on an order placed by any customer represented by sales rep 3.

This request involves traveling through the entire database. We begin by locating part BT04. If the part does not exist, we will issue an error message and terminate our processing. If it does exist, we examine in turn each order line that it owns (within *PART-ORDLNE*). For each of these order lines we find first the order that owns it (within *ORDERS-ORDLNE*), followed by the customer who owns the order (within *CUSTOMER-ORDERS*), and finally the sales rep who owns the customer (within *SLSREP-CUSTOMER*). Once we have found the sales rep, we can check to see whether the sales rep number is 3. If it is, we can terminate the process and print the answer "YES." If it is not, the process continues. When we have examined all the order lines owned by the part without ever encountering sales rep 3, we can print the answer "NO." The code is thus:

```
        MOVE 'BT04' TO PART-NUMBER.
        OBTAIN ANY PART.
        IF ERROR-STATUS = '0326'
            print error message - 'NO SUCH PART'
          ELSE
            MOVE 'NO' TO IS-THERE-A-MATCH
            OBTAIN NEXT ORDLNE WITHIN PART-ORDLNE
            PERFORM OBTAIN-AND-CHECK-ORDER-LINES
                UNTIL ERROR-STATUS = '0307'
                OR THERE-IS-A-MATCH
            IF THERE-IS-A-MATCH
                print 'YES'
              ELSE
                print 'NO'.
                .
                .
                .

    OBTAIN-AND-CHECK-ORDER-LINES.
        OBTAIN OWNER WITHIN ORDERS-ORDLNE.
        OBTAIN OWNER WITHIN CUSTOMER-ORDERS.
        OBTAIN OWNER WITHIN SLSREP-CUSTOMER.
        IF SLSRNUMB = 3
            MOVE 'YES' TO IS-THERE-A-MATCH.
        OBTAIN NEXT ORDLNE WITHIN PART-ORDLNE.
```

## Updating Multiple Occurrences

Often you will need to make many changes to the database. The following is an example of this process.

**Example 18:** Change all credit limits to $800 for customers of sales rep 3 whose credit limit is now $500 and whose balance is not over their credit limit.

We first attempt to locate sales rep 3. If we are unsuccessful, we issue an error message. If we are successful, we can step through each customer owned by sales rep 3 (within *SLSREP-CUSTOMER*) until reaching the end of the chain, in which case ERROR-STATUS will not be zero. For each customer we encounter, we will check whether he or she meets the desired criteria: a credit limit of $500 and a balance that does not exceed the credit limit. If he or she does fulfill these conditions, then we move the new credit limit into the UWA and modify the record.

```
MOVE 3 TO SLSRNUMB.
OBTAIN ANY SLSREP.
IF ERROR-STATUS = '0326'
    print error message - 'NO SUCH SALES REP'
  ELSE
    OBTAIN NEXT CUSTOMER WITHIN SLSREP-CUSTOMER
    PERFORM OBTAIN-AND-MODIFY-CUSTOMERS
        UNTIL ERROR-STATUS = '0307'
        .
        .
        .

OBTAIN-AND-MODIFY-CUSTOMERS.
    IF CREDLIM = 500
        AND BALANCE NOT > CREDLIM
        MOVE 800 TO CREDLIM
        MODIFY CUSTOMER.
    OBTAIN NEXT CUSTOMER WITHIN SLSREP-CUSTOMER.
```

**Example 19:** Change all credit limits to $800 for all customers whose credit limit is $500 and whose balance is not over their credit limit.

Example 4 demonstrated the logic of processing all customers within the database. Although in that example we only retrieved data, the same process could be used for update. The logic for the update would be:

```
OBTAIN FIRST CUSTOMER WITHIN DISTAREA.
IF ERROR-STATUS = '0326'
    print error message - 'NO CUSTOMERS'
  ELSE
    PERFORM OBTAIN-AND-MODIFY-CUSTOMERS
        UNTIL ERROR-STATUS NOT = '0307'
        .
        .
        .

OBTAIN-AND-MODIFY-CUSTOMERS.
    IF CREDLIM = 500
        AND BALANCE NOT > CREDLIM
        MOVE 800 TO CREDLIM
        MODIFY CUSTOMER.
    OBTAIN NEXT CUSTOMER WITHIN DISTAREA.
```

You will recall that Example 4 demonstrated an approach to processing all customers in the event of a system-owned set in which the *CUSTOMER* record was the member record type. That same logic would apply equally well here.

## SAMPLE IDMS APPLICATION PROGRAM

We now turn our attention to a sample IDMS application program. This program is designed to add records of various types to the Premiere Products database. You should recognize many of the individual routines in the program, since they are similar to the examples we have already considered. Before we look at the program itself, we need to look at some code that will automatically be inserted into the program prior to compilation. We will also look at the way IDMS commands are converted to subroutine calls. Once we have done so, we will examine the various divisions in the program to see the special features that are included for programs that access an IDMS database.

### Code Inserted or Converted Prior to Compilation

The crucial portion of the code that will be inserted in the working-storage section is shown in Figure 9.20a. It contains the special registers, such as ERROR-STATUS, as well as all the records and fields from the subschema. This forms the user work area (UWA) that we discussed earlier.

```
01  SUBSCHEMA-CTRL.
        03   PROGRAM-NAME          PIC X(8) VALUE SPACES.
        03   ERROR-STATUS          PIC X(4) VALUE '1400'.
        03   DBKEY                 PIC S9(8)
        03   RECORD-NAME           PIC X(16) VALUE SPACES.
        03   AREA-NAME             PIC X(16) VALUE SPACES.
        03   ERROR-SET             PIC X(16) VALUE SPACES.
        03   ERROR-RECORD          PIC X(16) VALUE SPACES.
        03   ERROR-AREA            PIC X(16) VALUE SPACES.
             .
             .
             .
01  ORDLNE.
        02   NUMBORD               PIC 9(4).
        02   QUOTPRCE              PIC 9(4)V9(2).
        02   FILLER                PIC X(6).
01  PART.
        02   PARTNUMB              PIC X(4).
        02   PARTDESC              PIC X(20).
        02   UNONHAND              PIC 9(4).
        02   ITEMCLSS              PIC X(2).
        02   WRHSNUMB              PIC 9(2).
        02   UNITPRCE              PIC 9(4)V9(2).
        02   FILLER                PIC X(2).
01  ORDERS.
        02   ORDNUMB               PIC 9(5).
        02   ORDDTE                PIC 9(6).
        02   FILLER                PIC X(5).
```

**Figure 9.20a**

Portion of WORKING-STORAGE code inserted by IDMS

*(continued)*

**Figure 9.20a**

(continued)

```
01  CUSTOMER.
    02  CUSTNUMB                PIC 9(3).
    02  CUSTNAME                PIC X(20).
    02  CUSTADDR                PIC X(20).
    02  BALANCE                 PIC 9(5)V9(2).
    02  CREDLIM                 PIC 9(5).
    02  FILLER                  PIC X(1).
01  SLSREP.
    02  SLSRNUMB                PIC 9(2).
    02  SLSRNAME                PIC X(20).
    02  SLSRADDR                PIC X(20).
    02  TOTCOMM                 PIC 9(5)V9(2).
    02  COMMRATE                PIC V9(2).
    02  FILLER                  PIC X(5).
```

A second portion of code is copied into the program as a result of the COPY IDMS SUBSCHEMA-BINDS command. This code is shown in Figure 9.20b. This code will fill in the special register, called PROGRAM-NAME, with the appropriate name. It also includes necessary BIND commands, which will cause IDMS to determine the precise addresses of the indicated records in working storage. This information is essential when IDMS transfers data between the database and the UWA.

**Figure 9.20b**

Code inserted
as result of
COPY IDMS
SUBSCHEMA-BINDS

```
COPY IDMS SUBSCHEMA-BINDS.
MOVE 'PGM100  ' TO PROGRAM-NAME
BIND RUN-UNIT
BIND ORDLNE
BIND PART
BIND ORDERS
BIND CUSTOMER
BIND SLSREP.
```

The final portion of code that is inserted is shown in Figure 9.20c.

**Figure 9.20c**

Code inserted as
result of COPY
IDMS STATUS

```
COPY IDMS IDMS-STATUS.
**********************************************************************
IDMS-STATUS                                               SECTION.
**********************************************************************
IDMS-STATUS-PARAGRAPH.
        IF DB-STATUS-OK GO TO ISABEX.
        PERFORM IDMS-ABORT.
        DISPLAY '***********************'
                ' ABORTING - ' PROGRAM-NAME
                ', '             ERROR-STATUS
                ', '             ERROR-RECORD
                ' **** RECOVER IDMS ****'
                UPON CONSOLE.
        DISPLAY 'PROGRAM NAME ------ ' PROGRAM-NAME.
        DISPLAY 'ERROR STATUS ------ ' ERROR-STATUS.
        DISPLAY 'ERROR RECORD ----- ' ERROR-RECORD.
        DISPLAY 'ERROR SET -------- ' ERROR-SET.
        DISPLAY 'ERROR AREA ------- ' ERROR-AREA.
        DISPLAY 'LAST GOOD RECORD -- ' RECORD-NAME.
        DISPLAY 'LAST GOOD AREA ---- ' AREA-NAME.
        DISPLAY 'DML SEQUENCE--------' DML-SEQUENCE.
        ROLLBACK.
        CALL 'ABORT'.
ISABEX. EXIT.
```

It is inserted as a result of the COPY IDMS IDMS-STATUS command. This code is used to test the ERROR-STATUS register. If ERROR-STATUS contains zero, no action will be taken. If it contains anything other than zero, the contents of many other special registers will be displayed to assist in determining the problem, the transaction in process will be rolled back, and the program will abort. We will see precisely how this is used when we look at the details of the program.

Another thing happens prior to compilation. All IDMS data manipulation commands are converted to subroutine calls. Figure 9.21a shows the conversion of the BIND RUN-UNIT command and Figure 9.21b shows the conversion of the STORE SLSREP command. This conversion is all automatic and programmers need not concern themselves with the details of this conversion or of the subroutine calls that are inserted.

```
*     BIND RUN-UNIT
                MOVE 0001 TO DML-SEQUENCE
                CALL 'IDMS' USING SUBSCHEMA-CTRL
                              IDBMSCOM (59)
                              SUBSCHEMA-CTRL
                              SUBSCHEMA-SSNAME;
```

**Figure 9.21a**

Subroutine call inserted for BIND RUN–UNIT

```
*     STORE SLSREP.
                MOVE 0010 TO DML-SEQUENCE
                CALL 'IDMS' USING SUBSCHEMA-CTRL
                              IDBMSCOM (42)
                              SR101.
```

**Figure 9.21b**

Subroutine call inserted for STORE SLSREP

## Environment Division

The complete program is shown in Figure 9.22 on the following pages. At various places in the program you will see entries in square brackets. These simply indicate the type of commands that should be inserted at that portion. For example, after INPUT-OUTPUT SECTION, there is such an entry that indicates that information about any necessary files should be inserted at this position.

The only special entries in the Environment Division are in the IDMS-CONTROL SECTION. Here you enter the mode of the program. This is used to indicate whether the program is to be run in a batch or on-line environment. In addition, if the program is to be run on-line, the mode is used to indicate the communications control program that will be used.

**Figure 9.22**

Update program

```
IDENTIFICATION DIVISION.
PROGRAM-ID.        PGM100.
AUTHOR.            DATABASE CLASS.
DATE-WRITTEN.      FALL, 1991.
DATE-COMPILED.
REMARKS.               THIS PROGRAM LOADS THE PREMIERE PRODUCTS
                       DATABASE.

ENVIRONMENT DIVISION.

CONFIGURATION SECTION.

SOURCE-COMPUTER.   IBM-370.
OBJECT-COMPUTER.   IBM-370.

INPUT-OUTPUT SECTION.

   [Any necessary file information goes here.]


IDMS-CONTROL SECTION.
PROTOCOL.                          MODE IS [mode of program]

DATA DIVISION.

SCHEMA SECTION.
DB  SSCHDIST  WITHIN SCHDIST.

FILE SECTION.

   [Any necessary file descriptions go here]

WORKING-STORAGE SECTION.

* Flags
01  STATUS-FLAGS.
    05 IS-THERE-A-MATCH         PIC X(3).
       88 THERE-IS-A-MATCH                      VALUE 'YES'.
    05 IS-THERE-MORE-INPUT      PIC X(3).
       88 THERE-IS-MORE-INPUT                   VALUE 'YES'.
       88 THERE-IS-NO-MORE-INPUT                VALUE 'NO'.
    05 RECORD-TYPE              PIC 9(1).
       88 SLSREP-RECORD                         VALUE 1.
       88 CUSTOMER-RECORD                       VALUE 2.
       88 ORDERS-RECORD                         VALUE 3.
       88 PART-RECORD                           VALUE 4.
       88 ORDLNE-RECORD                         VALUE 5.

* Work variables
01  W-SLSREP.
    05 W-SLSRNUMB               PIC 9(2).
    05 W-SLSRNAME               PIC X(20).
    05 W-SLSRADDR               PIC X(20).
    05 W-TOTCOMM                PIC 9(5)V9(2).
    05 W-COMMRATE               PIC V9(2).

01  W-CUSTOMER.
    05 W-CUSTNUMB               PIC 9(3).
    05 W-CUSTNAME               PIC X(20).
    05 W-CUSTADDR               PIC X(20).
    05 W-BALANCE                PIC 9(5)V9(2).
    05 W-CREDLIM                PIC 9(5).
    05 W-SLSRNUMB               PIC 9(2).

01  W-ORDERS.
    05 W-ORDNUMB                PIC 9(5).
    05 W-ORDDTE                 PIC 9(6).
    05 W-CUSTNUMB               PIC 9(3).
```

**Figure 9.22**

(continued)

```
01   W-PART.
     05  W-PARTNUMB              PIC X(4).
     05  W-PARTDESC              PIC X(20).
     05  W-UNONHAND              PIC 9(4).
     05  W-ITEMCLSS              PIC X(2).
     05  W-WRHSNUMB              PIC 9(2).
     05  W-UNITPRCE              PIC 9(4)V9(2).

01   W-ORDLNE.
     05  W-NUMBORD               PIC 9(4).
     05  W-QUOTPRCE              PIC 9(4)V9(2).
     05  W-ORDNUMB               PIC 9(5).
     05  W-PARTNUMB              PIC X(4).


PROCEDURE DIVISION.

*LEVEL-1-ROUTINES.

A000-MAINLINE.

   [Open any necessary files]

     COPY IDMS SUBSCHEMA-BINDS.
     MOVE 'PGM100' TO PROGRAM-NAME.
     BIND RUN-UNIT.
     READY  USAGE-MODE IS UPDATE.
     PERFORM IDMS-STATUS.
     MOVE 'YES' TO IS-THERE-MORE-INPUT.
     [Get record type and data for first add]
     PERFORM B000-MAIN-PROCESSING-LOOP
          UNTIL THERE-IS-NO-MORE-INPUT.
   [Close any necessary files]
     FINISH.
     PERFORM IDMS-STATUS.
     STOP RUN.


*LEVEL-2-ROUTINES.

B000-MAIN-PROCESSING-LOOP.

     IF SLSREP-RECORD
        PERFORM C000-ADD-SLSREP
      ELSE IF CUSTOMER-RECORD
        PERFORM C010-ADD-CUSTOMER
      ELSE IF ORDERS-RECORD
        PERFORM C020-ADD-ORDERS
      ELSE IF PART-RECORD
        PERFORM C030-ADD-PART
      ELSE IF ORDLNE-RECORD
        PERFORM C040-ADD-ORDLNE.
     [Get record type and data for next add]


*LEVEL-3-ROUTINES.

C000-ADD-SLSREP.
     MOVE W-SLSRNUMB OF W-SLSREP
                         TO SLSRNUMB.
     MOVE W-SLSRNAME    TO SLSRNAME.
     MOVE W-SLSRADDR    TO SLSRADDR.
     MOVE W-TOTCOMM     TO TOTCOMM.
     MOVE W-COMMRATE    TO COMMRATE.
     STORE SLSREP.
     IF ERROR-STATUS EQUAL '1205'
        [display 'SLSREP ALREADY EXISTS']
       ELSE
        PERFORM IDMS-STATUS.
```

*(continued)*

**Figure 9.22**

(continued)

```
C010-ADD-CUSTOMER.
    MOVE W-SLSRNUMB OF W-CUSTOMER
                          TO SLSRNUMB.
    OBTAIN ANY SLSREP.
    IF ERROR-STATUS EQUAL '0326'
       [display 'NO SLSREP FOR CUSTOMER']
      ELSE
        MOVE W-CUSTNUMB OF W-CUSTOMER
                          TO CUSTNUMB
        MOVE W-CUSTNAME    TO CUSTNAME
        MOVE W-CUSTADDR    TO CUSTADDR
        MOVE W-BALANCE     TO BALANCE
        MOVE W-CREDLIM     TO CREDLIM
        STORE CUSTOMER
        IF ERROR-STATUS EQUAL '1205'
           [display 'CUSTOMER ALREADY EXISTS']
          ELSE
            PERFORM IDMS-STATUS.

C020-ADD-ORDERS.
    [similar to C010-ADD-CUSTOMER]

C030-ADD-PART.
    [similar to C000-ADD-SLSREP]

C040-ADD-ORDLNE.
    MOVE W-ORDNUMB OF W-ORDLNE
                          TO ORDNUMB.
    OBTAIN ANY ORDERS.
    IF ERROR-STATUS EQUAL '0326'
       [display 'NO ORDER FOR ORDER LINE']
      ELSE
        MOVE 'NO' TO IS-THERE-A-MATCH
        OBTAIN NEXT ORDLNE WITHIN ORDERS-ORDLNE
        PERFORM C041-FIND-ORDER-LINE
            UNTIL THERE-IS-A-MATCH
            OR ERROR-STATUS = '0307'
        IF THERE-IS-A-MATCH
           [display 'ORDER LINE ALREADY EXISTS']
          ELSE
            MOVE W-PARTNUMB OF W-ORDLNE
                              TO PARTNUMB
            OBTAIN ANY PART
            IF ERROR-STATUS EQUAL '0326'
               [display 'NO PART FOR ORDER LINE']
              ELSE
                MOVE W-NUMBORD     TO NUMBORD
                MOVE W-QUOTPRCE    TO QUOTPRCE
                STORE ORDLNE
                PERFORM IDMS-STATUS.

C041-FIND-ORDER-LINE.
    OBTAIN OWNER WITHIN PART-ORDLNE.
    IF W-PARTNUMB OF W-ORDLNE = PARTNUMB
       MOVE 'YES' TO IS-THERE-A-MATCH
      ELSE
        OBTAIN NEXT ORDLNE WITHIN ORDERS-ORDLNE.

*SPECIAL-IDMS-ROUTINES.

COPY IDMS IDMS-STATUS.

IDMS-ABORT SECTION.
ABORT-EXIT.
    EXIT.
```

## Data Division

The first special feature of the Data Division is the SCHEMA SECTION. This functions in exactly the same way we discussed earlier. The only other special feature is the fact that the code shown in Figure 9.20a will be inserted in this division.

## Procedure Division

This program intentionally does not indicate where the input will come from. It could be from a transaction file; it could be obtained from a user through simple ACCEPT statements; or it could be from a CICS map. It really doesn't matter as far as the database update logic is concerned.

You'll notice that the main processing loop determines which type of record is to be added and then performs the appropriate paragraph. The logic in these paragraphs is similar to those of the examples discussed earlier so we won't examine these in detail here. There is one thing new, however, and that is the use of IDMS-STATUS.

Recall that the IDMS-STATUS section is inserted into the program as a result of the COPY IDMS IDMS-STATUS command (Figure 9.20c). When this routine is performed, any ERROR-STATUS other than zero will lead to termination of the program with appropriate information being displayed. It is critical that this be used in an appropriate fashion.

Consider the C000-ADD-SLSREP paragraph, for example. Notice that after the STORE SLSREP command, we have the following IF statement:

```
IF ERROR-STATUS EQUAL '1205'
    [display 'SLSREP ALREADY EXISTS']
  ELSE
    PERFORM IDMS-STATUS.
```

If a sales rep with the same number is already in the database, ERROR-STATUS will be 1205 and we will simply display an error message. If not, the program will perform the IDMS-STATUS routine. If ERROR-STATUS is zero, no special action will be taken. If there is some value other than zero (for example, 1211, which indicates that there is not enough space in the area to store the record), the program will be terminated and appropriate information will be displayed.

## Q & A

| | |
|---|---|
| Question: | What would happen if we replaced the IF statement with simply PERFORM IDMS-STATUS? |
| Answer: | As soon as we encountered a duplicate sales rep, the program would terminate, since ERROR-STATUS will not be zero. |

This is the general way we use IDMS-STATUS. We structure our logic so that we first test ERROR-STATUS for any non-zero values we expect to routinely encounter. If we don't get a value we expect, then we perform IDMS-STATUS. If in a particular case there is no non-zero ERROR-STATUS that we routinely expect, then we can simply perform IDMS-STATUS.

We will not discuss the program any further; however, take the time to go through the logic in it to make sure you understand how it works.

### IDMS/R

In 1983, an enhanced version of IDMS, called **IDMS/R (IDMS/RELATIONAL)**, was announced by Cullinet. All CODASYL facilities were retained and new relational features were added. Since this chapter is concerned with the CODASYL model, a review of these added features technically does not belong here. We do include such a review for two reasons, however. The first is that IDMS is one of the dominant CODASYL systems currently available, and this new component is an important part of the system. The second is that this represents a direction in which many DBMS vendors are moving (i.e., the enhancement of existing systems with relational-like facilities).

### Logical Record Facility (LRF)

Before discussing the feature that provides the relational capabilities themselves, we must first examine the Logical Record Facility (LRF). The LRF allows specification of logical records, or records that do not exist in the CODASYL database but can be derived from existing records and sets.

Suppose, for example, that a report were needed at Premiere Products that would list for a given sales rep his or her number and name, as well as the number and name of all the customers represented by the sales rep, together with the order number and date of all orders placed by each of these customers. Certainly this report could be produced by a program using a subschema that contained the *SLSREP* record, the *CUSTOMER* record, the *ORDERS* record, the *SLSREP-CUSTOMER* set, and the *CUSTOMER-ORDER* set. The program would, of course, need to navigate the database in an appropriate fashion to gather the required data. If, however, all the data were stored in a single file whose records contained *SLSRNUMB, SLSRNAME, CUSTNUMB, CUSTNAME, ORDNUMB,* and *ORDDTE* fields, no navigation would be required and the program would be much simpler. This is not to suggest that such a file would be appropriate. It would certainly suffer from a number of the update problems discussed in the chapter on normalization (chapter 6). It would certainly be handy for this report, however.

The LRF provides a mechanism for deriving such a record from data in the existing database. The subschema necessary for this particular record is shown in Figure 9.23. The record is called *SALES-CUSTOMERS* and contains the fields described earlier. It is termed a **logical record** (it does not actually exist physically in the database). The method for constructing such records is described in the PATH-GROUP. In Figure 9.23, the sales rep whose calc key matches the sales rep number of the request is found directly. Once this has been accomplished, each customer owned by this sales rep in the set *SLSREP-CUSTOMER* is obtained. For each of these customers, each order owned by the customer within the set *CUSTOMER-ORDERS* is also obtained.

```
ADD SUBSCHEMA NAME IS  SSCHCUST
    OF SCHEMA NAME SCHDIST.

ADD AREA NAME IS DISTAREA.

ADD RECORD NAME   SLSREP
    ELEMENTS ARE ALL..
ADD RECORD NAME   CUSTOMER
    ELEMENTS ARE ALL.
ADD RECORD NAME   ORDERS
    ELEMENTS ARE ALL..

ADD SET NAME      SLSREP-CUSTOMER.
ADD SET NAME      CUSTOMER-ORDERS.

ADD LOGICAL RECORD SALES-CUSTOMERS
    ELEMENTS ARE SLSRNUMB, SLSRNAME, CUSTNUMB, CUSTNAME,
        ORDNUMB, ORDDTE.

ADD PATH-GROUP OBTAIN SALES-CUSTOMERS
    SELECT FOR FIELDNAME-EQ SLSREP-NUMBER
        OBTAIN SLSREP WHERE CALCKEY IS SLSRNUMB OF REQUEST
        OBTAIN EACH CUSTOMER WITHIN SLSREP-CUSTOMER
        OBTAIN EACH ORDERS WITHIN CUSTOMER-ORDERS.
```

**Figure 9.23**

Partial subschema with a logical record

An application programmer can treat logical records as though they exist physically. The system will create these records when needed following the instructions specified in the subschema. When processing these records, the program need not concern itself with **database navigation**, which is a definite advantage.

### Automatic System Facility (ASF)

While implementing the LRF on top of IDMS gives some relational flavor to the system, it is the Automatic System Facility (ASF) that really represents the "R" in "IDMS/R." The ASF adds many new capabilities to those of the LRF.

Relations (termed relational records, or tables, within the ASF) are treated as LRF logical records. A table can be a *stored* table, in which case it is derived, when needed, from one or more existing tables. One interesting feature of the ASF is that stored tables can be derived; that is, a query is defined along with the definition of the stored relation. Executing the POPULATE command within the ASF causes the results of the query to be physically placed in the table. (By contrast, views do not exist in any permanent physical sense.) At any time, the table may be repopulated, in which case the previous contents of the table will be deleted and the query reexecuted. This type of stored table is called a derived stored table. A stored table that does not have such a defining query is called a basic stored table.

### Relationship to Network Databases

One of the unique features of IDMS/R is the relational-like access to network databases it offers. This is accomplished through views that are defined on an underlying network database. These views can then be manipulated in the same fashion as those views defined on relations (basic stored tables). The ASF thus supports not only a relational approach to database management, where the relations are the basic stored tables, but also relational access to network databases. This gives the potential for achieving the extra efficiency for which network systems in general and IDMS in particular are known.

## IDMS AND THE FUNCTIONS OF A DBMS

Obviously IDMS supports the storage, retrieval, and update of data. Through an integrated **data dictionary**, it furnishes a user-accessible **catalog** for data descriptions that far exceeds that of many of the other systems. It provides its own communications software (IDMS/DC), in addition to support for other communications programs, such as IBM's CICS. It provides several utility services, including services to initialize and/or update the directory, print a variety of reports concerning the structure of the database, load records into the database according to user formats, and restructure the database. We now consider the remaining functions individually.

## Logical Transactions

There are two important commands within IDMS that relate to support for logical transactions, shared update, and recovery: COMMIT and ROLLBACK. The COMMIT command will cause all changes to the database that the run unit (program) currently has in process to be made permanent and locks to be released. The ROLLBACK command causes all changes made since the last COMMIT to be undone and all locks to be released.

IDMS uses these two commands to provide support for **logical transactions**. While there is no BEGIN TRANSACTION command, the COMMIT command effectively marks both the end of one logical transaction and the beginning of the next. The READY command marks the beginning of the first transaction and the FINISH command marks the end of the last one. If, for some reason, not all the updates necessary for a single logical transaction can be completed, the ROLLBACK command, by undoing all the updates since the last **checkpoint** (i.e., all the updates since the start of the current transaction), will ensure that none of them is completed.

## Shared Update

IDMS uses shared and exclusive locks in supporting **shared update**. When an application program retrieves a record, the program is granted a **shared lock**. When the program attempts to update a record, the system attempts to **promote** the lock to **exclusive** status. Once this has been done, the update can be completed and no other program can acquire any type of lock on the record. Locks are automatically released by the COMMIT command, the ROLLBACK command, or the FINISH command. In addition, if a user is detected as having caused a deadlock, the system will cause an automatic rollback to be performed, in which case locks will be released.

## Recovery

Basically, IDMS supports the type of **recovery** described in chapter 2. During the recovery process it uses a journal containing **before** and **after images** of all changes, as well as information on **checkpoints**. These are not systemwide checkpoints, but individual ones for each of the application programs processing the database. The various types of recovery proceed in the manner described in chapter 2.

## Security

**Passwords** and **subschema** authorizations provide the primary **security** features in IDMS. Another security feature in IDMS is the **user-defined procedure**. (This is a procedure defined by users that will automatically be invoked by the DBMS at the appropriate time.) The database administrator could create such procedures to implement more sophisticated security features, perhaps even a dialogue with the user in which not one but several passwords must be given. Some of the passwords might be numbers calculated by a formula involving some always-changing entity, such as the date. In the case of a date, a password that worked one day would not work the next. The user would need to know the formula.

## Integrity

IDMS provides some **integrity** support. It provides features to ensure that data values are of the right type (numeric, alphabetic, etc.), that key values are unique, and that a MANDATORY AUTOMATIC set member cannot exist in the database without being related to its owner. Other features can be added by the organization through user-defined procedures. Such a procedure could, for example, ensure that a credit limit must be $300, $500, $800, or $1,000.

## Data Independence

Like many network and hierarchical systems, IDMS furnishes a moderate degree of **physical data independence**; (i.e., many changes can be made to the physical structure of the database that do not need to affect application programs). In some ways, IDMS furnishes slightly less than some of the other network systems. If, for example, the database at Premiere Products were reorganized so that the set **SLSREP-CUSTOMER** no longer had prior pointers, then the command FIND PRIOR WITHIN SLSREP-CUSTOMER would no longer be valid, and any program that contained such a command would have to be changed. In many systems this would not be the case.

Also, like most network and hierarchical systems, IDMS does not furnish a particularly high level of **logical data independence**; that is, changes to the logical structure of the database do require changes to application programs. This is due to the navigational nature of such systems. The addition or removal of a relationship (SET) can drastically affect the way some of the application programs must navigate their way through the database.

IDMS/R, on the other hand, furnishes a much higher level of data independence through the LRF and, more specifically, the ASF. Defining logical records through the LRF removes the navigational details from application programs and places these details in the subschema, specifically in the PATH-GROUP specifications. Thus, a change to the logical structure of the database may mean only a change to the access procedures specified in the path groups in the subschemas and not in the application programs themselves. Since databases defined through the ASF are really relational in nature, they achieve, in general, the added logical data independence furnished by the relational model.

## DIFFERENCES BETWEEN IDMS AND OTHER CODASYL SYSTEMS

While IDMS is similar to other CODASYL systems in most aspects, there are a few slight differences:

1. The concepts addressed in the schema and subschema DDL are the same. The form of some of the options is slightly different, however. For example, rather than

   ```
   LINKED TO PRIOR
   ```

   as in IDMS, some other CODASYL systems use the phrase

   ```
   SET IS PRIOR PROCESSABLE
   ```

2. Rather than ERROR-STATUS, most other CODASYL systems use the special register called DB-STATUS. The values for DB-STATUS are different from those for ERROR-STATUS, although they represent the same types of errors. The DB-STATUS value for not being able to find a record, for example, is 0502400, whereas the ERROR-STATUS value for the same condition is 0326. DB-STATUS fulfills exactly the same function as ERROR-STATUS, however; only the specific values differ.
3. Many other CODASYL systems do not have an OBTAIN command. In such systems, we replace the word OBTAIN with FIND, then immediately follow the FIND command with a GET command. This combination is equivalent to an OBTAIN command.
4. Since commands such as MODIFY and ERASE act on the current of run unit, some CODASYL systems allow you to omit the record name in the command, whereas IDMS requires that it be included. Thus, for example, in such systems, the

   ```
   MODIFY CUSTOMER
   ```

   command in IDMS would simply be

   ```
   MODIFY
   ```

You should be aware that the similarities far outweigh the differences. If you find yourself working with another CODASYL system after you have worked with IDMS, you should find it easy to make the transition.

## CHANGES IN THE 1978–1981 SPECIFICATIONS

The 1971–1973 specifications and most commercial CODASYL DBMS's do not fully support the three levels of schema described in the ANSI/SPARC model; consequently, they do not attain the level of data independence that is the goal of that model. The later specifications (see [3], [4], [5], and [7]) pushed the CODASYL model further in the direction of ANSI/SPARC by removing some of the physical aspects from the schema DDL and placing them in a separate facility. Some additional facilities were defined in the later specifications as well.

The 1978 specifications called for a DATA STORAGE DESCRIPTION LANGUAGE (DSDL), which included the Device Media Control Language (DMCL) from the earlier specifications as well as many new options. This language is used to specify the internal schema (using the ANSI/SPARC terminology) (i.e., to specify the mapping from the logical schema to physical storage). The portions of the 1971 schema DDL that were moved to the DSDL are some of those that described physical characteristics of the database, such things as the location mode of a record (CALC vs. VIA SET). In addition, more options are available than in the DMCL, including the ability to specify different types of indexes, the ability to split a record that is described as a single record in the DDL into two or more storage records in the physical database to improve performance, and so on.

The main changes we will discuss here, however, concern the DDL. As we said before, the location mode of a record is no longer specified in the DDL. In addition, there is a new clause, the RECORD KEY clause, in the record entry, which allows us to specify that one or more data items can be used as keys for the purpose of accessing record occurrences. A record key is specified as follows:

```
RECORD NAME IS SLSREP
    KEY SLSRNUMB IS ASCENDING SLSRNUMB
    DUPLICATES ARE NOT ALLOWED FOR SLSRNUMB.
```

or just

```
RECORD NAME IS SLSREP
    DUPLICATES ARE NOT ALLOWED FOR SLSRNUMB.
```

Basically, this indicates that no two occurrences of the *SLSREP* record will be allowed to have the same *SLSRNUMB*. It also gives us the basis for using the *SLSRNUMB* as a key to locate a specific occurrence. There is a corresponding DML command to do this:

```
OBTAIN ANY SLSREP USING SLSRNUMB.
```

Many of these keys can be declared within the same record type. We could choose to allow duplicates for some of them. We might state in the *CUSTOMER* record, for example, that

```
DUPLICATES ARE LAST FOR CUSTNAME.
```

This allows more than one customer to have the same name. It also allows us to find a customer rapidly, based on his or her name.

The STRUCTURAL CONSTRAINT clause is a new clause in the SET entry that can be used when the member record type contains as one of its fields the key of the owner record type. In this instance, we can use the STRUCTURAL CONSTRAINT clause to ensure that the two match. If we include in the *CUSTOMER* record, for example, the number of the sales rep who "owns" that customer, we could use the STRUCTURAL CONSTRAINT clause to make sure that a customer who is owned by sales rep 6 will not have a 3 in the sales rep field on the customer's record. In this example, the clause would read:

```
STRUCTURAL CONSTRAINT
    SLSRNUMB OF CUSTOMER EQUAL TO
    SLSRNUMB OF SLSREP.
```

Two additional changes to the SET entry are worth noting. The membership class FIXED is added as an option to the MANDATORY and OPTIONAL SET membership classes. We have already discussed this, since it is a feature of some existing systems (even though it was not technically part of the 1971 specifications). The other change is that a record type can now be *both* an owner record type *and* a member record type *in the same set*. This type is called a **recursive set**. The earlier specifications did not allow this type of set.

While the preceding changes enhance the CODASYL model, it is unclear whether they will find their way into commercial systems. The level of data independence has certainly been improved by these changes, but it is still not on a par with that of relational model systems. A program still must navigate the database and therefore must know all predefined paths (sets). A change of any substance to these predefined paths can require a major rewrite of the programs that access the database. Many CODASYL systems do offer query languages, which are far less procedural than COBOL and allow users to avoid much of the database navigation, but these languages are not standard (CODASYL did not propose specifications for a standard query language), nor are they appropriate for all applications.


## SUMMARY

In this chapter, we have studied one of the major models for database management systems, the CODASYL model. CODASYL (COnference on DAta SYstems Languages) appointed a task group, called the Data Base Task Group (DBTG) to develop a set of specifications for DBMS's. The report of this task group was formally presented in 1971. While these specifications were not adopted as a national standard, a number of commercial systems developed which adhered to them. Such systems are usually called CODASYL systems or DBTG systems. They fall within the general network model for DBMS's (i.e., their underlying data structures are simple networks). Even though some network model systems do not follow the CODASYL specifications, the term CODASYL has come to be synonymous with the network model for many people. Thus, if different people say they have a CODASYL system, a DBTG system, or a network model system, they often mean the same thing.

The terms "record" and "field" are used within CODASYL systems, just as they are used in ordinary processing. It is important to distinguish between a structure itself and a specific example of the structure, and we do this through the word **type**, which refers to the structure, and the word **occurrence**, which refers to a specific example of the structure. Thus, we can speak of a record of type *STUDENT*, which contains fields of type *STUNUMB* and *STUNAME*, and an occurrence of the *STUDENT* record, such as the following:

| 123 | John Smith |
|-----|------------|

Relationships are maintained in CODASYL systems by means of a construction called a set. A set type is a one-to-many association between record types. The record type that forms the "one" part of the association is called the owner record type, and the record type that forms the "many" part of the association is called the member record type. An occurrence of the set type is a single occurrence of the owner record type together with the many occurrences of the member record type that are related to it.

The schema is the overall logical structure of the database. It is conveyed to the computer through a language called the schema data definition language (or schema DDL). Physical aspects of the database are conveyed through the schema device/media control language (DMCL). A subschema is an individual user view of the database. It is conveyed through the subschema DDL. Since programs access the database through subschemas, various forms of the subschema DDL are tailored to different languages. The form presented here is tailored to COBOL.

Programs accessing the database do so through the normal commands present in the language in which the program is written and through additional commands specific to the processing of the database. These commands constitute the data manipulation language (DML). In CODASYL, these commands include CONNECT, DISCONNECT, ERASE, MODIFY, OBTAIN, STORE, and so on. The CODASYL DML is built around a concept called "currency." A variety of currency indicators or conceptual pointers are used to keep track of our position within the database. There is a currency indicator for each record type that indicates the last record of the same type that was accessed. There is another for each set type which indicates not only which occurrence of that set type was last accessed, but also its position within that set occurrence. There is also a currency indicator for the run unit (program) that indicates the last record of *any* type that was accessed. Various DML commands use and/or update these currency indicators.

We studied the CODASYL model by using one of the most popular CODASYL systems, IDMS. We looked at sample routines to handle a variety of tasks, as well as a sample application program. We also looked at IDMS/R (IDMS/RELATIONAL), which includes the full capabilities of IDMS, along with relational capabilities. These relational capabilities are furnished through the LRF (logical record facility) and the ASF (automatic systems facility). We discussed how IDMS furnishes the capabilities of a DBMS, as well as the differences between IDMS and other CODASYL systems.

While most commercial CODASYL systems follow the standards of the 1971 report (to which minor modifications were added in 1973), subsequent reports (1978, 1981) have proposed some significant changes to the model. Some physical characteristics have been moved from the DDL to the new Data Storage Description Language (DSDL), which also encompasses the DMCL from the earlier report. New clauses have been added to both the record and set entries. Whether these changes will find their way into existing commercial systems is uncertain.

# REVIEW QUESTIONS

1. Define the following and explain the relationship between them: CODA-SYL, DBTG, and DDLC.
2. Explain the difference between a record type and a record occurrence. Give an example of each.
3. Define the term SET as it is used within the CODASYL model. What purpose does this construction serve? Explain the difference between a set type and a set occurrence.
4. Define owner record type. Define member record type. What is the relationship between the number of owner occurrences and the number of set occurrences, if any? What is the relationship between the number of member occurrences and the number of set occurrences, if any?
5. What is a schema?
6. What is a subschema? What is the relationship between a schema and a subschema?
7. Define and briefly describe DDL, DML, and DMCL.
8. Describe LOCATION MODE. What is the difference between a location mode of CALC and a location mode of VIA SET? What factors would we consider in determining which of these two location modes to choose for a given record type?
9. Describe the effect of the SET IS PRIOR PROCESSABLE clause within the SET ENTRY. What are the benefits of picking this clause? What are the drawbacks?
10. Describe the INSERTION mode. Describe the differences between insertion modes of FIRST, LAST, NEXT, PRIOR, SORTED, and IMMATERIAL.
11. Describe the storage class. Describe the difference between the storage classes AUTOMATIC and MANUAL.
12. Describe the removal class. Describe the differences between the removal classes MANDATORY and OPTIONAL.
13. Describe the effect of the LINKED TO OWNER clause. What are the benefits of picking this clause? What are the drawbacks?
14. What purpose does the UWA serve when processing a CODASYL database? What does it contain?
15. Define ERROR-STATUS. How is this used within programs that access CODASYL databases?
16. Define currency indicator. Describe the various types of currency indicators available. How are they used?
17. What is the current of run unit? List the commands that act upon the current of run unit. List the commands that will change it.

18. How do COMMIT and ROLLBACK relate to the support of logical transactions in IDMS?
19. How do COMMIT and ROLLBACK relate to the support of shared update in IDMS?
20. Describe how the LRF furnishes logical data independence.
21. Describe the difference between the MODIFY command in IDMS and the MODIFY command in other CODASYL systems. How does the DBMS know which record is to be modified?
22. Describe the DSDL of the 1978 specifications. What is its relationship to the DDL and DMCL of the earlier specifications?

## EXERCISES

1. Suppose a department has many employees, and each employee works in many departments. Draw a data structure diagram showing how we would implement this many-to-many relationship within the CODASYL model. In which of your record types would you place the following fields?
   a. Employee name
   b. Department number
   c. Starting date (the date an employee began working for a department)
   d. Job description
2. A given user is concerned only with the *ORDERS* and *CUSTOMER* records. Within the *ORDERS* record, the only field required is the order number, which is to be called *ORDNUMB*. Within the *CUSTOMER* record, the only fields required are the customer's number, name, and address. The set, *CUSTOMER-ORDERS*, is also required for this user. Write an appropriate subschema.

Exercises 3 through 7 are based on the following information:
A database is needed to satisfy these seven requirements:

   (a) For a department, store its number (three digits) and name (twenty characters).
   (b) For an employee, store his or her number (four digits) and name (twenty characters).
   (c) For an insurance plan, store the plan number (four digits) and description (twenty characters).
   (d) For a job history record, store the job classification (twenty characters) and the starting date.
   (e) Each department can employ many employees but each employee works in exactly one department.

(f) Each insurance plan serves many employees but each employee is served by exactly one plan.

(g) Each employee can have several job history records but each job history record corresponds to exactly one employee.

3. Draw a data structure diagram for the database. Indicate the fields that would be a part of each record.

4. Write the schema DDL. Make whatever choices seem reasonable for LOCATION MODE, INSERTION, storage, and removal classes and indicate the effect of your choices.

5. What effect would the following four additional requirements have on the choices you made?

   a. An employee does not have to have an insurance plan.

   b. An employee must be in a department but is allowed to change from one department to another.

   c. When employees are printed by department, the order in which they appear should be the reverse of the order in which they have been placed in the database.

   d. When employees are printed by insurance plan, they should be listed alphabetically.

6. Give a full subschema (a subschema encompassing all records, fields, and sets) for the above schema.

7. Give a partial subschema for a user needing the department record, the employee record (called *EMP*), and the set between them. Give a subschema that includes a logical record, called *DEPT-EMP*, that consists of the department number, and department name together with the employee number and employee name for all employees in a given department.

In Exercises 8 through 23, write the code that will accomplish the required task. This code may be written in COBOL or pseudocode. An appropriate error message should be displayed for any problems that may arise. (The questions refer to the Premiere Products database.)

8. List the description and the number of units on hand for part BT04.

9. List the order number and date for all orders placed by customer 124.

10. If customer 124 currently has part BT04 on order, print "YES." If not, print "NO."

11. List the part number and description of all parts.

12. Store part BT05 (description "RANGE," units on hand 12, item class "AP," warehouse number 2, price $450).

13. Store order 12506 (date 9/05/91, customer number 412).

14. Change the description of part CA14 to "PAN."
15. Delete part CX11 only if there are no orders for this part.
16. Delete part CZ81 and any associated order lines.
17. Change the sales rep number for customer 256 to 12.
18. Add an order line for order 12491, part CA14 (number ordered – 1, quoted price – $19.95). If an order line for order 12491, part CA14 already exists, do *not* add this new order line.
19. Change the quoted price on the order line for order 12498, part AZ52, to $22.00.
20. Delete the order line for order 12504, part CZ81.
21. Determine whether sales rep 6 represents any customers who currently have any orders on file for any parts located in warehouse 2. If so, print "YES." If not, print "NO" (a highly useful query if there ever was one).
22. Change the quoted price on any order line for part BZ66 to $311.95.
23. Change the warehouse number for any part currently in warehouse 2 to 5.
24. ***** COMPUTER PROJECT *****

    If you have access to a CODASYL DBMS, do the following:
    a. Create a schema for your system for the Premiere Products database.
    b. Create a full subschema for your system for this database.
    c. Create the partial subschema described in the text for your system.
    d. Using the full subschema, write a program to populate the database (i.e., load data into the database). The input to this program should come from five separate files: *SLSREP, CUSTOMER, ORDERS, ORDLNE,* and *PART*. The record layouts for each of these files is shown in Figure 9.24 on the next page. The program should first add all sales reps, followed by the customers, orders, parts, and order lines in this order. Note that there are some additional fields that do not appear in the corresponding records in the schema and subschema. These are present for the purpose of identifying appropriate owner occurrences. In the *CUSTOMER* record, for example, the *SLSRNUMB* is present to allow us to identify the appropriate set occurrence within *SLSREP-CUSTOMER*.
    e. Create the files required for part d, using the data found in the tables for the relational model implementation of the Premiere Products database. (See Figure 3.1.) Using the program created in part d, add this data to the database.
    f. Write a program (or programs) to do the queries and updates described in Exercises 8 through 23.
    g. If your system has a query language associated with it, write programs using this query language to accomplish as many of the queries described in Exercises 8 through 23 as your system will handle.

**Figure 9.24**

Record layout for
update files

```
01    SLSREP.
      02    SLSRNUMB                    PIC 9(2).
      02    SLSRNAME                    PIC X(20).
      02    SLSRADDR                    PIC X(20).
      02    TOTCOMM                     PIC 9(5)V9(2).
      02    COMMRATE                    PIC V9(2).

01    CUSTOMER.
      02    CUSTNUMB                    PIC 9(3).
      02    CUSTNAME                    PIC X(20).
      02    CUSTADDR                    PIC X(20).
      02    BALANCE                     PIC 9(5)V9(2).
      02    CREDLIM                     PIC 9(5).
      02    SLSREP-NUMBER               PIC 9(2).

01    ORDERS.
      02    ORDNUMB                     PIC 9(5).
      02    ORDDTE                      PIC 9(6).
      02    CUSTNUMB                    PIC 9(3).

01    PART.
      02    PARTNUMB                    PIC X(4).
      02    PARTDESC                    PIC X(20).
      02    UNONHAND                    PIC 9(4).
      02    ITEMCLSS                    PIC X(2).
      02    WRHSNUMB                    PIC 9(2).
      02    UNITPRCE                    PIC 9(4)V9(2).

01    ORDLNE.
      02    NUMBORD                     PIC 9(4).
      02    QUOTPRCE                    PIC 9(4)V9(2).
      02    ORDNUMB                     PIC 9(5).
      02    PARTNUMB                    PIC X(4).
```

# REFERENCES

1] Bradley, James, *Introduction to Data Base Management in Business*, 2d ed. Holt, Rinehart & Winston, 1987.

2] Cardenas, Alfonso F., *Data Base Management Systems*, 2d ed. Allyn & Bacon, 1984.

3] CODASYL COBOL Committee, *Journal of Development*, 1978. Available from ACM.

4] CODASYL COBOL Committee, *Journal of Development*, 1981. Available from ACM.

5] CODASYL Data Description Language Committee, *DDL Journal of Development*, 1978. Available from ACM.

6] CODASYL Data Description Language Committee, *Journal of Development*, 1973. Available from ACM.

7] CODASYL Data Description Language Committee, *Journal of Development*, 1981. Available from ACM.

8] Data Base Task Group of CODASYL Programming Language Committee, *Report*, 1971. Available from ACM.

9] Date, C. J., *Introduction to Database Systems, Volume I*, 4th ed. Addison-Wesley, 1986.

10] Kroenke, David, and Dolan, Kathleen A., *Database Processing: Fundamentals, Design, Implementation*, 3d ed. SRA, 1988.

11] McFadden, Fred R., and Hoffer, Jeffrey A., *Data Base Management*, 2d ed. Benjamin Cummings, 1988.

12] Olle, T. W., *The CODASYL Approach to Data Base Management*, Wiley-Interscience, 1978.

13] Vasta, Joseph A., *Understanding Data Base Management Systems*, Wadsworth, 1985.

# The Hierarchical Model

## INTRODUCTION

In previous chapters the relational and CODASYL data models have been covered in detail. This chapter focuses on the hierarchical model to round out our study of the three data models. IBM's Information Management System (**IMS**) is one DBMS that is based on the hierarchical model. Since IMS has dominated the market for hierarchical model systems for the past two decades, it will be used to illustrate the concepts and implementation of the hierarchical model.

First released by IBM in 1968, IMS was the product of a joint venture with the aerospace company North American Aviation (now Rockwell International Corporation). Over the years IMS has been enhanced by additional features, improved performance, and the accommodation of developments in hardware. With thousands of enterprises relying on it to meet their database management needs, IMS remains a strong force in the marketplace.

IMS provides both database and data communications capabilities. The database access and manipulation component of IMS is called **Data Language/I (DL/I)**. DL/I is a separate component that can either stand alone in a batch-processing mode or be connected to other data communications products for on-line processing. DL/I follows the fundamental rules and constraints of the hierarchical model while providing additional features to extend its flexibility and usefulness.

Relational model DBMS's are based on a strong theoretical foundation; extensive research predated their first production release. CODASYL model DBMS's are based on a number of published specifications. Hierarchical model DBMS's have no comparable research or publication base on which to draw. Instead, a DBMS is held to be based on the hierarchical model if it represents data relationships in terms of hierarchies. In the next section we will discuss the hierarchical model, introduce the terminology associated with this model, and present specific terminology and capabilities associated with DL/I.

Next we will look at the data definition language of DL/I, then to the data manipulation language. We then examine the ways in which DL/I furnishes the functions of a DBMS. Finally, we contrast the three data models (hierarchical, CODASYL, and relational) in terms of their advantages and disadvantages.

## BASIC CONCEPTS AND TERMINOLOGY

Let's try a variation on Marvel College's requirements. This time we will use departments, faculty, majors, students, and the relationships between them to illustrate the basic concepts and terminology of the hierarchical model and of DL/I. Figure 10.1 shows the data structure diagram for these four entity types and for three one-to-many relationships. Each faculty member is employed by one department, and each department has many faculty members. Each student is related to the one faculty member who advises the student, while each faculty member advises many students. Finally, each major is offered by one department, and each department may offer many majors. Figure 10.2 shows one occurrence of this structure for the business department.

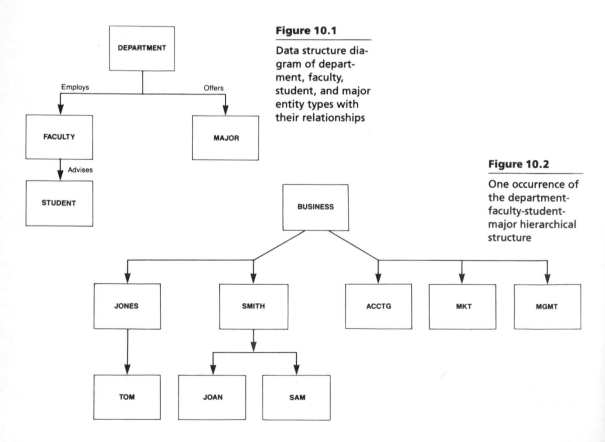

**Figure 10.1**

Data structure diagram of department, faculty, student, and major entity types with their relationships

**Figure 10.2**

One occurrence of the department-faculty-student-major hierarchical structure

In this structure, Jones is a faculty member advising Tom, Smith is a faculty member advising Joan and Sam, and accounting, marketing, and management are majors offered by the department.

## Hierarchical Model Concepts and Terminology

The **hierarchical model** supports a **tree** structure. The tree structure, however, is inverted, with a single root at the top and its branches leading toward the bottom, so it looks like the organizational chart, or hierarchy chart, of a typical enterprise. The terminology used for genealogical, or family, trees is also associated with the general hierarchical model.

A tree consists of **nodes**, connected by **branches**. The **root** node is at the top, and its **descendants** are below it. A **parent** node appears immediately above its **children**. In Figure 10.1 *DEPARTMENT, FACULTY, STUDENT,* and *MAJOR* are nodes connected by the branches *EMPLOYS, ADVISES,* and *OFFERS. DEPARTMENT* is the root, has descendants *FACULTY, STUDENT,* and *MAJOR,* and is the parent of *FACULTY* and *MAJOR. FACULTY* is the parent of *STUDENT. FACULTY* and *MAJOR* are children of *DEPARTMENT.* Finally, *STUDENT* is the child of *FACULTY.* In the hierarchical model, the branches are not named; these branches (*EMPLOYS, OFFERS,* and *ADVISES*) have been named merely for the sake of convenience in referencing the diagram.

In Figure 10.2, business is the root and the parent of faculty Jones and Smith and of the accounting, marketing, and management majors. Jones is the parent of Tom, and Smith is the parent of Joan and Sam. Jones, Smith, accounting, marketing, management, Tom, Joan, and Sam are children of their respective parents.

When viewing an occurrence of a tree structure like the one shown in Figure 10.2, *siblings*, or **twins**, are defined as children of the same node type with the same parent occurrence. Jones and Smith are siblings, sharing business as a parent. Accounting, marketing, and management are siblings, since they share business as a parent. Joan and Sam are siblings, sharing Smith as a parent. Though Smith and accounting share business as a parent, they are not siblings, since they belong to different node types. Likewise, though Tom is of the same node type as Joan and Sam, Jones and Smith are different parent occurrences, so Tom is not a sibling of Joan and Sam.

Each node contains one or more fields or attributes. The *FACULTY* node, for example, in addition to having faculty name, could also have the fields office location, phone number, and highest degree earned.

The following constraints apply to the hierarchical model:

1. There is a single root node, which is department in Figure 10.2. This restriction applies to the root node type, not to occurrences of the root. Business, biology, and psychology could exist as occurrences of the root node in the example database.

2. Each child node has a single parent node. Note that this is true for all children in Figure 10.2. If we needed additionally to represent a one-to-many relationship between *MAJOR* and *STUDENT*, we could not do it directly by simply adding a relationship between the two nodes. We could, however, retain the tree as structured and add a second, separate tree, with *MAJOR* as the root and *STUDENT* as its child. Or we could retain the tree as structured and combine major and student data into the *STUDENT* node, so that major data would appear in both the *MAJOR* and *STUDENT* nodes. Either solution results in duplicate data being stored in two different nodes. Note that this restriction prohibits many-to-many relationships directly in one tree, since we normally construct two one-to-many relationships, or a node with two parents, to represent these types of relationships.

3. Each node is accessed through its parent. Thus, to get to student Tom, we must first access business, then Jones, then Tom. This also means that a child node cannot exist without its parent or other ancestors. We could not add Tom as a student until we knew his advisor. Also, if faculty member Jones left and we deleted her node, we also would delete her children. Access, in other words, is along a **hierarchical path** from top to bottom.

The most common access method, and storage approach, is called **preorder traversal**, in which node occurrences are retrieved from top to bottom and left to right for each occurrence. For Figure 10.2, the preorder traversal path starts at business and travels in order to Jones, Tom, Smith, Joan, Sam, accounting, marketing, and management. Figure 10.3 shows this preorder traversal path more clearly. We have traced the preorder traversal path by enclosing the segment occurrences with a fingerlike circuit, starting at the root segment occurrence, traveling down the left side of the structure, and continuing around each segment occurrence until once again reaching the root segment occurrence. A preorder traversal path always forms this fingerlike pattern around a hierarchical structure occurrence.

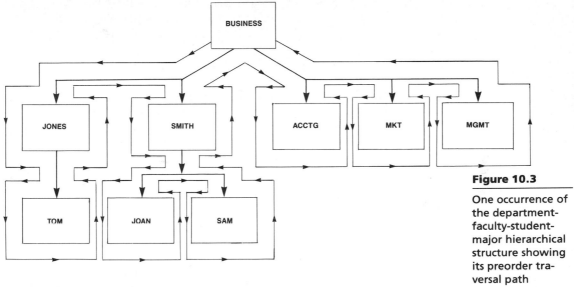

**Figure 10.3**

One occurrence of the department-faculty-student-major hierarchical structure showing its preorder traversal path

## DL/I Fundamental Concepts and Terminology

**DL/I Tree-related Terminology.** The terminology used in DL/I differs in several ways from that of the general hierarchical model. Specifically, DL/I uses the following terminology:

- A node is called a **segment**, so segments consist of logically grouped fields. The equivalent CODASYL term is *record*, and the equivalent relational term is *table* or *relation*. The segment at the top of the tree is the **root segment**. In Figure 10.1 the segments are *DEPARTMENT*, *FACULTY, STUDENT*, and *MAJOR*, with *DEPARTMENT* as the root segment.
- One tree structure occurrence of the root segment and all its descendants is called a **physical database record** (**PDBR**). Figure 10.1 is an example of one *PDBR type*, while Figure 10.2 shows a single *PDBR occurrence* of this PDBR type.
- The collection of all physical database records for a particular tree structure is called a **physical database**. So business and all its descendants from Figure 10.2, biology and all its descendants, and so on, constitute the physical database that is summarized in the tree structure of Figure 10.1.

**Figure 10.4**

Data structure diagram for building, room, and course entities

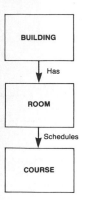

A number of different physical databases can exist under DL/I. Figure 10.4 shows the tree structure for a second possible physical database, with BUILDING as the root segment, *ROOM* as a child segment to *BUILDING* and a parent segment for *COURSE*, and *COURSE* as a child segment for ROOM. Many different courses are offered at different times in a particular room, and a particular course is offered in a single, specific room, so this is a one-to-many relationship. And a particular building has many rooms, another one-to-many relationship.

In DL/I each physical database is defined separately in a single database definition. This is where all segments, all fields within each segment, and all hierarchical relationships between segments are defined. This database definition is called a **database description**, or **DBD**. The process of defining a DBD is called a **DBD generation**, or **DBDGEN**. There would be one DBDGEN for the physical database in Figure 10.1 and a second DBDGEN for the physical database in Figure 10.4. Each DL/I physical database can have a maximum of 255 different segment types, and a single hierarchical path from the root segment to the bottommost segment is limited to fifteen segments.

**DL/I Logical Databases.**   A **logical database** is an individual user's, or program's, view of the database. It can be different from the physical database or databases. For example, a logical database could be one entire physical database, like the one shown in Figure 10.1, or a subset of one physical database, like the *DEPARTMENT* and *FACULTY* segments from Figure 10.1, or portions from two or more physical databases. The last of these three possibilities will be covered more fully in the next topic, which covers logical relationships. The primary restriction on a logical database is that its root segment must also be a root segment of a physical database.

Each logical database is defined through a **program specification block generation**, or **PSBGEN**. Defined in the PSBGEN are the fields and segments that constitute the logical database. In a particular logical database, for example, we could allow the user to update fields in certain segments and to access but not update fields in other segments. For example, in Figure 10.1, one logical database could provide:

- access to all fields in the *DEPARTMENT* segment, but no update privileges.
- update privilege to all fields in the *STUDENT* segment. If neither access nor update privileges are to be permitted to the *FACULTY* segment, it would still need to be defined in the PSBGEN so that the user could retrieve a particular *STUDENT* segment occurrence by traveling the hierarchical path from *DEPARTMENT* to *FACULTY* to *STUDENT*. In this case, we would define the *FACULTY* segment as having no access or update privileges. The *FACULTY* segment would be defined

as *key sensitive* to permit traveling the path from *DEPARTMENT* to *STUDENT*. If the user required access to only the *STUDENT* segment, then both the *DEPARTMENT* and *FACULTY* segments would be defined as key sensitive.

One occurrence of a logical database is called a **logical database record (LDBR)**. Based on the preceding paragraph and on Figure 10.2, one LDBR would be business, Tom, Joan, and Sam. Figure 10.5 shows the data structure diagram for this logical database and the occurrence just described. *FACULTY*, Jones, and Smith are in blue boxes indicating that access is permitted to these segments only for the purposes of the hierarchical path.

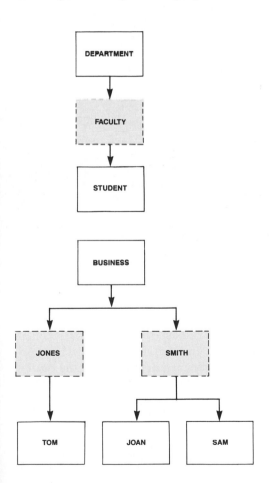

**Figure 10.5**

Data structure diagram for the business-student logical database and one logical database record occurrence

### DL/I Logical Relationships

In the general hierarchical model, each child node has a single parent. You will recall that if we need additionally to represent a one-to-many relationship between *MAJOR* and *STUDENT* in Figure 10.1, we cannot do it directly simply by adding a relationship between the two nodes.

DL/I, however, provides a facility called a **logical relationship** which overcomes this restriction through the use of **logical pointers**. There are several variations of logical relationships; we will discuss just two of them. The first variation is illustrated in Figure 10.6. This new data structure diagram has a logical relationship, shown with a blue line, between the *MAJOR* and *STUDENT* segments.

**Figure 10.6**

Logical relationship between major and student segments

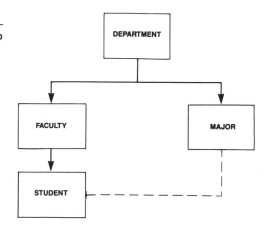

A logical relationship is a physical connection between two segments, and it is established through the DBDGEN process. Actually, three segments are needed for a logical relationship. In Figure 10.6, *FACULTY* is the **physical parent**, *MAJOR* is the **logical parent**, and *STUDENT* is a **physical child** to *FACULTY* and a **logical child** to *MAJOR*. Note that there is no arrowhead on the blue line. This is because, depending on user requirements and the resulting database design, there are two different ways to define this first logical relationship variation.

In the first case, suppose we needed to know only the student's major, given a particular student occurrence. Then we would define in the DBDGEN a **unidirectional** (or one-way) **logical relationship** from the *STUDENT* segment to the *MAJOR* segment. From this DBDGEN definition, DL/I adds a single pointer, actually the key of the *MAJOR* segment, to the *STUDENT* segment. Given a *STUDENT* occurrence, DL/I uses this logical pointer to retrieve the proper *MAJOR* occurrence. In Figure 10.7 the blue lines traveling from the occurrences of *STUDENT* to the occurrences of *MAJOR* show that Tom has a management major and both Joan and Sam have accounting majors. If we wish to travel from *MAJOR* to *STUDENT*, we cannot do so with these unidirectional logical pointers. The only way of accessing a *STUDENT* occurrence is through its physical parent of *FACULTY*.

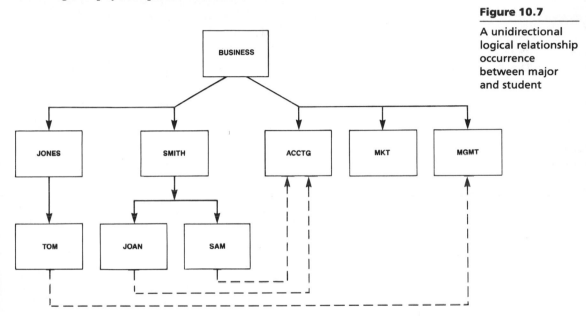

**Figure 10.7**

A unidirectional logical relationship occurrence between major and student

In the second case, suppose we also needed to access all students having a particular major from an occurrence of the *MAJOR* segment. Then we would define in the DBDGEN a **bidirectional** (or two-way) **logical relationship** between the *STUDENT* segment and the *MAJOR* segment. Retained in the *STUDENT* segment is the pointer we just described. A pointer is now added to the *MAJOR* segment. DL/I uses this new pointer to retrieve the first *STUDENT* occurrence for a particular *MAJOR*. To retrieve all other *STUDENT* occurrences for that *MAJOR*, DL/I uses a second pointer in the *STUDENT* segment (the third pointer overall) that connects each of the *STUDENT* occurrences for that *MAJOR*.

Suppose the *STUDENT* occurrences in Figure 10.2 were all accounting majors. Then in Figure 10.8 the first logical pointers for Tom, for Joan, and for Sam would all point to accounting, the logical parent to each of these *STUDENT* occurrences. If the logical pointer in the accounting occurrence pointed to Tom, the second *STUDENT* segment logical pointer for Tom might then point to Sam, the second logical pointer for Sam would point to Joan, and the second logical pointer for Joan would indicate the end of the chain.

**Figure 10.8**

A bidirectional logical relationship occurrence between major and student

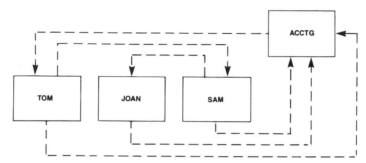

The second logical relationship variation involves a method for defining a logical database that consists of portions of two physical databases using logical relationships. Suppose each department were assigned a block of rooms in which to hold its classes, and only classes for a given department were held in the assigned block of rooms. Suppose further that we had defined the two physical databases shown in Figures 10.1 and 10.4 and needed to retrieve all rooms for a given department and to know which department had been assigned a given room. Figure 10.9 shows the logical database we would like to define. The blue line between the *DEPARTMENT* and *ROOM* segments again indicates that a logical relationship, defined in the DBDGEN, exists between the two segments. *DEPARTMENT* is the logical parent, and *ROOM* is the logical child. *BUILDING* is the physical parent of *ROOM*, and *ROOM* is the physical child of *BUILDING*. The possibilities for pointers discussed in the previous *MAJOR-STUDENT* example also pertain to this example.

**Figure 10.9**

Logical relationship between department and room segments in two different physical databases

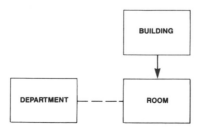

It is important to reemphasize that other variations are possible on the logical relationship capability. In summary, logical relationships allow a segment to have more than one parent segment and allow two or more physical databases to be considered part of the same logical database. DL/I, however, has a number of restrictions on the establishment of logical relationships. Following are a few that are of interest to us:

1. Every segment, except root segments, must have one physical parent segment.
2. A given segment can have at most one logical parent segment.
3. A root segment cannot be a logical child; however, it may be a logical parent.
4. A logical child segment cannot also be a logical parent segment.

Remember that both physical databases and logical relationships are defined explicitly in the DBDGEN process. A logical database, defined through a PSBGEN, must be defined in terms of existing physical databases and logical relationships already defined. In other words, the logical relationships, or user views, must be known in advance so that appropriate physical relationships can be established during the DBDGEN process.

Physical databases, logical databases, and logical relationships get very complicated when we study the full DL/I capabilities in these areas. We have chosen to touch on the main DL/I capabilities and to leave aside these areas of complexity.

## DL/I Physical Storage Structures

For each segment stored in the database, DL/I stores the data fields for the segment, logical pointers if necessary, and various control and identification information about the segment. The specific method of storing segments and hierarchical relationships between segments depends upon the particular *physical storage structure* chosen. DL/I has four physical storage structures: hierarchical sequential, hierarchical indexed sequential, hierarchical direct, and hierarchical indexed direct. IBM refers to these physical storage structures as access methods, and the following is a brief overview of each one.

**Hierarchical Sequential Access Method (HSAM).** An HSAM (**hierarchical sequential access method**) physical database stores segments sequentially in a **preorder traversal** structure. Figure 10.10 shows how the PDBR of Figure 10.2 would be stored using HSAM. The root segment is physically followed by its first child segment, which in turn is followed by its first child segment, and so on. This PDBR would be followed physically by the next PDBR, and so on. Stored in each segment is a segment identification field so that the segment type can be determined when segments are retrieved. This segment identification field is also present for each of the other DL/I access methods.

BUSINESS

JONES

TOM

SMITH

JOAN

SAM

ACCTG

MKT

MGMT

**Figure 10.10**

HSAM storage of a physical database record in preorder traversal order

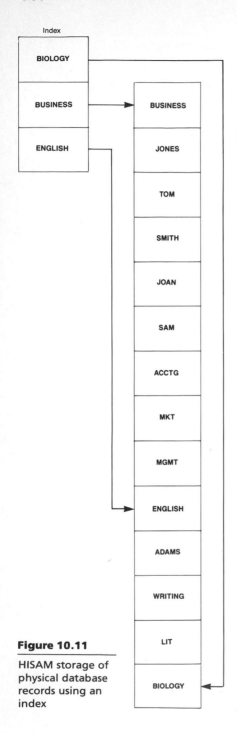

**Figure 10.11**

HISAM storage of
physical database
records using an
index

An HSAM database can be sequentially accessed only, and the database must be recreated if updates have to be made. Logical relationships cannot be defined. HSAM can be used either for disk or tape media; the other three access methods must be stored on disk. Since random access is not permitted under HSAM and since space requirements for HSAM are the least of the four access methods, HSAM is best suited to historical retention on tape of segments deleted from the production databases. These production databases are best stored using one of the other three access methods, since they permit random access.

**Hierarchical Indexed Sequential Access Method (HISAM).** A HISAM (**hierarchical indexed sequential access method**) physical database provides sequential and random access through an index to root segment occurrences and provides sequential access to dependent segment occurrences. Depending on which IBM operating system is used, either an **ISAM** or **VSAM** file organization (see the appendix) is employed for the root segment index.

Figure 10.11 shows the index entries for the root segment occurrences pointing to the start of their respective physical database records. Behind the scenes, the dependent segment occurrences may not necessarily be physically contiguous, as depicted in Figure 10.11; but the figure does represent the order in which dependent segment occurrences would be retrieved once a given root segment occurrence had been retrieved.

**Hierarchical Direct Access Method (HDAM).** An HDAM (**hierarchical direct access method**) physical database provides random access through a **hashing** technique to root segment occurrences. Access to dependent segment occurrences is through pointers stored in each segment. Either hierarchical or child-twin pointers may be used.

Figure 10.12 pictures the way in which hierarchical and child-twin pointers techniques would be used with the physical database record from Figure 10.2. Note that sequential access to the root segments is not possible unless a secondary index, which will be discussed just ahead, is also used.

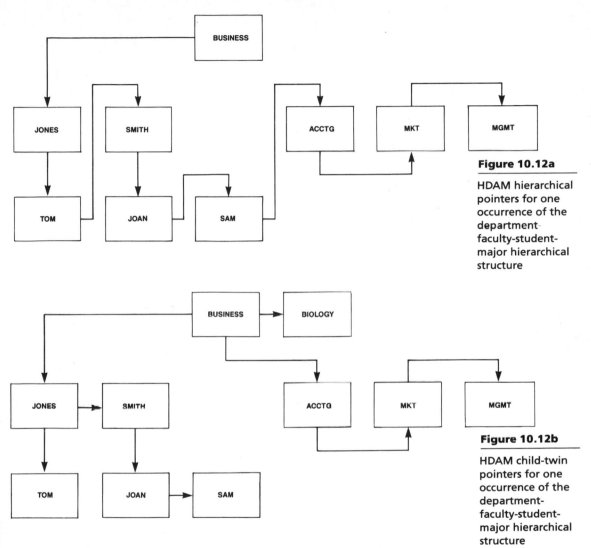

**Figure 10.12a**

HDAM hierarchical pointers for one occurrence of the department-faculty-student-major hierarchical structure

**Figure 10.12b**

HDAM child-twin pointers for one occurrence of the department-faculty-student-major hierarchical structure

**Hierarchical Indexed Direct Access Method (HIDAM).** A HIDAM (**hierarchical indexed direct access method**) physical database provides sequential and random access through an index to root segment occurrences. This is similar to the method used by HISAM; refer to Figure 10.11. The difference is that access to dependent segment occurrences is through either hierarchical or child-twin pointers stored in each segment. This is similar to the method used by HDAM; refer to Figure 10.12.

## DL/I Secondary Indexing

To permit random access through any of the hashing or indexed schemes used with HISAM, HDAM, and HIDAM, each root segment must have a primary key field defined during the DBDGEN process. We can also define a key or **sequence field** for nonroot segments. If a sequence field is used, DL/I arranges occurrences of that segment in order by that field. Even when using sequence fields, however, we still must travel the hierarchical path to reach a particular nonroot segment. But placing segments in some sequence makes updating and retrieval easier, as we shall see when we get to the data manipulation section of this chapter.

If we also need to randomly access the database through a nonroot segment, DL/I provides this capability through its **secondary indexing** feature. Secondary indexing is an **inverted file structure**. Figure 10.13 illustrates secondary indexing on the *MAJOR* segment. We are still able to randomly access, based on the root segment key values of biology, business, and English. With secondary indexing on the *MAJOR* segment, we can randomly access further, based on the major segment key values of accounting, marketing, management, writing, and literature.

## DL/I Fast Path

**Fast Path** is a DL/I feature supporting applications that require faster processing than can be obtained using the standard DL/I structures already described. The Fast Path feature obtains its greater efficiency through special transaction-processing facilities, through a special set of utilities, and through two special types of databases: the **main storage database** (MSDB) and the **data entry database** (DEDB).

An MSDB is a memory-resident database (the MSDB actually resides in virtual storage) consisting of root-only segments. It obtains its greater efficiency through this root-only restriction and through its memory-resident placement.

A DEDB resides on disk like normal DL/I databases but is restricted to a root segment and optionally up to seven child segment types. That is, a DEDB can be at most two hierarchical levels deep. Special storage techniques are used to assist in gaining greater efficiency in processing.

Both MSDB and DEDB have additional restrictions and characteristics. For more detail on the facets of Fast Path, see various IBM DL/I and IMS publications.

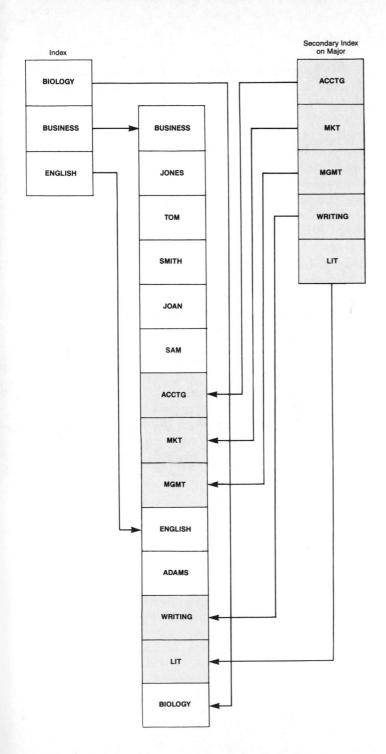

**Figure 10.13**

Example of a secondary index on the major segment

### Premiere Products Database

For a further example of DL/I concepts, consider the entities and relationships required for the Premiere Products database described in chapter 1. The basic entities and relationships are as follows:

- a sales rep entity, called *SLSREP*
- a customer entity, called *CUSTOMER*
- a one-to-many relationship from *SLSREP* to *CUSTOMER*
- an order entity, called *ORDERS*
- a one-to-many relationship from *CUSTOMER* to *ORDERS*
- a part entity, called *PART*
- a many-to-many relationship between *ORDERS* and *PART*

Designing a DL/I database to handle these requirements poses little difficulty except for the many-to-many relationship between *ORDERS* and *PART*. A variety of approaches are available for handling a many-to-many relationship in a DL/I database design. The design strategy chosen, of course, depends upon both the processing requirements and the performance needs of the system.

Figure 10.14 shows the data structure diagram for the DL/I design and the fields placed within each segment. There are two physical databases: *SALESDB* and *PARTDB*. The *SALESDB* physical database has *SLSREP* as the root segment, *CUSTOMER* as its child and the parent of *ORDERS*, and *ORDERS* as the child of *CUSTOMER*. The *PARTDB* physical database has *PART* as the root segment; there are no other physical segments in this database.

In this database design we have implemented the many-to-many relationship between *ORDERS* and *PART* by defining an *ORDLNE* segment that contains **intersection data** (i.e., fields related to a specific *PART* for a specific *ORDERS*). To form the connection between the two physical databases, we have defined a **bidirectional logical relationship** between *ORDLNE* and *PART*. *ORDERS* is the physical parent of *ORDLNE*, which is the physical child of *ORDERS*. *PART* is the logical parent of *ORDLNE*, which is the logical child of *PART*. *ORDLNE* is a segment serving a role similar to the CODASYL model link record approach. We have turned a many-to-many relationship, which DL/I cannot directly support, between *ORDERS* and *PART* into two one-to-many relationships, which DL/I can support through the use of a logical relationship. As we will see in the next section, there is more to the database design than what is shown in Figure 10.14, but the data structure diagram does represent the general approach to the Premiere Products design.

These databases for Premiere Products will be used to discuss DL/I's data definition and data manipulation languages in the following sections.

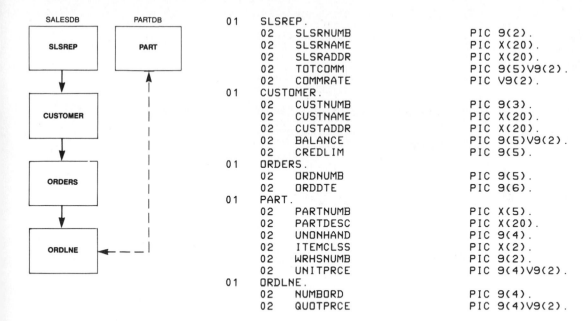

```
01    SLSREP.
      02    SLSRNUMB          PIC  9(2).
      02    SLSRNAME          PIC  X(20).
      02    SLSRADDR          PIC  X(20).
      02    TOTCOMM           PIC  9(5)V9(2).
      02    COMMRATE          PIC  V9(2).
01    CUSTOMER.
      02    CUSTNUMB          PIC  9(3).
      02    CUSTNAME          PIC  X(20).
      02    CUSTADDR          PIC  X(20).
      02    BALANCE           PIC  9(5)V9(2).
      02    CREDLIM           PIC  9(5).
01    ORDERS.
      02    ORDNUMB           PIC  9(5).
      02    ORDDTE            PIC  9(6).
01    PART.
      02    PARTNUMB          PIC  X(5).
      02    PARTDESC          PIC  X(20).
      02    UNONHAND          PIC  9(4).
      02    ITEMCLSS          PIC  X(2).
      02    WRHSNUMB          PIC  9(2).
      02    UNITPRCE          PIC  9(4)V9(2).
01    ORDLNE.
      02    NUMBORD           PIC  9(4).
      02    QUOTPRCE          PIC  9(4)V9(2).
```

**Figure 10.14**

Data structure diagram and fields in each segment for Premiere Products database

## DL/I DATA DEFINITION

We learned in the previous section that DL/I has physical databases and logical databases. A logical database is an application program's view of the physical databases. In this section we will discuss how to define physical and logical databases in DL/I.

### Physical Database Description

A physical database is defined with a **database description**, or **DBD**. The DBD consists of assembly language macro statements that are coded by the Database Administration group, assembled, and linked into an IMS load module library. This process is called a **DBD generation**, or **DBDGEN**, and occurs for each separate physical database required by the enterprise. A particular physical database goes through the DBDGEN procedure once, unless the physical structure of the database changes, in which case the macro statements would be changed and the DBDGEN procedure would be repeated.

The data structure diagram in Figure 10.14 shows two physical databases. Their corresponding DBDs are shown in Figure 10.15 on the next page. We will refer to Figure 10.15 in explaining each DBD statement type.

**Figure 10.15a**

DBD for the
*SALESDB* physical
database

```
 1   DBD        NAME=SALESDB,ACCESS=HDAM

 2   SEGM       NAME=SLSREP,PARENT=0,BYTES=51
 3   FIELD      NAME=(SLSRNUMB,SEQ,U),BYTES=2,START=1
 4   FIELD      NAME=SLSRNAME,BYTES=20,START=3
 5   FIELD      NAME=SLSRADDR,BYTES=20,START=23
 6   FIELD      NAME=COMMRATE,BYTES=7,START=43
 7   FIELD      NAME=TOTCOMM,BYTES=2,START=50

 8   SEGM       NAME=CUSTOMER,PARENT=SLSREP,BYTES=55
 9   FIELD      NAME=(CUSTNUMB,SEQ,U),BYTES=3,START=1
10   FIELD      NAME=CUSTNAME,BYTES=20,START=4
11   FIELD      NAME=CUSTADDR,BYTES=20,START=24
12   FIELD      NAME=BALANCE,BYTES=7,START=44
13   FIELD      NAME=CREDLIM,BYTES=5,START=51

14   SEGM       NAME=ORDERS,PARENT=CUSTOMER,BYTES=11
15   FIELD      NAME=(ORDNUMB,SEQ,U),BYTES=5,START=1
16   FIELD      NAME=ORDDTE,BYTES=6,START=6

17   SEGM       NAME=ORDLNE,POINTER=(LPARENT,LTWIN,TWIN),
                 PARENT=((ORDERS),(PART,PHYSICAL,PARTDB)),BYTES=14
18   FIELD      NAME=(PARTNUMB,SEQ,M),BYTES=5,START=1
19   FIELD      NAME=NUMBORD,BYTES=4,START=6
20   FIELD      NAME=QUOTPRCE,BYTES=6,START=10
```

**Figure 10.15b**

DBD for the
*PARTDB* physical
database

```
21   DBD        NAME=PARTDB,ACCESS=HIDAM

22   SEGM       NAME=PART,BYTES=38
23   LCHILD     NAME=(ORDLNE,SALESDB),PAIR=PORDLNE,POINTER=SNGL
24   FIELD      NAME=(PARTNUMB,SEQ,U),BYTES=5,START=1
25   FIELD      NAME=PARTDESC,BYTES=20,START=5
26   FIELD      NAME=UNONHAND,BYTES=4,START=25
27   FIELD      NAME=ITEMCLSS,BYTES=2,START=29
28   FIELD      NAME=WRHSNUMB,BYTES=2,START=31
29   FIELD      NAME=UNITPRCE,BYTES=6,START=33

30   SEGM       NAME=PORDLNE,POINTER=PAIRED,PARENT=PART,
                 SOURCE=((ORDLNE,SALESDB))
31   FIELD      NAME=(ORDNUMB,SEQ,M),BYTES=5,START=1
32   FIELD      NAME=NUMBORD,BYTES=4,START=6
33   FIELD      NAME=QUOTPRCE,BYTES=6,START=10
```

**DBD Statement.**  For each DBD there is one **DBD** macro **statement**, which is the first entry in the DBD (see lines 1 and 21). Using this statement, we give a name to the database with the NAME parameter. The name of the first database is *SALESDB*. *PARTDB* is the name of the second database. We also specify the physical storage structure in the DBD statement, using the ACCESS parameter. We have decided to use HDAM for the *SALESDB* database, and HIDAM for the *PARTDB* database.

**SEGM Statement.**  For each DBD there is one **SEGM statement** for each segment type in the database. We must start with the SEGM statement for the root segment (lines 2 and 22). The order of SEGM statements that follow the root determine the **hierarchical path** for the database (lines 8, 14, 17, and 30). Thus, SEGM statement order is important.

We name each segment, using the NAME parameter, and specify the size of each segment, using the BYTES parameter.

The PARENT parameter indicates the parent segment for a given child. *SLSREP* is the parent of *CUSTOMER* (line 8), and *CUSTOMER* is the parent of *ORDERS* (line 14). We can identify the root segment by coding PARENT = 0 (line 2) or by omitting the PARENT parameter (line 22).

The PARENT parameters for lines 17 and 30 are more complicated because these SEGM statements establish the **many-to-many** relationship between *ORDERS* and *PART* by means of the **bidirectional logical relationship** between *ORDLNE* and *PART*, shown in Figure 10.13. We want to be able to access occurrences of *ORDLNE* through either *ORDERS* or *PART*, access an occurrence of *ORDERS* from *ORDLNE*, and access an occurrence of *PART* from *ORDLNE*.

Figure 10.16 shows a way of viewing the relationships among *ORDERS*, *PART*, and *ORDLNE* to better understand the SEGM statements. *ORDERS* is the physical parent of *ORDLNE*, and *ORDLNE* is the physical child of *ORDERS*. *PART* is the logical parent of *ORDLNE*, and *ORDLNE* is the logical child of *PART*. The segment *PORDLNE* is called a **virtual segment**, since to the user it appears to physically exist even though, in fact, it does not. Figure 10.14 shows what actually exists, and Figure 10.16 shows what appears to exist and what must be defined in the SEGM statements.

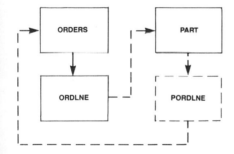

**Figure 10.16**

Conceptual view of the logical relationship for *ORDERS*, *PART*, and *ORDLNE* segments

The SEGM PARENT parameter for *ORDLNE* (line 17) has *ORDERS* as the physical parent segment and *PART* in the *PARTDB* database as the logical parent segment. The PHYSICAL subparameter means that *PARTNUMB*, the key to the *PART* segment, will be stored in the *ORDLNE* segment. It is not required that we store *PARTNUMB* in the *ORDLNE* segment, but we have chosen to do so. The POINTER parameter allows the database designer to specify the pointer types needed for that segment. In the case of *ORDLNE*, we have the following pointers:

- a logical parent pointer, subparameter of LPARENT, in each *ORDLNE* occurrence that points to its logical parent occurrence in the *PART* segment

- a logical twin pointer, subparameter of LTWIN, connecting the twin occurrences of *ORDLNE* for the same *PART* occurrence in *PARTNUMB* sequence
- a physical twin pointer, subparameter of TWIN, connecting the twin occurrences of *ORDLNE* for the same *ORDERS* occurrence in *ORDNUMB* sequence

The SEGM PARENT parameter for *PORDLNE* (line 30) and its LCHILD statement (line 23) should be studied together. The LCHILD statement immediately follows the SEGM for *PART* and defines *PORDLNE* in the PAIR parameter as being paired with *ORDLNE* in the *SALESDB* database; that is, they are one and the same. The POINTER parameter for the LCHILD statement creates in each *PART* occurrence a logical child pointer to the first *ORDLNE* occurrence in the logical twin pointer chain. The SEGM statement names this virtual segment as *PORDLNE*, specifies its virtual parent as *PART*, and identifies *PORDLNE* as being paired with the real segment of *ORDLNE* in the *SALESDB* database.

Since we are using HDAM and HIDAM, the two databases will have pointers connecting segment occurrences. We can choose to use hierarchical pointers for all segments, child-twin pointers for all segments, or hierarchical pointers for some segments and child-twin pointers for the other segments. A given segment type can have only one of the two pointer types. The choice between these two pointer types is made in the SEGM statement, using the POINTER parameter. The default is child-twin pointers if the POINTER parameter is not explicitly coded. Except for the *ORDLNE* and *PORDLNE* segments, we have chosen to use the default pointer types.

**FIELD Statement.**   We use the **FIELD statement** to define all fields for a given segment. There is one FIELD statement for each field in the segment. The FIELD statements follow the SEGM statement that names and defines the segment. The BYTES parameter defines the size of the field, and the START parameter defines the byte position in the segment where the field starts.

The NAME parameter provides the field name. Additionally, we can name one field per record as a *sequence* (or key) *field* (lines 3, 9, 15, 18, 24, and 31) by using the SEQ subparameter. If a sequence field is defined, then the segment occurrences will be stored in order by the sequence field. If U is specified for the sequence field, then DL/I ensures that only one segment occurrence with that sequence field value exists for a given parent occurrence. If M is specified for the sequence field, then multiple occurrences of that segment can have the same sequence field value for a given parent occurrence.

## Logical Database Description

A **logical database** is defined with a **program specification block**, or **PSB**. The PSB consists of assembly language macro statements that undergo a process similar to that undergone by the DBDGEN. The result of this process is called a PSB generation, or PSBGEN. For an application program to access the database, there must be a PSB defined for that program.

Figure 10.17a is an example PSB for the Premiere Products databases we have designed. Each PSB consists of one or more **program communication blocks** (**PCB**s). In each PCB (lines 1 and 7) we indicate that we are dealing with a database PCB, using the TYPE parameter, and give the name of the database, using the DBNAME parameter. The database name matches the name given in a previously defined DBD.

```
1   PCB        TYPE=DB,DBNAME=SALESDB
2   SENSEG     NAME=SLSREP,PROCOPT=G
3   SENSEG     NAME=CUSTOMER,PARENT=SLSREP,PROCOPT=G
4   SENFLD     NAME=CUSTNUMB,START=1
5   SENFLD     NAME=CREDLIM,START=51
6   SENSEG     NAME=ORDERS,PARENT=CUSTOMER,PROCOPT=(G,I,R,D)

7   PCB        TYPE=DB,DBNAME=PARTDB
8   SENSEG     NAME=PART,PARENT=0,PROCOPT=G

9   PSBGEN     LANG=COBOL,PSBNAME=SAMPLE
```

**Figure 10.17a**

PSB for a sample COBOL application program that will interact with a subset of the Premiere Products databases

We define the **sensitive segments** for this application program in the **SENSEG statements**. In the NAME parameter we give the name of the sensitive segment. This name must match the name of the applicable DBD given in the SEGM statement. We define the sensitive segments in hierarchical sequence and use the PARENT parameter to name the parent for the segment, as previously done in the DBD. Note that we can again indicate a root segment by coding PARENT = 0 or by omitting the PARENT parameter. We authorize the *processing options* allowable to the segment by using the **PROCOPT parameter**. A number of processing options can be chosen, among which are G for get (retrieval only), I for insert, R for replace, and D for delete.

The entire segment named in a SENSEG statement is accessible under the constraints of the PROCOPT parameter, except for those segments having SENFLD statements defined. If used, the SENFLD statements define the specific fields accessible for the preceding SENSEG statement. In our example we have two SENFLD statements (lines 4 and 5) that permit us to get values of only the *CUSTNUMB* and *CREDLIM* fields from the *CUSTOMER* segment. The other fields from the *CUSTOMER* segment, *CUSTNAME*, *CUSTADDR*, and *BALANCE*, cannot be accessed, since SENFLD statements are not defined for them. On the other hand, all fields for the *SLSREP*, *ORDERS*, and *PART* segments can be accessed, since their SENSEG statements are not followed by SENFLD statements.

We end the PSB with a PSBGEN statement (line 8), in which we specify the programming language, COBOL in this example, to be used with this PSB and give a name, SAMPLE, to the PSB. Other programming languages that can be specified are PL/I and Assembler.

Figure 10.17a is a PSB that allows the application program to access just the *SLSREP, CUSTOMER, ORDERS,* and *PART* segments, while Figure 10.17b is a PSB that allows access to all segments of the *SALESDB* and *PARTDB* databases.

**Figure 10.17b**

PSB for a sample COBOL application program that will interact with all segments of the Premiere Products databases

```
10    PCB         TYPE=DB,DBNAME=SALESDB
11    SENSEG      NAME=SLSREP,PROCOPT=(G,I,R,D)
12    SENSEG      NAME=CUSTOMER,PARENT=SLSREP,PROCOPT=(G,I,R,D)
13    SENSEG      NAME=ORDERS,PARENT=CUSTOMER,PROCOPT=(G,I,R,D)
14    SENSEG      NAME=ORDLNE,PARENT=ORDERS,PROCOPT=(G,I,R,D)

15    PCB         TYPE=DB,DBNAME=PARTDB
16    SENSEG      NAME=PART,PARENT=0,PROCOPT=(G,I,R,D)
17    SENSEG      NAME=PORDLNE,PARENT=PART,PROCOPT=(G,I,R,D)

18    PSBGEN      LANG=COBOL,PSBNAME=EXAMPLE
```

### DL/I Data Definition in an Application Program

Once the DBD's and the PSB's have been defined and the databases have been loaded, application programs are written to manipulate the databases. How do the DBD's and PSB's interact with the application programs?

Briefly, if we are using COBOL, we define in the LINKAGE SECTION of the DATA DIVISION the PCBs from our authorized PSB and a number of status flags and control values. The COBOL program communicates with DL/I through CALL statements that access the data areas established in the LINKAGE SECTION. We also define within the WORKING-STORAGE SECTION the **function code** and **segment search arguments** (**SSA's**), both discussed in detail in the next section. The function code tells DL/I the database manipulation required, and the SSA's tell DL/I the specific segment occurrence, or occurrences, desired.

The exact details of how all this works are not critical for gaining an appreciation of the DL/I data definition process. What is critical is the process of creating DBD's and PSB's in preparation for manipulating the databases.

### *DL/I DATA MANIPULATION*

The Premiere Products *SALESDB* and *PARTDB* databases defined in the previous section will be used to describe the data manipulation capability of DL/I. The EXAMPLE PSB defined in Figure 10.17b will also be used. Figure 10.18 illustrates the occurrences of the *SALESDB* and *PARTDB* databases that will be used:

- There are three occurrences of the *SALESDB* database with Rep 1, Rep 2, and Rep 3 being occurrences of the root segment *SLSREP*.

- *CUSTOMER* segment occurrences are Cust A and Cust B for Rep 1, Cust Z for Rep 2, and Cust D, Cust E, and Cust F for Rep 3.
- Cust A, Cust Z, Cust D, and Cust F have no *ORDERS* segment occurrences. Cust B has OR 11 as its single *ORDERS* segment occurrence, while Cust E has OR 25 and OR 55 as its *ORDERS* segment occurrences.
- There are two occurrences of the *PARTDB* database, with LOCK and GAUGE as occurrences of the root segment *PART*.
- *ORDLNE* has five occurrences: the physical child of OR 11 and the logical child of GAUGE, which is one and the same entity, has five units ordered; the physical child of OR 11 and the logical child of LOCK has two units ordered; the physical child of OR 25 and the logical child of LOCK has three units ordered; the physical child of OR 55 and the logical child of LOCK has six units ordered; and the physical child of OR 55 and the logical child of GAUGE has eight units ordered.

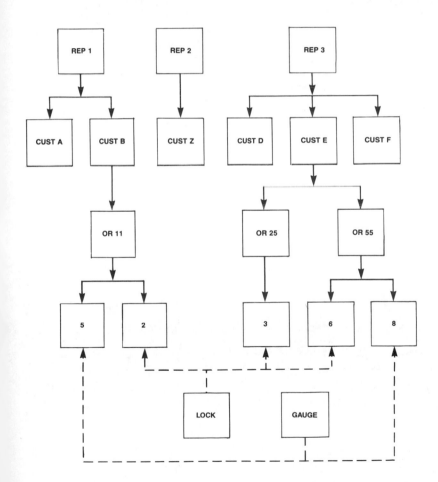

**Figure 10.18**

Three occurrences of *SALESDB* database, and two occurrences of *PARTDBD* database

An application program in a host language like COBOL interacts with the databases by using DL/I DML requests. A request is expressed as a CALL statement with a parameter list. The parameter list communicates to DL/I the following:

- the function code, or specific DL/I request
- the PCB being used
- the program record area, where DL/I places a retrieved segment occurrence or obtains one to place into the database,
- segment search arguments, which describe the segment(s) of the PSB to be manipulated

After executing the CALL, DL/I returns a value in the PCB's status code field. The application program tests this status code to determine the success or failure of the CALL statement just completed.

A summary of the DL/I function codes is shown in Figure 10.19. Rather than use the actual DL/I CALL syntax, we will use a simplified syntax to illustrate and explain each of these DL/I function codes.

| **Figure 10.19** | **Function Code** | **Description** |
|---|---|---|
| DL/I function code summary | GET UNIQUE (GU) | Direct retrieval of a segment occurrence that satisfies a given SSA |
| | GET NEXT (GN) | Sequential retrieval of the next segment occurrence using preorder traversal |
| | GET NEXT WITHIN PARENT (GNP) | Sequential retrieval of the next segment occurrence under current parent |
| | GET HOLD UNIQUE (GHU) | Same as GU, but allows subsequent DLET and REPL |
| | GET HOLD NEXT (GHN) | Same as GN, but allows subsequent DLET and REPL |
| | GET HOLD NEXT WITHIN PARENT (GHNP) | Same as GNP, but allows subsequent DLET and REPL |
| | DELETE (DLET) | Delete an existing segment occurrence |
| | REPLACE (REPL) | Replace an existing segment occurrence |
| | INSERT (ISRT) | Add a new segment occurrence |

## Get Unique (GU)

The **GET UNIQUE (GU)** function code is used for direct retrieval of a specific segment occurrence.

**GU Example 1:** Retrieving a Specific Root Segment

```
GU SLSREP (SLSRNUMB = 3)
```

This DL/I request retrieves the Rep 3 *SLSREP* root segment occurrence. In this example, GU is the function code, *SLSREP* is the segment name, *SLSRNUMB* is a field name within the *SLSREP* segment of the DBD, and "SLSREP (SLSRNUMB = 3)" is the segment search argument (SSA). This SSA is a *qualified SSA*, since the condition SLSRNUMB = 3 qualifies which specific segment occurrence is needed. After executing this request, the contents of the Rep 3 *SLSREP* segment occurrence are available for use by the application program. Since *SLSRNUMB* was declared as a unique field in the DBD, there is only one *SLSREP* segment occurrence with SLSRNUMB = 3. If, however, we had specified that *SLSREP* could have multiple occurrences with the same *SLSRNUMB* value, then this GU request would have retrieved the first occurrence having that *SLSRNUMB* value.

The **SSA** is a program data item whose value is "filled in" during execution of the program. For example, we would define the following:

```
03  SLSREP-SSA.
    05  FILLER              PIC X(19) VALUE
            "SLSREP   (SLSRNUMB = ".
    05  SLSREP-SSA-NUMBER  PIC 9(2).
    05  FILLER              PIC X     VALUE ")".
```

Then during execution of the program:

```
MOVE 3 TO SLSREP-SSA-NUMBER.
GU SLSREP-SSA
```

In all the examples that use SSA's, the equal (" = ") relational operator is used. DL/I, however, allows the use of these other relational operators: $> =$, $< =$, $>$, $<$, and NE.

**GU Example 2:** Retrieving a Specific Nonroot Segment

```
GU SLSREP    (SLSRNUMB = 3)
   CUSTOMER (CUSTNUMB = 'E')
   ORDERS    (ORDNUMB = 55)
```

For direct retrieval of a specific nonroot segment occurrence, SSA's are used to specify the hierarchical path to that segment occurrence. The three SSA's, "SLSREP (SLSRNUMB = 3)," "CUSTOMER (CUSTNUMB = 'E')," and "ORDERS (ORDNUMB = 55)," provide the hierarchical path to the OR 55 segment occurrence. After executing this DL/I request, the contents of the OR 55 *ORDERS* segment occurrence are available for use by the program. Only the *ORDERS* segment occurrence is retrieved; neither the *SLSREP* nor the *CUSTOMER* segment occurrences along the hierarchical path are retrieved.

Since the *SALESDB* is using HDAM, DL/I hashes on the *SLSRNUMB* of 3, goes directly to the Rep 3 *SLSREP* occurrence, sequentially searches *CUSTOMER* segment occurrences to find the one with *CUSTNUMB* of 'E', and then sequentially searches *ORDERS* segment occurrences to find the one with *ORDNUMB* of 55.

**GU Example 3:** Retrieving a Specific Nonroot Segment Using Unqualified SSA's

```
GU SLSREP
   CUSTOMER
   ORDERS      (ORDNUMB = 55)
```

Here we have omitted conditions for the first two SSA's, so DL/I will sequentially search the database until it finds the first *ORDERS* segment occurrence having an *ORDNUMB* of 55. DL/I ends up retrieving the same *ORDERS* segment, OR 55, that it did in the previous example. But since DL/I goes through the database sequentially, it typically takes more accesses and more time when we do not supply the SSA's. SSA's should be provided for each segment, if possible, to reduce overall processing time.

An SSA without a condition is called an *unqualified SSA*. The two unqualified SSA's in the example could be eliminated and OR 55 would still be retrieved. Thus, the following DL/I request is equivalent in that it produces identical results:

```
GU ORDERS (ORDNUMB = 55)
```

**GU Example 4:** Retrieving a Nonroot Segment Using All Unqualified SSA's

```
GU SLSREP
   CUSTOMER
   ORDERS
```

Since only unqualified SSA's are specified, DL/I sequentially searches from the first root segment occurrence and retrieves the very first *ORDERS* segment, OR 11 in Figure 10.18.

It is also possible to issue a GU command with no SSA's:

```
GU
```

In this case, DL/I retrieves the first root segment occurrence, Rep 1. In other words, this is a way to get to the start of the database at any time during processing.

**GU Example 5:** Root Segment With a Nonsequence Field SSA

```
GU SLSREP    (SLSRNAME = 'Jones, Mary')
```

An SSA does not have to consist of a sequence, or key, field. The sequence field for *SLSREP* is *SLSRNUMB*, and here *SLSRNAME* is being used for the *SLSREP* segment search field in the SSA. DL/I sequentially searches *SLSREP* segment occurrences until it finds the first one with a *SLSRNAME* of Mary Jones.

**GU Example 6:** Retrieving Multiple Segments With One Statement

```
GU SLSREP    *D(SLSRNUMB = 3)
   CUSTOMER  *D(CUSTNUMB = 'E')
   ORDERS     (ORDNUMB = 55)
```

In all previous GU examples, only the lowest-level segment occurrence was retrieved. In this example, one GU request is used to retrieve three segment occurrences: Rep 3, Cust E, and OR 55. An asterisk after the segment name indicates that one or more *command codes* will follow. In this case, the D command code is a **path call** requesting DL/I to additionally retrieve the occurrence of the segment named preceding the asterisk, both the *SLSREP* and *CUSTOMER* segments in the example. DL/I has several other command codes, but we will not discuss them further.

## Get Next (GN)

The **GET NEXT (GN)** function code retrieves the next segment occurrence sequentially in preorder traversal sequence. Typical use of the GN requires that a *current position* be established within the database prior to issuing the GN. The current position is the segment occurrence accessed by the most recently executed GU, GN, GNP, GHU, GHN, GHNP, or ISRT DL/I call.

There is one current position for each PCB. If the following requests were executed:

```
GU SLSREP     (SLSRNUMB = 1)
   CUSTOMER   (CUSTNUMB = 'B')
   ORDERS     (ORDNUMB = 11)
GU PART       (PARTDESC = 'LOCK')
```

then OR 11 would become the current position in the *SALESDB* database and LOCK would become the current position in the *PARTDB* database.

**GN Example 1:** Retrieval Without SSA's

```
GN
```

The effect of this DL/I request depends on the current position of the database. Let's assume the parameter list for this request points to the *SALESDB* PCB. If this is the very first DL/I request executed, then Rep 1, the first root segment occurrence, is retrieved. Recall that a GU request issued at any time without SSA's yields the same result. A GU always goes back to the start of the database, while the GN goes from the current position.

If we continued issuing this GN request, DL/I would retrieve in sequence every database segment occurrence from the current position of Rep 1. That is, DL/I would retrieve Cust A, Cust B, Or 11, the two *ORDLNE* segment occurrences for Or 11, Rep 2, Cust Z, and so on.

What if the application program needed to retrieve all descendant segment occurrences for a given *SLSREP* segment occurrence, for example, Rep 2? The program could issue a GU SLSREP (SLSRNUMB = 2) request to establish a current position at the needed root, followed by the execution of a loop issuing the GN request. But after Cust Z has been retrieved, there are no more descendant segments for Rep 2, so the next *SLSREP* segment occurrence of Rep 3 would be retrieved. How does the application program know this? A number of fields returned by DL/I, in addition to the status code and retrieved segment fields, can help. In particular, DL/I returns all sequence fields along the hierarchical path to the retrieved segment. Thus, after each segment occurrence is retrieved, the application program could check the SLSRNUMB-SEQUENCE-FIELD value and terminate the loop when it changed, as in the following:

```
GU SLSREP (SLSRNUMB = 2)
GN
PERFORM PROCESS-AND-GET-SEGMENTS
     UNTIL SLSRNUMB-SEQUENCE-FIELD NOT = 2.
    .
    .
    .
PROCESS-AND-GET-SEGMENTS.
   Process the segment occurrence.
   GN
```

**GN Example 2:** Retrieving All Occurrences of a Given Segment Type

To retrieve all root segments in the database, the program establishes a current position at the beginning of the database, using a GU request, then successively retrieves root segments, using a GN *SLSREP* request. The program checks the status code after each request and continues until the status code equals 'GB,' indicating the end of the database. The following illustrates the process:

```
GU
PERFORM PROCESS-ROOT-SEGMENTS
     UNTIL STATUS-CODE = 'GB'.
  .
  .
  .
PROCESS-ROOT-SEGMENTS.
     Process the root segment.
     GN SLSREP
```

A similar process is followed to retrieve all occurrences of a nonroot segment type. For example, to retrieve all *CUSTOMER* segment occurrences:

```
GU CUSTOMER
PERFORM PROCESS-CUSTOMER-SEGMENTS
     UNTIL STATUS-CODE = 'GB'.
  .
  .
  .
PROCESS-CUSTOMER-SEGMENTS.
     Process the CUSTOMER segment.
     GN CUSTOMER
```

**GN Example 3:** Retrieving Selected Occurrences of a Given Segment Type

Let's assume a customer can be serviced by more than one sales rep and that we want to retrieve all occurrences of Cust B in the database. The manner in which the program processes against the database is similar to that of the previous example, but it uses a qualified SSA to restrict retrieval to Cust B segment occurrences:

```
GU CUSTOMER (CUSTNUMB = 'B')
PERFORM PROCESS-CUSTOMER-SEGMENTS
     UNTIL STATUS-CODE = 'GB'.
  .
  .
  .
PROCESS-CUSTOMER-SEGMENTS.
     Process the CUSTOMER segment.
     GN CUSTOMER (CUSTNUMB = 'B')
```

### Get Next Within Parent (GNP)

The **GET NEXT WITHIN PARENT (GNP)** function code retrieves segment occurrences under the current parent in preorder traversal sequence. When a segment occurrence for the next parent is encountered, DL/I sets the status code to a value of "GE" to indicate that there are no more segment occurrences for the current parent. Either a GU or GN preceding the GNP establishes the current parent.

**GNP Example 1:** Retrieval Without SSA's

```
GU SLSREP (SLSRNUMB = 1)
GNP
PERFORM PROCESS-SEGMENTS
     UNTIL STATUS-CODE = 'GE'.
   .
   .
   .
PROCESS-SEGMENTS.
     Process the segment.
     GNP
```

The above retrieves all descendant segment occurrences under Rep 1 in hierarchical order: Cust A, Cust B, OR 11, and then the two *ORDLNE* occurrences. If GU SLSREP (SLSRNUMB = 1) is changed to GU CUSTOMER (CUSTNUMB = B), then OR 11 and the two *ORDLNE* occurrences are retrieved.

**GNP Example 2:** Retrieving Occurrences of a Given Segment Type

```
GU SLSREP (SLSRNUMB = 3)
    CUSTOMER
PERFORM PROCESS-CUSTOMER-SEGMENTS
     UNTIL STATUS-CODE = 'GE'.
   .
   .
   .
PROCESS-CUSTOMER-SEGMENTS.
     Process the segment.
     GNP CUSTOMER
```

The above causes DL/I to retrieve the three *CUSTOMER* segment occurrences under Rep 3: Cust D, Cust E, and Cust F. The GNP does not limit retrieval to the immediate child of the current parent. The application program, for example, could establish the current parent as Rep 3 and retrieve all *ORDERS* segment occurrences. OR 25 and OR 55 would be retrieved in the following example.

```
GU SLSREP (SLSRNUMB = 3)
   ORDERS
PERFORM PROCESS-ORDERS-SEGMENTS
     UNTIL STATUS-CODE = 'GE'.
   .
   .
   .
PROCESS-ORDERS-SEGMENTS.
   Process the segment.
   GNP ORDERS
```

## Get Hold

These three function codes work in precisely the same way as their counterparts without the HOLD. These HOLD versions must be used whenever a segment occurrence is to be changed or deleted. That is, prior to the use of a replace (REPL) or delete (DLET) function code, the segment occurrence to be replaced or deleted must be retrieved, using an appropriate GET HOLD.

## Delete (DLET)

Deleting a database segment occurrence is a two-step process. First, the segment occurrence to be deleted must be retrieved using one of the three GET HOLD function codes. Then the **DELETE (DLET)** function code is issued to remove that segment occurrence from the database. There must not be any intervening DL/I requests between these two steps. The following requests would remove Cust A from the database:

```
GHU SLSREP   (SLSRNUMB = 1)
    CUSTOMER (CUSTNUMB = 'A')
DLET
```

If the segment occurrence to be deleted has descendant segment occurrences, these occurrences will also be deleted. In the following example, not only is Cust B deleted, but OR 11 and its two *ORDLNE* occurrences are also deleted.

```
GHU SLSREP   (SLSRNUMB = 1)
    CUSTOMER (CUSTNUMB = 'B')
DLET
```

## Replace (REPL)

Changing the field values within a segment occurrence is a three-step process: the segment occurrence to be changed must be retrieved, using one of the three

GET HOLD function codes; the necessary changes are made to the field values within memory; the **REPLACE (REPL)** function code is issued to replace the retrieved segment occurrence in the database. The following changes the *ORDDTE* field value for OR 55 TO 021591:

```
GHU SLSREP (SLSRNUMB = 3)
    CUSTOMER (CUSTNUMB = 'D')
    ORDERS     (ORDNUMB = 55)
MOVE 021591 TO ORDDTE
REPL
```

There must not be any intervening DL/I requests between the GET HOLD and the REPL requests. Also, the value of a sequence field cannot be changed by using the REPL function code. Instead, the segment occurrence must be deleted, then added back to the database by using the ISRT function code.

### Insert (ISRT)

The **INSERT (ISRT)** function code is used to add a new segment occurrence to the database. Unlike the other database update functions of DLET and ISRT, a GET HOLD request is not issued prior to an ISRT request. Before a given segment occurrence can be added, the parent of that segment occurrence must already exist in the database. The segment occurrence is added in proper order, based on its sequence field. In the following example, the new *ORDERS* segment would be positioned under Cust E and between OR 25 and OR 55.

```
MOVE 40 TO ORDNUMB.
MOVE 090291 TO ORDDTE.
ISRT SLSREP    (SLSRNUMB = 3)
     CUSTOMER (CUSTNUMB = 'E')
     ORDERS
```

## DL/I AND THE FUNCTIONS OF A DBMS

In chapter 2 we discussed ten different functions of a DBMS. In this section we discuss how well DL/I, as a representative hierarchical DBMS, supports each of these ten functions.

DL/I adequately supports the following functions: a user-accessible catalog for data description; logical transactions; record-locking features to allow a shared update environment; full recovery services in the event of failure; and full utility services. These functions essentially operate as described in chapter 2, so they will not be discussed further here.

In the remainder of this section, we will briefly describe how well DL/I supports the following functions: storage and retrieval, security, data communications, integrity, and data independence.

## Storage and Retrieval

DL/I allows users to store, update, and retrieve data in a database. With both systems, although users do not need to know the exact internal structure of the database, some knowledge of the current structuring of the database is required by programmers and nontechnical end users for efficient processing.

In the case of DL/I, users must be able to navigate within the database through knowledge of the segments' hierarchical relationships and of key field and secondary indexing declarations. Structure changes are not accomplished easily in DL/I. Normally a reorganization of the database is required.

## Security

DL/I provides subschema and view capability through the program communication block (**PCB**). Access and update are limited to those segments and fields specified in the PCB.

DL/I also provides a full authorization system that restricts access to the system to authorized users. It also checks to make certain that a particular user can use a given transaction, and it can restrict transactions to specified terminals.

## Data Communications

DL/I can operate in a batch or an on-line mode. In the on-line mode, IMS/DC and CICS are the two teleprocessing monitors almost exclusively used.

## Integrity

DL/I handles data-type checking and uniqueness of primary keys (if defined as unique sequence fields). Also, because of its hierarchical structure, DL/I ensures that a child segment does not exist without its parent segment. However, if a parent segment is deleted, then all descendant segments are also deleted, so users must handle this situation themselves if this is not a proper action to be taken. Finally, users must create their own procedures to handle data verification.

### Data Independence

DL/I has some logical and physical data independence, although it falls far short of relational model systems in this area. Since the hierarchical structure of DL/I forces the user to navigate the database, changes within the hierarchical path used often necessitate procedural change by the user. For example, the addition of a new segment within the hierarchical path would require user procedural change. The addition of a new field to an existing segment within the hierarchical path would not require user procedural change unless the user needed access to the field. Logical and physical database changes outside the hierarchical path of the user obviously do not require user procedural change.

## COMPARISON OF THE THREE DATA MODELS

Now that the relational, CODASYL, and hierarchical data models have been described in detail, can we say which of the three is best suited to be the basis for a DBMS used to manage an enterprise's database? No universal answer is given by all database experts and by all enterprises utilizing a DBMS. Each data model has its proponents, and each enterprise can select from a large number of DBMS's conforming to each of the data models. A significant dollar investment has been made in each of the data models by vendors marketing DBMS's and by enterprises using these DBMS's.

Rather than abstractly deciding which is the best data model, it is more instructive to contrast the various models in terms of their respective advantages and disadvantages, some of which are inherent in the data models themselves; others are relative. Those advantages and disadvantages that are covered in this section are summarized in Figure 10.20.

**Figure 10.20**

Advantages and disadvantages of hierarchical, CODASYL, and relational data models

### Hierarchical Data Model Advantages

- Large current market penetration of IBM and DL/I
- Large number of available application packages
- Simplicity of hierarchical data model
- Good performance
- Good integrity support

### Hierarchical Data Model Disadvantages

- Difficulty in implementing nonhierarchical structures
- Problems adding/deleting segments
- Physical reorganization
- Minimal data independence
- Complexity
- Potential inefficient processing

## CODASYL Data Model Advantages

Figure 10.20

(continued)

- Longevity and availability of DBMS's for this model
- All data relationships may be modeled
- Standards exist for this model
- Good performance
- Data independence

## CODASYL Data Model Disadvantages

- Complex navigation
- Complexity

## Relational Data Model Advantages

- Simplicity
- High level of data independence
- Strong theoretical foundation

## Relational Data Model Disadvantages

- Performance needs improvement
- Referential integrity not supported

## Advantages of the Hierarchical Data Model

- IBM is the dominant force in the computer industry, and is committed to supporting the hierarchical data model through DL/I. IBM's continued support is based on the large number of enterprises using DL/I with large dollar investments in DL/I application systems. IBM's support means that enterprises can depend on future improvements in DL/I and can count on help in resolving current problems. DL/I is a proven DBMS in use since the late 1960s.

   The large base of knowledgeable enterprises, end users, programmers, and analysts for DL/I have formed organizations to address common problems and common needs and to interact as a common front with IBM in efforts to resolve them.
- A large number of application packages using DL/I are available, so an enterprise does not have to develop all its application systems internally.
- The hierarchical data model itself is simple, with a small number of commands needed to navigate the database. There are forms of each command available that make this model more nonnavigational than the CODASYL data model. For those applications having natural hierarchical relationships, the hierarchical data model lends itself simply to a database design solution.

- For application systems with fixed, predefined relationships that lend themselves to a hierarchical model or to an extended hierarchical model DBMS (like DL/I), performance is better than that provided by the relational model and no worse than that provided by the CODA-SYL model.
- Since adding a segment occurrence requires that the parent segment occurrence and other ancestors already exist in the database, integrity in this situation is provided.

## Disadvantages of the Hierarchical Data Model

- Many data relationships are not hierarchical. The biggest disadvantages of the hierarchical data model are the difficulty of representing many-to-many relationships and the limitation of allowing no more than one parent for a given segment type. Even in DL/I, where two parents — one physical, the other logical — are allowed, these constraints turn database design and performance tuning into challenging tasks. Solving these problems either creates unnatural data organization or introduces redundancy to the physical database.
- Even when the data relationships are hierarchical, the hierarchical data model can lead to problems. For example, if Premiere Products were to gain a new customer not associated with a sales rep, this customer could not be added to the database until he or she had been assigned to a sales rep. Or unintentional loss of data can occur when a segment is deleted, since all descendant segment occurrences are also automatically deleted.
- It is difficult to modify the structure of the physical database. Normally these modifications require reorganization and rebuilding of the physical database.
- There is minimal data independence. If a program is sensitive to segments that undergo physical restructuring either themselves or in relation to other hierarchical segments, the program will normally require modification.
- Powerful hierarchical DBMS's, such as DL/I, are complicated to understand and use. Premiums are paid to programmers, analysts, and designers who are competent in working effectively in the DL/I environment.
- Information requirements that do not follow the natural path of the hierarchy may be time-consuming to address. For example, if in Figure 10.1 a student were allowed to have more than one major and a report were needed for all students with their majors ordered by student number, then all student segment occurrences would need to be retrieved and sorted before the report could be produced.

## Advantages of the CODASYL Data Model

- CODASYL data model DBMS's have been available since the late 1960s, so a number of proven, successful DBMS's follow this model.
- There are no limitations on the types of data relationships that can be represented, in contrast to the hierarchical data model.
- The CODASYL data model is supported by various specification reports published by the Data Base Task Group and Data Description Language Committee.
- Performance is better than that of the relational data model and no worse than that of the hierarchical data model.
- This model supplies a degree of data independence in that an application program whose subschema does not reference a new record type or a changed record type does not have to be changed.

## Disadvantages of the CODASYL Data Model

- Application programs written to interact with CODASYL are complex in that they have to provide for navigation through the records and sets of the subschema used by the program.
- The CODASYL data model is not as natural as the relational data model and thus not as easy to understand and use.

## Advantages of the Relational Data Model

- The simplicity of the relational data model makes it easy to understand and use. The end user need not be concerned with the physical structuring of the database, so user requests can be nonprocedural in nature.
- This model supplies a high level of data independence, so both the physical and logical structures can be changed without affecting the application programs.
- The relational data model has a strong theoretical foundation. It is the focus of most database research today, which means that significant advances in database technology are most likely to occur with this model.

## Disadvantages of the Relational Data Model

- Poor performance is the biggest disadvantage of this model. Performance has improved, however, and is expected to improve more.

- Unlike the hierarchical and CODASYL data models, most relational DBMS's do not currently provide for referential integrity. A table record can be deleted without deleting dependent table records, and a table record can be added without the records it depends on in other tables being present. This is likely to be corrected in the near future.

## SUMMARY

In this chapter, we examined the hierarchical data model. The hierarchical model represents data relationships in the form of a tree structure. Each tree has a single root node at the top, with its descendants below it. Each child node has one parent node; each parent node can have multiple child nodes. Twin-node occurrences are children occurrences of the same node type with the same parent occurrence. Each node is accessed along a hierarchical path from top to bottom, beginning at the root node. Preorder traversal is an access method in which node occurrences are retrieved from top to bottom and left to right.

We discussed Data Language/I (DL/I), the database component of IBM's Information Management System (IMS). DL/I, in use since 1968, is an extended version of the hierarchical data model and is one of the most widely used DBMS's.

In DL/I a node is called a segment, and one tree structure occurrence is called a physical database record. The collection of physical database records for a given tree structure is called a physical database.

A DL/I logical database is an individual user view of the database. A logical database can be an entire physical database, a portion of one physical database, or portions of two or more physical databases.

DL/I permits the creation of linkages between segments, called logical relationships, which allow a segment to have both a physical parent segment and a logical parent segment. These linkages are made through pointer fields, which can form unidirectional or bidirectional logical relationships. The logical parent segment can be in the same physical database or in another physical database.

We studied DL/I's four physical database storage structures, called access methods. The hierarchical sequential access method (HSAM) stores segment occurrences sequentially in preorder traversal order. HSAM allows sequential access only and is used primarily for historical data retention. The hierarchical indexed sequential access method (HISAM) creates a separate index for the key field of the root segment. Both sequential and random access are permitted to the root segment, while access is sequential to dependent segments. The hierarchical direct access method (HDAM) uses a hashing technique for random access to the root segment. Either hierarchical or child-twin pointers provide access to dependent segments. The hierarchical indexed direct access method (HIDAM) allows sequential and random access through an index to the root segment and access to dependent segments through hierarchical or child-twin pointers. An inverted file structure, called secondary indexing, permits random access to nonroot segments.

A DL/I physical database is defined through a database description (DBD). The DBD defines all segments, fields, and hierarchical relationships, both physical and logical. A DL/I logical database is defined through a program specification block (PSB), in which program communication blocks (PCBs) define the sensitive segments accessible to a given program view.

DL/I segment retrieval is done through the GET UNIQUE, GET NEXT, GET NEXT WITHIN PARENT, and HOLD versions of these function codes. Segment updating is done through the DELETE, REPLACE, and INSERT function codes. These function codes can be used with or without segment search arguments (SSA's). The segment search argument forms can be qualified or unqualified.

We examined the manner in which DL/I furnishes the various functions of a DBMS. Finally, we compared the hierarchical, CODASYL, and relational data models by describing the advantages and disadvantages inherent in each model and relative to the two other models.

## REVIEW QUESTIONS

1. Define the following tree structure terms: node, branch, root, descendant, parent, child, and twin.
2. Explain the three constraints that apply to the general hierarchical model.
3. What is a hierarchical path? Compare it to preorder traversal access.
4. Explain the difference in DL/I between a physical database and a logical database.
5. Describe the method used by DL/I to allow a segment to have two parents. Include in your answer the name of this feature, the names of the parents, and an explanation of the unidirectional and bidirectional forms of this feature.
6. Explain the difference between the HSAM and HISAM access method.
7. Explain the difference between the HDAM and HIDAM access method.
8. What is a DBD? How does it differ from a DBD statement?
9. What is a virtual segment?
10. What is a PSB and how does it differ from a DBD?
11. How does a PCB relate to a PSB and to a DBD?
12. What is a SENSEG statement? How does it relate to a SEGM statement?

13. Which six DL/I function codes are used for retrieval? Which three are used for updating?
14. What is a segment search argument (SSA)? Name two situations in which an SSA is not used.
15. Explain current position. Which DL/I function codes establish current position?
16. Why would a GNP function code be used instead of a GN?
17. When is a GHU function code used instead of a GU?
18. What problem can occur if the DLET is not used carefully?
19. Which data model would you recommend? Justify your answer by listing its advantages over the other two data models.
20. Describe DL/I's security features.
21. What are some integrity shortcomings of DL/I?

## EXERCISES

1. Construct a data structure diagram that shows a virtual segment for the many-to-many relationship between *STUDENTS* and *COURSES*.
2. Construct an example of a qualified SSA and another example of an unqualified SSA, using the Premiere Products database. Use the DBD from Figure 10.15, the PSB from Figure 10.17b, and the occurrences in Figure 10.18.

Exercises 3 through 5 are based on the following information:
A database is needed to satisfy the following seven requirements:

(a) For a department, store its number (three characters) and name (twenty characters).
(b) For an employee, store his or her number (four characters) and name (twenty characters).
(c) For an insurance plan, store the plan number (four characters) and description (twenty characters).
(d) For a job history record, store the job classification (twenty characters) and starting date (six characters).
(e) Each department can have many employees, but each employee works in exactly one department.
(f) Each insurance plan serves many employees, but each employee is served by exactly one plan.
(g) Each employee can have several job history records, but each job history record corresponds to exactly one employee.

3. Draw a data structure diagram for the database. Indicate the fields that would be a part of each record.
4. Write the DBD for this physical database. Make logical choices for sequence fields. If more than one physical database is required and a logical relationship is needed, be sure to include the logical relationship properly in the DBD's.
5. Give a full PSB, permitting access to all segments for the DBD's defined.

Exercises 6 through 9 are based on Figure 10.21, which consolidates the data structure diagram and one physical database record for the example database used earlier in this chapter.

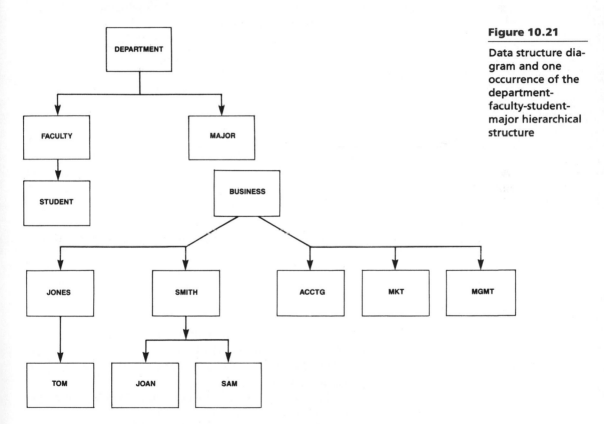

**Figure 10.21**

Data structure diagram and one occurrence of the department-faculty-student-major hierarchical structure

6. Write the DBD for this physical database. Assume there is one field per segment: DEPTNAME (fifteen characters), FACNAME (ten characters), STUNAME (twelve characters), and MAJNAME (eight characters) for segments named DEPT, *FACULTY, STUDENT,* and *MAJOR,* respectively. Assume that each field is a sequence field.

7. Give a full PSB permitting access to all segments for the DBD defined.
8. Which segment occurrences are retrieved with the following:

a. GU
   GN

b. GU DEPT
   GN STUDENT

c. GU DEPT
      FACULTY (FACNAME = 'Smith')
   GN STUDENT

d. GU DEPT
      FACULTY (FACNAME = 'Smith')
      STUDENT

e. GU STUDENT (STUNAME = 'Sam')
   GN
   GN

f. GU DEPT
      FACULTY (FACNAME = 'Smith')
   GNP STUDENT
   GNP STUDENT

9. Show the DL/I statements needed to perform the following actions:
   a. Retrieve all major segment occurrences.
   b. Delete 'Sam.'
   c. Delete all segments related to 'Jones.'
   d. Add student 'Paulette' to faculty 'Jones.'
   e. Modify major 'Mkt' so that it is called 'Finance' instead.

# REFERENCES

1] Atre, S., *Data Base: Structured Techniques for Design, Performance, and Management*, 2nd ed. John Wiley & Sons, Inc., 1988.
2] Date, C. J., *An Introduction to Database Systems, Volume I*, 4th ed. Addison-Wesley, 1986.
3] Hawryszkiewycz, I. T., *Database Analysis and Design*, SRA, 1984.
4] Hubbard, George U., "Computer-Assisted Hierarchical Database Design." In *Principles of Database Design Volume I: Logical Organizations*, S. Bing Yao. Prentice-Hall, 1985.
5] Kapp, Dan, and Leben, Joseph F., *IMS Programming Techniques: A Guide to Using DL/I*, Van Nostrand Reinhold, 1978.
6] McElreath, T. Jack, *IMS Design and Implementation Techniques*, Q.E.D. Information Sciences, Inc., 1979.
7] Tsichritzis, D. C., and Lochovsky, F. H., "Hierarchical Data-Base Management: A Survey," *ACM Computing Surveys* 8, no. 1 (March 1976).
8] Wiederhold, Gio, *Database Design*, 2d ed. McGraw-Hill, 1983.

# Physical Database Design

## INTRODUCTION

**Database design** takes place in two phases, **information-level design** and **physical-level design**. The goal of the information level is to produce a DBMS-independent design for a given set of user requirements. The design must be complete; that is, all user views must be included and all user requirements must be able to be satisfied. The design must also be correct. User views must be modeled correctly. All user restrictions must be present in the design and must be stated accurately. Some user restrictions, for example, "sales rep numbers are unique," will be implemented through primary keys. Others, such as "each customer in the database *must* have a sales rep," will be implemented through foreign keys. Still others, such as "credit limits are either 300, 500, 800, or 1,000," may be implemented through domain definitions or through stating them as special restrictions. The important point is that they must all be there, and must accurately reflect the actual restrictions of the organization. Finally, the information-level design must be clean. It must not contain any of the kinds of problems associated with non-3NF relations.

When the information-level design is complete, the physical-level design process, which is the subject of this chapter, can begin. The final information-level design is the input to the physical design process together with volume and usage figures, security requirements, recovery requirements, and characteristics of the DBMS that will be used to implement the system. Additionally, restrictions on data in the database form an important type of input to the physical process. If an information-level design does not include such restrictions, they must be listed separately as input to the physical design process. Since these restrictions are included in our information-level design, we do not need such a separate list.

The output of the process contains, at a minimum, a DBMS-processable schema; that is, a schema that can be implemented on the DBMS that will be used for the application. In addition, the output of this step may contain subschemas, program-design information, and information for the database administration and database operation functions. The subschemas produced will be subschemas necessary to support the individual user views. Program design information may contain tips for processing the database in the most efficient way to satisfy the requirements. It also *must* contain information concerning any restrictions that programs must enforce. (Remember, any restriction not enforcable by the DBMS must be enforced by the individual programs. Programmers must be aware of these restrictions.) Description of records, fields, relationships, domains, restrictions, program requirements, and so on, will be furnished to the database administration group for inclusion in the central data dictionary. Processing requirements and constraints will be furnished to operations.

One of the most important criteria for a physical-level design is adequate performance. We are concerned with such things as response time, system throughput, and utilization of disk space. It may very well be the case that some of the cleanness of the final information-level design is compromised in order to achieve adequate performance. Any such compromise must, of course, be thoroughly documented, and the data in the database must be closely monitored to ensure that it does not become inconsistent as a result of the compromise. (If the data is no longer in 3NF, inconsistencies are possible. Since programs must now enforce consistency, the possibility of a program error allowing inconsistent data in the database is very real.)

While some may treat the physical level of design as a single step, it usually works better to make it a two-step process. With this approach, the first step is to create a clean design for the particular type of DBMS that will be used. The result of the first step will be a legitimate implementation of the information-level design. No compromises will have been made, other than those forced upon us by the DBMS we are using. (If a portion of the information-level design contains foreign keys and our relational DBMS does not support foreign keys, for example, a compromise must be made. Likewise, if a portion of the information-level design could best be implemented using a recursive set and our CODASYL system does not support recursive sets, a compromise must be made.) However, we do not make any compromises that force our design to be in anything less than 3NF.

At this point, we have a legitimate design that can be implemented using our DBMS. The only remaining concern is adequate performance. If performance is not a major issue, we may not have to make any changes. If the database is relatively small, the demands may be light enough that spending more time in this part of the design process to improve the expected performance of the system would not be worthwhile. Often, however, this is not the case and a second step is necessary. In this step, we make changes to the design created in the first step to improve the performance of the overall application system being developed. This process is called **tuning**. Ideally, we want to *tune* the design so performance is optimal; that is, so that no other version of the design will produce better performance. In practice, this is almost an impossible task and we settle for tuning the design so the system will perform in an acceptable manner.

Finally, applications are designed, subschemas are created, program design information is created, and documentation is prepared for the various groups mentioned earlier. Once the system is in production, its performance will be periodically reviewed and some retuning may be necessary. The ideas and techniques used in the retuning are the same as those we will discuss in this chapter. In a way, retuning is easier than initial tuning, in that statistics on actual usage of the system can be gathered and used. In the original design process, we have no such statistics; rather, we have to deal with *predicted* usage patterns, and these are often imprecise.

We begin this chapter by discussing the process of creating an initial design for the type of DBMS in which we are interested. The process of creating such a design from our final information-level design is called **mapping**. We first focus on mapping to a relational model system, then on mapping to a CODASYL system. (These are the two types of systems most likely to be encountered in practice in the years to come). We also *briefly* discuss mapping to a hierarchical system. We next discuss the tuning step, the process of changing the design to improve performance. We also look at the problem of evaluating various alternative designs to determine the one whose performance is "best." Finally we discuss the process of designing the applications that will access the database.

## *MAPPING TO THE RELATIONAL MODEL*

An ideal **relational model** DBMS would include support for **primary keys** and **foreign keys**. **Nulls** would also be supported. In addition, there would be facilities to enforce restrictions on data in the database that were not merely consequences of primary and foreign key restrictions.

If we possess an ideal relational model DBMS, the mapping will be easy. Our final information-level design will effectively also be our physical-level design. The only potential difference between the two will be syntactical. Thus, the problem is merely to convert from the syntax of our information-level design to the syntax required for the DBMS. Unfortunately, most current DBMS's are not yet ideal. Thus, the methodology must address deficiencies in the DBMS.

## Methodology

The general methodology for mapping to a relational model DBMS is as follows:

1. Create the relations.
2. Implement the keys.
3. Implement nulls.
4. Implement special restrictions.

Each of these steps will now be addressed.

## Create the Relations

The relations in the physical design will be precisely those relations in the final information-level design. If the system supports domains, they should be used. If not, they should still be represented in the form of commentary for purposes of documentation in the physical design.

## Implement the Keys

Whatever facilities are present in the DBMS should be used. If the DBMS provides support for primary keys, primary keys should be implemented by the DBMS; if the DBMS provides support for foreign keys, foreign keys should be implemented by the DBMS; and so on. We need a way to implement these keys, however, in the event that they are *not* supported by the DBMS. If the DBMS does not provide the necessary support, that support must come from the programs that will access the database. This fact must be documented at this point, and this documentation must be furnished to any programmer who writes any program to access this database. It must indicate the restrictions to be enforced by the program, as well as tips on how most efficiently to implement them. With this in mind, we will discuss how each of the different types of keys should be treated in the event that support from the DBMS is lacking.

**Primary Keys.**   Programs must enforce the uniqueness of the primary key. They should also support efficient direct access, given a value for the primary key. The best way to accomplish both of these is to have the system create and maintain an index on the field or fields that constitute the primary key.

   If the system allows indexes to be specified as "unique," this should be done. The system will then at least enforce the uniqueness. If the system does not, then even this responsibility will fall on the shoulders of programmers.

To enforce uniqueness, programmers must attempt to find an existing record with a given key value before storing a new one, (e.g., before storing sales rep 4, the program should try to find sales rep 4 to determine if one already exists). Most mainframe systems do provide the option of specifying an index as unique, but many microcomputer systems do not.

**Alternate Keys.**   Since alternate keys by definition, are also unique, programs must enforce this uniqueness. The process described for the primary key also applies here.

**Secondary Keys.**   Since secondary keys are fields or combinations of fields that are of interest for retrieval purposes, the prime concern is supporting efficient retrieval given a value of the secondary key. The best way to do this is to create an index (not unique) on the fields that make up the secondary key.

**Foreign Keys.**   The process of supporting foreign keys in programs is much more involved than the processes required to support the other types of keys. To understand this process, consider the foreign key of *SLSRNUMB* within the *CUSTOMER* relation that must match the number of an actual sales rep in the *SLSREP* relation. Since *SLSRNUMB* is the primary key of the *SLSREP* relation, this primary key will be supported either through features of the DBMS or by programs, as described earlier. In addition, an index (not unique) will be built on the *SLSRNUMB* within the *CUSTOMER* relation.

When customer information is entered or modified, the program must check the *SLSREP* relation, using the primary key, *SLSRNUMB*, to ensure that the sales rep number entered for the customer is the number of a sales rep who actually exists in the database (unless it is null, and nulls are allowed, of course).

When an attempt is made to change the number of a sales rep in the *SLSREP* relation, the index on *SLSRNUMB* in the *CUSTOMER* relation will be used to determine whether there are any customers represented by this sales rep. If there are no such customers, the change is allowed. If there are customers represented by this sales rep, the action to be taken depends on the update restrictions for this foreign key. If update is restricted, the change is not allowed. If update cascades, the change is allowed, but then we must make a corresponding change for each customer represented by this sales rep. If update nullifies, the change is allowed, then the sales rep number for each customer currently represented by this sales rep is set to null.

When an attempt is made to delete a sales rep in the *SLSREP* relation, the index on *SLSRNUMB* in the *CUSTOMER* relation will again be used to determine whether there are any customers represented by this sales rep. If there are no such customers, the deletion is allowed. If there are customers represented by this sales rep, the action to be taken depends on the delete restrictions for this foreign key. If delete is restricted, the deletion is not allowed. If delete cascades, the deletion is allowed, but then each customer of this sales rep must also be deleted. If delete nullifies, the deletion is allowed, but then the sales rep number for all customers currently represented by this sales rep is set to null.

It should be pointed out that the processing just described may not be particularly complicated from a programming standpoint, particularly if a language like SQL is used. When it's time to change all the sales rep numbers of all customers currently represented by a given sales rep to the sales rep's new number, for example, all that is required is a single SQL command, such as:

```
UPDATE CUSTOMER
SET SLSRNUMB = NEWNUMB
WHERE SLSRNUMB = OLDNUMB
```

It is important that an index exists to make this process efficient, particularly if this operation is done with any frequency and if the number of customers is large.

Given a language like SQL, in which the processing just specified need not be overly cumbersome, and given the ability to create appropriate indexes to make the process reasonably efficient, it may seem as though the lack of support for foreign keys is not all that bad. The prime concern, however, is not the additional complexity in programs, but the fact that all programs must enforce these restrictions. If a single program does not, then the possibility of having data that violates our integrity constraints is very real. Further, we must disable the features of the system that allow users to enter data directly into the various relations, since this bypasses all the foreign key restrictions built into programs.

### Implement Nulls

No problem exists in this area if any fields that allow nulls were removed during the information-level design process to create entity subtypes. If, however, the final information-level design contains fields that are allowed to be null, and if the DBMS does not support nulls, then we must take special action. This action basically consists of two types. One type is to put the fields that are allowed to be null in separate relations, together with the key of the original relation, such as a relation with student number and dormitory number as its only attributes, student number being the key. This is really just the process of creating entity subtypes. In the preceding instance, we have created an entity subtype, namely, students who reside in dorms, which is a subtype of students. In many situations, this is the appropriate action. Often, this process will lead us to the realization that we do, in fact, have true entity subtypes. (You will note that this is an action usually taken during the information-level design. Sometimes, however, it can occur here.)

The other type of action is to support null fields by setting aside a certain value that will be treated as null by the programs accessing the database. An obvious choice would be space for character fields and zero for numeric fields. Sometimes these choices are, indeed, appropriate. Often, however, they are not. The value null is not a space or a zero. It means *unknown*. No real value can represent it. Further, in certain situations, zero might be a legitimate value for a given field. A customer might have a zero balance, whereas a null balance would mean that, for some reason, the customer's balance was not known, certainly a different situation. The best we can do is to determine a value the field can never legitimately assume. In one situation, zero might be appropriate; in another, –1 might be a better choice; in still another, we might choose 999999. The main concerns are, first, the ability to find such a "null" value and, second, the certainty that all programs accessing the database are aware of the meaning of this value and act upon it appropriately.

## Implement Special Restrictions

Any restrictions not already handled in other ways must be documented for programmers. The choice of style of documentation is not as important as the fact that these restrictions are all clearly documented in a fashion that will be useful to the programmers who must enforce them. They should be so organized that programmers can rapidly determine *all* the restrictions they must enforce.

## Example

Suppose we were given the **DBDL** design shown in Figure 11.1 on the next page. For simplicity, we have omitted format details for the various attributes. Neither are domains represented in this design. If they were, they would be used directly in a system that supports domains. Otherwise, they would appear only for documentation purposes. If a domain definition held any restrictions (credit limit must be 300, 500, 800, or 1,000), these would become special restrictions. In fact, this same restriction is represented as a special restriction in Figure 11.1.

Let's now create an appropriate physical design for a relational DBMS that corresponds to this information-level design. Let's assume we have a relational DBMS that does not support either primary or foreign keys but that does allow indexes to be specified as "unique;" that is, the system will prevent two rows in the table from having the same values in the columns on which the index is built.

**Figure 11.1**

**Sample DBDL**

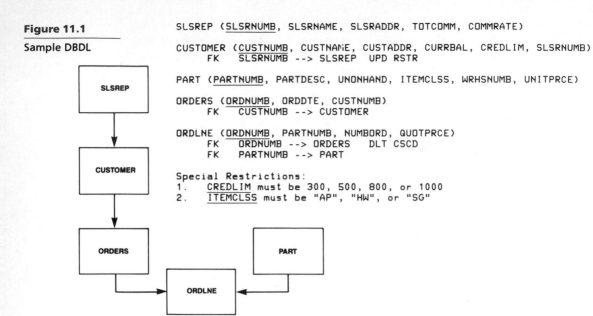

SLSREP (<u>SLSRNUMB</u>, SLSRNAME, SLSRADDR, TOTCOMM, COMMRATE)

CUSTOMER (<u>CUSTNUMB</u>, CUSTNAME, CUSTADDR, CURRBAL, CREDLIM, SLSRNUMB)
     FK   <u>SLSRNUMB</u> --> SLSREP  UPD RSTR

PART (<u>PARTNUMB</u>, PARTDESC, UNONHAND, ITEMCLSS, WRHSNUMB, UNITPRCE)

ORDERS (<u>ORDNUMB</u>, ORDDTE, CUSTNUMB)
     FK   <u>CUSTNUMB</u> --> CUSTOMER

ORDLNE (<u>ORDNUMB</u>, <u>PARTNUMB</u>, NUMBORD, QUOTPRCE)
     FK   <u>ORDNUMB</u> --> ORDERS   DLT CSCD
     FK   <u>PARTNUMB</u> --> PART

Special Restrictions:
1.   <u>CREDLIM</u> must be 300, 500, 800, or 1000
2.   <u>ITEMCLSS</u> must be "AP", "HW", or "SG"

1. *Create the relations.* Each relation in the DBDL representation becomes a relation in the design. These relations will be communicated to the DBMS, using whatever facilities are provided for this purpose.
2. *Implement the primary keys.* An index (unique) will be created for each primary key. In addition, enforcement of the primary keys will be listed in the set of restrictions that must be enforced by programmers.
3. *Implement the alternate keys.* In this example, there are none. If there were any, we would create an index (unique) on the alternate key and list the alternate key in the set of restrictions that must be enforced by programmers.
4. *Implement the secondary keys.* In this example, there are no secondary keys. If there were some, we would create an index (nonunique) on the secondary key. We would also document the existence of such an index for use in retrieval based on this secondary key.
5. *Implement the foreign keys.* For each foreign key, an index will be created. The foreign key will be listed in the set of restrictions that must be enforced by programmers.
6. *Implement nulls.* There are no fields within this design for which nulls are allowed; thus, the issue does not occur in this design. If it did, we would follow the steps given earlier.

7. *Implement special restrictions*. None of the special restrictions listed in the DBDL design can be supported directly by the DBMS. Thus, they must be included in the list of restrictions to be enforced by programmers. They can be listed in exactly the same form in which they are listed in DBDL.

The overall design is shown in Figure 11.2. Note that primary and foreign key restrictions are listed in separate categories and are not merely included with the special restrictions. This is owing to the special character and importance of these restrictions.

For additional information on creating physical designs for relational model systems, see [1], [2], [3], [4], [5], and [6].

———————— LIST OF RELATIONS ————————

SLSREP (SLSRNUMB, SLSRNAME, SLSRADDR, TOTCOMM, COMMRATE)

CUSTOMER (CUSTNUMB, CUSTNAME, CUSTADDR, CURRBAL, CREDLIM, SLSRNUMB)

PART (PARTNUMB, PARTDESC, UNONHAND, ITEMCLSS, WRHSNUMB, UNITPRCE)

ORDERS (ORDNUMB, ORDDTE, CUSTNUMB)

ORDLNE (ORDNUMB, PARTNUMB, NUMBORD, QUOTPRCE)

———— LIST OF FOREIGN KEY RESTRICTIONS ————

CUSTOMER
        FK    SLSRNUMB --> SLSREP        UPD RSTR

ORDERS
        FK    CUSTNUMB --> CUSTOMER

ORDLNE
        FK    ORDNUMB --> ORDERS        DLT CSCD
        FK    PARTNUMB --> PART

———————— SPECIAL RESTRICTIONS ————————

Special Restrictions:
1.    CREDLIM must be 300, 500, 800, or 1000
2.    ITEMCLSS must be "AP", "HW", or "SG"

**Figure 11.2**

**Relational model design (each primary key requires a unique index; each foreign key requires a non-unique index)**

## *MAPPING TO THE CODASYL MODEL*

The general methodology for mapping to a CODASYL model DBMS follows, with each of these steps being addressed.

1. Create records, fields, and sets.
2. Determine keys.
3. Determine location modes.

## Create Records, Fields, and Sets

The initial records in the physical design will be precisely the relations in the final information-level design. The fields for any record will be the attributes in the corresponding relation except for the foreign keys. (Remember that relationships in the CODASYL model are implemented through sets rather than foreign keys. Thus, there is no need for the foreign keys in our CODA-SYL design.) For each arrow in the data structure diagram, create a set. The record from which the arrow is pointing will be the owner record in the set and the record to which the arrow is pointing will be the member record.

## Determine Keys

We have already treated the foreign keys. We also need to treat the other three types of keys: primary, alternate, and secondary keys.

**Primary Keys.**   The primary key becomes, at least for now, the CALC key of the record, with duplicates *not* allowed. The only exception would be records in which all or part of the primary key has been removed as a foreign key. Such records will not have a CALC key.

**Alternate Keys.**   For any alternate keys, uniqueness must be ensured. We cannot make these CALC keys of the record in that this role has already been filled by the primary key. We must use some other features of the system. One of the two primary options would be to have the system maintain a unique index on this field (some systems designate such a field as a unique *alternate* key field). The other would be to create a system-owned set with this record as the member record type, sorted on this field. Duplicates must not be allowed within this set.

**Secondary Keys.**   By designating a field as a secondary key during the information-level design process, we are indicating that rapid retrieval based on a value in this field will be important. At this point, therefore, our task is to optimize retrieval on the field or fields that constitute this secondary key. The possibilities here are the same as those for alternate keys. The only difference is that we will not be ensuring uniqueness. The two main possibilities would thus be to have the system maintain an index (not unique) on this field. The second would again be to create a system-owned set with this record as the member record type, sorted on this field. In this case, duplicates must be allowed.

## Determine Location Modes

If a record has the primary key intact after the removal of foreign keys, then its **location mode** will be CALC on this primary key. If all or a portion of the primary key has been removed, then the location mode will be VIA SET. If the record participates as a member in more than one set, one of these will be chosen as the "VIA" set. At this point, it doesn't really matter which one. Factors influencing the choice will be discussed in the section on tuning the design for performance.

## Example

Let's suppose, again, we have been given the DBDL design shown in Figure 11.1. Now let's create an appropriate physical design for a CODASYL DBMS that corresponds to this information-level design. We will assume that we have a general CODASYL system.

1. *Create records, fields, and sets.* Each relation in DBDL becomes a record in the CODASYL design. The attributes of the relations (other than the foreign keys) become the fields in the records. The arrows in the data structure diagram become the sets. The records, fields, and sets are listed in Figure 11.3.

─────── **CODASYL RECORDS AND FIELDS** ───────

SLSREP (SLSRNUMB, SLSRNAME, SLSRADDR, TOTCOMM, COMMRATE)

CUSTOMER (CUSTNUMB, CUSTNAME, CUSTADDR, CURRBAL, CREDLIM, SLSRNUMB)

PART (PARTNUMB, PARTDESC, UNONHAND, ITEMCLSS, WRHSNUMB, UNITPRCE)

ORDERS (ORDNUMB, ORDDTE, CUSTNUMB)

ORDLNE (ORDNUMB, PARTNUMB, NUMBORD, QUOTPRCE)

─────── **CODASYL SETS** ───────

| SET | OWNER | MEMBER | COMMENT |
|-----|-------|--------|---------|
| SLSREP-CUSTOMER | SLSREP | CUSTOMER | |
| CUSTOMER-ORDERS | CUSTOMER | ORDERS | |
| ORDERS-ORDLNE | ORDERS | ORDLNE | |
| PART-ORDLNE | PART | ORDLNE | |

**Figure 11.3**

CODASYL records, fields, and sets

2. *Determine keys.* Primary keys are taken directly from the DBDL version at this point. Both parts of the primary key of *ORDLNE* were removed, so *ORDLNE* does not have a CALC key. For all other records, the primary key in the DBDL will be the CALC key of the record. There are no alternate or secondary keys in this example. If there were, they would be handled as just discussed.

3. *Determine location modes.* Any record whose primary key is intact after step three will have a location mode of CALC based on the primary key. Any record whose primary key has been either partially or completely removed will have a location mode of VIA SET. If there is more than one set to choose from, then one must be chosen. If there is not enough information to make an informed choice for the set, one may be chosen arbitrarily at this point. The result of this final step is shown in Figure 11.4.

For additional information concerning mapping to a CODASYL model, see [1], [3], [5], [6], and [7].

**Figure 11.4**

Updated list of records and fields (CALC keys underlined)

─────── CODASYL RECORDS AND FIELDS ───────

SLSREP (<u>SLSRNUMB</u>, SLSRNAME, SLSRADDR  TOTCOMM, COMMRATE)

CUSTOMER (<u>CUSTNUMB</u>, CUSTNAME, CUSTADDR, CURRBAL, CREDLIM)

PART (<u>PARTNUMB</u>, PARTDESC, UNONHAND, ITEMCLSS, WRHSNUMB, UNITPRCE)

ORDERS (<u>ORDNUMB</u>, ORDDTE)

ORDLNE (NUMBORD, QUOTPRCE)
       VIA ORDERS-ORDLNE

## MAPPING TO THE HIERARCHICAL MODEL

The main thrust of this chapter, as we noted, involves the process of physical design for a relational model DBMS or for a CODASYL DBMS. In this section, we will briefly touch on the process for hierarchical model systems.

When mapping to a hierarchical model system, the same rules discussed in the network model can also be applied to yield a network structure. This network must then be converted to a hierarchy or collection of hierarchies. In a system like IMS, for example, which supports logical child relationships between physical databases, the overall network could be replaced by physical databases, together with logical child relationships between them. Record types become segment types and sets become parent-child relationships. If a record type requires direct access (a CALC record in the CODASYL version), then either the corresponding segment should be the root of a physical database (which gives direct access capabilities), or some other feature should be used to provide the access.

In designs for hierarchical systems, the same final rule applies that applied to the models covered earlier: whatever the DBMS won't support must be handled by the application programs themselves and this fact *must* be documented.

For additional information concerning mapping to the hierarchical model, see [1], [3], [5], and [6].


## TUNING FOR PERFORMANCE

By applying one of the techniques described in the previous sections, we have created a legitimate, clean design that can be implemented using the DBMS that has been chosen. At this point, we begin the process of **tuning** the design, or making changes to improve the performance of the final system. To effectively accomplish this tuning, we must know the kinds of changes we can make to a design, the advantages and disadvantages associated with each type of change, and, finally, a way to choose between alternative designs created in this process. In this section, we will discuss the types of changes that can be made, together with the associated advantages and disadvantages. In the next section, we will examine the problem of choosing from among various alternative designs we might produce.

The changes discussed will be grouped according to whether they apply to a relational model system, a CODASYL system, or any system.


### Relational Model

**Splitting Relations.**   A relation may be split into two or more relations that each have the same key as the original relation and that collectively contain all the columns of the original relation. For example, the relation

```
CUSTOMER (CUSTNUMB, CUSTNAME, CUSTADDR, CURRBAL, CREDLIM,
          SLSRNUMB)
```

could be split into the two relations

```
CUSTADDR (CUSTNUMB, CUSTNAME, CUSTADDR)
```

and

```
CUSTFIN (CUSTNUMB, CUSTNAME, CURRBAL, CREDLIM, SLSRNUMB)
```

(Figure 11.5 shows a sample extension of the relation *CUSTOMER* with data from the Premiere Products database. Figure 11.6 shows sample extensions of the relations *CUSTADDR* and *CUSTFIN* with the same data.) The original relation could be reconstructed, when needed, by joining these two relations on the customer number.

**Figure 11.5**

*CUSTOMER* relation for Premiere Products

CUSTOMER

| CUSTNUMB | CUSTNAME | CUSTADDR | CURRBAL | CREDLIM | SLSRNUMB |
|---|---|---|---|---|---|
| 124 | Adams, Sally | 481 Oak,Lansing,MI | 418.75 | 500 | 3 |
| 256 | Samuels, Ann | 215 Pete,Grant,MI | 10.75 | 800 | 6 |
| 311 | Charles, Don | 48 College,Ira,MI | 200.10 | 300 | 12 |
| 315 | Daniels, Tom | 914 Cherry,Kent,MI | 320.75 | 300 | 6 |
| 405 | Williams, Al | 519 Watson,Grant,MI | 201.75 | 800 | 12 |
| 412 | Adams, Sally | 16 Elm,Lansing,MI | 908.75 | 1000 | 3 |
| 522 | Nelson, Mary | 108 Pine,Ada,MI | 49.50 | 800 | 12 |
| 567 | Baker, Joe | 808 Ridge,Harper,MI | 201.20 | 300 | 6 |
| 587 | Roberts, Judy | 512 Pine,Ada,MI | 57.75 | 500 | 6 |
| 622 | Martin, Dan | 419 Chip,Grant,MI | 575.50 | 500 | 3 |

**Figure 11.6**

Result of splitting *CUSTOMER* relation

CUSTADDR

| CUSTNUMB | CUSTNAME | CUSTADDR |
|---|---|---|
| 124 | Adams, Sally | 481 Oak,Lansing,MI |
| 256 | Samuels, Ann | 215 Pete,Grant,MI |
| 311 | Charles, Don | 48 College,Ira,MI |
| 315 | Daniels, Tom | 914 Cherry,Kent,MI |
| 405 | Williams, Al | 519 Watson,Grant,MI |
| 412 | Adams, Sally | 16 Elm,Lansing,MI |
| 522 | Nelson, Mary | 108 Pine,Ada,MI |
| 567 | Baker, Joe | 808 Ridge,Harper,MI |
| 587 | Roberts, Judy | 512 Pine,Ada,MI |
| 622 | Martin, Dan | 419 Chip,Grant,MI |

CUSTFIN

| CUSTNUMB | CUSTNAME | CURRBAL | CREDLIM | SLSRNUMB |
|---|---|---|---|---|
| 124 | Adams, Sally | 418.75 | 500 | 3 |
| 256 | Samuels, Ann | 10.75 | 800 | 6 |
| 311 | Charles, Don | 200.10 | 300 | 12 |
| 315 | Daniels, Tom | 320.75 | 300 | 6 |
| 405 | Williams, Al | 201.75 | 800 | 12 |
| 412 | Adams, Sally | 908.75 | 1000 | 3 |
| 522 | Nelson, Mary | 49.50 | 800 | 12 |
| 567 | Baker, Joe | 201.20 | 300 | 6 |
| 587 | Roberts, Judy | 57.75 | 500 | 6 |
| 622 | Martin, Dan | 575.50 | 500 | 3 |

*ADVANTAGES:* Even if a user accesses only certain columns within a relation, the remaining columns must still be transported from disk to memory. If the relation contained only the columns required by this user, his or her processing would be more efficient (less data to transport for each occurrence of the relation, more occurrences of the relation placed in a block on disk). If this user has very heavy processing requirements, the whole system may benefit through the creation of a relation tailored to his or her needs and a separate relation containing all the other columns. Additionally, splitting can be used for security purposes. In the preceding example, financial details have been separated from address details. The financial relation may not even be available to users who are not authorized to access financial data, in which case an added measure of security is provided.

*DISADVANTAGES:* Any user requiring data from both relations needs to do a join operation to obtain the required data. Since the relations in question will be joined on their primary keys, this type of join will be fairly efficient. It still requires extra activity, however, that would not be required if the relations had not been split. In many cases, any benefits obtained by the splitting are negated by the additional overhead experienced by this type of user. Another disadvantage is that the primary key must appear in both relations and an index must be created on this primary key for both relations. Thus, there is a potentially significant increase in the space that is required for the database.

**Combining Relations.**   Combining relations is exactly the opposite of splitting them. If two or more separate relations exist that have the same primary key, they may be combined into a single relation. For example, we could combine

```
CUSTADDR (CUSTNUMB, CUSTNAME, CUSTADDR)
```

and

```
CUSTFIN (CUSTNUMB, CUSTNAME, CURRBAL, CREDLIM, SLSRNUMB)
```

producing

```
CUSTOMER (CUSTNUMB, CUSTNAME, CUSTADDR, CURRBAL, CREDLIM,
          SLSRNUMB)
```

Since this process is exactly the opposite of the previous one, the same discussion of advantages and disadvantages applies here, only with the roles reversed.

**Denormalizing.** Even though relations in 3NF are desirable to prevent the types of problems discussed in chapter 6, we will occasionally make compromises in this area for the sake of performance. By "denormalizing," we mean converting relations that are in 3NF to something less than 3NF. This process introduces the problems alluded to previously, but it can decrease the number of disk accesses required by certain types of transactions, thus potentially increasing the overall efficiency of the system. The advantages of this increased efficiency must, of course, be weighed against the disadvantages associated with not being in 3NF. There are some database professionals who feel that no increase in performance can outweigh these disadvantages. Others, however, feel that there are times when performance requirements can necessitate such compromises.

**1NF.** We might choose to convert relations into non-1NF relations. As an example, consider the combination of *ORDERS* and *ORDLNE* within the Premiere Products database, as shown in Figure 11.7. If we have a system that will support repeating groups in some fashion (many will not), we could choose to combine these into a single *ORDERS* relation with repeating groups for the order lines, as shown in Figure 11.8. Since each row in this new relation represents an order, together with all the order lines for the order, by accessing this single row we might have all the information about the order that we need. If we need to find any further information about the parts on each of the order lines, we would require further disk accesses, but, even in this case, we wouldn't need to go through the *ORDLNE* relation to get there.

**Figure 11.7**

*ORDERS* and *ORDLNE* relations for Premiere Products

ORDERS

| ORDNUMB | ORDDTE | CUSTNUMB |
|---------|--------|----------|
| 12489 | 90291 | 124 |
| 12491 | 90291 | 311 |
| 12494 | 90491 | 315 |
| 12495 | 90491 | 256 |
| 12498 | 90591 | 522 |
| 12500 | 90591 | 124 |
| 12504 | 90591 | 522 |

ORDLNE

| ORDNUMB | PARTNUMB | NUMBORD | QUOTPRCE |
|---------|----------|---------|----------|
| 12489 | AX12 | 11 | 14.95 |
| 12491 | BT04 | 1 | 402.99 |
| 12491 | BZ66 | 1 | 311.95 |
| 12494 | CB03 | 4 | 175.00 |
| 12495 | CX11 | 2 | 57.95 |
| 12498 | AZ52 | 2 | 22.95 |
| 12498 | BA74 | 4 | 4.95 |
| 12500 | BT04 | 1 | 402.99 |
| 12504 | CZ81 | 2 | 108.99 |

**ORDERS**

| ORDNUMB | ORDDTE | CUSTNUMB | PARTNUMB | NUMBORD | QUOTPRCE |
|---------|--------|----------|----------|---------|----------|
| 12489 | 90291 | 124 | AX12 | 11 | 14.95 |
| 12491 | 90291 | 311 | BT04<br>BZ66 | 1<br>1 | 311.95<br>402.99 |
| 12494 | 90491 | 315 | CB03 | 4 | 175.00 |
| 12495 | 90491 | 256 | CX11 | 2 | 57.95 |
| 12498 | 90591 | 522 | AZ52<br>BA74 | 2<br>4 | 4.95<br>22.95 |
| 12500 | 90591 | 124 | BT04 | 1 | 402.99 |
| 12504 | 90591 | 522 | CZ81 | 2 | 108.99 |

**Figure 11.8**

Result of combining *ORDERS* and *ORDLNE* relations for Premiere Products (creating a non-1NF relation)

*ADVANTAGES:* As discussed before, the advantage is that certain kinds of retrieval are more efficient. In this case, the retrieval of an order and all the associated order lines will be more efficient than it would be with a separate *ORDLNE* relation.

*DISADVANTAGES:* One disadvantage of the non-1NF structure is that many systems do not support repeating groups. Even if a system does support them, there are problems that make them unattractive. Usually, a fixed number of occurrences of the repeating group (in this case a fixed number of order lines) must be specified. Once this has been done, any order with fewer order lines is wasting space, and any order with more order lines than this maximum number causes a real problem. In addition, certain types of processing (such as listing for a given part all the orders on which it is present) become considerably more complex.

**2NF.** We might choose to convert relations into non-2NF relations. If, in the Premiere Products database, the only part information we needed when processing all the order lines for a given order were the part description, we might choose to include the part description in the *ORDLNE* relation, as shown in Figure 11.9 on the next page. The relation is not in 2NF, since part description depends only on the part number, which is just a portion of the key for the *ORDLNE* relation. This procedure would, however, permit us to obtain the description of the part on a given order line without requiring that we access the *PART* relation.

**Figure 11.9**

Including description in *ORDLNE* relation (creating a non-2NF relation)

ORDLNE

| ORDNUMB | PARTNUMB | PARTDESC | NUMBORD | QUOTPRCE |
|---------|----------|----------|---------|----------|
| 12489 | AX12 | IRON | 11 | 14.95 |
| 12491 | BT04 | STOVE | 1 | 402.99 |
| 12491 | BZ66 | WASHER | 1 | 311.95 |
| 12494 | CB03 | BIKE | 4 | 175.00 |
| 12495 | CX11 | MIXER | 2 | 57.95 |
| 12498 | AZ52 | BASEBALL | 2 | 22.95 |
| 12498 | BA74 | SKATES | 4 | 4.95 |
| 12500 | BT04 | STOVE | 1 | 402.99 |
| 12504 | CZ81 | WEIGHTS | 2 | 108.99 |

*ADVANTAGES:* Again, certain types of retrieval become more efficient. In the example, the process of listing for a given order all the order lines within the order, giving the part number, description, number ordered, and quoted price, is more efficient, since this query will no longer involve the PART relation as it would with the original design.

*DISADVANTAGES:* The fact that the relation is not in 2NF creates redundancy and update problems.

**3NF.**   We might choose to convert relations into non-3NF relations. If, in the Premiere Products database, we frequently need to retrieve both the number *and the name* of the sales rep who represents a particular customer, we might choose to store the sales rep's name as part of the *CUSTOMER* relation, as shown in Figure 11.10. This relation is not in 3NF. It would, however, allow us to obtain the name of the sales rep who represents a customer at the same time we retrieve the customer without requiring any further accesses.

**Figure 11.10**

Including *SLSRNAME* in *CUSTOMER* relation (creating a non-3NF relation)

CUSTOMER

| CUST NUMB | CUSTNAME | CUSTADDR | CURRBAL | CRED LIM | SLSR NUMB | SLSRNAME |
|-----------|----------|----------|---------|----------|-----------|----------|
| 124 | Adams, Sally | 481 Oak,Lansing,MI | 418.75 | 500 | 3 | Jones, Mary |
| 256 | Samuels, Ann | 215 Pete,Grant,MI | 10.75 | 800 | 6 | Smith, William |
| 311 | Charles, Don | 48 College,Ira,MI | 200.10 | 300 | 12 | Brown, Sam |
| 315 | Daniels, Tom | 914 Cherry,Kent,MI | 320.75 | 300 | 6 | Smith, William |
| 405 | Williams, Al | 519 Watson,Grant,MI | 201.75 | 800 | 12 | Brown, Sam |
| 412 | Adams, Sally | 16 Elm,Lansing,MI | 908.75 | 1000 | 3 | Jones, Mary |
| 522 | Nelson, Mary | 108 Pine,Ada,MI | 49.50 | 800 | 12 | Brown, Sam |
| 567 | Baker, Joe | 808 Ridge,Harper,MI | 201.20 | 300 | 6 | Smith, William |
| 587 | Roberts, Judy | 512 Pine,Ada,MI | 57.75 | 500 | 6 | Smith, William |
| 622 | Martin, Dan | 419 Chip,Grant,MI | 575.50 | 500 | 3 | Jones, Mary |

Another type of change that would create non-3NF relations is the inclusion of the number of the sales rep who represents the customer in the *ORDERS* relation, as shown in Figure 11.11. Since customer number determines sales rep number but is not an alternate key for the *ORDERS* relation, this relation is no longer in 3NF. If, given an order, there is a need to find the sales rep who corresponds to the order without finding the customer, or if, given a sales rep, there is a need to find all the orders that correspond to that sales rep without finding the corresponding customers, retrieval will be more efficient with this new structure. Without it, we would have to go through the *CUSTOMER* record to get from the *ORDERS* record to the *SLSREP* record (or vice versa), even though customer data was not needed for the retrieval.

ORDERS

| ORDNUMB | ORDDTE | CUSTNUMB | SLSRNUMB |
|---------|--------|----------|----------|
| 12489   | 90291  | 124      | 3        |
| 12491   | 90291  | 311      | 12       |
| 12494   | 90491  | 315      | 6        |
| 12495   | 90491  | 256      | 6        |
| 12498   | 90591  | 522      | 12       |
| 12500   | 90591  | 124      | 3        |
| 12504   | 90591  | 522      | 12       |

**Figure 11.11**

Including *SLSRNAME* in *ORDERS* relation (creating a non-3NF relation)

*ADVANTAGES:* Once again, certain types of retrieval become more efficient. In the first example, the process of listing for a given customer data that includes the name of the customer's sales rep will be more efficient, since this query will no longer involve the *SLSREP* relation as it would with the original design. In the second example, listing information that involves the relationship between sales reps and orders without requiring any customer data will be more efficient, since no customer data need be retrieved along the way.

*DISADVANTAGES:* The fact that the relation is not in 3NF creates redundancy and update problems.

**Creating Indexes.**   Processing that involves finding occurrences of relations based on values in certain columns can be enhanced if there is an index on these columns. This type of processing includes accessing the database based on a primary key (finding information about a sales rep given the sales rep's number), accessing the database based on a secondary key (finding the name of all customers who have a $500 credit limit), and joining two relations together (joining the sales rep and the customer relations based on matching sales rep numbers). If we anticipate the need for such processing, we should strongly consider creating an appropriate index.

*ADVANTAGES:* The existence of such an index will greatly expedite the database retrieval that must take place.

*DISADVANTAGES:* An index involves overhead. The index itself occupies space on the disk. Further, any change made to the database that affects the index (adding new rows, deleting old rows, changing a value in a column on which the index is built) requires updating the index. Trying to build indexes on all combinations of columns, as some people have tried to do, will create a system that works wonderfully for retrieval purposes but disastrously when it comes to update.

## CODASYL Model

**Splitting or Combining Records.**  The same discussion of splitting or combining relations applies equally well to the CODASYL model. Records could be split or combined for exactly the same reasons. The same discussion of advantages and disadvantages applies.

**Denormalizing.**  The discussion concerning denormalizing also applies as well to the CODASYL model as it does to the relational model. The same discussion of advantages and disadvantages applies.

**System-owned Sets.**  A **system-owned set** (also called a **singular set**) is one in which the owner is specified as "SYSTEM." There is only one occurrence of such a set. It consists of a single chain through all the member occurrences. If the member record type is *CUSTOMER*, for example, this occurrence would be a single chain linking all customers. A requirement to list all customers could then be satisfied by retrieving all the member occurrences within this set, as demonstrated in Example 5 of chapter 9. Without such a set, we might very well need to sequentially scan the entire database, picking up just the customers for our report, as in Example 4 of chapter 9.

Is sequentially scanning the database just to retrieve customers a bad idea? From a programming standpoint, the answer is no. The code in Example 4 of chapter 9 is almost identical to that in Example 5. In terms of efficiency, however, there can be a big difference. To illustrate this difference, suppose that the database consists of 100 pages, there are 1,000 customers, the DBMS reads one page at a time, and we want to produce a report listing all the customers.

## Q & A

| | |
|---|---|
| Question: | How many disk accesses will be required if we sequentially scan the entire database? |
| Answer: | The DBMS would begin by reading the first page into memory. Each record on this page is examined to determine whether it is a customer. Once a customer is found, the DBMS returns it to the program. When the program requests the next customer, the DBMS continues scanning the page already in memory. This does not require another disk access. Only when the complete page has been examined will the DBMS read the next page. In this process, each page is read exactly once. Since there are 100 pages, there would be 100 disk accesses. |
| Question: | How many disk accesses will be required if we use a system-owned set? |
| Answer: | The DBMS would begin by reading the first member within this set. Assuming that the location mode for the *CUSTOMER* record is CALC (as it almost certainly would be), this customer would be located on the page determined by applying the hashing function to the customer number. The request to retrieve the next customer would require another disk access unless, by chance, the hashing function happened to have produced the same page for both customers. Since it is highly unlikely that two consecutive customers would be placed on the same page, most requests for the next customer would probably require an additional disk access. Thus, we would expect close to 1,000 disk accesses to retrieve the 1,000 customers in the database. |

From these calculations, it might appear that system-owned sets are actually less efficient. This is not necessarily the case. For example, suppose we want to list all the sales reps in the database. Suppose, as before, the database contains 10 pages and suppose there are twenty sales reps. The same analysis we used for customers would show that retrieving all twenty sales reps using a sequential scan would require 100 disk accesses, whereas retrieving them using a system-owned set would only require twenty disk accesses. In this case, a system-owned set would clearly be beneficial.

*ADVANTAGES:* If there are substantially fewer occurrences of a given type of record than there are pages in a database, using a system-owned set can make retrieval of all occurrences of the record much more efficient than a sequential scan.

*DISADVANTAGES:* There is an extra set to maintain. In addition, if the number of occurrences of the record is large in relation to the size of the database, using the system-owned set is actually less efficient than a sequential scan.

**Adding Sets.**    In the discussion on changes to a relational database, an example was given in which it was necessary to retrieve data on sales reps and related orders but not on the customers in between. A change to the structure to make this retrieval more efficient was discussed. A similar change can be made to a CODASYL database by adding an extra set, in this example a set in which the owner is *SLSREP* and the member is *ORDERS*. The new structure is shown in Figure 11.12.

**Figure 11.12**

Including additional set

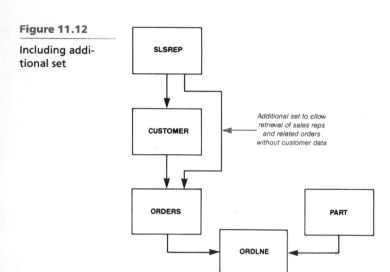

*Additional set to allow retrieval of sales reps and related orders without customer data*

ADVANTAGES: Retrieval of sales rep data and related order data that does not require intermediate customer data will be more efficient, since less data must be retrieved.

DISADVANTAGES: There is an extra set to maintain. Added pointer space is required in the database which is technically unnecessary (all required processing could still be done in the absence of this set). There may also be a problem with consistency of data. If order 12489 is owned by customer 124 in CUSTOMER-ORDERS and customer 124 is, in turn, owned by sales rep 3 in SLSREP-CUSTOMER, but order 12489 is owned by sales rep 6 in SLSREP-ORDERS, the data is inconsistent.

**Including Key of Owner in Member Record.**    Including the key of an owner record in a member record (e.g., including the number of the sales rep in the customer record in the Premiere Products database) is unnecessary in a CODASYL system. The relationship between sales reps and customers is accomplished through the set *SLSREP-CUSTOMER*, not by having the sales rep number as a field within the customer record. It is only within the relational model that such an inclusion would be necessary.

There is a reason why we might choose to make such an inclusion, however. A given type of transaction that requires directly retrieving customer data *and* the customer's sales rep's number, but no other sales rep data, would be more efficient. In processing such a transaction there would then be no need to find the owner within *SLSREP-CUSTOMER* after retrieving the customer. (The set would now be termed "inessential.") If the volume of this type of transaction is sufficiently large, such a change might be warranted.

*ADVANTAGES:* The advantage has already been discussed. The processing of certain types of transactions becomes more efficient.

*DISADVANTAGES:* Since including the presence of the key of the owner within the member record is technically unnecessary, it is a waste of space. Further, the value in this field had better agree with the value of the key in the owner record. This makes the update of the key of the owner record a more complex process. Not only would the sales rep number in the *SLSREP* record need to be changed, but also the sales rep number in the customer records of those customers whom the sales rep represents would need to be changed. Also, most CODASYL systems will not enforce consistency in values between the owner record and the member records, although the later CODASYL specifications do include a CHECK clause within the SET definitions that will cause the system to enforce such consistency.

**Changing CALC Record to VIA SET.**   If the primary key of a record was left intact after removing the foreign keys, the methodology indicated that the location mode of the record was to be CALC on this primary key. If there is a need to access records of this type, which are directly based on the foreign key, with any frequency, this is probably an appropriate choice. If, however, records of this type are usually accessed some other way, we might consider changing the location mode from CALC to VIA SET. In the Premiere Products database, for example, if orders are usually accessed through the customer who placed the order rather than directly, we could make the location mode of the ORDER record as VIA *CUSTOMER-ORDERS*. This will then cause each order to be placed as close as possible to the customer who placed the order. In turn, retrieving a customer and all the orders placed by the customer becomes a very efficient process. However, we have lost the ability to directly retrieve an order based on the order number alone.

*ADVANTAGES:* One advantage has already been mentioned. Retrieving a customer and all associated orders becomes more efficient. Another advantage is that since the order record is no longer CALC, there is no need for the CALC chain pointer and, thus, less storage space is required for each order.

*DISADVANTAGES:* The disadvantage has also already been mentioned. Retrieving an order directly based on the order number is no longer possible. Any transaction requiring such a retrieval will have to include some type of search of the database, rather than a simple FIND ANY command. This not only makes the logic involved in the transaction more complicated, but also makes processing such a transaction less efficient.

**Changing VIA SET Record to CALC.** Consider the link record, *ORDLNE*, within the CODASYL version of the Premiere Products database. The process of finding the order line for order 12491, part BZ66, entails more than a simple FIND command. Rather, it requires a search routine, as shown in chapter 9. Further, the attempt to store a second order line for order 12491, part BZ66, will *not* be rejected by the DBMS, since no duplicates clause is being violated. Thus, the burden of ensuring that duplicate order lines are not stored in the database falls to the programmers, something we would like to avoid.

A change to the design can be made that will both simplify the direct retrieval of an order line and allow the DBMS to reject duplicates. To accomplish both of these objectives requires two changes. First, we include the keys of both owner records, *ORDERS* and *PART*, within the *ORDLNE* record. Second, instead of a location mode of VIA SET, the *ORDLNE* record will be CALC on the concatenation of *ORDNUMB* and *PARTNUMB*, with duplicates not allowed. With this change to the design, filling in both the order number and the part number and then executing the command

```
FIND ANY ORDLNE
```

allows us to directly find a specific order line. In addition, an attempt to store a second order line for order 12491, part BZ66, will be rejected by the DBMS as a duplicate.

The general process entails including the keys of one or more owner records in the member record, as discussed earlier, and making the location mode of the member record CALC on these included keys.

*ADVANTAGES:* Advantages include both those discussed previously for including keys of owner records within member records and those just discussed. With this change, it will be possible to find a given order line directly, and the DBMS will be able to reject duplicate order lines.

*DISADVANTAGES:* Those disadvantages presented in the discussion of including keys of owner records within member records also apply here. The problem of wasted space tends to be even worse in this case, however. We are probably including the keys of *two* owner records, not just one. In addition, since the record is now CALC rather than VIA SET, each record occurrence must also include a calc chain pointer. If Premiere Products happened to have six character order numbers and twelve character part numbers, and if pointers were three bytes long, each order line record would now contain an extra twenty-one bytes. Multiply this by the number of order lines in the database, which can be sizable, and we may have more wasted space than we can tolerate.

Another disadvantage concerns the characteristics of the CALC location mode as opposed to those of VIA SET. If the *ORDLNE* record is stored VIA *ORDERS-ORDLNE*, order lines will be clustered as closely as possible to the orders that own them. This will make transactions that retrieve first an order and then all the associated order lines very efficient. It may be, for example, that a given order and its six order lines are all stored on the same page and thus can all be retrieved with a single disk access. This clustering is lost if the *ORDLNE* record is CALC, since order line occurrences will then be distributed around the database in positions determined by application of the hashing function to the calc key.

**Changing the Set in the VIA SET.**    If the procedure explained earlier for producing a CODASYL design has indicated that the location mode of a particular record is to be VIA SET, the set mentioned must be one in which the record participates as a member. If there is more than one such set, one of them must be chosen. The procedure indicates that we may pick any of them. At this point, we might decide not to use the one we chose earlier and instead pick another possibility.

The important thing to keep in mind in making such a decision is that occurrences of the record will be placed as closely as possible to the owner occurrence *within the set that we choose*. If we choose, for example, to use VIA *ORDERS-ORDLNE* as a location mode for the *ORDLNE* record, order lines will be placed near the order that owns the order line. If we choose to use VIA *PART-ORDLNE*, they will instead be placed near the part that owns them. Thus, the real question is, *Which arrangement will be more beneficial to the overall processing of the system?*

Processing that uses the set we choose will be more efficient than processing that uses the other set. If we choose to use *ORDERS-ORDLNE*, then processing an order and all the associated order lines will be much more efficient than processing a part and all its associated order lines. Thus, one factor to consider in the decision is which type of processing to make more efficient. Another factor to consider is the average number of member occurrences in each of these sets. If the number in one set is much larger than the number in another, we might want to avoid this set. If the average number of member occurrences in *ORDERS-ORDLNE* is five, for example, and the number of member occurrences in *PART-ORDLNE* is 1,000, we might choose to use *ORDERS-ORDLNE*. Trying to cluster 1,000 order lines near a part can cause problems. Not only will such a large number of order lines require several pages of the database to house them, thus causing much of the benefit of the clustering to be sacrificed, but it also tends to fill several pages, thus causing problems the next time something needs to be stored in this portion of the database.

**Prior Pointers.**   In any set, we might choose to include prior pointers. Prior pointers occupy space and constitute another field that must be updated whenever data in the database is changed. On the other hand, prior pointers make the process of finding the prior occurrence within a set efficient. This process is used not only when a FIND PRIOR WITHIN set-name command is executed, but also during a deletion. If customer 405 is deleted in Figure 11.13, for example, the prior customer, 311, must point to the next customer, 522. Since any set has to contain next pointers, finding customer 522 is a simple matter for the DBMS. On the other hand, if the system does not contain prior pointers, finding customer 311 is not a simple matter at all, particularly if the number of member occurrences is large. It requires searching sequentially all the way around the chain. Thus, deletion is also more efficient.

**Figure 11.13**

Deleting customer 405

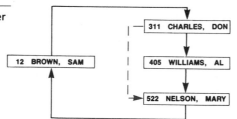

Most of the time, prior pointers are a good choice. Some systems even require their use, in which case we don't even have to address this issue during database design. Even if the DBMS does not require their use, some designers consider them so valuable that they always automatically include them in the design.

**Owner Pointers.**   In any set, we might also choose to include owner pointers. Owner pointers also occupy space and constitute another field that must be updated whenever data in the database is changed. On the other hand, owner pointers lend efficiency to the process of finding the owner occurrence within a set. For any set in which we need to find the owner with any frequency, we should probably choose owner pointers. In addition, some systems require the presence of owner pointers to find the owner. While the inclusion of owner pointers is perhaps not as universally appropriate as the inclusion of prior pointers (if prior pointers are the right choice 95 percent of the time, owner pointers would be the right choice 75 percent of the time), some database designers automatically include owner pointers in their designs. In addition, some systems require owner pointers in all sets.

### Any System

There are a number of tuning options that apply to any type of system.

**Encoding Data.**   In the information level of design, we may have decided to encode certain data items. There are only two real decisions to make here.

1. Do we really want to encode the data?
2. If so, will we store the codes in the database or elsewhere?

The advantage of encoding data is that it saves space. The disadvantage is that an extra step is necessary to retrieve any encoded data. First of all, the code itself is retrieved along with all the other data being retrieved. After this has taken place, the value for which the code stands must also be retrieved. If the data had not been encoded, this second step would be unnecessary. At this point, we may decide not to encode after all because of the additional overhead incurred during retrieval, choosing, instead, to put up with the additional storage cost incurred by not encoding.

Assuming we decide to encode, the next question is, *Where will the codes themselves be stored?* They might be stored in the database, and, in general, this would probably be appropriate. If the codes are more global to the enterprise than the data in this database, however, they should probably be external to the database, perhaps in a keyed file in which the key is the code and the record contains the value that has been encoded. By saying the code is more global to the enterprise, we mean that these codes are, or will be, used in other applications that do not use the database we are designing.

**Including Derivable Data.**    In the information level of design, we said we would include attributes that could be derived from other attributes. For example, in a *PART* relation that contains attributes *UNONHAND* and *COST*, we would include the attribute *OHVALUE* (on hand value), which is the product of *UNONHAND* and *COST*. In the *STUDENT* relation, the attribute *TOTCRED* (total number of credits), which can be computed by summing the number of credits for each of the courses in which the student has a passing grade, would be included. We must be sure we document the manner in which result is to be obtained, of course.

In the actual implementation, however, there are other considerations. If we store an attribute that is computable from other attributes, we are creating redundancy, update problems, and the possibility of inconsistency in the database. This would certainly make a good argument against storing the attribute. (If *UNONHAND* is 10 and *COST* is 15, but *OHVALUE* is 125, the information is inconsistent. The reason we have this problem is that a relation containing such derived data is technically not in 3NF. In this example, the concatenation of *UNONHAND* and *COST* determines *OHVALUE*. Yet, creating a separate relation containing *UNONHAND*, *COST*, and *OHVALUE* does not seem to be a particularly attractive alternative.)

In spite of these arguments, there are two situations in which we really should include the attribute. If the DBMS we are using supports the notion of *virtual* attributes (i.e., an attribute is not physically stored, rather the formula for computing it is applied whenever the attribute is requested), then the problems mentioned previously disappear. The second situation arises when the computation is complicated; that is, when it involves processing a large number of occurrences in the database. In this case, we may decide to store the result for the sake of efficiency. Suppose every time we needed the *TOTCRED* for a given student we had to sum the number of credits for all the courses he or she had successfully completed. We would have introduced a great deal of overhead, perhaps *more* than we can endure. As an aside, if we do decide to store the *TOTCRED* as a part of the *STUDENT* relation, we should create a utility program that periodically will verify that these numbers are correct; for example, that we didn't inadvertently update the *TOTCRED* for a particular student so that it no longer matches the figure obtained by summing the number of credits from the individual courses.

**General Physical Characteristics.**   Depending on the DBMS, it may be possible to make other changes to the physical characteristics of the database. We may be able to adjust the blocking factor and/or page size; we may be able to choose different access methods or a different hashing function. A complete treatment of all the possibilities is beyond the scope of this text. To determine which changes can be made, as well as the physical ramifications of the various options, it is necessary to have a thorough knowledge of the DBMS being used.

For additional information concerning tuning for performance, see [1], [3], [5], [6], and [7].

## ANALYZING SPACE AND PROCESSING REQUIREMENTS

The previous section included many choices that could be made to change the database design so as to affect the performance characteristics of the overall application. With so many choices to make in so many areas, the number of possible physical designs that can be derived from a single information-level design is extremely large (seemingly infinite). How can we possibly determine which design is best?

In many cases, knowing the advantages and disadvantages associated with certain compromises will make the appropriate choice obvious. It may well be clear that the advantages will be beneficial to our application and the disadvantages will be something that we can easily live with. By making these choices early in the physical design process, we can drastically reduce the overall number of possible alternatives we must consider. In some cases, however, it will not be clear which choice is the most beneficial. When this happens, we will need a mechanism to allow us to choose from among the remaining possibilities.

If we must choose from two or more physical designs, two distinct factors must be considered. The first is storage space. How much space will be needed by a database using this design if it is to support the required volume of data?

The second factor is performance. How well will the system perform if this design is chosen? Both factors are important. Since computations on storage space and performance depend on the characteristics of the DBMS that will be used, we cannot offer one exclusive technique that will always work. Rather, we will give some guidelines to follow. Before applying these guidelines to a given situation, however, it is essential to be familiar with the characteristics of the DBMS.

## Space Requirements

Several different components must be considered when determining the size of a database. We must consider the space occupied by the data itself; the space occupied by pointers and/or indexes; the space occupied by system data; the space wasted by the DBMS; and the space intentionally wasted by the users of the system. In making these determinations, we should include not only the volumes given to us as current requirements by the users, but also volumes for projected growth.

**Space Occupied by the Data Itself.** For each record in the database, the record length can be calculated. It is the sum of the lengths of the individual fields. We must, of course, take into account the storage characteristics of the DBMS we are using in order to determine how much space an occurrence of a specific field will occupy. Character data will occupy one byte per character unless the system supports special compression techniques. There are so many ways to store numeric data that we really need to consult the manual for the given DBMS to determine which alternatives we might specify and the amount of storage each would require.

Once the total record length for a given record type has been calculated, this figure can be multiplied by the number of occurrences expected to be stored in the database in order to arrive at the total storage required by all occurrences of records of this type. When these figures have been calculated for each record type in the design, they are added together to give the total storage requirements for data in the database.

**Pointers (CODASYL only).** In CODASYL systems, pointers embedded within records are used to maintain set relationships unless the pointer array option is chosen. (Since pointer arrays behave more like indexes, they will be discussed along with them.) To calculate the amount of pointer space required for a given record type, we need to know how many pointers will be embedded in this type of record and how much space is occupied by each pointer. We find the amount of space occupied by a pointer in the manual. Four bytes is a relatively common size, although three bytes is also common for databases that are not tremendously large. To calculate the number of pointers embedded, we need to understand the following.

1. For any set in which the record participates as either an owner or member, there will be a pointer to the next member occurrence within the set.
2. For any set in which the record participates as either an owner or member and for which prior pointers are requested, there will be a pointer to the prior member occurrence within the set.
3. For any set in which the record participates as a member and for which owner pointers are requested, there will be a pointer to the owner occurrence within the set.
4. If the location mode of the record is CALC, the record will have a pointer for the CALC chain.

We can thus calculate the number of pointers embedded in a given record type. Multiplying this figure by the size of these pointers will give the amount of space devoted to pointers within a single occurrence of this record type. This number can be multiplied by the number of occurrences of this record type that we expect to store in the database to get the total amount of pointer space for all records of this type. When we have made this calculation for each type of record in the database, we can add these numbers together to obtain the total amount of pointer space required in the database.

**Indexes.** Indexes are sometimes built on various fields or combinations of fields. When this is the case, the index, even though it is external to the database itself, takes up space and must be included in our computation of the total space requirements.

The ability to make a precise computation really depends on knowledge of the structure of the index used by the given DBMS. We can make a good guess at the total space required, however, even if we don't have knowledge of this precise structure. We add the length of the field (or the combined lengths of the fields) on which the index is built to the length of a single pointer. This figure is then multiplied by the number of occurrences of the record in question. The final result should be a reasonable guess for the space required by the index. (This computation is based on the simple index structure illustrated in Figure 11.14 in which each entry is simply a value for the field or fields on which the index is built, together with a pointer to the record on which the value occurs. In reality, the index structure will be much more sophisticated than this, and usually some type of B-tree.)

**System Data.** By system data, we mean data stored within the database that contains special information about a page or record. We do not mean schema, subschema, or data dictionary information, which occupy a small amount of space compared to the amount of space occupied by the actual database.

**CUSTNUMB INDEX**

| CUST<br>NUMBER | RECORD<br>LOCATION |
|:---:|:---:|
| 124 | 1 |
| 256 | 2 |
| 311 | 3 |
| 315 | 4 |
| 405 | 5 |
| 412 | 6 |
| 522 | 7 |
| 567 | 8 |
| 587 | 9 |
| 622 | 10 |

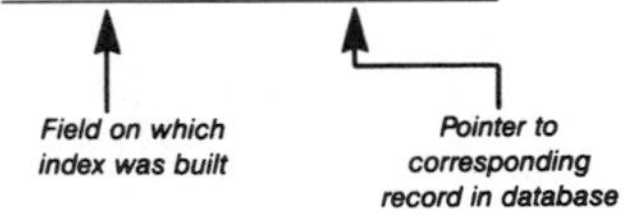

*Field on which index was built*      *Pointer to corresponding record in database*

**Figure 11.14**

Sample index

**Space Wasted by System.**    The database structure supported by the DBMS will, in general, cause some space to be "wasted" at any time. For example, if a page has only fifty bytes of available space remaining and the shortest record that can be stored on that page is seventy bytes long, the fifty bytes cannot be used and this space will be wasted.

**Space Intentionally Wasted by Users.**    Often, during the creation of a design, wasted (unused) space will be built in intentionally. Sometimes, extra space will be assigned as a safety factor in case the requirements have been underestimated. If hashing is to be used, extra space must be assigned or system performance will suffer drastically (see the discussion of hashing in the appendix). As a rule of thumb, if hashing is used, the database should be no more than 80 percent full.

## Example

To illustrate the process, let's assume we have a CODASYL system on which we are implementing the schema shown in Figure 11.15 on the next page. An examination of the manual for this DBMS has produced the following pertinent information:

1. A database is divided into pages of 4,096 bytes each.
2. Any record occurrence must be contained within a single page.
3. Eight bytes per page are devoted to system data. An additional four bytes per page are devoted to the header of the CALC chain.
4. Four bytes per record occurrence are devoted to system data.
5. Pointers for a database of the size we are implementing are three bytes each.
6. Numeric data occupies one byte per digit. Alphanumeric data occupies one byte per character.

**Figure 11.15**

Premiere Products
schema DDL

```
ADD SCHEMA NAME IS SCHDIST
     USER IS SD00
          REGISTERED FOR ALL
          RESPONSIBLE FOR UPDATE.

ADD FILE NAME IS DISTFILE ASSIGN TO DISTFILE.

ADD AREA NAME IS DISTAREA PAGE RANGE IS 1 THRU 1000
     WITHIN FILE DISTFILE.

ADD RECORD NAME IS SLSREP
     LOCATION MODE IS CALC USING SLSRNUMB
          DUPLICATES ARE NOT ALLOWED
     WITHIN AREA DISTAREA.

     02    SLSRNUMB                   PIC 9(2).
     02    SLSRNAME                   PIC X(20)..
     02    SLSRADDR                   PIC X(20).
     02    TOTCOMM                    PIC 9(5)V9(2).
     02    COMMRATE                   PIC V9(2).

ADD RECORD NAME IS CUSTOMER
     LOCATION MODE IS CALC USING CUSTNUMB
          DUPLICATES ARE NOT ALLOWED
     WITHIN AREA DISTAREA.

     02    CUSTNUMB                   PIC 9(3).
     02    CUSTNAME                   PIC X(20).
     02    CUSTADDR                   PIC X(20).
     02    BALANCE                    PIC 9(5)V9(2).
     02    CREDLIM                    PIC 9(5).

ADD RECORD NAME IS ORDERS
     LOCATION MODE IS CALC USING ORDNUMB
          DUPLICATES ARE NOT ALLOWED
     WITHIN AREA DISTAREA.

     02    ORDNUMB                    PIC 9(5).
     02    ORDDTE                     PIC 9(6).

ADD RECORD NAME IS PART
     LOCATION MODE IS CALC USING PARTNUMB
          DUPLICATES ARE NOT ALLOWED
     WITHIN AREA DISTAREA.

     02    PARTNUMB                   PIC X(4).
     02    PARTDESC                   PIC X(20).
     02    UNONHAND                   PIC 9(4).
     02    ITEMCLSS                   PIC X(2).
     02    WRHSNUMB                   PIC 9(2).
     02    UNITPRCE                   PIC 9(4)V9(2).

ADD RECORD NAME IS ORDLNE
     LOCATION MODE IS VIA ORDERS-ORDLNE
     WITHIN AREA DISTAREA.

     02    NUMBORD                    PIC 9(4).
     02    QUOTPRCE                   PIC 9(4)V9(2).
```

```
ADD SET NAME IS SLSREP-CUSTOMER
     ORDER IS SORTED
     MODE IS CHAIN          LINKED TO PRIOR
     OWNER IS SLSREP
     MEMBER IS CUSTOMER
          LINKED TO OWNER
          MANDATORY AUTOMATIC
     ASCENDING KEY IS CUSTNAME
          DUPLICATES ARE LAST.

ADD SET NAME IS CUSTOMER-ORDERS
     ORDER IS LAST
     MODE IS CHAIN          LINKED TO PRIOR
     OWNER IS CUSTOMER
     MEMBER IS ORDERS
          LINKED TO OWNER
          MANDATORY AUTOMATIC.

ADD SET NAME IS ORDERS-ORDLNE
     ORDER IS LAST
     MODE IS CHAIN          LINKED TO PRIOR
     OWNER IS ORDERS
     MEMBER IS ORDLNE
          LINKED TO OWNER
          MANDATORY AUTOMATIC.

ADD SET NAME IS PART-ORDLNE
     ORDER IS LAST
     MODE IS CHAIN          LINKED TO PRIOR
     OWNER IS PART
     MEMBER IS ORDLNE
          LINKED TO OWNER
          MANDATORY AUTOMATIC.
```

**Figure 11.15**

(continued)

Also, an interview with the users has produced the following information concerning volumes:

1. There are twenty sales reps.
2. There are 1,000 customers.
3. There are 2,000 orders on file at any one time.
4. On the average, each order has four order lines.
5. There are 5,000 parts.

Note we have not been given the specific number of order lines to expect. It is common for users to think in the terms indicated in the preceding list. They have the feeling that an average order has a certain number of order lines. All we need to do, of course, is multiply the number of orders (2,000) by the average number of order lines per order (four) to determine that there are 8,000 order lines. We will use this figure in our computations.

We are now ready to determine the number of pages that should be devoted to this database. The first step is to compute the amount of space occupied by records of each type. To do this, we calculate the total length of the record and multiply this figure by the number of occurrences of the record we expect will be in the database. It doesn't matter whether we do the computations for data and pointers separately, then combine at the end or combine at the beginning. In this case, we will combine at the beginning. The following are the computations for each record type.

**1. Determine Record Lengths    SLSREP.** The *SLSREP* record is CALC, so it contains a CALC chain pointer. It participates as the owner in *SLSREP-CUSTOMER*, in which prior pointers are requested. It participates as the member in no sets. There are thus three pointers in each occurrence of the record: CALC chain, next within *SLSREP-CUSTOMER*, and prior within *SLSREP-CUSTOMER*. The data fields total fifty-one bytes (two for *SLSRNUMB*, twenty for *SLSRNAME*, twenty for *SLSRADDR*, seven for *TOTCOMM*, two for *COMMRATE*).

**CUSTOMER.** The *CUSTOMER* record is CALC, so it contains a CALC chain pointer. It participates as the owner in *CUSTOMER-ORDERS*, in which prior pointers are requested. It participates as the member in *SLSREP-CUSTOMER*, in which prior and owner pointers are requested. There are thus six pointers in each occurrence of the record: CALC chain, next within *CUSTOMER-ORDERS*, prior within *CUSTOMER-ORDERS*, next within *SLSREP-CUSTOMER*, prior within *SLSREP-CUSTOMER*, and owner within *SLSREP-CUSTOMER*. The data fields total fifty-five bytes.

**ORDERS.** The *ORDERS* record is CALC, so it contains a CALC chain pointer. It participates as the owner in *ORDERS-ORDLNE*, in which prior pointers are requested. It participates as the member in *CUSTOMER-ORDERS*, in which prior and owner pointers are requested. There are thus six pointers in each occurrence of the record: CALC chain, next within *ORDERS-ORDLNE*, prior within *ORDERS-ORDLNE*, next within *CUSTOMER-ORDERS*, prior within *CUSTOMER-ORDERS*, and owner within *CUSTOMER-ORDERS*. The data fields total eleven bytes.

**PART.** The *PART* record is CALC, so it contains a CALC chain pointer. It participates as the owner in *PART-ORDLNE*, in which prior pointers are requested. It participates as the member in no sets. There are thus three pointers in each occurrence of the record: CALC chain, next within *PART-ORDLNE*, prior within *PART-ORDLNE*. The data fields total thirty-six bytes.

**ORDLNE.** The *ORDLNE* record is not CALC, so it does not contain a CALC chain pointer. It participates as the owner in no sets. It participates as the member in *ORDERS-ORDLNE* and *PART-ORDLNE*. In both of these sets, prior and owner pointers are requested. There are thus six pointers in each occurrence of the record: next, prior, and owner within *ORDERS-ORDLNE*, and next, prior, and owner within *PART-ORDLNE*. The data fields total ten bytes.

**2. Determine Total Space Required**   The preceding figures are used in calculating space requirements. The calculations are shown in Figure 11.16. The first column gives system data per record occurrence. In all cases, this is four bytes. The second column, which lists the total of the data fields, and the third column, which lists the number of pointers within a record occurrence, have been discussed. The fourth column gives the space occupied by the pointers. It is obtained by multiplying the number of pointers by the length of a pointer, in this case three bytes. The total amount of space is figured by adding the system data, user data, and space for pointers, and is given in bytes. Multiplying the total space for a single record by the expected number of occurrences gives the space required for all occurrences of the record type. Finally, adding all these numbers together gives the total space required to store the data and associated pointers, in this case 645,240 bytes.

**Figure 11.16**

Space calculations

| RECORD TYPE | SYSTEM DATA | USER DATA | # OF PTRS | SPACE PTRS | TOTAL SPACE | # OF OCCUR. | SPACE REQUIRED |
|---|---|---|---|---|---|---|---|
| SLSREP | 4 | 51 | 3 | 9 | 62 | 20 | 1,240 |
| CUSTOMER | 4 | 55 | 6 | 18 | 77 | 1,000 | 77,000 |
| ORDERS | 4 | 11 | 6 | 18 | 33 | 2,000 | 66,000 |
| PART | 4 | 36 | 3 | 9 | 49 | 5,000 | 245,000 |
| ORDLNE | 4 | 10 | 6 | 18 | 32 | 8,000 | 256,000 |
| | | | | | | TOTAL -- | 645,240 |

**3. Determine Number of Pages Required**   We now have all the information we need to calculate the number of pages to reserve for this database. It may seem that all we need to do is divide the total number of bytes required by 4,096, the number of bytes per page. If we go ahead and do this, however, we are overlooking three critical points.

First, let's assume that eight bytes per page are devoted to system data and another four to the header for the CALC chain. Thus, only 4,084 (4,096 – 8 – 4) bytes are actually usable for data.

Second, since any record occurrence must be contained within a single page, we will have some wasted space. If, for example, we attempt to store a customer record on a page on which fewer than seventy-seven bytes remain available, we will be unsuccessful. If fewer than thirty-two bytes (the length of the shortest record) remain on a page, we will be unable to store records of any type and the space will be wasted. How should we calculate the amount of space on a page that is truly available?

A valid but conservative method is to subtract from the 4,084 bytes one less than the length (in bytes) of the longest record. In this example, the longest record is the customer record, which is seventy-seven bytes in length.

Thus, we subtract seventy-six from 4,084, which yields 4,008. The rationale is that this much of the page will be usable. If fewer than 4,008 bytes are currently used, we will be able to store any occurrence of any type record on the page. This is a conservative approach, because even if more than 4,008 bytes are stored, records of some types may still fit on the page. If, for example, 4,020 bytes were used on a particular page, we could still store a *SLSREP* record (sixty-two bytes), an *ORDERS* record (thirty-three bytes), a *PART* record (forty-nine bytes), or an *ORDLNE* record (thirty-two bytes). Thus, on many pages, more than 4,008 bytes may be used. Rather than use the longest record, we could attempt to use some kind of average record length, for example, to obtain a slightly more realistic picture. Let's assume for now, however, that we do adopt this conservative technique. Thus, the practical amount of data that will fit on a page for this database is 4,008 bytes.

We still have a problem. If we divide 645,240 bytes by 4,008 bytes/page, we obtain 161 pages. If we reserve only 161 pages, however, and try to store the amount of data the users indicate they require, the database will effectively be 100 percent full. This figure would be pure disaster for the hashing that takes place for all CALC records. Ideally, for hashing, the database should be no more than 80- to 85-percent full. Thus, as a final step, we solve the equation

$$161 = .80 \times$$

yielding about 200. If we indeed have 161 pages worth of data and we reserve 200 pages, then the database will be about 80-percent full, and satisfactory performance from the hashing routines should be achieved.

Now let's summarize the process. Once the total number of bytes has been calculated, the following steps are applied:

1. Subtract the amount of space occupied on a page by any system data from the total amount of space for a page. In the example, this gave a figure of 4,084 bytes.
2. Subtract from this figure one less than the length (in bytes) of the longest record. In the example, this gave a figure of 4,008 bytes. This is a conservative approach. A slightly more realistic approach would be to use an average (or possibly a weighted average) of the record lengths of all types of records.
3. Divide the total number of bytes needed for the database by this figure. This result gives the number of pages necessary for a database that is full (in our example, 161 pages).
4. Calculate the number of pages needed so this figure represents about 80 percent (or potentially as much as 85 percent, but no more) of the total.
5. Plan for growth.

This completes the example. The only crucial aspect not covered in the algorithm itself is growth. The calculations here do not build in any growth factor. We don't change the procedure to accommodate growth, however. The easiest way to ensure that the database will support both current needs *and* a certain growth rate for some period of time is to increase the initial requirements to cover the projected growth.

## Performance

Estimating the relative performance of two different designs is not a simple task. We will investigate one methodology for attempting to do so. We will also discuss the limitations of this methodology and suggest other factors that might be considered to improve the picture. For an example, we will use the CODASYL database represented in Figure 11.15, together with the volume requirements given in the example on calculating space requirements.

**Logical Record Accesses (LRA's).**   This methodology relies heavily on logical record accesses (LRA's) and was proposed by Teorey and Fry in [7]. Each time a record from the database is retrieved, even if the record already happens to be in main memory, a logical record access occurs. Thus, LRA's do not take into account any buffering that might take place. If a record to be read is already in main memory, a logical record access occurs, but not a **physical record access**. It is, of course, the physical record accesses that really give the picture. Measuring physical record accesses involves difficulties, however, which will be addressed after the discussion of the methodology. By calculating LRA's, we are effectively simulating a system in which there is no buffering at all; every time a record is retrieved from the database, another disk access is required.

**Calculating LRA's.**   The first step in the methodology is to calculate the number of LRA's required for each application. We consider each transaction or report in the system and calculate the number of LRA's it requires. To do this, it is necessary to know the structure of the database, the number of occurrences of various types of records in the database and the algorithm that will be used to satisfy the request. The algorithms can be documented in different ways. Pseudocode, flow charts, action diagrams, or any number of other approaches are all legitimate. What is important is not how the algorithms are documented but rather how we then determine the number of LRA's required to process the given transaction or produce the given report. To illustrate the process, consider the following applications.

1. For a given customer, list his or her number, name, and address.
2. For a given sales rep, list his or her number and name, together with the number, name, and address of each customer he or she represents.
3. For a given customer, list his or her number and name, the number and name of the sales rep who represents the customer, and the number and date of each order placed by the customer. In addition, for each order line on each of these orders, list the part number, description, number of units ordered and quoted price.
4. For each customer, list his or her number and name, and the number and name of the sales rep who represents the customer.
5. Store a new customer. In this transaction, the user will enter a customer number. At this point, the system will verify that no customer with this number currently exists. The user will then enter the number of the sales rep to represent this customer. The system will ensure that such a sales rep does exist. In addition, the name of the sales rep will be displayed. Finally, the user will enter the remaining data (name, address, etc.) for this customer. The system will now store the new customer.

Let's now calculate the number of LRA's required for each of the five applications.

1. Since the *CUSTOMER* record is CALC, we should be able to retrieve information about a given customer directly. Thus, this application requires one LRA for the *CUSTOMER* record type and none for all the others.
2. Since the *SLSREP* record is also CALC, retrieving information about a given sales rep requires one LRA for the *SLSREP* record type. At this point, however, we must retrieve information about all customers represented by this sales rep. The appropriate way to do this is to find all the member occurrences in *SLSREP-CUSTOMER* owned by this sales rep. There will be one LRA for each customer in this chain. Thus, we need to determine, on the average, how many customers are owned by a given sales rep. Since there are twenty sales reps and 1,000 customers, an average sales rep would represent fifty (1,000/20) customers. Thus, this application will also require fifty LRA's for the *CUSTOMER* record type.
3. For reasons mentioned earlier, retrieving the given customer requires one LRA for the *CUSTOMER* record type. Calculating the number of LRA's required to find the sales rep who owns this customer is trickier.

The answer depends on whether the set *SLSREP-CUSTOMER* contains owner pointers. If it does, as in our example, the answer is simple. Since there is a pointer directly to the desired sales rep, one LRA for the *SLSREP* record type is all that is required. If not, then to find the sales rep, the system must work its way around the remainder of the chain, starting with the given customer until encountering the sales rep. To determine the number of LRA's required in this case, we assume, as stated before, that an average occurrence of *SLSREP-CUSTOMER* contains fifty customers. We also assume that the customer we are processing will be, on the average, about halfway around this chain. Thus, twenty-five LRA's of the *CUSTOMER* record type and finally, one LRA of the *SLSREP* record type would be required to determine the sales rep who represents the customer in this case.

Retrieving all the orders for this customer requires processing a complete occurrence of *CUSTOMER-ORDERS*. Since there are 1,000 customers and 2,000 orders, we would expect a customer to own, on the average, two orders. Thus, we must add two LRA's for the *ORDERS* record type. For each order, we are to retrieve all order lines. Since the average order contains four order lines and we are retrieving two orders, we will ultimately retrieve eight (two times four) order lines. Finally, since the part description is required along with the data for each order line, when we have retrieved an order line we must also retrieve the part that owns it in *PART-ORDLNE*. Since this set includes owner pointers, this process requires one LRA for the *PART* record. Since we have eight LRA's for the *ORDLNE* record type, we will also have eight LRA's for the *PART* record type. If *PART-ORDLNE* did not include owner pointers, the procedure explained earlier for finding the sales rep who represents a customer would apply.

4. Since the set *SLSREP-CUSTOMER* contains owner pointers, retrieving the sales rep who represents the customer, once we have retrieved a customer, requires a single LRA for the sales rep record type. But how do we retrieve all customers? If there were a system-owned set in our schema in which the member was *CUSTOMER*, we could retrieve all the members in this set. Since this would entail retrieving each customer, and there are 1,000 customers, this would give 1,000 LRA's of the customer record type.

In the absence of such a set, we must scan the entire database, looking for customers. (Even though we use the command FIND NEXT CUSTOMER WITHIN AREA-DISTRIBUTION, the system must still retrieve each record occurrence.) Thus, the process requires twenty LRA's of the *SLSREP* record type, 1,000 LRA's of the *CUSTOMER* record type, 2,000 LRA's of the *ORDERS* record type, 8,000 LRA's of the *ORDLNE* record type, and 5,000 LRA's of the *PART* record type. (A system-owned set would certainly have benefited this application!) Additionally, for each of the 1,000 customers, an additional LRA of the *SLSREP* record will then be required to obtain the sales rep who represents the customer. There will then be 1,020 LRA's for the sales rep record (twenty LRA's during the sequential scan, plus an LRA of a sales rep record whenever a customer is encountered).

5. When the customer number is initially verified, there will be a single LRA of the *CUSTOMER* record type. When the sales rep number is verified, there will be a single LRA of the *SLSREP* record type. Finally, when the customer is added, there will be another LRA of the *CUSTOMER* record type (in this case for output) to add the customer to the database.

At this point, the customer must be placed in the occurrence of *SLSREP-CUSTOMER*. Since the order of this set is sorted, the member occurrences along the chain must be examined sequentially to determine the location at which to insert the new customer (unless the set is stored using the pointer array mode, in which case the analysis would take that into account). Since the average occurrence of *SLSREP-CUSTOMER* contains fifty customers, and we would expect to have to search about half the chain, we would expect to require about twenty-five LRA's to determine the position at which to insert this customer. Finally, the customers on either side of the new customer must have their pointers updated, requiring two additional LRA's for the *CUSTOMER* record type. In total, this application requires one LRA for the *SLSREP* record type and twenty-nine LRA's for the *CUSTOMER* record type (one to attempt to read the customer initially, one to add the customer to the database, twenty-five to find a position at which the customer should be inserted into the occurrence of *SLSREP-CUSTOMER*, and two to adjust the pointers of the customers on either side of the new customer in the set occurrence).

This scenario depicts the customer being added before the position in the chain is known. If things truly happened in this fashion, the customer's record would have to be updated later, once the position had been determined to make the customer point to the correct next and prior occurrences in the set. In reality, the customer would not be added until this information was known. This fact, however, does not alter any of the numbers listed in the previous paragraph.

The numbers just calculated are shown in Figure 11.17. As you can see, the computations depend on numbers of occurrences of the various record types, the structure of the database, options chosen within the schema (set insertion, for example), and knowledge of the algorithm used in each application. A change to the structure of the database, a change in the options within the schema, or a change in the algorithms used will affect the results. In particular, the addition of a system-owned set in which the member is the customer record type will greatly improve the number of LRA's required for application four. In the exercises at the end of this chapter, you will be asked to redo the computations on the assumption that some of these changes have been made.

◄──────────── LRA's ────────────►

| APPLICATION | SLS REP | CUST OMER | ORDERS | PART | ORDER LINE | TOTAL |
|---|---|---|---|---|---|---|
| 1 | | 1 | | | | 1 |
| 2 | 1 | 50 | | | | 51 |
| 3 | 1 | 1 | 2 | 8 | 8 | 20 |
| 4 | 1020 | 1000 | 2000 | 5000 | 8000 | 17020 |
| 5 | 1 | 29 | | | | 30 |

**Figure 11.17**

Calculation of number of Logical Record Accesses (LRA's)

**Assigning Weights.** Now that LRA's have been calculated, we attach a weight, or measure of importance, to each application. This weight might be simply the number of times a given application occurred in a set period of time, such as a day. Suppose, for example, that application one occurred once every ten minutes; application two occurred once a week; application three occurred once every hour; application four occurred once every month; and application five occurred five times a day. Suppose also that the company were operating five days per week, eight hours per day. Figure 11.18 incorporates these figures.

◄──────────── LRA's ────────────►

| APPLICATION | SLS REP | CUST OMER | ORDERS | PART | ORDER LINE | TOTAL | WEIGHT | WEIGHTED TOTAL |
|---|---|---|---|---|---|---|---|---|
| 1 | | 1 | | | | 1 | 48 | 48 |
| 2 | 1 | 50 | | | | 51 | .2 | 10.2 |
| 3 | 1 | 1 | 2 | 8 | 8 | 20 | 8 | 160 |
| 4 | 1020 | 1000 | 2000 | 5000 | 8000 | 17020 | .05 | 851 |
| 5 | 1 | 29 | | | | 30 | 5 | 150 |

1219.2

**Figure 11.18**

Weighting the LRA calculations

The weights assigned in this case represent the frequency per day that an application is run. For applications not run every day, we still calculate the frequency. Application four runs once a month. Figuring a month as twenty working days yields a weight of 1/20, or .05. The higher an application's weight, the more we are going to prefer a design that reduces the number of LRA's it requires. Occasionally, an application that runs infrequently needs extremely rapid response time. If this is the case, the weight just calculated will be inappropriate. The needs of this application will be given a much lower priority in the choice of a design than will the needs of the jobs that run more frequently. The simplest solution is to increase the weight given to this application. This is why we intentionally call the column "WEIGHT" and not "FREQUENCY" or "FREQUENCY PER DAY."

**Obtaining Comparison Figures.**   The critical column in Figure 11.18 is the weighted total. This is the number of LRA's for each application, multiplied by the weight. It is the total at the bottom of this column that we will compare to totals from other designs.

The process then involves performing computations similar to those performed previously for each design alternative, then comparing the final figures. If one alternative design has a figure substantially lower than that of another, we can be reasonably confident that it is a better design. Many times this will be the case. Some pitfalls await us, however, if we rely completely on this approach.

**Potential Problems.**   The first potential problem concerns record length. If we are concerned only with LRA's, a design in which we have combined several record types and relaxed the requirement for 3NF may be unfairly rewarded by this methodology. There are bound to be substantially fewer LRA's. If we have such designs in the collection we are analyzing, we can include another factor, called **transport volume**, meaning the volume of data that is *actually* transported. As with the use of LRA's, in calculating this figure we assume that when a record is retrieved, it requires a disk access. We further assume that this record, and this record alone, is transported to main memory. With this in mind, we multiply the LRA's required for a given record type by the length of the record (including pointers). Since the customer record is seventy-seven bytes long (see Figure 11.16), the fifty LRA's for the customer record required by application two will cause 3,850 (77 * 50) bytes of data to be transported. These figures are then added in the same fashion as LRA's and multiplied by the appropriate weights. This gives us an additional check on the design process. If one design is substantially better in terms of the total number of LRA's, we should ensure that it will not be substantially worse in terms of total transport volume.

A second concern was mentioned earlier. It is not logical record accesses but physical record accesses that tell the story. Ideally, we would like to apply the same procedure but replace LRA's with PRA's. Unfortunately, it is not that simple.

Consider, for example, the process of retrieving an order and the four order lines associated with the order. If the order line record is stored VIA *ORDERS-ORDLNE*, these order lines will be clustered as closely to the order that owns them as possible. If, in fact, they end up on the same page as the order, one PRA will suffice to retrieve the order and all four order lines. On the other hand, if the page on which the order is located is full before all the order lines have been stored, they will not be on the same page and more than one PRA will be required. Thus, we have to take a probabilistic approach to analyzing the storage of data within the database. We need to determine the likelihood of all order lines being on the same page as the order, or, if this is not likely, how many order lines we expect to find on the same page, how many on the next page, and so on. Further, there may well be enough buffers in memory to hold not just a single page of the database but, perhaps, twenty pages. To analyze whether another retrieval request actually necessitates another PRA, we need to determine the probability of the required data being on one of the twenty pages currently held in memory. If so, no PRA is required. (For further information on the subject, see [7].)

A third problem concerns the methodology itself. While it seems ideally suited to CODASYL or hierarchical systems that are inherently navigational, what about inverted file systems or relational systems that are inherently non-navigational? The methodology can be used fruitfully with such systems if the LRA's analyzed included indexes; the index in this case will be considered just another type of record.

For other information concerning the analysis of space and performance requirements, see [1], [3], [5], [6], and [7].

## MARVEL COLLEGE EXAMPLE

We will now illustrate the ideas in this chapter by applying them to the database design for Marvel College. We completed the information-level design in chapter 8. The final design is shown in Figure 11.19 on the next page. Figure 11.20 on page 583 shows the domain definitions and Figure 11.21 on page 584 relates the attributes to these domain definitions. We will map this to a relational model system and to a CODASYL system. We will also analyze both space and processing requirements.

**Figure 11.19**

Final information-
level design for
Marvel College

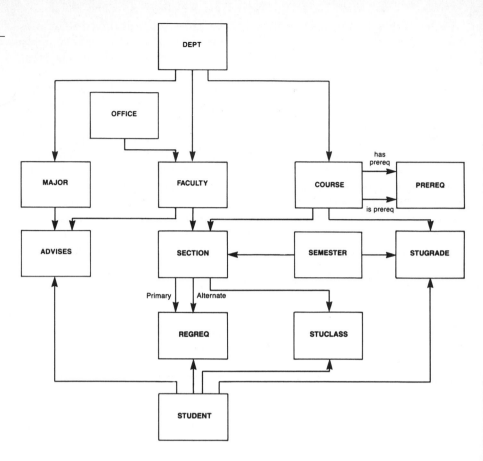

```
DEPT (DEPTCODE, DEPTNAME, LOCATION)

STUDENT (STUNUMB, STUNAME, LOCADDR*, LOCCITY*, LOCSTATE*,
         LOCZIP*, PRMADDR, PRMCITY, PRMSTATE, PRMZIP,
         CRDTAKEN, CRDEARND, GPA, TOTPNTS, CLSSSTND)

OFFICE (OFFNUMB, PHONE)

FACULTY (FACNUMB, FACNAME, FACADDR, FACCITY, FACSTATE, FACZIP,
         OFFNUMB, CURRANK, STRTDATE, DEPTCODE)
     FK  OFFNUMB --> OFFICE
     FK  DEPTCODE --> DEPT

MAJOR (MAJNUMB, MAJDESC, DEPTCODE)
     FK  DEPTCODE --> DEPT

ADVISES (STUNUMB, FACNUMB, MAJNUMB)
     FK  STUNUMB --> STUDENT   DLT CSCD
     FK  FACNUMB --> FACULTY
     FK  MAJNUMB --> MAJOR

COURSE (DEPTCODE, CRSNUMB, CRSTITLE, NUMBCRED)
     FK  DEPTCODE --> DEPT
```

```
PREREQ (DEPTCODE, CRSNUMB, PRERDEPT, PRERCRS)
    FK DEPTCODE, CRSNUMB --> COURSE DLT CSCD
    FK PRERDEPT, PRERCRS --> COURSE DLT CSCD

SEMESTER (SEMCODE, STRTDATE, ENDDATE, EXSTDATE, EXENDATE,
          WITHDATE)

STUGRADE (STUNUMB, SEMCODE, DEPTCODE, CRSNUMB, GRADE, CRDEARND,
          GRDPNTS)
    FK  STUNUMB --> STUDENT  DLT CSCD
    FK  SEMCODE --> SEMESTER
    FK  DEPTCODE, CRSNUMB --> COURSE

SECTION (SEMCODE, SCHDCODE, DEPTCODE, CRSNUMB, SECTLETT, TIME,
         ROOM, FACNUMB, CURENROL, MAXENROL)
    FK  SEMCODE --> SEMESTER
    FK  DEPTCODE, CRSNUMB --> COURSE
    FK  FACNUMB --> FACULTY

STUCLASS (SEMCODE, SCHDCODE, STUNUMB, GRADE*)
    FK  SEMCODE, SCHDCODE --> SECTION  DLT CSCD
    FK  STUNUMB --> STUDENT  DLT CSCD

REGREQ (STUNUMB, PRIMCODE, ALTCODE*, SEMCODE)
    FK  STUNUMB --> STUDENT  DLT CSCD
    FK  SEMCODE, PRIMCODE --> SECTION DLT CSCD
    FK  SEMCODE, ALTCODE* --> SECTION DLT CSCD
```

**Figure 11.19**

(continued)

**Figure 11.20**

Domain definitions
for final design

```
***************************** DOMAIN DEFINITIONS *****************************
```

| DOMAIN | TYPE | DESCRIPTION | RESTRICTIONS |
|---|---|---|---|
| ADDRESS | C(25) | ADDRESSES (STREET) | |
| CITY | C(25) | CITIES | |
| CLASS_STANDING | D(1) | CLASS STANDINGS | MUST BE 1 FOR FRESHMAN, 2 FOR SOPHOMORE, 3 FOR JUNIOR OR 4 FOR SENIOR |
| COURSE_ DESCRIPTION | C(25) | COURSE DESCRIPTIONS | |
| COURSE-NUMBER | D(3) | COURSE NUMBERS | |
| CREDITS | D(3) | NUMBER OF CREDITS | |
| DATE | D(6) | DATES | HAS FORM YYMMDD |
| DEPARTMENT CODE | C(3) | DEPARTMENT CODES | |
| DEPTNAME | C(25) | DEPARTMENT NAMES | |
| ENROLLMENT | D(3) | COURSE ENROLLMENTS | |
| FACULTY_NUMBER | D(4) | FACULTY NUMBERS | |
| GPA | D(3,2) | GRADE POINT AVERAGES | MUST BE BETWEEN 0.00 AND 4.00 |
| GRADE | C(1) | GRADES | MUST BE "A", "B", "C", "D", "F", OR "I" (INCOMPLETE) |
| GRADE_POINTS | D(3) | GRADE POINTS | OBTAINED BY MULTIPLYING THE NUMBER OF CREDITS OF "A" BY 4, THE NUMBER OF CREDITS OF "B" BY 3, OF "C" BY 2, OF "D" BY 1 AND ADDING THE RESULT |
| MAJOR_NUMBER | D(3) | MAJOR NUMBERS | |
| MEETING_TIME | C(20) | MEETING TIMES | IDENTIFIES START AND ENDING TIMES AND DAYS OF THE WEEK |
| NAME | C(25) | PERSON NAMES | |

*(continued)*

**Figure 11.20**

(continued)

| DOMAIN | TYPE | DESCRIPTION | RESTRICTIONS |
|--------|------|-------------|--------------|
| NUMBER_OF CREDITS | D(1) | NUMBER OF CREDITS GRANTED BY A COURSE | MUST BE BETWEEN 1 AND 5 |
| PHONE_NUMBER | D(4) | OFFICE PHONE NUMBERS | MUST BEGIN WITH A 3 |
| RANK | C(9) | FACULTY RANKS | MUST BE "INSTRUCTOR", "ASST PROF", "ASSO PROF", OR "PROFESSOR" |
| ROOM | C(7) | ROOM NUMBERS | CONSIST OF 3 DIGIT NUMBER AND 3 CHARACTER BUILDING ABBREVIATION, ("110 NSB") |
| SCHEDULE_CODE | D(4) | SCHEDULE CODES (CODES THAT UNIQUELY IDENTIFY SECTIONS OF COURSES IN A GIVEN SEMESTER | |
| SECTION_LETTER | C(1) | SECTION LETTERS | |
| SEMESTER_CODE | C(4) | SEMESTER CODES | HAS FORM SSYY WHERE SS IS EITHER FA FOR FALL, WI FOR WINTER, OR SU FOR SUMMER AND YY IS THE YEAR |
| STATE | C(2) | STATES | |
| STUDENT_NUMBER | D(9) | STUDENT NUMBERS | |
| ZIP | D(9) | ZIP CODES | |

**Figure 11.21**

Relation and attribute definitions for final design specifying underlying domains

******************* RELATION AND ATTRIBUTE DEFINITIONS *******************

| RELATION | ATTRIBUTE | DOMAIN | COMMENTS |
|----------|-----------|--------|----------|
| ADVISES | | | |
| | STUNUMB | STUDENT_NUMBER | |
| | FACNUMB | FACULTY_NUMBER | |
| | MAJNUMB | MAJOR_NUMBER | |
| COURSE | | | |
| | DEPTCODE | DEPARTMENT_CODE | |
| | CRSNUMB | COURSE_NUMBER | |
| | CRSTITLE | COURSE_TITLE | |
| | NUMBCRED | NUMBER_OF_CREDITS | Number of credits offered by the course |
| DEPT | | | |
| | DEPTCODE | DEPARTMENT_CODE | |
| | DEPTNAME | DEPTNAME | |
| | LOCATION | ROOM | |
| FACULTY | | | |
| | FACNUMB | FACULTY_NUMBER | |
| | FACNAME | NAME | |
| | FACADDR | ADDRESS | |
| | FACCITY | CITY | |
| | FACSTATE | STATE | |
| | FACZIP | ZIP | |
| | OFFNUMB | ROOM | |
| | CURRANK | RANK | |
| | STRTDATE | DATE | |
| | DEPTCODE | DEPARTMENT_CODE | |

**Figure 11.21**

(continued)

| RELATION | ATTRIBUTE | DOMAIN | COMMENTS |
|----------|-----------|--------|----------|
| MAJOR |  |  |  |
|  | MAJNUMB | MAJOR-NUMBER |  |
|  | MAJDESC | MAJOR-DESCRIPTION |  |
|  | DEPTCODE | DEPARTMENT-CODE | Department offering the major |
| OFFICE |  |  |  |
|  | OFFNUMB | ROOM |  |
|  | PHONE | PHONE-NUMBER |  |
| PREREQ |  |  |  |
|  | DEPTCODE | DEPARTMENT-CODE | Department for the course |
|  | CRSNUMB | COURSE-NUMBER | Number for the course |
|  | PRERDEPT | DEPARTMENT-CODE | Department for the prerequisite |
|  | PRERCRS | COURSE-NUMBER | Number for the prerequisite |
| REGREQ |  |  |  |
|  | STUNUMB | STUDENT-NUMBER |  |
|  | PRIMCODE | SCHEDULE-CODE | Primary request |
|  | ALTCODE | SCHEDULE-CODE | Alternate request (if one exists) |
|  | SEMCODE | SEMESTER-CODE |  |
| SECTION |  |  |  |
|  | SEMCODE | SEMESTER-CODE |  |
|  | SCHDCODE | SCHEDULE-CODE |  |
|  | DEPTCODE | DEPARTMENT-CODE |  |
|  | CRSNUMB | COURSE-NUMBER |  |
|  | SECTLETT | SECTION-LETTER |  |
|  | TIME | MEETING-TIME |  |
|  | ROOM | ROOM |  |
|  | FACNUMB | FACULTY-NUMBER |  |
|  | CURENROL | ENROLLMENT |  |
|  | MAXENROL | ENROLLMENT |  |
| SEMESTER |  |  |  |
|  | SEMCODE | SEMESTER-CODE |  |
|  | STRTDATE | DATE | Starting date for semester |
|  | ENDDATE | DATE | Ending date for semester |
|  | EXSTDATE | DATE | Starting date for exams |
|  | EXENDATE | DATE | Ending date for exams |
|  | WITHDATE | DATE | Last date to withdraw from courses |
| STUDENT |  |  |  |
|  | STUNUMB | STUDENT-NUMBER |  |
|  | STUNAME | NAME |  |
|  | LOCADDR | ADDRESS | Local street address |
|  | LOCCITY | CITY | Local city |
|  | LOCSTATE | STATE | Local state |
|  | LOCZIP | ZIP | Local zip code<br>  *Note if no local address, use<br>    permanent address as local<br>    address. |
|  | PRMADDR | ADDRESS | Permanent street address |
|  | PRMCITY | CITY | Permanent city |
|  | PRMSTATE | STATE | Permanent state |
|  | PRMZIP | ZIP | Permanent zip code |
|  | CRDTAKEN | CREDITS | Number of credits taken |
|  | CRDEARND | CREDITS | Number of credits earned |
|  | GPA | GPA | GPA (total points divided by<br>  number of credits taken) |
|  | TOTPNTS | GRADE-POINTS | Total points (4 for each credit<br>  of A, 3 for each B, and so on) |
|  | CLSSSTND | CLASS-STANDING | Class standing - determined by<br>  number of credits earned; if<br>  <30, standing is 1, if >= 30<br>  and < 60, standing is 2, if<br>  >= 60 and < 90, standing is 3,<br>  if >= 90, standing is 4 |

*(continued)*

**Figure 11.21**

(continued)

| RELATION | ATTRIBUTE | DOMAIN | COMMENTS |
|----------|-----------|--------|----------|
| STUGRADE | | | |
| | STUNUMB | STUDENT_NUMBER | |
| | SEMCODE | SEMESTER_CODE | |
| | DEPTCODE | DEPARTMENT_CODE | |
| | CRSNUMB | COURSE_NUMBER | |
| | GRADE | GRADE | Grade received in course |
| | CRDEARND | CREDITS | Credits earned in course - will be the number of credits offered by the course if grade is A, B, C, D;  will be 0 if grade is F |
| | GRDPNTS | GRADE_POINTS | Points earned in course (4 for each credit if grade is A, 3 for each credit if grade is B, and so on) |
| STUCLASS | | | |
| | SEMCODE | SEMESTER_CODE | |
| | SCHDCODE | SCHEDULE_CODE | |
| | STUNUMB | STUDENT_NUMBER | |
| | GRADE | GRADE | |

## Mapping to the Relational Model

We will assume that the relational model system to be used supports primary keys but not foreign keys. The collection of relations will be precisely the collection of relations in the final information-level design. Further, since the system supports primary keys, these will not require any special treatment. The collection of relations is shown in Figure 11.22.

**Figure 11.22**

Collection of relations in design for a relational model DBMS

DEPARTMENT (DEPTCODE, DEPTNAME, LOCATION)

STUDENT (STUNUMB, STUNAME, LOCADDR*, LOCCITY*, LOCSTATE*, LOCZIP*, ADDR, STATE, ZIP, CRDTAKEN, CRDEARND, GPA, TOTPNTS, CLSSSTND)

OFFICE (OFFNUMB, PHONE)

FACULTY (FACNUMB, FACNAME, ADDR, CITY, STATE, ZIP, OFFNUMB, CURRANK, STRTDATE, DEPTCODE)

MAJOR (MAJNUMB, MAJDESC, DEPTCODE)

ADVISES (STUNUMB, FACNUMB, MAJNUMB)

COURSE (DEPTCODE, CRSNUMB, CRSTITLE, NUMBCRED)

PREREQ (DEPTCODE, CRSNUMB, PRERDEPT, PRERCRS)

SEMESTER (SEMCODE, STRTDATE, ENDDATE, EXSTDATE, EXENDATE, WITHDATE)

STUGRADE (STUNUMB, SEMCODE, DEPTCODE, CRSNUMB, GRADE, CRDEARND, GRDPNTS)

```
SECTION (SEMCODE, SCHDCODE, DEPTCODE, CRSNUMB, SECTLETT,
         MEETTIME, MEETPLCE, FACNUMB, CURENROL, MAXENROL)

STUCLASS (SEMCODE, SCHDCODE, STUNUMB, GRADE*)

REGREQ (STUNUMB, PRIMCODE, ALTCODE*, SEMCODE)
```

**Figure 11.22**

(continued)

The foreign key restrictions must be enforced by programmers. These restrictions are shown in Figure 11.23. For efficiency, an index (nonunique) will be created on each of these foreign keys.

```
FACULTY
     FK   OFFNUMB --> OFFICE
     FK   DEPTCODE --> DEPARTMENT

MAJOR
     FK   DEPTCODE --> DEPARTMENT

ADVISES
     FK   STUNUMB --> STUDENT   DLT CSCD
     FK   FACNUMB --> FACULTY
     FK   MAJNUMB --> MAJOR

COURSE
     FK   DEPTCODE --> DEPARTMENT

PRERFQ
     FK DEPTCODE, CRSNUMB --> COURSE DLT CSCD
     FK PRERDEPT, PRERCRS --> COURSE DLT CSCD

STUGRADE
     FK   STUNUMB --> STUDENT   DLT CSCD
     FK   SEMCODE --> SEMESTER
     FK   DEPTCODE, CRSNUMB --> COURSE

SECTION
     FK   SEMCODE --> SEMESTER
     FK   DEPTCODE, CRSNUMB --> COURSE
     FK   FACNUMB --> FACULTY

STUCLASS
     FK   SEMCODE, SCHDCODE --> SECTION   DLT CSCD
     FK   STUNUMB --> STUDENT   DLT CSCD

REGREQ
     FK   STUNUMB --> STUDENT   DLT CSCD
     FK   SEMCODE, PRIMCODE --> SECTION DLT CSCD
     FK   SEMCODE, ALTCODE* --> SECTION DLT CSCD
```

**Figure 11.23**

Foreign key restrictions in design for a relational model DBMS (each foreign key requires a nonunique index)

The fields that must allow nulls are the local address fields, the *GRADE* field in the *STUCLASS* relation, and the *ALTCODE* field in the *REGREQ* relation. In each of the character fields in this group, blank can be used to represent null without causing any problem. In the single numeric field, *LOCZIP*, we can use zero to represent null.

There are no secondary or candidate keys in this design.

## Mapping to the CODASYL Model

To create a design for a CODASYL system, we create a record type for each relation in the final information-level design. Initially, the attributes of each relation are the fields in the corresponding record. Foreign keys are removed, and sets are created to fulfill the same role. (If relation B contains a foreign key identifying relation A, the foreign key is removed and a set is created in which A is the owner and B is the member.) Finally, any record with its primary key intact at the end of this process is assigned a location mode of CALC on this primary key. All others are assigned a location mode of VIA SET. (If there is more than one choice for the set, one is chosen arbitrarily at this point.)

The results obtained by applying this procedure to the final information-level design for Marvel College are shown in Figures 11.24 and 11.25. The records and the corresponding fields are shown in Figure 11.24. Any record with a field (or combination of fields) underlined as the key will be CALC on this key. All others will be VIA SET, using the indicated set. Note that two of the record types, *ADVISES* and *PREREQ*, contain no fields, a perfectly acceptable situation.

**Figure 11.24**

CODASYL records (CALC keys underlined)

```
DEPARTMENT (DEPTCODE, DEPTNAME, LOCATION)

STUDENT (STUNUMB, STUNAME, LOCADDR*, LOCCITY*, LOCSTATE*,
         LOCZIP*, ADDR, STATE, ZIP, CRDTAKEN, CRDEARND, GPA,
         TOTPNTS, CLSSSTND)

OFFICE (OFFNUMB, PHONE)

FACULTY (FACNUMB, FACNAME, ADDR, CITY, STATE, ZIP,
         CURRANK, STRTDATE)

MAJOR (MAJNUMB, MAJDESC)

ADVISES ()
    VIA S_STUDENT_ADVISES

COURSE (CRSNUMB, CRSTITLE, NUMBCRED)
    VIA S_DEPARTMENT_COURSE

PREREQ ()
    VIA S_HAS_PREREQ

SEMESTER (SEMCODE, STRTDATE, ENDDATE, EXSTDATE, EXENDATE,
         WITHDATE)

STUGRADE (GRADE, CRDEARND, GRDPNTS)
    VIA S_STUDENT_STUGRADE

SECTION (SCHDCODE, SECTLETT, MEETTIME, MEETPLCE, CURENROL,
         MAXENROL)
    VIA S_SEMESTER_SECTION

STUCLASS (GRADE*)
    VIA S_SECTION_STUCLASS

REGREQ ()
    VIA S_STUDENT_REGREQ
```

The sets are shown in Figure 11.25. The name of the set, the owner record type, and the member record type are listed for each set. Each set is assumed to be AUTOMATIC and MANDATORY unless otherwise noted. In this design, the only exception is *ALTERNATE*, which is MANUAL, since the corresponding foreign key is allowed to be null. Each set will include both owner and prior pointers. Set insertion modes may be assigned arbitrarily at this time.

———————————————— CODASYL SETS ————————————————

**Figure 11.25**

CODASYL sets

| SET | OWNER | MEMBER | COMMENT |
|---|---|---|---|
| OFFICE_FACULTY | OFFICE | FACULTY | |
| DEPARTMENT_FACULTY | DEPARTMENT | FACULTY | |
| DEPARTMENT_MAJOR | DEPARTMENT | MAJOR | |
| STUDENT_ADVISES | STUDENT | ADVISES | |
| FACULTY_ADVISES | FACULTY | ADVISES | |
| MAJOR_ADVISES | MAJOR | ADVISES | |
| DEPARTMENT_COURSE | DEPARTMENT | COURSE | |
| HAS_PREREQ | COURSE | PREREQ | |
| IS_PREREQ | COURSE | PREREQ | |
| STUDENT_STUGRADE | STUDENT | STUGRADE | |
| SEMESTER_STUGRADE | SEMESTER | STUGRADE | |
| COURSE_STUGRADE | COURSE | STUGRADE | |
| SEMESTER_SECTION | SEMESTER | SECTION | |
| COURSE_SECTION | COURSE | SECTION | |
| FACULTY_SECTION | FACULTY | SECTION | |
| SECTION_STUCLASS | SECTION | STUCLASS | |
| STUDENT_STUCLASS | STUDENT | STUCLASS | |
| STUDENT_REGREQ | STUDENT | REGREQ | |
| PRIMARY | SECTION | REGREQ | |
| ALTERNATE | SECTION | REGREQ | MANUAL |

It should now be a simple matter to create the schema DDL for the chosen CODASYL system, using the information given in Figures 11.24 and 11.25. Specific details concerning the format of the individual fields can be obtained from the information provided by the domain list (Figure 11.20) and by the list in Figure 11.21 that shows corresponding fields and domains.

We also need to document any special restrictions, such as the foreign key restrictions shown in Figure 11.23, together with any other restrictions programmers must enforce. The diagram in Figure 11.19 is effectively a data structure diagram for this design.

## Calculating Space Requirements

Using the initial CODASYL design for Marvel College, we will illustrate the calculation of space requirements. We'll assume that the CODASYL system we're using has the characteristics discussed in the material on calculating space requirements. We will also assume that PRIOR and OWNER pointers have been requested for all sets.

Let's suppose the following physical requirements have been obtained for the system at Marvel College: There are twenty-five departments offering 750 different courses; 300 faculty members housed in 250 different offices; thirty-five different majors available; and 6,000 students. On the average, half the students have a double major. A perusal of the catalog produces an estimate of 300 prerequisites that must be stored in the database. General grades must be kept in the database for twenty semesters (it is estimated that this will mean storing up to 150,000 grades). Since registration requests are retained for one semester beyond the one in which the request was made, 12,000 registration requests could be in the database at any time. Also, at any time, the database must be able to hold information concerning 1,600 sections of courses. Total enrollment in all these sections would be approximately 30,000 students. (In calculating this figure, we count students once for each section in which they are enrolled. Thus, a student enrolled in five courses will be counted five times.)

A translation of the above information into numbers of occurrences for each of the record types in the design gives:

```
DEPARTMENT - 25
COURSE - 750
FACULTY - 300
OFFICE - 250
MAJOR - 35
STUDENT - 6000
ADVISES - 9000 (half of the students have two majors)
PREREQ - 300
SEMESTER - 20
STUGRADE - 150,000
REGREQ - 12,000
SECTION - 1,600
STUCLASS - 30,000
```

The calculation for the required size of the database, given these requirements, is shown in Figures 11.26 and 11.27. In Figure 11.26, the number of pointers for each record type is calculated. The first column gives the number of calc chain pointers in each occurrence. Each CALC record has a calc chain pointer; other records do not. Thus, this number is either one or zero. The next column indicates the number of sets in which the record participates as the owner. For each of these sets the record will contain two pointers, and the next column gives the result of multiplying by two the number of sets in which the record is the owner. (Remember that prior and owner pointers will be picked for all sets. Since owner records do not contain owner pointers, each owner record will contain two pointers, a next pointer and a prior pointer. Each member record, in contrast, will contain three, a next pointer, a prior pointer, and an owner pointer.)

The next column gives the number of sets in which the record participates as a member, and the following column gives the result of multiplying this number by three. The final column gives the total number of pointers for the record type.

| RECORD TYPE | CALC PTR | OWNS SETS | # OF PTRS | MEMBER SETS | # OF PTRS | TOTAL PTRS |
|---|---|---|---|---|---|---|
| ADVISES | 0 | 0 | 0 | 3 | 9 | 9 |
| COURSE | 0 | 4 | 8 | 1 | 3 | 11 |
| DEPARTMENT | 1 | 3 | 6 | 0 | 0 | 7 |
| FACULTY | 1 | 2 | 4 | 2 | 6 | 11 |
| MAJOR | 1 | 1 | 2 | 1 | 3 | 6 |
| OFFICE | 1 | 1 | 2 | 0 | 0 | 3 |
| PREREQ | 0 | 0 | 0 | 2 | 6 | 6 |
| REGREQ | 0 | 0 | 0 | 3 | 9 | 9 |
| SECTION | 0 | 3 | 6 | 3 | 9 | 15 |
| SEMESTER | 0 | 2 | 4 | 0 | 0 | 5 |
| STUDENT | 1 | 4 | 8 | 0 | 0 | 9 |
| STUGRADE | 0 | 0 | 0 | 3 | 9 | 9 |
| STUCLASS | 0 | 0 | 0 | 2 | 6 | 6 |

**Figure 11.26**

Calculations giving the number of pointers for each record type

| RECORD TYPE | SYSTEM DATA | USER DATA | # OF PTRS | PTRS SPACE | TOTAL SPACE | # OF OCCUR. | SPACE REQUIRED |
|---|---|---|---|---|---|---|---|
| ADVISES | 4 | 0 | 9 | 27 | 31 | 9,000 | 279,000 |
| COURSE | 4 | 31 | 11 | 33 | 68 | 750 | 51,000 |
| DEPARTMENT | 4 | 35 | 7 | 21 | 60 | 25 | 1,500 |
| FACULTY | 4 | 105 | 11 | 33 | 142 | 300 | 42,600 |
| MAJOR | 4 | 28 | 6 | 18 | 50 | 35 | 1,750 |
| OFFICE | 4 | 11 | 3 | 9 | 24 | 250 | 6,000 |
| PREREQ | 4 | 0 | 6 | 18 | 22 | 300 | 6,600 |
| REGREQ | 4 | 0 | 9 | 27 | 31 | 12,000 | 372,000 |
| SECTION | 4 | 38 | 15 | 45 | 87 | 1,600 | 139,200 |
| SEMESTER | 4 | 34 | 5 | 15 | 53 | 20 | 1,060 |
| STUDENT | 4 | 144 | 9 | 27 | 175 | 6,000 | 1,050,000 |
| STUGRADE | 4 | 7 | 9 | 27 | 38 | 150,000 | 5,700,000 |
| STUCLASS | 4 | 1 | 6 | 18 | 23 | 30,000 | 690,000 |
| | | | | | | | 8,340,710 |

**Figure 11.27**

Space calculations

```
Effective page length = 4096 - 12 (used by system) - 174 (1
                            less than the length of the longest
                            record)
                      = 3910

Number of pages in 100% full database = 8,340,710 / 3910
                                      = 2134

Number of pages in 80% full database = 2134 * 1.25
                                     = 2668
                                     = 2700 (rounded)

Required database size is 2700 pages.
```

Figure 11.27 shows the actual calculations. The first column gives the number of bytes of system data for each record type. In each case, this number is four. The second column gives the number of bytes of data in records of each type. The third column gives the number of pointers and is taken directly from Figure 11.26. Assuming each pointer is three bytes long, these numbers are each multiplied by three, giving the number of space occupied by these pointers. The results are stored in the fourth column. Adding system data, user data, and space for pointers yields the total space (in bytes) required for a single record of each type. These numbers are stored in the fifth column. The sixth column represents the number of occurrences of records of each type that must be stored in the database (see the preceding list). Multiplying the figures in the fifth and sixth columns yields the total space required by all occurrences of records of each type. These figures are stored in the final column.

The total of figures in the final column (8,340,710) represents the total amount of space that will be required to store all occurrences of all records. To convert this into a number of pages for the database, three additional steps are required. First, the effective page length is calculated. From the total space on a page (4,096 bytes), we subtract the amount of space required on each page for general system data (twelve bytes). Next, we subtract a number that is one less than the length of the longest record. (See the discussion of these calculations earlier in the chapter if the reason for doing this is not clear to you.) In this example, the result is 3,910. Dividing this figure into the total number of bytes required produces the number of pages required for a database that is *totally full*, in this case 2,134 pages. Finally, assuming we desire the database to be about 80-percent full, we multiply this figure by 1.25, obtaining a size of about 2,700 pages.

## Calculating LRA's

To illustrate the process of calculating LRA's, we will perform the particular calculation for the number of LRA's required to produce the time schedule.

The first step in the production of the time schedule is to locate the appropriate semester. Since the *SEMESTER* record is CALC, this requires one LRA of the *SEMESTER* record.

At this point, each section owned by that semester must be accessed. Since the 1,600 sections mentioned in the requirements are for two semesters, we would expect the semester we just found to own approximately 800 sections. Thus, 800 LRA's of the *SECTION* record are required.

For each of these 800 sections accessed, we must find the faculty member who owns the section. Since owner pointers are included in all sets in this design, finding the faculty member who owns a section requires only a single LRA. Thus, 800 LRA's of the *FACULTY* record are required to find the faculty members who own each of the 800 sections.

For each of these 800 sections accessed, we must also find the course that owns the section. Again, since owner pointers are included in all sets in this design, finding the course that owns a section requires only a single LRA. Once a course has been found, the department that owns the course must also be located. As before, this requires only a single LRA. Therefore, finding the courses that own each of the 800 sections and the departments that own each of these courses requires 800 LRA's of the *COURSE* record and 800 LRA's of the *DEPARTMENT* record.

In total, one LRA of the SEMESTER record, followed by 800 LRA's each of the *SECTION, FACULTY, COURSE,* and *DEPARTMENT* records, is required, for a grand total of 3,301 LRA's.

To calculate associated transport volume, we multiply the number of LRA's of each record type by the associated record length. In this case, the computation would be

```
TRANSPORT VOLUME =   1 *    53            (SEMESTER)
                 + 800 *    87            (SECTION)
                 + 800 *   142            (FACULTY)
                 + 800 *    68            (COURSE)
                 + 800 *    60            (DEPARTMENT)
                 = 53 + 69,600 + 113,600 + 54,400 + 48,000
                 = 285,653 (bytes)
```

Once all the LRA's and corresponding transport volumes have been calculated for a given design alternative, they are multiplied by the appropriate weights, and the weighted figures are added together. Regarding the time schedule, the weight will probably be quite low, since the report is run infrequently (once per semester).

The final figures obtained in this process for each design alternative are compared, as are the figures concerning the amount of space required for the database by each of the design alternatives.

To illustrate the effect of a change to the design on LRA's and transport volume, let's assume we've decided to include the name of the faculty member who teaches a given section as part of the section record. This will add an extra twenty-five bytes to the data portion of each occurrence of the section record, thus adding 40,000 bytes (25 * 1600) to the space required for the database. It means that once an occurrence of *SECTION* is accessed, there is no longer a need to access the *FACULTY* record. Removing the 800 LRA's of the *FACULTY* record from the computations results in 2,501 LRA's being required to produce the time schedule. The new calculations for transport volume would be

```
TRANSPORT VOLUME =    1 *    53          (SEMESTER)
                   + 800 *  112          (SECTION)
                   + 800 *   68          (COURSE)
                   + 800 *   60          (DEPARTMENT)
                 = 53 + 89,600 + 54,400 + 48,000
                 = 192,653 (bytes)
```

These calculations reflect the new record length of each occurrence of *SECTION* as well as the fact that occurrences of *FACULTY* no longer need to be accessed in the production of the report. Thus, fewer LRA's are required and transport volume is decreased. The disadvantages of such a change include the increase in the size of the database and the problems associated with the fact that names of faculty members would be stored redundantly.


## *SUMMARY*

In this chapter, we studied the physical level of database design, the process of designing the database that will be implemented on a particular DBMS. Before this phase of design can begin, the information level of design must be completed. The final information-level design provides the input for the physical-level design process. Whereas the goal of the information level was a clean design, free of problems and capable of satisfying each individual user's needs, during the physical design another criterion is added: satisfactory performance.

We saw that physical design is best done in two phases. The first phase consists of creating a legitimate design for the DBMS that will be used, one that retains as much of the character of the information-level design as possible. We discussed in detail how to accomplish this for a relational model system and for a CODASYL system and briefly indicated how it would be done with a hierarchical system. The second phase consists of tuning this design to achieve optimum (or close to optimum) performance. This process consists of making changes to the design to improve it. We discussed the types of changes that could be made at this point to produce other possible designs, together with the advantages and disadvantages of the changes. A thorough understanding of the pros and cons will often make decisions concerning some of the possible changes obvious.

After making all the obvious changes, however, we will often be faced with a number of possibilities where it is not clear whether the change is wise. We are thus faced with a number of potential alternative designs. We discussed how to attempt to choose the best design from among them. To this end, we examined the process of calculating the size of a database given an actual design and projected volumes of occurrences of various entities. We discussed the process of acquiring estimates on performance through the use of logical record accesses (LRA's) as well as the strengths and weaknesses of this approach. We reviewed some ways of overcoming the weaknesses of this approach when necessary.

Finally, we illustrated the ideas in this chapter by applying them to the final information-level design that we created for Marvel College in chapter 8.

## REVIEW QUESTIONS

1. Describe the process of mapping an information-level design to a design for a relational model system. Describe in detail how the relations and keys are determined. Describe how special restrictions will be handled.
2. Describe the process of mapping an information-level design to a design for a CODASYL system. Describe how records, fields, and sets are determined. Describe how location modes are assigned.
3. Describe the general process of mapping to a hierarchical system.
4. What factors should be considered when calculating the total space required by a database?
5. Define logical record access (LRA). What is the difference between a logical record access and a physical record access? Which one gives a more accurate picture of the true performance that might be expected from a system? Why do we choose to use LRA's? What is meant by a weighted total of LRA's? What is transport volume? Why is transport volume sometimes considered in the process of choosing a design?

## EXERCISES

1. Illustrate mapping to the relational model by mapping the design you created in Exercise 3 of chapter 7 to the relational model.
2. Illustrate mapping to the relational model by mapping the design given in Example 5 of chapter 7 to the relational model.
3. Illustrate mapping to the relational model by mapping the design given in Example 6 of chapter 7 to the relational model.
4. Illustrate mapping to the CODASYL model by mapping the design you created in Exercise 3 of chapter 7 to the CODASYL model.
5. Illustrate mapping to the CODASYL model by mapping the design given in Example 5 of chapter 7 to the CODASYL model.
6. Illustrate mapping to the CODASYL model by mapping the design given in Example 6 of chapter 7 to the CODASYL model.

In Exercises 7 through 12, illustrate each suggested change to a relational model design, using your solution to Exercises 1, 2, or 3 as examples. Give an example of such a change, together with a reason you might consider for making the change and a reason for which you might choose not to make the change. If no example in the design illustrates such a change, discuss the change in general terms.

7. Splitting relations.
8. Combining relations.
9. Creating non-1NF relations.
10. Creating non-2NF relations.
11. Creating non-3NF relations.
12. Creating indexes.

In Exercises 13 through 22, illustrate each suggested change to a CODASYL model design, using your solution to Exercises 4, 5, or 6 as examples. Give an example of such a change, together with a reason for which you might consider making the change, and a reason for which you might choose not to make the change. If no example in the design illustrates such a change, discuss the change in general terms.

13. Splitting records.
14. Combining records.
15. Using system-owned sets.
16. Adding sets.
17. Including the key of the owner in a member record.
18. Changing a CALC record to VIA SET.
19. Changing a VIA SET record to CALC.

20. Changing the set in the VIA SET.
21. Requesting prior pointers.
22. Requesting owner pointers.

In Exercises 23 and 24, illustrate the suggested change to any model design, using your solution to Exercises 1, 2, or 3 as examples. Give an example of such a change, together with a reason for which you might consider making the change, and a reason for which you might choose not to make the change. If no example in the design illustrates such a change, discuss the change in general terms.

23. Encoding data.
24. Including derivable data.

Exercises 25 through 27 pertain to the CODASYL schema shown in Figure 11.15. In each exercise, you are to make the indicated change to the schema, then redo the calculations shown in Figures 11.16, through 11.18 concerning the size of the database and the weighted total of LRA's.

25. Add a system-owned set in which the member is the *CUSTOMER* record and in which prior pointers are requested.
26. Include the number and name of the sales rep who represents a customer in the *CUSTOMER* record.
27. Include the number and description of the part in the *ORDLNE* record.
28. \*\*\*\* *SPECIAL PROJECT* \*\*\*\*
    This project pertains to the Premiere Products database you designed in Exercise 14 of chapter 8. Using the final information-level design you created in that exercise, create an initial design for a relational system. Create an initial design for a CODASYL system.

# REFERENCES

1] Atre, S., *Data Base: Structured Techniques for Design, Performance, and Management*, 2nd ed. John Wiley & Sons Inc., 1988.
2] Date, C. J., and White, Colin J., *A Guide to DB2*, 3d ed. Addison-Wesley, 1989.
3] Hawryszkiewycz, I. T., *Database Analysis and Design*, SRA, 1984.
4] Kroenke, David, and Dolan, Kathleen A., *Database Processing: Fundamentals, Design, Implementation*, 3d ed. SRA, 1988.
5] Martin, James, *Managing the Data Base Environment*, Prentice-Hall, 1983.
6] McFadden, Fred R., and Hoffer, Jeffrey A., *Data Base Management*, Benjamin Cummings, 1985.
7] Teorey, Toby J., and Fry, James P., *Design of Database Structures*, Prentice-Hall, 1982.

# The Fourth-Generation Environment

## INTRODUCTION

Since the early 1950s, firms have been using computerized application systems. An **application system** is a collection of programs that together fulfill some specific function. Examples include common business application systems, such as payroll, accounts receivable, and inventory control, as well as more specialized application systems, such as airline reservations. It is only during the past few decades, a relatively short period of time, that firms have been using computers, yet computers and application systems have already undergone significant improvements in terms of speed, cost, capability, reliability, and ease of use. These improvements are due to the advances in both hardware and software technology. Let's briefly trace the progression of these advances.

### Hardware Generations

Computer experts usually characterize each major hardware advance by its primary electronic component, and each major advance is commonly referred to as a generation. The first generation of computers used vacuum tube components. A switch to transistor components in the late 1950s led to the second computer generation, which lasted until the mid-1960s. Through the remainder of the '60s, the third computer generation relied upon integrated circuits. Since the beginning of the '70s, we have been in the fourth computer generation, in which thousands of circuits are placed on a single chip using large-scale integration (LSI) or very-large-scale integration (VLSI) technology. (Figure 12.1 on the next page summarizes the hardware generations.) Improvements continue to occur as chip circuitry becomes more densely packed and as the functions performed by the hardware components become more sophisticated.

**Figure 12.1**

Hardware
generations

## Hardware Generations

1. First generation – vacuum tubes
2. Second generation – transistor components
3. Third generation – integrated circuits
4. Fourth generation – thousands of circuits on a single chip using large-scale integration (LSI) or very-large-scale integration (VLSI)

Each successive hardware generation has brought an increase in speed as the circuits have become more densely packed and more sophisticated. The reduction in size, improved manufacturing methods, and increased competition have also led to successive reductions in cost.

At the same time, peripheral devices have matured from the punched-card and simple printer configurations of the early generations to the terminal and laser printer technology of today. Magnetic disk has become the predominant secondary storage device for storing a firm's data.

## Software Generations

Major developments have also occurred in the software available to interact with advancing hardware technology. Each major software development is also referred to as a generation, though the time spans of the software and hardware generations do not exactly overlap. Figure 12.2 lists the software generations.

**Figure 12.2**

Software
generations

## Software Generations

1. First generation – machine language
2. Second generation – assembly language
3. Third generation – high-level languages, such as FORTRAN, COBOL, and many others
4. Fourth generation – high-productivity languages encompassing a variety of components that work together to form a single integrated environment

**First and Second Software Generations.**   Machine language was the single programming language available for use with the earliest computers. This first software generation was replaced in the '50s by assembly language, a more productive and less error-prone symbolic programming language equivalent to machine language. Both these first two generations of programming languages were executed on computers either with simple operating systems or with no operating system at all. Only one program at a time could be processed by the computer in a batch-processing mode. There were no database management systems, and data communications was in its infancy. Compared to the software environments of today, the first two software generations were primitive; but they did offer definite improvements over the alternative of manual processing.

**Third Software Generation.**   The introduction of high-level programming languages, such as FORTRAN in 1957 and COBOL in 1960 (and hundreds of others over the years), signaled the start of the third software generation. These languages have command structures that are closer to English in syntax than are machine and assembly languages, and so are considered to be at a higher level than the first- and second-generation programming languages. In addition, a single third-generation command translates to many machine-language instructions. This feature, plus the English-like syntax, led to significant productivity gains in the development and maintenance of application programs. In addition, industry-wide standards for languages like COBOL allowed programs in these languages to be *portable*, meaning that the same program could run on various brands of computers with minimal alteration.

Programs in high-level languages do not execute as rapidly as those written in machine and assembly language. The enormous demand for new programs, however, and changes to existing programs would have required larger numbers of programmers than could be supplied. In addition, the continued increase in programmer salaries combined with the continued decrease in hardware cost and increase in hardware speed made the use of high-level languages more cost effective.

The third-generation software environment saw the development of mature operating systems with multiprogramming capabilities (two or more programs executing concurrently) which, together with data communications, provided alternatives to batch processing. **Transaction processing**, for example, allows users to enter their own data and query the database through terminals.

Database management systems got their start and flourished during this third software generation. Vendors of these DBMS products eventually added capabilities in such areas as query languages, report writers, and data dictionaries.

New methods of developing software appeared during the '70s. Structured analysis and design, top-down methodologies, structured programming, and other software engineering techniques helped improve the quality and maintainability of programs and helped increase programmer productivity. Also, top-quality packaged software became more readily available for common business functions. Thus, packaged software became a viable alternative to the in-house development of common application systems.

**Fourth Software Generation.**    Within the past few years we have entered the fourth software generation. A DBMS that manages a firm's database is at the heart of this environment. Several other components are integrated with the DBMS. Functioning together, the DBMS and these other components constitute a **fourth-generation environment**. Since the DBMS is the foundation of this environment, the fourth-generation environment and its components are worthy of study in this book on database and are covered in this chapter. (There is another term commonly used for a fourth-generation environment. Since one of the main purposes for such an environment is to allow the rapid creation of application systems, people often use the term **applications generator** for a fourth-generation environment.)

In the next section, we will investigate some of the fundamental motivations for this environment, provide an overview of its components, and discuss the information center concept. We then turn to the data dictionary component, in many ways the hub of the environment. Following this we look at other fourth-generation environment components, such as program generators, report writers, screen generators, and query languages. At this point we turn to fourth-generation languages, as well as the process of prototyping an application system using the various components of the fourth-generation environment. Finally, we will look at some of the emerging innovations in the fourth-generation environment that are leading us into the fifth-generation environment.

## OVERVIEW OF THE FOURTH-GENERATION ENVIRONMENT

Both traditional forms of application languages and the traditional system development life cycle used during the first three software generations are undergoing fundamental changes as we emerge into the fourth-generation environment. Before discussing the fourth-generation environment and its components, we will first explore the reasons why these changes are occurring.

### Motivation for the Fourth-Generation Environment

Of course, change has been the only constant in the computer field since its inception. Innovative developments occur almost daily in hardware and software technology. This innovation is being shaped by the demands of the marketplace more now than ever. Several factors (see Figure 12.3) have forced development of the fourth-generation environment.

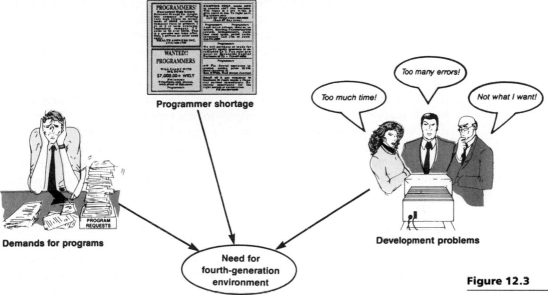

**Figure 12.3**

Factors forcing development of fourth-generation environment

**Programmer Shortage.** First, the effective use of programming languages from the first three software generations requires well-trained programmers. This has posed a chronic problem, as there have never been enough such programmers to meet the demand. Additionally, this demand has edged salaries for programmers higher and higher. As a result, firms in need of programmers have been seeking alternate means for developing application systems.

**Increased Demand for Programs.** Second, the demand by firms for application programming work has increased consistently over the years. Long-time users of computers experience an ongoing need for maintenance and enhancement changes to existing programs. These users have a constant backlog of new application system requests as they find more and more practical uses for their computers.

The demand for application programming work has accelerated over the past few years with the proliferation of computers, especially the low-cost microcomputers used by smaller firms and individuals. Interestingly, it was the development and continued improvement of the electronic *spreadsheet* capability that has been one of the principal causes of growth in the microcomputer area. The spreadsheet is a fourth-generation software tool that lends itself well to use by nontechnical users. Thus a software innovation has been fueling the sales of microcomputer hardware. This is a recurring phenomenon, as advancing hardware has made possible innovative types of software, and as advancing software has extended the research and development boundaries of hardware technology.

The shortage of programmers and the consistent, increased demand for computerization by firms have combined to force more and more nontechnical people to develop their own applications. This in turn has led to a need for easier-to-use software. Both hardware manufacturers and software vendors have a vested interest in this development. The third-generation environment matured to the point where it could no longer sustain the significant sales and profit increases these companies had grown used to. A low-cost, easy-to-use fourth-generation environment has provided a means of selling new products to existing computer users and a way to exploit new computer markets. Frequently, however, it has been new, start-up companies that have taken the lead in developing innovative capabilities in the fourth-generation environment; VisiCorp's VisiCalc spreadsheet (the first electronic spreadsheet ever developed) is just one example.

**System Development Problems.**   The problems inherent in the traditional way of developing computer application systems are the third major cause of the transition to the fourth-generation environment. Usually called the *system development life cycle*, the traditional software development approach is a multiphased methodology in which analysis of the users' requirements is followed up with the design and eventual implementation of a computer solution that satisfies these requirements. The major problems with the system development life cycle center around the time it takes to develop a system, the quality of the delivered system, and the degree to which the delivered system satisfies user requirements.

First, using third-generation programming languages, it takes much too long to develop a system of even moderate complexity. Many months or a year or two can elapse between the start of system development and the production use of the system. Users become impatient, and requirements often change during development. Meanwhile, the backlog of other developmental work increases. Users have been known to postpone requesting new developmental work because of the large backlog; this unrequested work is often referred to as the *invisible backlog*.

Second, it is virtually impossible to create error-free systems using conventional third-generation languages. Though systems of exceptional quality are occasionally developed, they are rare indeed. Errors can range from ones that are irritating nuisances to ones that can compromise the database by allowing unacceptable values to occur or by altering values illegally. Many, if not most, systems suffer from a variety of errors across this range. Systems are simply too complex to be developed error-free with traditional approaches. Various structured methodologies do help to minimize errors, but they do not eliminate them.

Third, when systems are completed and installed, they more often than not fall short of the users' desires. Even if a system has been perfectly developed, according to the written specifications prepared during the analysis phase, the user often finds the result less than satisfactory.

"Users don't know what they want until you give them what they asked for" is a famous comment that describes this user satisfaction problem. Though the statement may appear on the surface to be accusatory, there is justification for it. Imagine what it would be like if you were a user trying to picture how a future system would operate, and all you had to go on was a document consisting of written specifications filled with charts and diagrams. You would have to approve these specifications at the end of the analysis phase. It would be similar to what you would have to go through if the builder for your new home required you to approve construction on the sole basis of a written description of what was needed in the home, without any blueprints or a model home to review at the same time. The house would be bound to turn out differently in many ways from the way you pictured it.

## What is the Fourth-Generation Environment?

To overcome these problems, the computer industry has worked to develop a hardware/software environment that is easier to use and more productive than that of preceding generations. The new environment has also become more integrated as software vendors have tied together more and more tools to work in concert with one another. The software now handles a great deal of the procedural work, so that the programmer and user can concentrate on the problems being solved instead of having to come up with the method of solution. As a result, the quality of the developed system is better, there are fewer errors, and the interface between the user and the computer is much improved.

If the first three software generations can be called the age of the programmer, then the fourth software generation is the age of the user and the analyst. Although programmers are still integral to the functioning of the information systems department, more and more software tools are simple enough to be used both by users and analysts. In the following paragraphs of this section, we will give an overview of the fourth-generation tools, from the perspective first of the programmer, then of the user. In later sections of this chapter, each of the tools will be covered in greater depth.

**The Programmer's Fourth-Generation Environment.**　Figure 12.4 on the next page shows a fourth-generation, multi-user environment from the perspective of the programmer. The programmer sits at an interactive workstation, which is either a terminal or a personal computer serving as a terminal. From this single workstation the programmer performs all the work required to develop and maintain an application system. For example, the programmer can key in a high-level language program written in COBOL, test the program, document it, and request that the completed program be migrated from the test environment to the production environment.

**Figure 12.4**

Programmer's
fourth-generation
environment

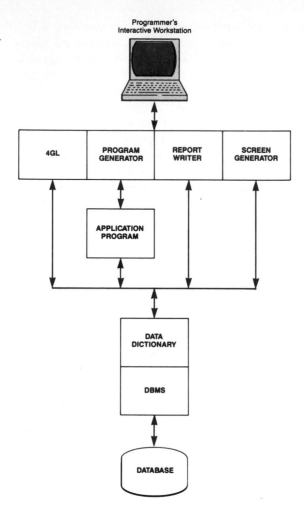

The programmer can also use any of the fourth-generation software tools shown in Figure 12.4 to develop a program solution for a particular problem. The core components of this environment are a DBMS and a **data dictionary**. Although the DBMS may conform to any of the data models we have studied, it is becoming increasingly common for the DBMS to follow the relational model. The data dictionary component permits the programmer to fully define all relations and characteristics of all attributes.

The other components interact with the data dictionary and the DBMS in carrying out their functions. Either a **fourth-generation language (4GL)**, a **program generator**, a **report writer**, or a **screen generator** can be used to rapidly create an application program. Combinations of these tools and others can be used to solve a given problem. The tools, in other words, are intended to be used with ease either together or alone, according to the requirements of any particular situation.

**The User's Fourth-Generation Environment.** Easier-to-use, more productive, and more highly integrated software products for use by programmers and other computer experts represent part of the fourth-generation environment. The other part of the environment consists of tools for use by nontechnical people, that is, the users themselves.

Figure 12.5 shows a typical fourth-generation environment for a user connected to a mainframe computer.

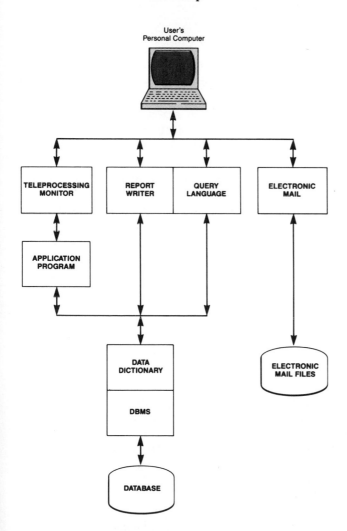

**Figure 12.5**

User's mainframe fourth-generation environment

The user's personal computer acts as a terminal to the host mainframe computer. Programmer-created application programs are managed by a **teleprocessing monitor**, which also manages the use of the terminals connected to the production mainframe environment. The user can create ad hoc reports, using either the report writer or query language facilities. All these software capabilities are again interfaced through the core components of the data dictionary and a DBMS. Additionally, the user can communicate with other mainframe users through an electronic mail software capability.

The software tools shown in Figure 12.5 are just a few of those available to users in today's fourth-generation environment. The full complement of tools is best explained in the context of the **information center** concept.

### The Information Center

There are two general categories of user computer-processing requirements. The first category consists partly of those requirements best handled by programs created and maintained by the information systems department. These programs interact with databases that require central control or must be shared by multiple users. Also in this first category are those requirements that have complex functions; these are best handled through programs constructed by an experienced computer programmer.

The second category of user computer-processing requirements consists of simple reports and queries or simple stand-alone information systems. Though these requirements can be handled by programmers, more firms today are having the users themselves handle them. Users have the best understanding of their total business requirements, their problems, and their information-processing needs. If easy-to-use software products are available for their use, it is most productive for the firm to have users solve their simplest information needs.

The **information center** serves as an adjunct to the information systems department and is designed to allow users to productively satisfy their own needs for information. An information center is typically staffed by information systems personnel who are experts in the use of the tools (software products) of end-user computing. The function of the information center is to make these software tools available to users and to train users to use the tools effectively. Users are encouraged to solve their own information needs with the tools and to use the information center as a resource for assistance whenever necessary.

The information center was first introduced by IBM Canada in 1972 as a way to help overcome the various third-generation problems described earlier in this section. The great majority of firms now use the information center concept, though it is not always referred to in this way by every firm. Some firms have multiple information centers. For example, if there are large numbers of users at several decentralized locations, each location may have its own information center. A large university may have one information center for academic end-user computing and one for administrative end-user computing. A large corporation may have one specialized information center for use by the marketing and production staffs, and another for use by financial analysts and accountants.

If a user had access to the mainframe environment shown in Figure 12.5, the information systems department staff who developed the application program would be responsible for training the user in its use and for creating the user manual for the program. On the other hand, the information center staff would be responsible for training the user in the use of the report writer, query language, and electronic mail facilities.

The responsibilities of the information center, however, extend beyond the mainframe environment. The use of the personal computer is widespread throughout most firms today, and the information center provides training and support for a full line of personal computer software tools.

Frequently, the data the user wants to manipulate on a personal computer already exists in the mainframe central database. The data does not have to be

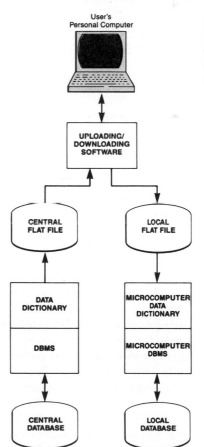

**Figure 12.6**

Downloading from the central database to a local database

reentered manually on the personal computer; Figure 12.6 shows an alternate method that is gaining in popularity. The required data is extracted from the central database into a flat file on the mainframe computer through the use of a normal DBMS capability, such as a report writer, query language, or utility. Special *uploading/downloading* software is then used to transfer the flat file from disk storage on the mainframe computer to hard disk or floppy disk storage on the personal computer. This process of transferring data from a mainframe computer to a personal computer is called **downloading**. Finally, the batch-loading facility of the microcomputer DBMS can be used to place the file onto the local database for processing by the user. If data exists on the local database and is needed on the central database, the entire process shown in Figure 12.6 can be reversed; the uploading/downloading software can be used to transfer data from the personal computer to the mainframe computer. This process is called **uploading**.

Once the user has the required data on the personal computer either through downloading or data entry, a large number of software tools can be used to manipulate the data. Figure 12.7 shows a typical complement of tools.

**Figure 12.7**

User's local fourth-generation environment

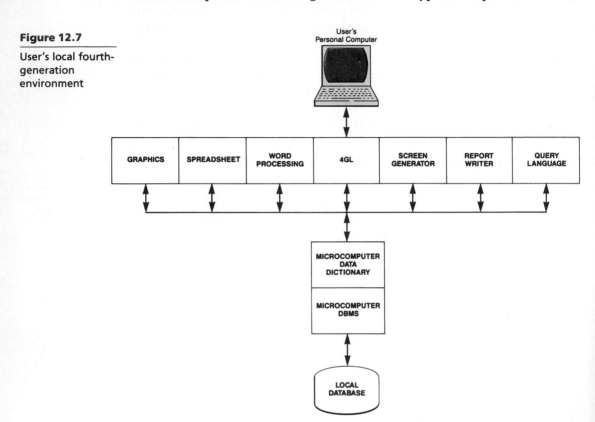

Again, the core components consist of a DBMS and a data dictionary integrated with the DBMS. The other tools are available as stand-alone products or can be bundled together as one integrated product. All these software tools (graphics, spreadsheet, word processing, fourth-generation language, screen generator, report writer, and query language) will be discussed further in later sections of this chapter.

Recently another alternative to the configuration shown in Figure 12.7 has become available, as shown in Figure 12.8. In this case, the DBMS run on the user's personal computer is capable of accessing either a local database or the mainframe database. This access is often transparent to the user; that is, the user may not even be aware of which database he or she is accessing. Both are accessed in exactly the same fashion.

As you can see, the information center staff must be fluent in a wide variety of hardware, software, and data communications functions.

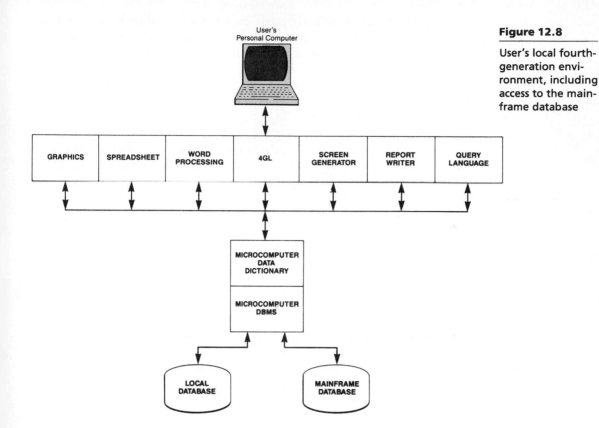

**Figure 12.8**

User's local fourth-generation environment, including access to the mainframe database

Increasingly, information centers are establishing guidelines and policies for the proper management of user computing within the firm. For example, it may be that only specific brands and models of personal computers are recommended for purchase by user departments. Likewise, users may be required to make their choice of specific software tools from among those recommended by the information center staff. In this way, a degree of compatibility between user-developed application systems is guaranteed.

## THE DATA DICTIONARY

Most database management systems today have a data dictionary component. A **data dictionary** is a central storehouse of data about the entire firm's data. It is a database, or set of files, containing the definition, characteristics, structure, and usage of data within a firm. Often the word *metadata* is used as a synonym for "data about data," so that a data dictionary can be viewed as a storehouse of a firm's metadata.

A distinction is frequently made between a data dictionary and a data directory. In this context, a data dictionary contains the fundamental definitions, characteristics, and uses of data; that is, it describes what the data is; and a data directory contains additional information about the data, such as where it is stored and how it is stored. For our purposes, this distinction is not necessary, and we will consider the data dictionary to be the comprehensive storehouse about a firm's data.

A **data dictionary system** is a system that stores, maintains, and reports on the contents of the firm's data dictionary. It is a set of programs to manage the data dictionary capability. This is the **catalog** function of a DBMS described in chapter 2. As we proceed through this section, we will see that the data dictionary system provides information both to the users of the database environment and to the database environment itself. A data dictionary system may be a manual system or a computer-based system. Since most firms today use computer-based data dictionary systems, we will restrict our discussion to them.

## Data Dictionary Content

The data dictionary is capable of storing a wide variety of documentation about a firm's data. Figure 12.9 lists a representative range of information stored in a comprehensive data dictionary. A data dictionary documents not only the firm's data but also the processes acting on the data and the environment in which the data exists.

**Figure 12.9**

Representative range of information stored in the data dictionary

```
Data
        Field
        Group
        Record
        File
        File Relationships
        User Views
        Database
Processes
        Program
        Report
        Screen
        Transaction
        Job
Environment
        System
        Department (People)
        Terminal
        Communication Line
        Disk Storage
        Processor
        Operating System
```

**Data Dictionary Field Entries.**    The data itself is documented from the field level to the database level. For each level the data dictionary entities and the relationships between entities at that level are defined, as well as the relationships between entities at different levels. (Note that entity is used in this section to refer to each of the items shown in Figure 12.9; for example, field, group, file, program, report, system.) For example, for each field we would store the following information:

1.  Name of the field and any synonyms or aliases. For example, we might have a field in the data dictionary named "Customer Current Balance." Users within the firm might refer to this same field by using synonymous names, such as "Outstanding Balance," "Customer Outstanding Balance," "Current Balance," "Customer's Receivable Balance," and "Amount Owed." All these alternative names should be documented in the data dictionary. In addition, the names by which the field is known within programs (CURRBAL within a COBOL program or CRBAL within an Assembler program, for example), within database entities (CRRBAL within a DL/I DBD or CURRBAL within a DB2 relation), or anywhere else within the firm should appear in the data dictionary.
2.  Description and definition
3.  Type (character, alphabetic, or numeric)
4.  Representation (integer, zoned decimal, or packed decimal)
5.  Length (number of bytes, number of characters, or number of decimal positions)
6.  Output format for printing and display purposes
7.  Default value
8.  Validation rules (criteria indicating which values may be entered in the field)
9.  Derivation formula if a calculated value
10. Number of occurrences if a repeating field
11. Responsible users (which department or user(s) are primarily responsible for initial entry of the field value and for maintenance of the field value)
12. Security (security codes for updating vs. retrieval)
13. Key information (Is this a primary, candidate, foreign, or secondary key? If so, for which relations? What are the rules for nulls, update, deletion, and other restrictions?)
14. If multiple or decentralized databases are used, where specifically is this field located?
15. Frequency of use and frequency of update

In addition, a large number of relationships must be documented for the field. For example, which groups, records, user views, and databases contain this field? Which programs retrieve or update this field? Which reports, screens, and transactions include this field? Where specifically is this field located, that is, what medium is used to store this field and where exactly within the record is it stored?

**Data Dictionary Report Entries.**   As you have seen, there is a great deal of information that must be stored in the data dictionary for each field. Fields are just one of the entities from Figure 12.9 that are documented in the data dictionary, however. Rather than explain everything that would be placed in the data dictionary for each entity in Figure 12.9, we will select one other entity, *reports*, as an illustration. For each report we would store in the data dictionary the following information:

1.  The report name
2.  Frequency of print
3.  Number of copies and report distribution
4.  Any special form required for production of the report
5.  The report format, including the sequence of fields, their exact positioning and format, subtotals and grand totals required
6.  All calculations
7.  Rules for excluding or including records and fields
8.  The program name that produces the report, and the job name that includes that program's execution
9.  Transactions used or created by the report program
10.  The system that includes this report

**Maintenance of Data Dictionary Information.**   For each of the other entities shown in Figure 12.9, and for each entity's relationships to other entities, the data dictionary would contain information that is relevant and important. A considerable amount of information has to be entered into the data dictionary. Too much, it may seem; however, all this information and more must be collected during the development and maintenance lifetime of an information system. Prior to the advent of the data dictionary capability, all this information appeared in written documents that were difficult to correct and maintain. Consequently, the documentation of an information system was often suspect and, therefore, seldom referenced during the system's production life.

Storing all documentation in the automated data dictionary rather than in written documents means that the documentation of an information system can be more easily and more accurately maintained. The entry of documentation into the data dictionary for an information system begins during its conceptual level design, continues through the external and internal level designs, and is modified as necessary during its production life. Most firms will not enter all the data for all their information systems into the data dictionary. Instead, only those information systems whose data is stored in the firm's database are normally documented in the data dictionary. The database administration group is the department within the firm responsible for managing the data dictionary capability and for making this type of decision.

## Types of Data Dictionaries

Data dictionaries can be categorized in a number of ways. First, a data dictionary that is **free-standing** runs independent of a specific DBMS. This type is sometimes also called an *independent*, or *stand-alone*, data dictionary. Most data dictionaries are not free-standing; rather, they are **integrated** (sometimes called *dependent*) data dictionaries that run only in conjunction with specific DBMS products.

The trend is toward the integrated data dictionary, and many database management systems have one. However, most integrated data dictionaries do not handle all the items shown in Figure 12.9. Fields and files are usually documented, but not to the extent described previously.

Another way of categorizing data dictionaries is to distinguish between the active data dictionary and the passive data dictionary. A **passive** data dictionary is simply a documentation tool for users of the environment. Information can be entered and maintained, then reported in a variety of ways. There is no interaction between the data dictionary and other environmental components, such as programs and the database.

An **active** data dictionary likewise serves as a documentation tool for users of the environment, but it also interacts with the other software components in the environment. The DBMS, programs, and query languages, for example, will not function unless the proper information is stored in the data dictionary and then funneled to these other software components. That's why a data dictionary of this type is described as active: it is actively involved in driving the other software components. The trend is for most of the newer data dictionaries to be active, integrated data dictionaries.

## Functions of Data Dictionary Systems

Data dictionary systems typically support a number of functions. The most common functions, described in the following paragraphs, are entry and maintenance, control and management, reporting, and software environment interaction.

**Entry and Maintenance.**   First, a data dictionary system must allow for the entry and maintenance of entities and their characteristics. This capability is implemented in some systems with a keyword language through batch-processed programs. In other, more prevalent systems, the entry and maintenance are accomplished through menus and data entry screens in an on-line mode of processing.

Some data dictionary systems permit users to extend the standard capabilities of the system. One way of doing this is by having the system handle additional entities and their characteristics and relationships. Imagine, for example, that a given data dictionary system does not permit the entry and maintenance of user views as a standard part of its functions. If the system allows us to extend its data maintenance capabilities, then we can define the user view and determine what data about user views we want maintained. From this point forward, we could enter and maintain this additional data within the data dictionary system.

**Control and Management.**   A data dictionary integrated with the DBMS most often has its data structured as a part of the database. Granted, this is a special part of the database. However, the normal authorization and recovery services of the DBMS are used to protect the data dictionary against unauthorized update and access and to recover the data in the event of damage. Also, ad hoc questions can be answered through normal query facilities and all other standard capabilities of the DBMS are available for use.

A free-standing data dictionary system normally has built-in security features. The degree to which concurrency control, recovery services, and other management and control functions exist in a free-standing system depends upon the particular data dictionary system.

**Reporting.**   The data dictionary system must also be able to provide a wide range of reports to the users of the environment. These users represent a wide cross section of the firm. They include the members of the database administration group; programmers, analysts, designers, and others within the information systems department; users; and auditors. Each user group requires reports that address their particular viewpoint and informational needs. Though some reports can be helpful to multiple user groups, each group also has unique reporting needs.

To meet these varying user needs, a data dictionary system should be capable of producing a combination of standard reports and user-defined reports. The standard reports are a fixed part of the system, while the user-defined reports are generated through a report writer component within the data dictionary system.

Some of the standard reports that can be produced by most data dictionary systems are as follows.

1. Lists of all fields in the database, alphabetized by field name. Particularly useful versions are lists of field names with their descriptions, lists of field names with their synonyms, and lists of field names along with the user area responsible for maintenance of the field within the database.
2. Reports by user area of the fields for which each has entry and maintenance responsibility. Information that often appears includes field name, length, default values, derivation formula, validation rules, and the names of the other user areas that have access to the field.
3. Reports showing relations and the fields contained within each relation. These reports could be ordered by application system or alphabetically by relation or for selected relations. Normally, the primary key field(s) will be identified.
4. Detail reports showing all characteristics of fields, records, user views, programs, or any other selected item stored in the data dictionary.
5. Cross-reference reports showing, for example, all the relations, screens, reports, programs, systems, and users using a field. These reports are especially helpful to programmers involved in the task of performing maintenance on a production application system.
6. Cross-reference reports that show for each user department the fields, user views, reports, screens, and transactions it uses.

Other reports besides these may be created as standard informational output from the data dictionary system. Also, most data dictionary systems permit screen output of information similar to that already described, either through standard on-line options or through query facilities. Finally, if a powerful enough report writer capability functions in conjunction with the data dictionary, any type of desired report can be generated, as long as it is based on the data stored in the data dictionary. These user-defined reports are limited only by the imagination of the users working with the report writer capability.

**Software Environment Interaction.**   If we are working with a passive data dictionary, then entries made to the data dictionary do not cascade to the other software components in the environment; also, entries made to the other software components have no effect on the data dictionary. This means, for example, that the field-level documentation placed in the data dictionary also must be directly entered into the programs and database DDL in an appropriate form. This is not a productive use of the database administrator's time and the programmer's time. Furthermore, inconsistencies may exist between the data dictionary documentation and the data definitions in the other software components. When they do, users rely on the data definitions in the programs and the database and learn to mistrust the documentation in the data dictionary. Often, as a result, the data dictionary system eventually becomes obsolete.

The most exciting data dictionary function involves the interaction of the data dictionary system with the rest of the software environment. This interaction can occur in many ways.

With some data dictionary systems, the interaction occurs by means of output generated by the data dictionary system. This output then serves as input to the other software components. Figure 12.10 illustrates such a data dictionary system. The data dictionary system is shown creating a file of extracted data definitions. Actually, this file is more likely to be multiple files. For example, one file would consist of data definitions in a form that could be directly copied into a COBOL or fourth-generation language program. Another file would contain the schema that directly feeds into the DBMS. Still another file would contain a subschema, user view, DL/I PSB, or some other DBMS control block appropriate to the specific DBMS. The report writer and query language facilities would interact with the DBMS and use the control block and parameter information supplied by the data dictionary system.

**Figure 12.10**

Interface between the data dictionary and the other software components occurring prior to execution

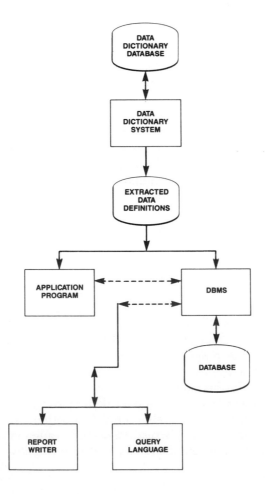

Users could even execute reports and queries that were created by the data dictionary system, fed to the DBMS, then stored in a user library on disk.

This form of interaction is called a **bridge facility** or a **static interface**, since the interaction occurs prior to the execution of the DBMS. The files created by the data dictionary system must be integrated with the appropriate software component; that is, the COBOL program must be compiled with its supplied data definitions; the fourth-generation language program must be compiled or interpreted with its supplied data definitions; the DL/I PSB must be assembled; and so on.

Some data dictionary systems have a bridge facility that goes in the opposite direction. In this case, the data dictionary system extracts data definitions from application programs and from existing databases and on the basis of these definitions constructs entries in the data dictionary. This is a useful feature if databases and programs exist in the production environment prior to the installation of the data dictionary system; it saves considerable data entry time and ensures consistency.

One of the problems with the bridge facility is that it can be bypassed by users. Entries can be made directly into the data dictionary, and duplicate entries can be made directly into the other software components. When this occurs, there is no guarantee of consistency.

The problem of inconsistency is overcome by another type of data dictionary system, one that furnishes what is called a **dynamic interface** or a **run-time interface**. Such a system is shown in Figure 12.11.

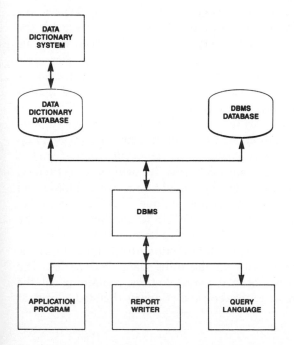

**Figure 12.11**

Interface between the data dictionary and the other software components occurring during execution

This is a true active data dictionary system that is fully integrated with a DBMS. All entries for data definitions and other system documentation are made in one place only, in the data dictionary. The DBMS obtains its database definitions directly from the data dictionary database. Since the interaction between the DBMS and the data dictionary occurs during the execution of the DBMS, any data definition changes made to the data dictionary are automatically reflected in the executing DBMS. Software components that interact with the DBMS, such as application programs and the report writer and query language facilities, can obtain their data definitions as late as the time of their execution. This ensures the consistency of data definition throughout the entire software environment.

The tradeoff for this high degree of consistency is the extra time it takes during execution for the DBMS to interact with the data dictionary database. We are actually trading off consistency for productivity. In another sense, however, people are *more* productive as a result of the gain in consistency, even though the DBMS is less productive during its execution. A reduction in the productivity of the computer environment versus an increase in the productivity of the people interacting with it is a common tradeoff.

It is impossible for the creators of data dictionary systems to anticipate all the types of processing that a particular firm might like its data dictionary system to perform. Therefore, some data dictionary systems have an *exit capability* that allows users to program their own routines to interact with the system. This is another way in which the standard capabilities of the data dictionary system may be extended to meet the specific requirements of a firm. There are various applications of the exit capability. It may be used, for example, by the database administrator to create a routine that extends the standard security facility of the data dictionary system. This can make the system more secure or can make the security control approach compatible with the approach already used by the firm. It may also be used to create a routine that provides more complex validity in checking for a field than is ordinarily provided by the data dictionary system.

There is one other important way in which a data dictionary system may interact with the software environment, and that is when a firm ends up having more than one data dictionary system. This can occur when a firm has multiple database management systems, each with its own data dictionary. For example, on the mainframe computer there might be a central DBMS and several application packages, each using its own unique DBMS and data dictionary. The firm might be shifting from one DBMS to another or might be introducing a fourth-generation language containing its own data dictionary.

Ideally, in such instances, one of the data dictionaries is targeted as the central dictionary that interfaces with all the other data dictionaries. The interface can be handled in one of two ways. Entries containing all the required information can be made to the central dictionary, then fed to each of the other dictionaries; or entries can be made primarily to one of the subsidiary dictionaries, with a notation made in the central dictionary indicating in which dictionary the detailed definitions of that entity can be found.

## Commercial Data Dictionary Systems

Hundreds of data dictionary systems are available on the market today. Many DBMS products have data dictionary systems that can be purchased or leased from the vendor selling the system. In addition, a number of data dictionary systems can be procured from third-party software companies for use with each DBMS.

Since the number of data dictionary systems is large and constantly growing, we will not try to provide a survey of these systems here. For a good background on commercially available systems, see [1]. Also, companies like Datapro and Auerbach are good sources of more current descriptions and evaluations of data dictionary systems.

## *FOURTH-GENERATION ENVIRONMENT COMPONENTS*

The data dictionary and DBMS are the core components of the **fourth-generation environment**. What are the other components? You will get different answers to this question depending on which expert you ask. There is even disagreement over what software generation we are currently in, though most experts believe we are in the fourth and on our way to the fifth.

Besides a lack of agreement on what constitutes this environment, there are no standards for its components. Even some of the terminology is not standardized. Multiple terms may apply to the same component or concept, and a single term may be used in different ways by different people. This is to be expected, since the components are undergoing constant refinement and improvement. The establishment of standards at this point would only constrain the creative research and development efforts currently under way.

The lack of standardization does cause problems, however. Different products are difficult to compare and evaluate, since there is nothing to use as a benchmark. Also, if a firm develops a large number of application systems using a given set of products, then decides to switch to another line of products, the process is a costly and difficult one, since the applications have to be redeveloped using the different languages of the new components.

Despite the lack of agreement on fourth-generation environment components, there is a general consensus that several components are part of the environment, and it is these components and their capabilities that we will describe. We will use a generic approach, since the lack of standardization, the large number of available products, and the list of new products being released almost continually prohibit us from an examination of specific software products. For further information on specific products, see [9] and [12] as well as many popular computer periodicals.

In this section we are going to describe such tools as report writers, query languages, screen generators, program generators, and teleprocessing monitors. In the next section, we will cover fourth-generation languages and the process of prototyping.

### Report Writer

A **report writer** is a tool intended to facilitate the process of developing reports. There are two main categories into which current report writers fall: language-oriented report writers and visually-oriented report writers. To create a report using a language-oriented report writer, we type an appropriate command in the language. When we use a visually-oriented report writer, we describe the layout of the report by positioning various elements on some sort of report design screen.

**Language-oriented Report Writers.**   The languages used by report writers are nonprocedural. A **nonprocedural language** specifies *what* has to be accomplished but not *how* to accomplish it. Contrast this with a **procedural language**, in which the programmer, or other user, must specify in detail how to accomplish the solution to the problem. Languages like COBOL, Pascal, Assembler, and FORTRAN are procedural.

In most cases, the report generated by the report writer is printed on paper, but it can also be output to a terminal screen or to a disk file. A report writer is sometimes called a *report generator*.

Let's take a look at the two relations, *SLSREP* and *CUSTOMER*, shown in Figure 12.12. The attribute names are listed at the top of each column. These are the same names used in the data dictionary for each attribute. Figure 12.13 shows a report writer request that we want to execute against the data contained in these two relations. Each request statement has been numbered for convenience of reference; numbering of statements is not normally required. The generated report is shown below the request. Note that there is information in the generated report that was not specified in the request. For example, both the date and page number appear on the first line of the report. These are examples of the defaults inherent in the report writer. Since the majority of reports need the date and page number printed, they will appear on the first line of each page unless suppressed by the requester. If necessary, they may be repositioned elsewhere on the page.

**SLSREP**

| SLSRNUMB | SLSRNAME | SLSRADDR | TOTCOMM | COMMRATE |
|---|---|---|---|---|
| 3 | Jones, Mary | 123 Main,Grant,MI | 2150.00 | .05 |
| 6 | Smith, William | 102 Raymond,Ada,MI | 4912.50 | .07 |
| 12 | Brown, Sam | 419 Harper,Lansing,MI | 2150.00 | .05 |

**CUSTOMER**

| CUSTNUMB | CUSTNAME | CUSTADDR | CURRBAL | CREDLIM | SLSRNUMB |
|---|---|---|---|---|---|
| 124 | Adams, Sally | 481 Oak,Lansing,MI | 418.75 | 500 | 3 |
| 256 | Samuels, Ann | 215 Pete,Grant,MI | 10.75 | 800 | 6 |
| 311 | Charles, Don | 48 College,Ira,MI | 200.10 | 300 | 12 |
| 315 | Daniels, Tom | 914 Cherry,Kent,MI | 320.75 | 300 | 6 |
| 405 | Williams, Al | 519 Watson,Grant,MI | 201.75 | 800 | 12 |
| 412 | Adams, Sally | 16 Elm,Lansing,MI | 908.75 | 1000 | 3 |
| 522 | Nelson, Mary | 108 Pine,Ada,MI | 49.50 | 800 | 12 |
| 567 | Baker, Joe | 808 Ridge,Harper,MI | 201.20 | 300 | 6 |
| 587 | Roberts, Judy | 512 Pine,Ada,MI | 57.75 | 500 | 6 |
| 622 | Martin, Dan | 419 Chip,Grant,MI | 575.50 | 500 | 3 |

**Figure 12.12**

*SLSREP* and *CUSTOMER* relations

```
1   PRINT SALES REP, CUSTOMER NAME, CUSTOMER #, CURRBAL
2   PRINT GRAND TOTAL RESERVE (CURRENCY)
3       MATCH ON REP NUMBER
4       IN ORDERS BY ASCENDING SALES REP, CUSTOMER NAME
5       ALL TOTALS FOR CURRBAL
6       COUNT BY SALES REP
7       CALCULATE RESERVE = 2.5% * CURRBAL
8       TITLE "CLIENT LIST BY SALES REPRESENTATIVE"
```

**Figure 12.13**

Report writer request and the report it produces based on the *SLSREP* and *CUSTOMER* relations

```
11/27/91        CLIENT LIST BY SALES REPRESENTATIVE          PAGE  1

                                    CUSTOMER      CURRENT
            SALES REP    CUSTOMER NAME    NUMBER      BALANCE

            Brown, Sam    Charles, Don      311       $200.10
                          Nelson, Mary      522         49.50
                          Williams, Al      405        201.75

            SALES REP TOTAL:  3                        $451.35

            Jones, Mary   Adams, Sally      124        418.75
                          Adams, Sally      412        908.75
                          Martin, Dan       622        575.50

            SALES REP TOTAL:  3                      $1,903.00

            Smith, William  Baker, Joe      567        201.20
                          Daniels, Tom      315        320.75
                          Roberts, Judy     587         57.75
                          Samuels, Ann      256         10.75

            SALES REP TOTAL:  4                        $590.45

            GRAND TOTALS:                            $2,944.80

                  RESERVE   $73.62
```

Statement one in the request specifies which attributes should be printed on a detail level. *CUSTOMER NAME* is a synonym for the attribute *CUSTNAME* used in the relation and defined in the data dictionary. *SALES REP* is a synonym for *SLSRNAME*, CUSTOMER # is a synonym for *CUSTNUMB*, and BALANCE is a synonym for *CURRBAL*. Because these synonyms are all stored in the data dictionary, they can be used without further definition.

Statements two and seven are closely related. In statement seven we define a temporary field, named RESERVE, that is calculated during the generation of the report. In statement two we specify that the calculated grand total RESERVE value should be printed at the end of the report and should be formatted in normal currency form. The formats of the other values printed are based on the defaults established in the data dictionary.

Since we are obtaining data from two different relations, statement three specifies the manner in which the two relations should be joined. REP NUMBER is a synonym for *SLSRNUMB*.

Statement four indicates the sequence for the report. Statement five specifies that subtotals and a grand total should be printed for the CURRBAL attribute. Statement six states that a count of the number of detail lines printed for a given sales rep should appear on the report whenever the SALES REP changes in value. The last statement provides the report title.

Notice that the SALES REP name prints on the report only when it changes in value. This is another example of the default concept employed in the report writer. The column headings are another set of defaults built into the data dictionary; these would be the output-heading characteristics for their respective attributes.

It would take a few hundred statements in a procedural high-level language to produce this same report. In our example we have let the nonprocedural report writer and the DBMS determine how to produce the report. We only need to describe the report we want; both the report writer and the DBMS work in conjunction with the data dictionary to accomplish the task we define. A report writer can easily handle more complex processing than we have indicated.

The language is easy to read and learn. Either a programmer or an end user can create the report writer request. Most firms train their end users to produce ad hoc reports using this capability. To obtain greater machine efficiency, however, most predefined reports are still generated by high-level language programs written by programmers.

Report writers are not a recent innovation — they have been around for the past twenty years. As they have evolved along with the software environment, report writers have become easier to use and have been better integrated with the data dictionary and the DBMS.

**Visually-oriented Report Writers.** In a visually-oriented report writer, we describe the layout of the report by placing elements in the positions where we would like them to appear. The report writer in dBASE IV, which we discussed in chapter 5, is an example of such a report writer. Remember that the report design screen consists of a number of bands that correspond to the various portions of a report. (See Figure 12.14.)

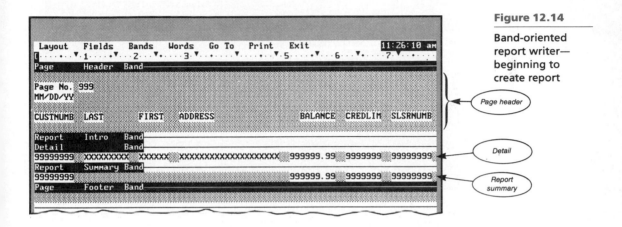

**Figure 12.14**

Band-oriented report writer— beginning to create report

To create a report, we add new elements, move existing elements, delete existing elements, and so on, until the layout on the screen matches that of the report we want. Figure 12.15 illustrates the results of making such changes. If we want to group records on our report, we can do so by introducing two new bands: group intro bands and group summary bands. Figure 12.16 on the next page illustrates a report layout containing these additional bands. (If you want to see what this report would look like, refer back to Figure 5.15.)

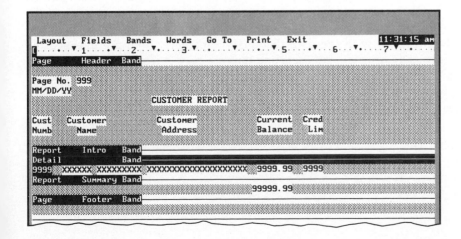

**Figure 12.15**

Report layout has been modified

**Figure 12.16**

Group bands have
been added

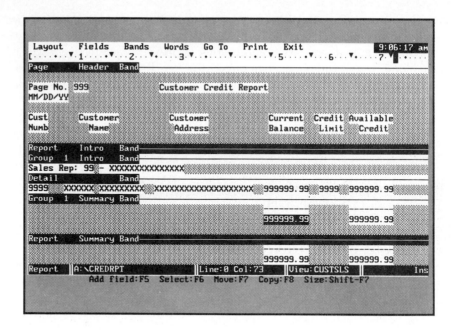

## Query Language

A **query language** is a nonprocedural language for retrieving information from a database. The retrieved information is typically displayed on a screen but may also be printed on paper or output to a disk file. Query language is a misleading term, since many query languages allow nonretrieval manipulation of the database by way of addition, deletion, and change commands.

Structured Query Language (SQL) and Query-by-Example (QBE) are two examples of query languages. Chapter 3 offers numerous examples of queries using each of these languages, so we will not provide further examples of them here.

A query language is similar in many ways to a report writer. Both are firmly integrated with the data dictionary capability. Both are intended for nontechnically oriented end users and thus are easy to learn and use. Both are nonprocedural; a small number of statements can accomplish a great deal. The report writer example request in Figure 12.13 and SQL are *command-driven languages*, which means that language commands, or statements, must be entered according to the precise syntax of the language. Some of the newer report writers and query languages are *menu-driven languages*, which means the user is prompted to respond to choices presented on a screen in a menu- or form-oriented manner. Though both are frequently used for ad hoc processing, either a report writer request or a query may be stored in a library file and executed repeatedly over a period of time.

Many report writers and many query languages can be processed in batch or on-line modes. However, the main objective of a report writer is to produce a hard-copy report, while that of a query language is to display retrieved information on a screen. Consequently, report writers tend to be more compatible with batch processing, and query languages are more on-line oriented. Report writers tend to have more sophisticated output-formatting capabilities, while query languages are built for rapid response.

Other differences between a report writer and a query language are more subtle. Often a product is advertised by a software vendor as a query language when it might be advertised more appropriately as a report writer, and vice versa.

### Screen Generator

A **screen generator** is an interactive facility for creating and maintaining display and data entry formats for screen forms. The screen generator allows you to define how the screen is to be *painted*; that is, how literals are displayed on-screen and how color and other visual attributes are handled. It permits you to define the placement of variable data that the user is to enter or that is to be displayed. Through its interaction with the data dictionary, the screen generator performs validation on values entered by the user. Table lookups, calculations, interaction with the DBMS, and a user exit facility are other functions handled by the screen generator. *Screen painter* and *screen mapper* are two other names for a screen generator.

A screen generator should be easy to use. Some of the older screen generators are batch-oriented, but almost all the newer ones are interactive. To illustrate one possible approach to an interactive screen generator, suppose we wanted to use one to create the Customer Maintenance data entry form shown in Figure 12.17 on the next page. The areas in boxes are for values to be entered or displayed as necessary. The literals outside the boxes will be painted on the screen when the form first appears.

**Figure 12.17**

Data entry screen
to be created
through use of a
screen generator

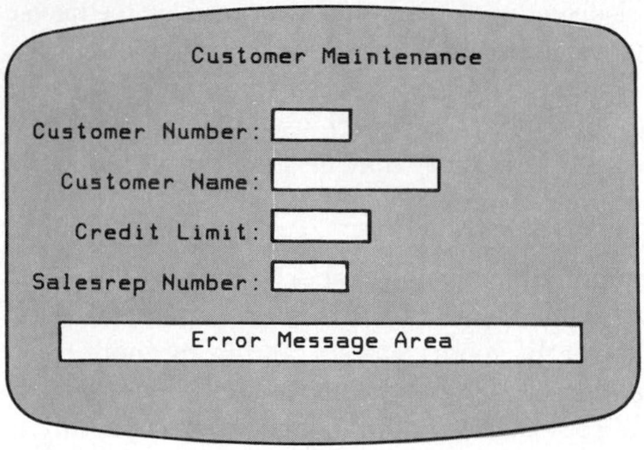

```
                 Customer  Maintenance

    Customer  Number: [      ]

      Customer  Name: [            ]

      Credit  Limit: [      ]

   Salesrep  Number: [    ]

            [   Error  Message  Area            ]
```

Figure 12.18 is the main menu for the interactive screen generator. Option one for element maintenance lets us define the literal and variable value areas on the screen. Option two lets us define color blocks on the screen and manipulate these blocks once they have been defined. Option three allows us to move an entire form on the screen, store the form in a library, combine separate forms together, and otherwise manipulate entire forms. Option four terminates the screen-generator session.

**Figure 12.18**

Main menu for the
screen generator

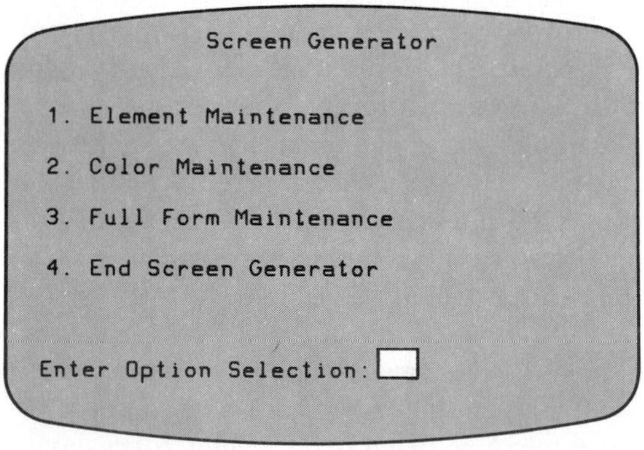

```
                 Screen  Generator

    1.  Element  Maintenance

    2.  Color  Maintenance

    3.  Full  Form  Maintenance

    4.  End  Screen  Generator


    Enter  Option  Selection: [  ]
```

We start building the Customer Maintenance form by selecting option one for element maintenance. The element maintenance menu shown in Figure 12.19 is then displayed by the screen generator. We are building a new form, so we select option one to create a new element.

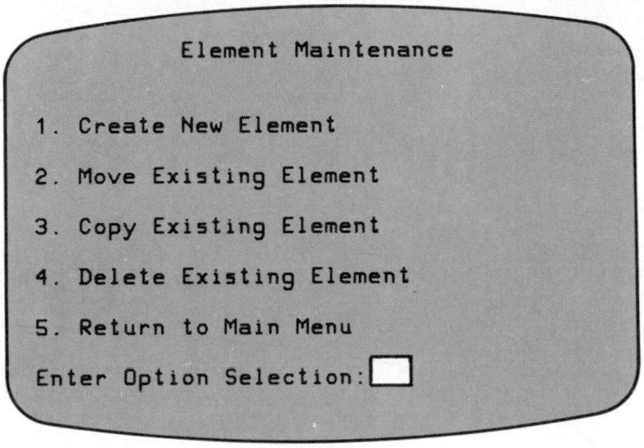

**Figure 12.19**

Element mainte-
nance menu for
the screen
generator

A similarly formatted menu appears next. On this menu we choose to define a literal on the screen. A blank screen then appears. On the blank screen we use the cursor control keys on the keyboard to move the cursor to the exact position we want to begin the placement of the literal Customer Maintenance. Once the cursor has been properly positioned, we enter this literal. We continue to alternate repositioning the cursor and entry of literals until we have fully defined the literal values we want painted on the screen. When we are finished with the literals, we press the enter key and are returned back to the screen in Figure 12.19 for our next choice.

If at any point we aren't sure how best to proceed, we can use a keyboard function key to invoke a *help facility* that will explain our options and the actions we can take. When we have finished using the help documentation, the screen generator returns us back to the exact spot we were at prior to invoking the help facility.

Each of the boxed-in areas in Figure 12.17 is defined separately in a similar fashion. We make choice one ("create new element") in Figure 12.19, then specify that we are defining a variable area on the form, in this case for the boxed-in area for Customer Number. We are then prompted by the screen generator to enter the data dictionary field name or the calculation or our exit routine name for the variable field area we are defining. We also have the option of specifying special screen attributes for the screen area, such as blinking, reverse video, underlining, or color. The screen generator presents us with the screen with the literals we have defined on it. We position the cursor where the variable Customer Number starts and press the Enter key.

The creation of the rest of the Customer Maintenance form follows in a similar manner. The screen generator creates a "program" that may need to be compiled or assembled, or that may be in a form ready for execution. Figure 12.20 on the next page shows the generated screen form with sample user-entered data filled in.

**Figure 12.20**

Data entry screen filled in with user-entered data

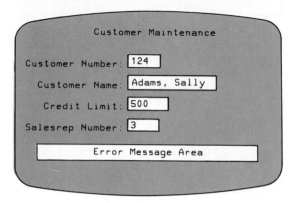

There are other approaches to the process, such as the one used in dBASE IV. With this approach, we manipulate the screen directly to produce the form we want. We usually begin with a simple form containing the desired fields. (See Figure 12.21.) We then modify the layout on the screen to produce the one we want. (See Figure 12.22.) We then add other visual characteristics, such as the boxes shown in Figure 12.23.

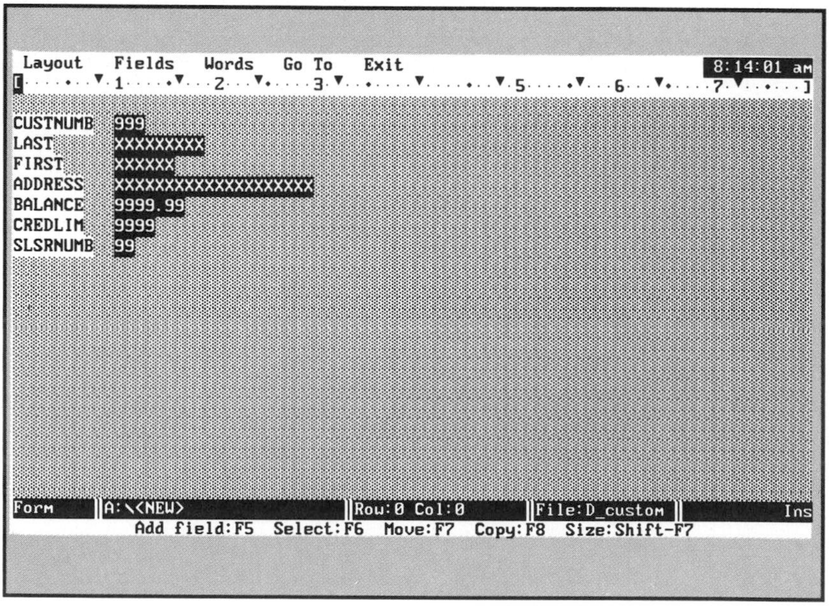

**Figure 12.21**

Beginning to create a form

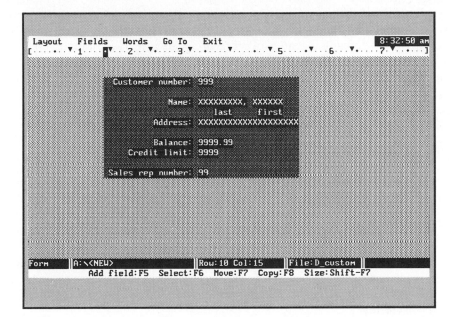

**Figure 12.22**

Fields have been
modified and
moved

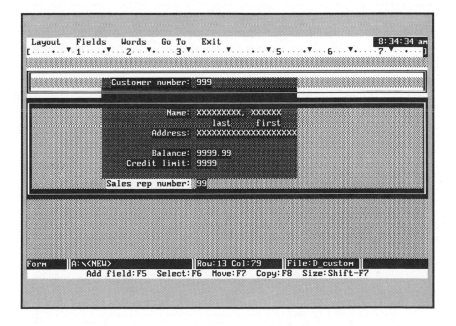

**Figure 12.23**

Other attributes
have been added

Regardless of the specific approach taken by an individual screen generator, the process is easy and we can see our progress each step of the way. We can define the form in a matter of minutes, whereas it takes hours to create a program to handle the same processing. Testing time is minimal, compared to the length of time it takes to debug a high-level language program. Overall, using a screen generator is a much more productive approach than the traditional methods of creating screen forms.

## Special Components

There are some special components often included in a fourth-generation environment. These include:

1. A facility to assist us in developing menus to tie together the various screens, reports, and updates
2. A facility to assist us in including on-line help in our application systems
3. A facility to assist us in supporting windows in our application systems

**Menu Facility.**   The typical menus used in application systems in the past contained a list of choices, each preceded by a number or letter. To make a selection from the list, a user typed the number or letter preceding the desired choice and pressed Enter. Including this type of menu in an application system was not a particularly difficult task. It is much more common now, however, to see such things as "horizontal bar" and "pull-down" menus. (See Figure 12.24.) Selecting certain options from these menus may in turn cause "pop-up" menus to appear on the screen. (See Figure 12.25.) (If you don't remember the definitions of these various types of menus, refer to chapter 5.)

**Figure 12.24**

Menus

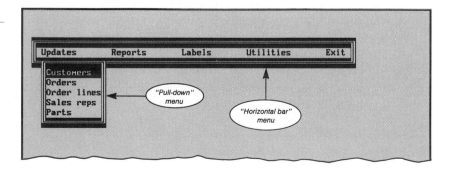

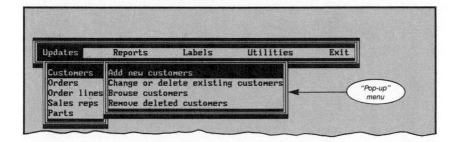

**Figure 12.25**

Menus

Writing programs to support these types of menus can be a time-consuming process. Users, however, have come to expect them, since many of the software packages they frequently encounter employ this style. For this reason, a menu facility, a facility to assist us in creating and implementing these menus, can be an important component of the fourth-generation environment. We have already seen such a facility when we looked at dBASE IV in chapter 5.

Using this facility, we first create a horizontal bar menu with the options we want (see Figure 12.26) by simply typing the options in the appropriate locations. We can then create the various pull-down menus in exactly the same fashion. (See Figure 12.27 on the next page.) Once we have done this, we simply indicate the action to be taken when the user selects any of the options. At this point, we are done. dBASE then creates the programs to support our menu structure for us.

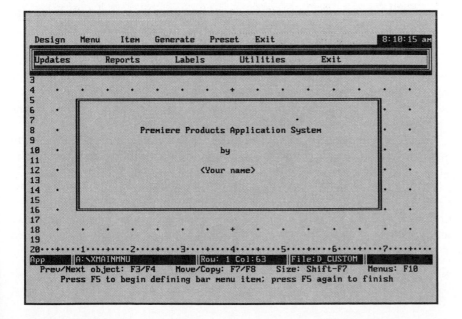

**Figure 12.26**

Application Design screen

**Figure 12.27**

Application Design
screen

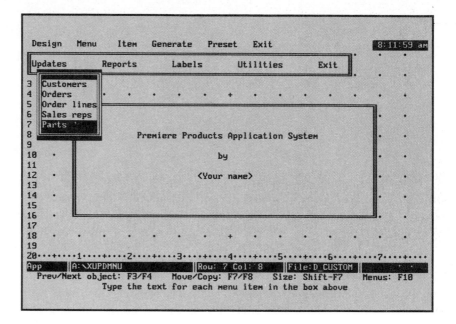

**Help Facility.** Many software packages include on-line help. To obtain help on a particular function, the user only needs to press a certain key. It would be nice to include such help in the application systems we create.

There are actually two different types of help we might include in our systems. When a menu is on the screen, we can include a message line at the bottom of the screen. The message line will contain a more detailed description of the currently highlighted menu option. This type of help is restricted to a single line, however. The other type of help allows us to use an entire screen to provide the necessary information to the user of our system. To obtain this type of help, the user presses a special key, often F1. The screen on which the user is working disappears and is replaced with the help information that we have created. Once the user has viewed this information and pressed Enter, the original screen reappears.

Some fourth-generation environments include a facility to allow us to easily include such help information in the application systems we create. Figure 12.28 illustrates such a facility. In this figure, which illustrates the help facility included in the dBASE IV applications generator, we are in the process of creating a message line prompt. Using another option, we could describe a full screen of help text. In either case, the use of the help information we specify will be automatically included in the application programs generated for us by dBASE IV.

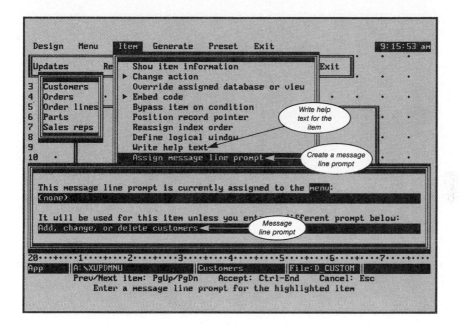

**Figure 12.28**

Application Design screen

**Window Facility.** The chances are very good that you have used some software product that made use of *windows*. Perhaps while you were working on a particular task, you pressed a special key, and a box, often called a window, appeared on the screen allowing you to carry out a different operation. Depending on the size of the window, a portion of your original screen may still have been visible. When you finished the other operation, you pressed some other key. At this point, the window disappeared and you were returned to your original screen.

We might want to build the use of windows into our application systems. For example, suppose a user is making a change to customer 567 using the form shown in Figure 12.29 on the next page and that the user wants to change the sales rep number for this customer from 12 to 16. Suppose the user realizes at this point that there is no sales rep 16. Normally, the user would have to:

1. Exit from the process of updating customers.
2. Return to the menu.
3. Select the option for adding sales reps.
4. Add sales rep 16.
5. Exit from the process of adding sales reps.
6. Return to the menu.
7. Select the option for updating customers.
8. Begin the update for customer 567 from scratch.

**Figure 12.29**

Customer form

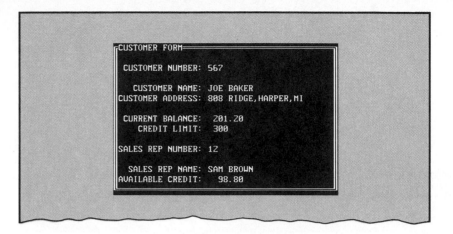

In an environment using windows, however, the scenario could be much different. In this case the user would:

1. Press a special key to bring the sales rep form to the screen.
2. Add sales rep 16. (See Figure 12.30.)
3. Press a key to return to the customer update process.
4. Complete the update for customer 567. (See Figure 12.31.) The user would *not* need to begin the update from scratch, but could simply resume the update from the point where he or she left off.

**Figure 12.30**

Customer and sales rep forms

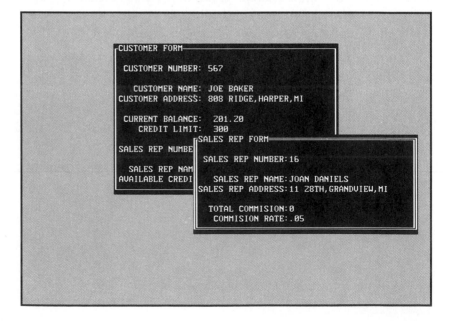

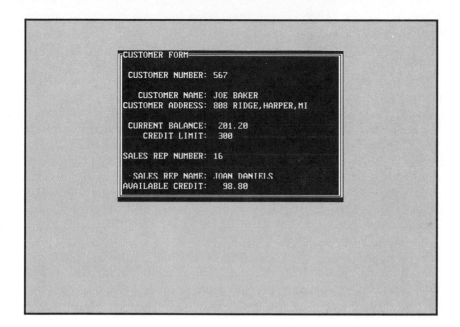

**Figure 12.31**

Customer form

This type of approach can make users much more productive. Building the logic to handle windows into our application programs can be very cumbersome, however. Using a window facility, we simply specify the contents of the various windows we want along with where and how they are to be used. The system handles all the other details for us.

## Program Generator

A **program generator** is a language facility that generates a second- or third-generation language program. The objective of a program generator is to allow a programmer to more productively create and maintain programs written in traditional languages.

A *precompiler* language is one type of program generator. It combines its own unique language features with those of the target language. Another reason for its name is that it is compiled, and the output of the compilation is a source program in the target language.

There are a number of precompiler languages that generate COBOL programs. In these cases, the program is coded in the precompiler language, which is then compiled to create a COBOL program. Either the original precompiler language version of the program or the generated COBOL program can be maintained. The precompiler language increases productivity partly through the use of abbreviated names for data definitions, paragraphs, and so on. When it is compiled into COBOL, fuller names are substituted for the abbreviated names. Another way these languages save time is by automatically providing the standard portions of a COBOL program that remain the same from program to program. Yet another productivity aid is the use of precoded modules with parameters for commonly encountered routines.

One alternative to a program generator is the *skeletal program*. A skeletal program is the skeleton of a high-level language program. High-level languages, such as Pascal and COBOL have language statements that are fixed from program to program. These statements are already provided in the skeleton program. Normally, a number of different skeleton programs exist for the different common types of programs that need to be created. For example, there may be skeleton programs to produce a report from a file, to update a file in batch mode, to update a file in on-line mode, and so on. Each of these skeletons would have the standard routines already included for programs of that type.

The skeleton serves as the starting point for the program to be created. The skeleton is copied, then an editor is used to manipulate the language statements to tailor them for the specific problem solution. Statements are added as necessary to complete the solution. The skeleton eliminates the bother of a great deal of the program coding that is repetitive from program to program.

### Teleprocessing Monitor

One of the functions of a DBMS is to provide integration with support for data communication. It is the purpose of a teleprocessing monitor to handle this function. A **teleprocessing (TP) monitor** is a system software product that controls a host computer's terminal communications and the application programs executed by the terminal users. The type of processing managed by a TP monitor is called **transaction processing**.

All major mainframe DBMS's have a TP monitor component. In addition, most DBMS's work with a number of other TP monitors. IBM's CICS (Customer Information Control System) is the dominant TP monitor in the marketplace today.

Figure 12.32 provides an overview of the relationship of the TP monitor to the DBMS. The TP monitor and the DBMS are placed in their own main memory areas when the production system is started up. The TP monitor scans the terminal network, asking one terminal after the other if it has a transaction to submit. This process is called *polling*. (Sometimes a *front-end processor*, which is a mini- or microcomputer connected to the terminal network, handles this polling function instead.) The TP monitor queues the transaction and schedules the application program that handles that transaction type. When main memory becomes available, the program is loaded from the application program library and the program processes the transaction. All database program requests are handled by the DBMS.

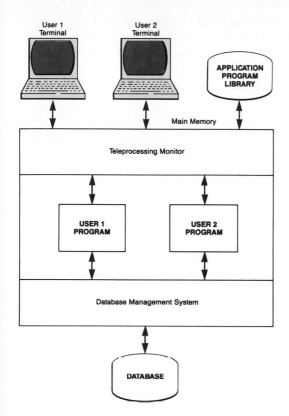

**Figure 12.32**

Use of a tele-
processing monitor
to manage termi-
nals and applica-
tion programs

When the application program completes its execution, program output back to the terminal is passed to the control of the TP monitor. The TP monitor then communicates the output back to the proper terminal.

To perform its functions, the TP monitor must have a great deal of knowledge about the environment it is managing. For example, it must know which communication lines it controls, the type of terminal attached to each line, which application program handles each specific type of transaction, and which users are authorized to use specific terminals and transactions. These facts are stored in tables that are under the control of the TP monitor.

Since multiple users may be authorized to use the same type of transaction, the TP monitor must allow for concurrent use of the same application program and must have an authorization services function to control access. Also, it must provide recovery services for the terminal network and the application programs it manages. The TP monitor handles other functions as well, but the functions already mentioned should give you an appreciation for the complexity of the job it does.

Earlier we said that most DBMS products work with a number of different TP monitors. Not just any DBMS and TP monitor will function together properly, however. Both are complicated software products, and there is some overlap in the functions performed by each. Each must be specifically programmed to interface and function in synchronization with the other.

## FOURTH-GENERATION LANGUAGES AND PROTOTYPING

The fourth-generation environment consists of a DBMS, a data dictionary, and the components described in the previous section. Other components, such as spreadsheets, graphics, modeling tools, and decision-support systems, are also included in the fourth-generation environment as well, but we will not discuss them here.

We have to discuss one other major component of this environment. It is called a **fourth-generation language**, or 4GL, and is discussed in this section along with the prototyping process.

### Fourth-Generation Languages

Each of the other components of the fourth-generation environment is easily defined, and software products can be categorized according to whether they have the characteristics of a given component. It is a different story with 4GLs. There is no common agreement as to what a 4GL is and is not. Let's review two of the more popular definitions and descriptions.

A definition frequently encountered is similar to one presented by Paquette and Sardinas. (See [13].) According to them, a 4GL is a complete family of components rather than a single programming language. These components must be easy and productive to use, since end users have to be able to work with them comfortably.

James Martin (see [9]) implies that it should take approximately one-tenth the amount of time to develop a 4GL program as it does to develop an equivalent high-level language program. Martin also places all current nonprocedural languages and some other types of products in the category of 4GL and suggests that *high-productivity language* be used instead of 4GL to more clearly describe these languages.

Many software vendors tout as 4GLs products that range from fairly simple report writers, query languages, and programming languages to comprehensive families of products that handle every conceivable function. 4GL, or fourth-generation language, has a nice state-of-the-art sound, and probably helps market a vendor's product.

Calling a particular software product a 4GL, however, does not tell us anything about what the product does. It would be more helpful if a product were given a category name like Vendor A's ADA compiler, Vendor B's report writer, Vendor C's nonprocedural programming language, Vendor D's tele-processing monitor, Vendor E's DBMS, or Vendor F's data dictionary. The categorization of each of these products would then give a clue as to its general functional capabilities.

Though we will not attempt to give a precise definition for a 4GL, it may be helpful to talk about what we think should be in one. A 4GL should be a programming language that integrates all the other fourth-generation environment components and complements them by providing any functions not already contained in them. From this description, it is clear a 4GL has both procedural and nonprocedural aspects.

For an example of what we mean by a 4GLs integration capability, suppose we needed to use a TP monitor and a relational DBMS, both integrated with a data dictionary, to process a user's terminal transaction. We would create a screen form using a screen generator. The 4GL program would contain a nonprocedural statement to handle the input from the terminal by way of the TP monitor, an SQL statement to access the database, and another nonprocedural statement to send the output back to the terminal, again under the control of the TP monitor. Thus the 4GL would be integrating into one program the functions performed by the other components.

As an example of how the 4GL would complement the other components by providing additional functionality, suppose data validation were required beyond what the data dictionary and screen generator could provide. Then the previous scenario would need to include some procedural statements to perform these validity checks through a user exit from the screen-generator component.

Some products considered to be 4GLs function approximately along the lines we have just described. We are not endorsing these products, however, just because they follow our concept of what a 4GL should do. Products, and families of products, should be evaluated by what they do, not by what they are called. For more information on 4GLs, see [4], [8], [9], [10], [11], [12], [13], and [14].

## Prototyping

More and more frequently, the collection of components that constitute the fourth-generation environment is being called an *application development system*, while the environment itself is being called the *integrated development environment*. Though these terms may be more descriptive, "fourth generation" is still the phrase most in favor today.

When we put all the fourth-generation components together into an integrated package, the result is a set of high-productivity tools for developing and maintaining application systems. Some firms use these tools in place of traditional languages within the programming phase of the system development life cycle, thus realizing a dramatic decrease in the amount of time needed to program the information system.

However, firms may encounter two major problems when they use these tools simply as a replacement for traditional languages. First, the fourth-generation tools may often be less efficient when executing on the computer. That is, certain programs can take longer to execute and may result in more database accesses and higher usage of other system resources. The lowered machine efficiency makes sense when you consider that some of the tools are interpretive languages rather than compiled languages. Also, these tools are still in their embryonic stage, so they are not as efficient as they eventually will be. Some application systems require a performance level higher than that which can be obtained through the fourth-generation tools, so they are still developed with traditional languages. Even assembly language is used in some cases to gain the highest performance level possible.

The second problem centers on the degree of user satisfaction with the developed production system. If we follow the system development life cycle by continuing to use written specifications as the basis for user requirements, this problem will be maintained; the user must continue to picture the final information system by means of the abstract written specifications. Earlier in this chapter we discussed the difficulties inherent in this approach. (See Figure 12.33.) The prototyping process is shown in Figure 12.34 and described on page 644.

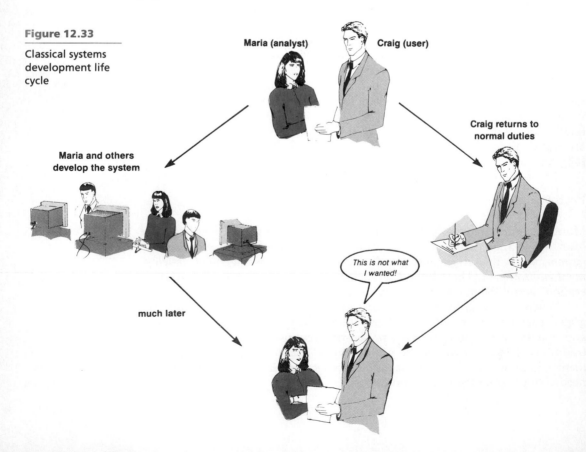

**Figure 12.33**

Classical systems development life cycle

Maria (analyst)    Craig (user)

Craig returns to normal duties

Maria and others develop the system

*This is not what I wanted!*

much later

**Figure 12.34**

Prototyping

Rather than use the fourth-generation tools as a replacement for traditional languages during the programming phase, many firms have begun using them as an aid in determining the user requirements during the analysis phase. Then in place of written specifications as an abstract model for the information system, the fourth-generation tools are used to build an actual working version of the system. The system is constructed in an iterative fashion. The system developers first build an initial system they feel satisfies user requirements. This is done rapidly, using the highly productive fourth-generation tools. This initial system is then given to the users to work with, which provides feedback on the system's functioning with respect to the user's particular needs. Users are encouraged to be highly critical of the system, and the system undergoes repeated change and critique until they are completely satisfied with it.

When the iterative cycle is completed, the result is a complete, functioning system. The working version of the system is called a **prototype**, and the process of creating the system in this manner is called **prototyping**. (See Figure 12.34.) This process and result resemble the procedure used in the engineering world, where a less-expensive prototype is created to eliminate the bugs before the final product is designed and produced.

When we prototype an application system, we end up with an application system that satisfies user requirements. People can more easily visualize what they will be getting when they work with a functioning system than they can by reading a written document. Developing a system that satisfies the needs of the users is the ultimate aim of any system development life cycle methodology, and prototyping is very successful in attaining this goal.

If the application system does not demand high performance, then the prototype can serve as the final version of the system and subsequent steps of the system development life cycle can be bypassed. If one of the tools available is an *automatic documentation* component, the user and operations manuals can be generated directly from the completed prototype. All in all, the process results in significant savings in time, money, and frustration.

If the system demands a performance level higher than can be obtained from the fourth-generation tools, then the prototype serves as the definition of the users' requirements. The remaining steps of the system development life cycle are then followed to design, develop, and implement the information system through the use of traditional programming languages.

Bernard Boar, in his landmark book on prototyping (see [3]), gives an example of the quantity of work that can be accomplished quickly by using fourth-generation tools. In only six weeks two prototypers were able to create a medium-sized application system. Using traditional programming languages, it would have taken many multiples of the six weeks to develop this same application system.

The high productivity components of the fourth-generation environment have made it possible to prototype application systems. For further details on the benefits, problems, and process of prototyping, see [3], [4], [9], and [10].

## EMERGING SOFTWARE TOOLS

Much of the research and development effort in software technology continues to center around improvements and advancements in fourth-generation and earlier-generation concepts and tools. There are software tools already available that are considered to be part of the fifth-software generation. **Fifth-generation software** is characterized chiefly by concepts and methods from the field of artificial intelligence. **Artificial intelligence** is the capability of a computer-based system to perform functions normally associated with intelligent human behavior. Examples of these functions include the ability to learn, reason, and draw inferences in solving problems.

Natural languages are one such example of fifth-generation software. A **natural language** allows a user to communicate with a computer in human language form by using ordinary English words. The user is not bound by an artificial computer language that has its own syntax and vocabulary. Let's look at a few examples of querying a database through a fictitious (but representative) natural language called NL.

1. Find the name of customer 256.

```
User: What is the nme of customer 256?
Computer: I don't recognize "nme."  Did you mean "name"?
User: Yes.
Computer:      NAME
          Samuels, Ann
```

2. Find the names of all the customers of sales rep 6.

```
User: Give me the names of the customers of sales rep 6.
Computer:      NAME
          Samuels, Ann
          Daniels, Tom
          Baker, Joe
          Roberts, Judy
```

3. Of the names found in the previous query, which ones have a credit limit of $300?

```
User: Which ones have a credit limit of 300?
Computer:      NAME
          Daniels, Tom
          Baker, Joe
```

One final note: if the user had placed the term *small customer* in the dictionary and had defined it as a customer whose credit limit is $300, then that last query could have been formulated as "Which ones are small customers?"

Natural languages rely upon the entries in the data dictionary and on an auxiliary dictionary of common words the language understands. They are not typically built to recognize every conceivable English-like communication a user might enter. Too much processing overhead would be incurred, owing to today's technology, and in many cases there would be great uncertainty on the part of the natural language processor as to the intent of the user. Furthermore, for repetitive processing requests, it is more efficient to use more productive language techniques.

While we are on the subject of more natural interfaces with computers, it should be pointed out that some users interact with computers through pictures and voice input. Picture-oriented input involves the use of special screen symbols, called *icons*, that serve as representations of the functions they perform. The use of a *mouse* or *touchscreen* to select the desired function is popular with this form of interface. Because of the inefficient nature of this processing and its limited vocabulary, however, *voice input* and *output* are principally used in specialized applications.

Another area associated with fifth-generation software is knowledge-based software. A **knowledge-based system** consists of a knowledge database of both data and rules, and it can draw inferences from the stored knowledge. Many natural language systems are actually knowledge-based systems, according to this definition.

One special type of knowledge-based system is the expert system. An **expert system** is a knowledge-based system dedicated to a specific field of expertise. One example of an expert system is Mycin, which was developed by the Stanford University Medical Experimental Computer Facility to diagnose and prescribe treatments for meningitis and bacteremia infections. Mycin has been highly successful in diagnosing these type of infectious diseases and in prescribing treatment for them.

Expert systems are being used to store the knowledge and reasoning rules of an expert in a given specific field. The system is then used by a novice in the field to ask the same questions the expert would ask and to explain to the novice how the conclusions are reached. Thus, expert knowledge and reasoning can be transferred to those who are less expert in a specific field.

**CASE (computer-aided software engineering)** tools represent another type of software tool that is becoming increasingly popular. These tools are designed to automate various phases of the systems life cycle. The heart of a CASE product is the same data dictionary we discussed earlier. In addition, some CASE products offer assistance in the database design process. For further information on CASE tools and their role in the system development process, see [15].

In the next few years we will see some stabilization in fourth-generation environment components, as well as the continued emergence of fifth-generation products. These developments should make computers easier to use, and the job of developing and maintaining application systems more productive and more accurate. For details on the topics in this section, see [9].

## SUMMARY

In this chapter, we discussed hardware and software generations and saw that we are currently in the fourth generation for both hardware and software. We pointed out that there is considerable interest in developing improved fourth-generation software tools. A shortage of programmers, the increased demand for programs, and the problems inherent in the traditional system development life cycle are the major factors fostering this interest. The life cycle problems include the large amount of time required, the imperfections in the developed system, and the failure of the developed system to completely satisfy user requirements.

We discussed the large number of diverse products that have been developed to improve the productivity of the developers and users of information systems. Some of the fourth-generation tools are intended primarily for the use of programmers, while other tools are excellent aids to user interaction with the computer environment.

We discussed the manner in which the information center provides user-oriented software tools and training for users in their operation both initially and on an ongoing basis. The tools exist on central mainframe computers and on personal computers. The downloading of data from the mainframe to the personal computer and the uploading from the personal computer to the mainframe aid the user in productively moving from environment to environment.

We investigated the data dictionary, a central storehouse of data about all the firm's data. It contains a wealth of data that is of interest to the users of the software environment and to the environment itself. A data dictionary system stores, maintains, and reports on the contents of the firm's data. Data dictionaries may be free-standing or integrated; active or passive. Most newer data dictionaries are active and integrated. The data dictionary system must handle entry and maintenance of its data; control and management of its functioning; reporting; and integration with the software environment. It can interact with the software environment with a bridge facility or with a runtime interface.

The data dictionary and the DBMS are the core components of the fourth-generation environment. The other components of this environment that we discussed include report writers, query languages, screen generators, menu facilities, help facilities, window facilities, program generators, teleprocessing monitors, and fourth-generation languages, all of which tend to be nonprocedural, highly productive, and easy to use. When used together in the prototyping process, these integrated tools can help to rapidly develop an information system. The prototype may end up being the final product, or it may be the basis for the design phase of the system development life cycle.

Finally, we pointed out that, while work proceeds on the fourth-generation environment components, fifth-generation products based on artificial intelligence research are also being released. Natural languages, knowledge-based systems, and expert systems are three examples of fifth-generation components.

## REVIEW QUESTIONS

1. What programming language was used during the first software generation? During the second software generation?
2. What is an application system? What is an application generator? What is another name for an application generator?
3. Name two benefits of high-level programming languages that were not offered by the earlier languages.
4. Name three principal factors that motivated the development of fourth-generation environment components.
5. What is an information center?
6. What is uploading? What is downloading? Sketch the manner in which data flows during these processes.
7. What is a data dictionary? What is metadata?
8. What is a data dictionary system?
9. Name at least five entities maintained in a data dictionary.
10. What data is maintained in a data dictionary for each field?
11. What is the difference between a free-standing and an integrated data dictionary? What is the difference between an active and a passive data dictionary?
12. What four functions does a data dictionary system perform?
13. What is a data dictionary bridge facility? How does this compare with a runtime data dictionary interface?
14. How does a procedural language differ from a nonprocedural language?
15. What is a report writer? Briefly describe two different types of report writers.
16. What is a query language?
17. What is a screen generator? What does "painted" mean in this context?
18. What is a menu facility? Why is it important?
19. What is a help facility? Why is it important?
20. What are windows? What is a window facility? Why is it important?
21. Name and describe two types of program generators.
22. What two areas are controlled by a TP monitor?
23. What is prototyping?
24. What is artificial intelligence?
25. How do icons fit in with user data entry? 26. What is an expert system?

# EXERCISES

1. If the computer system you use for this course has fourth-generation environment tools, draw a diagram showing the relationships between them. Use Figures 12.5 and 12.7 as guidelines.
2. If your DBMS has a data dictionary capability, briefly describe its type (free-standing or integrated, active or passive) and say which field characteristics can be documented.
3. Figure 12.13 shows a generic report writer request and the report it produces. Use the report writer (or query) capability on your computer system to produce this same report.
4. After completing Exercise 3, create the same report using a high-level language with which you are familiar. What time savings did you experience using the two different methods?
5. Use your computer system's screen generator capability to produce a data-entry screen similar to the one in Figure 12.20.
6. Determine whether your system has each of the following. If so, discuss the way the facility would be used and the savings that would result from using it.
   a. A menu facility
   b. A help facility
   c. A window facility

# REFERENCES

1] Allen, Frank W., Loomis, Mary E. S., and Mannino, Michael V., "The Integrated Dictionary/Directory System," *ACM Computing Surveys* 14, no. 2 (June 1982).

2] Atre, S., *Data Base: Structured Techniques for Design, Performance, and Management*, 2nd ed. John Wiley & Sons Inc., 1988.

3] Boar, Bernard H., *Application Prototyping: A Requirements Definition Strategy for the 80s*, John Wiley & Sons Inc., 1984.

4] Codd, E. F., "Codd Stresses Importance of Shared Data and Sublanguages," *ComputerWorld* (24 February 1986).

5] Garcia, Beatrice, "The Information Center Adapts to Corporate America," *ComputerWorld* (28 October 1985).

6] Gillenson, Mark L., *Database: Step-by-Step*, 2nd ed. John Wiley & Sons Inc., 1989.

7] Horwitt, Elizabeth, "Redefining the Information Center," *Business Computer Systems* (September 1985).

8] Leavitt, Don, "Fourth-Generation Programming: The End-User Environment," *Software News* (April 1985).

9] Martin, James, *Fourth-Generation Languages, Volume I, Principles*, Prentice-Hall, 1985.

10] Martin, James, *Fourth-Generation Languages, Volume II, Representative 4GLs*, Prentice-Hall, 1986.

11] Mimmo, Pieter, "4GL Part One: Power to the Users," *ComputerWorld* (8 April 1985).

12] Mimmo, Pieter, "4GL Part Two: Power from the Products," *ComputerWorld* (15 April 1985).

13] Paquette, Laurence R., and Sardinas, Joseph L., "Productivity Tools Past, Present and Future," *Data Management* (June 1985).

14] Rowe, Lawrence A., "Tools for Developing OLTP Applications," *Datamation* (1 August 1985).

15] Shelly, Gary B., Cashman, Thomas J., Adamski, Joseph J., and Adamski, Judy, *Systems Analysis and Design*, boyd & fraser, 1991.

# *Database Administration*

## *INTRODUCTION*

You've come a long way in your study of database management. You've studied a large number of technical concepts, issues, strategies, and choices. If you take them a step at a time, you should now feel comfortable with database principles. We need to discuss next how database capabilities are managed and controlled within an enterprise.

The resources of an enterprise include money, materials, machines, and personnel. You are probably familiar with the enterprise's need to manage these resources. Data and information are other resources of an enterprise. Data represents facts and figures about the first four resources and about external entities, such as customers/clients and suppliers. Information, on the other hand, is data organized in a manner that provides specific meaning to executives of the enterprise about all the other resources and about the external entities. Many executives have little direct contact with all of these resources and external entities; their view of the enterprise is acquired primarily from information they receive about them. To these executives, information about the enterprise and the enterprise itself are often one and the same.

Recognizing data and information as resources naturally leads to the conclusion that they must be managed in a way similar to that in which the other resources of the enterprise are managed. Data must be gathered and processed into meaningful information in an accurate, cost-effective, and controlled manner for the enterprise to meet its goals and objectives in producing goods and services. Where does data come from, and where is information used? Data originates from many sources, both internal and external to the enterprise. Likewise, many people and organizations, internal and external to the enterprise, make use of the information produced. Figure 13.1 on the next page lists a few of the many sources of data and destinations of information. Just as many departments within the enterprise play a role in the management and control of money, materials, machines, and personnel, so do many departments participate in the management and control of data and information.

**Figure 13.1**

Sources of data
and destinations
of information

| INTERNAL: | | EXTERNAL: | |
|---|---|---|---|
| | Budgeting | | Shareholders |
| | Research and Development | | Lenders |
| | Purchasing and Receiving | | Suppliers |
| | Inventory Control | | Marketing |
| | Production | | Customers |
| | Distribution | | Competitors |
| | Order Entry | | Unions |
| | Sales Analysis | | Community Relations |
| | Billing | | Local Government |
| | Accounts Receivable | | State Government |
| | Cash Receipts | | Federal Government |
| | Accounts Payable | | Governmental Agencies |
| | Fixed Assets | | |
| | Payroll | | |
| | General Ledger | | |

Though many departments fit into the flow of resources, an enterprise gives primary responsibility for the management and control of particular resources to specific departments. The finance and accounting departments administrate money, for example, while the human resources department administrates personnel. In this chapter we will study database administration, the department that has primary responsibility for the management and control of the data and information resources of an enterprise.

We first discuss the background of database administration. We will explain why it is an important part of the organization and why it is necessary for optimal use of a DBMS. We also need to review how database administration has evolved from the time of inception in order to gain a perspective on typical organizational concerns, and on problems involved with the central management and control of data. Finally, we will describe a few of the ways an enterprise positions database administration in the organizational structure. The remaining sections of the chapter describe the functions performed by database administration: administrative functions, application functions, and technical functions.

## BACKGROUND OF DATABASE ADMINISTRATION

### Early Development

Prior to the use of computers, and even in the early days of their use, each department in an organization was responsible for its own data. Though corporate policies and procedures dictated how expenses, budgets, and other data should be processed, it was nonetheless left to each department to handle its own data. No central group was responsible for the overall data processing rules. If specific procedures were required for the capture, storage, processing and retention of data relating to expenses, it was the job of the accounting department to establish them. Likewise, it was up to the payroll department to formulate the procedures for the capture, storage, processing, and retention of the hours worked by each employee within a department. But once these procedures had been established and standardized, there was no further centralization of data processing; each department was on its own.

Recall from earlier chapters that when database management systems were introduced and used by companies for the first time in the '60s and '70s, several advantages were highlighted to justify their use. Among these were the minimization of data duplication; the economies of scale inherent in large, shared, centralized bases of data; the ability to easily form relationships among data elements and records; and the comprehensive reporting capabilities available, given these other advantages. But with these benefits came new responsibilities: additional considerations of security, disaster recovery, efficient data access, and user education, to name a few. Though accounting and payroll, for example, continued to be responsible for the formulation of standard procedures for processing data under their jurisdiction, central databases necessitated central management and control of the stored data. The standard procedures now had to be updated to reflect this comprehensive, central data storage.

Along with the introduction of DBMS into the enterprise also came the creation of a group of personnel referred to as **database administration (DBA)**, which was given the responsibility of maintaining and controling the DBMS environment. Since the DBMS was a product of the technical world of computers, DBA was placed within the information systems department. The exact positioning of this group was based on the company's management philosophy, its then-existing organizational structure, its maturity in the use of computers, its size, and the specific responsibilities and authority placed in the hands of DBA. (Some books say "the DBA," but mean database administration as an individual, while we mean it as a group; others use DBA to refer to the database administrator, the individual who has chief responsibility for this group.)

The formation of DBA under the information systems department was a natural development, since the responsibilities of the group were initially viewed as technical in nature. For example, DBA handled physical database design; security; backup and recovery; database reorganization; and the creation and enforcement of application programming standards and documentation related to database processing. In the execution of these technical functions, DBA functioned reasonably well. As with any new technology, however, there were the normal false starts and problems to be resolved. As experience with the new DBMS technology increased and as DBA recovered from these initial problems, it proved to be a necessary and important function of the organization for the purpose of managing the technical aspects of the DBMS environment.

## Maturing of Database Administration

Many of the first applications developed in the new DBMS environment were stand-alone systems, such as general ledger, fixed assets, inventory control, purchasing, and payroll. A stand-alone system is not integrated with other application systems. This meant that one of the most powerful features of a DBMS, the ability to form relationships between the enterprise's data groups, was not being utilized. The next step then in the use of a DBMS was to integrate applications that formed the required business relationships between records of different applications. By attempting to integrate applications, information systems and the DBA group were also addressing the problem of redundant data storage, which is an inefficient, costly, and inconsistent way for an enterprise to manage its information.

The integration of applications requires that information systems and each user area look upon data and information as a corporate resource. This view of data and information was a novel concept back in the early '70s. Each user had been taking a proprietary view of data: "This is my data, that is your data." And each programmer and systems analyst within information systems had a similar viewpoint: "This is my program, that is your program;" and, "This is my application, that is your application." Now DBA was asking the enterprise to look at data, programs and applications on a more global, enterprise level. The results were as you might expect: inconsistencies between users in their views of data meanings, and conflicts in resolving these differences; lack of cooperation by some users in working with information systems; the inability of some programmers and systems analysts to make the transition from the application view of data to an enterprise view of data; and frustration over the inability to make rapid progress on data integration.

At this critical stage, some enterprises successfully overcame the problems of data integration and made the transition to true DBMS environments, while other enterprises continued to struggle. What were the factors that enabled some enterprises to succeed? They are, in fact, the same factors that determine which enterprises will succeed today.

## Achieving a Successful DBMS Environment and DBA Group

Several factors influence the degree of success an enterprise achieves in its use of DBMS technology. Very important is the ability of the DBA group to perform the functions for which it is responsible. These functions will be discussed in subsequent sections of this chapter. For now, let's focus on the organizational factors that establish the proper climate for the DBMS environment and for the DBA group. The factors necessary for success are summarized in Figure 13.2; the following paragraphs explain them.

## Organizational Factors Necessary for DBMS Success

1. Top-level management commitment and involvement
2. Data and information requirements planning
3. Authority vested in DBA
4. Proper selection of people to staff DBA
5. Realistic, flexible view of DBMS and DBA
6. Action-oriented and results-oriented approach
7. Improved information to users

**Figure 13.2**

Organizational factors necessary for DBMS success

**Top-level Management Commitment and Involvement.**   The first and most important factor is top-level management commitment and involvement. Enterprises that have a successful DBMS environment take the concept of DBMS very seriously. Besides supporting the viewpoint that data and information are resources of the entire enterprise, top-level management gets involved, educates itself about the benefits of database technology, endorses the database concept with all its implications, and communicates its belief in database to the rest of the organization. Though top-level management commitment and involvement do not guarantee success (no single factor or combination of factors can), their absence does guarantee at best an ineffective DBMS environment and at worst (and more commonly), failure.

**Data and Information Requirements Planning.**   Top-level management also has a key role to play with regard to the second factor, data and information requirements planning. It is important for top-level management to oversee the creation of a plan that documents the data and information needs for the entire enterprise. This should be done prior to implementing applications into the DBMS environment. The plan provides the overall framework that will guide subsequent application development. It ensures that the overall requirements of the enterprise are always kept in mind as each application is developed. The DBA group normally acts as the developer of this plan, as we will see in the next section. But the support of top-level management is crucial to the success of the planning process. Top-level management must initiate, review, and approve the plan. It must also make certain that the plan is kept current by the DBA group, since business requirements change over time.

**Authority Vested in DBA.**   The third factor is a strong DBA group, and it is essential to the success of the DBMS environment. It must administer the appropriate set of functions, or responsibilities. But the DBA group can derive its true strength only by being given full authority over these functions by top-level management. For example, when the DBA group institutes standards and procedures under management approval, it must be allowed to enforce them fully. If any dispute arises, management must intervene on the side of the DBA group to reinforce the authority granted to it. In other words, to function properly, the DBA group needs as much muscle as any other functioning group within the organization. Though this may seem obvious, it is frequently ignored in the everyday life of the enterprise. The placement of the DBA group organizationally within the enterprise affects its clout, as we will discuss further in the last portion of this section.

**Proper Selection of People to Staff DBA.**   DBA plays the leading role in the administration of the data and information resources of an enterprise. This is a complex responsibility. Accordingly, DBA needs a talented blend of people who can do the job effectively. The proper selection of people to staff DBA is the fourth factor necessary for the success of the DBMS environment and the DBA group. Most carefully chosen must be the head of DBA, who must have credibility within the organization and must command the respect of the others. This person takes the leading role in interactions with top and middle management and directs the functions of DBA while dealing with complex technical decisions. A most difficult, and necessary, person to find.

**Realistic, Flexible View of DBMS and DBA.**   The fifth factor for success is the need for the enterprise to take a realistic, flexible view of both DBMS and DBA. Though computers are sometimes thought of as miracle workers, it is best to think of DBMS as just another tool to aid the organization in meeting its goals and objectives. As such, a DBMS should be called upon to do some things and not others. One misconception held by many experts in the late '60s and early '70s was the belief that all data of an enterprise would eventually reside within a single, central, corporate database. Instead of a single, central corporate database, successful enterprises recognize that common organizational data is best stored centrally, while other data may be stored in satellite databases, or under traditional file-processing techniques, or through entirely manual means.

Taking a realistic, flexible view of both DBMS and DBA pays off in a number of other ways. For example, application software packages are an economical and practical solution to many business problems. The best package solution in a given situation may require the use of a database model different from the one currently used by the enterprise. Successful enterprises weigh the difficulties and costs of additional technical tools against the benefits that will be derived from the desired package and make decisions on a case-by-case basis. Likewise, the trends toward distributed processing and increased use of microcomputers require a realistic, flexible approach.

**Action-oriented and Results-oriented Approach.**   The sixth factor for success is an action-oriented and results-oriented approach to data and information processing. Successful enterprises plan properly, but they get the job done. Having selected and installed a DBMS, successful enterprises develop applications in small, manageable chunks. They use appropriate productivity tools, like 4GLs, and take advantage of prototyping to ensure accurate requirements definition. They take the necessary steps to ensure that the DBMS will enhance, rather than intrude on, the data and information resources. Getting the job done goes a long way toward providing both the user and the technical staffs with a sense of excitement and satisfaction about their work.

**Improved Information to Users.**   Finally, successful enterprises use DBMS technology to provide improved information to users. This, in the end, is the principal objective, and attaining it in a cost-effective manner is the true measure of success.

## DBA Organizational Placement and Structure

As we mentioned earlier, when DBA was first introduced, each enterprise determined its exact positioning, based on the management philosophy of the enterprise, its then-existing organizational structure, its maturity in terms of computer utilization, its size, and the specific responsibilities and authority placed in the hands of DBA. These same factors still form the basis for DBA's positioning. Though DBA fits into the organizational structure of an enterprise in many ways, the size of the information systems department generally determines its placement. A brief study of a few common placements based on the size of the information systems department will illustrate some of the possibilities.

In the smallest installations, the DBA technical functions are spread over the entire information systems department. Usually, there is no separate DBA group. Figure 13.3 shows a representative organization chart for a small installation.

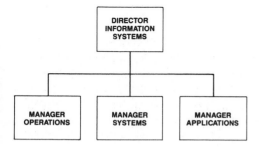

**Figure 13.3**

Organization chart for a typical small enterprise

The director of information systems is the chief executive over the information systems area. Three managers report to the director and lead groups that handle different functional responsibilities. The operations group runs the computer and such peripheral devices as line printers. It also schedules the execution of batch jobs, distributes printed output, and serves as the first line of contact when users have problems with their operational computer applications. The systems group installs and supports systems software, such as the operating system, language and editor processors, and the DBMS. The applications group analyzes, designs, programs, tests, installs, and maintains application software, such as payroll and inventory control.

In this small installation, the management and control responsibilities for the DBMS environment are distributed among the three groups. The operations group coordinates the use of the DBMS, schedules batch database jobs, and monitors throughput and response times. The systems group handles performance improvements and physical database reorganizations. The applications group does database design and creates standards for testing, documentation and programs.

Administrative and application functions normally handled by DBA in larger installations are either not done at all or are the responsibility of the applications group along with either a user coordinator of information systems activity or a steering committee of users. We will describe these administrative and application functions in detail in the next two sections.

When the information systems department is slightly larger, or if a small organization does form a DBA group, the DBA group consists of a single individual called the **database administrator**. The database administrator reports to the director of information systems either in a line capacity on a level with the other three groups or from a staff-level position, as shown in Figure 13.4. It is impossible for a single individual to be responsible for all the DBA functions. Consequently, the other three groups continue to perform a number of database management and control functions, while the database administrator serves in a consulting or advisory capacity. He or she establishes standards and serves as a control point to ensure conformance to these standards. Users interact with the database administrator, for example, with regard to database planning, security, and performance.

In larger enterprises, the DBA group consists of the database administrator in a manager position along with a number of other personnel. Either one of the two organizational structures shown in Figure 13.4 is a common placement of the DBA group. It is at this point that all the typical administrative, application, and technical functions associated with DBA become the responsibility of this group and are no longer handled by the other information systems groups. Specialization occurs as individual experts within DBA concentrate on separate areas, such as documentation and standards, performance, user interaction, database design, and security administration. The database administrator position is a varied, challenging, and important one. Figure 13.5 lists some suggested qualifications for the database administrator position in a typical enterprise. Note that the position demands a combination of management, technical, and interpersonal skills.

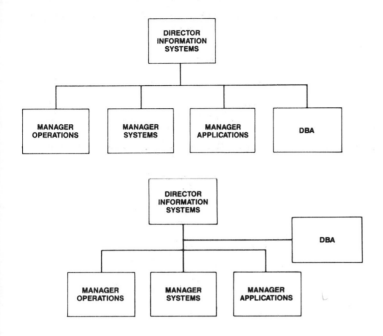

## Suggested Position Qualifications

### Formal Education:

M.S. in Information Systems, Computer Science, or Accounting; MBA; or equivalent experience.

### Skill Prerequisites:

Must be able to work well with people at all levels of management.

Must be capable of thorough investigation of implications of database changes.

Must have mature judgment.

Must be able to communicate effectively orally and in writing.

Must thoroughly understand the business and its data needs.

### Experience:

Minimum of five years experience as a system designer and programmer; at least two years on large-scale integrated systems.

Experience in large database systems.

Minimum of two years supervisory experience of five or more subordinates.

Application-oriented background.

In the past several years, some of the largest enterprises have expanded the role of DBA to give it responsibility for all the data of the enterprise, not just the data under the control of the DBMS. The expanded function continues to be called DBA in some cases but has also been named *data administration* or *information resource management*, and is placed higher in the organizational structure to reflect its increased importance. The head of the group may hold a director position that places him or her on an equal level with the head of information systems, or may be placed at an even higher level of the organization. This is to ensure that the group has sufficient authority to match its more significant role.

In some of these larger enterprises, there continues to be a DBA group within information systems to perform the technical DBA functions, while the data administration, or information resource management, group performs the majority of the administrative functions. The application functions are then appropriately allocated between the two groups. Just as a single, central database has usually proved unworkable, a single group that carries out all DBA functions is not necessarily the best approach in these larger enterprises.

Thus there is no one standardized placement in an enterprise for the DBA function. What is right for one enterprise may be wrong for another. The factors for success mentioned earlier in this chapter should be kept in mind when organizing and staffing DBA; they must be satisfied no matter what its organization and placement.

Since a DBA group within the information systems department is still the most common placement, we will use this structure as the basis of our discussion of the DBA functions in the next three sections. We will assume that there is no additional data administration group and that all functions are handled by the DBA group. You will notice as we discuss each function that there is overlap between some of the functions and that some functions could be placed equally well in one of the other categories. We will first discuss the administrative functions of DBA, followed by the application functions, then finally the technical functions. We will concentrate on the most prevalent and most important responsibilities of DBA. Not all DBA groups deal with all these responsibilities, but some other DBA groups go well beyond them.

## DBA ADMINISTRATIVE FUNCTIONS

Before the introduction of a DBMS, an enterprise does not have a database administrator or a DBA group. Ideally, in the transition to a DBMS environment, the database administrator, or chief candidate for that position, is involved in the transition process. This is not always the case. Many enterprises involve the information systems department in the initial stages of the decision-making process, but give no thought to the need for a database administrator or DBA group or for the management and control activities necessary in a DBMS environment. Instead, they evaluate and select the DBMS by means of a task force consisting of executives, key users, and representatives from the information systems department. It is only after the DBMS has been selected that the functions of DBA begin to be shaped and the position of database administrator is created and staffed. The development of the first application under the new DBMS environment may already be under way or may even have been completed before the database administrator begins functioning.

Again, this is not ideal. Fewer mistakes are likely to be made if a functioning database administrator is involved at the beginning of the DBMS evaluation and selection process. At the very least, a number of the administrative functions typically handled by the DBA should be identified and assigned to existing information systems personnel. We will assume that a database administrator or DBA group is in place from the very beginning of the DBMS evaluation and selection process as we discuss DBA functions in this section and in the following two sections.

In this section we will focus on the administrative functions performed by the DBA group. Functions of a planning or policy nature have been placed in the administrative category. Figure 13.6 is a summary of these functions. At the end of this section, we will give an example of the type of requirements that frequently arise to complicate the job of DBA and make the DBMS environment a most challenging one.

**DBA Administrative Functions**

1. Top-level education and commitment
2. Enterprise planning
3. Hardware/software requirements
4. Policy formulation

Figure 13.6

DBA administrative functions

## Top-Level Education and Commitment

As we saw earlier in this chapter, the most important factor for a successful DBMS environment is top-level management commitment and involvement. The database administrator (we will use DA, a nonstandard acronym, for the individual who heads the database administration, or DBA, group) must take the lead in educating these executives about the major functions of a DBMS. (See chapter 2.) These functions are best explained in nontechnical business terms. It isn't necessary to turn the executives into technical experts, but they have to appreciate what a DBMS can do for the enterprise. And they must be familiar with the complexities of a DBMS. These complexities should be equated with the policies and procedures required to control and minimize their impact.

The DA should justify the proposed new database technology on a cost-benefit basis. Only in this way can top-level management be supplied with a realistic understanding of the price to be paid for shifting to the database technology. Progress has a price, and there is a price to be paid in managing and controlling the data and information resources. Not only is there an initial outlay, there are also recurring costs. The initial costs of database include the following:

1. DBMS software itself
2. DBMS software tools, such as query languages, 4GLs, and performance monitors, if they are not bundled with the DBMS software
3. Teleprocessing monitor, if they are not included with the base DBMS software
4. Additional hardware, especially disks, terminals, and additional memory
5. Technical and user training
6. Planning and start-up activities
7. Facility preparation charges for additional hardware
8. DBMS installation and integration
9. Overhead for developing the first application

The recurring costs of database include:

1. Software maintenance
2. Hardware maintenance and depreciation
3. Ongoing training
4. DBA personnel
5. Teleprocessing/communications maintenance
6. Supplies
7. Computer system overhead

The costs associated with a database processing environment must be balanced by the benefits derived from its utilization. Benefits are often more difficult to quantify than costs. But since database represents significant capital and operating expenses to the enterprise, the benefits must be carefully identified and quantified to justify the investment. The benefits typically obtained through the use of database include:

1. Reduced program development costs
2. Reduced program maintenance costs
3. Reduced user costs in obtaining ad hoc information through queries
4. Ease of providing integrated information
5. More accurate data and information (i.e., improved integrity)
6. Improved security
7. Information users need rather than information the information systems department can provide

Even if the known costs exceed the quantifiable benefits, the move to database proves to be a sound, economical choice in the long run because of improved information and improved control over the data and information resources, factors which make the enterprise more competitive and better able to provide employee and customer satisfaction. Though not easily quantified, these are usually things that count most to an enterprise.

Once the DA has educated top-level management and has justified the use of a DBMS on a cost-benefit basis, it is crucial for him or her to obtain a solid commitment for DBMS use. This commitment has to be ongoing, so the DA must continue to educate, inform, communicate to, and sell top-level management as improvements and refinements are made to the DBMS environment and to the administration of the data and information resources. Any serious problems that arise should be quickly and completely reported to the appropriate executives so the communication line remains accurate and unbiased. If the DA is honest, considerate, enthusiastic, competent and professional in dealing with management and others in the organization, the successes of database will overshadow any unavoidable difficulties.

### Enterprise Planning

Another administrative function of DBA is planning on an enterprise-wide basis. Successful use of database technology depends at least as much on skilled planning as on technical sophistication.

Action in the absence of planning is certain to result in failure. On the other hand, conducting planning effort after planning effort without taking any action also produces poor results. Obviously, planning must be completed before installing a DBMS, but how much planning and what kind of planning? Much depends upon the management philosophy of the organization. The planning process can be lengthy and formal, involving all functional areas and organizational levels of the enterprise. Or it can be short and informal, involving just a few key members of the enterprise. Both extremes work when handled properly.

An example of a popular, widely used planning methodology is *Business Systems Planning (BSP)*, created by IBM and offered for the first time in the mid-'70s. BSP provides a step-by-step process for developing a comprehensive plan of an organization's information requirements. For more information about BSP, see [7], [11], and [12].

No matter which approach is used for planning, the DA must produce at a minimum a plan that documents the following:

1. Overall goals and objectives of the enterprise
2. Primary business functions
3. General data and information requirements
4. Application system priorities

**Overall Goals and Objectives of the Enterprise.**   The overall goals and objectives of the enterprise should already be available from the organization's business plan. If a business plan does not exist, the DA must meet with top-level management to determine these goals and objectives. Their importance lies in the fact that they help the DA understand the direction of the enterprise and help identify potential new business functions that may be necessary in the future. For example, Premiere Products may be planning to use excess warehouse capacity to stock super gismos for Red Robin Inc., starting a year from now. When the company starts this new venture, it wants to be able to segregate the inventory data of Red Robin from its own inventory data. If a study of current data and information needs were conducted with lower-level management, this requirement would most likely not be uncovered. Interaction with top-level management is necessary in order to discover these types of plans.

Another reason for knowing the enterprise's goals and objectives is that they give an indication of planned future growth. It would be important to know that an enterprise planned to double its number of customers over the next three years or to start construction of its first satellite production plants in two years. In the former case, plans would have to be made for sufficient storage capacity in the new DBMS environment. In the latter case, meetings would have to be held to discuss the need for distributed processing of data.

By focusing on the executives of the enterprise, the DA is taking a top-down approach to planning. A top-down approach provides perspective in terms of where the enterprise is now and where it will be going in the future. The insight, knowledge and perspective of top-level management is important for creating a proper plan and for obtaining the support of the enterprise's executives.

**Primary Business Functions.**   The DA needs to identify and document the primary business functions of the enterprise. For example, the DA for Marvel College would find that among the school's many business functions were general ledger, accounts payable, admissions, student records processing, and alumni processing. Knowledge of the primary business functions is necessary to provide the list of possible application systems under the DBMS. Some of these business functions may already be processed with a computer, while others may not. It is important to know the scope of the enterprise in preparation for the transition to database.

**General Data and Information Requirements.**   The DA must start to develop the **conceptual data level**, or global enterprise view of data. How thorough a job is done will depend on the individual organization. Based on the DA's determination of the primary business functions however, he or she will at least document the principal entities, which would be *students*, *faculty*, and *classes*, for example, in the case of Marvel College. If using BSP, for instance, the DA would ideally completely define all entities and all data elements for the enterprise; but time constraints, organizational philosophy, and shortage of personnel may preclude such thoroughness.

**Application System Priorities.** The enterprise must evaluate each business function and then decide which functions should be developed under the DBMS and when. Often a user committee is formed to do the preliminary evaluation and the results are presented to top-level management for their review. These executives make necessary modifications based on their strategic perspective. The DA takes this approved priority list and creates an implementation timetable. Unless a thorough plan has been created by means of a methodology like BSP, the timetable is tentative; the information systems department must analyze the detailed requirements of each application as it is developed, and only then can the timetable be definite.

The first application to be implemented under the DBMS must be carefully selected. The choice should be influenced by the fact that the transition to the DBMS environment is a learning experience for everyone in the enterprise. The application should be of small to medium size, but under no circumstances should it be any larger. If the application is of some significant size, then it is best to develop it a piece at a time, using a phased approach. Mistakes may be made with the new technology, and it is easier to recover from mistakes or misunderstandings with a smaller, less complex application. Many experts claim you should plan to throw away the first application developed, since you will end up throwing it away whether you planned to do so or not.

Quick-payback applications are good first choices. These are applications of a manageable size whose benefits far exceed their costs, both developmental and ongoing. The decision to select them is not only smart and economical, it also gets the database environment initiated on a positive note.

## DBMS Evaluation and Selection

DBA is responsible for the evaluation and selection of the DBMS. To oversee this responsibility, DBA sets up a checklist like the one shown in Figure 13.7 on the next page. (This checklist applies specifically to mainframe or microcomputer DBMS's that follow the relational model, since this is the direction in which most organizations are currently headed. Typically, if an organization is going to use a DBMS that is purely hierarchical or CODASYL, the DBMS is already in place. If this is not the case, a category called "Choice of Data Model" would have to be added to the list.)

**Figure 13.7**

DBMS evaluation
checklist

1. Data Definition
   a. Data types
      (1) Numeric
      (2) Character
      (3) Date
      (4) Logical (T/F)
      (5) Memo
      (6) Money
      (7) Other
   b. Support for nulls
   c. Support for primary keys
   d. Support for foreign keys
   e. Unique indexes
   f. Views

2. Data Restructuring
   a. Possible restructuring
      (1) Add new tables
      (2) Delete old tables
      (3) Add new columns
      (4) Change layout of existing columns
      (5) Delete columns
      (6) Add new indexes
      (7) Delete old indexes
   b. Ease of restructuring

3. Nonprocedural Languages
   a. Nonprocedural languages supported
      (1) SQL
      (2) QBE
      (3) Natural language
      (4) Own language. Award points on the
          basis of ease of use as well as
          the types of operations (joining,
          sorting, grouping, calculating various
          statistics) which are available in the
          language. SQL can be used as a standard
          against which such a language can be judged.
   b. Optimization done by one of the following:
      (1) User, in formulating the query
      (2) DBMS (through built-in optimizer)
      (3) No optimization possible. System will only do
          sequential searches.

4. Procedural Languages
   a. Procedural languages supported
      (1) Own language. Award points on the
          basis of the quality of this language
          both in terms of the types of statements
          and control structures available and
          the database manipulation statements
          included in the language.
      (2) COBOL
      (3) FORTRAN
      (4) C
      (5) Pascal
      (6) BASIC
      (7) Other
   b. Can nonprocedural language be used in
      conjunction with the procedural language
      (e.g., could SQL be embedded in
      COBOL programs)?

5. Data Dictionary
   a. Types of entities
      (1) Tables
      (2) Columns
      (3) Indexes
      (4) Relationships
      (5) Programs
      (6) Other
   b. Integration of data dictionary with other
      components of the system

6. Shared Update
   a. Level of locking
      (1) Column
      (2) Row
      (3) Table
   b. Type of locking
      (1) Shared
      (2) Exclusive
      (3) Both
   c. Responsibility for handling deadlock
      (1) Programs
      (2) DBMS (automatic rollback of transaction
          causing deadlock)

**Figure 13.7**

(continued)

7. Backup and Recovery Services
   a. Backup facilities
   b. Journaling facilities
   c. Recovery facilities
      (1) Recover from backup copy only
      (2) Recover using backup copy and journal
   d. Rollback of individual transactions

8. Security
   a. Passwords
      (1) Access to database only
      (2) Read or write access to any column or combination of columns
   b. Encryption
   c. Views
   d. Difficulty in bypassing security controls

9. Integrity
   a. Support for entity integrity
   b. Support for referential integrity
   c. Support for data-type integrity
   d. Support for other types of integrity constraints

10. Limitations
    a. Number of tables
    b. Number of columns
    c. Length of individual column
    d. Total length of all columns in a table
    e. Number of rows per table
    f. Number of files that can be open at the same time
    g. Types of hardware supported
    h. Types of LANs supported
    i. Other

11. Documentation
    a. Clearly written manuals
    b. Tutorial
       (1) Written
       (2) On-line
    c. On-line help available
       (1) General help
       (2) Context-sensitive help

12. Vendor Support
    a. Type of support available
    b. Quality of support available
    c. Cost of support
    d. Reputation of support

13. Performance
    a. Tests comparing the performance of various DBMSs in such areas as sorting, indexing, reading all rows, changing data values in all rows, and so on, are available from a variety of periodicals.
    b. If you have special requirements, you may want to design your own benchmark tests that could be performed on each DBMS under consideration.

14. Additional software tools
    a. 4GLs
    b. Application generators
    c. User-oriented query languages
    d. User-oriented report writers
    e. Other

15. Compatability between mainframe and microcomputer DBMS
    a. Ease of transferring data
    b. Consistency

16. Cost
    a. Cost of basic DBMS
    b. Cost of any additional components
    c. Cost of any additional hardware required
    d. Cost of network version (if required)
    e. Cost and types of support

17. Future Plans
    a. What does vendor plan for future of system?
    b. What is the history of the vendor in terms of keeping the system up-to-date?
    c. When changes are made in the system, what is involved in converting to the new version?
       (1) How easy is the conversion?
       (2) What will it cost?

18. Other Considerations (fill in your own special requirements)
    a. Special purpose reports

DBA must evaluate each prospective purchase of a DBMS in terms of all the categories shown in the figure. An explanation of the various categories follows.

1. **Data definition.** What types of data are supported? Is support for nulls provided? What about primary and foreign keys? The DBMS will undoubtedly provide indexes, but is it possible to specify that an index is unique and then have the system enforce the uniqueness? Is support for views provided?

2. **Data restructuring.** What type of database restructuring is possible? How easy is it to do this restructuring? Will the system do most of the work or will the DBA have to create special programs for this purpose?

3. **Nonprocedural languages.** What type of nonprocedural language is supported? The possibilities are SQL, QBE, natural language, or a DBMS built-in language. If one of the standard languages is supported, how good a version is provided by the DBMS? If the DBMS furnishes its own language, how good is it? How does its functionality compare to that of SQL?

   How does the DBMS achieve optimization of queries? Either the DBMS itself optimizes each query; the user must do so by the manner in which he or she states the query; or no optimization occurs. Most desirable, of course, is the first alternative.

4. **Procedural languages.** What types of procedural languages are supported? Are they common languages, such as COBOL, Fortran, BASIC, Pascal, or C, or does the DBMS come with its own language? In the latter case, how complete is the language? Does it contain all the required types of statements and control structures? What facilities are provided for accessing the database? Is it possible to make use of the nonprocedural language while using the procedural language?

5. **Data dictionary.** What kind of data dictionary support is available? Is it a simple catalog, or can it contain more, such as information about programs and the various data items these programs access? How well is the data dictionary integrated with other components of the system (for example, the nonprocedural language)?

6. **Shared update.** Is support provided for shared update? What is the unit that may be locked (column, row, or table)? Are exclusive locks the only ones permitted or are shared locks also allowed? (A shared lock permits other users to read the data; with an exclusive lock, no other user may access the data in any way.) How is deadlock handled? Will the DBMS take care of it, or is it the responsibility of programs to ensure that it is handled correctly?

7. **Backup and recovery services.** What type of backup and recovery facilities are provided? Can the DBMS maintain a journal of changes in the database and use the journal during the recovery process? If a transaction has aborted, is the DBMS capable of rolling it back (that is, undoing the updates of the transaction)?

8. **Security.** What type of security features does the system make available? Are passwords supported? Do passwords simply regulate whether a user may access the database, or is it possible to associate read or write access to a combination of columns with a password? Is encryption supported? Does the system have some type of view mechanism that can be used for security? How difficult is it to bypass the security controls?

9. **Integrity.** What type of integrity constraints are supported? Is there support for entity integrity (the fact that the primary key cannot be null)? What about referential integrity (the property that values in foreign keys must match values already in the database)? Does the DBMS support data-type integrity (the property that values which do not match the data type for the column into which they are being entered are not allowed to occur in the database)? Is there support for any other types of constraints?

10. **Limitations.** (This category is usually more relevant if we are selecting a microcomputer DBMS.) What limitations exist with respect to the number of tables, columns, and rows per table? How many files can be open at the same time? (On some microcomputer DBMS's, each table and index is in a separate file. Thus, a single table with three indexes, all in use at the same time, would account for *four* files. Problems may arise if the number of files that can be open is relatively small and many indexes are in use.) On what types of hardware is the DBMS supported? What types of **local area networks (LANs)**?

    (A local area network is a configuration of several computers all hooked together, thereby allowing users to share a variety of resources. One of these resources is the database. In local area network, support for shared update is important, since many users may be updating the database at the same time. The relevant question here, however, is not how well the DBMS supports shared update, but which of the LANs can be used in conjunction with this DBMS?)

11. **Documentation.** How good are the manuals? Are they easy to use? Is there a good index? Is a tutorial, in either printed or on-line form, available to assist users in getting started with the system? Is on-line help available? If so, is it general help or context-sensitive? (Context-sensitive help means that if a user is having trouble and asks for help, the DBMS will provide assistance for that particular problem at the time the user asks for it.)

12. **Vendor support.** What type of support is provided by the vendor, and how good is it? What is the cost? What is the vendor's reputation for support among current users?

13. **Performance.** How well does the system perform? This is a tough one to answer. One way to determine relative performance is to look into benchmark tests that have been performed on several DBMS's by various periodicals. Beyond this, if an organization has some specialized needs, it may have to set up its own benchmark tests.

14. **Additional software tools.** What additional software tools, such as 4GLs, application generators, user-oriented query languages, and report writers, are available? How easy are these tools to use? How well are they integrated with the DBMS?

15. **Compatibility between mainframe and microcomputer DBMS's.** If both a mainframe DBMS and microcomputer DBMS's will be used, how compatible are they? Is it easy to transfer data from one to another? Are they consistent in the way they operate?

16. **Cost.** What is the cost of the DBMS and of any components the organization is planning to purchase? Is additional hardware required and, if so, what is the associated cost? If the organization requires a special version of the DBMS for a network, what is the additional cost? What is the cost of vendor support, and what types of support plans are available?

17. **Future plans.** What plans has the vendor made for the future of the system? This information is often difficult to obtain, but we can get an idea by looking at the performance of the vendor with respect to keeping the existing system up-to-date. How easy has it been for users to convert to new versions of the system?

18. **Other considerations.** This is a final, catch-all category that contains any special requirements not covered in the other categories.

Once each DBMS has been examined with respect to all the preceding categories, the results can be compared. Unfortunately, this process can be difficult, owing to the number of categories and their generally subjective nature. To make the process more objective, a numerical ranking can be assigned to each DBMS for its performance in each category (for example, a number between zero and ten, where zero is poor and ten is excellent). Further, the categories can be assigned weights. This allows an organization to signify which categories are more critical to it than others. Then each of the numbers being used in the numerical ranking can be multiplied by the appropriate weight. The results are added up, producing a weighted total. The weighted totals for each DBMS can then be compared, producing the final evaluation.

How does DBA arrive at the numbers to assign each DBMS in the various categories? Several methods are often used. It can request feedback from other organizations that are currently using the DBMS in question. It can read journal reviews of the various DBMS's. Sometimes a trial version of the DBMS can be obtained, in which case members of the staff can give it a hands-on test. In practice, all three methods are sometimes combined. Whichever method is used, however, it is crucial that the checklist and weights be carefully thought out; otherwise, the findings may be inadvertently slanted in a particular direction.

## Policy Formulation

The final administrative function of DBA is the creation of policies that set the stage for effective, controlled, and safe database processing. The DA must consider the capabilities of the selected DBMS to formulate these policies. These policies deal with security, disaster and contingency planning, and user billing, and a number of standards and procedures must be developed in support of them; these will be discussed next, along with other standards and procedures.

**Security.**   The provision for **security** facilities is one of the functions of a DBMS we discussed in chapter 2. The protection of data in the database against intentional or accidental access, modification, and destruction is a key function of the DA. The DA takes advantage of facilities available within the DBMS and supplements them with non-DBMS facilities, as necessary, to secure the data and information resources of the enterprise. No protection system is foolproof, so the objective is to minimize the enterprise's exposure to possible security violations and to maximize its ability to discover and recover from security violations. The benefits obtained from elaborate security measures must be weighed against the degree of difficulty in their implementation by authorized personnel.

Security considerations are important to all enterprises, even those that have neither a DBMS nor computers. Security is a complex area. The amount of publicity in the popular media concerning security violations demonstrates the importance of security to business, the public and the government, as well as the fact that it is an imperfect science at best. We will highlight several of the most important facets of security. The discussion of disaster and contingency planning which follows is closely related.

First, information systems personnel who require access to the database must be barred from incurring either inadvertent or intentional security violations. Operations personnel who tend the computers and peripheral devices do not need to access the database directly through normal DBMS methods. However, they are responsible for both scheduling and executing backups of the database, so they must be in physical contact with the equipment. Failure to properly back up the database can jeopardize database integrity and result in loss of critical data in the event that recovery must occur. Also, uninformed or disgruntled employees may cause physical harm to the equipment. With regard to the former, DBA should review computer logs to ensure that scheduled backups are occurring according to schedule; with regard to the latter, close supervision minimizes the potential for physical harm.

Application programmers do need to interact directly with the database as they develop and maintain programs, as do systems programmers as they install and maintain systems software. Software bugs, deletion of production programs, and the intentional introduction of fraudulent or destructive code into programs are representative of potential security problems. DBA must enforce strict testing of programs. Testing and production environments should exist apart from one another, and application programmers should have access only to the test environment. DBA should transfer tested versions of programs into the production environment only after both DBA and the users have verified the quality of the software test results.

Separation of functions within the information systems department is most important. One person should not be responsible for too many functions, and each person's work should be subjected to a system of checks and balances. In smaller information systems departments, where full separation of functions may not be feasible, careful selection and supervision of each employee and frequent reviews of employees' work by an audit group from outside the information systems department can serve the same purpose.

A second important facet of security is the proper control of user access and modification of data. Access should be given only to those users who require it, and each user's privileges should be limited according to what he or she needs to accomplish. Procedures and documentation that explain how to gain access to the database environment and to specific data should be issued only to authorized personnel and should be safely stored away when not in use.

Many elaborate methods have been devised to restrict access to authorized users. Voice recognition devices, fingerprint verification devices, and badge readers are three of the successfully used techniques. To control the opportunity for remote access to the total computer environment, some organizations require the user to call into the computer center and give a special user code. Using this code, the security clerk then contacts the registered location of that user and makes the connection between the user terminal and the computer from the computer center end of the communications link. This approach minimizes the chance of a hacker or other unauthorized person gaining access on a remote processing basis.

The most widely used approach to user security remains user entry of special codes to gain access. The DA gives a unique user identification code to a given user. This code is tied to a profile for that user that indicates which programs, records, and data elements he or she is permitted to access. In certain cases the user will be allowed read-only access; in other instances the user will be able to change specific data. Besides supplying an identification code, the user typically must enter a password. The user creates the password and changes it periodically. Together, the user identification code and password link the user to his or her profile for subsequent authorized processing. Since the DA knows the user identification code, the use of the password, which is known only to the user, protects somewhat against security violations by the DA and the DBA staff. It is important for the user to select a nonobvious password, to keep the password secret, and to change it periodically.

Subschemas and active data dictionaries provide controls over what users can and cannot access. Encryption of data disguises data in the event that someone is able to gain unauthorized access to the database. Another control is the use of data change logs, or activity logs, employed by DBA to audit activity against the database. It has been proven many times that any security system can be circumvented by individuals who are smart enough and who wish to do so. After-the-fact reviews of these logs can minimize tampering with the security system and with data. The importance of audits conducted by both internal and external auditors cannot be overemphasized. The system of checks and balances should be as comprehensive as possible.

Though the DA and the DBA staff fall neither in the information systems processing nor in the user category, limitations should also be placed on their ability to interact with the DBMS environment. Because of the number of critical duties allotted to it, DBA ends up having a great deal of access and control over the database. In many enterprises it has primary responsibility for security in the DBMS environment, but it would be better to assign this responsibility to a separate security officer who would report to someone outside the information systems department and outside the DBA group. It would be the security officer's job to create and distribute user identification codes. The security officer would also review the activity logs and perform other security tasks but would not perform any of the other normal duties of DBA. This separation of functions would better provide a more secure DBMS environment.

The third facet of security is physical security. Physical security is a concern not just in database processing but also non-DBMS and non-computer environments, and the steps taken on behalf of physical security there are just as important in a DBMS environment. User areas need to control access to terminals, to important source documents, and to reports. Locks can be placed on terminals so that only users with keys can use them. Critical source documents, which contain confidential data or which must be legally retained for audit or governmental purposes, should be locked away in fire-resistant, bomb-proof safes or storage vaults. The same is true for critical reports.

In the early days of computers, enterprises often liked to showcase their computer facilities. Few limitations were imposed on who could walk through rooms where hardware was located. If there were restrictions, then the computers might be located in glass-enclosed rooms. Many buildings were constructed before computers were purchased, so no planning had gone into safe placement of the computers. Computers would be situated wherever there was room: in the basement, near the reception area, or in an open, high-traffic area. These various choices of locale left organizations vulnerable to problems with physical security. Sabotage, theft of hardware, fire, and such natural disasters as floods and tornadoes are a few examples of problems that have occurred.

Today, organizations carefully plan their computer facilities so as to eliminate or minimize such threats to physical security. The computer hardware is placed away from high-traffic areas and away from the threat of flood and other natural disasters, in rooms that provide strict access control. Only authorized employees are allowed entry, and entry is obtained through the use of badge readers, access codes, voiceprints, fingerprints, and other personal forms of identification. The computer room is provided with excellent fire and humidity protection and is isolated from the threat of sabotage.

In the absence of a separate security officer, DBA must always take the lead in formulating workable policies that take advantage of the security facilities built into a given DBMS. These policies must undergo reviews and approvals by appropriate executives of the enterprise. For further details on this subject, see [5].

**Security and the DBMS.** DBA should utilize whatever security facilities are present in the DBMS, such as passwords, encryption, and/or views. Some DBMS's, especially some of the microcomputer DBMS's, lack some of the crucial security facilities. Any features the DBMS lacks should be supplemented by DBA through the use of special programs. Figure 13.8 shows security features of the DBMS both with and without DBA. In Figure 13.8a, only the security features of the DBMS stand between the users and the database. In Figure 13.8b, on the other hand, for the users to access the database, they must first pass through special security features created by DBA, then through the security features of the DBMS. DBA could, for example, create a dialogue that would ask a user a series of questions, each of which must be answered correctly, before the user could access the database. DBA could also create a special feature where passwords would vary from one day of the week to another.

**Passwords.** One security feature we have mentioned, passwords, deserves further attention. Sometimes people think that simply establishing a password scheme will ensure security. After all, Tim can't gain access to Pam's data if he doesn't know her password (assuming, of course, that Tim doesn't have a password of his own that allows access to the same data).

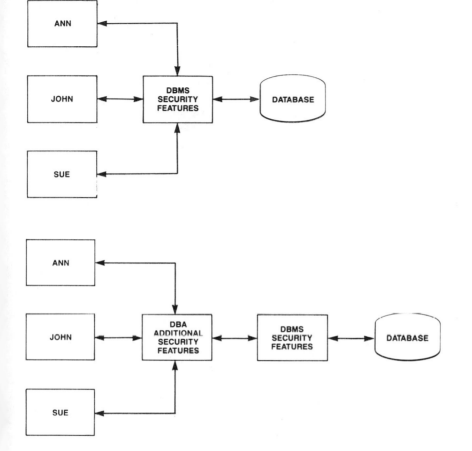

**Figure 13.8a**

Security features
of DBMS as sole
security mechanism

**Figure 13.8b**

Security features
of DBMS supple-
mented by DBA

But what if Tim observes Pam entering her password? What if he guesses her password? You might think this sort of occurrence is so unlikely that there is nothing to worry about. In fact, it is not so unlikely. Many people often choose passwords that they can remember easily. A very common choice, for example, is the name of a family member. So if Pam is a typical user, Tom might very well be able to obtain her password just by trying names of family members. Other users choose unusual passwords (or have such passwords assigned to them), but, in order to remember them, they often have these passwords written down somewhere. Without giving it much thought, such users may be careless about the paper on which a password is written, giving people like Tim still another vehicle for obtaining one. Figure 13.9 on the next page illustrates the careless use of passwords.

It is up to DBA to educate users on the use of passwords. The pitfalls we have just discussed should be stressed, as should precautionary measures, including the need for frequent changes of passwords.

**Figure 13.9**

Careless use of
passwords

**Disaster and Contingency Planning.**   Closely related to security issues is disaster and contingency planning. Taken together, security and disaster and contingency planning help protect the organization from accidental and intentional damage to data. In the event that damage does occur, procedures for recovery and reconstruction must be part of the disaster and contingency plans. Owing to its management and control responsibilities for the database, DBA must take an active role in the formulation of these plans.

A key element in any such plan is redundancy. In chapter 2 we discussed the functions of a DBMS. Among these functions were recovery from failure plus certain utility services, such as journaling and backup/recovery. These are all integral parts of disaster and contingency planning, and they provide a degree of redundancy to database activity. Given a failure, backups of the database permit reconstruction and limit the damage. Journals can then make the database current with the most recent transactional activity. Care must be taken with the database backups. If the backups are stored near the computers and a catastrophe in the form of a fire or bomb occurs, for example, destroying or severely damaging the data storage devices (disks), there is a chance that the backups also will be damaged. Thus, backups should be stored outside the computer room itself, either in the same building in a fire/bomb-proof vault, or off the premises in another facility.

Some enterprises need to keep their computers functioning no matter what problems occur. Airlines, for example, can switch quickly to duplicate backup computers in the event of a malfunction in the main computer. Other companies contract with firms using hardware and software similar to their own so that in the event of a catastrophe they can temporarily use these other facilities.

Total loss of an enterprise's data or computers can have a crippling effect, so proper attention to disaster and contingency planning is a major function of DBA.

**Supplementing DBMS Recovery Procedures.**  Many mainframe DBMS's contain all the required features to support backup and recovery as we discussed in chapter 2. Some mainframe systems and many of the microcomputer systems do not. For example, many microcomputer DBMS's lack facilities to maintain a journal (or log) of changes in the database. Thus, recovery is usually limited to copying the most recent backup over the live database. This means that any changes made since this backup have to be redone by the users. If this presents a major problem (and it usually does), DBA may decide to supplement the DBMS facilities. A typical solution would be to have each program that updates the database also make appropriate entries in a journal (see Figure 13.10a), then make use of this journal in the recovery process. (See Figure 13.10b.) In this case, the database is first recovered by copying the backup version over the live database; and then it is brought up-to-date through a special DBA-created program that updates the database with changes recorded in the journal.

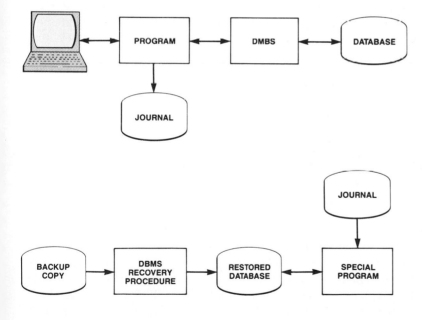

**Figure 13.10a**

Programs involved in database processing also maintain a journal

**Figure 13.10b**

Journal is used in recovery

**User Billing.**  Investment in computer hardware and software is a capital investment; so is the purchase of a DBMS. An enterprise also expends funds during the development of applications to run under the DBMS and on a continual basis once the application becomes functional. In a number of enterprises, the costs of developing and maintaining an application are charged back to the user areas served by that application. Database processing environments that provide the capability for integration, user queries, and other sophisticated functions complicate the billing process; the DA must help formulate fair user billing schemes in these instances.

A number of charge-back billing methods are feasible for operational applications. One method involves charging the user a fixed amount per month independent of the amount of computer resources used by the application in that same month. This fixed amount is determined in advance on a periodic basis, most often annually, and holds for the entire period as determined. A review is conducted of charges vs. resources used and adjustments are proposed and renegotiated going into the next billing period. This method is simple to implement, and the negotiation process is an interesting exercise, as you might expect.

A second billing method involves charging a variable amount per month, based on the computer resources used during that month. This method is often called **resource utilization billing**. Computer resources are used as factors in devising a formula. The computer's operating system continuously tracks, captures, and files away the computer resources used by each application. Some of the computer resource factors used in the billing formula are the amount of permanent disk used for the part of the database associated with the application; the amount of temporary disk used for transaction and sort files, for example; the total amount of time during which terminals are connected to and in active use with the computer system; the amount of CPU time used by executing programs; the number of tapes mounted on drives for use with the application; the amount of main memory used during the period; and the number of lines of printed output for that application. Many other factors may be considered; the preceding list is typical.

On the surface this second method appears to be the most equitable way of billing for services that are provided to a given user area for its applications. There is a major drawback, however: resources used will vary from day to day and even from hour to hour, given equivalent work accomplished. For example, a heavier load on the computer system (i.e., more users and more complicated processing needs), will require more terminal connect time and more temporary disk accesses to page a program in and out of main memory for a given amount of work. Therefore, the user is charged more when there is a heavier load on the computer system, even if the same amount of work is accomplished. One school of thought suggests that this method is fair, because users who perform their work during heavy-use periods may force the enterprise to spend more in upgrades to accommodate the heavier system load. So these users should pay more, according to the proponents of resource-utilization billing. Others feel this is unfair. Unless the formula automatically adjusts for this type of variation, resource-utilization billing varies too much to suit its opponents. Automatic adjustment, however, complicates the formula and makes it incomprehensible to all but selected experts. Much research and applied work continues to be done in this area.

A third approach to billing for operational applications is also a formula method. The user area is billed for the month on the basis of user-related volume factors. Marvel College, for example, may charge its alumni office for its alumni processing system on the basis of the number of alumni records, the number of queries made, and the number of output lines printed. These factors are simple and clear both to users and technical personnel. There is a correlation between the number of alumni records, the number of queries made, and the number of output lines printed vs. the amount of work done by the computer environment, so this method appears to be a reasonable approximation of the resource-utilization method. It is not exact, however, since five queries could be simple and take just moments to complete or could be complex and require many hours of computer resources. In either case, the user would be billed the same amount with this method. On the other hand, one query executed under a light system load would result in the same charges as the same query executed an hour later under a much heavier system load.

Before leaving the subject of user billing, we should say something about charging users who sponsor the first few projects to develop applications under the new DBMS environment. Charges to these pioneers should be equitable but not overly burdensome. There are fixed costs associated with a computer environment. When there are few users, the proportionate share of the costs will be considerably higher than they will be when there is a full complement of users and applications. A certain portion of these fixed costs could be allocated to overhead expense and distributed across the enterprise to lessen the penalty for being a pioneer.

## Complications to DBMS Processing

There is a particular type of user requirement that can complicate the job of DBA, and that is twenty-four-hour-a-day processing. We are discussing this here because it affects the administrative, application, and technical functions of DBA. There are other complicating requirements as well, such as distributed databases and dual database environments, which will be discussed in the next chapter. We will limit our discussion of twenty-four-hour-a-day processing to a review of its impact on database backups.

Making a complete backup of a database requires users to stop update activity under normal circumstances. Otherwise, transactions that update multiple database records may update one record prior to its being copied, while a related record may be updated after it has been copied. This will cause those records to be out of synch with one another. Extremely large databases need several hours to complete the backup cycle. This means that users cannot perform any update processing during the time required for the backup. For an enterprise whose update activity occurs over a limited geographical area and whose database is not very large, finding the necessary few hours of time overnight to do the backups is not a problem.

Multinational enterprises with worldwide offices often need access to their centralized database twenty-four hours a day, since some office or offices are always open and need to access the database. For such an enterprise there is no window of time during which overnight backups can be done. Doing backups only on the weekend is a solution; the tradeoff is that if recovery is needed, the most recent backup could be a week old. The amount of time to recover from that backup and all journals for the week would make the database unavailable for a long, possibly prohibitive, period of time.

Even if this potential outage does not cause a problem, many legal requirements force an enterprise to keep a backup copy of their database as of the end of each month. More often than not, month end occurs in the middle of the week, so we are now back to our original problem of making a backup at a time when the enterprise needs access to the database. There are two solutions to this problem. One is to make the system unavailable to users until backups have been completed when month end occurs in the middle of the week. A second solution is to factor the need for twenty-four-hour-a-day processing into the design of the database. This can be a tricky design problem, but it is not an unsolvable one. For example, the database design might end up being structured predominantly on an office basis. Then, instead of using the standard DBMS utility backup facility against the entire database, a special backup program would be written to selectively back up individual offices as they closed.

Every enterprise is different, and each one's overall application requirements will be unique. Interesting problems of the type just discussed are encountered frequently enough to make DBA's job most interesting and challenging.

## DBA APPLICATION FUNCTIONS

DBA has to perform a number of application functions. We include in the application category those functions directly related to DBA's interaction with users and with information systems personnel. Figure 13.11 shows a summary of the application functions we will discuss in this section.

| **Figure 13.11** | **DBA Application Functions** |
|---|---|
| DBA application functions | 1. Standards and procedures |
| | 2. Data dictionary management |
| | 3. Training |
| | 4. Overall coordination |
| | 5. Database loading |

## Standards and Procedures

Related to the policy formulation role of DBA is its responsibility for standards and procedures. DBA must create, publish, and enforce standards and procedures that control and enhance database processing, and that conform to established policies. These standards and procedures must be developed in a nondisruptive manner. The ability of users to get their job done must not be adversely affected. The standards and procedures must not become a bottleneck to information systems development and maintenance tasks and must not place an inordinate burden on system designers.

Standards and procedures are already in place when an enterprise acquires a DBMS. So the task of DBA is to develop new ones, or to modify existing ones, which integrate DBA functions and database processing into the functioning enterprise. These standards and procedures should be communicated to all departments and personnel that will be impacted by them. Most importantly, they must be enforced. They must also be periodically evaluated and revised as necessary.

An example of a user-related procedure is the process a user must follow to obtain a user identification code to access the database. The procedure should specify who is eligible; what forms need to be filled out; what authorizations are required; who receives and approves the request; how a rejected request is handled; how an approved request is communicated back to the requester; and how the user identification code is to be handled.

An example of a standard is the naming standard for data items, records, and files defined in the data dictionary. This standard describes the conventions used for naming and gives examples of them.

Other standards and procedures that need to be created include those for:

1. Program testing
2. Application program coding and design
3. Performance (terminal response time and report distribution)
4. Change control — both user requests for change and the procedure programmers follow in making program changes
5. Documentation, including user, operations, program, and database

In large enterprises certain members of DBA would handle standards and procedures on a full-time basis. In smaller organizations the responsibility would be spread out among a number of DBA staff members.

## Data Dictionary Management

In chapter 12 we covered the concept and role of the **data dictionary** in the DBMS environment. The management and control of the data dictionary is another application function of DBA and is one of its primary responsibilities.

DBA must create naming convention standards and procedures for using the data dictionary. It creates the data definitions, including, for example, the data validation rules. It defines the user views, which describe access to and ownership of data. It handles entry into and maintenance of the data dictionary. Documentation of the data dictionary and the creation and distribution of informational reports from the data dictionary are other responsibilities of DBA. Finally, DBA must establish procedures for auditing the content, standards, and procedures associated with the data dictionary environment.

Whether data not stored in the database should be defined in the data dictionary is a question that has to be addressed and formulated into policy by DBA and the enterprise. Most companies aim for inclusion of all data definitions, but concentrate initially on defining only that data stored in the database.

## Training

A third application function of DBA is training. DBA will conduct training on the use of the data dictionary, on how to access the database, and even in some technical areas, such as how database users and programmers can efficiently use the database. In addition, DBA coordinates vendor training of information systems and user areas. DBA also ensures that applications programmers and analysts properly train users and operations personnel.

## Overall Coordination

A fourth application function of DBA is the overall coordination of the database environment. There are a number of database management and control functions handled by personnel outside DBA and that have to be coordinated by DBA; we will highlight a few of them.

The operations group performs database backup and recovery processing, but DBA decides how often and when these functions should be scheduled and verifies that they have been executed properly. If recovery has to be undertaken, DBA ensures that operations notifies all users of the fact and of how long the recovery process will take. DBA also periodically ensures that backup and journal tapes are created safely and stored properly, in case they need to be used in recovery.

When a problem occurs, DBA must be sure that the right people are involved in the solution. If it is a hardware or systems software problem, DBA helps coordinate the involvement of the hardware or software vendors and the systems group. If it is an application software problem, DBA coordinates the involvement of the users and the applications group. If application software corrections are necessary, DBA coordinates the user review of the test results and transfers the correction to the production environment.

When users have special one-time processing needs or extensive query requirements against the database, DBA coordinates the users so their needs are met without unduly affecting the performance of the database environment.

When the applications group develops a new application system or enes an existing one, conflicting needs may arise if multiple users are involved. DBA helps to resolve these user conflicts. It also helps the applications group determine whether data already exists in the database to satisfy new informational requirements.

These are just a few examples of the extensive coordination role played by DBA.

## Database Loading

Database loading is a fifth application function of DBA. DBA has a major role to play in the initial loading of data into the database for a new application. DBA must verify that everything is ready, (i.e., that sufficient hardware is available to store the data and to handle the additional system load; that software has been tested and transferred from the test to the production environment; that documentation has been published and distributed; that training has taken place; that the data dictionary reflects the new data definitions; and so on).

If everything is in place, existing data must now be loaded into the database. If the application is a conversion from a nondatabase computer environment, special programs created by the applications group must be ready to automatically convert the data to its proper database form. These programs must be executed and their results verified before users can begin processing against the database. Often extremely long periods of time are required to execute these programs, so DBA must fit them into the schedule, frequently over a weekend. Should problems occur, they must be rapidly resolved or, failing this, the former application must be ready to be resumed as a contingency measure until the problems can be corrected.

Even when the data is converted from another computerized form, new data items and records may be present and must now be added to the automatically converted data. The users will complete this entry of new data using the normal transactions of the new application or transactions specially created for this purpose. Because of the volume of data entry involved, it may be necessary to hire temporary help and lend extra terminals to users from other areas of the enterprise in order to shorten the elapsed time required for data entry. The problem becomes even more severe when the former application was a manual one and all data must be entered manually through terminals.

If the project being completed is for an enhancement to an existing database application, there may be new data requirements. It may be necessary to reorganize the database to accommodate these new data requirements. All activities described for a new application may then need to be performed.

## DBA TECHNICAL FUNCTIONS

We finish this chapter with a discussion of the technical functions performed by DBA. Figure 13.12 shows a summary of the technical functions we will examine. These are no less important than the administrative and application functions discussed in the previous two sections. In fact, the technical functions must be performed extremely well to set the stage for smooth database functioning and for satisfied users and information systems personnel. If this is done, DBA usually does not hear from the users of the database environment. If it is not, you can be sure DBA will receive many communications, none favorable, from the users.

**Figure 13.12**

DBA technical functions

**DBA Technical Functions**

1. DBMS support
2. Test/production environments
3. Database design
4. DBMS performance
5. Keep current with technology

### DBMS Support

DBA is responsible for the DBMS. This responsibility includes the evaluation and selection activities already discussed under administrative functions. Once the DBMS has been selected and delivered to the enterprise, DBA continues to have primary responsibility for it.

DBA installs the DBMS, with vendor assistance. Should options be available, such as which DBMS features should be memory resident and which should be paged in from disk, the DBA chooses them. If these options must be changed in the future, DBA makes the changes.

If there is a separate teleprocessing monitor or separate communications packages or protocols, DBA ensures that the DBMS is properly connected to them. If the enterprise uses both a mainframe computer and micros, **downloading** of data from the mainframe to the micros and **uploading** of data from the micros to the mainframe may be required, in which case, DBA selects the appropriate hardware and software links to enable this data transfer to occur.

When a new version of the DBMS is released by the vendor, DBA reviews the corrections and improvements it contains, determines whether and when the organization should install it, and coordinates its implementation. If intermediate corrections are sent by the vendor, DBA handles their inclusion into the DBMS.

A DBMS, both the software itself and the database it manages, is everchanging. DBA makes sure that change takes place in a progressive, controlled manner.

## Test/Production Environments

The actual database and hardware/software environment for the users is called the production environment. This environment should be strictly controlled by DBA. With just two exceptions, only authorized users should have access and modification rights to the database. When problems occur, corrections or reconstructions must take place; and sometimes loading of new applications or reorganizations to the database must take place. In the case of these exceptions, DBA should handle the database activity or should closely control another area's interaction with the database.

Programmers should not have access to the production environment. A second, separate, environment, called the test environment, should be used by programmers for developing new programs and maintaining existing programs. All programs should be completely tested in the test environment. When they are ready, the test results and documentation should be reviewed and approved by the user and by DBA. If they are acceptable, DBA notifies affected users that new or corrected features will now be available, then transfers the programs to the production environment.

There are enough complexities in a DBMS environment; controlling the production environment should not be one of them. A separate test environment reduces the complexity of the production environment by providing an extra measure of control.

## Database Design

In earlier chapters we covered logical and physical database design thoroughly. You will recall that the **ANSI/SPARC** model has three levels: **conceptual** (the global enterprise view of data), **external** (the individual user view of data), and **internal** (what is seen by the machine). DBA takes on the primary design responsibility for two of these levels, the conceptual and internal, and a major advisory role for the external level.

DBA is responsible for the conceptual design. As part of its administrative planning function, DBA analyzes the enterprise's requirements and creates the conceptual design. This should be done before application development begins. When the job is done thoroughly, the conceptual design contains all entities, data elements, relationships, and keys representing the data and information requirements of the enterprise. This becomes the model for all subsequent application development. The requirements for each individual application are measured against the conceptual model so that the external and internal level designs will be compatible with long-term data and information needs.

Taking into consideration the requirements of each user involved with the application, the systems analysts and designers within the applications group develop the external level design during system development. DBA reviews this design and recommends change when necessary. Design changes may be necessary to avoid redundancy with data already in the database, for example, or to allow for future database requirements. Following the approval of the external level design, DBA creates the data dictionary entries and communicates these user views to the appropriate users and information systems personnel.

DBA uses the existing production database structure and the additional requirements from the new external level design to create the internal level, or physical, design. The issues, problems, tradeoffs, and steps involved in this physical design were discussed in chapter 11. In summary, DBA determines the physical access methods to be used and allocates physical storage for the database.

It is not just new or revised user views that may force a change to the existing physical design. Performance problems, new versions of the DBMS, new hardware, new programming languages, unforeseen growth, and better DBA understanding of DBMS capabilities are some of the other reasons for changing the physical design. Physical design changes should not cause changes to the external level design. If an extreme situation occurred and the external level design did have to be changed, it would have to be done carefully so users could still enter and maintain their data productively and could continue to easily obtain the information they needed.

Many DBA groups use automated software aids and system software tools during design activities. For example, Data Designer was the first powerful computerized tool to assist in the design process. Given a number of user views, Data Designer produces a consolidated, normalized design and generates reports on its results. This eliminates a considerable amount of manual work on the part of DBA. See [3], [10], and [11] for more details on the Data Designer processor. Some of the physical design aids are discussed in the next topic.

## DBMS Performance

DBMS performance deals with the ability of the total hardware and software environment to serve the users in a timely, responsive, and cost-effective manner. Funding normally is a constraint, so the challenge involves getting the best possible performance from the available funds. Part of DBA's performance function is planning for optimal performance. The other part is monitoring performance and taking corrective action to enhance service to users.

**Performance Planning.**   DBMS performance begins with proper sizing of the hardware environment. By **sizing** we mean the process of evaluation that determines whether the enterprise has, for example, adequate CPU speed, adequate memory, sufficient disk capacity, sufficient printer capacity, and enough communications ports to meet the workload demands the total DBMS environment will encounter. DBA bases the sizing on estimates for a large number of factors, such as the number of records of each entity type, the number of terminal users, the number of on-line transactions to be processed per day, the amount of work each terminal user needs to accomplish per day, the number of batch jobs and transactions per batch job, and the length of scheduled and ad hoc reports. These factors are then matched against terminal response and batch throughput expectations to obtain the proper system sizing.

Sizing may sound like a simple process, but it is very complex, and there is no guarantee the resulting environment will optimally meet the enterprise's expectations. To understand some of the complexity, consider the load placed on the system over time. In sizing the system, consideration must be given to the average vs. peak system loads. For example, printer capacity must be sufficient to handle the daily report volumes, but how much excess capacity would be required if daily, weekly, monthly, quarterly, semiannual, and annual reports all had to be produced the same day? Most enterprises allow these peak load reports to be printed over several days, or have the reports printed by a service company. In this way, excess printer capacity can be kept to a minimum, and so can costs.

Another issue involved in sizing complexity is expectations for terminal response during peak loads. Should the system be sized under the assumption that response time will be allowed to degrade substantially during peak loads? That is, if an average number of terminal users expect a response to a transaction within two seconds, should the system be allowed to take twenty seconds to give the same response when all terminal users are interacting with the system? Should it be allowed ten seconds? Five? Two? Questions like these must be answered before adequate sizing plans can be completed.

**Performance Monitoring and Tuning.**  Once an operational DBMS environment has been established, the enterprise must be able to add new applications with minimal disruption to the applications already functioning. **Prototyping** can be used to help identify the impact of the new application and provide a benchmark of its expected performance. But only when the new application becomes fully operational in the production environment can its performance truly be evaluated.

Another concern is the changing nature of applications as they mature in a DBMS environment. As the volume of business increases, so does the transactional and print load on the system. As users become more knowledgeable about capabilities, they want to schedule additional reports and enter more queries of a more complex variety. What was once the predicted usage pattern against the database changes as users request different information. In other words, change is inevitable. And change may cause performance problems: poorer transactional response, the delivery of reports later than scheduled, and so on.

Waiting for complaints from users is one way of discovering performance problems, but it is not the best method. Users experiencing these problems become dissatisfied, and a problem may take a long time to solve even after the user has complained. It is far better for DBA to anticipate potential problems.

DBA must monitor system performance and tune the system to maintain a proper level of performance. A number of software tools are available with operating systems and with DBMS's to assist DBA in measuring performance. Some enterprises develop additional software tools to supplement available performance-monitoring tools. All these tools provide DBA with volume and performance statistics on both an average and peak-load basis. These statistics include:

1. The number of terminal users
2. The number of transactions per transaction type
3. The time it takes an application transactional program to execute
4. The number of database accesses per transaction
5. The number of database accesses per database record type
6. The number of database accesses per disk pack
7. The database pages having high access rates
8. The transactional response time
9. The user terminal connect time
10. The number of ad hoc queries processed and their characteristics in terms of number of database accesses, record types accessed, response message lengths, and response time
11. The time it takes an application batch program to execute
12. The number of database accesses per batch program

The preceding list will give you an understanding of the wide range of statistics that needs to be reviewed for potential performance problems. A variety of actions can be taken, depending on the nature of the problem.

The most extreme solution is to buy hardware, either additional or replacement, that is faster or has more capacity than the present configuration. A faster CPU, additional main memory, an additional processor, an added disk pack, and an extra channel for the secondary devices are a few examples of possible hardware enhancements.

Procurement of more hardware is just one way to change a DBMS environment. Data can be taken from the database that is accessed the most and distributed among several disks and channels to balance the data transfer more evenly, thus minimizing channel contention and improving performance. Also, if many terminals are connected through low-speed communication lines, upgrading to faster lines will improve response times.

The database itself can be tuned to improve performance. It may need to be redistributed so records that are frequently accessed at the same time by given transactions can be clustered. It may be necessary to change the access methods to introduce redundancy to improve performance. Any of these database tuning techniques may require reorganization of the physical database, a task that must be carefully planned and executed. Any logical database changes that result from database restructuring must be coordinated along with the physical database changes.

If specific application programs are causing problems, they should be reviewed for potential redesign and rewrite. Streamlining the most frequently used, most inefficient programs can produce a marked improvement in overall system performance. Reviewing groups of programs for possible redesign can also be helpful. If, for example, two batch application programs are both accessing the same data to produce two separate reports, combining their functions into one program that makes one pass against the data can improve performance twofold. Further, it may be possible to reschedule batch jobs so they will either run less frequently or at times of low user transactional activity.

At some point, data becomes obsolete, and if not periodically purged from the database and placed in archival storage, can interfere with system performance. Users typically are provided with transactional capabilities to remove obsolete data, but they often assign these transactions a low priority. DBA needs to periodically review database usage patterns and see to it that obsolete data is transferred to archival storage. The data can always be reconstructed from the archives, should it be needed at a future time.

Other performance tuning options are available. The options described here should give you an idea of the complex nature performance monitoring and tuning can be.

## Keep Current with Technology

DBA needs to stay current with hardware and software innovations that could positively affect the DBMS environment. DBA must keep abreast of current industry efforts in database development. For example, recent strides in database design and in the use of 4GLs and prototyping should be studied for possible use by the enterprise. New features of the DBMS that are offered by the vendor should be evaluated by DBA and implemented as required. Since change is inevitable, DBA must keep alert to those changes that will improve the technical DBMS environment.

## *SUMMARY*

In this chapter, we examined the role database administration (DBA) plays in managing and controlling the database for an enterprise. We briefly traced the historical development of DBA and its importance in a DBMS environment. We considered the factors that make for a successful DBMS environment and DBA group, and explored some of the possible placements and structures for the DBA function.

In discussing the functions of DBA, we divided them into three categories: administrative, application, and technical functions.

A summary of the administrative functions, those involving overall, top-level management and control of the DBMS environment, that we examined is as follows:

1. Top-level education and commitment
2. Enterprise planning
3. Hardware/software requirements
4. Policy formulation

We then covered the application functions of DBA, those involving direct interaction with the database users and with personnel from the information systems department. They include:

1. Standards and procedures
2. Data dictionary management
3. Training
4. Overall coordination
5. Database loading

Finally, we examined the technical functions of DBA. These functions directly involve management and control of the technical aspects of the database environment. They include:

1. DBMS support
2. Test/production environments
3. Database design
4. DBMS performance
5. Keeping current with technology

## REVIEW QUESTIONS

1. What are six resources an enterprise needs to manage?
2. Give definitions for data and information that clearly distinguish the difference between the two.
3. List five internal sources of data for an enterprise and five external destinations of information.
4. In which department was the DBA function usually placed in the early days of DBMS's? Why?
5. Discuss the factors that influenced an enterprise's placement of DBA in the organization during the early days of DBMS's.

6. List the seven organizational factors required for DBMS success.
7. Which of the seven organizational factors required for DBMS success is the most critical? Why?
8. Who normally develops the data and information requirements plan?
9. Is the development of a single, central corporate database a realistic goal? Justify your answer.
10. A typical information systems department is divided into operations, systems, and applications groups. What are the functions of each group?
11. Name five skills a database administrator must possess.
12. What is the difference between database administration and data administration? What is another name for data administration?
13. What are four administrative functions of DBA?
14. Name nine of the initial costs in preparing a DBMS environment.
15. Name seven recurring costs of a DBMS environment.
16. Name eight benefits typically considered in justifying a DBMS on a cost/benefit basis.
17. What is Business Systems Planning?
18. What four areas must a plan cover at a minimum?
19. Name two reasons for DBA needing to know the overall goals and objectives of an enterprise.
20. Of the conceptual, external, and internal data level designs, which is a DBA administrative function?
21. What are attractive choices for the first application to be developed in a DBMS environment?
22. With which three areas does DBA concern itself in the formulation of policies?
23. What is meant by separation of functions?
24. Name four means employed by users to gain authorized access to a database.
25. What is the function of a security officer?
26. Name three different charge-back billing techniques.
27. Name some factors used in a resource-utilization billing formula?
28. What are the positive and negative aspects of resource-utilization billing?
29. What are five application functions of DBA?
30. List five standards and procedures for which DBA is responsible.
31. What are five technical functions of DBA?
32. Explain why an enterprise should have separate test and production environments?
33. What role does DBA play in each of the conceptual, external, and internal data levels?
34. What is meant by sizing?
35. What types of performance statistics are received and reviewed by DBA?

# EXERCISES

1. Interview a database administrator in your local area and determine how the functions performed by this DA compare with those discussed in this chapter.
2. If your school has a information systems department or a computer center, diagram its organization and determine which functions covered in this chapter are handled by the different groups or individuals.

# REFERENCES

1] Atre, S., *Data Base: Structured Techniques for Design, Performance, and Management*, 2d ed. John Wiley & Sons, 1988.
2] Cardenas, Alfonso F., *Data Base Management Systems*, 2d ed. Allyn & Bacon, 1985.
3] Database Design Inc. Information on Data Designer is available from Database Design Inc., 2020 Hogback Rd., Ann Arbor, MI 48104.
4] Date, C. J., *An Introduction to Database Systems, Volume II*, Addison-Wesley, 1983.
5] Fernandez, Eduardo B., Summers, Rita C., and Wood, Christopher, *Database Security and Integrity*, Addison-Wesley, 1981.
6] Gore, Marvin, and Stubbe, John, *Elements of Systems Analysis*, 3d ed. William C. Brown Co. Publishers, 1983.
7] IBM Corporation. *Business Systems Planning, Information Systems Planning Guide*, 2d ed. IBM Corporation, 1978.
8] Kroenke, David, and Dolan, Kathleen A., *Database Processing: Fundamentals, Design, Implementation*, 3d ed. SRA, 1988.
9] Lyon, John K., *The Database Administrator*, John Wiley & Sons, 1976.
10] Martin, James, *Managing the Data-Base Environment*, Prentice-Hall, 1983.
11] Martin, James, *Strategic Data-Planning Methodologies*, Prentice-Hall, 1982.
12] McFadden, Fred R., and Hoffer, Jeffrey A., *Data Base Management*, 2d ed. Benjamin Cummings, 1988.
13] Tsichritzis, Dionysios C., and Lochovsky, Frederick H., *Data Base Management Systems*, Academic Press, 1977.
14] Vasta, Joseph A., *Understanding Data Base Management Systems*, Wadsworth, 1985.
15] Wiederhold, Gio, *Database Design*, 2d ed. McGraw-Hill, 1983.

# Distributed Systems and Other Current Trends

## INTRODUCTION

During the 1970s, database processing typically consisted of a mainframe computer that supported users through terminals connected directly to the mainframe. The mainframe would run a DBMS, which would manage databases on disk. In many organizations today, this is still the way database processing occurs, and it is perfectly appropriate. There are, however, three main alternatives to this scenario: distributed databases, database machines, and database systems for microcomputers. While each of these is a major topic in itself and a complete treatment is beyond the scope of this text, we will examine the basic ideas involved here.

The centralized approach to data processing, by which users access a central computer through terminals, was cost effective in the 1970s. The advent of reasonably priced minicomputers and microcomputers, however, facilitated the placement of computers at various locations within an organization, which meant that users could be served directly at those various locations. These computers were hooked together in some kind of network that allowed users to access data not only in their local computer but anywhere along the entire network. Thus, distributed processing was born. In the next section, we will examine the issues involved in **distributed databases**, the database component of distributed processing.

It has been common practice for some time to use special front-end computers to off-load communications functions from a host mainframe computer. Recently, **back-end machines** have appeared to off-load database access functions from a host computer. Such computers, often called **database computers** or **database machines**, form the subject of the second section.

693

Two specialized types of systems are becoming increasingly important. Object-oriented systems treat data as objects, complete with the actions that can occur on the objects. Knowledge-based systems use draw inferences from the facts already contained in the database to deduce new facts. The third section focuses on object-oriented systems. The final section discusses the concepts involved in knowledge-based systems.

## DISTRIBUTED SYSTEMS

### Description

Suppose Premiere Products has many locations (or sites) around the country. For the most part, each location has its own sales reps and customer base, and each location maintains its own inventory. Instead of using a single, centralized mainframe computer accessed by all the separate locations, Premiere Products is considering installing a computer at each site. If it did so, each site would maintain its own data concerning its sales reps, customers, parts, and orders. However, occasionally an order at one site might involve parts from another site. Also, customers from one site might occasionally place orders at another site. Thus, the computer at each site would have to be able to communicate with the computers at all the other sites. The computers would have to be connected in some kind of **communications network**. (See Figure 14.1.)

Distributed databases fall within the realm of database management and are involved in the networks just described. While there is some disagreement on a precise definition for distributed databases, the following is a good, general description:

> *Definition:* A **distributed database** is a database that is stored on computers at several sites of a computer network and in which users can access data at any site in the network.

On the basis of this definition, we can go on to describe a distributed database management system:

> *Definition:* A **distributed database management system** (DDBMS) is a DBMS capable of supporting and manipulating distributed databases.

Communication between computers in the network is achieved through **messages**; that is, one computer sends a message to another. The word "message" is used here in a fairly broad sense. It could mean a request for data. It could be used to indicate a problem. For example, one computer could send a message to another computer indicating that the requested data was not available. Finally, a message could be the data itself.

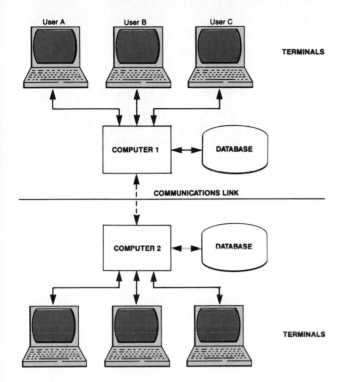

**Figure 14.1**

Communications
network

Although we are not going to discuss the mechanics of sending a message, it is important to be aware that the length of time required to send one message depends on the length of the message together with the characteristics of the network. There will be a fixed amount of time, sometimes called the access delay, required for every message. In addition, the time for each message must include the time it takes to transmit all the characters. The formula is as follows:

```
Communication time = access delay +
                           (data volume / transmission rate)
```

We will discuss an example a little later in this section that is similar to one given by Date (see [3]) in which he assumes an access delay of one second and a transmission rate of 10,000 bits per second. Assuming that a message consists of 1,000 records, each of which is 100 bits long, the communication time would be as follows:

```
Communication time = 1 + (1,000 * 100) / 10,000
                   = 1 + 100,000 / 10,000
                   = 1 + 10
                   = 11 seconds
```

To transmit a ten-byte message would take:

```
Communication time = 1 + 10 / 10,000
                   = 1 + .001
                   = 1.001 seconds or, for practical
                             purposes, 1 second
```

As you can see, in short messages the access delay can become the dominant feature. Thus, in general, a small number of lengthy messages is preferable to a large number of short messages.

This form of communication is substantially slower than accessing data on a disk. In a centralized system, design decisions are made to minimize disk accesses, but, in general, in a distributed system, it is more important to minimize messages.

**Location Transparency.**   The definition of a distributed database says nothing about the *ease* with which users access data that is stored at another site. Still, systems that support distributed databases should enable a user to access data at a **remote site** (a site other than the one at which the user is currently operating) just as easily as he or she accesses data at the **local site** (the site at which the user is working). Response times for accessing data stored at a remote site may be much greater, but except for this difference, it should feel to a user as though the entire database is stored at his or her location. This property is called **location transparency** and is one of the major objectives of distributed systems.

**Replication Transparency.**   Sometimes, in a distributed database, data will be duplicated (technically called **replicated**) at more than one site, for performance reasons. (Accessing data at the local site is much more efficient than accessing data at remote sites, because it does not involve the added communication discussed earlier.) If, for example, the sales reps at Premiere Products have customers at all locations and sales rep information must be accessed frequently, the company might very well choose to store sales rep data at all its locations.

While this replication of data can improve the efficiency of certain types of processing, it creates update problems and causes associated problems with data consistency. If we increase the total commission of one of the sales reps at Premiere Products, the update must be made at each of the locations at which data concerning this sales rep is stored. Not only does this make the update process more cumbersome, but should one of the copies of data for this sales rep be overlooked, there would be inconsistent data in the database.

Ideally, the DBMS should handle this problem for us. Any work to keep the various copies of data consistent should be done behind the scenes; the user should be unaware of it. This property is called **replication transparency**.

**Fragmentation Transparency.**    When customers at each Premiere Products site are stored at that site, we have what is termed **data fragmentation**. A system supports data fragmentation if a logical object, such as the collection of all records of a given type, can be divided among the various locations. The main purpose of data fragmentation is to place data at the site where it is most often accessed.

Fragmentation can occur in a variety of ways. Assume, for example, Premiere Products has four sites called S1, S2, S3, and S4. Also assume that an additional column in the *CUSTOMER* table, called *SITENUMB*, identifies the primary site with which a customer is associated.

Using a SQL-like language illustrated by Date (see [3]), we could define the following fragments:

```
DEFINE FRAGMENT F1 AS
     SELECT CUSTNUMB, CUSTNAME, CUSTADDR, CURRBAL, CREDLIM,
               SLSRNUMB, SITENUMB
          FROM CUSTOMER
          WHERE SITENUMB = 'S1'
DEFINE FRAGMENT F2 AS
     SELECT CUSTNUMB, CUSTNAME, CUSTADDR, CURRBAL, CREDLIM,
               SLSRNUMB, SITENUMB
          FROM CUSTOMER
          WHERE SITENUMB = 'S2'
DEFINE FRAGMENT F3 AS
     SELECT CUSTNUMB, CUSTNAME, CUSTADDR, CURRBAL, CREDLIM,
               SLSRNUMB, SITENUMB
          FROM CUSTOMER
          WHERE SITENUMB = 'S3'
DEFINE FRAGMENT F4 AS
     SELECT CUSTNUMB, CUSTNAME, CUSTADDR, CURRBAL, CREDLIM,
               SLSRNUMB, SITENUMB
          FROM CUSTOMER
          WHERE SITENUMB = 'S4'
```

Each of these fragment definitions indicates what is to be selected from the global *CUSTOMER* relation that will be included in the fragment. Note that the global *CUSTOMER* relation will not actually exist in any one place. Rather, parts of it will exist in four pieces. These pieces, or fragments, will be assigned to locations. Here, fragment F1 is assigned to site S1, fragment F2 is assigned to S2, and so on. The effect of this assignment is that each customer is stored at the site at which he or she is a customer.

The Premiere Products data shown in Figure 14.2 on the next page is used as the basis for the fragmentation illustrated in Figure 14.3 on the next page. Creation of the complete *CUSTOMER* relation entails taking the union of these four fragments.

**Figure 14.2**

Customer data for
Premiere Products
including
*SITENUMB*

CUSTOMER

| CUSTNUMB | CUSTNAME | CUSTADDR | CURRBAL | CREDLIM | SLSRNUMB | SITENUMB |
|---|---|---|---|---|---|---|
| 124 | Adams, Sally | 481 Oak,Lansing,MI | 418.75 | 500 | 3 | S1 |
| 256 | Samuels, Ann | 215 Pete,Grant,MI | 10.75 | 800 | 6 | S1 |
| 311 | Charles, Don | 48 College,Ira,MI | 200.10 | 300 | 12 | S4 |
| 315 | Daniels, Tom | 914 Cherry,Kent,MI | 320.75 | 300 | 6 | S2 |
| 405 | Williams, Al | 519 Watson,Grant,MI | 201.75 | 800 | 12 | S3 |
| 412 | Adams, Sally | 16 Elm,Lansing,MI | 908.75 | 1000 | 3 | S1 |
| 522 | Nelson, Mary | 108 Pine,Ada,MI | 49.50 | 800 | 12 | S3 |
| 567 | Baker, Joe | 808 Ridge,Harper,MI | 201.20 | 300 | 6 | S2 |
| 587 | Roberts, Judy | 512 Pine,Ada,MI | 57.75 | 500 | 6 | S2 |
| 622 | Martin, Dan | 419 Chip,Grant,MI | 575.50 | 500 | 3 | S4 |

FRAGMENT F1

**Figure 14.3**

Fragmentation
of customer data
by site

CUSTOMER

| CUSTNUMB | CUSTNAME | CUSTADDR | CURRBAL | CREDLIM | SLSRNUMB | SITENUMB |
|---|---|---|---|---|---|---|
| 124 | Adams, Sally | 481 Oak,Lansing,MI | 418.75 | 500 | 3 | S1 |
| 256 | Samuels, Ann | 215 Pete,Grant,MI | 10.75 | 800 | 6 | S1 |
| 412 | Adams, Sally | 16 Elm,Lansing,MI | 908.75 | 1000 | 3 | S1 |

FRAGMENT F2

CUSTOMER

| CUSTNUMB | CUSTNAME | CUSTADDR | CURRBAL | CREDLIM | SLSRNUMB | SITENUMB |
|---|---|---|---|---|---|---|
| 315 | Daniels, Tom | 914 Cherry,Kent,MI | 320.75 | 300 | 6 | S2 |
| 567 | Baker, Joe | 808 Ridge,Harper,MI | 201.20 | 300 | 6 | S2 |
| 587 | Roberts, Judy | 512 Pine,Ada,MI | 57.75 | 500 | 6 | S2 |

FRAGMENT F3

CUSTOMER

| CUSTNUMB | CUSTNAME | CUSTADDR | CURRBAL | CREDLIM | SLSRNUMB | SITENUMB |
|---|---|---|---|---|---|---|
| 405 | Williams, Al | 519 Watson,Grant,MI | 201.75 | 800 | 12 | S3 |
| 522 | Nelson, Mary | 108 Pine,Ada,MI | 49.50 | 800 | 12 | S3 |

FRAGMENT F4

CUSTOMER

| CUSTNUMB | CUSTNAME | CUSTADDR | CURRBAL | CREDLIM | SLSRNUMB | SITENUMB |
|---|---|---|---|---|---|---|
| 311 | Charles, Don | 48 College,Ira,MI | 200.10 | 300 | 12 | S4 |
| 622 | Martin, Dan | 419 Chip,Grant,MI | 575.50 | 500 | 3 | S4 |

While this type of fragmentation is certainly common, there are other possibilities. The following illustrates another type:

```
DEFINE FRAGMENT F1 AS
    SELECT CUSTNUMB, CUSTNAME, CUSTADDR, SLSRNUMB, SITENUMB
        FROM CUSTOMER
        WHERE SITENUMB = 'S1'
            OR SITENUMB = 'S2'
DEFINE FRAGMENT F2 AS
    SELECT CUSTNUMB, CURRBAL, CREDLIM SITENUMB
        FROM CUSTOMER
        WHERE SITENUMB = 'S1'
            OR SITENUMB = 'S2'
DEFINE FRAGMENT F3 AS
    SELECT CUSTNUMB, CUSTNAME, CUSTADDR, SLSRNUMB, SITENUMB
        FROM CUSTOMER
        WHERE SITENUMB = 'S3'
            OR SITENUMB = 'S4'
DEFINE FRAGMENT F4 AS
    SELECT CUSTNUMB, CURRBAL, CREDLIM, SITENUMB
        FROM CUSTOMER
        WHERE SITENUMB = 'S3'
            OR SITENUMB = 'S4'
```

This fragmentation is illustrated in Figure 14.4 on the next page. In this case, to create the complete *CUSTOMER* relation, fragments F1 and F2 should be joined on *CUSTNUMB*, fragments F3 and F4 should be joined on *CUSTNUMB*, and, finally, the union of these two intermediate results should be taken.

Again, users should not be aware of the underlying activity, in this case the fragmentation. They should feel as if they are using a single central database. If users are unaware of fragmentation, we say the system has **fragmentation transparency**.

**FRAGMENT F1**

**Figure 14.4**

Alternative
fragmentation of
customer data

CUSTOMER

| CUSTNUMB | CUSTNAME | CUSTADDR | SLSRNUMB | SITENUMB |
|---|---|---|---|---|
| 124 | Adams, Sally | 481 Oak,Lansing,MI | 3 | S1 |
| 256 | Samuels, Ann | 215 Pete,Grant,MI | 6 | S1 |
| 315 | Daniels, Tom | 914 Cherry,Kent,MI | 6 | S2 |
| 412 | Adams, Sally | 16 Elm,Lansing,MI | 3 | S1 |
| 567 | Baker, Joe | 808 Ridge,Harper,MI | 6 | S2 |
| 587 | Roberts, Judy | 512 Pine,Ada,MI | 6 | S2 |

**FRAGMENT F2**

CUSTOMER

| CUSTNUMB | CURRBAL | CREDLIM | SITENUMB |
|---|---|---|---|
| 124 | 418.75 | 500 | S1 |
| 256 | 10.75 | 800 | S1 |
| 315 | 320.75 | 300 | S2 |
| 412 | 908.75 | 1000 | S1 |
| 567 | 201.20 | 300 | S2 |
| 587 | 57.75 | 500 | S2 |

**FRAGMENT F3**

CUSTOMER

| CUSTNUMB | CUSTNAME | CUSTADDR | SLSRNUMB | SITENUMB |
|---|---|---|---|---|
| 311 | Charles, Don | 48 College,Ira,MI | 12 | S4 |
| 405 | Williams, Al | 519 Watson,Grant,MI | 12 | S3 |
| 522 | Nelson, Mary | 108 Pine,Ada,MI | 12 | S3 |
| 622 | Martin, Dan | 419 Chip,Grant,MI | 3 | S4 |

**FRAGMENT F4**

CUSTOMER

| CUSTNUMB | CURRBAL | CREDLIM | SITENUMB |
|---|---|---|---|
| 311 | 200.10 | 300 | S4 |
| 405 | 201.75 | 800 | S3 |
| 522 | 49.50 | 800 | S3 |
| 622 | 575.50 | 500 | S4 |

**Homogeneous vs. Heterogeneous.** Since a distributed database management system (DDBMS) effectively contains a local DBMS at each site, an important property of such systems is that they are either homogeneous or heterogeneous. A **homogeneous DDBMS** is one that has the same local DBMS at each site. A **heterogeneous DDBMS** is one that does not (i.e., there are at least two sites at which the local DBMS's are different). There are, of course, many more problems associated with heterogeneous systems than with homogeneous ones. This important subject is the focus of much research activity. No completely heterogeneous systems exist at this point, but advances are being made in this direction.

## Advantages

As compared with a single centralized database, distributed databases offer some advantages (shown in Figure 14.5) as well as some disadvantages (shown in Figure 14.6).

### Advantages to Distributed Databases

1. Local control of data
2. Increasing capacity
3. System availability
4. Added efficiency

**Figure 14.5**

Advantages to distributed databases

### Disadvantages to Distributed Databases

1. Update of replicated data
2. More complex query processing
3. More complex treatment of concurrency
4. More complex recovery measures
5. More difficult management of data dictionary
6. Database design is more complex

**Figure 14.6**

Disadvantages to distributed databases

**Local Control of Data.**   Since each location can retain its own data, it can exercise greater control over that data. With a single centralized database, on the other hand, the central data processing center that maintains the database will usually not be aware of all the local issues at the various sites served by the database.

**Increasing Capacity.**   In a properly designed and installed distributed database, the process of increasing system capacity is often simpler than in a centralized system. If the size of the database at a single site becomes inadequate, potentially only the local database at that site needs to be changed. Further, the capacity of the database as a whole can be increased by merely adding a new site.

**System Availability.**   When a centralized database becomes unavailable for any reason, *no* users are able to continue processing. In contrast, if one of the local databases in a distributed database becomes unavailable, only users who need data in that particular database are affected; other users can continue processing in a normal fashion. In addition, if the data has been replicated (another copy of it exists in other local databases) potentially all users can continue processing. (Processing for users at the site of the unavailable database will be much less efficient, since data that was formerly obtained locally must now be obtained through communication with a remote site.)

**Additional Efficiency.**   As we saw earlier, the fact that data is available locally means the efficiency with which that data can be retrieved is much greater than with a remote centralized system.

## Disadvantages

**Update of Replicated Data.**   It is often desirable to replicate data, both for the sake of performance and to ensure that the overall system will remain available even when the database at one site is not. Replication can cause severe update problems, most obviously in terms of overhead. Instead of one copy being updated, several must be, and since most of these copies are at sites other than the site instigating the update, communication overhead must be added to the update overhead.

There is another, slightly more serious problem, however. Let's assume that data at five sites must be updated, and that the fifth site is currently unavailable. If all updates must be made or none at all, the whole update fails. Thus, data is unavailable for update if even one of the sites that is the target of the update is not available. This certainly contradicts earlier remarks about *additional* availability. On the other hand, if we do not require all updates to be made, the data will be inconsistent.

There is a compromise strategy that is often used. One copy of the data is designated the **primary copy**. As long as the primary copy is updated, the update is deemed complete. It is the responsibility of the primary copy to ensure that all the other copies are in sync. The site holding the primary copy sends update transactions to all other sites to accomplish the update and notes whether any sites are currently unavailable. If it discovers an unavailable site, the primary site must try to send the update again at some later time and continue trying until successful. This strategy overcomes the basic problem, but it obviously incurs more overhead. Further, if the primary site itself is unavailable, the problem remains unresolved.

**More Complex Query Processing.** The issues involved in processing queries can be much more complex in a distributed environment. The role of an efficient optimizer becomes even more crucial than in a single centralized database. The problem stems from the difference between the time it takes to send messages between sites and the time it takes to access a disk. As we saw earlier, the minimizing of message traffic is extremely important.

To illustrate the problems involved, we will consider two queries. The first query is: List all parts in item class "SG" and whose price is more than $100.00.

For this query, we will assume that (1) the *PART* table contains 1,000 rows and is stored at a remote site; (2) there is no special structure, such as an index, which would be useful in processing this query; and (3) only ten of the 1,000 rows in the *PART* table satisfy the conditions. How would we process this query?

One solution would involve retrieving each row from the remote site and examining the item class and price to determine whether the row should be included in the result. For each row, this solution would require two messages: a message from the local site to the remote site requesting a row, followed by a message from the remote site to the local site containing either the data or, ultimately, an indication that there is no more data. Thus, in addition to the database accesses themselves, this strategy would require 2,000 messages.

A second solution would involve sending a single message from the local site to the remote site requesting the complete answer, followed by a single message from the remote site back to the local site containing all the rows in the answer. The second message might be quite lengthy, especially where many rows satisfied the conditions, but this solution would still be a vast improvement over the first one. (Remember, a small number of lengthy messages is preferable to a large number of short messages.)

The net result is that systems that are only record-at-a-time-oriented can create severe performance problems in distributed systems. If the only choice is to transmit every record from one site to another as a message, then examine it at the other site, the communication time can become intolerable. Systems that permit a request for a set of records, as opposed to an individual record, will inherently outperform record-at-a-time systems. This includes both a relational system in which the message sent could be an SQL query, for example, and a relational-like system, such as IDMS/R with its logical record facility.

A second query that illustrates the importance of an efficient optimizer is: List the order number of all orders placed on 9/02/91 which contain any parts in item class "SG" whose unit price is more than $100.00.

This time let's assume that (1) the *PART* table contains 1,000 rows and is stored at a remote site; (2) the *ORDERS* table contains 100 orders, ten of which were placed on 9/02/91; (3) the *ORDLNE* table contains 1,000 order lines, 100 of which correspond to orders placed on 9/02/91 (both are stored at the local site); and (4) only two of these order lines correspond to parts that meet the conditions.

## Q & A

**Question:**     List five strategies we can use to satisfy this query.

**Answer:**          (Others are possible as well.)

1. Move the *PART* relation from the remote site to the local site and process the query at the local site. This entails moving 1,000 rows (and potentially some indexes) over a communications line before processing begins.

2. Move the *ORDERS* and *ORDLNE* relations from the local site to the remote site, process the query there, and send the result back to the local site. This entails moving 100 orders, 1,000 order lines, and perhaps some index records, then processing the query, and finally moving the two rows in the result back to the local site.

3. Join the *ORDERS* and *ORDLNE* relations at the local site and select only those rows in which the *ORDDTE* is 9/02/91. For each row selected, determine whether the part meets the given conditions by sending a message to the remote site. For each row this process involves two messages, a message to the remote site requesting data and a message back containing the response. Thus, 200 messages will be required altogether.

4. Select all parts that meet the conditions at the remote site. For each row selected, examine all order lines for the part at the local site to determine whether any are for orders placed on 9/02/91. For each row this will entail two messages, a message from the remote site to the local site requesting that order lines for the given part be examined to see which ones were placed on 9/02/91, followed by a message carrying the response back to the remote site. Twenty messages will be required. (Actually, there would be two more messages in this example, an initial one from the local site to the remote site to request that the indicated processing begin and a final message sending the results from the remote site back to the local site.)

5. Select all parts that meet the conditions at the remote site. Move the result to the local site. Complete processing at the local site. This involves moving ten records from the remote site to the local site. This could be done with a single message, however.

In what follows, we will concentrate on the factors that affect the time it takes to send the required messages, not on factors affecting disk accesses. In [3], Date gave a similar example and calculated the time it would take for each formulation, given the figures discussed earlier in this section (a one-second access delay and a transmission rate of 10,000 bits per second). The example he gave involved suppliers, parts, and shipments, which correspond to orders, parts, and order lines in our example. The volumes used in his example correspond to 10,000 orders, 100,000 parts, ten of which meet the indicated conditions, and 1 million order lines, 100,000 of which corresponded to orders placed on 9/02/91.

Using these volumes, Date obtained the following requirements for communication time for the strategies listed earlier:

```
Strategy                 Communication Time
   1                         16.7 minutes
   2                          2.8 hours
   3                          2.3 days
   4                         20 seconds
   5                          1 second
```

Quite a variation! Yet each strategy is a legitimate way to process the query. Since the optimizer should choose the strategy, an efficient optimizer is absolutely critical to the success of a distributed system.

**More Complex Treatment of Concurrency.** **Concurrency** in a distributed system is treated in basically the same way as it is treated in nondistributed systems: **shared** and **exclusive locks** are acquired; locking is **two-phase** (locks are acquired in a **growing phase**, during which no locks are released, and then all locks are released in the **shrinking phase**); **deadlocks** must be detected and broken; and offending transactions must be **rolled back**. The primary distinction lies not in the kinds of activities that take place but in the additional level of complexity created by the very nature of a distributed database.

If all the records to be updated by a particular transaction occur at one site, the problem is essentially the same as in a nondistributed database. However, the records may be stored at a number of different sites, and, if the data is replicated, each occurrence may be stored at several sites, each requiring the same update to be performed. Assuming each record occurrence has replicas at three different sites, an update that would affect five record occurrences in a nondistributed system might affect twenty different occurrences in a distributed system (each occurrence together with its three replicas). Further, these twenty different occurrences could conceivably be stored at twenty different sites.

The fact that there are more occurrences to update is only part of the problem. Assuming each site keeps its own locks, several messages must be sent for each record to be updated: a request for a lock; a message indicating that either the record is already locked by another user or that the lock has been granted; a message indicating the update to be performed; an acknowledgment of the update; and, finally, a message indicating that the record is to be unlocked. Since all of these messages must be sent for each record and the number of records can be much larger than in a nondistributed system, the total time for an update can be substantially longer in a distributed environment.

There is a partial solution to this problem. It involves the use of the primary copy mentioned earlier. You will recall that one of the replicas of a given record occurrence was designated as the primary copy. If this is done, then merely locking the primary copy rather than all copies will suffice. This will cut down on the number of messages concerned with the process of locking and unlocking records. The number of messages may still be large, however, and the unavailability of the primary copy can cause an entire transaction to fail. Thus, even this partial solution presents problems.

As in a nondistributed system, deadlock is a possibility. Here there are two types, **local deadlock** and **global deadlock**. Local deadlock can be detected at one site. If two transactions are each waiting for a record held by the other at the same site, this fact can be detected from information internal to the site (the waiting-for information only at that site). Another possibility is that one transaction might require a record held by another transaction at one site, while the second transaction required a record held by the first at a different site. In this case, neither site would contain information individually to allow this deadlock to be detected; this is a global deadlock, and it can be detected only through global waiting-for information. Maintaining such global waiting-for information, however, necessitates many more messages.

As you can see, the various factors involved in supporting shared update greatly add to the communications overhead in a distributed system.

**More Complex Recovery Measures.**   While the basic **recovery** process is the same as the one described in chapter 2, there is a potential problem. You will recall that each transaction should be either **committed** and made permanent or aborted and **rolled back**, in which case *none* of its changes will be made. In a distributed environment, with several local databases being updated by an individual transaction, the transaction may be committed at some sites and rolled back at others, thereby creating an inconsistent state in the global database. This *cannot* be allowed to happen.

This possibility is usually prevented through the use of the principle of **two-phase commit**. The basic idea of the two-phase commit is that one site, often the site initiating the transaction, will act as **coordinator**. In the first phase, the coordinator sends messages to all other sites requesting they prepare to commit the transaction; in other words, they prepare all resources required to commit the transaction. They do not commit at this point, however, but send a message to the coordinator that they are ready to commit. If for any reason they cannot secure the necessary resources, or if the transaction must be aborted at their site, they send a message to the coordinator that they must abort. The coordinator waits for replies from all sites involved before determining whether to commit the transaction. If all replies are positive, the coordinator sends a message to each site to commit the transaction. At this point, each site *must* proceed with the commit process. If any reply is negative, the coordinator sends a message to each site to abort the transaction and each site *must* follow this instruction. In this way, consistency is guaranteed.

While a process similar to the two-phase commit is essential to the consistency of the database, there are two problems associated with it. For one thing, as you may have noticed, many messages are sent in the process. For another, during the second phase, each site must follow the instructions from the coordinator; otherwise, the process will not accomplish its intended result. This means the sites are not as independent as we might like them to be.

**More Difficult Management of Data Dictionary.**   The distributed environment introduces further complexity to the management of the **data dictionary** or **catalog**. Where should the data dictionary entries be stored? There are several possibilities:

1. Choose one site and store the complete data dictionary at this site and this site alone.
2. Store a complete copy of the data dictionary at each site.
3. Distribute (possibly with replication) the dictionary entries among the various sites.

While storing the complete dictionary at a single site is a relatively simple approach to administer, retrieval of information in the dictionary from any other site will suffer because of the communication involved. Storing a complete copy at every site solves the retrieval problem, since any retrieval can be completely satisfied locally. Since this approach involves total replication (every occurrence is replicated at every site), it suffers from severe update problems. If the dictionary is updated with any frequency, the update overhead will probably be intolerable. Thus, some intermediate strategy is usually implemented.

One fairly obvious partitioning of the dictionary involves storing dictionary entries at the site at which the data they describe is located. Interestingly, this approach also suffers from a problem. If a user is querying the dictionary in an attempt to access an entry not stored at the site, the system has no way of knowing where the data is. Satisfying this user's query may well involve sending a message to every other site, which involves a considerable amount of overhead.

A modification of this idea is actually used in the system called R*, a distributed system developed by IBM. Dictionary entries are stored at each site for all data items currently stored there, as well as data items that were originally stored there. If the *PART* table was originally stored at site A but has now been moved to site B, dictionary entries concerning the *PART* table will be stored at site A (as the originating site) and site B (as the site at which the data is currently located). When a data item is originally defined, R* creates a unique name for it that includes, among other things, the identification of the site at which the item was created. (Users may assign local names to these items that are more convenient than the system-generated name.) When the dictionary is queried, if the query cannot be satisfied locally, the system-generated name is used to determine the site at which the item originated. A message is then sent to that site requesting the appropriate dictionary entry. This entry *will be* at this site, even though the data may have been moved to another site, since the site of origination always maintains a dictionary entry for such an item. This strategy overcomes some of the problems discussed in the previous paragraph.

**Database Design is More Complex.** The distributed environment adds another level of complexity to database design. The information level of design is unaffected by the fact that the system is distributed, but, during the physical level phase of design, an additional factor must be considered, and that is communication. In a nondistributed environment, one of the principal concerns during the physical design is disk activity, both numbers of disk accesses and volumes of data to be transported. While this is also a factor in the distributed environment, there is another important factor to consider: communication activity. Since transmitting data from one site to another is *much* slower than transferring data to and from the disk, in many situations this will be the most important factor of all.

In addition to the standard issues encountered for nondistributed systems, possible fragmentation and/or replication must be considered during the physical level of database design. The process of analyzing and choosing among alternative designs must include any message traffic necessitated by each alternative. While much has been done concerning database design for distributed systems, much work remains. See [1] for a discussion of distributed database design issues.

## Rules for Distributed Systems

C. J. Date has formulated twelve rules that distributed systems should follow (see [2]). The basic goal of these systems is that a distributed system should feel like a nondistributed system to the user; that is, the user need not be aware that the system is distributed. The rules are as follows:

1. **Sites should be autonomous.** No site should depend on another site to function.
2. **No master site.** There should not be reliance on a single site (often called a master site) to control specific types of operations. A system, for example, in which one of the sites was in charge of transaction management would violate this rule.
3. **No need for planned shutdowns.** Performing functions, such as adding sites, changing versions of DBMS's, modifying hardware, should not require planned shutdowns of the entire distributed system.

4. **Location transparency**. Users should not need to be concerned with the location of any specific data in the network. It should feel to users as though the entire database is stored at their location.

5. **Fragmentation transparency**. Users should not be aware of any fragmentation that has taken place. They should feel as if they are using a single central database.

6. **Replication transparency**. Users should not be aware of any replication that has taken place. Any work to keep the various copies of data consistent should be done behind the scenes; the user should be unaware of it.

7. **Query processing**. We have already discussed the complexities of query processing in a distributed environment. It is critical that the DDBMS (specifically, the optimizer) be able to process these queries efficiently.

8. **Transaction management**. We have already discussed the complexities of transaction management and the need for the two-phase commit protocol. It is essential that the DDBMS effectively manage this activity.

9. **Not dependent on specific hardware**. Since installations typically have a number of different types of hardware, it is desirable that the distributed system is able to integrate these various types. Without this, users would be restricted to only the data stored on similar machines.

10. **Not dependent on a specific operating system**. Even though the hardware in use may be the same, there may be different operating systems in use. For the same reasons that it is desirable for a distributed system to support various types of hardware, it is also advantageous for it to support various operating systems.

11. **Not dependent on a specific network**. Since different sites within an organization may employ different communications networks, it is desirable for a distributed system to support the various types of networks within the organization and not to be restricted to a single type.

12. **Not dependent on a specific DBMS**. Another way of stating this requirement is the DDBMS should be heterogeneous; that is, capable of supporting local DBMS's that are different. This is a difficult task. In practice, the way it will be accomplished is for each of the local DBMS's to be capable of "speaking" a common language. As you might guess, this common language will, in all probability, be SQL.

Suppose, for example, DBMS A is running at site A and DBMS B is running at site B. Suppose further that DBMS A and DBMS B are different. Finally, suppose that a user at site A requires some data from site B. Without a common language, this would be very difficult. Since DBMS B is different from DBMS A, DBMS B might very well not recognize the type of request for data that DBMS A would send to it. If, however, DBMS A could formulate the request as an SQL command, and if DBMS B is capable of recognizing and processing SQL commands, then the differences in the DBMS's won't matter.

For other information on distributed systems, see [1], [2], [3], [4], [7], [8], and [9]. For further information on Date's twelve rules, see [2].

## *DATABASE COMPUTERS*

### General Description

Your computer may very well have a *front-end*. This is a computer that handles communication with terminals for the main computer, which is often called the host computer. This computer sits between the user and the host computer, hence the term front-end. (See Figure 14.7.) Without a front-end (see Figure 14.8), every character you type on your terminal is acted upon by the main computer, and every response you see on your screen is received directly from the main computer. Much of this work can be handled by the front-end, thus freeing the host computer for other activities.

**Figure 14.7**

Host computer
with front-end

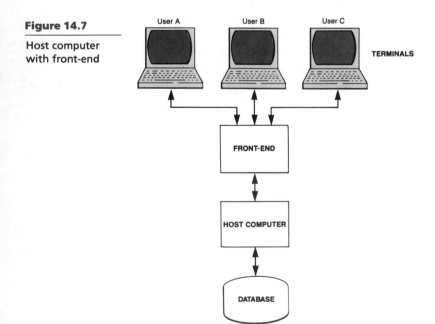

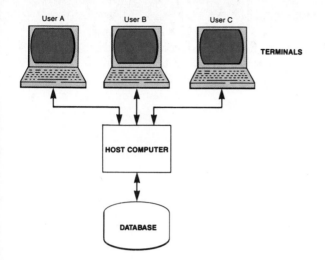

**Figure 14.8**

Host computer
without front-end

**Figure 14.9**

Host computer
with front-end
and back-end

Within the past few years, vendors have developed specialized computers called **database computers**, or **database machines**, whose sole purpose is handling database accesses. One of the best known of these is the Intelligent Database Machine (IDM) developed by Britton-Lee.

Since these computers sit between a host computer and the disk on which a database resides, they have come to be called **back-end computers**. (See Figure 14.9.) When a database computer is used, the host computer will communicate with it whenever access to a database is required. The database computer then begins the task of retrieving data from the database or updating data in the database to satisfy the request received from the host computer. While this activity is taking place, the host computer is free to accomplish other tasks or to serve other users. When the database computer has finished its job, it notifies the host computer. In addition, it will send any data that was retrieved to the host computer.

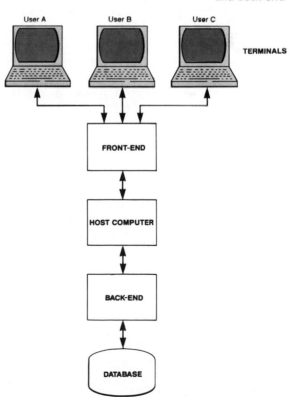

### Advantages and Disadvantages

For every advantage obtained by using database computers, there is a corresponding disadvantage. Both are listed in Figure 14.10.

**Figure 14.10**

Advantages (and disadvantages) to database computers

**Database Computer Advantages/Disadvantages**

1. Performance       4. Simplicity
2. Security          5. Reliability
3. Flexibility

**Performance.**    Since the host computer can perform other operations while the database computer is performing a database operation, parallel processing is possible and improvements in overall system performance can be achieved. Further, since the database computer exists *only* to perform database operations, this computer, together with its operating system, can be tailored specifically to optimize these operations, potentially achieving still further improvements in performance.

On the other hand, every database operation that must be performed requires not only disk accesses on the part of the database computer but also communication between the host computer and the database computer. This communication would not be required if the host computer were performing all the database accesses itself. In some cases, this additional communication will negate the performance benefits mentioned earlier. This is especially true if the request to the database computer entails retrieving or updating only a single row or record in the database. For this reason, a record-at-a-time-oriented DBMS is not particularly well suited for use in a database computer.

**Security.**    If the host computer is maintaining the database, the potential exists for bypassing the DBMS and other facilities within the operating system in order to gain access to the database. Certainly there will be operating system facilities to protect the database and the database can be **encrypted**, but the possibility of this type of access still exists. If a database computer is used, it stands between users and the database. (See Figure 14.9.) It is not a computer on which users can run any programs directly, nor can they directly access its operating system, so it is much more difficult for a user to bypass the controls.

Users can, however, attempt to fool the database computer into believing that they are legitimate users making a database request. The database computer is an obvious point of attack, and this presents a potential weakness in security.

**Flexibility.** Figure 14.9 illustrates a single host computer connected to a single database computer, but the approach is really much more flexible. Several host computers can be connected to a single database computer, permitting sharing of the database and database operations among the several hosts. The database computer, however, can easily become a bottleneck in the whole process. In addition, if the database computer fails, so does the entire system.

Another alternative is to connect a single host computer to several database computers. This permits an even higher degree of parallelism, which may dramatically improve performance in systems that are heavily database-oriented. This structure becomes essentially a distributed system, so many of the problems associated with distributed systems also apply here.

**Simplicity.** Unlike a host computer, a database computer exists for one purpose: to satisfy database requests. The hardware and operating system of such a computer can thus be dedicated to this purpose. Most functions that a host computer operating system must support do not need to be present in a database computer operating system. The database computer is thus much simpler than the host computer. Among other things, this means that there is less to go wrong.

On the other hand, the overall system is more complex than one in which a database computer is not used. Extra hardware is connected together in a fairly sophisticated fashion. One of the challenges in a configuration in which one component is handling one specialized function is to balance the load appropriately. While the host computer is processing at peak capacity, the database computer may be almost idle, if too little of the work requires elaborate database accesses. On the other hand, while the host computer is working far short of capacity, if most of the work requires heavy database accesses the database computer may be saturated, thus creating a bottleneck.

**Reliability.** Because of the simplicity of a database computer and its operating system, database computers are potentially more reliable than host computers; fewer things can go wrong in the operating system. But this reliability may, in some cases, be offset by the potential for things to go wrong on account of the additional hardware and software!

For additional information concerning database machines, see [3], [4], and [8].

## OBJECT-ORIENTED SYSTEMS

### What is an Object-Oriented System?

In the last few years, some computing professionals have begun promoting an **object-oriented** approach to the system-development process. There are also object-oriented programming languages. An **object** is some unit of data along with the actions that can take place on that object. A *customer* object, for example, would consist of the data relevant to customers (number, name, balance, and so on) together with the actions that can take place on customer data (*add-customer*, *change-credit-limit*, *delete-customer*, and so on).

The primary emphasis in the object-oriented approach is on the *data* rather than the actions. The actions are defined as part of the data definition. They can then be used whenever they are required. In contrast, in the more traditional, non-object-oriented approach, the actions are created as part of data manipulation, rather than data definition. In other words, they appear in the programs that date the database rather than as part of the schema.

There are also object-oriented database management systems that are starting to appear. It's too early to tell what impact these systems will have on database processing in industry. Nevertheless, you should still be familiar with the general ideas. In particular, you should have a general understanding of the five key concepts in object-oriented systems:

1. Objects
2. Classes
3. Methods
4. Messages
5. Inheritance

### Objects and Classes

Let's illustrate these terms by examining an object-oriented representation of the Premiere Products database. (See Figure 14.11.) Actually, there is a slight variation of the Premiere Products database. There is a column labeled *ALLOC* in the *PART* table that represents the number of units of a given part that are currently on order (allocated).

Figure 14.12 on page 716 shows a representation of this database as a collection of objects. (**Note:** This is just one approach to representing objects. There are many different ways of doing so. They all represent the same general features, however.) At first glance, it doesn't look much different from the relational model representation we are used to working with. (Figure 14.13 on page 716.) If you look closer, however, you'll see some differences.

**SLSREP**

| SLSRNUMB | SLSRNAME | SLSRADDR | TOTCOMM | COMMRATE |
|---|---|---|---|---|
| 3 | Jones, Mary | 123 Main,Grant,MI | 2150.00 | .05 |
| 6 | Smith, William | 102 Raymond,Ada,MI | 4912.50 | .07 |
| 12 | Brown, Sam | 419 Harper,Lansing,MI | 2150.00 | .05 |

**CUSTOMER**

| CUSTNUMB | CUSTNAME | CUSTADDR | CURRBAL | CREDLIM | SLSRNUMB |
|---|---|---|---|---|---|
| 124 | Adams, Sally | 481 Oak,Lansing,MI | 418.75 | 500 | 3 |
| 256 | Samuels, Ann | 215 Pete,Grant,MI | 10.75 | 800 | 6 |
| 311 | Charles, Don | 48 College,Ira,MI | 200.10 | 300 | 12 |
| 315 | Daniels, Tom | 914 Cherry,Kent,MI | 320.75 | 300 | 6 |
| 405 | Williams, Al | 519 Watson,Grant,MI | 201.75 | 800 | 12 |
| 412 | Adams, Sally | 16 Elm,Lansing,MI | 908.75 | 1000 | 3 |
| 522 | Nelson, Mary | 108 Pine,Ada,MI | 49.50 | 800 | 12 |
| 567 | Baker, Joe | 808 Ridge,Harper,MI | 201.20 | 300 | 6 |
| 587 | Roberts, Judy | 512 Pine,Ada,MI | 57.75 | 500 | 6 |
| 622 | Martin, Dan | 419 Chip,Grant,MI | 575.50 | 500 | 3 |

**ORDERS**

| ORDNUMB | ORDDTE | CUSTNUMB |
|---|---|---|
| 12489 | 90291 | 124 |
| 12491 | 90291 | 311 |
| 12494 | 90491 | 315 |
| 12495 | 90491 | 256 |
| 12498 | 90591 | 522 |
| 12500 | 90591 | 124 |
| 12504 | 90591 | 522 |

**ORDLNE**

| ORDNUMB | PARTNUMB | NUMBORD | QUOTPRCE |
|---|---|---|---|
| 12489 | AX12 | 11 | 14.95 |
| 12491 | BT04 | 1 | 402.99 |
| 12491 | BZ66 | 1 | 311.95 |
| 12494 | CB03 | 4 | 175.00 |
| 12495 | CX11 | 2 | 57.95 |
| 12498 | AZ52 | 2 | 22.95 |
| 12498 | BA74 | 4 | 4.95 |
| 12500 | BT04 | 1 | 402.99 |
| 12504 | CZ81 | 2 | 108.99 |

**PART**

| PARTNUMB | PARTDESC | UNONHAND | ITEMCLSS | WRHSNUMB | UNITPRCE | ALLOC |
|---|---|---|---|---|---|---|
| AX12 | IRON | 104 | HW | 3 | 17.95 | 11 |
| AZ52 | SKATES | 20 | SG | 2 | 24.95 | 2 |
| BA74 | BASEBALL | 40 | SG | 1 | 4.95 | 4 |
| BH22 | TOASTER | 95 | HW | 3 | 34.95 | 0 |
| BT04 | STOVE | 11 | AP | 2 | 402.99 | 2 |
| BZ66 | WASHER | 52 | AP | 3 | 311.95 | 1 |
| CA14 | SKILLET | 2 | HW | 3 | 19.95 | 0 |
| CB03 | BIKE | 44 | SG | 1 | 187.50 | 4 |
| CX11 | MIXER | 112 | HW | 3 | 57.95 | 2 |
| CZ81 | WEIGHTS | 208 | SG | 2 | 108.99 | 2 |

**Figure 14.11**

Premiere Products
sample data

**Figure 14.12**

Object-oriented
representation of
Premiere Products
database

```
SLSREP      OBJECT

Slsrnumb: Slsrep-numbers
Slsrname: Names
Slsraddr: Addresses
Totcomm:  Commissions
Commrate: Commission-rates
CUSTOMER: CUSTOMER OBJECT; MV


CUSTOMER OBJECT

Custnumb: Customer-numbers
Custname: Names
Custaddr: Addresses
Currbal:  Balances
Credlim:  Credit-limits
SLSREP:   SLSREP OBJECT; SUBSET[Slsrnumb, Slsrname]


PART OBJECT

Partnumb: Part-numbers
Partdesc: Part-descriptions
Unonhand: Units
Itemclss: Item-classes
Wrhsnumb: Warehouse-numbers
Unitprce: Prices
Alloc:    Units
ORDLNE:   ORDLNE OBJECT; MV


ORDERS OBJECT

Ordnumb:  Order-numbers
Orddte:   Dates
CUSTOMER: CUSTOMER OBJECT; SUBSET[Custnumb, Custname, Slsrnumb]
ORDLNE:   ORDLNE OBJECT; MV


ORDLNE OBJECT

Ordnumb:  Order-numbers
Partnumb: Part-numbers
Numbord:  Units
Quotprce: Prices
```

**Figure 14.13**

Underlying rela-
tions for Premiere
Products database

```
SLSREP (SLSRNUMB, SLSRNAME, SLSRADDR, TOTCOMM, COMMRATE)

CUSTOMER (CUSTNUMB, CUSTNAME, CUSTADDR, CURRBAL, CREDLIM, SLSRNUMB)
     FK   SLSRNUMB --> SLSREP   UPD RSTR

PART (PARTNUMB, PARTDESC, UNONHAND, ITEMCLSS, WRHSNUMB, UNITPRCE, ALLOC)

ORDERS (ORDNUMB, ORDDTE, CUSTNUMB, SLSRNUMB)
     FK   CUSTNUMB --> CUSTOMER
     FK   SLSRNUMB --> SLSREP

ORDLNE (ORDNUMB, PARTNUMB, NUMBORD, QUOTPRCE)
     FK   ORDNUMB --> ORDERS    DLT CSCD
     FK   PARTNUMB --> PART
```

1. For each entity (*SLSREP, CUSTOMER,* and so on) there is an *object* rather than a relation.
2. The properties (attributes) are listed vertically under the object names. In addition, each property is followed by the domain with which the property is associated.
3. Objects can contain other objects. The *SLSREP* object, for example, contains as one of its properties, the *CUSTOMER* object. The letters *MV* following the *CUSTOMER* object indicate it is multivalued. In other words, a single occurrence of the *SLSREP* object can contain multiple occurrences of the *CUSTOMER* object. Roughly speaking, this is analogous to a relation containing a repeating group.
4. An object can contain just a portion of another object. The *CUSTOMER* object, for example, contains the *SLSREP* object. The word SUBSET indicates, however, that it only contains a subset of the object. In this case, it only contains two of the properties: *SLSRNUMB* and *SLSRNAME.*

Notice that two objects can each appear to contain the other. The *SLSREP* object, for example, contains the *CUSTOMER* object, and the *CUSTOMER* object contains the *SLSREP* object (or at least a subset of it). The important thing to keep in mind here is that users deal with *objects*. If the users of the *CUSTOMER* object require a sales rep's number and name, they will be part of this object. If the users of the *SLSREP* object require data about all the customers of the sales rep, then the *CUSTOMER* object is viewed as part of the *SLSREP* object. This is not to imply, of course, that the data will be physically stored in this fashion. Rather this is the way it appears as far as users are concerned.

Objects can contain more than one other object. Consider the *ORDERS* object, for example. It contains the *CUSTOMER* object and the *ORDLNE* object, with the *ORDLNE* object being multivalued. Nevertheless, to users of this object, *ORDERS* is a single unit.

Technically, what we have defined are not objects, but classes. The term *class* refers to the general structure (like the word *type* as we have used it earlier in the text). The term *object* really refers to a specific occurrence of a class. Thus, *SLSREP* is a class, whereas the data for sales rep 12 would be an object. Often, however, we don't need to bother with this distinction and we use the words almost interchangeably.

## Methods and Messages

The actions defined for an object (class) are called **methods**. Figure 14.14 shows two methods associated with the *ORDERS* object. The first, *ADD-ORDER*, is used to add an order. The data for the order is to be found in *W-ORDERS*.

**Figure 14.14**

Methods for Premiere Products database

```
METHODS

ADD-ORDER (W-ORDERS)
     Add row to ORDERS table
          ORDNUMB  := W-ORDNUMB
          ORDDTE   := W-ORDDTE
          CUSTNUMB := W-CUSTNUMB
     For each order line in W-ORDERS DO
          Add row to ORDLNE table
               ORDNUMB  := W-ORDNUMB
               PARTNUMB := W-PARTNUMB
               NUMBORD  := W-NUMBORD
               QUOTPRCE := W-QUOTPRCE
          Update PART table (WHERE PARTNUMB = W-PARTNUMB)
               ALLOC     := ALLOC + W-NUMBORD

DELETE-ORDER (W-ORDNUMB)
     Delete row from ORDERS table (WHERE ORDNUMB = W-ORDNUMB)
     For each order line (WHERE ORDNUMB = W-ORDNUMB) DO
          Delete row from ORDLNE table
          Update part table (WHERE PART.PARTNUMB = ORDLNE.PARTNUMB)
               ALLOC     := ALLOC - NUMBORD
          .
          .
          .
```

## Q & A

Question:    Describe the steps in this method.

Answer:      The steps accomplish the following:

1. Add an appropriate row to the *ORDERS* table.
2. For each order line, add an appropriate row to the *ORDLNE* table.
3. For each order line, update the *ALLOC* value for the appropriate part.

The other method, *DELETE-ORDER*, is used to delete an order. The only data required as input to this method is the number of the order to be deleted.

Q & A

---

Question:        Describe the steps in this method.

Answer:          The steps accomplish the following:

1. Delete the order with the indicated number from the *ORDERS* table.
2. For each *ORDLNE* on which the order number matches the indicated number, delete the order line.
3. Also for each such order line, add the *NUMBORD* value to the *ALLOC* value for the corresponding part. (With this order deleted, the parts are no longer allocated.)

---

(**Note**: The methods we have illustrated are fairly complicated, each involving many separate updates. Many methods are much simpler.)

These methods are defined during the data definition process. To actually execute the steps indicated in a method, we send what is termed a **message** to the object. A message is a request to execute the method. As part of sending the message, we must send the required data (for example, full order data for *ADD-ORDER*, only the order number for *DELETE-ORDER*). The whole process is similar to the process of calling a subroutine in a standard programming language.

## Inheritance

One of the key features of the object-oriented approach is **inheritance**. For any class, we can define a subclass (like the subtypes we discussed in database design). Every occurrence of the subclass is also considered to be an occurrence of the class. The subclass *inherits* the structure of the class as well as the methods. In addition, we can define additional properties and methods for the subclass.

As an example, suppose Premiere Products has a special type of order. It has all the characteristics of other orders. In addition, it contains a freight amount and a discount that are calculated in a special way. Rather than create a new class for this type of order, it will be a subclass of *ORDERS*. In that way, it automatically has all the properties of *ORDERS*. It has all the same methods, including the appropriate updating of *ALLOC* whenever orders are added or deleted. The only thing we would have to add would be those properties and methods that are specific to this new type of order, thus greatly simplifying the whole process.

### Object-Oriented Database Design

There are some database designers who use an "object-oriented" approach to database design. Usually, this means the design process is oriented toward objects. Each user view is designed and documented using some object-oriented representation. These objects still need to be normalized, however, and converted to a representation appropriate for the selected DBMS.

(**Note:** Some proponents of the object-oriented approach claim that there is no need to normalize. Nothing could be further from the truth. Failure to normalize object-oriented designs leads to precisely the same problems we discussed in the chapter on normalization. It is still a critical step.)

For additional information concerning object-oriented systems, see [2] and [5]. For additional information concerning object-oriented database design, see [6].

## KNOWLEDGE-BASED SYSTEMS

### What is a Knowledge-Based System?

Another important trend, database systems based on logic, has emerged recently. In such systems, the database initially contains a number of basic facts and we have the capability of deriving or deducing additional facts from those already in place. There are several terms that have been used for such systems. The list includes:

1. Knowledge-based system
2. Expert DBMS
3. Deductive DBMS
4. Logic database

We will use the term *knowledge-based system* in this text. The ideas are the same regardless of the terminology.

We will begin the discussion by examining one way in which knowledge can be represented. We will then discuss a way to deduce additional facts from those already present. Next, we will look at the use of recursive expressions in deducing facts. Finally, we will examine the way in which a typical corporate database, like the Premiere Products database, can be represented using a knowledge-based system. (This is not to say we would particularly want to do so. The types of database systems we have encountered throughout the text are much better for processing such a database.)

## Representing Knowledge — Predicates

There are several ways to represent knowledge. We will investigate one approach. In this, the underlying facts are represented through predicates. A **predicate** is a function whose value is either true or false. Consider the following predicates, for example.

```
female(X)
parent(X,Y)
```

The first of these, *female*, is a function that is true if $X$ is a female and false otherwise. The second, *parent*, is true if $X$ is a parent of $Y$ and false otherwise. As an example, consider the following "facts." In other words, each of the following evaluates to True.

```
female(Theresa)
female(Maria)
female(Sara)
female(Susan)
female(Dana)
parent(Maria,Theresa)
parent(Juan,Theresa)
parent(Theresa,Adam)
parent(Theresa,Bill)
parent(Michael,Adam)
parent(Michael,Bill)
parent(Adam,Susan)
parent(Adam,Dana)
parent(Sara,Susan)
parent(Sara,Dana)
```

(In these examples, we will assume for simplicity that names are the unique identifier of people. Thus, wherever we see the name Sara, for example, we know it is the same person.)

Q & A

---

Question:       Use this data to answer the following questions.

1. Who are Adam's parents?
2. Who is Susan's grandmother?
3. Who is Bill's brother?
4. Who are Maria's descendants?

Answer:         1. Theresa and Michael.
2. Theresa.
3. Adam.
4. Theresa, Adam, Bill, Susan, Dana.

---

If a statement contains only constants (no variables), it is called a **ground axiom**. Thus, all the above statements are ground axioms. The ground axioms give us the base data with which to begin. We can see from these ground axioms, for example, that Theresa, Sara, Dana, and Susan are the females; Michael is the parent of Adam and Bill; and so on.

### Deductions — Defining New Predicates

Notice that

```
female(Sara)
parent(Sara,Susan)
```

are both true. From these facts we can deduce the additional information that Sara is Susan's *mother* (she is one of Susan's parents and is female). We can represent this deduction by defining a new predicate, *mother*, as follows:

```
mother(X,Y) :- parent(X,Y),female(X)
```

In this notation we have defined a new formula, *mother*. *Mother* is true for a particular combination X,Y, provided X is the parent of Y and X is a female. By using NOT, we can construct a similar formula for father:

```
father(X,Y) :- parent(X,Y),NOT female(X)
```

Since

```
parent(Adam,Dana)
```

is true and

```
female(Adam)
```

is not, we know that

```
father(Adam,Dana)
```

is true; that is, Adam is Dana's father.

What about determining grandparents from the data? By looking at it, we can see that Theresa is Adam's parent and Adam is Dana's parent. From this, we know that Theresa is Dana's grandmother, but how would we define a *grandmother* function? We do it as follows:

```
grandmother(X,Y) :- parent(X,Z),parent(Z,Y),female(X)
```

This notation indicates that X is the grandmother of Y provided there is some person Z such that X is the parent of Z, Z is the parent of Y, and also Z is a female.

Given that we have already defined the *mother* function, we could do it more simply as

```
grandmother(X,Y) :- mother(X,Z),parent(Z,Y)
```

## Recursive Predicates

We can also define what are called recursive predicates. These are predicates that appear on both sides of the predicate's definition. For example, consider the following:

```
descendant(X,Y) :- parent(Y,X)
descendant(X,Y) :- parent(Z,X), descendant(Z,Y)
```

As you might have guessed this is a predicate for determining descendants. It states that there are two ways of determining whether *descendant(X,Y)* is true (X is a descendant of Y). It is true if *parent(Y,X)* is true (Y is X's parent). It is also true if there is a Z such that both *parent(Z,X)* (Z is X's parent) and *descendant(Z,Y)* (Z is a descendant of Y) are true. In this definition, the name of the predicate, *descendant*, appears on both sides; in other words, it contains itself as part of its own definition.

How does this work? In particular, we know from looking at the data that Dana is a descendant of Maria. (Maria is Theresa's parent; Theresa is Adam's parent, and Adam is Dana's parent.)

First, since

```
parent(Maria,Theresa)
```

we know that

```
descendant(Theresa,Maria)
```

Since

```
parent(Theresa,Adam)
descendant(Theresa,Maria)
```

we know that

```
descendant(Adam,Maria)
```

Finally, since

```
parent(Adam,Dana)
descendant(Adam,Maria)
```

we know that

```
descendant(Dana,Maria)
```

### Premiere Products Database as a Knowledge Base

How does this method of representing facts relate to a production database like the one for Premiere Products? To simplify the discussion, suppose the Premiere Products database is as shown in Figure 14.15. Notice that we are only looking at two of the tables and only at certain columns in those tables. Further, we have shortened some of the column names as well as the names within the data.

**Figure 14.15**

Premiere Products
sample data

SLSR

| SNUM | SNAME |
|------|-------|
| 3 | Jones |
| 6 | Smith |
| 12 | Brown |

CUST

| CNUM | CNAME | CRED | CSNM |
|------|-------|------|------|
| 124 | Sally | 500 | 3 |
| 256 | Ann | 800 | 6 |
| 311 | Don | 300 | 12 |
| 315 | Tom | 300 | 6 |
| 405 | Al | 800 | 12 |
| 412 | Sally | 1000 | 3 |
| 522 | Mary | 800 | 12 |
| 567 | Joe | 300 | 6 |
| 587 | Judy | 500 | 6 |
| 622 | Dan | 500 | 3 |

We will have predicates for each column. For example, for the columns in the *SLSR* table, we will have an *SNUM* predicate and an *SNAME* predicate. The ground axioms for these predicates will be

```
SNUM( 3)    SNAME(Jones)
SNUM( 6)    SNAME(Smith)
SNUM(12)    SNAME(Brown)
```

These indicate that the sales rep numbers currently in the database are 3, 6, and 12, and also that the sales rep names are Jones, Smith, and Brown. Next, we need a predicate, *SLSR*, to tie all the data together. The ground axioms for this predicate are the following

```
SLSR( 3, Jones)
SLSR( 6, Smith)
SLSR(12, Brown)
```

The ground axioms for the *CNUM, CNAME,* and *CRED* predicates are:

```
CNUM(124)   CNAME(Sally)   CRED( 300)
CNUM(256)   CNAME(Ann  )   CRED( 500)
CNUM(311)   CNAME(Don  )   CRED( 800)
CNUM(315)   CNAME(Tom  )   CRED(1000)
CNUM(405)   CNAME(Al   )
CNUM(412)   CNAME(Sally)
CNUM(522)   CNAME(Mary )
CNUM(567)   CNAME(Joe  )
CNUM(587)   CNAME(Judy )
CNUM(622)   CNAME(Dan  )
```

We will not have ground axioms for *CSNM,* since this is a foreign key that must match a sales rep number from the sales rep table. (We will see how to specify this as an integrity constraint.) The ground axioms for the *CUST* predicate are:

```
CUST( 124, Sally, 500, 3)
CUST( 256, Ann, 800, 6)
CUST( 311, Don, 300, 12)
CUST( 315, Tom, 300, 6)
CUST( 405, Al, 800, 12)
CUST( 412, Sally, 1000, 3)
CUST( 522, Mary, 800, 12)
CUST( 567, Joe, 300, 6)
CUST( 587, Judy, 500, 6)
CUST( 622, Dan, 500, 3)
```

### Integrity in the Premiere Products Knowledge Base

We specify integrity constraints through appropriate predicates.

1. **Domain constraints**. If $SLSR(X, Y)$ is true, then $X$ should be a sales rep number (should come from the domain of sales rep numbers) and $Y$ should be a sales rep name (should come from the domain of sales rep names). We can specify these constraints with the following predicates:

```
SNUM(X) :- SLSR(X,Y)
SNAME(Y) :- SLSR(X,Y)
```

The first indicates that whenever $SLSR(X,Y)$ is true, $SNUM(X)$ is also true; that is $X$ is indeed a sales rep number. Similarly, the second indicates that $Y$ must be a sales rep name.

2. **Primary key constraints.** To specify the uniqueness of the primary key, we use a predicate like the following:

```
X=Y  :- SLSR(Z,X),SLSR(Z,Y)
```

This specifies that if $SLSR(Z,X)$ and $SLSR(Z,Y)$ are both true, (that is, sales rep number $Z$ is associated with sales rep name $X$ and sales rep name $Y$), then $X$ must be equal to $Y$. In other words, a sales rep number is associated with one unique sales rep name.

3. **Foreign key constraints.** We can specify the fact that a foreign key must match the primary key in some other table by using a predicate similar to the following:

```
SNUM(W)  :- CUST(X,Y,Z,W)
```

This indicates that if a combination of $X$, $Y$, $Z$, and $W$ makes $CUST$ true, the fourth value, $W$, which is the customer's sales rep number, must also make $SNUM$ true. This forces the value of $W$ to match the primary key of some row in the $SLSR$ table. At the present time, for example, the only possible values for sales rep number in the $CUST$ table are 3, 6, or 12, since these are the only sales rep numbers currently in the $SLSR$ table.

### Views in the Premiere Products Knowledge Base

In the first knowledge base we examined, we had two predicates, *female* and *parent*. We later defined a predicate *mother* that was constructed from *female* and *parent* data. Thus, *mother* was a view in the same sense as the views we discussed within the relational model. We could construct views for the Premiere Products database in a similar fashion. Suppose, for example, we want to construct a view, $SMCST$, consisting of the customer number and name for all customers whose credit limit is $300. We could do this with the following predicate:

```
SMCST(X,Y)  :- CUST(X,Y,Z,W), Z=300
```

This indicates that if there are values of $X$, $Y$, $Z$, and $W$ that make $CUST$ true, and if $Z$ (the credit limit) is 300, then $SMCST(X,Y)$ is also true.

For additional information concerning knowledge-based systems, see [2] and [10].

## SUMMARY

Conventional database processing consists of a single mainframe computer, which supports several users and accesses a database through a DBMS stored and designed to operate on that computer. In this chapter, we have briefly examined two alternative modes of database processing: distributed systems and database computers.

We saw that a distributed database is a database stored on several computers hooked together in some kind of network. A user at any site can access data at any site. A distributed database management system is a DBMS capable of supporting and manipulating distributed databases. We investigated some of the advantages and disadvantages associated with the use of distributed databases and contrasted them with a single mainframe computer that services many sites.

We examined database computers. A database computer, or database machine, is a computer designed to handle the database operations for some mainframe, called the host computer. When the host computer requires access to a database, this request is sent to the database computer. While the database computer is acting on this request, the host computer can accomplish other tasks. Once the database computer has completed its task, the host is notified and any data retrieved is sent to the host. We also investigated the advantages and disadvantages associated with the use of database computers.

We next turned to two other current trends: object-oriented and knowledge-based systems. We saw that object-oriented systems deal with data as **objects**. Each of the properties of an object is associated with a **class** (domain). The key concept is that the actions that manipulate an object are defined as part of the definition of the object. These actions are called **methods**. To cause a particular method to be executed, we send a **message** to the object. Finally, we can define subclasses that **inherit** both the structure and methods of another class.

In knowledge-based systems, facts are stored in the database in some fashion. We saw how to represent these facts through **predicates**, functions that evaluate to either true or false. Predicates that only involve constants are called **ground axioms** and form the base data in the database. From these ground axioms other predicates can be constructed to derive additional facts. We saw that we can use recursive predicates, predicates that contain themselves as part of their definition. Finally, we saw how a typical corporate database can be represented using a knowledge-based system.

## REVIEW QUESTIONS

1. How does the area of database management relate to computer networks?

2. What is a distributed database? Can we use this name to describe a system in which each location has only its own private database that cannot be accessed by anyone else?

3. What is a distributed database management system? How does it differ from database management systems discussed earlier in the text?

4. What is a message? Why are messages important in designing distributed databases and in optimizing queries? Give examples of three different types of messages.

5. What is meant by a local site? By a remote site?

6. What is location transparency?

7. What is replication? Why is it used? What benefit is derived from using it? What are the biggest potential problems?

8. What is replication transparency?

9. What is data fragmentation? What purpose does it serve?

10. What is fragmentation transparency?

11. Explain why each of the following features of distributed systems is advantageous:
    a. Local control of data
    b. Ability to increase system capacity
    c. System availability
    d. Increased efficiency

12. Why is query processing more complex in a distributed environment? Why are record-at-a-time systems not particularly well-suited to query processing in a distributed environment?

13. Why is the treatment of concurrency more complicated in a distributed environment? What is meant by local deadlock? By global deadlock?

14. Describe the principle of two-phase commit. How does it work? Why is it necessary?

15. Describe the various possible approaches to storing data dictionary entries.

16. What additional factors must be considered during the information-level design process if the design is for a distributed database?

17. What additional factors must be considered during the physical-level design process if the design is for a distributed database?

18. What is meant by a front-end? What purpose does it serve? What is meant by a back-end? What purpose does it serve? What other terms are used to describe a back-end?

19. Describe the positive and negative aspects of database computers in each of the following areas:
    a. Performance
    b. Security
    c. Flexibility
    d. Simplicity
    e. Reliability
20. What is the main difference between the object-oriented approach and the more traditional approach?
21. What is an object? What is a class? How do classes relate to objects?
22. What is a method? What is a message? How do messages relate to methods?
23. What is inheritance? What are the benefits to inheritance?
24. What is a knowledge-based system? What are some other terms for it?
25. What is a predicate? Give an example?
26. What is a ground axiom? What type of information is conveyed by ground axioms? Give an example of a ground axiom. Give an example of a predicate that is not a ground axiom.
27. What is a recursive predicate? Give an example.
28. How is the data contained in the tables of a relational database represented in a knowledge base?
29. How do we represent the following types of integrity constraints in a knowledge base?
    a. Domain constraints
    b. Primary key constraints
    c. Foreign key constraints
30. How can views be represented in a knowledge base?

---

## EXERCISES

1. If the access delay is one second and the transmission rate is 10,000 bits per second, how long would it take to send 500 records if each record were 100 bits long and:
   a. Each record were sent in a separate message?
   b. All 500 records were sent in a single message?
2. Assume that orders are to be stored at the same site(s) where the customers who placed those orders are stored. Define appropriate fragments to match the first fragmentation scheme for customers shown in the text.

3. Create a definition for the *FACULTY* object in the Marvel College database. (See chapter 1.) Include all the attributes in the *FACULTY* table, as well as the department number and name, and the number and description of the insurance plan for the faculty member. Include both speaking topics and job history information (both multivalued).

4. Define a method called *ADD-FACULTY* for the *FACULTY* object. This method should add a faculty occurrence together with as many occurrences of speaking topics and job history information as desired.

5. Define a method called *DELETE-FACULTY* for the *FACULTY* object. This method should delete the faculty member identified by *W_FACNUM*, along with all associated occurrences of speaking topics and job history information.

6. Define the following predicates. They concern the knowledge base concerning persons and parents.
   a. *sibling(X, Y)* (*X* and *Y* are siblings; that is, they have at least one parent in common).
   b. *brother(X, Y)* (*X* is the brother of *Y*; that is, they are siblings and *X* is a male).
   c. *daughter(X, Y)* (*X* is the daughter of *Y*).
   d. *maleanc(X, Y)* (*X* is a male ancestor of *Y*).

# REFERENCES

1] Ceri, Stefano, and Pelagatti, Giuseppe, *Distributed Databases Principals and Systems*, McGraw-Hill, 1984.

2] Date, C. J., *Introduction to Database Systems, Volume I*, 5th ed. Addison-Wesley, 1990.

3] Date, C. J., *Introduction to Database Systems, Volume II*, Addison-Wesley, 1983.

4] Goldstein, Robert C., *Database Technology and Management*, John Wiley & Sons, 1985.

5] Kim, Won, and Lochovsky, Frederick H., *Object-Oriented Concepts, Databases, and Applications*, Addison-Wesley, 1989.

6] Kroenke, David, and Dolan, Kathleen A., *Database Processing: Fundamentals, Design, Implementation*, 3d ed. SRA, 1988.

7] Larson, James A., and Rahimi, Saeed, *Tutorial: Distributed Database Management*, IEEE Computer Society Press, 1985.

8] McFadden, Fred R., and Hoffer, Jeffrey A., *Data Base Management*, 2d ed. Benjamin Cummings, 1988.

9] Mohan, C., *Tutorial: Recent Advances in Distributed Database Management*, IEEE Computer Society Press, 1984.

10] Ricardo, Catherine, *Database Systems: Principles, Design, and Implementation*, Macmillian, 1990.

# File and Data Structures for Database Processing

## INTRODUCTION

**Data independence** is one of the functions of a DBMS. Data independence means that users in a database environment should be unaffected by changes to the logical and physical structures of the database. The DBMS should shield users from these changes. In theory, users should not be concerned with the internal or physical level of the database. Instead, they should be concerned with data on the conceptual and external levels of the **ANSI/SPARC** model.

It is true that the DBMS and the operating system file access routines handle the job of storing and retrieving data from the physical database. It is not true, however, that users, particularly programmers and other technical personnel, do not need to be knowledgeable about the logical and physical structures of the database. Programmers, for example, need to know the logical structure of CODASYL and hierarchical model database management systems to navigate their way around the database. And database administrators need to know both the logical and physical structures available with their particular DBMS and must choose appropriate options if they wish to obtain optimal performance and flexibility from the database.

In this appendix we will discuss the fundamentals of file and data structures for database processing. The appendix can serve as a refresher for those students who have taken a data structures course as a prerequisite to this database course. Other students will be able to gain a sufficient level of understanding to appropriately apply these fundamentals to the rest of the book.

We assume that the student is familiar with the fundamentals of disk storage and access. Furthermore, we do not attempt to exhaustively cover file and data structure topics; there are books of several hundred pages each devoted to these topics. Rather, we will concentrate on general concepts and on some commonly encountered data structures in database processing.

We first discuss the fundamental concepts of file and data structures as they relate to database processing. We then focus on the three basic file organizations of sequential, direct, and indexed. Finally, we turn our attention to data structures, specifically, inverted files, linked lists, and the B-tree structure.

## FUNDAMENTAL CONCEPTS

The database we will use throughout this appendix is shown in Figure A.1. It consists of a CUSTOMER file and an ORDERS file. Both files are stored on a secondary storage device; we assume this device to be a disk unit throughout this appendix.

**Figure A.1**

**Sample CUSTOMER and ORDERS files**

CUSTOMER File

| CUSTNUMB | CUSTNAME | BALANCE | CREDLIM |
|---|---|---|---|
| 124 | Adams, Sally | 418.75 | 500 |
| 256 | Samuels, Ann | 10.75 | 800 |
| 311 | Charles, Don | 200.10 | 300 |
| 315 | Daniels, Tom | 320.75 | 300 |
| 405 | Williams, Al | 201.75 | 800 |
| 412 | Adams, Sally | 908.75 | 1000 |
| 522 | Nelson, Mary | 49.50 | 800 |
| 567 | Baker, Joe | 201.20 | 300 |
| 622 | Martin, Dan | 575.50 | 500 |

ORDERS File

| ORDNUMB | ORDDTE | CUSTNUMB |
|---|---|---|
| 12489 | 90291 | 124 |
| 12491 | 90291 | 311 |
| 12494 | 90491 | 315 |
| 12495 | 90491 | 256 |
| 12498 | 90591 | 522 |
| 12500 | 90591 | 124 |
| 12504 | 90591 | 522 |

The sample CUSTOMER file contains nine records; "124, Sally Adams, 418.75, 500" is the first record, "256, Ann Samuels, 10.75, 800" is the second record, and so forth. Each record in the CUSTOMER file contains four fields: a CUSTNUMB that has a unique value for each record, the CUSTNAME of that customer, and the BALANCE and CREDLIM for that customer.

The sample ORDERS file contains seven records; "12489, 90291, 124" is the first record. Each record in the ORDERS file contains three fields: an ORDNUMB that has a unique value for each record, the ORDDTE of the order, and the CUSTNUMB of the customer who placed the order.

We begin this section by describing the steps that must be taken to access data in the database. This is followed by discussions of blocking, clustering, record access alternatives, page addresses, and keys.

## Accessing Data

**Logical Transaction.** A user at a terminal interacts with the environment through the use of logical transactions. A **logical transaction**, or, simply, a transaction, is a user request to accomplish a single task, such as adding a customer, deleting an order, or increasing a customer's credit limit. Though the user pictures the transaction as a single interaction with the database, many more interactions typically are occurring behind the scenes.

Suppose the user enters an order with an *ORDNUMB* of 12505 for *CUSTNUMB* 522 with an *ORDDTE* of 91391 and for an amount of $200.00. This constitutes one transaction to the user, who wants the new order added to the *ORDERS* file only if this customer has sufficient remaining credit. The transaction is submitted to an application program, as shown in Figure A.2.

**Logical Record.** The application program processes the transaction by interacting with the DBMS on a logical record basis. A **logical record** represents an individual application program's (or user's) view of a data record in the database. For the sample database shown in Figure A.1, we will assume that each of the nine *CUSTOMER* records and each of the seven *ORDERS* records is a logical record, though this is not always the case. The application program does not directly access the database; instead, it requests that the DBMS store and retrieve data for it within the database.

To continue with our sample transaction, the application program performs the following logical record accesses in processing the single order transaction against the database:

1. Retrieve the *CUSTNUMB* 522 logical record from the *CUSTOMER* file and verify that the remaining credit of 750.50 (*CREDLIM* of 800 minus *BALANCE* of 49.50) covers the 200.00 for this order.
2. Add a new logical record with *ORDNUMB* of 12505, *ORDDTE* of 91391, and *CUSTNUMB* of 522 to the *ORDERS* file.
3. Change the *BALANCE* to 249.50 and store this changed *CUSTOMER* logical record in the *CUSTOMER* file.

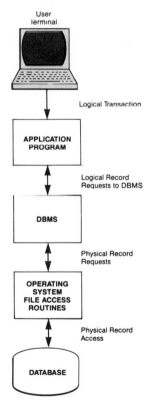

**Figure A.2**

Software component interaction to access physical database records

Thus, the single transaction results in three logical record accesses to the database. A given transaction could result in fewer or more logical record accesses, depending on the work to be accomplished. Most of the time in this appendix we will simply say *record* when we are referring to a logical record.

**Physical Record.**   Each logical record request from the application program is submitted to the DBMS, which determines which physical record or records need to be accessed, then submits appropriate physical record requests to the operating system file access routines. A **physical record** is one unit of data transferred between memory and disk. It is the function of these operating system file access routines to transfer the data to and from disk and memory.

The number of physical record accesses required for the sample order transaction depends upon the characteristics and current status of the database. The attempt to resolve the question of how many physical record accesses are required would be premature at this point. We will come back to it later.

One significant point can be made now, however. One of the most important goals of a database environment is to minimize the number of physical record accesses required against the database. Transferring physical records between memory and disk is a time-consuming task, and keeping processing time to a minimum is an important consideration. The greater the number of physical record accesses needed, the worse the performance of the database environment. Keep this in mind as we probe deeper into file and data structures for database processing.

## Blocking

Suppose a user submits a logical transaction to display all customers by name with their current balances in the same sequence in which they exist in the *CUSTOMER* file. To satisfy this request, the application program needs to request that the DBMS retrieve all *CUSTOMER* records from the database. However, the application program requests these records one at a time, asking for the first record, then each succeeding one until the end of the *CUSTOMER* file is reached.

Each request for a record would require a separate access to the *CUSTOMER* file if each logical record were a separate physical record. In this case, the display of all *CUSTOMER* records shown in Figure A.1 would require nine separate accesses to the database by the DBMS and operating system file access routines.

But a physical record can be larger than one logical record and, with rare exceptions, always is. Suppose each physical record is sized large enough so that it can contain three *CUSTOMER* records or seven *ORDERS* records, as shown in Figure A.3. Each separate group of three *CUSTOMER* records and each separate group of seven *ORDERS* records is treated as a unit, or **block**. Block and physical record are treated synonymously, so that an entire block of data is transferred as a single unit between memory and disk. What this means is that only three disk accesses are required instead of the previous nine. We say that the **blocking factor**, or number of logical records in a block, is three for the *CUSTOMER* file and seven for the *ORDERS* file.

When the application program requests the first logical record, the entire first block is transferred from disk to memory. When it requests the second and third logical records, disk accesses are not required; the DBMS simply does a transfer within memory of the next logical record to the application program.

**Figure A.3**

Blocking of the sample *CUSTOMER* and *ORDERS* files

CUSTOMER File

| CUSTNUMB | CUSTNAME | BALANCE | CREDLIM | Block |
|---|---|---|---|---|
| 124 | Adams, Sally | 418.75 | 500 | |
| 256 | Samuels, Ann | 10.75 | 800 | 1 |
| 311 | Charles, Don | 200.10 | 300 | |
| 315 | Daniels, Tom | 320.75 | 300 | |
| 405 | Williams, Al | 201.75 | 800 | 2 |
| 412 | Adams, Sally | 908.75 | 1000 | |
| 522 | Nelson, Mary | 49.50 | 800 | |
| 567 | Baker, Joe | 201.20 | 300 | 3 |
| 622 | Martin, Dan | 575.50 | 500 | |

ORDERS File

| ORDNUMB | ORDDTE | CUSTNUMB | Block |
|---|---|---|---|
| 12489 | 90291 | 124 | |
| 12491 | 90291 | 311 | |
| 12494 | 90491 | 315 | |
| 12495 | 90491 | 256 | 4 |
| 12498 | 90591 | 522 | |
| 12500 | 90591 | 124 | |
| 12504 | 90591 | 522 | |

Figure A.4 on the next page demonstrates this process. The operating system file access routines transfer an entire block to a data buffer area under the control of the DBMS. A **buffer** is a memory area holding one or more blocks of data. When the application program requests the next *CUSTOMER* record, the DBMS transfers that record from its data buffers to the *CUS-TOMER* logical record area in the application program. If the application program also processes *ORDERS* records, it would have an additional *ORDERS* logical record area, as shown in the figure.

**Figure A.4**

Data movement
between the physi-
cal database and
the logical compo-
nents in memory

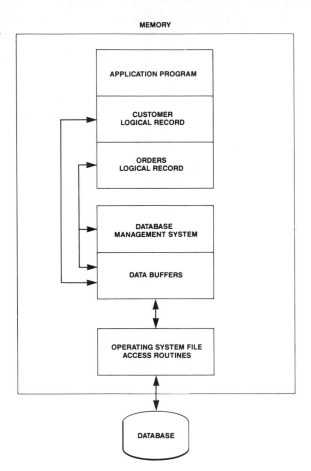

The important consideration is that the number of disk accesses has been
reduced to a third of its former level, and system performance has been pro-
portionately improved. If the blocking factor for the *CUSTOMER* file is nine,
then only one physical disk access is required and a further speedup in file
processing has been achieved. The larger the blocking factor, the fewer the
number of disk accesses required.

Also, the database administrator can normally control the number of
blocks held in the DBMS data buffers. The larger this number is, the greater
the likelihood is that the next logical record is already in memory. If so, then
no disk access is required and performance is again improved.

For larger blocking factors and a larger-sized buffer, there is a tradeoff:
more memory is required. As the cost of memory has decreased and as memory sizes have increased, it has become more practical to manage increasingly
larger sized blocks and buffers.

## Clustering

When dealing with a file-processing environment, it is appropriate to talk about different block sizes and different blocking factors for each separate file. A DBMS, however, manages data in a more general way. All blocks are the same size, regardless of the data contents of the block. In a database environment, a block is frequently referred to as a **page**, so that page, block, and physical record all mean the same thing.

Also, in a file-processing environment, each block contains only logical records from the same file. A single block contains *CUSTOMER* records or *ORDERS* records, but not both. (We will not deal with those cases in which one file contains records of various types differentiated by application programs through record type codes, nor will we deal with variable-length records. Though important subjects, they are not relevant here.)

In a database environment, on the other hand, each page can contain different types of logical records. A single page can consist of *CUSTOMER* records only, *ORDERS* records only, or a combination of *CUSTOMER* and *ORDERS* records. The database administrator who configures the physical DBMS should have control over how records are grouped into pages, and most DBMS's do permit this type of control. Essentially, you want to place into the same page on disk, or in a page close by, those records frequently used together in order to minimize the number of pages accessed and the time needed to access them. This grouping process based on usage patterns is called **clustering**.

If *CUSTOMER* records are most frequently processed in *CUSTNUMB* sequence and *ORDERS* records in *ORDNUMB* sequence, then the clustering shown in Figure A.5a on the next page is appropriate. This figure is identical to Figure A.3 except that it has been redrawn with less detail to focus on the concept of record clustering. To process all *CUSTOMER* records, only three pages need to be accessed. To process all *ORDERS* records, only one page is accessed. This is an example of *intrafile clustering*: the clustering applies to individuals files. What if *CUSTOMER* records are most frequently processed in *CUSTNAME* sequence? It would then be appropriate to cluster the *CUSTOMER* file in *CUSTNAME* order, rather than *CUSTNUMB* order.

The usage pattern, on the other hand, might be that a given *CUSTOMER* record and its *ORDERS* records are frequently processed together. Then the clustering method shown in Figure A.5b on the next page would be selected. This is called *interfile clustering*: the clustering applies to multiple files. Now only four pages are accessed to process all *CUSTOMER* records in *CUSTNUMB* sequence, along with their individual *ORDERS* records.

**Figure A.5a**

Intrafile clustering
based on logical
record type

```
                                          Page
          CUSTOMER    124  record
          CUSTOMER    256  record         1
          CUSTOMER    311  record

          CUSTOMER    315  record
          CUSTOMER    405  record         2
          CUSTOMER    412  record

          CUSTOMER    522  record
          CUSTOMER    567  record         3
          CUSTOMER    622  record

          ORDERS  12489  record
          ORDERS  12491  record
          ORDERS  12494  record
          ORDERS  12495  record           4
          ORDERS  12498  record
          ORDERS  12500  record
          ORDERS  12504  record
```

```
                                          Page
          CUSTOMER     124  record
          ORDERS  12489  record
          ORDERS  12500  record           1
          CUSTOMER     256  record

          ORDERS  12495  record
          CUSTOMER     311  record         2
          ORDERS  12491  record
          CUSTOMER     315  record

          ORDERS  12494  record
          CUSTOMER     405  record         3
          CUSTOMER     412  record
          CUSTOMER     522  record

          ORDERS  12498  record
          ORDERS  12504  record           4
          CUSTOMER     567  record
          CUSTOMER     622  record
```

**Figure A.5b**

Clustering based
on an interrecord
relationship

# Q & A

**Question:**    Show why the intrafile clustering of Figure A.5a could require as many as eighteen page accesses to accomplish the same results just described.

**Answer:**    If the DBMS buffer is big enough to hold only one page at a time, then the retrieval of *CUSTOMER* pages would alternate with the retrieval of the *ORDERS* page. This is necessary to determine whether a given *CUSTOMER* has any orders on file.

We cannot simultaneously cluster the same file in two or more ways. We have to choose either the intrafile clustering of Figure A.5a or the interfile clustering of Figure A.5b. If our sample database had a third file, however, it could be clustered on an intrafile basis while the *CUSTOMER* and *ORDERS* files were clustered on the interfile basis of Figure A.5b. In other words, separate files can be clustered in different ways but a given file cannot be clustered in two different ways.

If usage patterns change so that performance suffers, clustering changes may correct this problem. The database administrator needs to continually review this area for potential change. If clustering changes must occur, it is best if individual programs do not have to be changed; that is, if true data independence exists within the DBMS.

For more details on clustering, see [9].

## Record Access Alternatives

There are two different ways to access records in a file: sequentially and randomly. **Sequential access** requires that records be stored or retrieved in a predetermined order, while random access does not.

**Sequential Access.**   *Physical sequential access* is one type of predetermined order. For the *CUSTOMER* file in Figure A.1, *CUSTNUMB* 124 is the first physical record and *CUSTNUMB* 622 is the last physical record. Using physical sequential access to retrieve records from this file, we need to start at the physical beginning of the file and proceed in physical order, record by record. If we are using physical sequential access and need to retrieve just a single record from the file, all records physically preceding the needed record must be retrieved before we can reach the desired record.

*Logical sequential access* is a second type of predetermined order. An example of this for the *CUSTOMER* file shown in Figure A.1 is accessing the records in *CUSTNAME* sequence by starting at Sally Adams (*CUSTNUMB* 124), then accessing Sally Adams (*CUSTNUMB* 412), then Joe Baker, and so on, until ending with Al Williams. Notice that this file is in physical order by *CUSTNUMB* so that access by *CUSTNAME* could not represent physical sequential access.

**Random Access.**   With **random access**, the storage and retrieval of records is not based on any predetermined order. Records are stored in the file as they occur, so they can later be retrieved directly, without the necessity of accessing other records in the file. Since records are directly accessed, random access is also frequently called *direct access*. If we were to randomly access records from the *CUSTOMER* file, for example, we might first need to access Mary Nelson, then Ann Samuels, then Dan Martin.

**Choice of Access.**   Sequential access is appropriate when we need to access all or most of the records in a file. Also, if a file contains few enough records to fit in one page or very few pages, then sequential access may be acceptable, since the file's pages probably already reside in the memory buffers. In all other cases, random access is the appropriate access technique.

Random access and logical sequential access techniques are available only because there are special ways of structuring files and databases to accommodate them. These structures are the topics in all remaining sections in this appendix. Before ending this section on fundamental concepts, we need to discuss page addresses and keys.

## Page Addresses and Keys

In a file processing environment, the operating system keeps track of each file in terms of its size, starting position on disk, block size, locations on disk, and a number of other factors. In a database environment, the operating system keeps track of the pages on disk allocated to the database, while the DBMS controls what data is located where within these allocated pages. Each page (or block) on disk has a unique address, called the *page number*, which can be used to store or retrieve the data in that page. In addition to the use of the page number, there are a number of other possible addressing techniques. The use of a relative record number is one of them. The **relative record number** is the number of a record relative to the start of the file. All the examples in this appendix use either the page number or the relative record number as the address for storing and retrieving a logical record on disk. When the page number is used, multiple logical records will be stored in each page.

To use random access to store and later retrieve a particular record, we need some mechanism for transforming the value of a field (or group of fields) within the record into a page address. In most cases, a primary key is used as the basis for this transformation. A **primary key** is a field (or group of fields) that has a unique value for each record. Therefore, it can uniquely distinguish one record in the file from any other record in the file. For example, *CUSTNUMB* could serve as a primary key for the *CUSTOMER* file, and *ORDNUMB* could be a primary key for the *ORDERS* file.

Frequently, we need to randomly retrieve records in a file through the value of a field other than the primary key. For example, we might want to retrieve all customers whose *CREDLIM* is 800. A field that allows access in this fashion is called a **secondary key**.

A third type of key in file and database processing is a sequence key. A **sequence key** is a field (or group of fields) within a record that determines the order of records within the file. From the appearance of the *CUSTOMER* file in Figure A.1, *CUSTNUMB* serves as the sequence field, since the records are in physical order on the basis of this field. If this file also allowed logical sequential access based on the *CUSTNAME* field, then *CUSTNAME* would also be a sequence field for the file. Some DBMS's refer to a sequence key as a *sequence field*.

## *FILE ORGANIZATION*

**File organization** refers to the physical structure of a file on disk. The three available file organization techniques are **sequential**, **direct**, and **indexed**, and will be discussed in this order.

Each of these file organizations is used by a DBMS in some form. Sequential organization is used for journal files; for backup copies of the database; for certain extract files passed to batch application programs; for batch transaction files; and for certain forms of data storage within the database. Both direct and indexed organization are techniques used by a DBMS for storage of data within the database.

A file organization, together with the set of possible access techniques for that organization, constitute an **access method**. Each access technique defines the steps involved in storing and retrieving specific records through either sequential or random access. As we discuss each file organization, we will describe the access techniques possible for that organization, thereby describing the complete access method.

### Sequential Organization

For **sequential organization**, records are stored in physical sequence as they occur during processing. Two different types of sequential organization are possible. If records are stored in no special sequence except chronological (that is, time occurrence or arrival sequence), the file is called a *pile*. Figure A.6a shows the *CUSTOMER* file organized as a pile. Note that the records are not in order by *CUSTNUMB*, nor are they in order by any other field. Journal files, backup copies, batch transaction files, and certain types of archive files would typically call for the use of a pile.

```
                               Page
┌──────────────────────────────┐
│ CUSTOMER    405  record      │
│ CUSTOMER    256  record    1 │
│ CUSTOMER    311  record      │
│                              │
│ CUSTOMER    622  record      │
│ CUSTOMER    124  record    2 │
│ CUSTOMER    567  record      │
│                              │
│ CUSTOMER    522  record      │
│ CUSTOMER    412  record    3 │
│ CUSTOMER    315  record      │
└──────────────────────────────┘
```

**Figure A.6a**

Sequential organization showing record arrival sequence: a pile

The second type of sequential organization is applicable with certain kinds of database storage and with master files in a file-processing environment, where a large percentage of the records usually need to be accessed.

This type is usually implied when sequential organization is indicated for a file. A file with this type of sequential organization has all its records stored in sequence key order. The sequence key is normally a primary key. Figure A.6b illustrates the *CUSTOMER* file with this type of sequential organization. The sequence key is *CUSTNUMB*, which is also the primary key for the file.

Only sequential access can be used with a sequentially organized file; random access is not possible. (*Caution:* the word "sequential" describes both a type of file access and a type of file organization. We will be careful in this appendix to make clear which meaning of the word we are using.) If one specific record needs to be retrieved from the file, all records physically preceding that record must be retrieved first to get to it. Thus, sequential organization is not suited for an on-line environment, which requires rapid access.

When records are sequentially accessed in a sequentially organized file, records can be added to the end of the file. If changes need to be made to an existing record, that record can be updated and rewritten to the same physical location. But if a new record must be inserted anywhere in the middle of the file, the entire file must be recopied to a new physical location, with the new record properly positioned. Physically deleting an existing record also requires that the file be recopied to a new physical location; the deleted record may not be output to the new version of the file. Figure A.6c demonstrates the addition and deletion process: *CUSTOMER* records 256 and 522 from Figure A.6b have been deleted; *CUSTOMER* record 600 has been added. Additions, deletions, and changes to a sequentially organized master file are normally collected in a transaction file in the form of a pile. The transaction file is sorted and processed against the current version of the master, thereby creating the new version of the master, which incorporates the effects of the additions, changes, and deletions.

**Figure A.6b**

Sequential organization showing the more typical primary key sequence

```
                                          Page
     CUSTOMER   124  record
     CUSTOMER   256  record          1
     CUSTOMER   311  record

     CUSTOMER   315  record
     CUSTOMER   405  record          2
     CUSTOMER   412  record

     CUSTOMER   522  record
     CUSTOMER   567  record          3
     CUSTOMER   622  record
```

**Figure A.6c**

The previous file after deleting records 256 and 522 and adding 600

```
                                          Page
     CUSTOMER   124  record
     CUSTOMER   311  record          1
     CUSTOMER   315  record

     CUSTOMER   405  record
     CUSTOMER   412  record          2
     CUSTOMER   567  record

     CUSTOMER   600  record
     CUSTOMER   622  record          3
```

Sequential organization is extremely useful in terms of storage on disk, since only the logical records themselves need to be stored. No additional physical structure fields need to be stored, so the file is as compact as possible in disk usage.

## Direct Organization

Direct organization gives exceptional performance in an on-line environment, where random access is required. For **direct organization**, each record is stored and retrieved at a disk address on the basis of a formula that is applied to the value of a field in the record. (If the field used for the formula is alphanumeric, we assume it is converted to a number before being used in the formula.) Two different types of direct organization are possible, one using key-addressing techniques and the other using hashing techniques.

**Key-Addressing Techniques.** With **key-addressing** techniques, the formula is applied to the primary key field and results in a unique **relative record number**. Figure A.7a provides an example of this technique. We have now given *CUSTNUMB*, the primary key field, values 1 through 9, respectively, for each of the nine *CUSTOMER* records. The value of *CUSTNUMB* is used to store the record in the same-valued relative record position in the file. Retrieving a record, say, *CUSTNUMB* 8, simply means reading the record whose relative record number is 8. The formula in this example uses the primary key field value without any change.

|  |  |  | Relative<br>Record<br>Number | Page |
|---|---|---|---|---|
| CUSTOMER | 1 | record | 1 | |
| CUSTOMER | 2 | record | 2 | 1 |
| CUSTOMER | 3 | record | 3 | |
| CUSTOMER | 4 | record | 4 | |
| CUSTOMER | 5 | record | 5 | 2 |
| CUSTOMER | 6 | record | 6 | |
| CUSTOMER | 7 | record | 7 | |
| CUSTOMER | 8 | record | 8 | 3 |
| CUSTOMER | 9 | record | 9 | |

**Figure A.7a**

Direct organization using a key-addressing technique: the relative record number equals the *CUSTNUMB*

Figure A.7b on the next page provides a second example of the key-addressing technique. In this case, a true formula is used. For *CUSTNUMB* 19, we subtract 3 from the *CUSTNUMB* value of 19 and divide the resulting value of 16 by 2, giving 8 as the relative record number to be used. Again, each primary key value results in a unique relative record number used for file access. Notice that it takes just one file access to store and retrieve a specific record. Increased speed of file access is a distinct advantage of the key-addressing technique for direct organization.

**Figure A.7b**

Direct organization using a key-addressing technique: the relative record number determined from the formula (*CUSTNUMB – 3*) / 2

| | | | Relative Record Number | Page |
|---|---|---|---|---|
| CUSTOMER | 5 | record | 1 | |
| CUSTOMER | 7 | record | 2 | 1 |
| CUSTOMER | 9 | record | 3 | |
| CUSTOMER | 11 | record | 4 | |
| CUSTOMER | 13 | record | 5 | 2 |
| CUSTOMER | 15 | record | 6 | |
| CUSTOMER | 17 | record | 7 | |
| CUSTOMER | 19 | record | 8 | 3 |
| CUSTOMER | 21 | record | 9 | |

In these first two examples, the primary key values behave nicely; the pattern maps the records to file storage locations without any wasted space. Usually, it is impossible to establish such a pattern. Our original *CUSTOMER* file example is typical of what we find in actual practice. Figure A.8 shows this file stored with the key-addressing technique, using the *CUSTNUMB* value as the relative record number. Once again, only one access is required to manipulate a given record. However, you will notice that only nine out of the first 622 storage locations are used in the figure. The unused storage locations, called *gaps*, must be reserved, even though they are not being used. There is usually a tradeoff between speed of access and wasted disk storage space when the key-addressing technique is applied.

**Figure A.8**

Direct organization using a key-addressing technique: the relative record number equals the *CUSTNUMB*

| | Relative Record Number |
|---|---|
| | 1 |
| | 2 |
| | 3 |
| . | |
| CUSTOMER 124 record | 124 |
| . | |
| CUSTOMER 256 record | 256 |
| . | |
| CUSTOMER 311 record | 311 |
| . | |
| CUSTOMER 315 record | 315 |
| . | |
| CUSTOMER 405 record | 405 |
| . | |
| CUSTOMER 412 record | 412 |
| . | |
| CUSTOMER 522 record | 522 |
| . | |
| CUSTOMER 567 record | 567 |
| . | |
| CUSTOMER 622 record | 622 |

Unless we have a primary key that can be directed into a compact mapping to relative record numbers, the key-addressing technique is not a wise choice for direct organization. Though it is a fast access method, it leaves many gaps, which wastes disk storage. In our three examples, the records end up stored in sequence by primary key, but sequential access is time-consuming, owing to the necessity of retrieving and bypassing the gaps in order to reach the actual records. Finally, if we were to decide to change the key-addressing formula we were using, the file would most certainly need to be reorganized and may no longer be in primary key sequence.

For example, instead of using the *CUSTNUMB* value as the relative record number, let's use a formula in which the first digit of *CUSTNUMB* is added to the last two digits. Figure A.9 shows the results of this change to our formula. The file requires reorganization to place the nine *CUSTOMER* records into seventy-two storage locations, rather than the 622 we had before.

Programs have to be changed to use the new formula, and the records are no longer stored in primary key sequence. Finally, what happens if a record with a *CUSTNUMB* of 553 is added to the file? It should be stored using a relative record number of 58, but the *CUSTOMER* 256 record is already stored there! Direct organization is still possible, but now we must switch from a key-addressing technique to a hashing technique.

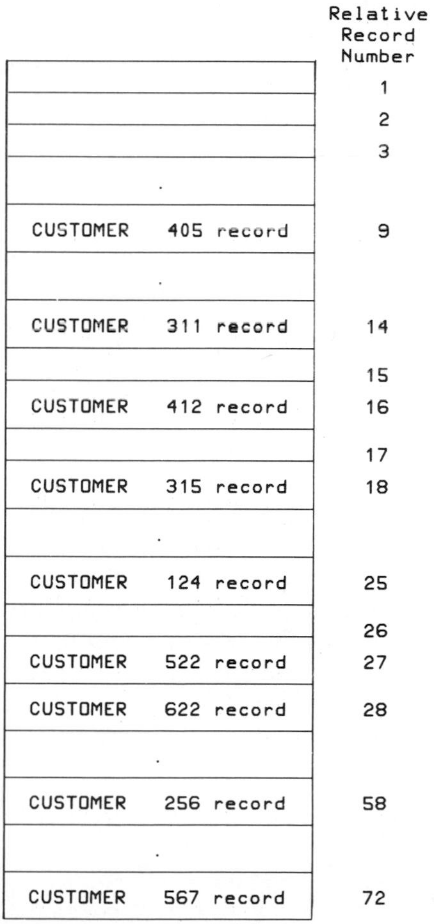

| | Relative Record Number |
|---|---|
| | 1 |
| | 2 |
| | 3 |
| CUSTOMER   405 record | 9 |
| CUSTOMER   311 record | 14 |
| | 15 |
| CUSTOMER   412 record | 16 |
| | 17 |
| CUSTOMER   315 record | 18 |
| CUSTOMER   124 record | 25 |
| | 26 |
| CUSTOMER   522 record | 27 |
| CUSTOMER   622 record | 28 |
| CUSTOMER   256 record | 58 |
| CUSTOMER   567 record | 72 |

**Figure A.9**

Direct organization using a key-addressing technique: the relative record number determined from the formula (last two digits of *CUSTNUMB* + first digit of *CUSTNUMB*)

**Hashing Techniques.**   **Hashing techniques** are similar to key-addressing techniques in that a formula is applied to a field in the record (again, usually the primary key field), resulting in a value used as the disk address for storing and retrieving the record. The difference is that hashing does not guarantee a unique storage address. The formula can produce two or more records with the same resulting value. Also, the stored records are normally not in primary key sequence. So why use a hashing technique? The answer is that this technique allows us to efficiently utilize disk storage while attempting to retain the fastest possible random access (no more than one disk access) for on-line processing. Fast random access is possible only if we can minimize the effects of duplicate results from the formula.

Hashing techniques are sometimes called *randomizing techniques*. The formula used to transform the primary key into a disk address is also known as a *hashing algorithm*, a *hashing routine*, a *randomizing routine*, or, simply, a **hash function**. The hash function is chosen so the records are spread as evenly as possible throughout the file, but the stored records usually end up stored in no particular sequence.

When we attempted to add a new record having *CUSTNUMB* 553 to the *CUSTOMER* file in Figure A.9, we saw that the result of the hash function yielded a relative record number of 58. Since the *CUSTNUMB* 256 record already is stored there, we now have two records that need to be stored in the same disk location. When two or more records end up with the same hash function value, we have what is called **collision**. And the two records, the ones with *CUSTNUMB* 256 and 553, are called **synonyms**, since they have the same hash function value. Before we discuss different methods of managing the collision problem, we will review two commonly used hashing techniques.

**Folding Hashing Technique.**   The hash function used in Figure A.9 is an example of the **folding method**. This method involves taking the primary key value, dividing the digits of it into two or more groups, and adding these groups of digits together. The resulting sum is used as the disk address. In effect, we take a somewhat large primary key value and transform it into a smaller number, used as a disk address. This is true of all hashing techniques because we are dealing with large primary key values, such as Social Security numbers and bank account numbers. Our objective is to map each primary key value into as small a disk address space as possible while minimizing the collision problem. Note that none of the nine records in Figure A.9 has a synonym; however, we are utilizing only 12.5 percent (9 out of 72) of the available space. This percentage is frequently referred to as the *packing density*, or *load factor*, of the file.

Question:          What would be the packing density of the nine records in Figure A.9 if we changed the hash function to be the sum of the first two digits of *CUSTNUMB* and the last digit of *CUSTNUMB*? Would any collisions occur with this new folding method?

Answer:                 The packing would be 14 percent (9 out of 64), and no collisions would occur. The transformations would be:

| CUSTNUMB | Relative Record Number |
|----------|------------------------|
| 124      | 16                     |
| 256      | 31                     |
| 311      | 32                     |
| 315      | 36                     |
| 405      | 45                     |
| 412      | 43                     |
| 522      | 54                     |
| 567      | 63                     |
| 622      | 64                     |

**Division-Remainder Hashing Technique.** The **division-remainder method** employs a formula in which the primary key value is divided by a fixed, preselected number and the remainder of this division is used as the disk address. Research has proven that the number selected for the division should be a prime number and that the division-remainder method is one of the very best hashing techniques. Since the remainder could be zero, we will add 1 to the remainder in our examples of this method.

Figure A.10 on the next page demonstrates the division-remainder method, using the same *CUSTOMER* file records and a divisor of 29. We have added 1 to the results of the formula to produce the relative record number. The nine *CUSTOMER* records fit into twenty-nine storage locations, a 31-percent packing density.

**Figure A.10**

Direct organization
with a hashing
technique using
the division-
remainder method
and a divisor of 29

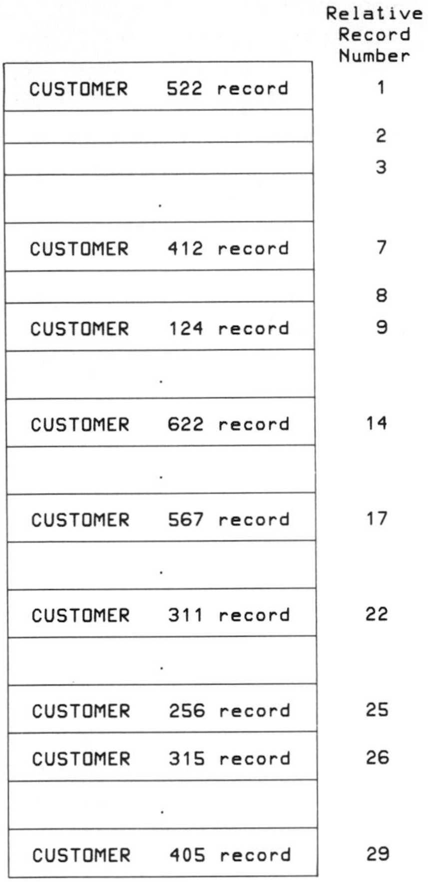

| | Relative Record Number |
|---|---|
| CUSTOMER    522 record | 1 |
| | 2 |
| | 3 |
| . | |
| CUSTOMER    412 record | 7 |
| | 8 |
| CUSTOMER    124 record | 9 |
| . | |
| CUSTOMER    622 record | 14 |
| . | |
| CUSTOMER    567 record | 17 |
| . | |
| CUSTOMER    311 record | 22 |
| . | |
| CUSTOMER    256 record | 25 |
| CUSTOMER    315 record | 26 |
| . | |
| CUSTOMER    405 record | 29 |

There are no collisions in this example, but that does not guarantee none in the future. For instance, if we attempt to add the record whose *CUSTNUMB* was 625, the hash function produces a value of 17. Thus, the *CUSTOMER* 567 record is a synonym for this new record, so collision results.

**Collision Management.** No matter how well we choose our hashing algorithm, we are going to have to face the problem of collisions and how best to manage them. A variety of techniques is used to minimize the number of collisions and to minimize the effects of collision when it does occur.

You will recall that a DBMS stores records in pages holding multiple records and that each page has a unique page number, or address. Rather than use a relative record number for storing and retrieving records, hashing techniques use the page number for locating records. With this approach, a page is often called a *bucket*, and each record location within a page is called a *slot*.

In Figure A.11, seven pages have been allocated, and each page can store three *CUSTOMER* records. The division-remainder method is used with a divisor of 7 (again we add 1 to the result to obtain the page number). The *CUSTOMER* 315 and 567 records both hash to page one, but both records can be stored with room for one additional record in the future. What we have done is minimized the effects of collision, since it will now cause a problem only when we attempt to store an additional record in a page that is full with three records.

| | | Page |
|---|---|---|
| CUSTOMER 315 record<br>CUSTOMER 567 record | | 1 |
| | | 2 |
| | | 3 |
| CUSTOMER 311 record | | 4 |
| CUSTOMER 256 record<br>CUSTOMER 522 record | | 5 |
| CUSTOMER 124 record | | 6 |
| CUSTOMER 405 record<br>CUSTOMER 412 record<br>CUSTOMER 622 record | | 7 |

**Figure A.11**

Collision resolution using page addresses

If we enlarge the size of each page so that it holds more records, the effects of collision will be reduced further. The file in Figure A.11 has a packing density of 42 percent (9 out of 21, the maximum number of records that can be stored). If we enlarge each page so it holds four records and keep the number of pages and our hash function the same, the packing density reduces to 32 percent (9 out of 28). This demonstrates that the more we try to eliminate collision, relying strictly on larger page sizes, the less efficiently we are utilizing disk space.

When a page becomes full and a further collision occurs on that page, there are a number of methods for dealing with the new record. One method involves using a **linear search** for storing and later retrieving the record. If we find that the page is full when we attempt to add a new record to it, we place the record in the next page that has an available record slot.

Let's assume we need to add two new records to those shown in Figure A.11. These records are for customers 623 and 630, both of which hash to page one. The *CUSTOMER* 623 record is placed into page one, since there is room for one more record, and the *CUSTOMER* 630 record is placed into page two, the next page having an available record slot. Figure A.12 shows the result of these additions. When later retrieving the *CUSTOMER* 630 record, we employ the division-remainder hash function and get a value of 1. Page one is retrieved, and when we find that the *CUSTOMER* 630 record is not located there, page two is retrieved and the record is found.

**Figure A.12**

Collision resolution using a linear search

| | | Page |
|---|---|---|
| CUSTOMER   315 record<br>CUSTOMER   567 record<br>CUSTOMER   623 record | | 1 |
| CUSTOMER   630 record | | 2 |
| | | 3 |
| CUSTOMER   311 record | | 4 |
| CUSTOMER   256 record<br>CUSTOMER   522 record | | 5 |
| CUSTOMER   124 record | | 6 |
| CUSTOMER   405 record<br>CUSTOMER   412 record<br>CUSTOMER   622 record | | 7 |

The advantage of the linear search method is that records that hash to the same address will end up clustered together in the same page or in nearby pages. But what happens if there are many records that hash to the first three pages, so that when we store the *CUSTOMER* 630 record, it must be stored in page four or even a later page? Multiple file accesses are required to obtain the requested record. This procedure is inefficient but does not affect performance too badly if only a few accesses are required.

But what happens when we are asked to retrieve the *CUSTOMER* 616 record, which hashes to page one, and the first five pages are filled with *CUSTOMER* records? We have to retrieve each of these pages and check each record before we will know for sure that this record does not exist. And the problem can be even worse for large-sized files with high packing densities. We may have to search through thousands of pages before we store or retrieve the correct record or find that such a record does not exist.

There is another method of managing collisions that helps overcome these problems. It involves the use of a separate **overflow area** for storing records that cannot be placed in the exact page specified by the hash function. Figure A.13 demonstrates the use of a separate overflow area consisting of pages eight and nine. These two pages are in addition to the seven pages, normally called the *prime area*, that we have been using in our examples. Rather than store the *CUSTOMER* 630 record in page two, as we did with the linear search method, we store this record in page eight, the first of the two overflow pages. Now when we retrieve the *CUSTOMER* 630 record, we employ the division-remainder hash function, getting a value of 1. Page one is retrieved, and when we find that the *CUSTOMER* 630 record is not located there, page eight is retrieved and the record is found.

Both with the linear search and the overflow area method, exactly two accesses were required to retrieve the *CUSTOMER* 630 record. So both methods appear to be equally efficient. However, the overflow area method proves to be more efficient in the long run. When collision occurs with the linear search method, the record is placed in the closest nearby page. This may tend to cause collision for a future record that hashes to that same page. Also, if we can keep the number of collisions to a minimum, it will be faster to search through a smaller overflow area than to search through the prime area, where records that properly hash to a given page are intermingled with records placed in that page because of collision management.

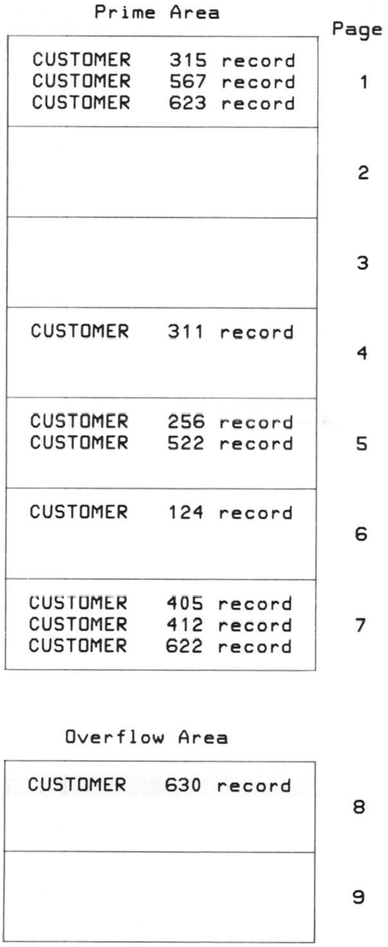

The efficiency of both the linear search and the overflow area method can be improved through the use of a **pointer chain** (also known as a *synonym chain* or a *collision chain* when using direct organization). Each page has a field, called a pointer, that serves as an indicator of whether collision has occurred on that page. On the next page in Figure A.14, pages two through six have a pointer value of zero, meaning that no collision has occurred on any of these pages. Both

**Figure A.13**

Collision resolution using overflow pages

```
        Prime Area                    Page

   CUSTOMER    315 record
   CUSTOMER    567 record              1
   CUSTOMER    623 record

                                       2

                                       3

   CUSTOMER    311 record
                                       4

   CUSTOMER    256 record
   CUSTOMER    522 record              5

   CUSTOMER    124 record
                                       6

   CUSTOMER    405 record
   CUSTOMER    412 record              7
   CUSTOMER    622 record

        Overflow Area

   CUSTOMER    630 record
                                       8

                                       9
```

pages one and seven have a pointer value of 8, meaning that collision has occurred on both these pages and that the synonym records for both pages have been stored in page eight in the overflow area. The use of a pointer chain helps to minimize the number of pages that have to be searched when collision occurs.

**Figure A.14**

Collision resolution
using overflow
pages and a
pointer chain

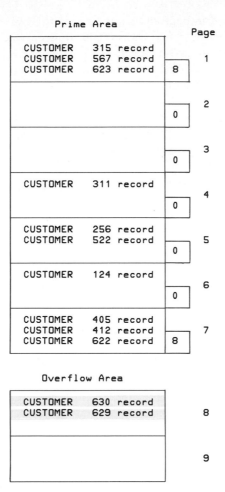

A number of other collision management techniques and variations are available; for further details, see [2], [7], [9], and [10].

**Direct Organization Summary.** Direct organization provides fast random access, but sequential access is inefficient and does not normally return records in primary key sequence. Key-addressing techniques, which require only one disk access, are most efficient, but are also impractical in most situations, owing to low packing densities and the need for large amounts of disk space.

Hashing techniques provide a reasonable tradeoff between very fast access and efficient use of disk space. Because of collisions, hashing techniques require on an average more than one disk access to store or retrieve a given record. The precise performance of a given hashing technique in a given application depends upon a number of factors, including the following.

1. The characteristics of the primary key used as the basis for the hash function.
2. The hash function that is chosen.
3. The collision management technique that is chosen.
4. The page size that is chosen, since larger page sizes tend to reduce the likelihood of a record needing to be placed outside its proper page.
5. The packing density, since higher densities will result more frequently in the need to place a record outside its proper page. Experts claim that the packing density should be no higher than 80 percent. Very low packing densities result in greater waste of disk storage, so that 40 percent to 80 percent is the typical range for effective packing density.

See [2], [5], and [7] for analyses of these performance factors.

## Indexed Organization

**Indexed organization** provides efficient access to records both sequentially and randomly; the logical records are stored in one file, called the *data file*, and there is a separate **index file** (or simply *index*) that contains records consisting of the key value and the address of the logical record having that key value. We say that the data file is *indexed by* the index file. Most operating systems restrict the type of indexed organization covered in this section to keys having unique values, or to primary keys. As a result, this type of index is often called a **primary index**. However, methods permitting the data file to be indexed by a non-unique secondary key will be discussed in the next section. In this case, we would have what is called a **secondary index**. Two general types of indexed organization are possible, one called indexed random organization and the other called indexed sequential organization.

**Indexed Random Organization.** An example of indexed organization is shown in Figure A.15a on the next page. The nine records of the *CUSTOMER* file are stored in the data file, and the index has one record, or entry, for each of the nine data file records. Each index record contains a *CUSTNUMB*, which is the primary key, and the page number, which indicates where the record having that *CUSTNUMB* value is located in the data file.

The index file obviously places additional space requirements on record storage. So why incur this additional overhead? One purpose is to allow sequential retrieval of the logical records. The logical records in the data file in Figure A.15a are not stored in primary key sequence, but the index records are stored in primary key sequence. By retrieving *CUSTOMER* records in the order specified by the index, we end up accessing them in logical sequence by *CUSTNUMB*. This form of indexed organization is called **indexed random organization** (also known as *indexed nonsequential organization*), since the data file records are in random sequence.

**Figure A.15a**

**Indexed random organization**

```
Index File              Data File
Key Address
                                                        Page
124    2         CUSTOMER    405  record
256    1         CUSTOMER    256  record            1
311    1         CUSTOMER    311  record
315    3
405    1         CUSTOMER    622  record
412    3         CUSTOMER    124  record            2
522    3         CUSTOMER    567  record
567    2
622    2         CUSTOMER    522  record
                 CUSTOMER    412  record            3
                 CUSTOMER    315  record
```

Since the logical records are not in sequence, there must be one index record for each logical record when we are using indexed random organization.

A second benefit of indexed organization is that we can randomly access records much faster than we could without the use of the index. Without it, we would have to sequentially access data file records if we wanted to randomly retrieve a specific record. Though we have to sequentially access the index to achieve the same result, the overall search time is substantially reduced. One reason for the more rapid random access is the relative sizes of data file records and index records. Data file records are usually large; in many applications, each logical record is hundreds or thousands of bytes in size. In the absence of an index, a considerable amount of time is required to sequentially retrieve each page and scan each logical record to find the one record needed randomly. On the other hand, each index record is very small. Typically the address is four bytes, so with the addition of the primary key length of three bytes in our example, we have a record size of seven bytes. Many index records can fit in one page of the index file, so fewer disk accesses are needed and the overall search time is considerably reduced.

Furthermore, if a large proportion of the index can fit into memory, the sequential search proceeds at memory speeds and requires a minimal number of disk accesses. And even faster search methods, such as a binary search, can be used to further reduce the search time to a very small fraction of a second.

Another advantage of using an index for random access applies to data files containing large numbers of records. As the number of logical records grows, the number of records in the index grows at the same rate. Index search time increases, but even more time would be spent searching through the data file. Additionally, once the index has grown to a point where it can no longer reside in memory, we can treat it as if it were a data file and create an index to the index.

Figure A.15b illustrates this process. The "level 2 index" is our original index, and the "level 1 index" is the new index to the original index. We now have a two-level index, more generally called a *multilevel index*. We call level 1 index a high-level index, and level 2 index a low-level index.

```
Level 1 Index   Level 2 Index              Data File                       Figure A.15b
Key Address     Key Address
                                   Page                          Page      Indexed random
  315    7        124    2                CUSTOMER  405  record            organization using
  567    8        256    1                CUSTOMER  256  record    1       a 2-level index
  622    9        311    1          7     CUSTOMER  311  record
                  315    3

                  405    1                CUSTOMER  622  record
                  412    3                CUSTOMER  124  record    2
                  522    3          8     CUSTOMER  567  record
                  567    2

                  622    2                CUSTOMER  522  record
                                          CUSTOMER  412  record    3
                                          CUSTOMER  315  record
                                   9
```

Since the key values in our original index are in sequence, we only need to have one record in the high-level index for each page in the low-level index, with the key being the highest-valued key in that low-level index page. This is called a *sparse index*, since it does not contain a record for each record in the low-level index, while the low-level index is called a *dense index*, since it has one record for each record in the data file. Now we can fit the high-level index in memory, search it, and retrieve the proper low-level index page, search the low-level index page in memory, and finally retrieve the data file page containing the record we need to randomly access. Two accesses to randomly retrieve a logical record! We have only nine records and three pages in our data file, so this may not seem too impressive; to fully appreciate the benefits of using an index for random access, picture a data file and low-level index requiring thousands of pages of disk storage. If necessary, the indexing structure can expand to many more levels than we have shown.

An additional advantage of indexed random organization is that we do not need to access the data file if all we need to know is whether a logical record having a specific primary key value exists. This question can be answered by restricting the search to the index. As a result, one less disk access is required.

A final advantage of indexed random organization is that the data file records do not need to be in sequence. When records are added and deleted, the data file update process is fairly simple. However, the programming to handle the indexes can become complicated. Fortunately, indexed organization is a standard feature on most computers. This means that index management is the responsibility of the operating system file access routines, not of the programmer.

**Indexed Sequential Organization.**    If indexed organization is being used and the data file records are in primary key sequence, we have **indexed sequential organization**. In Figure A.16a on the next page the *CUSTOMER* records are in sequence by the primary key of *CUSTNUMB*. The index looks the same as before. But must we continue to have one index record for each data file record? No! Since the data file records are in sequence, we need only one index record for each data file page. The index, therefore, is reduced in size and is stored as a sparse index. Figure A.16b depicts the index for indexed sequential organization.

**Figure A.16a**

Indexed sequential organization

```
Index File          Data File
Key Address
                                            Page
124    1      CUSTOMER   124  record
256    1      CUSTOMER   256  record
311    1      CUSTOMER   311  record         1
315    2
405    2      CUSTOMER   315  record
412    2      CUSTOMER   405  record         2
522    3      CUSTOMER   412  record
567    3
622    3      CUSTOMER   522  record
              CUSTOMER   567  record         3
              CUSTOMER   622  record
```

**Figure A.16b**

Indexed sequential organization with one index entry per page

```
Index File          Data File
Key Address
                                            Page
311    1      CUSTOMER   124  record
412    2      CUSTOMER   256  record         1
622    3      CUSTOMER   311  record

              CUSTOMER   315  record
              CUSTOMER   405  record         2
              CUSTOMER   412  record

              CUSTOMER   522  record
              CUSTOMER   567  record         3
              CUSTOMER   622  record
```

Fewer index records means a smaller-sized index, faster search times, and the need for fewer levels to the index as the data file grows in size. On the other hand, we can no longer determine the existence of a specific primary key value by searching only through the index, as we could with indexed random organization. Now the data file must be accessed with one additional disk access. But since fewer index pages and levels are required overall, in practice fewer disk accesses are required to the index, so in the end, indexed sequential organization turns out to be more efficient.

Since indexed sequential organization takes less space and performs better than indexed random organization, why would we ever want to use the latter? The answer is that it allows us to have the data file indexed by as many fields as we need. In other words, we can have a number of **secondary indexes**. Since the data file is in one sequence only, usually by the primary key, all secondary indexes must use indexed random organization or some other structure for relating a secondary key value to the record(s) containing that particular value.

If we need to sequentially retrieve records from an indexed sequential file by its primary index, it is not necessary to use the index. Since the data file is in primary key sequence, we simply retrieve data file pages in order. The index is used for random access retrieval only. But what happens to the primary key sequence of the data file when we attempt to add a new logical record to a page that is full? Where does the system insert the record, and what happens to the index? To answer these questions, we need to look into the data file management alternatives available under indexed sequential organization.

**Indexed Sequential Organization Data File Management.** One method for managing data file insertions under indexed sequential organization is the use of an **overflow area** and a **pointer chain**. Suppose we need to add the *CUSTOMER* 350 record to the example shown in Figure A.16b. Since all data file pages are full, a record must be placed in an overflow page, and a means must be established for locating the record placed in the overflow page. As Figure A.17a on the next page demonstrates, a separate overflow area and two new fields in each data file page have been added. One of the new fields is an overflow location pointer, which links the data file page to the next logical record in sequence located in the overflow area. The overflow location pointer consists of a page number and relative record number within that overflow page. The expression "4 1" for page two means that the next logical record can be found in the overflow area in relative record position 1 of page four. The other new field represents the highest key value associated with the given data file page that can be found in the overflow area, the *CUSTOMER* 412 record in our example. Note that the new *CUSTOMER* 350 record has been positioned in proper sequence in page two, and the *CUSTOMER* 412 record is the one that has been relocated to the overflow area. The "---" for data file pages one and three represents the fact that overflow has not occurred for these pages. Finally, this logical record insertion has resulted in no change to the index file.

When the *CUSTOMER* 410 record is now added, it must be stored in the overflow area, as shown in Figure A.17b on the next page. Since this record precedes the *CUSTOMER* 412 record already in the overflow area, the page two location pointer must be changed to indicate where the *CUSTOMER* 410 record is located, and a pointer chaining the *CUSTOMER* 410 record to the *CUSTOMER* 412 record must be added. The records in the overflow area are kept in arrival sequence, not logical sequence, and thus pointer chaining is required for the overflow area. The pointer associated with the *CUSTOMER* 412 record in the overflow area would be "---."

**Figure A.17a**

Indexed sequential
organization using
an overflow area
with a pointer
chain after adding
the *CUSTOMER* 350
record

**Figure A.17b**

Indexed sequential
organization using
an overflow area
with a pointer
chain after
*CUSTOMER* 350
and 410 have been
added

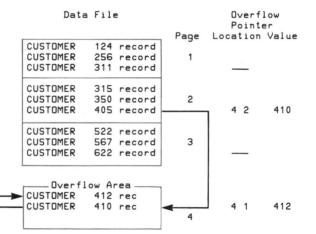

```
Figure A.17a

              Index File              Data File                    Overflow
              Key Address                                           Pointer
                                                        Page    Location Value
               311   1     CUSTOMER   124  record
               412   2     CUSTOMER   256  record         1
               622   3     CUSTOMER   311  record                  ───

                           CUSTOMER   315  record
                           CUSTOMER   350  record         2
                           CUSTOMER   405  record                  4 1      412

                           CUSTOMER   522  record
                           CUSTOMER   567  record         3
                           CUSTOMER   622  record                  ───

                          ──Overflow Area──
                           CUSTOMER       412  record

                                                         4


Figure A.17b

              Index File              Data File                    Overflow
              Key Address                                           Pointer
                                                        Page    Location Value
               311   1     CUSTOMER   124  record
               412   2     CUSTOMER   256  record         1
               622   3     CUSTOMER   311  record                  ───

                           CUSTOMER   315  record
                           CUSTOMER   350  record         2
                           CUSTOMER   405  record                  4 2      410

                           CUSTOMER   522  record
                           CUSTOMER   567  record         3
                           CUSTOMER   622  record                  ───

                          ──Overflow Area──
                           CUSTOMER       412  rec
                           CUSTOMER       410  rec                 4 1      412
                                                         4
```

As you can guess, performance degrades as more records are added to the overflow area and the pointer chains become longer. Periodically, the indexed file needs to be reorganized so that all records are placed in the data file in correct logical sequence and the index file is appropriately reconstructed.

When the overflow area technique is used with indexed sequential organization, usually the data file is initially built with gaps in each page. That is, each data file page is only partially filled with logical records, leaving empty record slots for use by future additions to the file. These gaps are called **distributed free space**. The use of distributed free space reduces the problem of overflow area chaining but does not eliminate the problem entirely. Low packing densities reduce the need for placing records in the overflow area and for chaining within the overflow area, but they do increase the size of the index and the number of levels to the index.

IBM's *indexed sequential access method* (ISAM) uses the overflow area technique on a more complicated basis, which relies on the physical characteristics of disk. For details on the ISAM approach, see [2], [4], and [7].

A second method for managing data file insertions under indexed sequential organization is the use of the **block-splitting** technique. To demonstrate this technique, we will again add the *CUSTOMER* 350 record to the file shown in Figure A.16b. Page two is where this new record should be stored, but there is no room left there. So page four, the next available empty page, is used, and the *CUSTOMER* 350 record plus the three records in page two are divided between the two pages. Figure A.18a shows the result. We have split the contents of the full page, or block, into two pages; and thus the term block splitting for this technique.

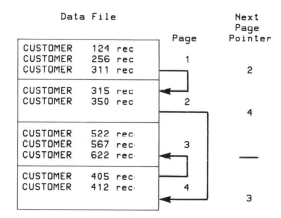

**Figure A.18a**

Indexed sequential organization using block splitting after adding the *CUSTOMER* 350 record

Adding the *CUSTOMER* 410 record presents no difficulty, as you can see in Figure A.18b on the next page. It is simply stored in page four, since there is room for one additional record. But now the page is full. It may seem that this technique would require us to split pages quite frequently. However, our examples are structured small in order to illustrate concepts; in reality, we would be storing a larger number of logical records in each page. If we were to store twenty *CUSTOMER* records in each page, then when we split the contents of one full page into two pages, there would be enough room to accommodate ten more records in each of the two pages.

**Figure A.18b**

Indexed sequential
organization using
block splitting
after *CUSTOMER*
350 and 410
records have been
added

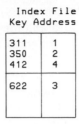

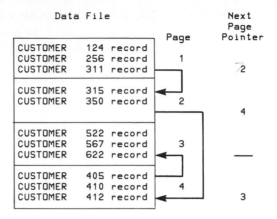

The index file has to change to reflect the added page in the proper sequence. This is shown both in Figure A.18a and A.18b. Although the logical records are no longer in logical sequence by page number, the index can be used as a guide for sequentially accessing data file records. Another technique frequently employed to avoid the necessity of using the index for sequential access is the addition of a field to each data file page. This field serves as a pointer to the next logical page in sequence. It is shown in the two A.18 figures as the "next page pointer," and arrows have been drawn to indicate the correct sequence of records by primary key.

Distributed free space can be used with the block-splitting technique when the indexed file is first created to delay the initial need to redistribute records. IBM's *virtual storage access method* (VSAM) uses both distributed free space and the block-splitting technique to manage its type of indexed sequential organization. For details on the VSAM approach for managing the data file, see [2], [4], and [7].

**Indexed Organization Summary.**   Indexed organization provides an efficient means of both sequentially and randomly accessing records. Random retrieval of records is faster than with sequential organization, though not as fast as with the best forms of direct organization. Extra disk storage space is required to store the index and possible pointers, and additions and deletions to the data file can be time-consuming.

We will investigate some further index structures in the next section when we discuss inverted files and tree structures.

## *DATA STRUCTURES*

The file organizations discussed in the previous section are sufficient to support traditional file-processing environments. They fall short, however, of totally supporting DBMS environments that in effect are managing many files and many relationships among these files. A DBMS, for example, has to be able to form relationships between records from different files, to handle secondary indexes having multiple records for each secondary key value, and to provide rapid response to both predefined and ad hoc requests. The DBMS must provide more sophisticated data structures for dealing with these common requirements. In this section we will discuss three of the data structures frequently utilized by DBMS's: inverted files, linked lists, and B-trees.

### Inverted Files

We've mentioned a number of times that secondary key access is important to users in a database environment. One file structure that can be used to represent secondary keys is **indexed random organization**, which was reviewed in the previous section. When indexed random organization is used in this way on a secondary key, we have what is called a **secondary index**. Figure A.15b shows indexed random organization applied to the *CUSTNUMB* field, but this organization works in the same way for any secondary key that has unique values for each record in the data file.

　　　When we use an index on a secondary key field in this fashion, we say we have *inverted on* that field, and the index formed to support that secondary key is known as an **inverted file**, or *inverted list*. We have inverted the normal role of a field in the record, since we find the record based on the field value instead of finding the field value after locating the record.

　　　We can use an inverted file structure (or index) on any secondary key in a logical record. Figure A.15b, however, is not sufficiently complex to illustrate how the index is structured when the secondary key has nonunique values across the data file. Our original *CUSTOMER* file, for example, consisted of *CUSTNUMB*, *CUSTNAME*, *BALANCE*, and *CREDLIM*. What if we need to randomly access *CUSTOMER* records, using *CREDLIM* as a secondary key? *CREDLIM* cannot serve as the primary key for the *CUSTOMER* file, since a given value appears in more than one record. Therefore, the index structure in Figure A.15b is not appropriate for handling the *CREDLIM* situation.

What we need is an index structure that handles secondary key values pointing to multiple data file records. The inverted file structure in Figure A.19 does exactly this. We now show both *CUSTNUMB* and *CREDLIM* for each of the nine logical records in the *CUSTOMER* file. The page numbers we have been using has been changed back to relative record numbers to simplify the discussion of this form of inverted file structure.

**Figure A.19**

Inverted file structure on *CREDLIM*

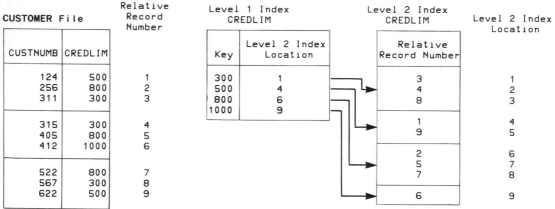

The inverted file for this example is a two-level index. The level 1 index consists of one record for each different secondary key value, *CREDLIM* in this example. Since *CREDLIM* has four different values (300, 500, 800, and 1,000), there are four records in the level 1 index, which is in sequence by *CREDLIM* value. Stored in each level 1 index record, along with the *CREDLIM* value, is a pointer to the level 2 index. This pointer indicates the position in the level 2 index that starts the list of relative record numbers with that secondary key value. For example, the *CREDLIM* value of 300 in the level 1 index points to location 1 in the level 2 index. The first three entries in the level 2 index, which are 3, 4, and 8, give the relative record numbers for the three *CUSTOMER* records having a *CREDLIM* of 300.

If we have inverted files for all fields in the *CUSTOMER* file, then we have a *fully inverted file*. If only some of the fields in the *CUSTOMER* file have inverted files, then we have a *partially inverted file*.

Inverted files can be used to answer certain queries without the need to access the data file. Examples of queries of this type are:

1. How many customers have a *CREDLIM* of 800?
2. How many customers have a *CREDLIM* between 500 and 800?
3. How many orders are there for *CUSTNUMB* 405?
4. How many orders having a *ORDDTE* more recent than 90591 are there for customers 256 and 567?
5. Are there any records that have a *BALANCE* greater than $750.00?

The retrieval of records is very efficient with an inverted file structure; such is the case with most indexing techniques. The tradeoffs are the space required to store the multilevel index and the extra time required to update the inverted files. Therefore, inverted files are created only for those fields critically needed for retrieval. For further information on inverted files, see [2], [7], and [9].

## Linked Lists

There are methods other than inverted files for managing secondary keys. Among them is the use of linked lists. Before considering how linked lists can be used in secondary key and other situations, we need to examine the basic concepts and terminology of the linked list structure and processing techniques.

A **linked list** consists of a field added to each logical record that has as a value the location of the next logical record in sequence. This field is called a link field or *pointer*, and the linked list is also known as a **pointer chain**, since pointers are used to chain records together. Suppose we take the *CUSTOMER* file from Figure A.19 and form a linked list to allow sequential access of the logical records based on increasing values of the *CREDLIM* field. Figure A.20a has the new pointer field added to each *CUSTOMER* record. There is an additional field external to the *CUSTOMER* records, which serves the function of pointing to the start of the linked list. This field is a *head pointer* and has a value of 3 in Figure A.20a. The value 3 represents the relative record number of the first *CUSTOMER* record in sequence. This record has a *CREDLIM* value of 300 for *CUSTNUMB* 311. The pointer field for this record links to relative record number 4, which is the next record in *CREDLIM* sequence. You can follow the chain of pointers until reaching *CUSTNUMB* 412, which has a *CREDLIM* value of 1,000 and is the last record in the chain. The pointer value of "---" signifies the end of the chain.

CREDLIM Head Pointer: 3

**CUSTOMER File**

| CUSTNUMB | CREDLIM | Pointer | Relative Record Number |
|---|---|---|---|
| 124 | 500 | 9 | 1 |
| 256 | 800 | 5 | 2 |
| 311 | 300 | 4 | 3 |
| 315 | 300 | 8 | 4 |
| 405 | 800 | 7 | 5 |
| 412 | 1000 | — | 6 |
| 522 | 800 | 6 | 7 |
| 567 | 300 | 1 | 8 |
| 622 | 500 | 2 | 9 |

**Figure A.20a**

Linked list with pointers for *CREDLIM*

What happens if we start in the middle of the linked list, say, at the *CUSTOMER* 622 record, and want to retrieve every *CUSTOMER* record in the order specified by the pointer field? We would not be able to do so, since the *CUSTOMER* 412 record does not point to any other record. Once we reached the end of the chain, however, we could use the value of the external head pointer to continue our circuit of the chain. Another more common approach is to have the last link field point to the first record in the chain, as shown in Figure A.20b. The pointer for the *CUSTOMER* 412 record now points to relative record number 3, which is the start of the chain. This refinement is called a *circular linked list* or *ring*.

**Figure A.20b**

Circular linked list
with pointers for
*CREDLIM*

CREDLIM Head Pointer:  3

CUSTOMER File

| CUSTNUMB | CREDLIM | Pointer | Relative Record Number |
|---|---|---|---|
| 124 | 500 | 9 | 1 |
| 256 | 800 | 5 | 2 |
| 311 | 300 | 4 | 3 |
| 315 | 300 | 8 | 4 |
| 405 | 800 | 7 | 5 |
| 412 | 1000 | 3 | 6 |
| 522 | 800 | 6 | 7 |
| 567 | 300 | 1 | 8 |
| 622 | 500 | 2 | 9 |

We can have as many linked lists as we need in the data file, just as we can have as many indexes as we need. In addition to the linked list for *CREDLIM*, we could create one for *CUSTNAME* and one for *BALANCE* in the *CUSTOMER* file. Each additional linked list takes additional storage space and requires extra time to update.

A linked list can be used as an alternative to the inverted file to represent **secondary keys** through a structure called a *multilist*. Figure A.21 shows a multilist constructed on the *CREDLIM* field as the secondary key. There is one index similar to the level 1 index we needed for the inverted file structure in Figure A.19. The multilist index has one record for each different secondary key value and is in order by the secondary key. Instead of pointing to a level 2 index, as with the inverted file, each multilist record has a head pointer that starts the chain for records having that particular *CREDLIM* value. For example, *CREDLIM* 500 in the index points to relative record number 1 for *CUSTNUMB* 124, whose pointer of 9 links to *CUSTNUMB* 622, which is the end of the chain.

**CUSTOMER File**

| CUSTNUMB | CREDLIM | Pointer |
|---------:|--------:|:-------:|
| 124 | 500 | 9 |
| 256 | 800 | 5 |
| 311 | 300 | 4 |
| 315 | 300 | 8 |
| 405 | 800 | 7 |
| 412 | 1000 | — |
| 522 | 800 | — |
| 567 | 300 | — |
| 622 | 500 | — |

Relative Record Number

| |
|:---:|
| 1 |
| 2 |
| 3 |
| 4 |
| 5 |
| 6 |
| 7 |
| 8 |
| 9 |

**CREDLIM Index**

| Key | Relative Record Number |
|:---:|:---:|
| 300 | 3 |
| 500 | 1 |
| 800 | 2 |
| 1000 | 6 |

**Figure A.21**

Multilist with *CREDLIM* as secondary key

If we have multiple secondary keys, we can use a separate multilist structure for each one. Each multilist would have its own index and its own linked list. Compared to the inverted file, the multilist's index is easier to create and maintain, since the level 2 index for the inverted file has a variable number of entries. On the other hand, the multilist pointers must be maintained, while there are no pointers within the logical records with the inverted file. Overall, the multilist is easier to maintain.

A major disadvantage of the multilist approach as compared to the inverted file is that answering the queries we posed earlier at the end of the inverted file discussion is more difficult and takes more time. The response to the query "How many customers have a *CREDLIM* of 800?" could be determined by means of the level 1 and level 2 index of the inverted file structure. To answer the same query with a multilist, we have to "walk" the chain from the multilist index through all the records that are linked together. And for more complicated queries, such as, "How many customers have a *BALANCE* over 500 and a *CREDLIM* of 800 or 1,000?" we have to traverse two separate multilist chains with multiple paths. With the inverted files, we can take the intersection of the indexes without having to access the data file.

The linked lists so far have been *singly linked lists* or *one-way linked lists*; the chains travel in one direction only. We can also have *doubly linked lists* or *two-way linked lists*. These have two sets of chains, one traveling in the forward direction we've seen so far, and the other traveling in a backward direction. Figure A.22 on the next page illustrates a doubly linked list on the *CREDLIM* field. The forward pointers are next pointers and the backward pointers are prior pointers. The additional external tail pointer is needed to start the prior pointer chain. Doubly linked lists make the job of maintaining the chains easier on additions and deletions, at the expense of additional space requirements.

**Figure A.22**

Doubly linked list
on *CREDLIM*

```
CREDLIM Head Pointer:  3
CREDLIM Tail Pointer:  6
```

**CUSTOMER** File

Relative
Record
Number

| CUSTNUMB | CREDLIM | Next Pointer | Prior Pointer | |
|---|---|---|---|---|
| 124 | 500 | 9 | 8 | 1 |
| 256 | 800 | 5 | 9 | 2 |
| 311 | 300 | 4 | 6 | 3 |
| 315 | 300 | 8 | 3 | 4 |
| 405 | 800 | 7 | 2 | 5 |
| 412 | 1000 | 3 | 7 | 6 |
| 522 | 800 | 6 | 5 | 7 |
| 567 | 300 | 1 | 4 | 8 |
| 622 | 500 | 2 | 1 | 9 |

Linked lists can be used to establish a relationship between records from
two different files. There is a **one-to-many relationship** between the *CUS-
TOMER* file and the *ORDERS* file. Each *CUSTOMER* record can have zero,
one, or more *ORDERS* records, while a given *ORDERS* record is owned by
only one *CUSTOMER* record. Figure A.23 shows the use of a doubly linked
list to tie together the records in this one-to-many relationship. Beginning with
a *CUSTOMER* record, the head pointer starts the chain in a forward direction
to the *ORDERS* records and the tail pointer starts the chain in a backward
direction to the *ORDERS* records. The next and prior pointers in the *ORDERS*
file link together *ORDERS* records for the same *CUSTOMER*. Note that we
have included the *CUSTOMER* records with the *ORDERS* records in the
pointer chains.

**CUSTOMER** File

| CUSTNUMB | CREDLIM | Head Pointer | Tail Pointer | Relative Record Number |
|---|---|---|---|---|
| 124 | 500 | 10 | 15 | 1 |
| 256 | 800 | 13 | 13 | 2 |
| 311 | 300 | 11 | 11 | 3 |
| 315 | 300 | 12 | 12 | 4 |
| 405 | 800 | 5 | 5 | 5 |
| 412 | 1000 | 6 | 6 | 6 |
| 522 | 800 | 14 | 16 | 7 |
| 567 | 300 | 8 | 8 | 8 |
| 622 | 500 | 9 | 9 | 9 |

**ORDERS** File

| ORDNUMB | CUSTNUMB | Next Pointer | Prior Pointer | Relative Record Number |
|---|---|---|---|---|
| 12489 | 124 | 15 | 1 | 10 |
| 12491 | 311 | 3 | 3 | 11 |
| 12494 | 315 | 4 | 4 | 12 |
| 12495 | 256 | 2 | 2 | 13 |
| 12498 | 522 | 16 | 7 | 14 |
| 12500 | 124 | 1 | 10 | 15 |
| 12504 | 522 | 7 | 14 | 16 |

**Figure A.23**

Doubly linked list
forming the rela-
tionship between
customers and
their orders

We could add another linked list to the *ORDERS* file, which would provide a pointer for each *ORDERS* record back to the *CUSTOMER* file. These pointers are called *parent pointers* or *owner pointers*, and would allow us to get directly back to the *CUSTOMER* record for a given *ORDERS* record without having to travel around the chain back to the *CUSTOMER* record. This can be a considerable time saver if the chain tends to be very long.

As with any file organization or data structure, our main concern is to minimize disk accesses. In addition to the use of linked lists for the *CUSTOMER* to *ORDERS* relationship, it would be ideal if *ORDERS* records were clustered in the same page as the owner *CUSTOMER* record. Some DBMS's permit this as an option at the time the database is defined.

For further details on linked lists, see [2], [7], and [9].

## Trees

We now turn to a discussion of one final data structure, called the **B-tree**. The B-tree is one of the most widely used data structures in database processing today. Its chief use is for the storage and management of indexes. The B-tree is a special form of the general tree structure, so we will begin our discussion by reviewing some of the terminology and concepts of trees.

**General Tree Terminology.** A **tree** is a structure that resembles the organizational, or hierarchy, chart of a business enterprise. It also resembles a genealogical, or family, tree. The tree is inverted, with a single root at the top and the tree's branches leading toward the bottom. Tree terminology is a mixture of botanical and genealogical tree terms.

A tree consists of *nodes* that are connected by *branches*. The single *root* node is at the top, and its *descendants* are below it. In Figure A.24, nodes appear in boxes, and branches are the connecting lines between boxes. Node A is the root, and all other nodes are its descendants. A node other than the root, together with all its descendants, comprises a *subtree* of the original tree. There are several subtrees in Figure A.24; nodes D, J, and K represent one subtree, as does node J by itself.

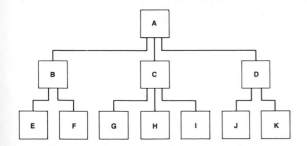

**Figure A.24**

Tree structure

A *parent* node appears immediately above its *children*. Every node has exactly one parent, except for the root, which does not have a parent. In Figure A.24, the root is the parent to its children B, C, and D. Node D is the parent of J and K, both of which are its children and only descendants. A node's *ancestors* consist of all nodes, including the root, which connect that node by branches directly back to the root. The ancestors of node G are nodes A and C, while node B has just the root as its ancestor.

A *leaf* node has no children. The leaves in Figure A.24 are E, F, G, H, I, J, and K. A *twin*, or *sibling*, is a node related to other nodes by virtue of its having the same parent. In Figure A.24 there are four sets of siblings: B, C, and D; E and F; G, H, and I; and J and K.

The root is defined to be at *level* 0, the root's children (B, C, and D in Figure A.24) are level 1, and so on down the tree. The *height*, or *depth*, of a tree is the maximum number of levels in the tree. Figures A.24 and A.25a show trees of height 3, while the tree in Figure A.25b is of height 4.

**Figure A.25a**

Balanced tree
structure

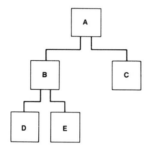

**Figure A.25b**

Unbalanced tree
structure

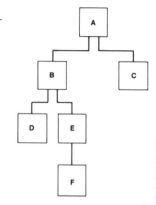

A *balanced tree* is one in which the height of each node's subtrees differs at most by one. Balanced trees are shown in Figures A.24 and A.25a, but Figure A.25b is an unbalanced tree, since the subtree starting from node B differs by two levels from the subtree starting from node C.

The **order**, or *degree*, of a tree is the maximum number of children a node can have. Figure A.24 has a tree of order 3 (node C has three children), whereas both trees in Figure A.25 are of order 2. A tree of order 2 is called a *binary tree*. A *multiway tree* is one in which a node may have more than two children, or a tree of order greater than 2.

You may be wondering about the purpose of all this tree terminology. Picture each node as a page of disk storage and each branch as a pointer forming a relationship between the pages. This is exactly what an index is. A tree structure is the overwhelming choice for the representation of index structures in file and database processing environments today.

Whatever organization or data structure is used for the index, our objective in randomly accessing a data file record is to minimize the number of disk accesses. If we use a tree structure for our index and each tree node is a page of disk storage, what we want to achieve is a balanced tree with as few levels as possible under the circumstances. One tree structure that does well with this constraint is the B-tree.

**B-Tree.** The B-tree was first described in a paper by Bayer and McCreight in 1972 (see [1]). It is a multilevel index, and each of its nodes is an index page having the following general format:

| Pointer 1 | Key 1 | Address 1 | Pointer 2 | Key 2 | Address 2 | Pointer 3 | . . . . . . |
|---|---|---|---|---|---|---|---|

Each "pointer" points to an index page at the next lowest level, each "key" is the value of a logical record key in the data file, and each "address" is the location in the data file of the logical record that has that "key" value. A key value/address combination will appear exactly once in some node of the B-tree for each key that exists in the data file. The maximum number of pointers in the page is the **order** of the B-tree, since the number of pointers determines the maximum number of children the node can have. A B-tree can be of any order, and a B-tree of order $n$ has the following properties:

1. The root is either a leaf or has at least two children.
2. Each node, except for the root and the leaves, has between $n/2$ and $n$ children.
3. All leaves appear on the same level.
4. A nonleaf node with $k$ children has $k-1$ keys.

Figure A.26 on the next page shows an example of a B-tree index of order 5. The root node is shown below:

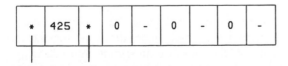

| * | 425 | * | 0 | - | 0 | - | 0 | - |
|---|---|---|---|---|---|---|---|---|

**Figure A.26**

B-tree of order 5

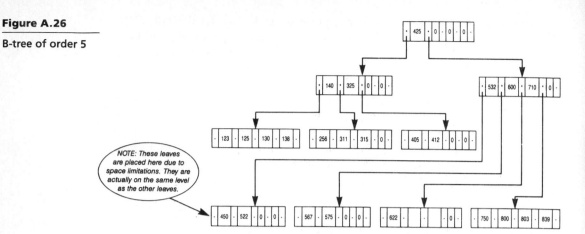

NOTE: These leaves are placed here due to space limitations. They are actually on the same level as the other leaves.

With reference to the first property in the list, this root has two children, pointed to by the root entries with a "*," which would actually be index page numbers. The other three pointers have a "–" entry to indicate (for illustrative purposes only) that they do not point anywhere. The "425" is a shorthand way of representing both the key value of 425 and its location in the data file. Any key value less than 425 can be found in the root's left subtree (pointed to by the leftmost root pointer), and any key value greater than 425 can be found in the root's right subtree (pointed to by the pointer to the right of "425" in the root). The three "0" entries have been inserted where key value/address combinations would be placed as needed. The root would be a leaf only if the data file contained zero through four logical records, since four is the maximum number of key value/address combinations that can be stored in the root without needing children node storage.

With reference to the second property, every node has between three (5 divided by 2) and five children. Leaves have no children within the index structure, which is why the property is worded the way it is. The root node will always have between two and five children, except when the root is a leaf and has no children at all.

All leaves are on the same level, in concordance with the third property. Therefore, the B-tree is a balanced tree.

Each node with two children has one key (key value/address combination); each node with three children has two keys; each node with four children has three keys; and each node with five children has four keys, though no example of the latter appears in Figure A.26. Each node can contain a maximum of four keys.

The key values are in sequence within each node. This is important to the way B-trees operate. Let's assume we wished to randomly access the record whose key value is 622. Starting at the root, we determine that 622 is greater than 425 and retrieve the node at the next level down within the right subtree.

Comparing 622 to the keys in this node, we find that it is between 600 and 710 and retrieve the child node indicated by the third pointer. Retrieving this leaf node, we find a match on the first key value and use the address associated with it to retrieve the page containing the logical record with a key of 622.

If we had wanted to randomly access the record whose key value is 623, we would have completed the exact same steps and found no such key value in the leaf node. This would have signified the absence of any record having this key value.

Finally, if the record we needed had a key value of 532, we would find its location after two accesses, one to the root and the other to the right subtree node directly beneath it. Most of the time only one access would be required, since the root would reside in memory with almost no exceptions.

## Q & A

**Question:** The great advantage of B-trees is not evident from the order 5 example in Figure A.26. It becomes apparent only when we look at B-trees of a realistic size. Before we do so, determine how many keys can be contained in a B-tree of order 5 in its first three levels, counting the root as one level.

**Answer:** The root can contain four keys and can have five children. Each of these five children can have four keys, for an additional total of twenty keys, and each child can have five children, for a total of twenty-five children on the third level (level 2, in tree terminology). Each of the twenty-five level 2 children can have four keys, for a final total of 100 keys. Adding four, twenty, and 100 gives a grand total of 124 keys that can be represented at a maximum.

A more realistically sized B-tree on a mainframe would probably use a page size of at least 4,096 bytes. Using 4,096 as the page size, let's determine the number of keys that can be represented in each page, the order of the B-tree, and the number of keys that can be represented at a maximum in the first three levels. We will assume that each index page pointer and each key address requires 4 bytes and that the key value itself requires 9 bytes.

If we add together the 4-byte index pointer, the 4-byte key address, and the 9-byte key, getting 17, we can use this value to divide into the 4,096 page size for a close approximation to the number of keys that can be stored in one page. We must realize that an additional 4 bytes will be consumed by the one additional index pointer (there is always one more index pointer than key value/address combination) and that the operating system or DBMS may need to use some of the bytes in the page for control purposes. Dividing 17 into 4,096, we have 240 keys for each node in the B-tree. The order of this B-tree is 241.

The root can hold 240 keys and can have 241 children. Each of these 241 children can hold 240 keys, for a total additional 57,840 keys. Since each of the 241 children on level 1 can have 241 children, there can be a maximum of 58,081 children on level 2. Each of these children can hold 240 keys, for a total of 13,939,440 level 2 keys. Adding 240 to 57,840 and the result of that to 13,939,440 gives a grand total of 13,997,520 keys that can be contained in our order 241 B-tree. This is the theoretical maximum. In practice, not all nodes would be full, and the number of keys would be smaller than our calculation.

If we again assume that the root resides in memory, what we are saying is that we can randomly access one record in a data file having up to 13,997,520 records with no more than three accesses (one to the level 1 index, one to the level 2 index, and one to retrieve the record from the data file). Three accesses is the worst case; some of the data file records could be retrieved with one or two. In common applications, more than three B-tree levels are seldom required.

B-trees have other advantages besides rapid access. First, insertions and deletions are reasonably efficient. Second, disk utilization is acceptable, with packing densities of at least 50 percent, since each node is at least half full. And third, the data file is maintained in sequence by primary key, so that sequential access by primary key is both possible and efficient.

Many variations of the B-tree and other multiway tree structures have been researched and implemented in DBMS environments. For further examples and details, see [2], [3], [5], [6], [8], [9], [10], and [11].

## SUMMARY

In this appendix, we focused on fundamental file processing concepts and on the file and data structures important in the study of a DBMS environment. A logical transaction, which is a user request to accomplish a single task, is processed by a program on a logical record basis against the physical records of a file or database. Logical records are grouped into blocks, which are also called pages or physical records.

We saw that grouping records based on usage patterns in the process called clustering allows control over the DBMS's responsiveness to the more common user requests. Clustering can be applied to records within a single file (intrafile) or to records from multiple files (interfile).

We next studied sequential and random access. Sequential access necessitates the storage and retrieval of records in a predetermined order, while random access permits the storage and retrieval of records in a direct fashion. Random access is used for rapid response in an on-line environment.

We examined the three major file organizations: sequential, direct, and indexed. Sequential organization permits sequential access only. The pile and the ordering of records by primary key value are the two common physical arrangements of records for sequential organization.

We saw that direct organization uses an algorithm to store and later retrieve records randomly in the file. Key-addressing techniques produce a unique physical storage location, but they are difficult to construct in practice and usually leave storage gaps which waste disk storage. Hashing techniques use a hash function algorithm that does not guarantee a unique disk storage location. When two or more records hash to the same storage location, they are called synonyms and we have collision. Different methods for resolving collision include the linear search and overflow area techniques; pointer chains are usable with both.

We discussed indexed organization, which provides an efficient means of sequentially and randomly accessing records. The logical records are stored in a data file and a separate index is used to locate records in the data file. Both primary and secondary indexes are possible. Indexed random and indexed sequential are two different forms of this type of organization. Indexed sequential organization must work at keeping records in sequence through the use of overflow areas and pointer chains, distributed free space, and block splitting.

The three data structures we covered were inverted files, linked lists, and B-trees. An inverted file is an index on a secondary key, which can have unique or nonunique values. Linked lists use pointers to chain together records within a single file or to establish a relationship between two files. The B-tree is widely used as a multilevel index structure and provides fast and efficient random and sequential processing.

## REVIEW QUESTIONS

1. Explain the difference between a logical transaction, a logical record, and a physical record.
2. What is blocking? Explain the tradeoffs involved in large blocking factors.
3. Explain the difference between intrafile and interfile clustering.
4. What is the difference between physical sequential and logical sequential access?
5. Define primary key, secondary key, and sequence key.
6. What is a pile? Name three situations in which a pile would be an appropriate organization.
7. What is the difference between the key-addressing and hashing techniques?
8. Describe two different hash function techniques. In general, which technique is better? Why?
9. How can a pointer chain be used for collision management?
10. How are both sparse and dense indexes used with indexed random organization?

11. Describe the use of distributed free space with the block-splitting technique.

12. What is the difference between a fully and a partially inverted file?

13. How does the multilist structure differ from an inverted file?

14. Define subtree, height, balanced tree, and order.

15. For a B-tree of order 7, how many children per node can there be at a maximum? For a two-level B-tree of order 7, how many keys can be stored at a maximum?

16. What are the advantages of the B-tree structure?

---

## EXERCISES

1. A hash function using the division-remainder method and a divisor of 37 is used to store records with these key values into a direct file with forty pages: 112, 186, 195, and 225. Which pages does each of these keys hash to? Does collision occur? If so, for which key values?

2. If a file with direct organization has twenty-five buckets and five slots per bucket, what is the packing density if seventy-five records are stored?

3. Imagine a data file of ten records with primary key values of 5, 10, 20, 25, 30, 50, 60, 70, 80, and 90. Construct an indexed sequential file for these records with a two-level index and two data records and three index records stored per page. Add one record that requires block splitting, and show the changes caused by its addition.

4. Imagine a data file of ten records with secondary key values of 10, 10, 20, 30, 30, 50, 60, 60, 60, and 60. Construct an inverted file to allow access to the data records.

5. Picture a data file of ten records with secondary key values of 10, 10, 20, 30, 30, 50, 60, 60, 60, and 60. Construct a multilist to allow access to the data records.

6. For a B-tree of order 7 that has three levels, calculate how many keys can be stored at a maximum. How many index pointers would there be at a maximum?

# REFERENCES

1] Bayer, R., and McCreight, E. M., "Organization and Maintenance of Large Ordered Indices," *Acta Informatica* 1, no. 3, 1972.

2] Bradley, James, *File and Data Base Techniques*, Holt, Rinehart & Winston, 1981.

3] Ellzey, Roy S., *Data Structures for Computer Information Systems*, SRA, 1982.

4] Gillenson, Mark L., *Database Step-by-Step*, John Wiley & Sons, 1985.

5] Knuth, Donald E., *The Art of Computer Programming* Vol. 3, *Sorting and Searching*, Addison-Wesley, 1973.

6] Lewis, T. G., and Smith, M. Z., *Applying Data Structures*, 2d ed. Houghton Mifflin, 1982.

7] Martin, James, *Computer Data-Base Organization*, 2d ed. Prentice-Hall, 1977.

8] Merrett, T. H., *Relational Information Systems*, Reston Publishing Co., 1984.

9] Teorey, Toby J., and Fry, James P., *Design of Database Structures*, Prentice-Hall, 1982.

10] Wiederhold, Gio, *Database Design*, 2d ed. McGraw-Hill, 1983.

11] Wirth, Niklaus. *Algorithms and Data Structures*, Prentice-Hall, 1986.

# Answers to Odd-Numbered Review Questions

*CHAPTER 1 — INTRODUCTION TO DATABASE MANAGEMENT*

1. Redundancy occurs when the same data item is stored in more than one place. For instance, several pieces of faculty data, such as a faculty member's name and address, may be stored in more than one file. This is wasteful of space and creates potentially severe update problems.

3. An entity is an object; an attribute is a property of an entity; and a relationship is an association between entities.

5. A database is a structure that can house information about multiple types of entities and about relationships among those entities.

7. The database contains information on relationships among the entities. Without this feature, we would no longer have the advantage of easily being able to follow relationships among entities.

9. A DBMS is a database management system. It is a software package whose fundamental function is to manipulate a database on behalf of the users of the database.

11. The APOLLO project.

13. Dr. E. F. Codd proposed the relational approach to database management.

15. When data is pooled into a single database, each user's data becomes available to other users (provided corporate policy permits this, of course). Thus, each user has access to more data than the file approach would provide, which means each user is able to obtain more information.

17. When redundancy is present, there is more than one copy of a single data item. If two or more copies of the same data item differ in value, inconsistency is present. If redundancy is eliminated, this inconsistency cannot occur. If redundancy is not eliminated but is carefully controlled, the possibility of inconsistency still exists, but the probability of its occurring is reduced.

19. Security is the prevention of access to the database by unauthorized users. One way to achieve security is through user views. Any data items not included in the user view for a given user will not be accessible to that user. Another way to achieve security is through the use of sophisticated password schemes.

21. Since programmers are freed from the details involved in the manipulation of the database, they can be more productive. The advent of fourth-generation languages associated with database management systems also allows programmers to be much more productive. Writing a program to accomplish a particular task in a fourth-generation language typically takes a fraction of the time it would take to write a program to accomplish the same task in a third-generation language (like COBOL).

23. The ANSI/X3/SPARC model contains external schemas (individual users' views of the database), conceptual schemas (the organization's view of the database), and internal schemas (the physical view of the database). Any of these can be changed without the others necessarily being affected, which promotes data independence.

25. A DBMS is a very complex product, and programmers and analysts have to master a great deal of information to effectively use the product. If the DBMS is not thoroughly understood, some crucial choices may be made incorrectly, spelling disaster for a project. In addition, the more complex a product is, the more likely it is to contain bugs, none of which can have a serious impact on processing.

27. Since the database is a considerably more complicated structure than a simple file, recovery is by nature more difficult. The problem is compounded by the fact that in a database environment, it is more likely for several users to be simultaneously updating the database than in a file-oriented environment.

## CHAPTER 2 — FUNCTIONS OF A DATABASE MANAGEMENT SYSTEM

1. The DBMS should handle all of the details of manipulating the database when users attempt to store, retrieve, or update data.

3. The DBMS must be aware of at least some of the information in the catalog in order to function. Therefore, if the information is not maintained by the DBMS or a related product, some of it must be kept in two different places, which creates redundancy problems.

5. A logical transaction is a sequence of steps that will accomplish what is perceived by the user as a single task. Changing the address of customer 124 is an example of a logical transaction, requiring the update of only a single record. Adding an order and all associated order lines is an example of a logical transaction requiring multiple updates.

7. When a transaction is committed, all of its updates are made permanent and available to other users. When a transaction is aborted, any updates already completed are undone.

9. A transaction might be aborted because a deadlock has occurred or because the data is faulty (e.g., after some of the updates have been completed, it is discovered that the next update cannot occur because there is nonnumeric data in a field that is supposed to be numeric). A transaction might be aborted because of a computer crash that occurs while the transaction is being processed.

11. Locking is the process of assigning locks to users on portions of the database to prevent other users from updating these portions for the period during which the user holds the lock.

13. Two-phase locking occurs when there are two distinct phases of locking: a growing phase, in which locks are acquired but no locks are released, and a shrinking phase, during which all locks are released and no further locks are acquired. Suppose user A releases a lock before successfully completing a transaction, at which time user B updates the record on which user A held the lock. If user A's transaction is later aborted, user A's updates will be undone. In the process, however, user B's update to the record on which A held and later released a lock will also be undone.

15. If a user holds a shared lock on a portion of the database, other users may read but not update this portion. If a user holds an exclusive lock on a portion of the database, no other user may access this portion in any way. If only exclusive locks are used, the action of a user reading data, which by itself does not cause a problem, will prevent all other users from accessing this portion of the database. This can create severe contention problems.

17. Records should be locked until the transaction has completed. This can, however, cause portions of the database to be unavailable for extended periods of time, so we will often unlock them as soon as we have read them. To prevent the lost update problem, we must check to see if a record we have previously read has been updated by someone else. If so, we will abort our transaction. If not, we can proceed with the update.

19. Recovery is the process of returning the database from an incorrect state to one that is known to be correct.

21. A backup copy of the database is made before the update is run. If the database is later damaged, the backup copy is then copied over the live copy and the update is rerun.

23. The journal is the record of updates to the database. For each update, a before image and an after image of the portion of the database affected by the update are typically stored in the journal. In addition, when a transaction is committed, a record of this fact is stored in the journal.

25. Forward recovery is the process of starting with a backup copy of the database that is no longer current and bringing it forward by effectively repeating the updates that have taken place. It is accomplished by first copying the backup copy of the database over the live copy, then applying the after images of committed transaction that are stored in the journal to the database. It is appropriate when damage has made the live copy of the database unusable.

27. If the transaction has just occurred, it can potentially be rolled back. If a period of time has intervened, rollback may not be practical, in which case the data is corrected by entering an offsetting transaction.

29. Security is the protection of the database from unauthorized access.

31. Since any user can access only the data present in his or her subschema, omitting records and/or fields from that user's subschema prevents him or her from having access to them.

33. A given user can take a given action on a given object. These actions are usually supported through the combination of subschemas and passwords.

35. Privacy is the right of an individual to have certain information concerning him or her kept confidential. It is through appropriate security measures that privacy can be ensured.

37. Integrity occurs when data in the database satisfies any constraints that have been placed on it. An integrity constraint is a condition that data in the database must satisfy or a condition under which certain types of processing must take place or must not take place.

39. Logical data independence occurs when changes to the logical structure of the database do not affect programs that access the database. This permits the database structure to be altered to keep pace with changing requirements without requiring massive changes to programs.

41. The DBMS should furnish services to assist in making changes to the database structure, to gather and report statistics concerning database usage, and so on.

## CHAPTER 3 — INTRODUCTION TO THE RELATIONAL MODEL

1. A relation is a two-dimensional table in which
   a. the entries are single-valued.
   b. each column has a distinct name, called the attribute name.
   c. all of the values in a given column are values of the same attribute.
   d. the order of columns is immaterial.
   e. each row is distinct.
   f. the order of rows is immaterial.
3. The primary key is the attribute or collection of attributes that uniquely identifies a given row. A foreign key is an attribute in one relation that is required to match the primary key of another relation. Foreign keys provide a mechanism for explicitly specifying relationships between different relations.
5. Suppose entity A is represented by relation A and entity B is represented by relation B. A one-to-many relationship from entity A to entity B is implemented by including the key of relation A as an attribute (actually a foreign key) in relation B.
7. Two relations are union-compatible if they have the same number of attributes and if the corresponding attributes have the same domain.


## CHAPTER 4 — RELATIONAL MODEL: ADVANCED TOPICS AND IMPLEMENTATION

1. Nulls are special values used for missing information. A column that can contain nulls can cause problems when selecting rows, when joining with other tables, or when calculating statistics using the column.
3. They furnish logical data independence. They allow different users to view the same data in different ways. By including only the columns a given user needs in his or her view, the database seems much simpler to the user, and the portion of the database not included in the view is not available to him or her, which furnishes a measure of security.
5. A view, although it may be defined as a join of several tables, is still perceived as a single table by the user of the view. For some users, this is sufficient. Others require more than a single table in their subschema (or external schema). Thus, a view is best characterized as a subset of a subschema. Some subschemas will be single views; others may consist of a collection of views.

7. Indexes speed up retrieval. The disadvantages of using indexes are that they must be updated when data in the database changes, which adds overhead, and that they occupy space that is technically not necessary.

9. The catalog is updated by the system when users make changes to the structure of tables or associated indexes. If users were to update the catalog directly and make any kind of mistake in the process, the catalog would not match reality. Since the system uses the catalog to access the tables, this situation would be disastrous.

11. SQL provides support for entity integrity and referential integrity, as well as for ensuring that a column can accept only certain specific values. Only versions of SQL that contain the integrity enhancement feature provide this support.

13. a. A system in which data is perceived by the user as tables is called *tabular*.
    b. A system that also supports the SELECT, PROJECT, and JOIN operations independently of any predefined access paths is called *minimally relational*.
    c. A system that supports the full relational algebra is called *relationally complete*.
    d. A system that supports the full relational algebra and the two integrity rules is called *fully relational*.

15. Embedded SQL commands in COBOL programs are identified to the precompiler by being preceded by EXEC SQL and followed by END-EXEC. Host variables are the normal COBOL variables (i.e., the nondatabase variables). They are distinguished from the database column names in embedded SQL commands by being preceded by a colon.

17. Like many other languages, COBOL is designed to process a single record at a time. There are no facilities in the language to handle a situation like the one created when a SELECT statement returns multiple records (rows). Cursors allow the result of such a SELECT statement to be presented to COBOL one row at a time.

19. When a COMMIT is executed, all locks are released. When a user is the victim in a deadlock situation, an automatic ROLLBACK occurs.

21. DB2 furnishes logical data independence through the view mechanism and the use of cursors. Both of these allow the underlying logical structure of the database to change without necessarily affecting the users of the database. Provided the same view or cursor can still be defined against the new structure, users really will be unaffected. DB2 furnishes physical data independence through automatic navigation. Since it is not the user but the DBMS that determines how the database is to be navigated to satisfy a request, the user does not need to be aware of any physical changes to the database structure (such as the addition or deletion of an index).

23. Security in INGRES is handled through the DEFINE PERMIT command, through which authority can be given to a user to take certain types of actions on certain rows or columns of a collection of tables. In addition, the authority can be specified to be in effect only during certain periods of time and at certain terminals. When a user who has had such authority defined enters a query, the query is modified to include any restrictions placed on him or her.

## CHAPTER 5 — MICROCOMPUTER DATABASE MANAGEMENT

1. A typical microcomputer DBMS contains a facility to assist us in the process of creating a database. Using this facility we indicate the names of the columns and critical information concerning the columns, such as the type of data a column can contain. This is all done through a form on the screen. The DBMS ensures we do not make any illegal entries for any of this information. The DBMS also gives us an automatic form we can use to populate the database. The same facility we use to create a database in the first place can also be used to change the structure of the database.

3. Grouping means putting together records that have the same value in a particular field or combination of fields. A group intro is a line or group of lines that will print before a group of records. A group summary is a line or group of lines that will print after a group of records.

5. Many microcomputer systems do not have a separate facility for creating labels. Instead, you must use the report facility. Since there are some special issues (e.g., label size, number of labels across the page) involved in producing labels that are not present in other reports, it is often easier to use a facility that is geared strictly for creating labels.

7. To update a single row of a database, use either the built-in form supplied by the DBMS or a custom form. To make the same change to all rows that satisfy some condition, use the feature of the DBMS supplied for this particular purpose. You will have to identify the change to be made, as well as the condition.

9. A custom form has a more pleasing appearance than the DBMS-supplied form. It can also be used to enforce certain integrity constraints. In dBASE IV, we create a form by using the form design screen. We place fields, prompts, and boxes in the position where we want them to appear on the actual form.

11. It is desirable for a microcomputer DBMS to include a programming language to supplement the built-in features of the DBMS. We would need to write programs whenever the built-in features were not sufficient for some task we needed to accomplish.

13. An applications generator often generates a program, so we could modify the program the generator created. We could also create a special, separate program to handle a certain task. We could then indicate to the applications generator that this program is to be executed when the user of the application makes a certain menu choice.

## CHAPTER 6 — NORMALIZATION

1. An attribute, B is functionally dependent on another attribute, A, (which may be a collection of attributes) if a value for A determines a single value for B at any time.

3. An attribute A (or collection of attributes) is a candidate key for relation R if all attributes in R are functionally dependent on A and no subcollection of the attributes in A also has this property.

5. A relation is in first normal form if it does not contain repeating groups. This is the same as the "normalized" relation of chapter 3.

7. A relation is in third normal form if it is in second normal form and the only determinants it contains are candidate keys. If a relation is not in third normal form, there is a determinant, B, that is not a candidate key. Since B is a determinant, there is at least an attribute, C, in the relation that depends on B. Since B is not a candidate key, a given value of B can occur in many rows in the table. Since C depends on B, the value of C in each of these rows must be the same, which creates redundancy and a variety of update problems concerning attribute C.

9. A relation is in fourth normal form if it is in third normal form and contains no multivalued dependencies.

## CHAPTER 7 — INTRODUCTION TO DATABASE DESIGN

1. The inputs to the design process that are useful during the information-level design are the reports that must be produced; the inquiries that must be supported; the output that must be sent to other systems; update transactions that must be processed; calculations that must be performed; restrictions that must be enforced; and synonyms used within the organization. The inputs useful during the physical-level design are the number of occurrences of the various entity types; the frequency with which reports will be printed; report lengths; response time requirements; and any special security conditions that must be enforced.

3. The goal of the information-level design is to satisfy the user requirements as cleanly as possible. The goal of the physical-level design is twofold: acceptable performance and retaining as much cleanness of the information-level design as possible.

5. The process of designing a database to support a complex set of requirements is too complex to be achieved in a single step. Separation of the overall problem into a consideration of user views is a method of breaking down the process into smaller, more manageable pieces.

7.  a. REPRESENT EACH USER VIEW AS A COLLECTION OF RELATIONS. A collection of relations that will support the user view is created.

   b. NORMALIZE THESE RELATIONS. The relations created in step 1 are converted to 4NF.

   c. REPRESENT ANY OTHER RESTRICTION. Any restrictions not covered in the previous steps are represented at this point.

   d. REPRESENT ANY OTHER RESTRICTION. Any restrictions not covered in the previous steps are represented at this point.

   e. MERGE THE RESULT OF THE PREVIOUS STEPS INTO THE DESIGN. The relations and restrictions for the user view are added to the cumulative design. Relations with identical primary keys are combined.

   The above steps are repeated for each user view.

## CHAPTER 8 — DATABASE DESIGN: ADVANCED TOPICS

1. Existing documents tell us nothing about additional requirements included in the new system for which the design is being completed. Further, the underlying assumptions and requirements are not always clear from the document itself. We need additional input from the users.

3. Processing information is used in the physical design process. Rather than interview the users in two separate steps, we try to obtain and document the information that is required for both steps in the design process.

5. The key question is whether there are independent many-to-many relationships among pairs of entities. If not, it is a true three-way, many-to-many-to-many relationship and should be implemented by creating a relation whose key is the concatenation of the primary keys for each of the entities. If there are independent many-to-many relationships, they should each be implemented by creating relations whose keys are the concatenations of the primary keys of the entities involved in the many-to-many relationship.

7. Derived data is data that can be derived or computed from other attributes. Since it is important information, we include it in the information-level design, but we carefully document how it is computed (perhaps as part of the domain definition). In the physical-level design, we would not want to include it, in general, since it causes redundancy and update problems. If the computation is complicated, however, and would involve significant overhead, we might include it for performance reasons.

9. To merge the relations that satisfy a given user's view into the cumulative design, the relations are first added to the cumulative collection. At this point, relations with common primary keys are combined. When relations are combined, all attributes of both relations appear, with any duplicated attributes removed. Relations should not be merged if they have been separated to represent subtypes. Such relations can be recognized by the fact that their primary key is also a foreign key. If two relations that have identical foreign keys within them are merged, there will be a problem if the foreign key restrictions do not agree (e.g., in one case, delete might cascade, and in the other, it might be restricted). Such conflicts must be resolved with the users before the design can be completed.

11. A computerized tool to assist in the database design process should accept as input functional or multivalued dependencies, or alternatively 3NF or 4NF relations. It should produce as output various reports and/or graphical representations of possible database designs. It should allow for user override of any decisions it might make. It should be iterative, allowing user interaction along the way to refine the design. In the physical-design part of the process, it should accept processing requirements and suggest alternative physical designs for specific systems that are optimal with respect to the given requirements.

13. A "bottom-up" methodology starts with a collection of specific user requirements and ultimately synthesizes a design from these requirements. A "top-down" methodology starts with a general overall database design representing the basic corporate entities and relationships and continually refines the design until a design that will satisfy the individual requirements is produced. A top-down methodology gives a global feel to the project; there is always an idea of where the project is headed, which is not true with a strict bottom-up approach. On the other hand, a bottom-up approach provides a rigorous way of handling each user requirement. With the top-down approach, a bad start in determining an initial design can cause problems at some later point in the process, but with a bottom-up approach, it is not necessary to have an initial overall design from which to proceed.

   DBDL, in its basic form, is an example of a bottom-up methodology. A simple modification can allow DBDL to provide the benefits of both types of methodologies. Before beginning the specific treatment of individual user views, the views are reviewed for the purpose of determining the basic entities and relationships that are present. At this point, each entity is represented by a relation. The primary key is the only attribute that needs to be listed for the relation. Additionally, foreign keys may be included for each of the one-to-many relationships, although this is not absolutely essential, since these foreign keys will emerge as the individual user views are treated later.

15. In a later article, Chen proposed a change to the E-R model. In the new version, only entities can have attributes. Further, entities that are introduced to implement many-to-many relationships have a special name; they are called composite entities and are represented as a diamond inside a rectangle.

## CHAPTER 9 — THE CODASYL MODEL

1. CODASYL (the COnference on DAta SYstems Languages) set up a task group, the DBTG (DataBase Task Group) to develop standards for database management systems. The DBTG, which published an initial report in 1971, became a permanent part of CODASYL in 1972. At that time, its name was changed to the DDLC (Data Description Language Committee).

3. A set type is a one-to-many association between record types. This is the construction that is used to implement relationships in the CODASYL model. A set type is the general structure. A set occurrence is a specific example of a set type. This would consist of a single occurrence of the record type that constitutes the "one" part of the association and all the occurrences of the "many" record type associated with it.

5. The schema is the overall logical view of a database.

7. The DDL (data definition language) is used to describe the logical characteristics of the database and of individual users' views of the database. The DML (data manipulation language) is used to manipulate the database. The DMCL (device media control language) is used to describe the physical characteristics of the database.

9. Including the SET IS PRIOR PROCESSABLE clause requests that prior pointers be maintained for this set. This in turn will make any process that involves finding a prior occurrence within a set occurrence more efficient. This includes not only attempting to find the prior occurrence in a program, but also the process of deleting record occurrences or disconnecting record occurrences from a set occurrence. In such an operation, the record immediately prior to the record that is to be removed must point to the record immediately after. Finding the record immediately after is easy, since the NEXT pointer points directly to it. The process of finding the record that is immediately prior can be very difficult and inefficient unless prior pointers are used. Thus, the inclusion of prior pointers makes this operation much more efficient. On the other hand, prior pointers require space and update operations must now also update prior pointers. Since prior pointers are technically not necessary (the same operations would be possible without them, just less efficient), both of these represent unnecessary overhead.

11. The storage class of a record within a set indicates whether the record is to be inserted into an occurrence of the set automatically during a STORE command. If the storage class is AUTOMATIC, the record will be inserted. If the storage class is MANUAL, it will not.

13. Including the LINKED TO OWNER clause in a set description requests that owner pointers be maintained within the member record occurrences in this set. This makes the process of finding the owner occurrence for any member occurrence much more efficient (there is no need to follow the rest of the chain to locate the owner if owner pointers exist). On the other hand, owner pointers occupy space and must be maintained by the system. Since they are technically not required, this represents unnecessary overhead.

15. The special register, ERROR-STATUS is used by the DBMS to notify the program of any problems that occurred when accessing the database. If anything abnormal occurred during the execution of any DML command, ERROR-STATUS will be set to a value that indicates the type of problem. Programs can then test ERROR-STATUS and take appropriate action.

17. The current of run unit is the last record of any type that was found or stored. It is the object of the GET, MODIFY, ERASE, CONNECT, DISCONNECT, and RECONNECT commands. The current of run unit is updated by the FIND and STORE commands.

19. When a COMMIT is executed, all locks are released. When a user is the victim in a deadlock situation, an automatic ROLLBACK occurs.

21. In IDMS, the MODIFY command must contain the name of the record to be modified, whereas in other CODASYL systems this is not required. In all CODASYL systems, including IDMS, the DBMS knows which record to modify since the record must be the current of run unit.


## CHAPTER 10 — THE HIERARCHICAL MODEL

1. A node is a record type or record occurrence. A branch is a one-to-many relationship between two nodes. The root is the topmost node in the hierarchy. A descendant is any node connected by branches beneath a given node. A parent is a node directly above another node, located where both nodes are connected by a branch (the "one" node in a one-to-many relationship). A child is a node directly below another node, located where both nodes are connected by a branch (the "many" node in a one-to-many relationship). Twins are two or more child node occurrences of the same node type, and have the same parent occurrence.

3. A hierarchical path is the top-to-bottom route taken in accessing (reaching) a given node occurrence. Access begins at the root node and proceeds

from parent to child occurrence until the required node occurrence is reached. Using preorder traversal, node occurrences are retrieved from top to bottom (following the hierarchical path) and from left to right.

5. DL/I logical relationships allow a segment to have two parents. The segment has both a physical parent and a logical parent. The unidirectional logical relationship is a one-way relationship going from the logical child segment to the logical parent segment. The bidirectional logical relationship retains the pointers from logical child to logical parent and additionally has a pointer connecting the logical parent to the first logical child occurrence, which then points to the next logical child, and so forth.

7. HDAM permits random access through hashing to root segment occurrences and access to dependent segment occurrences through pointers stored in each segment. Sequential access to root segments is not possible unless a secondary index is also used. HIDAM permits sequential and random access through an index to root segment occurrences and access to dependent segment occurrences through pointers stored in each segment.

9. In a logical relationship, a virtual segment is a segment that does not physically exist but appears to the user as if it did.

11. A PCB is a program communication block and is one of the components of a PSB. The PCB identifies, among other things, which database (by name) will be used; this database must have been previously defined through a DBD.

13. GU, GN, GNP, GHU, GHN, and GHNP are the six DL/I function codes used for retrieval. DLET, REPL, and ISRT are the three DL/I function codes used for updating.

15. The current position is the segment occurrence accessed by the most recently executed GU, GN, GNP, GHU, GHN, GHNP, or ISRT DL/I function code.

17. Use any of the hold versions of the retrieval function codes when you need to replace (REPL) or delete (DLET) the retrieved segment occurrence.

19. Various answers are possible. Use Figure 10.20 as a guideline for the relative advantages and disadvantages of each data model.


## CHAPTER 11 — PHYSICAL DATABASE DESIGN

1. Create a relation for each relation in the final information-level design. The attributes of each relation will be precisely the same as those in the information-level design. Implement the various keys, primary, candidate, secondary, and foreign, using features of the DBMS if such features exist. If not, document the fact that programs must enforce such features. Finally, document any other restrictions that programs must enforce.

3. The general process of mapping to a hierarchical system is similar to that of mapping to a CODASYL system. In fact, the same rules can be applied to produce an initial network. The sets in this network become the parent-child relationships. If the network created is not a hierarchy, it must be converted to a hierarchy or collection of hierarchies. In IMS, this would most likely be accomplished through the use of logical child relationships.

5. A logical record access is the access of any record occurrence in the database. Even if the desired occurrence is already in the system's buffers, a logical record access is considered to occur. In contrast, a physical record access occurs only when the disk is actually accessed. Physical record accesses thus give a better picture of the performance that might be expected from a system. However, they are much more difficult to calculate, so we often choose to use LRA's. A weighted total of LRA's is obtained by assigning each application a weight that is indicative of its importance in the system. The weight for each application is multiplied by the number of LRA's required for the application. The total of these figures is called the weighted total of LRA's. Transport volume is the amount of data actually transported. Transport volume can be used along with LRA's to give a better picture of performance. When any record is accessed, an LRA occurs, and the total amount of data included in the record is transported. Without examining the total transport volume (actually a weighted total calculated in the same manner as the weighted total of LRA's), we would reward designs that have a small number of very long records, since such designs are bound to require fewer LRA's.

## CHAPTER 12 — THE FOURTH-GENERATION ENVIRONMENT

1. Machine language during the first; assembly language during the second.

3. Select from the following: English-like syntax, greater productivity, and portability.

5. An information center is an information systems "department" whose function is to make available to users the tools they need to interact productively with the computer and to train these users in the use of these tools.

7. A data dictionary is a central storehouse of data about a firm's entire data. Metadata is used as a synonym for "data about data."

9. In the data category: field, group, record, file, file relationship, user view, and database. In the process category: program, report, screen, transaction, and job. In the environment category: system, department (people), terminal, communication line, disk storage, processor, and operating system.

11. A free-standing data dictionary runs independently of a specific DBMS. An integrated data dictionary must be used with a specific DBMS product or products. An active data dictionary interacts with the other software components in the environment, while a passive data dictionary does not.

13. A data dictionary bridge facility performs its interaction with the other software components prior to the execution of the DBMS, while a run-time interface occurs during the execution of the DBMS.

15. A report writer is a nonprocedural language for producing formatted reports from data in a database. The two types of report writers are language-oriented report writers, in which we specify the layout of the report by constructing appropriate commands, and visually-oriented report writers in which we manipulate objects on our screen to make the screen look like the report we want.

17. A screen generator is an interactive facility for creating and maintaining display and data entry formats for screen forms. "Painted" refers to how literals are displayed on the screen and how color and other visual attributes are handled.

19. A help facility is a feature that allows us to obtain help on the task on which we are working on the computer. Without such a facility we would need to stop what we were doing, find an appropriate manual and look up the information in the manual.

21. A precompiler combines its own language features with those of a typical programming language such as COBOL; the combined source code is compiled by the precompiler and then compiled by the programming language's compiler. A skeletal program is the skeleton of a high-level language program; a programmer adds language statements for the specific problem to be solved.

23. Prototyping is the process of rapidly creating a working version of the complete system.

25. Icons are special screen symbols that serve as representations of the functions they perform.


## CHAPTER 13 — DATABASE ADMINISTRATION

1. Money, materials, machines, personnel, data, and information.

3. Internal sources of data should be selected from purchasing, receiving, inventory, production, sales, distribution, billing, collection, and paying. External destinations of information should be selected from federal government, state government, local government, stockholders, vendors, advertising, lenders, customers, unions, competitors, and community. Other answers are possible.

5. Each company determined the exact position of DBA on the basis of its management philosophy, its then existing organizational structure, its degree of experience in the use of computers, its size, and the specific responsibilities and authority placed in the hands of DBA.

7. Top-level management commitment and involvement is the most critical, since without it the success of the DBMS environment will be limited.

9. This is not normally a realistic goal, since it represents a complex undertaking and may not be in the best interests of the firm to pursue.

11. Typical skills include interpersonal skills, mature judgment, communication skills, technical skills, and an understanding of the business and its data needs.

13. Top-level education and commitment, enterprise planning, hardware/software requirements planning, and policy formulation.

15. Seven of the recurring costs of a DBMS environment are software maintenance; hardware maintenance and depreciation; ongoing training; DBA personnel; TP and communications maintenance; various supplies; and computer system overhead.

17. Business System Planning is a widely used planning methodology created by IBM that provides a step-by-step process to develop a comprehensive plan for an organization's information requirements.

19. Knowledge of the overall goals and objectives of an enterprise helps the DA understand the direction of the enterprise and helps identify business functions that may be necessary in the future. It also gives an indication of planned future growth.

21. Quick-payback applications of a manageable size whose benefits far exceed their costs are always wise choices.

23. The distribution of responsibilities among several people with checks and balances on their work so that the potential for security problems can be minimized.

25. A security officer has primary responsibility for security in the firm.

27. Amount of permanent disk used; amount of temporary disk used; terminal connect time; CPU time; number of tape mounts; main memory used; and number of lines of print.

29. Five DBA application functions are standards and procedures, data dictionary management, training, overall coordination, and database loading.

31. Five DBA technical functions are DBMS support; test/production environments; database design; DBMS performance; and keeping abreast of technological changes.

33. DBA is responsible for the conceptual and internal data-level designs and serves in an advisory capacity to the systems analysts and designers for the external data-level design.

35. Among the many types of performance statistics are the following: number of terminal users; number of transactions per transaction type; program execution time; number of database accesses per transaction, per database record type and per disk pack; database pages with high access rates; transactional response time; user terminal connect time; ad hoc queries processed, and their characteristics; batch program execution time; and the number of database accesses per batch program.

## CHAPTER 14 — DISTRIBUTED SYSTEMS AND OTHER CURRENT TRENDS

1. Databases on computer networks may be split over several sites in the network, which requires a special type of database management system, called a distributed database management system to manage the data.
3. A distributed database management system (DDBMS) is a DBMS that is capable of supporting and manipulating distributed databases. In contrast, a DBMS does not have the capability of dealing with databases that are not completely contained on one machine.
5. The local site is the site at which the user is currently operating. A remote site is any other site in the network.
7. Replication is the storing of the same data item at more than one site in the network. It is done to speed access to data (data accessed at the local site does not require additional communication time). The benefit is that users at each of the sites where the replicated data is stored can access that data more efficiently than they could if the data were stored only at a remote site. The main problem concerns update: when replicated data is update, all copies of the data around the network must be updated.
9. Data fragmentation is the dividing of a logical object, like the collection of all records of a given type, among the various locations in a network. Its main purpose is the place data at the site where it is most often accessed.
11. a. Since each location can keep its own data, greater local control can be exercised over it.
    b. In a well-designed distributed system, capacity can often be increased at only one site rather than for the whole database. Capacity can be further increased through the addition of new sites to the network.
    c. Other users can continue their processing even though a site on the network is unavailable. In a centralized system, no users can continue processing if the database is unavailable.
    d. Data available locally can be retrieved much more efficiently than data stored on a remote, centralized system.

13. All the same issues are encountered when concurrency is treated in a centralized system, but two other issues are encountered as well: local deadlock, which means that two users at the same site are in deadlock, and global deadlock, which means that two users at different sites are in deadlock.

15. The complete data dictionary may be stored at a single site. A complete copy of the data dictionary may be stored at every site. The entries in the dictionary may be distributed among the sites in the network (possibly with replication).

17. In the physical-level design process, in addition to the usual factors, communication time must be considered in the choice of an optimum design.

19. a. Since the mainframe is free to perform other functions while the database computer is accessing the database, parallel processing is possible and improvements in performance can be achieved. On the other hand, if a database request only retrieves a single record, there is actually more overhead than before, since the mainframe sends a request to the database computer, which then accesses the database to retrieve the record and finally sends the retrieved record back to the mainframe. Without a database computer, the mainframe would simply have retrieved this record directly from the database on disk.

    b. If a host computer is managing a database, there exists the possibility for someone to bypass the DBMS and access the database directly. When a database computer is used, users must go through it to access the database; it is impossible to bypass it. On the other hand, the potential exists for users to fool the database computer into believing that they are legitimate users even though they are not. If they do so, these users will be able to access the database.

    c. The possibility exists of hooking several database computers to a single host computer. These options allow great flexibility in configuring systems to specific needs, but their implementation causes the system to become effectively a distributed system, which means it is susceptible to the problems associated with such systems.

    d. A database computer is a specialized machine built to serve a single purpose; consequently it is much simpler than a typical mainframe. On the other hand, the entire system, including both the host and the database computer, is more complex than a system in which a database computer is not used.

    e. Since database computers are much simpler than a typical mainframe, they are potentially more reliable; fewer things can go wrong. This reliability may be offset, however, by the presence of additional hardware and software, which can cause other things to go wrong.

21. An object is some unit of data along with the actions that can take place on that object. A class represents a general structure (like a domain). Each object is associated with a class, which effectively describes the structure of the object, as well as the methods that act upon it.

23. When one class is a subclass of another, it inherits the structure of the class, as well as the methods that apply to the class. This means that the structure and methods apply to the subclass automatically. The benefit to this is that we only need to define the structure or methods that were not inherited from the class. This makes the process of defining the subclass much easier.

25. A predicate is a function whose value is either true or false. An example is *parent*. If X is a parent of Y, *parent(X,Y)* is true, otherwise it is false.

27. A recursive predicate is a predicate that appears on both sides of the predicate's definition. An example is

    descendant(X,Y) :– parent(Y,X)
    descendant(X,Y) :– parent(Z,X), descendant(Z,Y)

which is true if X is a descendant of Y.

29. a. We represent domain constraints by setting up predicates that guarantee that whenever a tuple is part of the overall knowledge base, each attribute must be part of the appropriate domain. For example, SNUM(X) :– SLSR(X,Y) (where SNUM represents sales rep number and SLSR represents sales rep) is a predicate that states that whenever the tuple X,Y makes SLSR true, X must make SNUM true. In other words, the first value in any tuple for sales rep must be a legitimate sales rep number.

   b. For primary key constraints, we set up predicates that ensure the uniqueness. For example, to indicate the first attribute in SLSR is the primary key, we could use the predicate X = Y :– SLSR (Z,X),SLSR(Z,Y). This indicates that if two tuples begin with the same value, the other value or values must be the same; that is, the first attribute must be unique.

   c. For foreign key constraints, we create predicates to specify the fact that a foreign key must match the primary key in some other table. For example, to indicate the fourth attribute in CUST is a foreign key must be a legitimate sales rep number, we could use the predicate SNUM(W) :– CUST(X,Y,Z,W). This says that if a given collection of X, Y, Z, and W make CUST true, the value of W must also make SNUM true; that is, it must be the number of an existing sales rep.

## APPENDIX — FILE AND DATA STRUCTURES FOR DATABASE PROCESSING

1. A logical transaction is a user request to accomplish a single task. A logical record is an individual user's view of a data record in the database. A physical record is one unit of data transferred between memory and disk. A logical transaction may require the processing of multiple logical records, and a logical record may require the access of multiple physical records.

3. Intrafile clustering involves records from one file, while interfile clustering involves records from two or more files.

5. A primary key is a field(s) that has a unique value for each record in the file. Random access is permitted for a field that is a secondary key; this field does not have to be unique. A sequence key is a field that determines the order of records within the file. There may be more than one field in each case.

7. The formula applied with a key-addressing technique results in a unique disk address, while a hashing formula does not guarantee a unique address.

9. When collision occurs on a given page, a pointer field within the page indicates which page received the relocated record. If multiple collisions occur, the pointer field chains together the relocated records.

11. When an indexed file is initially created by means of the block-splitting technique and when full pages are split into two or more pages by means of this technique, each page is only partially filled, which leaves free space distributed throughout the file to allow for future additions to the file.

13. Both the inverted file and the multilist structures have an index, with one record for each unique key field value. For the inverted file, this index has a pointer to a lower-level index that contains the addresses of all records with that key field value. For the multilist, this index has a pointer to a logical record with that key field value. Each logical record has a pointer field that chains together all other fields with that particular key field value.

15. There can be seven children per node at a maximum. For a two-level B-tree, forty-eight keys can be stored at a maximum (the root can have six keys; each of the root's seven children can have six keys, or forty-two total level 1 keys; adding six and forty-two gives forty-eight keys).

**Abort a transaction** To undo all of the updates already completed for the *transaction*.

**Access method** A file organization, together with the set of possible access techniques.

**Active data dictionary** A data dictionary that documents the firm's data and that interacts with other software components.

**After image** A record of a portion of a database after a change has been made.

**Alias** An alternative name for a given table (used in SQL).

**ANSI** The American National Standards Institute.

**ANSI/SPARC** The American National Standards Institute/Standards Planning and Requirements Subcommittee.

**ANSI/SPARC model** A model of data proposed by *ANSI/SPARC* that includes external, conceptual, and internal schemas.

**Application generation** The process of developing an application system.

**Application generator** A Software tool that allows rapid development of an application system.

**Applied** When a database is changed to match either before or after images stored in a log or journal, we say these images have been applied.

**Artificial intelligence** A computer-based system that performs functions normally associated with intelligent human behavior.

**Attribute** A property of an entity.

**Authorization rule** A rule indicating the conditions (constraints) under which a given person or group (the subject) can take a certain type of action on a set of database entities (the object).

**B-tree** A widely used multilevel index structure in which multiple keys and pointers are stored in each tree node.

**Bachman diagram** A diagram of the records and sets in a network database. Also called a *data structure diagram*.

**Back-end computer** See *database computer*.

**Back-end machine** See *database computer*.

**Backup** A copy of a database. Used to recover the database when the database has been damaged or destroyed.

**Base table** An existing, permanent table in a relational database.

**Before image** A record of a portion of a database before a change was made.

**Bidirectional relationship** A two-way logical relationship in a DL/I database which uses pointers in the logical parent and child segments.

**Bill-of-materials relationship** In manufacturing, the relationship between a parent part and its component parts. The classic example of a many-to-many relationship between an entity and itself.

**Block** See *page*.

**Blocking factor** The number of logical records in a block or page.

**Boyce-Codd normal form (BCNF)** A relation is in Boyce-Codd normal form if it is in second normal form and the only determinants it contains are candidate keys. Also called third normal form in this text.

**Branch** The connection between two nodes in a tree structure.

**Bridge facility** A data dictionary software interface occurring prior to the execution of the DBMS. Also called a *static interface*.

**Buffer** A memory area holding one or more blocks of data.

**Candidate key** A minimal collection of attributes (columns) in a relation on which all attributes are functionally dependent but which was not necessarily chosen as the primary key, the main direct access vehicle to individual tuples (rows).

**Catalog** A source of information on the types of entities, attributes, and relationships in a database.

**Checkpoint** A time at which updates to the database which are in progress are made permanent. In some cases, systemwide checkpoints are used; in others, checkpoints pertain only to individual transactions.

**Children** Nodes that are direct descendants of other nodes in a tree structure.

**Ciphering** See *encryption*.

**Clustering** The grouping of logical records in a database on the basis of usage patterns.

**CODASYL** COnference on Data SYstems Languages. The group that developed COBOL and that proposed the CODASYL model for database management.

**CODASYL model** The model for database management systems proposed by CODASYL. Falls within the general network model of data. Not a standard, although it has been used in the development of many systems.

**Collision** The result of two or more records ending up with the same hash function value in direct organization.

**Commit** The process of completing all updates for a logical transaction, making them permanent, and making the results available to other users.

**Communications network** A number of computers configured in such a way that data can be sent from any one computer in the network to any other.

**Composite** In the entity-relationship model, an entity used to implement a many-to-many relationship.

**Compression** The packing of data on disk by, for example, removing trailing spaces and leading zeros.

**Concatenation** Combination of attributes. To say a key is a concatenation of two attributes, for example, means that a combination of values of both attributes is required to uniquely identify a given tuple.

**Conceptual schema** The global organizational view of data.

**Concurrent update** Multiple updates taking place to the same file or database at almost the same time. Also called *shared update*.

**Coordinator** In a distributed network, the site that directs the *two-phase commit* process. Often, it is the site that initiates the transaction.

**Cross-reference** A record used to implement a many-to-many relationship. Also called a *link record*.

**Currency** A concept used to indicate position within a CODASYL database.

**Currency indicator** A conceptual pointer maintained by a CODASYL DBMS to establish a current record of a run unit, record type, set type, or realm.

**Cursor** In embedded SQL, a pointer to a collection of rows returned by the query that defines the cursor. Used to allow the processing of the multiple rows returned by SQL in a record-at-a-time-oriented language.

**Data Base Task Group** The group originally appointed by CODASYL to develop specifications for database management systems.

**Data definition language** A language used to communicate the structure of a database to the database management system.

**Data dictionary** A central storehouse of data about the firm's data.

**Data entry database** A DL/I Fast Path database restricted to a root segment and up to seven child segment types.

**Data fragmentation** The process of dividing a logical object, such as the collection of records of a certain type, among various locations in a *distributed database*.

**Data independence** The property that allows the structure of the database to change without requiring changes to application programs.

**Data Language/I** See *DL/I*.

**Data manipulation language** A language used to manipulate the data in the database.

**Data model** A classification scheme for database management systems. A data model addresses two aspects of database management: *structure* and *operations*.

**Data structure diagram** A diagram of the records and sets in a network database.

**Database** A structure that can house information about multiple types of entities and about relationships among the entities.

**Database administrator** The individual responsible for the database. The head of database administration.

**Database computer** A computer whose sole purpose is to perform database activities on behalf of another computer. Also called *back-end computer*, *back-end machine*, or *database machine*.

**Database description** See *DBD*.

**Database design** The process of determining the content and arrangement of data in the database in order to support some activity on behalf of a user or group of users.

**Database Design Language (DBDL)** A relational-like language used to represent the result of the database design process.

**Database machine** See *database computer*.

**Database management system** A software package designed to manipulate data in a database on behalf of a user.

**Database navigation** The process of finding a path through the relationships in a database to satisfy a given request.

**Data communication** The process of sending data from one computer to another.

**DB2** A relational DBMS offered by IBM.

**DBA** Database administration. The individual or group responsible for the database. (Sometimes the acronym stands for database administrator.)

**DBD** A DL/I database description defining the physical database. DBD is an acronym for database description.

**DBDL** See *Database Design Language*.

**DBMS** Database management system.

**DBTG** The Data Base Task Group, the group originally appointed by CODA-SYL to develop specifications for database management systems.

**DDL** Data definition language.

**Deadlock** A state in which two or more users are each waiting for resources held by the other(s).

**Deadly embrace** Another name for deadlock.

**Defining query** The query used to define the structure of a view.

**Dependency diagram** A diagram indicating the dependencies among the attributes in a relation.

**Descendant** A node beneath another node in a tree structure.

**Determinant** An attribute that determines at least one other attribute.

**Differential file** A file of changes to be made to data in a database. This file is consulted first when users access a database to determine whether the records to be retrieved have been changed in any way.

**Direct access** Another name for *random access*.

**Direct organization** A physical file structure by which records are accessed at a disk address on the basis of a formula applied to the value of a field in the record.

**Distributed database** A database that is stored on computers at several sites of a computer network and in which users can access data at any site in the network.

**Distributed database management system** A database management system that is capable of manipulating distributed databases.

**Distributed free space** Unfilled record slots in a file reserved for future additions.

**Division-remainder method** A direct-organization hashing technique whose formula uses the remainder as the disk address.

**DL/I** Data Language/I, the database definition and manipulation component of IBM's hierarchical model DBMS, IMS.

**DML** Data manipulation language.

**Domain** A pool from which the values for an attribute must be chosen.

**Domain-key normal form** A relation is in domain-key normal form if every constraint on the relation is a logical consequence of the definitions of keys and domains.

**Downloading** Data transfer from mainframe to personal computer.

**Dynamic interface** A data dictionary software interface that takes place during the execution of the DBMS. Also called a *runtime interface*.

**Encryption** The transformation of data into another form before it is stored in the database. The data will be returned to its original form for any legitimate user accessing the database. Also called *encyphering* or *ciphering*.

**Encyphering** See *encryption*.

**Entity** An object (person, place, or thing) of interest.

**Entity integrity** The rule that no attribute that participates in the primary key may accept *null* values.

**Entity subtype** Entity A is an entity subtype of entity B if every occurrence of A is also an occurrence of B.

**Entity-relationship (E-R) model** A graphic model for database design in which entities are represented as rectangles and relationships are represented as diamonds connected by arrows to the entities they relate.

**Equijoin** A type of *join* in which both columns used in the join appear in the result.

**Essential set** A set that cannot be removed from a CODASYL database structure without incurring the loss of a relationship.

**Exclusive lock** A type of lock on a resource which prohibits other users from accessing the resource in any way.

**Existence dependency** In the *entity-relationship model*, a dependency in which one of the entities depends on the other for its existence.

**Expert system** A knowledge-based system dedicated to a specific field of expertise.

**Extension** The data in a relation at a given point in time. It can be visualized as a "filled-in" table.

**External schema** In the *ANSI/SPARC model*, the application program's view of the database.

**External view** The application program's view of the database.

**Fast Path** DL/I's high-speed capability.

**Fifth-generation software** Emerging software exhibiting functions of artificial intelligence.

**Fifth normal form (5NF)** A relation is in fifth normal form if every join dependency is implied by the candidate keys.

**File organization** Physical structure of a file.

**First normal form (1NF)** A relation is in first normal form if it does not contain repeating groups. (Technically this is part of the definition of a relation.)

**Flat file structure** A two-dimensional table.

**Folding method** A direct-organization hashing technique whose formula uses the sum of groups of the key's digits as the disk address.

**Foreign key** An attribute (or collection of attributes) in a relation whose value is required either to match the value of a primary key in another relation or to be null.

**Fourth-generation environment** Current software environments with a DBMS and data dictionary at their core and other software components integrated with these core components.

**Fourth-generation language (4GL)** A programming language with both procedural and nonprocedural features.

**Fourth normal form (4NF)** A relation is in fourth normal form if it is in third normal form with no multivalued dependencies.

**Fragmentation transparency** The property that means users do not need to be aware of any *data fragmentation* (splitting of data) that has taken place in a *distributed database*.

**Free-standing data dictionary** A data dictionary system that executes independently of a specific DBMS. Also called an *independent* or *stand-alone* data dictionary.

**Fully inverted file** A file in which inversion takes place on all fields.

**Fully relational** The expression used to refer to a DBMS in which users perceive data as tables, which supports all the operations of the *relational algebra*, and which supports *entity* and *referential integrity*.

**Functionally dependent** An attribute, B, is functionally dependent on another attribute, A (or possibly a collection of attributes), if a value for A determines a single value for B at any one time.

**Functionally determine** Attribute A functionally determines attribute B if B is *functionally dependent* on A.

**Global deadlock** *Deadlock* in a distributed system that cannot be detected solely at any individual site.

**Growing phase** A phase during an update in which new *locks* are acquired but no locks are released.

**Hash function** A formula used in direct organization to transform the primary key into a disk address. Also called a *hashing algorithm*, a *hashing routine*, or a *randomizing routine*.

**Hashing** A direct-organization technique for transforming a primary key to a disk address that does not guarantee a unique address.

**Heterogeneous DDBMS** A *distributed DBMS* in which at least two of the local DBMS's are different from each other.

**Hierarchical model** Tree-structured DBMS.

**Hierarchical path** The path followed in the process of accessing nodes in a tree structure.

**Homogeneous DDBMS** A *distributed DBMS* in which all of the local DBMS's are the same.

**Host language** A language such as COBOL in which database commands may be embedded.

**Hybrid system** A DBMS that combines features of two or more data models.

**ID dependency** In the *entity-relationship model*, a relationship in which one entity depends on the other for identification.

**IDMS** A CODASYL DBMS that is offered by Cullinet.

**IDMS/R** A DBMS with both CODASYL and relational features that is offered by Cullinet.

**IMS** A hierarchical DBMS offered by IBM.

**Index** A file relating key values and logical records with those key values. Also called an *index file*.

**Indexed organization** A physical file structure consisting of the data file and a separate index file.

**Indexed random organization** Indexed organization in which data records are not stored physically in primary key sequence.

**Indexed sequential organization** Indexed organization in which data records are physically stored in primary key sequence.

**Inessential set** A set that can be removed from a CODASYL database structure without incurring the loss of a relationship.

**Information center** The department in an enterprise which makes software tools available to users and trains them in their use.

**Information level of database design** The step during *database design* in which the goal is to create a clean DBMS-independent design that will support user requirements.

**INGRES** A relational DBMS that is offered by Relational Technology.

**Integrated data dictionary** A data dictionary system executing with one or more specific DBMS's. Also called a *dependent* data dictionary.

**Integrity** A database has integrity if all integrity constraints that have been established for it are currently met.

**Integrity constraint** A condition that data within a database must satisfy. Also, a condition that indicates types of processing that may or may not take place.

**Intension** The permanent part or structure of a relation. It can be viewed as the listing of attributes or columns in a relation.

**Internal schema** The view of the database as seen by the computer.

**Interrelation constraint** A condition that involves two or more relations.

**Intersection data** The data in a link record.

**Inverted file** A data structure for which an index has been created for a secondary key field. Also called an *inverted list*.

**Inverted file model** A DBMS that is based on an inverted file structure.

**Inverted list** See *inverted file*.

**ISAM** IBM's indexed sequential access method.

**Join** In the *relational algebra,* the operation in which two tables are connected on the basis of common data.

**Journal** A record of all changes to the database. Used to recover a database that has been damaged or destroyed. Also called a *log.*

**Journaling** The process of maintaining a *journal* or *log.*

**Key-addressing** A direct-organization technique for transforming a primary key to a unique disk address.

**Knowledge-based system** Fifth-generation software consisting of a database of data (knowledge) and rules that can draw inferences from the stored knowledge.

**Linear search** A collision-management technique that locates records in a nearby page.

**Link record** A record used to implement a many-to-many relationship. Also called a *cross-reference.*

**Linked list** A data structure that uses pointers to connect records in a logical sequence. Also called a *pointer chain.*

**Local deadlock** Deadlock that can be detected totally at one site in a distributed system.

**Local site** From a user's perspective, the site in a distributed system at which the user is working.

**Location mode** A two-part strategy consisting of one strategy for placing records in a database and a companion strategy for finding those records at some later time. Also called an *access method.*

**Location transparency** The property that means users do not need to be aware of the location of data in a *distributed database.*

**Lock granularity** The amount of the database that is locked when locks are acquired. Can be a field, record, page, or the entire database.

**Locking** The process of placing a lock on a portion of a database, which prevents other users from accessing that portion.

**Log** A record of all changes to the database. Used to recover a database that has been damaged or destroyed. Also called a *journal.*

**Logical data independence** The property that allows the logical structure of the database to change without requiring changes to application programs.

**Logical database** An individual user's view of the database.

**Logical record access (LRA)** The process of accessing any record in a database. A logical record access occurs whether or not the record happens already to be in memory. Used in estimating performance.

**Logical transaction** A sequence of steps or updates that will accomplish what is perceived by the user as a single task.

**Lower conceptual domain** The portion of an *entity-relationship* diagram in which *domains* are defined.

**Main storage database** A DL/I Fast Path memory-resident database restricted to root-only segments.

**Manual set** A set in a CODASYL database for which retention is manual. Member occurrences in such a set will automatically not be connected to a set occurrence by virtue of the STORE command.

**Many-to-many relationship** A relationship between two entities in which each occurrence of each entity type is related to many occurrences of the other entity type.

**Mapping** The process of creating an initial design for the DBMS that will be used in an application from the final information-level design.

**Member record type** In a CODASYL set, the record type that is the "many" part of the one-to-many relationship.

**Message** Data sent from one computer to another.

**Microcomputer DBMS** A DBMS that can be used on a microcomputer.

**Minimally relational** A DBMS in which users perceive data as tables and which supports at least the SELECT, PROJECT, and JOIN operations of the *relational algebra* without requiring any predefined access paths.

**Multidependent** If there is a *multivalued dependency* of attribute B on attribute A, B is multidependent on A.

**Multidetermine** If there is a *multivalued dependency* of attribute B on attribute A, A multidetermines B.

**Multimember set** A CODASYL set with more than one *member record type*.

**Multivalued dependency** In a relation with attributes A, B, and C, there is a multivalued dependency of attribute B on attribute A if a value for A is associated with a specific collection of values for B independently of any values for C.

**Natural join** A type of *join* in which only one of the columns used in the join appears in the result.

**Natural language** A language in which users communicate with the computer through the use of normal English questions and commands.

**Navigation** See *database navigation*.

**Network** A structure containing record types and explicit one-to-many relationships between these record types.

**Network model** A *data model* in which the structure is a network and the operations involve navigating the network (following the arrows in a data structure diagram).

**Node** A record in a tree or hierarchical structure. An index page in a B-tree data structure.

**Nonprocedural language** A language in which the user specifies the task to be accomplished rather than the steps necessary to accomplish the task.

**Nonkey attribute** An attribute that is not part of the primary key.

**Nonloss decomposition** A decomposition of a relation through projections which allows the original data to be reconstructed.

**Normal form** See *first normal form, second normal form, third normal form, Boyce-Codd normal form, fourth normal form,* and *fifth normal form*.

**Normalization** Technically, the process of removing repeating groups to produce a *first normal form* relation. Sometimes used to indicate the process of producing a *third normal form* relation, which is the goal of part of the database design process.

**Null** A special value meaning "unknown" or "not applicable."

**Occurrence** A specific example of a structure, such as the record for student Lee Adams. Distinguished from *type*, which means the structure itself (for example, the general student record).

**One-to-many relationship** A relationship between two entities in which each occurrence of the first entity type is related to many occurrences of the second entity type but each occurrence of the second entity type is related to only one occurrence of the first entity type.

**One-to-one relationship** A relationship between two entities in which each occurrence of the first entity type is related to one occurrence of the second entity type and each occurrence of the second entity type is related to one occurrence of the first entity type.

**Operation** One of the two components of a *data model*. The facilities given users of the DBMS to manipulate data within the database.

**Optimizer** The component of a DBMS that will select the best way to satisfy a query.

**Order** In a tree structure, the maximum number of children a node can have.

**Outer join** A type of *join* in which rows in one table that do not match rows in the other table are still included in the result.

**Overflow area** A separate area used in indexed organization and in collision management for direct organization. Records are placed and accessed in this area if they cannot be added at their optimal disk address.

**Owner record type** In a CODASYL set, the record type that is the "one" part of the one-to-many relationship.

**Page** The unit of data that is transferred between memory and disk. Also called *block* or *physical record*.

**Parent** A node that is located directly above another node in a tree structure is said to be the parent of the other node.

**Partial dependency** A dependency of an attribute on only a portion of the primary key.

**Partially inverted file** A file in which inversion takes place on only some of the fields.

**Passive data dictionary** A data dictionary providing documentation of the firm's data only.

**Password** A word that must be entered before a user can access certain computer resources.

**Physical data independence** The property that allows the underlying physical structure of the database to change without requiring changes to application programs.

**Physical level of database design** The step during *database design* in which a design for a given DBMS is produced from the final information level design.

**Physical record** See *page*.

**Physical record access (PRA)** The process of transferring a record from the database to the disk. Unlike a *logical record access*, a physical record access does not occur if the record happens already to be in memory.

**Pointer array** An alternative method for implementing *sets* in a CODASYL database. Permits more efficient implementation of sorted sets than the normal chain implementation.

**Pointer chain** See *linked list*.

**Preorder traversal** Top-to-bottom and left-to-right *hierarchical path* followed through a tree structure.

**Primary copy** In a distributed database with replicated data, the copy that must be updated in order for the update to be deemed complete.

**Primary index** For indexed organization, the index file based on the primary key.

**Primary key** A minimal collection of attributes (columns) in a relation on which all attributes are functionally dependent and which is chosen as the main direct access vehicle to individual tuples (rows). See also *candidate key*.

**Privacy** The right of an individual to have certain information concerning him or her kept confidential.

**Procedural language** A language in which the user must specify the steps necessary to accomplish a task instead of merely specifying the task itself.

**Program generator** A language facility that generates a second- or third-generation language program.

**Program specification block** See *PSB*.

**Promote a lock** To change the status of a lock from shared to exclusive.

**Prototype** A working version or model of an application system.

**Prototyping** The use of fourth-generation software that permits us to rapidly create an application system prototype.

**PSB** A DL/I program specification block used to define a logical database.

**QBE** Query-by-Example. A *data manipulation language* for relational databases in which users indicate the action to be taken by filling in portions of blank tables on the screen.

**Qualify** To indicate the relation (table) of which a given attribute (column) is a part by preceding the attribute name with the relation name. For example, *CUSTOMER.ADDRESS* indicates the attribute named *ADDRESS* within the relation named *CUSTOMER*.

**QUEL** A data manipulation language used by the INGRES DBMS.

**Query facility** A facility that enables users to easily obtain information from the database.

**Query language** A language that is designed to permit users to easily obtain information from the database.

**Query-by-Example (QBE)** See *QBE*.

**Random access** A type of access in which records are accessed directly without the need to access other records in the file. Also called *direct access*.

**Recovery** The process of restoring to a correct state a database that has been damaged or destroyed.

**Recursive set** A CODASYL set in which the owner and member records are of the same type.

**Redundancy** Duplication of data.

**Referential integrity** The rule that if a relation, A, contains a *foreign key* matching the primary key of another relation, B, then the values of this foreign key must either match the value of the primary key for some row in relation B or be null.

**Relation** A two-dimensional table in which all entries are single-valued.

**Relational algebra** A relational *data manipulation language* in which relations are created from existing relations through the use of a set of operations.

**Relational calculus** A relational *data manipulation language* which is based on the predicate calculus of mathematical logic.

**Relational database** A collection of relations.

**Relational model** A *data model* in which the structure is the *table* or *relation* and the operations strictly involve the data in these tables.

**Relationally complete** A term applied to any relational *data manipulation language* that can accomplish anything that can be accomplished through the use of the relational calculus. Also applied to a DBMS that supplies such a data manipulation language.

**Relationship** An association between entities.

**Relative record number** The number of a record relative to the start of a file.

**Remote site** From a user's perspective, any site other than the one at which the user is working.

**Replicated** Data that is duplicated at more than one site in a distributed database.

**Replication transparency** The property that means users do not need to be aware of any *replication* that has occurred in a *distributed database*.

**Report generator** See *report writer*.

**Report writer** A nonprocedural language for producing formatted reports from data in a database. Also called a *report generator*.

**Resource utilization billing** A technique for billing users of the computer environment on the basis of computer resources they use.

**Rollback** The process of undoing changes that have been made to a database.

**Root** The topmost node in a tree structure.

**Runtime interface** See *dynamic interface*.

**Save** A backup copy.

**Schema** A description of the overall structure of the database.

**Screen generator** An interactive facility for creating and maintaining display and data entry formats for screen forms.

**Second normal form (2NF)** A relation is in second normal form if it is in first normal form and no nonkey attribute is dependent on only a portion of the primary key.

**Secondary index** For indexed organization, an index file that is based on a secondary key.

**Secondary key** An attribute or collection of attributes that is of interest for retrieval purposes (and that is not already designated as some other type of key).

**Security** The protection of the database against unauthorized access.

**Segment** A node or record in a DL/I hierarchical structure.

**Self-describing** A term applied to a structure that contains a description of itself. To say a database is self-describing means that no external source need be consulted to determine the structure of the database.

**Sequence field** A DL/I *sequence key*.

**Sequence key** A field or group of fields within a record that determines the order of records within the file.

**Sequential access** A type of access in which records are stored and retrieved in a file in a predetermined order.

**Sequential organization** A physical file structure consisting of records that are stored in the physical sequence in which they occur during processing.

**Set** The CODASYL implementation of a one-to-many relationship.

**Shared lock** A type of lock that permits other users to access the resource for retrieval only.

**Shared update** Multiple updates taking place to the same file or database at almost the same time. Also called *concurrent update*.

**Shrinking phase** A phase during an update in which all locks are released and no new locks are acquired.

**Singular set** A CODASYL set with only one occurrence. Also called a *system-owned set*.

**Sizing** Determining the required levels of computer resources.

**Sorted set** A CODASYL set in which insertion is SORTED BY DEFINED KEYS.

**Special register** Special item available to users of CODASYL systems in application programs. The most important of the special registers is DB-STATUS, which is used by the DBMS to convey any error that occurred during processing.

**SQL** Structured Query Language. A very popular relational *data manipulation language* that is used in DB2 and many other DBMS's.

**Static interface** See *bridge facility*.

**Statistical database** A database intended to supply only statistical information.

**Structure** One of the two components of a *data model*. The manner in which the system structures data or, at least, the manner in which the users perceive that the data is structured.

**Structured Query Language (SQL)** See *SQL*.

**Subschema** An application program's view of the database.

**Synonyms** Two or more records having the same hash function value.

**System-owned set** A CODASYL set with only one occurrence. Also called a *singular set*.

**Table** Another name for a relation.

**Tabular** A DBMS in which users perceive data as tables but which does not furnish any of the other characterstics of a relational DBMS.

**Teleprocessing (TP) monitor** A system software product that controls a host computer's terminal communications and the application programs executed by the terminal users.

**Theta-join** A type of *join* in which the join condition is something other than equality.

**Third normal form (3NF)** A relation is in third normal form if it is in second normal form and if the only determinants it contains are candidate keys. (Technically this is the definition of Boyce-Codd normal form, but in this text the two are used synonymously.)

**Three-way logic** A type of logic in which, in addition to *"true"* and *"false,"* there is a third possibility: *"maybe."*

**Transaction** See *logical transaction*.

**Transaction processing** Processing that is controlled by a TP monitor.

**Transport volume** The volume of data that is transported from disk to memory (and memory to disk) during processing.

**Tree** A data structure that resembles a tree, with a single root at the top and its branches leading toward the bottom.

**Tuning** The process of changing aspects of a database design in order to improve performance.

**Tuple** The formal name for a row in a table.

**Twin** A node in a tree structure that has the same parent as another node is said to be the twin of the other node.

**Two-phase commit** An approach to the commit process in distributed systems in which there are two phases. In the first phase, each site is instructed to prepare to commit and must indicate whether the commit will be possible. After each site has responded, the second phase begins: If every site has replied in the affirmative, all sites must commit. If any site has replied in the negative, all sites must abort the transaction.

**Two-phase locking** An approach to *locking* in which there are two phases: a *growing phase*, in which new locks are acquired but no locks are released, and a *shrinking phase*, in which all locks are released and no new locks are acquired.

**Type** A structure itself (for example, a student record). Distinguished from *occurrence*, which means a specific example of a structure, such as the record for student Lee Adams.

**Unnormalized relation** A structure that satisfies the properties required to be a relation with one exception: repeating groups are allowed.

**Union-compatible** Two relations that have the same number of columns and in which corresponding columns have the same domain. Such relations can be combined with the *UNION, INTERSECTION,* and *DIFFERENCE* operations of the *relational algebra*.

**Update anomaly** An update problem that can occur in a database owing to a faulty design.

**Uploading** Data transfer from personal computer to mainframe.

**Upper conceptual domain** The portion of an *entity-relationship* diagram in which the entities and relationships are defined.

**User view** The view of data that is necessary to support the operations of a particular user.

**User-defined procedure** A procedure defined by users that will automatically be invoked at the appropriate time by the DBMS.

**Victim** In a deadlock situation, the deadlocked user whose transaction will be aborted to break the deadlock.

**View** An application program's or individual user's view of the database.

**Weak entity type** In the E-R model, an entity type that depends on another entity type for its existence.